The Dark Age
of Greece

to the people of Greece
καὶ κύντερον ἄλλο ποτ᾽ ἔτλης

♦ ♦ ♦
♦ ♦
♦

A. M. SNODGRASS

The Dark Age
of Greece

AN ARCHAEO-

LOGICAL SURVEY

OF THE ELEVENTH

TO THE EIGHTH

CENTURIES

BC

at the University Press
EDINBURGH

◆ ◆ ◆
◆ ◆
◆

© A. M. Snodgrass, 1971, 2000

Edinburgh University Press Ltd
22 George Square, Edinburgh

Facsimile origination by Brinnoven, Livingston
Printed and bound in Great Britain by the Cromwell Press

A CIP Record for this book is available from the British Library

ISBN 0 7486 1404 4 (hardback)
ISBN 0 7486 1403 6 (paperback)

Preface

◆ ◇ ◆
◆ ◆
◆

The method of this work is empirical. Its field is by no means new: the period of the early Iron Age is necessarily traversed more and more often by studies of Greek history, literature, religion, language, art and architecture, as knowledge broadens of the Bronze Age civilizations before it, and their common features with the Classical Greek world afterwards. In most of these studies it forms an unsatisfactory interlude, interrupting any pattern of continuous development, yet not providing the positive evidence needed to demonstrate a fundamental change of direction. It is hard to reach concrete conclusions about such a period. The commonest course is to make inferences from later literature and oral traditions; it is a legitimate one, since the traditions may contain much truth, and the literature is in some cases not so much later. Indeed, by drawing a dividing-line across Greek history at the end of the eighth century BC – a procedure which the archaeological findings might seem to justify – it is possible to admit the earliest extant written literature of Greece, the Homeric poems and the works ascribed to Hesiod, as contemporary testimony for the preceding age, and to draw on Late Geometric art for the same purpose.

But there is another possible approach: it is to examine the whole period in chronological sequence, scrutinizing the evidence as it comes, assembling the facts and endeavouring to face them. This sounds banal enough, but in this instance it involves abandoning the normal priorities of the historian, the literary scholar or the Classical archaeologist; for there is simply no direct answer to the questions that they would naturally, and rightly, consider most important. This method also entails an almost obsessional insistence on chronology. Much of the material that is available is trivial in itself and ambiguous as to the conclusions that can be drawn from it; yet this same material has some security as a basis for broader understanding of the period, in a sense in which no inference or analogy from better-known periods or regions can be secure.

Most scholars of this century have reached the conclusion that Greek civilization did pass through a true dark age, a time of some abjectness and gloom, during part or all of the period under consideration. That same conclusion is endorsed in this book, as my title suggests; it is based on the evidence presently available, and it is always theoretically possible that future discoveries will modify or radically detract from it. But it is, I think, a definite mistake to oppose such a conclusion on intuitive or even emotional grounds, from the conviction that the Greek genius was too strong to have suffered such a setback. To those who also believe in the underlying continuity of the Greek people, from Mycenaean times and before, down into the Classical period, as I do, it is if anything a greater tribute to their qualities to believe that catastrophe and recession on such a scale were endured and finally surmounted.

In writing of this period, at this time, several major disabilities and disadvantages must be acknowledged. A casual glance at the preliminary notices of archaeological discoveries, particularly in Greek periodicals of the last few years, will show that new evidence on this period is coming to light at a bewildering speed. Modern building-operations have very often been responsible for these discoveries; but since we may expect (and, up to a point, hope) that they will continue at the same pace, there is no real ground for thinking that the future will bring an opportune lull in which to take stock of the situation. An even more substantial objection is that pottery forms the basis of the archaeological material of this period, and that the most fruitful approach to it has always been that of the pottery-specialist, in whose field I am ill-qualified. Here I can only re-emphasize my obvious debt to the work of other scholars in this and other fields, and pay particular tribute to those colleagues who have generously imparted their wisdom in discussion as well as through their writings – Mr Vincent Desborough, Mr Nicolas Coldstream, Mr John Boardman, Professor E. L. Smithson, Professor John Cook and others; the enlightenment that I owe to them extends far beyond the field of pottery. Without their help, I could not have begun to write a work of this kind. I have also been perhaps too sparing in my acknowledgements to the only recent book which has taken this whole period as its central theme, Professor Chester G. Starr's perceptive and sympathetic work of 1961, *The Origins of Greek Civilization*, which has been a valuable guide throughout. I have learned much, too, from scholars whose main work is in other fields of prehistory, and especially from my colleagues Professor Stuart Piggott and Mr David Ridgway; and I gratefully acknowledge the help I received from Mr Joseph Alsop of Washington, DC, in the formulation of hypotheses about the early spread of iron which are advanced in Chapter 5.

Several scholars have kindly provided me with photographs used in their own publications: the late Mr J.K.Brock (nos. 10, 39, 41, 121, 122); Mr J.N.Coldstream (nos. 17, 24, 25, 26, 27, 31, 36, 37, 38, 40, 44, 45, 46, 47); Mr V.R.d'A.Desborough (nos. 1, 22, 23, 30, 35, 51, 53, 103); Dr L.H. Jeffery (no. 111); Professor Carlo Panseri (nos. 72 and 73); Mr D.W.R. Ridgway (no. 48); Dr C.-G.Styrenius (nos. 2 and 28); and Mr R.T. Williams (no. 137). A number of others were generous enough to let me publish illustrations from their excavations: Professor P.Amandry (no. 128); Mr J.Boardman (nos. 110, 132, 133 and colour plate 11); Dott.G. Buchner (nos. 49, 50, 65, 109); Professor A.Cambitoglou (no. 134); Professor John L.Caskey (no. 118); Professor J.M.Cook and Mr R.V. Nicholls (nos. 114 and 117); Professor Paul Courbin (nos. 85, 96, 126); Professor G.Kleiner (nos. 29 and 136); Professor L. Morricone (no. 34); Professor P.J.Riis and the Nationalmuseet, Copenhagen (nos. 54, 55); Mr Ph.Petsas (nos. 33, 60, 61, 62); Mr M.R.Popham (nos. 9, 32, 101); Mrs M.Seiradhaki (no. 11); and Professor Evelyn L.Smithson (no. 52 and colour plate 1). I also owe much to Mr Ridgway and Mr J.Touratsoglou for their good offices in obtaining photographs; and I am delighted to thank Mrs Morna Simpson for drawing many of the text figures, and Mr Walter Cairns of the Edinburgh University Press for much patience, tact and trouble.

A.M.SNODGRASS

Contents

◆ ◆ ◆
◆ ◆
◆

Illustrations

◆ ◆ ◆
◆ ◆
◆

Abbreviations

✦ ✦ ✦
✦ ✦
✦

A A Archäologischer Anzeiger (suppl. to *JdI*)

A A A Athens Annals of Archaeology

A A S O R Annual of the American Schools of Oriental Research

Act.A Acta Archaeologica (Copenhagen)

A D ’Αρχαιολογικὸν Δελτίον

A E ’Αρχαιολογικὴ ’Εφημερίς

Agora The Athenian Agora; results of excavations conducted by the American School of Classical Studies at Athens, i-ii (1953–65)

A I R R S Acta Instituti Romani Regni Sueciae

A J A American Journal of Archaeology

A J P American Journal of Philology

A M Mitteilungen des deutschen archäologischen Instituts, Athenische Abteilung

Ann. Annuario della Scuola Archeologica di Atene

Ant. Antiquity

Ant.J Antiquaries' Journal

A R Archaeological Reports (suppl. to *JHS*)

A S Anatolian Studies

B A S O R Bulletin of the American Schools of Oriental Research

B C H Bulletin de Correspondance Hellénique

Bd A Bollettino d' Arte

BICS Bulletin of the Institute of Classical Studies, University of London

B J b Bonner Jahrbücher

B S A Annual of the British School at Athens

C A H 2 Cambridge Ancient History, second edition

C B M W H.W.Catling, *Cypriot Bronzework in the Mycenaean World* (1964)

CRh *Clara Rhodos*

CVA *Corpus Vasorum Antiquorum*

Deiras J.Deshayes, *Argos, les Fouilles de la Deiras* (*Études Peloponnesiennes* 4, 1966)

EGA A.M.Snodgrass, *Early Greek Armour and Weapons* (1964)

EMF P.Ålin, *Das Ende der Mykenischen Fundstätten auf dem Griechischen Festland* (*Studies in Mediterranean Archaeology* 1, 1962)

EP *Études Peloponnesiennes*

Ergon Τὸ "Εργον τῆς 'Αρχαιολογικῆς 'Εταιρείας

FA *Fasti Archaeologici*

FGO Chr.Blinkenberg, *Fibules grecques et orientales* (1926)

Fortetsa J.K.Brock, *Fortetsa* (1957)

GBA E.T.Vermeule, *Greece in the Bronze Age* (1964)

GGA *Göttingische Gelehrte Anzeigen*

GGP J.N.Coldstream, *Greek Geometric Pottery* (1968)

GO J.Boardman, *The Greeks Overseas* (1964)

GP P.Jacobsthal, *Greek Pins and their connections with Europe and Asia* (1956)

GRBS *Greek, Roman and Byzantine Studies*

Hesp. *Hesperia*

HM H.L.Lorimer, *Homer and the Monuments* (1950)

IM *Istanbuler Mitteilungen*

JdI *Jarbuch des deutschen archäologischen Instituts*

JEA *Journal of Egyptian Archaeology*

JHS *Journal of Hellenic Studies*

JRS *Journal of Roman Studies*

Ker. W.Kraiker, K.Kübler, *Kerameikos, Ergebnisse der Ausgrabungen*, 1-6, 2 (1939 – 70)

LAAA *Liverpool Annals of Archaeology and Anthropology*

LMS V.R.d'A.Desborough, *The Last Mycenaeans and their Successors* (1964)

MA *Monumenti Antichi* (Reale Accademia dei Lincei)

Marb.WPr *Marburger Winckelmannsprogramm*

MEFR École française de Rome, *Mélanges Archéologie et d'Histoire*

MP A.Furumark, *The Mycenaean Pottery; Analysis and Classification* (1941)

NSc *Notizie degli Scavi*

Ol.ber. *Bericht über die Ausgrabungen in Olympia*, 1-8 (1937 – 67)

Ol.Forsch. *Olympische Forschungen* 1-6 (1944–66)

Op.Arch. Opuscula Archaeologica (in *AIRRS*)
Op.Ath. Opuscula Atheniensia
OPT Pitt-Rivers Museum, Oxford, *Occasional Papers on Technology*
PCPS Proceedings of the Cambridge Philological Society
PEQ Palestine Exploration Quarterly
PGP V.R. d'A.Desborough, *Protogeometric Pottery* (1952)
PPS Proceedings of the Prehistoric Society
Prakt. Πρακτικὰ τῆς ᾿Αρχαιολογικῆς ῾Εταιρείας
QDAP Quarterly of the Department of Antiquities, Palestine
RA Revue Archéologique
REG Revue des Études grecques
*RM Mitteilungen des deutschen archäologischen Instituts, Römische
   Abteilung*
SCE The Swedish Cyprus Expedition, 1-4, 3 (1934–62)
SS C.-G. Styrenius, *Submycenaean Studies* (1967)
Stud.Etr. Studi Etruschi
TAPA Transactions of the American Philological Association
WMBH Wissenschäftliche Mitteilungen aus Bosnien und Herʒegowinen
YCS Yale Classical Studies

Foreword to the new edition

✦ ✦ ✦
✦ ✦
✦

In the thirty-odd years since it was published, there has been no new edition of this book;[1] and it has long been out of print. To reissue it now, with the main text unchanged and with only this short foreword, may seem a presumptuous decision. I should first attempt to justify that decision. The book appeared near the outset of a pronounced re-orientation of attitudes in the archaeology of the English-speaking countries, and was in some respects typical of this new orientation. The search for an archaeology of process, which could construct a narrative that was independent, deriving neither from historical analogy, nor from the scanty documentary sources that could be brought to bear on such a period as that covered by this book, was then being conducted on every side. In purely prehistoric contexts, this took the form of the movement labelled 'New Archaeology' – a movement which pursued these goals much further, but whose heyday is now past. But the larger purpose of the reorientation is still very much alive today: the insistence that archaeological material can be used to explain change as well as to describe it; above all, that the rise and decline of cultures needs to be interpreted without that persistent recourse to a narrative of conquests and borrowings which characterised the archaeology of the preceding two hundred years and more. If the book is still consulted today, it is precisely because these tenets are not obsolete.

The book also stood at the beginning of a much more localised phenomenon: the exponential increase in study and field-work directed to the, hitherto neglected, period of Greece's past with which it dealt. This change is in one sense gratifying; but it is also one reason why, today, I find it an insurmountable task to try to produce an updated edition, which could make a claim to anything approaching comprehensiveness. The numbers of published sites, buildings, graves and sanctuary-deposits which are now available for consideration in a synthetic study of this period must have increased between five- and ten-fold since 1971. This order of increase is perhaps not entirely out of line with that in other archaeological fields, within and beyond the Greek and Mediterranean worlds; but it would make it a difficult task to embark on writing afresh such a synthesis today – and positively intimidating to think of doing so within a framework adopted for that selection of the evidence which happened to be available thirty years ago.[2]

This prompts the immediate question: is that framework then obsolete? Here, one may begin with my choice of title, incorporating the phrase 'The dark age'. Despite the fact that I still strongly maintain the position implied by that phrase, I nevertheless regret not having named the book, say, *The Early Iron Age of Greece*. For one thing, such an alternative title would have underlined one message of the book (Chapter 5), that in the case of Greece (unlike those of many other cultures in later prehistory) the 'Iron Age' is not a mere convenience-label, but actually means what it suggests – a cultural epoch in which iron had become the main metal for practical use. But, more importantly, it would have avoided presenting such a tempting target for the attempts to use later discoveries to dilute, modify, or reject outright[3] the view that a prolonged period of cultural, economic and social regression had engulfed Greece after the fall of the Mycenaean civilisation. Today, not a year passes without a claim that some new find, or some newly revealed evidence of continuity, has invalidated the belief in such a period of 'darkness'. Yet it remains beyond question that the *material* picture presented by this period is still generally devoid of many of those important attributes which can be found in the record of both the preceding and, still more obviously, the ensuing ages.

A more interesting question, not often enough addressed directly, is whether, despite the modesty of these physical traces, Greek society nevertheless retained many of the archaeologically invisible institutions, practices and aspirations of the Mycenaean age, or anticipated those whose existence is confirmed by later historical records. Even if it were shown to have done so, however, explanations on a profound level would still be needed to account for this drastic impoverishment in the archaeological record;

above all, for the *quantitative* impoverishment which, along with others, I attribute primarily to depopulation. Here, nothing in the past three decades has served to bring about a change in this quantitative picture, relative to the periods before and after, except to reinforce it. Further, the geographical concentration of the new finds, as of the old, serves to underline the disparity between those regions of Greece which possessed an Aegean seaboard, and those which did not (the 'advanced' and 'backward' regions of Chapter 7, pp. 374–6, but with the former now emphatically joined by Euboea, on the strength of the remarkable finds since published from Lefkandi and elsewhere).[4]

Perhaps the least-cited chapter of the book has been the first, in which the evidence of literature and epigraphy is used to demonstrate that the explicit concept of a 'dark age' was unknown to the Greeks of historical times, and is essentially a finding of early twentieth-century scholarship: only the implicit argument, from the silence and apparent ignorance of the Greeks of any names or episodes which we would date between the eleventh and the eighth centuries, can be cited as ancient support for this modern construct. Yet only a 'neo-fundamentalist' view, of the kind that has begun to re-emerge since the appearance of the first volume of Martin Bernal's *Black Athena* in 1987, would maintain that Greek archaeology (and other branches of scholarship) should be primarily constrained by the testimony of Greek literature, and contradict it at their peril; a modern discipline, in my view, is by definition one that does not tolerate the imposition of such a strait-jacket. In this chapter, as is to be expected with a topic centred on written evidence, there is less need for urgent updating than in any other part of the book, with the exception of a passage on the evidence for the Phoenicians in the west (p. 18) which is now seriously defective and outdated.

With the chapters on the pottery series (2) and on chronology (3), a new edition would have contained much new material, but only a handful of cases where the account would have been substantially rewritten. These latter would include Euboea, Phokis and Lokris (pp. 71–3), where entire ceramic sequences have been filled in, rather than merely reinforced at points already attested; and Thrace and the northern Aegean (p. 90), where a pottery series linked at many points with that of the central regions of Greece has recently emerged. As a result of these and other advances, the list of regional pottery styles has been considerably lengthened and refined in recent decades. In the chronological chapter, less reliance would today be placed on the evidence from the Philistine sites (pp. 107–9) as a secure terminus for cross-dating to the Aegean. Conversely, a new discovery of great potential importance was the excavation of part of a Middle Protogeometric Greek krater, in a context perhaps datable to around 1000 BC, at Tell Hadar on the Sea of Galilee.[5] On the broader question of the duration of the Early Iron Age, a case has been made for down-dating the closing centuries of the Bronze Age by more than a century, which would reduce the interruption in the documented record; but it has been matched by a parallel proposal to bring down the dates of the end of the Geometric style and the Archaic period, which would leave a similar gap unfilled.[6] Each case seems to me to rest on evidence rather weaker than that for the orthodox chronology; and scientific dating methods, which will eventually give a definitive answer, have so far acted to confirm the existence of a substantial lapse of time between the last datable constructions of the Bronze Age civilisations and the first undertakings of the reviving historical cultures.

From this point on, I think it will be preferable not to appraise the content chapter by chapter, but to address certain central theses put forward in 1971, most of which have since given rise to extended debate. I begin, however, with an argument which subsequent scholarship has so far passed over in almost complete silence: it first arises in pp. 179–83 of Chapter 4, and is then discussed in a broader context in Chapter 7, pp. 383–6. This is the suggested parallel, and the more tentative hint of continuity, between the Middle Helladic and Early Iron Age cultures of mainland Greece. Here is an idea which seems to me to have gained considerably in strength with the passage of the years, particularly through the major extension of field-work in peripheral regions of the Mycenaean world like Phokis, Lokris and Aetolia. There, a picture is emerging of whole areas where the reflections of Mycenaean culture were faint and fleeting at best; and where as a result the material features of Middle Helladic times appear to merge directly and uninterruptedly into those of the post-Mycenaean period, which so closely resemble them. The implications of this continuity are far-reaching, and I plan to return to them in future publications. It is enough to say here that this new material offers not merely a strengthening of the evidence, but the potential for an explanation, for many of the material features, hitherto seen as revivals or regressive adaptations, of the Early Iron Age culture of the Greek mainland.

The study of Early Iron Age cemeteries, and of burial generally, has been greatly enriched by new publications and syntheses, devoted to Attica (especially), to the Argolid, Euboea, Epirus, Crete and the far West.[7] The new cemetery publications have, not surprisingly, added enormously to the volume of iron finds, as well as of pottery: three examples that stand out in this category, by no means only on grounds of size, are the partial publication of the array of cemeteries at Lefkandi in Euboea; of the first group of tombs from the huge cemetery at Pithekoussai on Ischia; and of the equally huge North Cemetery at Knossos.[8] With the iron objects (though much less so with the pottery), the striking feature has been that the *typological* range has been so little extended: instead, the main effect has been greatly to enrich the existing categories of weapons, tools and jewellery.

At the same time, this access of new material leads naturally on to a more contentious issue, the hypothesis of a shortage of bronze, affecting important areas of Greece during the earlier part of the dark age, advanced in this book (Chapter 5, pp. 237–9). On the one hand, the new grave-finds have only served to reinforce the appearance of an overwhelming dominance of iron at this time; on the other, later study of evidence from other parts of the Mediterranean world has shown that some of the phenomena used to support the hypothesis, such as the intermittent use of iron to make fibulae, also occur outside Greece, in circumstances where there is little sign that access to bronze had been cut off. Here too it should be said that a quite different line of explanation has been advanced, to the effect that the much-increased deposition of iron in early tombs reflects, rather, the temporary prestige that iron enjoyed, and a certain social exclusiveness in access to its use.[9] Strict control over the necessary technical knowledge could still 'ration' the distribution of iron, so that even the widespread availability of iron ore is not a conclusive argument against this latter explanation; but it does have to be reconciled with the fact (reinforced by new analyses from Cyprus and elsewhere) that early iron objects show the invariable presence of carburisation and other techniques designed to ensure their *practical* effectiveness. In any case, neither the explanation based on the posited shortage of bronze, nor that of an exclusive exploitation of iron by a controlling élite, can be applied to more than a brief transitional phase: presently bronze objects return in a steady trickle and finally, by the later eighth century, in a flood. Nothing in all this has detracted from the view that the initial adoption of iron, whatever the precise social circumstances of its occurrence in Greece, represents one of the major technological advances in human history. What it rather reveals is a profound difference of views about the nature of Greek society at the period in question. To this vexed question we should now turn.

The picture presented in my book was a strongly egalitarian one: see especially Chapter 7, pp. 380–3. Neither in the contents of the numerous graves, nor in the rarer surviving architecture and settlement-finds, could I detect any signs of marked social stratification. Since then, a number of scholars have found reason to conclude otherwise. The most important of such arguments is without doubt that first advanced by Ian Morris in his book of 1987 (cited in n. 7): that the surviving burial record, especially from Athens but probably more widely, is representative only of a select minority of the population. In other words, formal burial had *itself* become a privilege, not universally extended – specifically, not to poorer adult males, or to many women or children. The period of this exclusiveness extends, in Athens, from roughly the beginning of the Attic Protogeometric period to the end of the Middle Geometric, some 300 years on the orthodox chronology. This radical insight is supported by a wide range of arguments and I am in no doubt that it is soundly based. The implication is, to put it somewhat crudely, that my 'egalitarian' interpretation arose from applying an inappropriate standard of material wealth: the 'impoverished' burials of these centuries still represent something beyond the reach of the majority. But, obviously enough, this conclusion serves further to reinforce the impression that the overall level of disposable wealth was strikingly low. If it is objected that this poverty applies only to the provision of burial goods, which are a matter of cultural preference, then it is reasonable to ask for counter-evidence from other contexts.

Just such evidence has, in many opinions, been forthcoming from the site of Lefkandi. Not only has the progressive publication of the cemeteries here (see n. 8) revealed a recurrent pattern of fairly rich grave-goods, unmatched in any of the sites that I had studied, and calling into question the case for the isolation of Greece at this period (see pp. 246–9, 328, 368–80); but the discovery of the unique building at the Toumba site has also revealed architecture of a scale and pretension which has surprised everyone – and this at a date probably in the tenth century BC. A preliminary account of this find was given in 1982, and a full publication has since appeared.[10] Its owners – or, in the excavators' opinion, the honorands of its construction – are reasonably identified in the couple buried, also with unique accoutrements, below its floor. As this last sentence implies, controversy has arisen over the purpose of the building, whether domestic or commemorative; but its architectural importance remains largely unaffected by that. Twice the size of any structure known from the Greek world within two centuries or more on either side of its date, it surely represents, together with a handful of the richest graves from Early Iron Age Greece, the very apex of the social pyramid. Yet some qualifications apply, parallel to those in the case of the reappraisal of early Greek burials. In its size and in the provision of a (timber) colonnade or veranda running most of the way round it, it stands out clearly from the pattern previously recognised; but in its materials and construction it does not. The apsidal plan and mud-brick walls, on a socle of uncut stones and reinforced by timber uprights, are entirely typical of the day: so is the roof, probably thatched, which had been at least partly laid when the whole structure was – perhaps deliberately – destroyed. While greatly extending the picture of the aspirations of the building practices of its time, it leaves the range of those practices largely unchanged. No more than its contemporaries was it a 'monumental' structure, in the sense of being built for durability. Its importance lies rather in the light it throws on the issue of social differentiation – and perhaps on the separate question of regional disparity.

A feature of the Lefkandi grave-goods which has already been alluded to is their geographical range of origins: for well over a century, from the date of the Toumba building down to the abandonment, around 825 BC, of the cemeteries so far excavated, grave after grave produces evidence of contact with a wide area of the Eastern Mediterranean. It is more likely than not that the carriers of these exotic goods were themselves Euboeans; but even if they were not Greeks at all, this would still be enough to show that Lefkandi was a regular calling-point for ships from much further east. This is an extremely important new finding, and it is not an entirely isolated one. At Kommos on the southern coast of Crete, a sequence of temples of non-Greek form has been excavated which, with some accompanying imports, point firmly in the direction of a Phoenician presence at the site.[11] Belief in the isolation of the entire Aegean world, even for the relatively short period for which I had posited it, can no longer be sustained.

Yet almost as striking is the fact that, after thirty further years of archaeological discovery, the evidence of external contacts remains so clearly concentrated in geographical terms; indeed, the new finds serve to accentuate this. Even when we combine the more or less direct evidence of imports (and of the decidedly rarer exports outwards from the Aegean) with the much less secure arguments from the adoption of new practices which *could* have had an external inspiration, the list of regions affected remains fairly short: Attica, the Argolid, central Euboea, Thessaly, the central Cyclades, Crete and the south-western coast of Asia Minor. Some of these regions are represented by no more than one or two sites. As already remarked (above, p. 3), they share the common feature of possessing a seaboard on the Aegean itself. The greater part of the Greek peninsula, to the west and north-west, remains as unaffected as before.

So far, discussion has been largely confined to the discoveries made by recent excavation and to their interpretation. Something must be added about the results obtained by the much newer technique of intensive surface survey, which began to be widely applied in Greece about a decade after the appearance of the book. Quite large areas of the Greek landscape have now been covered by teams of field-walkers, searching for the traces of past activity, of all periods, left on the surface – in northern and central Greece, the Peloponnese and the islands. Several of these projects have already generated major publications.[12] Their findings in respect of this period are strikingly concordant. Some thousands of 'sites', large and small, known and unknown, have been identified in what is today the open countryside; in many cases, they show several periods of activity or occupation, extending from the Palaeolithic to early modern times. Yet the Early Iron Age is one of a small number of periods – the earlier Neolithic, the Middle Bronze Age, the Early Byzantine period – whose traces are very seldom present. Broadly speaking, it is only in the larger settlements, often with occupation both in the Bronze Age and in historical times, where pottery or other remains datable to this time are found: even there, they are usually present in small quantities. This is a negative finding of direct importance. It suggests that the Early Iron Age population, such as it was, had not been scattered into isolated pockets across the landscape, but was nucleated, probably to a greater degree than before or after. Hitherto, it was possible to argue that the fugitive quality of Early Iron Age remains in the excavation record was the result of looking in the wrong locations: now, on the contrary, it seems that they are most likely to occur in just the kind of site which would be selected for excavation. The implications for the general level of population at this period are obvious: not only is the number of sites known to be in occupation remarkably low, as was already clear; but the quantity of material in the sites that *were* inhabited is nearly always overshadowed by that from the Bronze Age or the Archaic period.

There is a further debate whose light plays around the edges of all discussion of this period, but which has not yet been mentioned. This is the relationship between the modern archaeological concept of the 'dark age' on the one hand, and the world portrayed in the Homeric poems on the other.

My treatment of this issue (in Chapter 7, pp. 388–94 and 434–6) has been justly criticised for concentrating on physical features, to the exclusion of institutions. But it may be unnecessary to reopen this apparently unending debate here. In a study of periodisation in early Greek history, Ian Morris has written that, in the 1970s, 'there was a classic example of the paradigm shift . . . with hardly any sustained debate in print, the archaeological model quietly swept the field.'[13] Whether or not one welcomes this outcome, it is hard to question its reality. There seems today to be an unspoken consensus that the Early Iron Age is as much the archaeologists' property, to be evaluated primarily in archaeological terms, as is, say, the Bronze Age – something which I remember hearing openly contested in the 1960s. Even a chronologically late phenomenon like the incidence of cult at prehistoric tombs, briefly treated in this book (Chapter 4, pp. 192–4), which belongs close to the end of this period and has clear implications for Greek religion of historical times, has since given rise to an extensive literature, predominantly of an archaeological kind;[14] and the same can be said of the archaeological study, on a scale much larger still, of the early Greek sanctuary-finds.

It will by now be clear what the main changes in emphasis would have been, had a full rewriting of this book proved possible. There would have been less emphasis on isolation, but even greater on continuity from the past, especially from the pre-Mycenaean age. As a consequence of this last point, there would have been a detectable shift in the balance of emphasis between different regions of Greece, with closer attention paid to the culture of the less advanced regions which may represent the norm of responses to the breakdown of Mycenaean civilisation, and a background against which the few prominent sites stand out in contrast. Again as a consequence, there would have been even more stress on regional differences. There would have been major concessions on the stratification of Greek society, but based on the archaeological finds and their interpretation, not on any revision of views as to the historical applicability of the Homeric evidence.

My over-riding reason for not attempting the task is, however, a feeling that it is time for study and discussion to advance beyond the level on which the book was written. It is now clear that the 'dark age', at any rate in terms of the simple lapse of time, will not go away. It must be either radically reinterpreted, or explained as it is. For those archaeologists who believe in its current interpretation, one urgent task (as I argued in 1987 – see n. 1) is to explain its long duration: to throw light on the process – often repeated in history – whereby a culture and a people with major attainments behind them, of a highly visible kind archaeologically, and with even more obvious ones ahead of them, were content for some centuries to pass during which there would not be, materially speaking, anything comparable to show. There should also be greater stress on the search for positive aspects of the choices made at this time: adaptation, physical mobility, economic change and the mere adjustment of social priorities need to be measured against decline, deprivation and depopulation. These are surely the directions in which research must now turn, and I welcome the signs that it is beginning to do so.

A.M. Snodgrass
September, 1999

Notes

1] The greater part of the text was in fact written in 1968. The Rumanian edition, *Grecia: Epocii Intunecate* (trans. M. Gramatopol, Bucharest, 1994) appeared without alteration to the main text. My nearest approaches to a reassessment of the whole field have been a short paper 'The Greek Early Iron Age: A Reappraisal', in *Dialogues d'Histoire ancienne* 9 (1983), 73–86; and Chapter 6 of my book *An Archaeology of Greece* (Berkeley and Los Angeles, 1987), 'The Early Iron Age of Greece' (pp. 170–210).

2] It is significant that works by other scholars, treating the period (or a large part of it) at a similar level of detail, have tended to die away in recent years: see notably J. Bouzek's *Homerisches Griechenland* (Prague, 1969), which actually antedated my book but was not available in the West in time to be assimilated, either in my own work or in that of V. R. d'A. Desborough, *The Greek Dark Ages* (London, 1972); J. N. Coldstream, *Geometric Greece* (London, 1977); C. T. Syriopoulos, *I metabatikí hróni: apó tís Mikinaïkís eis tín Arhaïkín períodon, 1200–700 p.Khr.* (Athens, 1983). Presently began the appearance of composite volumes (which still continue): edited by S. Deger-Jalkotzy, *Griechenland, die Ägäis und die Levante während der 'Dark Ages'* (Vienna, 1983); by R. Hägg, *The Greek*

Renaissance of the Eighth Century BC (Stockholm, 1983); by D. Musti, *La Transizione dal miceneo all'alto archaico* (Rome, 1991); and by S. Langdon, *New Light on a Dark Age: Exploring the Culture of Geometric Greece* (Columbia, MO/London, 1997). The latter end of the period is extensively treated in a triple number of Annuario, 59–61 (1981–3), devoted to the Conference 'Grecia, Italia e Sicilia nell' VIII e VII secolo a.c.'. Later single-author treatments have been more summary: W. D. E. Coulson, *The Greek Dark Ages: A Review of the Evidence and Suggestions for Future Research* (Athens, 1990); R. Osborne, *Greece in the Making, 1100–479 BC* (London/New York, 1996). A volume on this period by Dr Oliver Dickinson (as a sequel to his *The Aegean Bronze Age* (Cambridge, 1994)) is promised for the near future.

3] Most memorably, by J. K. Papadopoulos in *Journal of Mediterranean Archaeology* 6 (1993), pp. 196–7: 'Greek civilization . . . would certainly be better served if the spectre of the Dark Age, a phantom that has haunted the "musty confines of Cambridge" . . . for too long, is finally laid to rest.'

4] A point well brought out by the table in n. 15 (p. 1471) of A. Schnapp's review article, *Annales: Économies, Sociétés, Civilisations* 29 (1974), 1465–76.

5] For a preliminary notice, see A. Mazar in V. Karageorghis (ed.), *Cyprus in the Eleventh Century BC* (Nicosia, 1994), at p. 48.

6] See, respectively, P. James and others, *Centuries of Darkness: A Challenge to the Conventional Chronology of Old World Archaeology* (London, 1991); and E. D. Francis and M. Vickers, 'Greek Geometric Pottery at Hama and its Implications for Near Eastern Chronology', *Levant* 17 (1985), 131–8, one of a series of articles by the same authors.

7] Note especially, among others too numerous to list here, G. Krause, *Untersuchungen zu den ältesten Nekropolen am Eridanos in Athen* (Hamburg, 1975); I. Morris, *Burial and Ancient Society* (Cambridge, 1987); J. Whitley, *Style and Society: The Changing Face of a Pre-Literate Society, 1100–700 BC* (Cambridge, 1991); R. Hägg, *Die Gräber der Argolis in submykenischer, protogeometrischer und geometrischer Zeit* 1: *Lage und Form der Gräber* (Uppsala, 1974); P. Courbin, *Tombes géométriques d'Argos* 1 (Paris, 1974); I. Vokotopoulou, *Vitsa: tá nekrotafeía mías Molossikís komís* 1–3 (Athens, 1986); and the three works mentioned in the next note.

8] M. R. Popham and others (ed), *Lefkandi* i: *The Iron Age Settlement and Cemeteries* (London, 1979–80); *Lefkandi* iii: *The Early Iron Age Cemetery at Toumba: Plates* (London, 1996); G. Buchner and D. Ridgway, *Pithekoussai* 1 (Rome, 1993); J. N. Coldstream and H. W. Catling (eds), *Knossos North Cemetery: Early Greek tombs* 1–4 (London, 1996).

9] Ian Morris, 'Circulation, Deposition and the Formation of the Greek Iron Age', *Man* 24 (1989), pp. 502–19.

10] M. R. Popham, P. G. Calligas and L. H. Sackett (eds), *Lefkandi* ii: *The Protogeometric Building at Toumba*: 1, *The Pottery*, with R. W. V. Catling and I. S. Lemos (London, 1990); 2, *The Excavation, Architecture and Finds*, with J. Coulton and H. W. Catling (London, 1993), especially pp. 49–59, 97–101 on the interpretation of the building.

11] For a convenient summary, see J. W. Shaw, 'Phoenicians in Southern Crete', *AJA* 93 (1989), pp. 165–83.

12] Notably, J. F. Cherry, J. L. Davis and E. Mantsourani, *Archaeology as Long-Term History: Northern Keos in the Cycladic Islands* (Los Angeles, 1991), especially pp. 245–7; A. Rizakis (ed.), *Paysages d'Achaie: le bassin du Peiros et la plaine occidentale* (Athens, 1992), esp. pp. 167–8; H. Lohmann, *Atene: Forschungen zur Siedlungs- und Wirtschaftsstruktur des klassischen Attika* (Cologne/Weimar/Vienna 1993), esp. p. 36; M. H. Jameson, C. N. Runnels and T. H. van Andel, *A Greek Countryside: The Southern Argolid from Prehistory to the Present Day* (Stanford, 1994), esp. pp. 372–4; W. G. Cavanagh and others, *The Lakonia Survey* ii: *The Archaeological sata* (London, 1996) (note the hiatus between Chapters 13 and 14); C. B. Mee and H. Forbes (eds), *A Rough and Rocky Place: The Landscape and Settlement of the Methana Peninsula*, Greece (Liverpool, 1997), esp. p. 57.

13] I. Morris, 'Periodization and the Heroes', in M. Golden and P. Toohey (eds), *Inventing Ancient Culture: Historicism, Periodization and the Ancient World* (London/New York, 1997), pp. 96–131, at p. 123.

14] See, most comprehensively, C. Antonaccio, *An Archaeology of Ancestors: Tomb Cult and Hero Cult in Early Greece* (Lanham, MD, 1995).

1

The Concept of a Dark Age

◆ ◆ ◆
◆ ◆
◆

'There is a far-off island of knowledge, or apparent knowledge; then darkness; then the beginnings of continuous history.' These words of Gilbert
Murray's, appearing first in 1907,[1] fittingly embodied a doctrine which is
largely the property of the present century. The period between the fall of
the Mycenaean civilization and the rise of Archaic Greece, once its general
nature and broad chronological limits had been agreed upon, was coming
naturally to attract the name of a dark age[2]; but this rough delineation had
only really become possible with the advent of modern archaeological
methods. For the ancient authors all, in one way or another, fall short of
giving the sequence of events that is described by Murray's words; and to
scholars of earlier generations – even perhaps to some of Murray's contemporaries – the use of such an absolute term as 'dark age' would have seemed
tendentious. Even today, the name – originally applied to Greece and the
Aegean – is used only sparingly by students of those civilizations further
to the East which, at the same period, seem to have experienced a parallel
course of events to that in Greece; while there are several scholars who, on
various grounds, would question the aptness of the term even for the
Aegean. On a superficial level, there is no denying that the archaeologist,
with his sequence of a Mycenaean period, a dark age, and an Archaic period,
is using a different language from that which served the ancient Greeks for
describing their own past. Nevertheless, in tracing the growth of this conception the proper place to begin is with the Greeks themselves. For their
view of what was, to them, the comparatively recent past does at times
embrace elements of the modern theory. The fact that no ancient author
explicitly combines these elements, to give a coherent picture of a dark age,
is not in itself proof that the Greeks did not know of, or believe in, such a
period. Earlier generations of scholars, who did not themselves envisage

A

such a picture, were not inclined to look for traces of it in the ancient literature.

But first, the basic elements of the modern doctrine of the dark age may be stated, at the risk of anticipation. To begin with, there is the matter of the passage of time: the solid fact that, between the end of the Mycenaean civilization (whether we equate that event with the positive signs of destruction, or with the later and vaguer point at which identifiably Mycenaean cultural traits disappear), and the rise of the Hellenic world to a level which we can *see* to be roughly comparable, several centuries elapsed. This fact, slow to emerge, is now universally accepted; what is debated is the competence of our evidence for determining cultural level. It is one thing to prove that a long period of time elapsed between two comparatively well-explored cultural phases, and another to show that that period was dark. Mere lack of information about a period makes it dark in one sense for us; but we must not confuse this sense with the darkness real and serious enough to have been apparent to the people who lived at the time. It is this alone which gives true meaning to the phrase 'dark age', and it is this which cannot be accepted without positive and laborious proof. The modern doctrine would hold that the following characteristics were present in the post-Mycenaean period: first, a fall in population that is certainly detectable and may have been devastating; secondly, a decline in or loss of certain purely material skills; thirdly, a similar decline or loss in respect of some of the more elevated arts, of which the apparent loss of the art of writing is the most striking to us, although to contemporaries this need by no means have been so; fourthly, a fall in living-standards and perhaps in the sum of wealth; fifthly, a general severance of contacts, commercial and otherwise, with most peoples beyond the Aegean area and even with some of those within it. To these features, some would add a growth of acute insecurity. If all of these could be proved to be characteristic of this period, no one would dispute the aptness of the name 'dark age'. Our first purpose is to see how far, if at all, Greek literature reflects awareness of such a picture.

THE LITERARY EVIDENCE

The Homeric poems, for all the uncertainties and provisos which must attend discussion of them, will be agreed to show a consistent attitude on one point. The Trojan War and its aftermath, which form their subject-matter, are represented as having happened in 'better' times, in a heroic age long since passed. The favourite illustration of this is perhaps the poet's reference (*Iliad* XII, 447) to a hero's throwing a stone 'which two men of today could scarcely have lifted'; but throughout the *Iliad* and *Odyssey* there are passages which describe the prowess and wealth of the characters in a way apparently designed to impress an age which was unaccustomed to such standards. But in this respect the Homeric poems are merely an unusually fine example of a widespread tendency to weave legends – not always enshrined in literary form – around a heroic past. Not only may these legends exaggerate or distort the historical realities, and thus overstate the difference between the past age and the present one; but, equally important, it is not a necessary precondition of such legends that there should be any sharp historical decline from the period remembered as a heroic age to the period when the legends grow up. Sir Maurice Bowra in his comparative study, *The Meaning of a Heroic Age*,[3] points out that many different circumstances can lead to the establishment of this kind of concept; conquest or disaster may be the commonest preludes to it, but there are also known cases where migration, political change or religious conversion appear to have provided the impetus. Since the memory of the Greek heroic age was apparently for a long time kept alive by the settlers in Ionia, to whose tradition Homer was almost certainly heir, the attitude of the Homeric poems to the past could, even today, be ascribed as plausibly to migration as to any catastrophic fall in material standards. Neither the one influence nor the other is really detectable in the poems; even if Homer had positively stressed the poverty or misery of his own times, which he does not, one could have pointed out that within the context of the heroic age itself, Nestor more than once recalls the greater days of his own youth, two generations previously (see especially *Iliad* I, 260). The *laudator temporis acti* is too deeply engrained in human nature to be taken as a reliable independent witness, whether he speaks through the mouth of the poet or of one of his characters. Homer consistently avoids overt reference to events and circumstances at or after the fall of his heroic society; inferences that can be extracted from his text by later scholars are another matter. The poems 'ignore the movements of people in the period after the fall of Mycenae'; they portray 'a period of stability',[4] even where analysis suggests that that period must be post-Mycenaean. This is why a reading of the Homeric poems is not enough to suggest either that a dark age had descended on, and still enveloped, the world in which the poems were shaped; or that such an age had come and gone in the interval since the heroic age.

Hesiod is in a very different case. One of the most famous of all his passages is that which describes the five races or generations of man (*Works and Days*, 110f.). After the depiction of the primitive races of Gold and Silver, there follow in turn the race of Bronze, fierce warriors with bronze weapons and bronze houses; the race of Heroes, the contemporaries of the expedition of the Seven against Thebes and the Trojan War; and then: 'I wish that I could no longer be among the men of the Fifth Race, but had either died sooner or been born later. For now it is the race of Iron . . .'. The presence of the race of Heroes, in what is almost certainly an older sequence, is clearly anomalous, and must be the result of an interpolation, probably by Hesiod himself, possibly by a predecessor. Although it is not specified whether the Heroes used bronze or iron, the sequence of Hesiod's last three races is tolerably well confirmed by the archaeological evidence of metallurgical practice, a fact whose significance is questionable.[5] But it remains to be asked how far Hesiod's picture provides grounds for the modern theory of a dark age. He speaks disparagingly, in moral rather than material terms, of the race of Iron among whom he says he lives, by comparison with what had gone before. But when did he live? The answer of most recent scholarship is that he flourished after the end of what can reasonably be called the dark age; perhaps the most general point of agreement would be that he was alive in 700 BC, whether the greater part of his life extended before or after that date. This is a date at which many of the skills and arts lost in the post-Mycenaean period had returned to Greece; at which foreign contacts in almost every direction except that of Egypt had been resumed; at which the art of writing had certainly been revived; and at which there is every sign that the population was speedily increasing. Hesiod does not explicitly acknowledge any of these signs of returning prosperity, and may not even have regarded them as such; but he nevertheless hints – in so far as his language does not merely reflect the influence of Epic – at the presence of some of them in the *Works and Days* : as when he treats sea-borne commerce as a serious (if inferior) alternative to agriculture (lines 617-94); when he shows familiarity with the idea of a walled city (246); and perhaps in the far-flung geographical references in the *Theogony*. If the accepted dating of Hesiod is sound – and it depends on criteria wholly different from those which we have mentioned – then we must look rather to local or personal explanations for his gloomy picture of the race of Iron: his father's unfortunate choice of land to settle on, the remoteness of his situation in the hills of southern Boeotia, or the private injustices he had evidently suffered. The tempo of events at this period, which in many ways seems to us startlingly rapid, was apparently too slow, at least in Askra, to attract the notice of Hesiod. The *Works and Days* suggests, as the Homeric poems clearly imply, the poet's knowledge that the better past was at some considerable remove of time; but this in itself does not betoken a dark age.

The early poets were, of course, much nearer to the critical events than the first extant Greek prose-writers, but it is the latter who provide the more fruitful field of enquiry in respect of the dark age. Not only were the historians among them expressly concerned with such questions as this, but the passage of time could itself prove an ally to these later writers. It is notoriously difficult to place current or very recent periods in their historical perspective; later generations, provided that they have the necessary evidence, can make comparisons with the succeeding, as well as the preceding, age. In the pages of Herodotus, it is true, we shall look largely in vain for such historical interpretations of the remoter past; this although in the opening chapters of the *Histories* he goes out of his way to consider events of the heroic age, before and including the Trojan War, as a potential source of the great conflict between the Greeks and Persians (I, 1-5). But Herodotus makes isolated observations that are of great relevance to our purpose. One, in these opening chapters, is that 'the cities which in ancient times were great, have most of them become small; and those which in my time were great, were formerly small' (I, 5, 4) – an obvious enough conclusion for any Greek who was familiar with legend and the Epic poets, and one from which he might infer a major upheaval in the state of things which had prevailed in the heroic age. But such a *bouleversement* was in any case not a matter of doubt among educated Greeks of the Classical period; it was the sort of thing that saga and folk-memory could apprehend more clearly than a prolonged dark age; it did not necessarily lead to a dark age, and we may doubt whether anybody thought that it had. Also valuable is Herodotus' observation 'I believe that Hesiod and Homer belong four hundred years before me in time, and not longer' (II, 53, 2). Much of the interest of the statement lies in the last three words. They suggest that Herodotus is dissenting from a common opinion which favoured an earlier dating for the poets; the suggestion is reinforced by the next sentences, which disagree with the accepted view on an allied matter, and then repeat that the dating proposed for Hesiod and Homer is the historian's own personal opinion. Since Herodotus accepted the more or less orthodox view that the Trojan War had taken place about 800 years before his time, that is in the thirteenth century BC (II, 145, 4), his down-dating of Homer to the ninth century becomes a significant step. He is purposely dissociating the Homeric poems, by a long period of time, from the events which formed their subject-matter, and anyone who does this is faced with the difficulty of finding events to place in the intervening space. Scholars in the nineteenth century, who had mistakenly rejected this opinion of Herodotus' in pursuit of a much earlier date for Homer, found themselves revising their view in the face of new evidence, and thus treading the same path that Herodotus had apparently followed.[6] It is not chance that this process, in the later case, coincided with the acceptance of the idea of a dark age; but it was hardly possible for Herodotus to take any steps along this road. To him, and perhaps to others in his time, it was an accepted fact that the sea-power of Minos of Crete, and therefore presumably the Trojan War which happened 'in the third generation after his death' (VII, 171, 1), belonged in an age too early to be called human history; Herodotus specifically implies this in III, 122, 2. If the heroic period could be dismissed as being beyond the frontiers of true knowledge, then the immediately post-heroic period was no longer in a special case.

Nevertheless, the problems of the Classical historians on this issue must have been intense; particularly for those writers – perhaps the majority – who more or less followed Herodotus in his later dating of Homer, but who did not share his scepticism about the heroic age. The heroic age had left nothing worth remembering later than about two generations after the Trojan War, and there was little if any of the historical age which could be placed before Homer; if the interval was neither 'heroic' nor 'historical' what could it have been like? In the century after Herodotus, Theopompus of Chios widened the gap and accentuated the difficulty by bringing Homer down to the seventh century, so that he no longer stood even at the dawn of the 'historical' period. It may have been partly in reaction to this quandary that some later scholars fell back once again on a much earlier date for Homer, though they mainly based their conclusions on internal evidence from the poems. Eratosthenes, for example, placed the Homeric poems only a century after the Trojan War; Aristarchus made Homer contemporary with the Ionian migration, which meant a generation or so later than that, according to Greek chronological tradition, but would still leave Homer within the eleventh century BC by our reckoning. Even the naïve view that Homer was an actual contemporary of the Trojan War found a surprising number of adherents.[7] This is, however, a digression from the main theme; Herodotus had set a problem and the Greeks, down to late in antiquity, did not apparently consider it solved. But one Greek at least, Thucydides, tried to face the problem squarely.

The 'Archaeology' at the beginning of Thucydides' history is an enthralling piece of writing, as an intellectual exercise as much as for its content. The care with which steps in the reasoning are enumerated, and the evidence sometimes specifically cited, suggests that a systematic enquiry into the remoter past was a thing as unfamiliar to fifth-century readers as it is precious to us. Thucydides shows that he subscribes to a similar tradition about the chronology of events in the heroic age to that of Herodotus; on Homer he does not commit himself more precisely than to say that he lived 'much later than the Trojan War' (1, 3, 3), but this gives him broadly the same starting point as Herodotus. Unlike his predecessor, however, he sets out to give in these chapters a continuous, if broad, narrative of events from well before the Trojan War to well after Homer; so that we are given, however incidentally, a picture of the period designated by our phrase 'dark age'. What is this picture like?

Many of the phrases which stand out from Thucydides' narrative are consonant with the modern picture. There is talk of the smallness of cities, and of general weakness and poverty, in ancient times; of the lack of communication or trade; of piracy and insecurity, and the need to carry arms; of migration, disturbance, and hard-earned pacification. But on closer examination, many of these comments are seen to apply to a period far earlier than our 'dark age'. This closer examination is needed, because the sequence of the events in the narrative is not easy to follow, let alone their position in absolute chronology; and this vagueness in turn derives from one of the basic features of the whole 'Archaeology', its indivisibility. Thucydides' story is one of a consistent, if extremely slow, progress; there is no 'crest' in the heroic age followed by a 'trough' in the dark age, partly because one of his aims is to modify the poets' assessment of the achievements of the heroic age. Where we can isolate passages that relate to post-heroic times, and compare them with what in Thucydides' view had gone before, there is a complete lack of distinction between the two. The first remarks on the unsettled state, poor resources and weak communications of Greece, introduced in chapter 2 with the vague word 'formerly' (πάλαι), seem to refer to the very earliest times; but Thucydides illustrates their effects by linking them, with an unbroken chain of causation, to the Ionian migration which he knew to be well after the Trojan War (cf. 1, 12, 4). Again, in chapter 3, where Thucydides is stressing the tribal and local divisions within Greece in the period *before* the united enterprise of the expedition to Troy, Homer's failure to use the common name 'Hellene' or the contrasting term 'barbarian' is apparently taken to show that these divisions persisted until Homer's own times, which are 'much later' than the Trojan War. Then in chapter 5 the discussion of piracy, which is set in the context of Minos' reign and even earlier, is extended to cover robbery on land; in the following chapter this leads naturally to the topic of insecurity, and we are told that 'all Greece used to carry arms'; but the word used is σιδηροφορεῖν, literally 'to carry iron', an uncomfortable anachronism for a historian who knew and trusted Homer, and one which suggests an almost intentional vagueness over the distinction of the bronze-using contemporaries of Minos from their iron-armed successors. At the end of chapter 8 Thucydides concedes that it was an increase in prosperity among the early Greeks which ultimately made possible the expedition to Troy; and although he devotes the next three chapters to a rigorous assessment of Agamemnon's armament by the higher standards of fifth-century Greece, he is careful to warn his readers against rejecting the poets' testimony along with their opinions. We need not doubt that the final achievement of the heroic age 'surpassed those before it' (1, 10, 1); what was the aftermath like?

The first sentence of chapter 12 tells all: '. . . Since even after the Trojan War, Greece was still too involved in migration and settlement for quiet growth to take place'. The use of the words 'even' and 'still' shows that, to Thucydides if not his readers, the post-heroic age was merely an appendage to the far longer period of unrest that had gone before. Its advent is marked not by any change in kind or in level of existence, but only by further movements of population. The 'revolutions and factions' which Thucydides speaks of are illustrated by events confined to the eighty years after the Trojan War, and culminate in the Dorian conquest of the Peloponnese; on Thucydides' own reckoning, we are at this point still within the twelfth century BC (cf. V, 112, 2). What follows is vaguer; the pacification of Greece, whose deferment was mentioned in the first sentence of the chapter, is achieved 'with difficulty and at great length', and makes possible the Ionian migration and Greek colonization in the West. Thucydides ends by driving home to his readers the point that these last events came after the Trojan War, a hint of the extreme vagueness about chronology which must have prevailed in his day.

From the very beginning of chapter 13, with the mention of increased revenues and the rise of tyranny, we clearly move into the full Archaic period; the account of the dark age is over, within a few sentences of having begun.[8] Thucydides is under no illusion as to the lapse of time involved; he has acknowledged it with his words 'at great length' in chapter 12. By his summary treatment he suggests that, for him too, the period after the coming of the Dorians was a dark age, in the limited sense that he knew no more about it than anyone else. In another way, however, his account adds an important new dimension to the classical picture of the dark age. Even if the idea was his alone, the notion of a steady improvement in conditions from far back in the Bronze Age down to the Archaic period, with no set-back at the end of the heroic age, is a far-reaching one. So far from beginning with a set-back, the period that we would call the dark age was for Thucydides an improvement on its predecessor. Since his main criteria are pacification, and its fruits in the shape of material growth and colonization abroad, the post-Dorian age (as presented by Thucydides) is on all counts preferable to what went before (again, as presented by Thucydides).

Steady improvement suggests continuity; and there is a strong indication, in one of Thucydides' arguments hereabouts, that he believed in a degree of continuity between heroic and Classical Greece that would be quite unacceptable to modern minds. In chapter 10, 1 he draws attention to the small size and comparative insignificance of Mycenae, but says how wrong it would be to conclude from this that the expedition to Troy could not have been on the scale described by the poets. In a penetrating study of the argument at this point,[9] R. M. Cook shows that Thucydides' words imply, among other things, that he regards the ruins visible in the fifth century as a yardstick for judging Agamemnon's Mycenae. It is true that some architectural remains of the heroic age must still have been visible in his time – the fortification-walls, the Lion Gate, perhaps one or two beehive tombs – but the city whose ruins Thucydides had seen was primarily Classical Mycenae, sacked by the Argives when he himself was a small boy. The notion that Agamemnon's Mycenae had itself been sacked much earlier, at the end of the heroic age; that its extent was not confined to the circuit of standing walls; that it had lain in ruins until the Classical city had grown up on the levelled débris – all this seems utterly absent from Thucydides' account. He would have said that Classical Mycenae, unlike Classical Athens, had not progressed since heroic times; the possibility that it had had to make a fresh start apparently lay outside his field of surmise.

For Herodotus, the ninth-century Homer had stood at or near the beginning of continuous history; most of what went before him, including presumably some of the post-heroic age, had to be segregated as something other than history, and Homer's evidence for it was of very questionable value. Thucydides, surprisingly, is bolder or more credulous here. Homer, dated to roughly the same period, is treated with much more respect as a historical source, and on other independent grounds Thucydides is disposed to accept the Greek traditions about the heroic age as reliable. Even so remote a figure as Minos, whose sea-empire had been a particular object of Herodotus' uncertainty (p. 6 above), is accepted without question, together with some details of his achievement (1, 4; cf. 1, 8, 2).

By accepting these traditions, Thucydides is able to present the past in such a way as to conform with his model, which is the ostensibly simple one of a steady progress towards peace and prosperity, but which is buttressed by economic and other arguments of some sophistication. He gives us, indeed, the earliest of the many scientific models of the past on which history, and more recently archaeology, have so often depended since.[10] His model is as deeply subjective as many of its successors; one of its signs of weakness is the point with which we have been concerned, the fact that it can provide so little to say about the four-hundred-year period after the coming of the Dorians. This alone, however, is not reason enough for rejecting it; and if we prefer a different version, it had better be supported by arguments at least as convincing as Thucydides'. If Thucydides sees no line of demarcation at the beginning of what we would call the dark age, then for Hesiod, to whom we may return for a moment, there is no line at the end.[11] The gloom of the race of Iron is still with him, in spite of the faint signs of material improvement, and on the whole he expects things to get worse, not better. These authorities are agreed, it seems, only in that none of them subscribes to the modern view of a recession, a period of weakness, and a recovery, between the heroic and Classical ages. If there is a ghost of the modern notion in Homer's disparagement of 'what men are like now', it is a ghost only.

CHRONOGRAPHY

A rather different, and perhaps more substantial, impression can be extracted from ancient evidence of a different kind. So far we have considered the Classical writers only where they are consciously describing the past, or reconstructing it by means of continuous narrative. But there were other, and older, expedients by which the past could be penetrated or, at worst, invented. Some seem more respectable than others today, but in antiquity the valuations may have been reversed; some indeed are used by Thucydides in the same chapters that we have been discussing, and will be mentioned presently. Most prominent is the use of pedigrees, and of a system of chronography based on the generations recorded in a pedigree.[12] The faith which the Greeks placed in this method was perhaps not entirely misplaced. It is possible for a man to record the successive generations of his ancestors – even to record them truthfully – over a long period. A Muslim who today traces his ancestry back to the Prophet is covering more than twice the range of time that Hecataeus of Miletus claimed to span with his pedigree of fourteen human ancestors and a fifteenth divine one.[13] Continuous literacy is not a necessary condition for the survival of such genealogies.

Further, over a long period of years the average length of generation should
settle down to something near the universal average of about thirty years, or
else three to a century; the longer the pedigree, the better the theoretical
chance of an accurate conversion from generations into years, provided that
one can trust the reality of each name in the series. But when it can be shown
that an excessive number of years has been allowed to each generation, or
when, in the case of royal pedigrees, lengths of reign and the attribution of
events to regnal years begin to appear, then suspicion, or something stronger, is justified. Both these faults apply to the genealogies of the Spartan
kings, which were preserved down to Classical times and are retailed by
Herodotus.[14] Their importance lies in the fact that orthodox early Greek
chronology seems to have been very largely founded upon them. King
Leonidas, who succeeded his brother Cleomenes and fell at Thermopylae
in 480, was reckoned 20th in line of descent from Heracles, son having succeeded father in every case except the last. Since the orthodox dating for
Heracles, also supported by Herodotus (11, 145, 4), was at the end of the
fourteenth century, the *average* length of generation on which the Spartan
genealogies were based must have been forty years, an impossibly high
figure which the Greeks (including Herodotus when he thought about it
(11, 142, 2)) soon came to reject. The genealogies are suspect on other
grounds. There were two dynasties at Sparta, the Agiads and the Eury-
pontids, and the awkward necessity to derive the ancestry of both from
Heracles led to a plausible expedient: in the fifth generation after Heracles,
twin sons had been born to the king, and their sons in turn were Agis and
Eurypon, eponyms of the two lines. The preceding kings are shadowy
figures with the faintest claims to reality, and the successors are not above
reproach: on Eurypon's side there occur a few suspiciously allegorical
names – Soös (the safe), Prytanis (the president) and Eunomos (the law-
abiding). These may well have been inserted to cover the fact that the
Eurypontid line had arrived in Sparta some generations later than the
Agiad, so that extra names were needed in order to achieve parity. Some
time before the date when Eratosthenes wrote, in the third century BC, an
elaborate annalistic structure had also been hung on the bare pedigrees;
the kings were provided with reigns to an exact number of years, steadily
and improbably high, and important events were allocated to them.

Much of this construction must obviously be rejected. It would hardly
be over-sceptical to jettison the whole list of regnal years, and all the kings
in the list before Agis and Eurypon. If we then substituted for the forty-year
generation a normal one of about thirty years, and concentrated attention

on the better-attested Agiad line, Agis at the fourteenth generation before Leonidas would have flourished rather before 900 BC. The 'range' of the pedigree would then roughly conform to several other examples of which we know: that of the Philaids at Athens, who in the mid-sixth century BC claimed twelve ancestors, the first of which was said to be Ajax; that of Hecataeus of Miletus, who at a somewhat later date alleged fourteen human ancestors (p. 10 above); that of Heropythus of Chios, whose genealogy, inscribed in the fifth century, lists fourteen ancestors; that of the Asclepiads of Xos, who in the late fifth century reckoned themselves in the nineteenth generation from Asclepius, son of Apollo.[15] These pedigrees, re-interpreted in a modern way, thus suggest the presence of some kind of barrier to this type of recollection in the region of the tenth century BC. But before we accept, even tentatively, such a conclusion, there is a curious fact to be explained away: that the accepted Greek dating of the main events of the heroic age, which is intimately bound up with the early part of the Spartan and other pedigrees, seems in the light of modern evidence to have been startlingly accurate. Herodotus' date for the Trojan War (about 1250 BC) and Eratosthenes' rather more popular one (1183) are both close enough to the archaeological date, estimated as that of the sack of the city now called Troy VII A, for a group of modern scholars to return to each of them like repentant prodigals. Great architectural works at Mycenae and Pylos conform to the traditional dates for Atreus and Nestor. The tradition that Thebes was sacked by the Epigoni at a date slightly before the Trojan expedition has also received general support from the excavation of the site. Earlier still, there are synchronisms at least as striking (p. 14 below). If these traditional dates, as most scholars seem to assume, were reached only by the ramshackle structure of the Spartan pedigree, with forty years to its generation, then their accuracy is a remarkable coincidence. There is indeed only one truly consistent reaction for a scholar who accepts this hypothesis: A. R. Burn in 1935[16] brought the date of the Fall of Troy down to c.1010, in line with his re-interpretation of the generation-lengths – a course both bold and honest, but one which could hardly be followed today in the light of recent archaeological evidence. Perhaps, therefore, another explanation of the phenomenon should be considered : that the dating of the Trojan War, and thence of the whole heroic age, was independently arrived at by the use of some other, perhaps Oriental source; and that the pre-existing structure of pedigrees was, so to speak, hung from it and stretched, as it had to be if it were to reach down into Classical times and give contemporaries a respectable ancestry going back to the heroic age.

The false forty-year generation would then be a by-product, not a cause, of the dating of the heroic age. There is some support for this suggestion in the fact that Eratosthenes, for one, apparently took his date for the Fall of Troy from Ctesias, who claimed, however falsely, to derive it from Oriental documentary sources;[17] Eratosthenes is also said to have used an Egyptian Pharaoh-list as one of his sources.[18] Even on this explanation, however, one would guess that the accuracy of Eratosthenes' date was to a large extent determined by luck; and it is in any case hard to imagine that Herodotus or his predecessor Hecataeus, who both wrote well before Ctesias, could have carried out any such research in establishing their date for the Trojan War. Yet there are pedigrees of the Classical period which, however energetically stretched, cannot be made to reach back to a plausible date for the Trojan War: one, which has the interest of having been apparently known to Herodotus (VI, 35, 1), is that of the Philaids at Athens (see p. 12 above); it passes in only twelve generations from the mid-sixth century back to Ajax and Troy. All this evidence gives a suggestion, if no more, that the old view of the total dependence of early Greek chronography on the Spartan royal pedigrees is exaggerated; there were sources which, disreputable or otherwise, had the merit of independence, and we cannot know the extent to which they were used.

But, whether or not one believes in the possibility of an independently-reached date for the Fall of Troy, the pedigree of forty-year generations and, *a fortiori*, the events ascribed to a generation or reign on such a basis, must remain chronologically valueless. Yet the more credible sections of a pedigree may be salvaged, and rationalized in the manner suggested for the Agiad tree (p. 12 above). Merely to establish a vague date for the beginning of a pedigree can give valuable historical evidence, as Wade-Gery (n. 15) showed in the case of Heropythus of Chios, whose genealogy might reasonably be inferred to go back to the Ionian migration and no further; Hecataeus' first human ancestor may be somewhat earlier than Heropythus' first recorded one, but should still be within the tenth century. Whichever one prefers of the views discussed earlier, it is clear that the method of chronography by pedigree in Greece particularly failed to illuminate the long period of twilight at and after the fall of Mycenae, the twelfth and eleventh centuries BC.

This impression becomes clearer when we consider the Parian Marble, an inscribed chronicle set up in 264/3 BC which offers dates for a series of prehistoric and historical events, expressed in years before the date of its erection.[19] The events are also placed in relation to Athenian history by giving the name of the king, or in the case of later events the magistrate, at Athens; the early part of the chronicle keeps in close harmony with a pedigree for the Athenian kings which, with lengths of reigns, is preserved for us elsewhere. The Marble is thus basically another piece of genealogical reconstruction in its earlier reaches, and it should be looked at in this light. The document begins with the earliest events, and its first salvo of long-range shots must be accounted remarkable either in luck or in accuracy. The first ten 'epochs', which embrace the prelude to the heroic age in Attica, the Argolid and Boeotia, are located in the sixteenth century BC, the century to which archaeologists are unanimous in dating the beginning of the Aegean Late Bronze Age, with its sudden access of wealth and activity on the Greek mainland.[20] The correspondence is more remarkable: the first entry dates the reign of Cecrops at Athens to 1582; the beginning of the Late Helladic period on the Greek mainland is located 'by a tidy approximation or conjecture', but quite independently, at c.1570. The voyage of Danaus from Egypt to the Argolid, which should be more directly connected with the opening of the heroic age at Mycenae, is admittedly placed rather late at 1511. Thereafter, the epochs become more thinly distributed and, on the whole, a shade less plausibly dated; but the placing of the Fall of Troy in 1209, and the consequent date for the events indirectly connected with it, have at least as good a claim to archaeological confirmation as those of Herodotus or Eratosthenes (see p. 12). But a striking change follows; after 26 epochs have been allocated to rather less than 400 years, there ensue a further four centuries in which only four events are recorded; and three of these are given datings which are by modern lights totally unacceptable. The date for the Ionian migration, 1087, if perhaps a shade early, is by far the most plausible of the group. Next are recorded the lifetimes of the poets Hesiod and Homer, at 937 and 907 respectively; the relative order, no less than the high absolute dating, would find few supporters today. Finally, and most objectionable to all, the institution of coinage, and probably of weights and measures, by Pheidon of Argos is placed in 895, a date between two and three hundred years too early. The next date on the Marble, that of the colonization of Syracuse, was also probably elevated to an impossible degree. In the distribution of this group of dates we may detect a sign, not only of the almost total dearth of information about the post-heroic age, but also perhaps of the first and most natural reaction to it: the tendency to push known events upwards, or occasionally downwards, into the gap so as to achieve a more evenly spread series of dates. This weakness is a recurrent one, and has operated as insidiously in modern archaeological and historical scholarship in connection with the dark age as ever it did among Classical writers. Be that as it may, we can draw two main conclusions from the series of dates on the Parian Marble: that chronological information was much more abundant for the sixteenth to twelfth centuries B C than for the eleventh to eighth; and that what there was was somehow, perhaps by pure luck, also more accurate for the earlier period than for the later. If we are right in imputing to the chroniclers a deliberate tendency to move events into the gaps, then by the third century B C there must have been an awareness in Greece that the post-heroic age was suspiciously and intolerably empty. The germ of this is perhaps present in Thucydides, but this would be an explicit reaction, and one from which posterity could have learned.

Such a lesson, however, would immediately be obscured by consideration of another document, a text that is unique both in the period it purports to cover and in its method of doing so. This is the List of Thalassocracies recorded in Eusebius and Jerome, which J. L. Myres[21] derived from a fifth-century document published about the time of the Peloponnesian War, and regarded as a genuine and, in its latter part, accurate record of the changes in tenure of supremacy at sea between 1184 and 480 B C. A minority of scholars has accepted his views, while another minority has strongly criticized them; that the commonest attitude has been one of hesitant neutrality is suggested by R. M. Cook, who has himself called the theory of the Thalassocracies 'very improbable'.[22] Certainly, at any period such a picture could only be a simplified and summary reflection of the state of affairs. Here it will be enough to say that the List, while giving a fairly recognizable picture of the final century of its period, in which the approximate years 580 to 480 are distributed among the last six Thalassocrats, presents a very different spectacle for the six centuries before that. This section of the List can be made to square with historical *possibility* only by drastic emendation of the text, or else by what one of the defenders of the List has called 'heroic surgery'.[23] Even then, we are left in the realms of pure surmise if we try to find any real worth in the uppermost reaches of the List. But the question of real historical value should be sharply distinguished from the question of conformity to Greek historical beliefs. Whether or not Myres' arguments for a fifth-century origin for the List are sound – and this seems the weakest part of his case – most of the List can be shown, piecemeal, to conform to Greek beliefs of *some* period. The picture that it presents is one of the dark age and the Archaic period as a homogeneous whole, both as a field of knowledge and in terms of its subject-matter, the

actual maritime situation. It is just as confident and precise in its enumer-
ation of the earlier Thalassocrats as in that of the later. It therefore tacitly
rejects the possibility of a dark age, even in the limited sense of an unknown
age; and it was natural for later scholars, using it without the aid of the
archaeological evidence by which it is principally judged today, to do the
same – even at the cost of deserting the viewpoint of Herodotus (cf. p. 6),
who shared few of the assumptions behind the List.

OTHER TYPES OF EVIDENCE

We have not exhausted the methods of approach to their past which ancient
writers used. Legend in general was of course a medium of the first importance, but it could only be given a chronological or historical force by use of
the methods we have been discussing, normally by making equations between the generations of different pedigrees. When such methods are
applied today, and the legends then attached to absolute dates (whether
based on ancient or modern authority), the result is clear: an intense 'heroic
age' of some three generations' length appears located in the later years of
Mycenaean civilization, with the Trojan War placed towards the end of it,
and with its essence enshrined above all in Epic. This is flanked by an earlier
heroic age of several generations of mistier figures, whose human member-
ship is heavily interspersed with deities; and by an aftermath of three or four
generations of somewhat inferior personages, remembered chiefly for their
participation in migrations or resistance to them.[24] Then for a time there is
virtually silence, as one would expect if the concept of the heroic age was to
grow up, if there was to be promoted that 'belief in the past as more
adventurous and more glorious than the present'.[25] When legends re-
appear, they tend to be independent of the Epic tradition, and to group
themselves round figures whose connections are downwards into history,
and not upwards into heroic times. The same lesson might therefore be
drawn from a study of Greek legend as from the dates on the Parian Marble:
that there was an 'empty' period in the Greeks' remembrance of their past.
But on the other hand, a chronological function was hardly one of the staple
requirements of Greek legend, and probably few people ever thought of it
in this light. If they did, they may have had ready explanations of the uneven
distribution of the legends in their temporal setting: for example, the
Thucydidean doctrine of the gradual pacification of Greece, which put an
end to the essentially warlike background of the heroic age.

Of the other potential means of access to their past, the Greeks made
rather rare use, so that there is scarcely need to discuss them at length. Two
of the more scientific methods are employed by Thucydides in the same

chapters that we were discussing earlier: arguments from archaeological evidence, and arguments from contemporary analogy.[26] Both of these methods lend themselves to abuse, and Thucydides was rare among Classical Greeks in trying to use them to reach the historical truth. Archaeological evidence, in particular, normally appears in Classical literature and history as a weapon for propaganda: the chance excavation of graves, and often the transportation of their contents, are recurrent themes, and the aim is usually to prove the antiquity or authenticity of a city's past achievements, or else to use the discovery as a talisman of success in some current enterprise. Plutarch and Aelian's story of Solon and the graves on Salamis (*Solon*, x, 3 : Aelian *VH* v, 14 and v11, 19) is a typical example; we may also recall Cleisthenes' exhumation and re-interment at Sicyon of the bones of Melanippus, and the Spartan and Athenian appropriations, from their graves abroad, of the bones of Orestes and Theseus respectively.[27] Next to human bones, excavated written documents were the favourite instrument for this manipulation of history; we read of a whole series running from Acousilaus of Argos, who in the late sixth century is said to have based his faked genealogies on 'bronze tablets' excavated by chance, down to the Emperor Nero's tendentious interpretation of some documents, exposed at Knossos by an earthquake in A D 66, as Phoenician. In a separate category were the false dedications, connected with or even inscribed by legendary figures, which appeared in many Greek temples and shrines, and in which the Temple of Athena at Lindos specialized to a degree which placed it beyond all rivals. But occasionally the evidence of antiquities was enlisted in the cause of scientific enquiry: it appears in the pages of Herodotus, who mentions the architectural remains of the site called The Camps in the Nile Delta (11, 154, 7), given to his Greek mercenaries by Psammetichos 1 in the mid-seventh century, and abandoned about a hundred years later. Thucydides in his opening chapters uses such evidence twice: in the passage on the ruins of Mycenae whose reasoning we discussed earlier (p. 9), and in the obscurer question of the 'Carian' graves on Delos;[28] in each case his purpose is honest and scientific. Arguments from contemporary analogy were also used by both these historians; in Thucydides' case, particularly arguments from contemporary barbarian or semi-barbarian peoples to past Greeks – again, an exemplary procedure. It might perhaps have been possible for the use of one of these two methods to lead Thucydides, or some later Greek, to infer the existence of a 'dark age' in his people's past, but it is hardly surprising that this did not happen. The handling of archaeological evidence in antiquity could not be expected to be accurate; similar

B

sporadic archaeological finds, and anthropological observations, took place in Greece throughout the nineteenth century without such a theory being formulated.

The other, and final, type of evidence conspicuously used by Thucydides in the course of his argument about early Greece, and by others elsewhere, is that of Homer and 'the Old Poets'. These formed an obvious enough source for a Classical historian to tap, but it was evidently one often neglected, even when the prestige of the Epic poems as fountainheads of moral and practical wisdom stood at its greatest height; greater attention to Homer's actual words, for example, would surely have saved Greek and Roman antiquaries from the heresy of making him an exact contemporary of the Trojan War. On the other hand, there may be 'hidden' references to Homer, which lie behind ancient theories not expressly said to depend on him. The best chance of detecting such dependence would seem to be given when the theory is apparently mistaken in point of fact, and can be traced to no other source. A good example, if the case could be proven, would be that of the Greek beliefs about early Phoenician penetration and settlement in the western Mediterranean. Rhys Carpenter, in 1958, put forward the argument that the antiquity of the Phoenician settlements in the West had been consistently exaggerated by Greek tradition from at least the time of Thucydides, and subsequent archaeological discoveries have, in the main, served to confirm the soundness of this view.[29] The explanation he suggested was this: that the Greeks' respect for Homer compelled them to accept his picture of the heroic age as an accurate one, free of anachronisms; Homer's repeated mention of the Phoenicians, especially in the *Odyssey*, therefore inevitably led to the belief that the Phoenicians were active in these waters from heroic times on. There are certain difficulties about Carpenter's view: for example, it falls short of explaining why the Phoenicians, who even in the *Odyssey* are only seen on the outer fringes of the Aegean, and whose activity further west than Ithaka is little more than hinted at by Homer, should later be credited with achievements far more extravagant both in temporal and in spatial distance. But it might still be possible for these extravagances to have grown from the original core of the Homeric passages; and even if we decline, as too simple an expedient, to attribute the whole responsibility for these traditions to Homer, it still seems likely that Homer's testimony would be called in to buttress a tradition of this sort, particularly a weakly-based one.[30] In either case, it would involve the Greeks' treating Homer as a historical authority to illuminate the period of the dark age.

To try to sum up the testimony of extant ancient literature, on a subject with which it is nowhere explicitly concerned, may seem misguided. But there are two recurrent attitudes to that portion of their past which fell between the end of the heroic age and the dawn of continuous, documented history, which we can detect on the part of the Greeks. One group of attitudes may be classed together only in so far as it attempted to reconstruct, by some means, a scheme for the past which would draw this period into a continuous panorama of time, extending far beyond it. This was a natural reaction for the Greeks who believed, rightly, that they were racially descended from the inhabitants of Greece in the heroic age. We see it at its simplest in Hesiod's description of the Five Races, a piece of myth-making which must in part go back to an earlier and perhaps foreign source, but which also registers a sharp qualitative decline, and comes near to suggesting that a dark age had succeeded the heroic age. His despairing picture could not long remain acceptable to Greeks, however. The scientific model of Thucydides' opening chapters, although we may see it as a fifth-century answer to Hesiod, and although its underlying doctrine of progression directly contradicts Hesiod's basic attitude, still treats the past as a continuous field of knowledge, and expressly acknowledges its debt to Homer and the 'Old Poets' (of whom Hesiod may be one) on no less than five occasions (cf. n.26). This same attitude to the past is also present in the older and less scientific approach of the genealogists and mythographers, who claimed to bridge the post-heroic age with pedigrees; we hear that two of the earliest exponents, Acousilaus of Argos and Hecataeus of Miletus, were in fact preoccupied, to different degrees, with the interpretation or re-interpretation of Hesiod, and of other early poets. Even the List of Thalassocracies, with its glib summary of seven centuries of sea-power, shares the same assumptions for the period it covers. Why this period begins only with the Fall of Troy is another question; the studied omission of the most famous of all Thalassocrats, Minos, ill accords with the emphasis placed by Thucydides on the early Cretan sea-power, and is a serious objection to Myres' view that Thucydides used the List or something like it. The Parian Marble, finally, transparently fails to fill the gap which the List of Thalassocracies covers so speciously, but its list of epochs seems designed with a similar end in view. One of the features common to these authorities is that the Dorian Invasion, which looms so large in almost all modern discussions of the dark age, as a kind of milestone marking its inception, is given a much less conspicuous place by those of the sources which mention it; it is simply recorded as one migration among many, with several predecessors (and at least one successor) of comparable importance and similar nature. There may be a lesson for modern scholarship here.

Divergent as their attitudes are, the authorities we have considered may be grouped together as 'continuum-theorists', in that they offered, or pretended to offer, a continuous account of the course of events, at least in some particular field, from heroic times down to the Archaic or Classical periods. They are opposed, therefore, to that view of the past which drew a sharp line across it, an upper limit of real history, at a certain not too distant point. If we call this latter view Herodotean, we should remember that such a name would be based practically on a single passage in the *Histories* of Herodotus (III, 122, 2), who elsewhere confidently offers information, including approximate dates, for events which lay far beyond his historical limit. But one of the themes of his work, from the opening chapters onwards, is its deliberate concentration on the historical epoch rather than the remoter past. The line of division would no doubt be drawn at, or rather before, the time of Homer; but Herodotus himself coupled this attitude with a view of Homer that he seems to have reached entirely on his own – that Homer wrote at a comparatively late date, and was so unreliable as a historical source that he could be suspected of being mistaken in so fundamental a theme of the *Iliad* as the presence of Helen at Troy (II, 116-20; and compare II, 23). Such a view can hardly have recommended itself to the majority of fifth-century Greeks, and one may doubt whether Herodotus' accompanying theory of the limits of true history was any more popular; certainly it is harder to trace in contemporary and later literature than the 'continuum-theories'. On the specific subject of the post-heroic age, however, it could afford to avoid dogma as its rivals could not. A demonstration that there had been a drastic and unprecedented fall in the level of civilization at the end of the heroic age would have been distressing to most of the continuum-theorists; to the Herodotean view it was a matter of indifference.

One reason for dwelling at length on the ancient theories of early Greek history is simply that the evidence used, and indeed the theories themselves, remained constant in essentials right down to the last decades of the nineteenth century. In the Victorian attitude to early Greece, the dominant force was the same view that we have called 'Herodotean'. George Grote, and others after him, repudiated the idea of a historical knowledge of any period before the first Olympiad in Greece; when confronted with the empty centuries that followed the supposed 'Heroic Age', Grote's answer was that 'when we make what appears to me the proper distinction between legend and history, it will be seen that a period of blank time between the two is perfectly conformable to the conditions under which the former is generated'.[31] Once again Homer (in so far as one could refer to him by a personal name in this heyday of the analyst school) had taken his place at the beginning of Greek history; if his date was necessarily vague, that mattered little so long as his testimony was treated with almost total incredulity.

The more recent part of the story need not long detain us. The archaeo-logical unveiling of the heroic age began with Schliemann's discoveries in the 1870s, but this brought no swift comprehension of the full sequence of events. By slow and hotly-debated steps, the chronology of the two main styles of painted pottery known from early Greece, the 'Mycenaean' and the 'Dipylon', was agreed on: far from overlapping, as some had at first main-tained, the two periods were found to be separated by an interval of time, a discovery which gave birth to the modern notion of the dark age. Looking back, one finds the most conspicuous statement of the theory appearing, perhaps a shade prematurely, in the first edition of Gilbert Murray's *The Rise of the Greek Epic*. Soon the dark age had become an article of orthodox dogma; perhaps its apogee came with the description of this period in 1933, by one of the noted scholars of the day, as 'the poorest and darkest epoch in all Greek history except for the Stone Age'.[32] But there were already dissidents then, and they have become more numerous since. Perhaps the most important tenet of the dark age theory, the belief in the loss of the art of writing and the subsequent period of illiteracy in Greece, between the disuse of the Linear B script and the adoption of the alphabet, has been called into question; others have doubted the validity of the archaeological evidence on which knowledge of the dark age is otherwise almost entirely based; others again have seen the Homeric poems as witnesses offering evidence for every period in succession from the sixteenth century BC to the end of the eighth (or possibly even later), including – perhaps to a marked degree – the centuries just after the fall of the Mycenaean civilization.[33] This last theory is perhaps incompatible with the view of these years as a period of abject gloom and obscurity; in this respect, it compensates for another major tendency in recent Homeric scholarship, the steady lowering of the date at which the *Iliad* and *Odyssey* are believed to have reached their final form, which would otherwise tend to dissociate Homer from the dark age. All in all, a consensus is perhaps as far away today as it was in the fifth century BC.

Notes

1] In *The Rise of the Greek Epic* (1st edition), 29

2] The term (and perhaps the conception) seem to have remained a speciality of English-speaking scholars. An alternative name, the 'Greek Middle Ages', was adopted by Eduard Meyer in his *Geschichte des Alterthums*, II (1893), 249f. and used by A. Furtwängler in his *Antike Gemmen* (1900); it was taken over in English by A. R. Burn in *The World of Hesiod* (1936), but seems to have dropped out of favour in both languages; cf. H. Bengtson, *Griechische Geschichte* (1950), 51, n.3, who himself later refers to a 'dark period of transition' (61). On the use (or misuse) of the term in the contemporary Near East, see W. F. Albright in *The Aegean and the Near East*, ed. S. Weinberg (1956), 144-64; and for an earlier period, in the Anatolian Bronze Age, A. Goetze in *Iraq* 25 (1963), 124. A distinction from the Dark Ages after the fall of the Western Roman Empire (a more familiar and geographically far more widely applicable use of the name) is best served by the use of the singular form, and perhaps of small letters

3] 37th Earl Grey Memorial Lecture (1957), especially 15-23

4] M. I. Finley, *Historia* 6 (1957), 136

5] See especially J. Gwyn Griffiths in *Journal of the History of Ideas* 17 (1956), 109-19; H. C. Baldry, *ibid.* 553-4 would rightly modify some of his conclusions. For recent datings of Hesiod, G. S. Kirk in *Hésiode et son Influence* (Fondation Hardt, *Entretiens* VII (1960)), 63; M. I. Finley, *The World of Odysseus* (1956), 34-5; H. T. Wade-Gery, *The Poet of the Iliad* (1952), 1

6] See E. R. Dodds, *Fifty years of Classical scholarship* (1954), 5

7] For a summary of the ancient views, see G. Raddatz in Pauly-Wissowa, *Real-encyclopädie* VIII, 2 (1913), 2206-13

8] Elsewhere, at VI, 2, 5, Thucydides does name one event which he would date to this obscurer period, the migration of the Sicels to Sicily 'about 300 years before any Greeks came to Sicily', i.e. about 1030 BC

9] *BSA* 50 (1955), 266-7

10] See Stuart Piggott, *Ancient Europe* (1965), 5f., for a critique of such models

11] It is also true, as Mr M. C. Stokes has shown me, that Hesiod is (perhaps deliberately) vague about the transition from the race of Heroes to the race of Iron, and about the relationship, or lack of it, between them; whereas in the previous cases he has explicitly distinguished each race from its predecessor in terms of lineage

12] For an excellent account, see chapter 11 of E. J. Forsdyke's *Greece before Homer* (1956)

13] Hdt. II, 143, 4

14] Hdt. VII, 204; VIII, 131, 2. See especially A. R. Burn, *JHS* 55 (1935), 130f., Wade-Gery, *op. cit.* (n.5), 27-9, and G. L. Huxley, *Early Sparta* (1963), 19-24 and 102 n.71

15] H. T. Wade-Gery, *The Poet of the Iliad* (1952), 8f., fig. 1, and 88-94; cf. the conclusions of W. G. Forrest, *A History of Sparta* (1968), 20-3, 27

16] *JHS* 55 (1935), 131, 146

17] Forsdyke, *op. cit.* (n.12), 35, 68-78

18] See F. Jacoby, *Apollodors Chronik* (*Philologische Untersuchungen* 16 (1902)), 19-21 and 399f., frag. 117

19] Forsdyke, *op. cit.* 50-61

20] See F. H. Stubbings in *CAH*, revised edition, vol. I, ch. vi, 70, 74 and vol. II, ch. xiv, 12

21] *JHS* 26 (1906), 84-130

22] *JHS* 66 (1946), 69-70 and n.26

23] A. R. Burn in *JHS* 47 (1927), 167

24] Cf. the table in Myres, *Who were the Greeks?* 344-5 and N. G. L. Hammond in *CAH*, revised edition, vol. II, ch. xxxvi, (fascicle 13), 22-50

25] Bowra, *op. cit.* (n.3), 15

26] R. M. Cook, *BSA* 50 (1955), 266f. and n.29

27] Forsdyke, *op. cit.* 109 (Hdt. I, 68; Plutarch, *Theseus* XXXVI); 142 on Acousilaus; 154 on Nero; 44f. on Lindos

28] I, 8, 1; on this see most recently *JHS* 84 (1964), 113

29] Carpenter, *AJA* 62 (1958), 35-6; cf. 68 (1964), 178; Lepcis Magna and Sabratha, *AJA* 69 (1965), 123f., 152; Motya, *Annual of the Leeds University Oriental Society* 4 (1962-63), 109, 118. J. Heurgon's attribution of an eighth-century date to the Punic cemetery near Almuñécar in S. Spain (*JRS* 56 (1966), 2) seems controverted by the excavator's report, *Madrider Mittheilungen* 4 (1963), 9-38, but the settlement at 'Cortijo de los Toscanos' (*AA* 79 (1964), 476-

93) could go back to the late eighth century, and there are striking new discoveries at the Rio Tinto mines, reported in *Antiquity* 43 (1969), 124-31. However, the very high dating sometimes given to the first Punic ivories in Spain is shaken by the closely analogous finds in a seventh-century context on Samos – see J. Boardman, *Gnomon* 39 (1967), 845-6 and *The Greeks Overseas* (1964), 219. By contrast, see below, pp. 334-6, for the antiquity of Greek trading and colonial activity in the West.

30] I prefer this view to the older theory that Homer's 'Phoenicians' were a confused memory of the Minoans or other Bronze Age peoples – see M. P. Nilsson's criticisms, *Homer and Mycenae* (1933), 131-2. The recent claim that widespread Phoenician trading activity did actually take place over much of the Mediterranean in the Late Bronze Age (see G. F. Bass in *Transactions of the American Philosophical Society* 57, 8 (1967), 74-8, 164-7, etc.) would naturally affect this argument, but it remains largely unsubstantiated

31] *History of Greece*, 1st ed. (1846), II, 45

32] M. P. Nilsson, *Homer and Mycenae* 246

33] On literacy, see A. J. B. Wace in the introduction to Ventris and Chadwick, *Documents in Mycenaean Greek* (1956); for predecessors in this view, see e.g. J. P. Harland, *AJA* 38 (1934), 90. On the archaeological evidence, R. M. Cook, *Antiquity* 34 (1960), 179; on Homer, M. I. Finley, *The World of Odysseus* (1956), esp. 51, and *Historia* 6 (1957), 159; G. S. Kirk in *Museum Helveticum* 17 (1960), 192-3 and *PCPS* 187 (1961), 38f.

2

The Regional Pottery-styles

◆ ◆ ◆
◆ ◆
◆

For the study of any period, a chronological framework is desirable; and an era which spans three centuries or more, and stands near the boundaries of true history, is too long to be treated *en bloc*. Yet it needs constantly to be emphasized, even today, that it is unsafe to generalize about the dark age of Greece, to infer conditions from one phase of it to others. Equally salutary, if of somewhat less recent growth, is the realization that we cannot make inferences from one *area* to others. The 'horizontal' and the 'longitudinal' divisions alike are of fundamental importance in the understanding of this period.

Both kinds of division are largely made possible by the use of one aid, the classification of pottery-styles. It was by this means, originally, that the very existence of the dark age as a period of time was established; and it is this which still holds out the best prospects for interpreting the period aright. Geographically, it underlines some of the regional characteristics within Greece. Chronologically, it should at the very least save us from the ultimate pitfall of mistaking causes for effects, and *vice versa*; and perhaps also from the commoner one of illustrating tendencies and generalities with examples taken from a different set of circumstances. A detailed chronology, even a relative one, may never be achieved for the early Iron Age in Greece; but this should not prevent us from aspiring to one.

A pottery series is an elusive thing: more so than one would gather from the modern archaeological syntheses, which often build on generations of search, trial and error in the classification of the pottery of a culture. There are many conditions to be satisfied before a series can be well enough established to serve as an accurate chronological instrument. In the period that concerns us, the best aid, that of well-stratified occupation-sites, is almost entirely absent; its place has to be taken by graves. The resultant difficulties are much increased by another factor, the prevalence of regionalism and localism in Greece at this time. This is one of the most important characteristics of the period, and its effect on the chronological problems is profound. Whereas in the Aegean Late Bronze Age, down to about 1200 BC at any rate, the establishment of relative and absolute chronologies for the Mycenaean pottery series – in so far as this has been achieved – has made possible conclusions about the whole Mycenaean world, the pottery of early Iron Age Greece, even if its analysis progresses equally far, will do no such thing. An agreed series for Attic Protogeometric gives no indication of the dating of the pottery-series in those regions which are independent of Attic influence, and only very vague ones for the schools whose relationship to Attic, though undoubted, is of debatable nature. At an earlier period, in the eleventh century BC, it is clear that within Attica itself, two areas whose centres of settlement and production cannot have been more than twenty miles apart were at the same time using pottery of two independent classes, not directly related to each other.[1] To draw up a relative chronological scheme, let alone an absolute one, for Greece in the eleventh, tenth, ninth and eighth centuries is thus no simple task; for many regions, it is even difficult to tell whether or not there are gaps in the pottery-series.

But pessimism must not be carried too far. The horizontal divisions between the periods of the early Iron Age are neither simple nor continuous, but they exist. It is usually possible to draw a distinction between each main style, its predecessor and its successor, even though there are invariably transitional styles. But the longitudinal divisions, by locality, are in a sense stronger; they break up the horizontal lines into shorter sections, often set at different levels. It is especially hard to draw these lines of division, of either type, when they divide not two known fields from one another, but the known from the unknown; such a situation, as we shall see, is all too common.

TERMINOLOGY

The nomenclature of the pottery-styles of the early Iron Age, and the application of the names, have now reached a stage of fairly general agreement, in spite of the acknowledged inadequacy or unsuitability of some of the terms themselves. The duration of the early Iron Age in Greece is fixed by the placing in time of the two pottery-styles which form its termini. The 'Mycenaean' and the 'Dipylon' – the latter soon replaced by the more serviceable term 'Geometric' – were early identified as distinct ceramic phases, and they have remained acceptable names for their periods; when, gradually and after much confusion, it became clear that there were at least two intervening transitional stages, a decadent after-life of the Mycenaean style giving way to an austere forerunner of the full Geometric style, it seemed equally natural to name them 'Submycenaean' and 'Protogeometric'. Originally all these names were based on the pottery, there being in some cases little else to apply them to; the process of extending a name from a pottery-style to cover a whole era of culture, and of giving a provisional duration in years to each era, has created misleading situations, as later discoveries about the pottery itself have shown. The most important case in point is that of Submycenaean, which will be discussed presently (pp. 30-3). 'Protogeometric' and 'Geometric' are in a rather better case. For one thing, the names rightly suggest that they apply basically to the pottery alone; for another, they are applied to periods when there were strong unifying traits in the pottery of large areas of the Greek world. It should be emphasized that, in all essentials, these two styles are merely successive phases of the same movement; both represent 'Geometric' pottery in its broadest sense. This means that, although there are clear stylistic and technical advances which mark them off from what had gone before, it is harder to distinguish them from each other, and to define in words the scope of 'Protogeometric'.[2] Desborough has suggested the fundamental characteristics that such a style should possess: it must be based on a Geometric system of decoration, and it should be the direct forerunner, in its own locality, of a subsequent Geometric school; or, failing such a school, it must be reasonably close to other local styles which have already been named Protogeometric.

This perfectly acceptable convention nevertheless brings anomalies, not least in terms of chronology. There are regional Protogeometric styles which satisfy the definition and yet lie partly or wholly outside the time-span of other Protogeometric styles. There are other examples whose title to the name is questionable on different grounds: the outstanding example is the school which flourished in central Crete, for it retains to a remarkable degree the decorative vocabulary of the preceding Late Minoan and Sub-minoan styles, and keeps certain Bronze Age shapes of vessel in use throughout its duration. But to revive a more accurate name for this school – such as 'Central Cretan pre-Geometric' which was once proposed for it – would today only lead to confusion. At a later date, long after full Geometric styles had been adopted in many areas of Greece, there occurred a further phase at Knossos which may still be described as 'Protogeometric' by virtue of the technique of clay and varnish, and of a few vase-shapes, which are

see 39

taken over from the preceding period. This phase has been christened 'Protogeometric B', but with great reluctance; its title to the name is doubly indirect.[3] Another example of a problematical style is that centred upon a single vase-type, produced in several regions. The low-footed skyphos with compass-drawn pendent semicircles round the body was inevitably *see 26* classed as Protogeometric, both on account of its main decorative motif, which is one of the very commonest in Protogeometric, and because its shape probably developed from an Attic Protogeometric type of skyphos with a high conical foot, and concentric circles instead of semicircles. But when the examples of the low-footed shape are examined in their context, the evidence points uniformly to a date at or after the end of Protogeometric, not only in Attica but sometimes in the very areas where they are being produced. Here again, an accurate if even less euphonious term has been suggested, 'Sub-protogeometric', which may conceivably prevail in the end.[4]

Because Geometric pottery has come to be associated with a primitive era at the dawn of Greek history, its presence is often taken as a sign that something in the nature of a dark age is still prevalent. In fact Greece had witnessed, before the end of *any* local Geometric style, a renaissance in almost every field of life; here as elsewhere, the landmarks of the major changes in pottery-style prove misleading as the termini of eras. But to this must be added the element of regional variation: there are differences of fifty years and more in the dates at which different areas of Greece repudiated the abstraction of Geometric vase-decoration, usually under the new influence of Oriental art. The year 700 BC, long ago estimated to be the rough date at which the Geometric style came to an end, at least in Athens, continues to 'exercise a fascination over the minds of scholars' as the proper date for this change of style all over Greece.[5] Yet it has become clear that this picture is far from the truth, even for some areas near the heart of Greek culture: it is salutary to recall that Geometric pottery of some kind was still in partial or general use alike in the Sparta of Tyrtaeus, the Argos of Pheidon, the Ionia of Callinus or the Cyclades of Archilochus. The latest Geometric or 'Subgeometric' style is closer in time to Pericles than it is to the Protogeometric.

We have surveyed the main terms used of the pottery of early Iron Age Greece, and it is time now to consider the pottery itself. Here certain limitations must be established straight away. Pottery retains its vital function of providing a chronological framework on which to hang any other scraps of knowledge that we can muster; it also provides one of the elements of regional difference; it also allows of a few social and economic inferences, within a circumscribed range. But once it is used to shape our whole picture of Greece in the dark age, it becomes not helpful but dangerous. The major divisions and changes of pottery-style are not always the best divisions of cultural eras. We have already seen an important instance of this, in that the dark age of Greece, in any meaningful sense of the term, does not end with a major change in the style of pottery-decoration; presently, when we come to consider its beginnings, we shall find that there are problems of the same kind there (pp. 30-3). If pottery provides no valid outer termini for a period, it may be doubted whether the internal divisions according to pottery-style will be any more meaningful. The element of regionalism further weakens the temporal content of ceramic phases: even when we adopt such a simple term as 'Protogeometric Greece', we are using an ambiguous, perhaps almost meaningless expression. We cannot even take the phrase, by transference, to refer to a stage in metallurgical progress or funerary practice, as prehistorians often can, without being faced by insurmountable anomalies. A Classical archaeologist who used the term 'Black-figure Greece' would stand in no greater risk of being misled.

This is one reason why I believe that a close analysis of the morphological and decorative developments of Greek pottery in the early Iron Age would be out of place in this book. A more important one is that such a survey would in any case be beyond my powers; what I offer instead is something inferior, an interpretative summary of others' researches. And here I must acknowledge an outstanding debt to two colleagues, Mr Vincent Desborough and Mr Nicolas Coldstream, who have both freely discussed their findings with me, and whose books provide the detailed analyses of early Greek pottery which I cannot pretend to offer.

The Latest Bronze Age Styles and the Problem of Submycenaean

The beginnings of the Iron Age in Greece certainly lie in the eleventh century BC. Whether or not we equate this time with the beginning of the true dark age, it is a fact that the immediately preceding period of decline belongs entirely to the Mycenaean age; indeed, now that the relative succession of pottery-styles has become clearer, the most remarkable quality of this Mycenaean twilight epoch is shown to be its persistence and forcefulness. The mere fact that pottery shaped and decorated in the Mycenaean tradition, and no other painted pottery, continued to be produced, will not serve as a conclusive cultural indicator; but when we find that, throughout the twelfth century and even into the eleventh, a substantial number of Mycenaean settlements remain in occupation; that the signs of fire and destruction which marked the years shortly before 1200 seldom now appear; that the time-honoured funerary practices of family interment in chamber-tombs, and more rarely in tholos-tombs, persist; that the traditional Mycenaean dress-ornaments and female clay figurines are still found – when faced with all this, we are bound to conclude that Mycenaean culture, if moribund, is not yet dead. The faint historical light thrown on Greece in the thirteenth century by the references in Hittite and Egyptian documents, and by the Linear B tablets, has gone; but it does not follow that Greece has yet entered a dark age, any more than the early Mycenaean period from the Shaft-graves to the fall of Knossos was a dark age.

I have given above an incomplete and indeed one-sided account of the Mycenaean III C period; there is another and darker side to the story, but it is the pottery that we are concerned with here, and in this we can see signs of what is still recognizably Mycenaean vitality for much of the period. The Argolid, the heart-land of Mycenaean culture, had received the heaviest blows in the era of destruction, but is also witnessed perhaps the most powerful recovery: the men who painted the Warrior Vase, and who developed and diffused the highly competent pottery of the Close 1 Style, were hardly living in a dark age. The destruction of the granary at Mycenae itself, perhaps about 1150, often treated as the last nail in the coffin of Mycenaean civilization, is isolated and has no measurable effect on the development of events; indeed, a recent authority has suggested that the burning may have been merely due to accident. Occupation was resumed at Mycenae, while at nearby sites like Argos and Asine it was apparently uninterrupted; Tiryns, once thought to have been almost extinguished in the earlier destruction of about 1200, has now been found to have housed a major settlement of Mycenaean III C date.[6] Other areas of Greece had different experiences: in several, notably Achaea, the island of Kephallenia, Eastern Attica, the Cyclades and the Dodecanese, there are positive signs of an increase of Mycenaean population in the twelfth century, caused perhaps by the incursion of refugees from more troubled areas. Intermittent contacts with each other, and with other outlying areas of the Mycenaean world, were maintained; a new settlement on the island of Chios was made; Cyprus receives its greatest infusion of life from the Mycenaean world in the twelfth century, and an architectural revival and some fine work in metal and ivory are the results. By contrast, Messenia and Laconia appear to have suffered so heavily from destruction and depopulation

1. The 'Close Style' of the Argolid in Mycenaean III C: stirrup-jar
from tomb 5 at Asine. Height 23·5 cm; earlier 12th century BC.

around 1200 that they can almost be said to have entered a dark age then,
over a century before the rest of Greece; in Western Attica, too, several
sites seem to be deserted. Thessaly presents a unique picture: the palace at
Iolkos was destroyed, but apparently at a slightly later date than the palaces
further south; elsewhere in Thessaly, and even in the settlement surrounding the palace itself, there is no destruction and almost all the sites, except
for a few in the north, remain in occupation. Crete, finally, having never
been in any real sense a part of the Mycenaean world, had been immune to
some of the vicissitudes of the last two centuries; she presents in the twelfth
century the aspect of a peaceful island, assimilating perhaps at least one
wave of Mycenaean settlers, by no means devoid of artistic activity, in touch
with the Dodecanese and Cyprus, and even able to influence the outstanding pottery-style of the mainland at this time, the Close Style of the
Argolid.[7]

When can the element of the new and the unknown, which should mark
the end of Mycenaean culture, first be detected? Already in Mycenaean
III C pottery we have the signs of a significant new phenomenon, a variegated style with different local manifestations, in place of the fairly uniform

pottery of III B. After this, we shall be more ready to find Mycenaean culture terminating at different moments in different areas of Greece; and this is what happens. If there were a class of pottery which could be shown, throughout Greece, to stand in the relation of a degenerate aftermath to Mycenaean pottery, then a clear temporal horizon would exist. Such a class was believed to have been found in the pottery named Submycenaean, and the name was widely applied by other scholars besides archaeologists for this reason. But in 1964 Desborough put forward strong arguments for the view that the 'Submycenaean' pottery did not after all represent a separate chronological entity, so much as a geographical variant.[8] It was, he showed, suspiciously narrow in its distribution, being largely confined, in its fully characterized form, to two excavated cemeteries, on the island of Salamis and in the Kerameikos at Athens. Here in Western Attica the pottery of the latest fully Mycenaean class, Furumark's 'III C I c', is curiously absent: the settlement material from the west slope of the Acropolis at Athens extends only into the earlier part of Mycenaean III C, while the chamber-tomb burials on and near the Acropolis slopes stop even earlier. Elsewhere, and most significantly in the still quite well-populated Argolid, there was a supposed chronological gap, with little or no 'Submycenaean' available to fill it, between the latest Mycenaean (Furumark's III C I c) and the earliest Protogeometric material. Yet there were apparent signs of a direct connection between these two phases at Argos. These and other considerations led Desborough to conclude that the 'gap' in the series at Argos might after all be non-existent; that something approaching continuity between the latest Mycenaean and the earliest Protogeometric may have existed, not only in Argos but in several other regions where Submycenaean material was barely represented, but where the other two phases were found. If this is so, then the Submycenaean of Athens and Salamis, which in both cases is the earliest style represented at a newly-established cemetery, must be moved upwards in time so as to overlap almost entirely with the latest Mycenaean at Argos and elsewhere; it can hardly be pushed downwards relatively, since as we shall see it is succeeded by a Protogeometric style at least as early as its counterparts elsewhere. This move will also have the effect of reducing the presumed earlier 'gap' in the Western Attic series (above). 'Submycenaean', then, does not represent an aftermath of decay following on the fall of Mycenaean civilization all over Greece. On the contrary, it marks an important variant style, developed mainly in the very restricted area of Western Attica at a time when the rest of Greece was ceramically speaking almost static, even though the development was on a downward slope; and, more important, it was directly ancestral to the much greater innovations of Protogeometric, which in Attica grows directly from it by continuous and well-attested stages.

Such are the implications of Desborough's theory. But it must be said that it has already been challenged by J. Deshayes, one of the French excavators of Argos during the 1950s, who has now published his findings at the Deiras cemetery on the edge of the town;[9] and, apparently independently, by C.-G. Styrenius in his *Submycenaean Studies*. To these scholars, 'Submycenaean' remains a major chronological entity in Argos and elsewhere as well as Western Attica; Deshayes believes that its earliest stages are represented in the Deiras cemetery in two distinct phases, and that the pottery of both phases antedates the finds from Salamis and the Kerameikos. He further argues that a third and latest period of Submycenaean, corresponding with the Salamis and Kerameikos cemeteries, is represented not indeed at Deiras but elsewhere in Argos, in the graves from the area of the modern town, near the Museum and the Classical theatre, to which may be added a group recently found in Tripolis St (below, p. 151). Now there are several quite distinct points involved here. Deshayes' first contention is primarily a question of nomenclature, as he himself shows by equating the first of his three phases with Furumark's III c I c; but this terminological difference must not be allowed to mask the main conflict, which arises from Deshayes' other argument. Here there are two considerations which, to me, stand decisively in the way of Deshayes' view, and support that of Desborough. First, the duration of the two Attic Submycenaean cemeteries, each with more than a hundred graves, must cover a substantial period of time; especially since, as has been observed,[10] the scope of the Salamis burials seems to extend over an earlier period than that of the first ones at the Kerameikos. By compressing these burials into a single phase, represented even on his own account by immeasurably fewer burials at Argos, Deshayes has strained the evidence to make it conform with his theory. Second, and hardly less significant, is the fact that Desborough himself, after close examination of the pottery from the Argos town graves to which Deshayes refers, concluded that 'almost every one of these tombs shows the influence of Protogeometric from the very beginning';[11] in other words, that the Argos material from outside the Deiras cemetery should belong largely or entirely later than the Attic material with which Deshayes groups it. On this considered judgment, the evidence from Argos would point, on Deshayes' argument, to the conclusion that there is a substantial gap in time in the Argive series, between the

2. Later Mycenaean III c: stirrup-jar from Deiras chamber tomb xxix at Argos, probably contemporary with the Submycenaean of Western Attica. Height, less restored base, 13·6 cm; *c.* 1100 bc.

latest Deiras material and the earliest from the town site: it is not clear that the new Tripolis St graves (p. 151) would do much to fill this gap. The unlikelihood of such a lacuna, and the difficulty of compressing the two Attic cemeteries into the short compass which Deshayes suggests, incline one to think that Desborough's conclusion was nearer the truth: Western Attic Submycenaean must largely overlap in time with the latest Deiras material.

The original choice of the term 'Submycenaean' thus seems, in the light of after events, unfortunate. But there would be difficulties in transferring the name to a broader class of material, quite apart from the confusion caused by a change in terminology. Much of Mycenaean III c pottery belongs to a period when, as we have seen, a measure of peace and even recovery prevailed in many areas of Greece, and strong Mycenaean characteristics are still prevalent; the period as a whole does not invite the name 'Submycenaean', which indeed few would now propose to apply to it. As for the III c I c phase of Furumark's classification, which Deshayes has in effect put forward as a candidate for this name, the difficulty here is that it is

c

not nearly so sharply distinguished, in terms of ceramic style, from the preceding phases as is the case with Attic Submycenaean; nor is its advent marked in the same way by external events, such as the adoption of new cemetery-sites. The final level of destruction at Mycenae, for example, falls not at the opening of this phase, but well before the end of the preceding Mycenaean III c I b period. The truth is that there is no really satisfactory dividing-line within the series of the Mycenaean III c style. It is better, therefore, to accept the present terminology, even if this means that we can no longer use the expression 'Submycenaean Greece' with reference to any archaeological criteria. The most important lesson is once again that the pottery-series, while fairly reliable in giving the relative sequence of periods, is here shown to be defective at more than one point as an indicator of the broader division of time into major eras.

QUALITIES OF THE SUBMYCENAEAN STYLE

What, then, are the qualities of the Submycenaean style? Our material for judging it is slight, being derived from two cemeteries of poorly-furnished graves (although there is some unpublished settlement-material from the Athenian Agora); the Kerameikos group produced barely a hundred pots, the Salamis burials only about sixty that can be traced today. Very little pottery from other parts of Greece can be exactly classed with this material in the matter of shape or decoration; only a few finds from other parts of the city of Athens materially extend the Submycenaean class. But occasional vases or collections of pottery, some of them very recent finds, have appeared elsewhere in Greece, which are close enough to the Submycenaean of Western Attica to be judged contemporary with it, but which with the present precision in terminology are better classed as late Mycenaean III c.[12] The limitations of such evidence as this are clear enough: the range and quality of vases included in small single burials may be far from representative of the abilities of the epoch; certain vase-types can be seen throughout Greek history to have funerary connections, while others tend to be excluded from such use; temporary shortages may discourage people from interring their finer earthenware in a grave. But when over two hundred graves from an extended period of time have been excavated, some of them very markedly richer than others, it is reasonable to judge the period by them, at least relatively to other periods which provide a similar type of evidence.

On this showing there can be only one verdict on the Submycenaean pottery: it is narrow in range and utterly derivative. When in 1941 Furumark published his analysis of the vase-shapes in use in the different phases

3. Submycenaean: amphoriskos from Submycenaean grave 47 at the Kerameikos, Athens. Height 8 cm; *c.* 1100 BC.

of Mycenaean civilization, he was able to find 108 types assignable to III C 1, as against twelve for III C 2 (his name for Submycenaean). Of the III C 1 shapes, at least ninety are definitely found in graves, and well over thirty of these appear in graves of the latter part of the period, which may thus be contemporary with the Attic cemeteries. This is a striking difference; and while later finds and publications have added a few shapes to the Submycenaean repertoire, others have been subtracted by the process of reclassification of styles referred to earlier. It remains true that there are only five common shapes in the graves, three or four others which occur more than once, and a few isolated rarities. None of the shapes is really new; few show even a significant development in form from their Mycenaean forerunners. The commonest of all vessels in Submycenaean graves, the miniature amphora with flaring neck, had only recently become so predominant numerically, but its importance must have been slight; most specimens stand well under six inches in height, and are shaped and painted in a perfunctory way. They represent a rather unsuccessful scaling-down of the Mycenaean amphora with handles on the body, the scale of the handles being disproportionately large; their vogue dies out at the close of the Submycenaean period, when the spread of cremation in Attica created the

3

4, 5. The degeneration of a characteristic Mycenaean shape (cf. nos. *1* and *2*): stirrup-jars from Submycenaean grave 81 (*4*, height 20·6 cm; *c.* 1100 BC) and from Protogeometric grave 1 (*5*, restored height 13 cm; *c.* 1050 BC), at the Kerameikos, Athens.

need for a larger jar to hold the ashes of the deceased. The next two com-
4 monest shapes bear a complementary relationship; they are the stirrup-vase
6 or false-necked jar, and the lekythos. Both were narrow-necked vessels for
holding and pouring oil; but the stirrup-vase, having been one of the very
commonest Mycenaean shapes, becomes rarer as the Submycenaean style
5 progresses and dies out almost at once after its end in Attica, whereas the
lekythos, a rarer Mycenaean form, apparently becomes commoner at the
cf. 13 expense of the stirrup-vase whose function it usurps; it is unusual for both
to be found in a Submycenaean grave. The two remaining favoured shapes
are the deep rounded bowl or skyphos with a high foot, and the jug or
7 oenochoe with trefoil-shaped mouth. Both had become popular rather late
in the Mycenaean period, but their antecedents are there.[13]
The other shapes are all relatively rare in the graves: a small, more or less

6, 7. Submycenaean: lekythos from grave 87 (*6*, height 11·1 cm) and oenochoe from grave 19 (*7*, height 20 cm), at the Kerameikos, Athens. Both *c.* 1100 BC.

globular jug; the one-handled cup, of which three varieties have turned up in small numbers; the full-sized amphora with handles running from shoulder to neck, found in four Kerameikos graves, three of which were cremations, with the amphora serving to hold the ashes; the amphora with horizontal handles on the body, of which the Kerameikos produced a fine example with a lid; the pilgrim-flask, the flat-based pyxis or situla, and the ring-flask, the last two known only from fragments – so far, all are shapes known from the later Mycenaean world. But there was also a curious two-handled, flat-based bottle or lekythos from a late grave, which was unlike *8* Mycenaean shapes but for which parallels could be found in Late Bronze Age Cyprus; and, from one point of view most interesting of all, a group of hand-made vases – three jugs or pitchers of varying sizes, an amphoriskos and three small pyxides with their lids. Perhaps the most striking thing about these hand-made vessels is their comparative rarity; but this may apply only to graves, from which all our evidence comes. They are

8. Late Submycenaean bottle from grave 97 at the Kerameikos, Athens. Height 9·7 cm; rather before 1050 B C.

commoner in female graves; presumably they are products of domestic industry, but they need not necessarily have been made by the women as has been suggested.[14] The settlement levels and wells of the Athenian Agora region, however, somewhat broaden the range of Submycenaean shapes (see below, n.16).

The most general tendency of Submycenaean shapes, discernible in those which are commonest like the stirrup-vase, is an apparent gradual 'sagging', the result of the widest part of the vase being brought down from the shoulder to about the middle of the body. It is interesting that a similar effect can be observed in some late vases of Mycenaean III C I style; Furumark explained this as an anticipation of the tendencies of Submycenaean, but in the light of Desborough's observations it can now be seen as a parallel and contemporary development. Nor is this the only such resemblance.[15] But quite a substantial proportion of Submycenaean vases show actual incompetence on the part of the potter; there are stirrup-vases and lekythoi with asymmetrical shapes (the result of the literal sagging of the clay before firing), or with inefficiently-joined handles. The worst of the hand-made pots are deplorable. Such lapses are only worth pointing out because they are untypical of both Mycenaean and later Greek pottery, particularly that included in graves. Once again, the latest III C I pottery

9. Later Mycenaean III C: bowl in the manner of the 'Granary Class' from a grave at Lefkandi in Euboea. Height *c.* 12 cm; 11th century BC.

does show some deterioration in technique too, but it is more obvious in the settlement-material than in that from graves. The standards of Submycenaean seem lower in this respect, as in the matter of repertory of shapes with which we began. Potters in other parts of Greece were still making and, equally important, putting into graves a whole range of shapes that seem to be beyond the ken of Submycenaean craftsmen – the pithos, the large amphora, tall jugs with both plain and beaked mouths, jugs with a side-spout, askoi, straight-sided cups, stemmed kylikes, kalathoi, high-footed skyphoi – even this list is not exhaustive.[16]

The same qualities, of narrowness and dependence on Mycenaean prototypes, are apparent in the decoration of Submycenaean pots. The range is perhaps a little wider, but the dependence more complete. Decorative elements are taken, not only from the unambitious 'Granary class' of the mid-twelfth century and later, which had provided almost the whole basis for the jejune range of Submycenaean shapes, but also from the rather earlier 'Close Style' in which a high standard of decoration had been achieved. In many cases the motifs are lax and muddled memories of their prototypes; one or two examples are surprisingly competent and even elaborate. It can be argued that some of these last are not strictly Submycenaean – not without a hint of circularity, unless there is a suspicion that they are not locally made.[17] The simplest forms of decoration are taken over from the Granary class along with the corresponding vase-shapes: the horizontal wavy line, the row of languettes, the all-over black glaze. The remainder show the influence, more or less indirect, of the more ambitious Close Style, and the Salamis graves, which seem to belong to the earlier phases of Submycenaean, show a wider range of these motifs than is found in the Kerameikos material.[18]

Judged from their pottery alone, the Submycenaean communities of Western Attica present a consistent if gloomy picture. First, they are isolated: the known exports of Attic Submycenaean, and the known examples of non-Attic vases in the Submycenaean cemeteries, are few indeed. This is the more remarkable when one considers that there was at least one thriving community, less than twenty miles away, burying its dead in the chamber-tomb cemetery of Perati during part of this same period; a community which, in pottery and other fields, shows abundant signs of being in touch with other areas in and beyond the Aegean world. Secondly, the shape and decoration of Submycenaean pottery are almost totally dependent on Mycenaean models; apart from the few hand-made vases, which are a new departure, only the isolated flat-bottomed bottle (p. 37) shows any signs of derivation from other than Mycenaean sources. Thirdly, the repertoire of the Submycenaean potters seems to have been very narrow; only a selection of later Mycenaean shapes is found. The pattern of this evidence suggests communities of Mycenaean survivors, including few if any outside elements and with no artistic inspiration other than that of their own past, out of touch with contemporary and parallel communities in other parts of Greece, served by potters who were narrow in their range, and perhaps few and overworked; and who passed their limited expertise on to successors who were long without any other source of technical knowledge. But such a picture is, I emphasize, based exclusively on the pottery; part of its interest lies in the fact that a different, even contradictory impression can be derived from the other sources of evidence which we shall examine later.

THE SUBMINOAN STYLE

The Subminoan style of Crete is only very loosely comparable with Submycenaean, and on the whole less problematical. First, there are no tight geographical limits on the extent of Subminoan: the pottery is spread widely if thinly over the island of Crete, including its little-explored western end.[19] Further, from every point of view (not only that of the pottery) Subminoan appears as a period eminently well-named, in which the Minoan way of life continued, not uninterrupted nor yet undiluted by outside influences, but with the native element heavily preponderant.

10. Subminoan: krater (height 20cm) and jar (height 20·5 cm) from tomb *Π* of the Fortetsa cemetery, Knossos. Both *c*. 1000 BC.

The known material of the Subminoan class was for a long time very slight, scarcer even than Submycenaean; when Furumark studied the evidence in 1944 only a handful of sites had produced usable material, and that in very small quantities. But already it included pottery from settlements as well as graves, and was spread over a representative area of Crete; and since then a number of new sites have yielded Subminoan, in some cases too recently for it to have been fully published.[20] Clearly there is no such isolation as is detectable in the Submycenaean style; Subminoan includes, besides the expected shapes and motifs of Minoan character, others which seem to be derived from the contemporary styles of mainland Greece. These include some of the vase-shapes known in the later stages of Mycenaean III C in the Argolid and elsewhere, some of which are absent from the Submycenaean of Western Attica[21]; the types which do appear in Submycenaean are also present in Subminoan. So too in decorative motifs Subminoan is not nearly so circumscribed as Submycenaean; some of its choicer products are indeed tasteful as well as elaborate. And there is evidence for trade with, and influence from, Cyprus at this period, which does not stop at vase-shapes.[22] But perhaps the most noteworthy feature of the Subminoan style is its long duration. When we come to consider the evidence in detail in the next chapter (p. 128), we shall find it hard to avoid the conclusion that Subminoan remained current for something approaching two hundred years in

10

11. 'Transitional': kalathos in the peculiar local style of Karphi in east central Crete, recalling, particularly in its shape, the Late Minoan pottery of earlier centuries. Height 11·5 cm; *c.* 1100 BC.

all parts of Crete, and in some areas for perhaps nearly three hundred. Furthermore, the half-hearted 'Protogeometric' style of Central Crete (p. 26) contains a still strong element of Subminoan survival. Altogether the durability of Minoan – and indirectly of Mycenaean – cultural traits in Crete seems to have been unusually strong.

It is also possible to argue for an analogy between Submycenaean and Subminoan, of a significant kind: just as in mainland Greece the former style coexisted in time with other regional styles, also of more or less degenerate Mycenaean type, so in Crete there are sites which, in a period which must be in part contemporary with Subminoan, produce pottery which is distinguishable from it, although equally dependent on Minoan. In Crete these are the exception; but they include the important settlement-site of Karphi. Here the excavators classed the pottery as of an 'Intermediate' period; today this is often equated with Subminoan, which, chronologically speaking, may be partly correct; yet the pottery hardly observes the limits of the Subminoan style as found elsewhere in Crete. There are decorative elements in the Karphi material which have fairly close links *11* with the Late Minoan III B style which had generally come to an end in the late thirteenth century; some vases even have representational paintings in a style which recalls the Late Minoan II of fifteenth-century Knossos, and which may conceivably have survived over the intervening years in the medium of embroidered textiles. To extend the name of 'Subminoan' to this pottery might seem reasonable enough, but the trend today is, surely rightly, towards greater precision of terminology in these fields; Karphi, on this showing, is a so far unique site, and should be treated as such. Different but no less bewildering is the cemetery-site of Olous.[23] Here the pottery shows a fusion of old Minoan elements with an extraneous and apparently late type of jar, in most cases containing a cremation. The burials are almost impossible to date, but are surely partly or entirely contemporaneous with the Subminoan style which was being used on other sites in east central Crete, some of them very close to Olous. One lesson from mainland Greece seems therefore repeated in Crete, where the distances are smaller and the conclusion therefore more surprising: to transfer the name of a pottery-style to a substantial period of time over an extensive area, is to risk misinterpreting those sites which use a different style, but which are revealed by other evidence as being contemporary.

THE RISE OF PROTOGEOMETRIC AND THE ATTIC SERIES

With the exceptions that we have been considering, the Geometric system of decoration dominates all the local styles of painted, wheel-made pottery in Greece for the remainder of the early Iron Age. The isolation of an early phase within this era, the Protogeometric, has remained by far the most workable horizontal distinction within the period. If my treatment of this pottery becomes, from now on, more cursory, this is in part because it is the subject of detailed studies in English by Desborough and Coldstream (see p. 28); but such a course is in any case made necessary by the profusion of the material and of its local variations. The increase in the quantity of material seems to be relative as well as absolute; for one thing, far more vases on average are now included in each grave, even though single burials – mainly cremations now – continue to be the rule. Possibly this is foreshadowed in the latest stages of Attic Submycenaean: the two richest graves, numbers 108 and 113 in the Kerameikos, both belong towards the end of the period. On the other hand, the range of shapes, having increased sharply at the period of transition, is pared down thereafter; only towards the end of the Protogeometric period, when we find Attic potters imitating in clay objects whose natural material was wood, metal, leather or even wickerwork, is the momentum resumed in this direction.[24] The decoration of the vases, though often austere in nature, gradually increases its repertoire, so that analysis by single motifs is a far greater task than with Submycenaean. These factors, compounded by the considerable range of entirely distinctive local styles prevalent in Greece during the lifetime of the Protogeometric and Geometric styles, build up the extremely complex picture of Greek ceramic development during the remainder of the early Iron Age.

The central hypothesis of Desborough's study of Protogeometric, one widely held since the first systematic exploration of the Kerameikos cemetery in the 1920s, was that this style originated in Athens. This meant, in the first place, only that the earliest Protogeometric was produced in Athens, a hypothesis that has stood the test of time remarkably well. Desborough did however carry his conclusions a step further, and argued that the other Protogeometric schools of Greece not only developed later than Attic but were nearly all dependent on Attic Protogeometric, and indeed on an advanced stage of that style, for their inspiration and growth. Practically the only exceptions were the schools of Ithaca and Laconia, which showed barely any direct Attic influence; but the Protogeometric style in these areas was a phenomenon of largely local significance. Now in his second book twelve years later, Desborough has somewhat modified this latter argument.[25] An important reason for this was his own discovery that the Submycenaean style was a local variant, virtually confined to Western Attica; this disposed of the alleged gap in the pottery-series of other districts, where there was no Submycenaean. It therefore removed the grounds for believing, *a priori*, in a gap before the beginning of Protogeometric in these areas. In fact, fresh discoveries of both Mycenaean III c and Protogeometric pottery in areas outside Western Attica had already occurred in some numbers, and these made it far easier to believe in local continuity between these two styles. These new finds of Protogeometric also carry another implication: that the influence of Attic Protogeometric must have been diffused over Greece almost from the beginning of the style, and without any appreciable initial period of isolation. For Desborough still maintains the view, surely a sound one, that the technical and stylistic advances that produced Protogeometric cannot have been achieved independently in a number of different centres, but must have been carried through in one centre, Athens, and imitated more or less rapidly elsewhere. Where there are signs of a direct continuity with the preceding Mycenaean III c pottery of the locality, it is natural to believe that the adoption of Protogeometric took place fairly soon after its adoption at Athens; where there is an apparent stylistic gap, or an intervening phase characterized by a 'survival' style such as Subminoan, Protogeometric may have begun a century or more later.

12. Attic Protogeometric: belly-handled amphora from Protogeometric grave 18 at the Kerameikos, Athens. The figure of a horse
is a notable rarity at this date. Height 47·2 cm; *c.*975 BC.

What are these advances which distinguish Protogeometric from its
immediate predecessors, and indeed from everything that had gone before?
They are among the most clearly identifiable phenomena of the early Iron
Age; some of them can be seen on the actual surviving pots, others inferred
with certainty from them. The most fundamental perhaps is the adoption
of a faster wheel by the potter; this leads to shapes that are more disciplined,
less sagging and free of surface irregularities. The ovoid shape, with the
point of greatest diameter well over half-way up the body, becomes standard for all the closed vases in Protogeometric; and in sympathy with this, *12-14*
the main decoration tends to move upwards to the shoulder, or at least
not to extend below the level of the handle or handles. This decoration is
invariably grouped in a series of horizontal zones; there was nothing new
about this in itself – it had been characteristic of the later phases of
Mycenaean pottery, as well as of Submycenaean; what was new was the use

13, 14. Attic Late Protogeometric: lekythos from grave 40 (*13*) and
oenochoe from grave 48 (*14*), at the Kerameikos, Athens. Heights
c. 18 cm; *c.* 925 B C.

of this zonal system to accentuate the division of the pot into its component
parts, already stressed by the potter in shaping it: foot, body, shoulder,
neck, lip. The main decoration seldom occupied even a third of the surface
of these closed vases; the bulk of the pot was at first usually left plain in the
natural colour of the clay, but later tended to be covered in a plain black
wash; two or three thin horizontal black lines commonly marked the
transition to this plain area. The open vases, usually smaller and of a simple
shape, were painted on a similar principle except that the main decoration
here covered a larger part of the surface proportionately; the most notable
innovation was that of the potter, in introducing and steadily developing
a high foot, in the shape of a truncated cone, very clearly distinct from the
lower part of the body. The notion that each part of the pot had its own
proper, separate function to perform, but that in doing so it should nevertheless preserve a harmonious proportion to the pot as a whole; and that

15. The pottery from the double grave, Submycenaean 114, at the Kerameikos, Athens. The three vases on the right were with one burial and are Submycenaean in style; the five on the left were with the other, and are Early Protogeometric. Height of jug on extreme right, 16·7 cm; *c.* 1050 B C.

the main decoration had its own proper place on the pot, to which it should be confined – these are among the qualities that distinguish the new style.

But far more tangible are two new aids used in the actual technique of decoration, the compass and the multiple brush – at this stage used never separately but always in combination. The compass alone had been known *12-14* to the producers of Aegean Bronze Age decoration, but it is not very often detectable; the multiple brush, though long known among vase-painters in other parts of the ancient world, had not been adopted in the Aegean either with or without the compass, although there are several motifs on Mycenaean and Submycenaean pottery which seem to cry out for its use. The Protogeometric painters may have borrowed the use of the multiple brush on pottery from Cyprus, but the combination of the two aids was probably a pure innovation, and it is in no small degree responsible for the impression of control and symmetry which their products give.[26] In the Attic series, we can see the adoption of these new devices taking place almost before our eyes. Particularly interesting are, first, a double child-burial recently discovered on the fringes of the Kerameikos cemetery, *15* where the vases with one interment are still Submycenaean in character, while those with the other, presumably virtually contemporary burial have passed the transition into Protogeometric; and secondly a group of vases in Heidelberg from a single tomb on the south-west slope of the

Acropolis at Athens, which includes two lekythoi with hand-drawn concentric semicircles (already a favourite Submycenaean pattern), and a lekythos and a bottle with compass-drawn ones. Such explicit evidence as this supports Desborough's view that the change to Protogeometric, and to the use of compass and multiple brush, was made in Athens, and took place elsewhere in Greece not spontaneously but through Attic influence. A further consideration is the immediate and lasting mastery of the new aids which the Attic products show, in contrast to some other local Protogeometric schools. If it be suggested that these were simple techniques, in which a vase-painter could be expected to become adept as soon as he was given the instruments, then we can point to considerable evidence to the contrary: for example, the occasional habit of painters outside Athens, when drawing concentric semicircles with the compass and multiple brush, of carrying the curves round too far, and then cutting them off by painting a horizontal black band over the lower part; and more especially, an interesting transitional piece from Macedonia on which the same technical aids have been used in an experimental and not wholly competent way to draw sets of concentric circles (see below, p. 74).[27]

33

The aesthetic and technical superiority of the Attic Protogeometric school continues to assert itself, in this and other ways. We may note the uniquely clear contour given by the potter to his products, his wide repertoire of shapes, and his mastery of clay-preparation and firing which translated the painter's efforts into a beautifully clear-cut colour-scheme and, particularly in the case of the later dark-ground vases, gave the painted areas of the surface a lustrous black sheen. But the Attic school was merely the most important of a wide range of regional centres of pottery-production in the early Iron Age; and since there have been, proportionately speaking, only quite small additions to the Attic Protogeometric material since Desborough published his meticulous shape-by-shape study in 1952, we should now pass on to the full Geometric style in Athens, and briefly consider this before turning to the other regions of Greece. For the Geometric schools of Athens and many other centres build directly on the achievements of their Protogeometric predecessors; as has been pointed out, it is a mistake to treat Protogeometric as a separate style which develops, then wanes and dies out in the face of Geometric; the one is simply the logical culmination of the other.[28]

14

The Attic school retained its pre-eminence for much of the Geometric period, although changes in shape and technique were present from the first. For example, the lustre on the black paint becomes less marked by

16. Attic Protogeometric: high-footed skyphos from grave D at the
Kerameikos, Athens. Height 11·4cm; *c.*950 BC.

the middle Geometric period, and the Protogeometric habit of initially
coating the surface with a clay wash before painting is apparently dis-
continued. But more striking is the dismissal of several Protogeometric
shapes and features. The characteristic high conical foot of the open
Protogeometric vases – skyphoi, cups, kantharoi, kraters – is gradually *16*
dispensed with, and a whole range of new, squat forms comes into being. *17, 19, 20*
Two other important shapes, the lekythos which had been developed two
centuries earlier for a specific use (p. 36), and the older if less ubiquitous
jug, had served their turn and disappear for a time. Somewhat later, the
oenochoe with trefoil-shaped lip undergoes a change, the lower part of
the body being broadened and shortened to give the vase a flat-based, *31*
truncated appearance. The globular pyxis, at roughly the same time, sinks
to a flat, *torus*-like shape. However, in one of the important instances of a *18*
change in shape, that of the flat-based cup, the new form appears before
the end of Protogeometric; and at the same time a wide range of other
basic shapes – principally the krater and the four different varieties of
amphora – can be seen to carry on in an unbroken series from one style to
the other; while the kantharos, common in Geometric but once thought

D

17. Four vases – oenochoe, cup, two kantharoi – from Agora grave
XXVII at Athens (cf. nos. *19* and *20*), of the transition to Geometric.
Heights 24·4, 5·6, 8·7, and 12·4cm; *c.*900 BC.

15, top left to appear only late on in the Protogeometric series, has now been found in
a rather peculiar form in the transitional grave 114 of the Kerameikos.
For a long time afterwards, Attic Geometric potters were content to use
this revised and reduced repertory of shapes, the exceptions being few
and isolated. Real innovation in vase-shapes comes in only with the massive
wave towards the middle of the eighth century, when a dozen or more
fresh shapes appear, some of them, like the kotyle and the later aryballos,
plainly borrowed from other schools, others deliberate and basic modifications of old shapes.[29]

From one point of view, it is somewhat unfortunate that the study of
Attic Geometric pottery over the last thirty years has been heavily weighted
towards the partly representational style of its later phases, although
Coldstream's study may now rectify this. The intensive investigation of
workshops, and even of individual painters, which only becomes possible
at this period, has allowed the earlier stylistic development to fall rather
into the background. Perhaps the most influential study of recent years
was K. Kübler's publication, in 1954, of the all-important Geometric
graves in the Kerameikos; but his findings, and those of P. Kahane who
had previously contributed an important essay on this subject, have also
been seriously questioned, not only for their chronological results which
many believe to involve too high a dating, but for their whole stylistic
basis.[30] Kübler's extremely detailed study of the Kerameikos finds starts
from the standpoint of style; so much so, that it produces results which

18. Attic Middle Geometric: pyxis from Geometric grave 69 at the Kerameikos, Athens, showing the revival of plastic representational art in its horse-handle. Height 10·5 cm; *c.*775 BC.

19, 20. Attic Late Geometric: two low-footed skyphoi from Geometric grave 50 at the Kerameikos, with decoration showing the possible influence of Oriental art. Diameters 14·2 and 8·1 cm; *c.*750 BC.

seem quite anomalous in terms of the composition of grave-groups, vases in the same grave being given in several cases dates that differ by up to fifty years. This approach, coupled with his treatment of each vase-type singly, seems to some scholars to be a reversal of the proper procedure; they would prefer to take the grave-groups as the basis for the ceramic series. R. Hachmann's careful attempt to construct an alternative scheme on this principle, using grave-locations and changes in funerary custom as a further aid for grouping the graves, gives results which seem to me more convincing than Kübler's. The importance of this question rests in the fact that the Kerameikos cemetery gives a uniquely complete series for Attic Geometric, and Attic in turn provides the main stylistic framework for the other Geometric schools of Greece. Yet the Kerameikos remains purely a cemetery site; and even within that limitation it is evidently not fully representative of the ceramic achievements of Athens, particularly towards the end of the Geometric period; in cases where the Kerameikos is silent, it is still possible for scholars, by the combination of a different stylistic criterion and a different absolute chronology, to differ by over a century in their dating of the same Attic Geometric vase.

In spite of all this, the main tendencies of the period, in decoration as in the use of shapes, are sufficiently clear for our purpose. The legacy of the latest Protogeometric was a tendency towards plain dark-ground vases relieved by sparse ornament; earlier Geometric at times carried this practice to even more austere lengths, with decorative motifs, new or already familiar, present only in fragmentary form – groups of lines slanted in *17* alternate directions, parallel chevrons and above all the newly-revived maeander pattern.[31] Some such rectilinear motifs had always been present in Protogeometric alongside the compass-drawn ones; but the delight in the use of compass and multiple brush had evidently palled, and they give ground to rectilinear decoration from the beginning of Geometric. Concentric semicircles indeed largely fade away; circles survive, particularly *see 120* on larger vases where they are often given a place of honour, framed by rectangular panels. As time went on, the Attic painters gradually applied the straight-line motifs, especially the maeander, more confidently; less and less of the surface was left to the plain black glaze; and since many of the designs were composed of elements in outline, with hatching inside, while others were drawn in a line either finer in texture or rendered fainter by the lack of intense firing, the vases acquired by the middle of Geometric *eg. 21* a characteristic greyness in overall effect, in contrast to the stark *chiaroscuro* of Protogeometric. The decoration is not allowed merely to agglutinate;

21. Attic Middle Geometric: pedestalled krater in the Metropolitan
Museum of Art, New York. This vase is now usually placed at the head
of the great series of Geometric figured scenes. Height 99 cm;
c. 770-760 B C.

principles of subordination are firmly applied on the larger vases, and the
most important zones – the neck, the widest part of the body, and the handle-
zone if it does not coincide with either of these – are given dominant motifs,
drawn on a larger scale and sometimes also interrupting the zonal rhythm
of the design with vertical lines of division: by contrast, on Protogeometric
closed vases the shoulder had been the most important zone for decoration.
The multiple brush, retained in use for the concentric circles, is later applied
to straight and angular lines as well, the first freehand use of this instrument

in Greek pottery. Then, at a fairly advanced point in the style, representational figures make what was to be a permanent re-entry into vase-painting. Surprisingly, the Protogeometric painters had very occasionally introduced
12 an inconspicuously-placed silhouette figure of a horse on to their products, but the experiment had been a tentative, perhaps premature one. A few animal and human figures appear in the earlier part of Attic Geometric, still in an inconspicuous, if not apologetic treatment.[32] The Geometric figure-style only develops to fruition when the figures are given a whole zone, or a large part of one, to themselves; above all, on the great funerary
21 amphorae and kraters which were used as combined grave-markers and receptacles for libation in the later Geometric period. This use of vases as a medium for representational art will be considered in a later chapter (pp. 417-19, 431-4).

Supreme within Greece, Attic Geometric owed little or nothing to contemporary outside influences until its later stages; but it is nevertheless surprising to find how little it was exported at first. The earlier Geometric period indeed seems to witness a fall in the export of Attic ware after the Protogeometric (cf. below, p. 64), and even the material from Attica outside Athens is still not very copious. When Attic Geometric does begin to spread abroad, it shows a general bias towards the islands of the Aegean: to Delos, which has produced some of the earlier pieces but little that need be earlier than 800 B C, and to Aegina, Euboea, Siphnos, Thera, Samos, Kos, Crete, and beyond them to Smyrna; to Cyprus, where a notable krater of the earlier eighth century was found, as with other contemporary and later pieces, and to Syria; northwards, finds have occurred in Boeotia, Delphi, Kapakli in Thessaly and now perhaps Macedonia. But the bulk of these finds belong to the middle and later eighth century, when Greek trade had opened up quite broadly, and the proportion of Attic Geometric even on these sites is not impressive when compared with other imported wares. Elsewhere, Attic is often completely absent down to and after the end of Geometric: this is true of much of the Peloponnese, while further west there is only an allegedly Attic vase from Corcyra, others from Veii and Canale, and sherds from Syracuse and Megara Hyblaea.[33] But although sparingly exported, the vases of Geometric Athens had a detectable influence on other local schools of Greece, which presently became as wide as in the late Protogeometric period: the Geometric styles of Argos, Corinth, Boeotia, Euboea, the Cyclades, and later Crete and Rhodes all show its impact in differing degrees.

THE REGIONAL GROUPING OF THE POTTERY-STYLES

If Attic must still provide the framework on which our picture of the other styles is based, this will one hopes become less true as knowledge of the various local styles, in some cases only fractional today, is extended. Since there are so many local styles to be considered in early Iron Age Greece, it is almost essential to classify them in some way. The grouping here suggested is based on the character of the local Protogeometric style; for the break at the beginning of Protogeometric is from every point of view the most important one in ceramic terms, and the pattern which grew up in Greece thereafter is the result of revolution which in time covered almost the whole of Greece. On this reasoning, the local Protogeometric styles outside Attica seem to fall most naturally into three groups: (i) those which, although their inception must be in part due to Attic influence as we have seen, do also show connections with the preceding Mycenaean pottery of the locality, sometimes together with early stylistic traits of Protogeometric; and must therefore have begun not too long after the rise of Attic Protogeometric; (ii) those which show faint Mycenaean connections or none at all, and no early Protogeometric traits, but were indebted to later Protogeometric, either of the Attic or of some other school, and so may be assumed to have begun some time later; and (iii) those which seem to be of late but independent growth – a small group. But we should note the existence of a fourth group, consisting of the numerous areas where no Protogeometric worthy of the name appears to have developed. As with the Attic school, so here it seems best to carry our survey of each pottery-series down to the end of Geometric so as to give, however briefly, the span of each region's ceramic development within the remainder of the dark age.

(i) THE EARLY OR 'ADVANCED' STYLES

The first group of schools forms, together with Attic, the basis for the most constructive reasoning, since it is in these cases that we can most safely infer continuity of style in the pottery, and therefore continuity of occupation in at least the more important sites. This is not to say that continuity is excluded for the other groups; but it is quite unwarranted to assume that, for example, because a site has produced some Mycenaean III c pottery and some Protogeometric, continuous occupation is thereby proven for that site.[34] Unless further details are available, it is quite possible for a period of anything up to two hundred years' desertion to have intruded on such a site. In our first group, however, we have the

22. Argive Protogeometric: belly-handled amphora from grave P G 601 at Mycenae. Height 32 cm; *c.* 950 B C.

combination of a connection with the preceding Mycenaean of the locality, and a dependence on Attic for the first impulse of Protogeometric. These styles must clearly not begin before Attic Protogeometric, but if their rise is placed much later, anomalies will occur, with stylistic time-lags both before and after the change. It seems easiest to believe that these local schools began soon after the technical advances and changed tastes, of which they made use, had developed in Athens.

22   THE ARGOLID. We may begin this group with Argive. The Protogeometric style is represented most notably at Argos itself, where the French excavations have shown that, although there was a change in the location of the settlement and of the burials, and a change too in the type of interment, at the end of Mycenaean times, the interval of time between the end of the old and the beginning of the new was probably of the slightest; while the new, represented by the Protogeometric pottery, inaugurates a series that extends to the end of Geometric and beyond. Another important site for this style is Tiryns, where again there is evidence that the location of the cemetery was changed (in this case rather before the introduction of Protogeometric), but again with no sign of a significant chronological

gap, now that the Mycenaean III c occupation of Tiryns is fully attested (p. 29). The continuity or near-continuity of pottery-styles is thus assured by the finds at Argos and Tiryns, but this does not guarantee continuity of *occupation* in the other sites where Mycenaean III c and Argive Protogeometric are found. In the case of Mycenae itself, the graves recently discovered in the area of the Citadel House may prove to have filled the gap whose presence Desborough in 1964 still suspected;[35] but from the published evidence at the sites of Dendra, Asine and Nauplion, despite claims to the contrary, continuity of occupation is in varying degrees open to question. The fact of the seniority of Argive Protogeometric has been established, but it is difficult to say much more about the style as yet, until the Argos finds are published in full. But already in 1952 Desborough found evidence for close and direct imitation of Attic in the area, with a few imports from Attica also present; this conclusion was confined to the later stages of Protogeometric (and to the earlier Geometric), which was all that the evidence then available covered, but there is little doubt that it will prove valid for the beginning of Protogeometric as well, except perhaps in the matter of actual Attic imports, while the time-lag of the Argive style behind the Attic is likely to have been very small. It is noteworthy that a Protogeometric cup found on Aegina could be attributed to the Argive school.[36]

For Argive Geometric, the excavations at Argos are as important as for the preceding period, but with the difference that they have now been fully published, as far as the pottery is concerned. A grave-series has thus been revealed which spans the whole duration of the style, less fully than that of the Kerameikos in the case of Attic, but with the added asset of a settlement-site in close vicinity.[37] Besides the half-dozen sites known from the preceding period which remain inhabited, re-occupied Bronze Age sites like Berbati, Kandia, Lerna, the Argive Heraeum and Kalauria on the offshore island of Poros all help to contribute material for the Geometric of the Argolid. This style at first lives up to its respectable pedigree; it moves through a series of phases which seem to equate very well with those of Attic Geometric, and its nearness to Attic still ensures its superiority to most other Geometric schools. But the Attic mastery of the principle of *hypotaxis* is not present in Argive: the abstract decoration jostles together without much feeling for composition. The departures from Attic practice, which increase in Late Geometric, are hardly a success – as in the oversized maeanders, the step-maeander with its unsettling diagonal movement, or the massing together of thinner motifs in frenzied array, horizontal

23

23. Argive Early Geometric: neck-handled amphora from grave G 607
at Mycenae. Height 40cm; *c.* 875 BC.

giving way to vertical or zigzag to straight without any detectable aim
beyond that of covering the surface of the pot. Figure-scenes are also
adopted, showing only slight signs of the inspiration of Attic, but the
repertoire is smaller; notable is the painters' insistence on the horse, often
see 126 with its head held by a man. The apparent utter decline of Argive vase-
painting in the seventh century, and that after a long survival of sub-
Geometric decoration, comes as a surprise. Argive Geometric finds its
way to Tegea and Amyklai, to Aegina, Corinth, and in such quantity to
Perachora that it may betoken political control; more surprisingly it has
occurred at Eleusis, on Melos, and at a very late stage in Sicily; one or two
pieces from Delphi, Ithaka and Corcyra may be Argive.[38]
CORINTH. In Corinth a rather different picture unfolds. At the beginning,
the conclusions reached for the Argolid may be tentatively applied to
Corinthia; connections with the preceding Mycenaean are visible in the
latter region too, and at Old Corinth and Isthmia there is a possibility of

24. Corinthian Middle Geometric: pedestalled krater from a grave in
the Agora at Corinth. Height 49·5 cm; *c.* 800 B C.

fully continuous habitation. But, partly no doubt because of the paucity
of the Corinthian material, there is far less evidence for an independent
style of Protogeometric at Corinth; only a handful of vases belong to the
earlier stages of Protogeometric, while in the later part of the period there
is heavy borrowing from Attic. The relationship between Argive and
Corinthian Protogeometric, though real, is not so close as might have
been expected; but the material is too scanty to justify going beyond these
generalities. From the beginning of Geometric, however, this ceases to
be so; the material increases sharply in quantity, and we can see the rise
of an unpretentious school to a considerable degree of mastery. Corinthian
Geometric begins with the same inhibition of decoration as Attic and Argive,
but the modesty of the style remains striking even when it enters its middle
and later stages; there are no large-scale motifs to attract the attention, and   *24*

25. Corinthian Late Geometric: oenochoe from a well at Corinth.
Height 31·6cm; *c.*725 B C.

25

no real figure-style at all; when the taste for the dark-ground system wanes (which happens much later than in Attic), it is replaced by a pattern of plain horizontal stripes which often cover at least half the surface of the pot; even for the main field, simple linear motifs usually suffice; the vertical wavy line is a Corinthian speciality. The style was a paradise for the multiple brush, which was liberally used. Corinthian Geometric is finally significant for its early modification, from a purely Geometric style to one influenced by Oriental art, well before the end of the eighth century.

49, 5od
cf. 38

Before that happens, we have the spectacle of two new Corinthian shapes, the kotyle or rimless skyphos and the round aryballos, being imported or imitated, or both, by several centres in Greece, with Athens among the first. The characteristic conical oenochoe of the Geometric and later eras at Corinth may well be a Corinthian invention and not, as was long supposed, a derivative from an 'Argive monochrome' shape (see below, p. 96). At a comparatively early stage, Corinthian Geometric reached Megara, Aegina, Delphi, Smyrna, Crete, Thera, perhaps Rheneia, and above all Ithaka, where Corinthian potters may possibly have settled; somewhat later, its products reach Attic and the Argolid; and later still, after the beginning of the true 'Protocorinthian' style, Corinthian ware appears in quantity from the Levant to the far West – where indeed the earliest pieces, both in the Greek colony of Pithekoussai, and at Falerii   *49, 50b,d* and elsewhere in Etruria, arrive before this stage, perhaps around 750. S. Weinberg has suggested that one class of 'Corinthian' Geometric was in fact made at Aegina or some other centre outside Corinth, but the theory has not been very warmly received, and it is applied to a group not proportionately numerous or widely distributed.[39]

THESSALY. Next we should consider Thessaly, the home of perhaps the most important and the most individual school of Protogeometric outside Attica. It was discoveries in Thessaly which first occasioned the revision of Desborough's original hypothesis about the development of Protogeometric in Greece; a study of the Thessalian school was published by the former Ephor of this district, the late N. M. Verdelis, in 1958, and his conclusions were strongly supported by the discoveries of his successor, D. Theocharis, at the major site of Iolkos. Here, in an area adjoining the site of the Mycenaean palace, the near-continuity of occupation from Mycenaean III c – and that not apparently represented by the latest stage of the style – through into Protogeometric, was argued on stratigraphic grounds, quite independently of considerations of pottery-style.[40] Thessalian Protogeometric should therefore succeed the preceding Mycenaean very swiftly, presumably at much the same time as the rise of Protogeometric in Athens. Theocharis has even claimed an earlier rise for the Thessalian school, and Verdelis had already proposed that it developed in total independence of the Attic. It was here that Desborough could not agree with him (p. 44), since this required an independent adoption of the fast wheel, the compass and the multiple brush by Thessalian and by Attic potters. These advances transformed the ceramic art as the Mycenaeans had known it, and it seems too much to believe that they could have been hit on spontaneously by the Protogeometric potters in two centres little over a hundred miles apart. The most economical hypothesis remains that the Attic potters, who at once put these innovations to expert and far-reaching use, were the ones who devised or borrowed them and passed them on to other regions of Greece. But the potters of Thessaly must be credited with some notable independent achievements: among them, the conversion of some peculiar shapes from the repertory of Thessalian native hand-made ware – the jug with cut-away neck, the two-handled cup or kantharos with high-swung handles – into competent wheel-made versions with Protogeometric decoration; the development of the krater

26. The long-lived and widely produced shape of the low-footed
skyphos with pendent semicircles (see pp. 27, 70, 71, 79). This example
is from a grave on the island of Rheneia. Height 7·5 cm; *c.* 850 B C.

into an individual shape with a high, flaring foot; the development or
early adoption of a further range of shapes which cannot be traced to
Attic sources. It may be added that continuity of habitation is possible
at Gremnos in the far north of Thessaly, at the cemetery site of Gritsa
near Pteleon in the south, and conceivably at Neleia the harbour-town
of Iolkos, in addition to Iolkos itself; but the curiously heterogeneous
styles found in outlying sites, especially Marmariani, Halos and Theotokou, show that the area which later became Thessaly was hardly yet a
cultural unity in the Protogeometric or earlier Geometric periods.[41]

    Thessaly in the Geometric period falls strangely back into obscurity.
There is evidence that at the remoter sites, notably the cemetery of Marmariani, people adhered to the Protogeometric style long after it was
abandoned further south. A notable legacy to Thessaly was the low-footed
26   skyphos with pendent semicircles, whose peculiar position we considered
earlier (p. 27); this shape, together with others (notably amphoriskoi)
that make use of the same decoration, persisted for long enough (probably
down to at least 850 in Thessaly) to delay the adoption of Geometric
decoration in more than one class of vessel. There are no real traces in the
published material of earlier phases of Thessalian Geometric, unless we
27   count the peculiar style of Marmariani (cf. p. 330 and n. 39); but all the
while the native unpainted Thessalian ware, both hand- and wheel-made,
continued to represent a stronger tradition. From now on, one detects
a growing reluctance to copy the trends of vase-decoration further south,
which continues into the post-Geometric period: the later Geometric
style of Thessaly, which is still not very fully represented, may prove to
have survived for generations after the end of Attic and other schools of

27. Thessalian Geometric: pedestalled krater of the local school of
Marmariani in northern Thessaly. Height 36·5 cm; later 9th century B C.

Geometric. A few imports from Attica in the eighth century no doubt
helped to provide such fresh impulse as there was; but in general Thessaly
presents in the Geometric period a picture of the consolidation of the ideas
received earlier, and of the growth towards homogeneity from what had
been discordant local features; there is nothing to match the whole-hearted
adoption of Protogeometric.

THE CENTRAL CYCLADES. Two or three other local styles should also
be placed in this group. One is that of the island of Naxos in the Cyclades,
where again the evidence has very recently appeared. The settlement at
Grotta has produced successive building-periods of Mycenaean III c,
Protogeometric and Geometric date; as at Iolkos, the only possible

interruption – and that of the briefest duration – comes at the transition from what the excavator called the 'Submycenaean' level to the Protogeometric. The groups of tombs from the nearby Aplomata ridge confirm that the Protogeometric settlement must have succeeded the latest Mycenaean one almost without a break. What the subsequent Naxian Protogeometric was like is not yet clear; there appear to be links with Attic Submycenaean at the beginning, and with Thessalian Protogeometric later on; a probable Cycladic export of the Late Protogeometric period was found in Crete. At least there is no longer any doubt of the existence of an individual school of Protogeometric hereabouts; yet the finds from others of the central and southern Cyclades are in most cases not only later, but closely under the influence of Attic Protogeometric, and sometimes actual Attic imports; Desborough found this to be true of Paros, Amorgos, Siphnos and Thera, as well as the closer island of Aegina, and the recent finds on Kea have, not unexpectedly, shown the same characteristics; more surprisingly, most of the Protogeometric published from the large and comparatively distant island of Samos seems to be pottery of Attic type. But it should be mentioned that a solitary Protogeometric amphora from Melos has been shown to be of local manufacture.[42]

This early school whose existence is attested in Naxos came in the course of time to carry more of the neighbouring islands with it in joining the mainstream of Greek ceramic development: it was no doubt helped by a strong wave of Attic influence which spread over the Cyclades in the Middle Geometric phase. By the end, pottery was clearly being made on Paros, Thera and other islands besides Naxos, although it must be admitted that distinctions between the products of the various island schools are still often debated. Furthermore, the material from Andros, Delos and Rheneia shows that these islands, which in Protogeometric times had lain within the orbit of a distinct northern Cycladic style, now extended their contacts strongly towards the southern group. For the earlier stages of Geometric, it is still enough of a task to distinguish Cycladic from non-Cycladic: much of the now well-established Euboean Geometric school (p. 71) has been 'reclaimed' from the body of Cycladic, and in compensation some allegedly Attic products – probably too many – have been claimed for the Cyclades. That there was a genuine earlier Geometric style in these islands is shown by finds from Naxos, Delos and Rheneia, *see 121* Thera and perhaps Paros; there are also exports to Crete and even Athens at this time. Some of the later 'Cycladic' Geometric reported from Cyprus and Al Mina in the East, and from Pithekoussai and Megara Hyblaea in the

West, can be shown to have come from the Cyclades rather than Euboea. The influence of Attic Geometric is again strong on this style, and there are imported pieces on Delos, and later on Siphnos and Thera. In the later stages of Geometric it does become possible to distinguish the individual island schools, particularly those of Paros and Naxos which led to more clearly identifiable successors in the seventh century. The former may extend some way back into Geometric, if the 'Aa' group of vases from Delos is rightly classed as Parian; while the Naxian school rises to large vases with bird- and animal-friezes. A recent school of island Geometric to emerge is that of Andros. Later still develops the sometimes overrated school of Thera, distinguished by the red and grey impurities in the volcanic clay of that island; some hint of its backwardness is given by the presence of a series of belly-handled amphorae still entirely in the Attic Protogeometric tradition, but in a late Geometric context; Theran Geometric is scarcely exported at all. That there was a Melian school of Geometric, as of Protogeometric (p. 64), may now be taken as established.[43]

ELIS. The Protogeometric style of Elis makes that region at least a candidate for inclusion in this group. Here there are sites – Olympia and Agios Andreas – where continuity of occupation is at least a possibility, while at Ancient Elis itself tombs have been discovered which belong, if not to Submycenaean, at least to an early stage of the local Protogeometric. The vases appear to be of poor workmanship, but the links   *28* with the Attic series are evident. At present there is no site where a continuous ceramic series can be followed through from full Mycenaean to Protogeometric, but unless it can be shown that this area developed its Protogeometric style after a marked time-lag, or a prolonged survival of Mycenaean, it is easiest to see in the pottery from the Ancient Elis tombs a sign of very early contact with Attica; the bronzes from these tombs (p. 234) certainly favour an early date, and a grave at Palaiopyrgo (Salmone) was similarly dated on its discovery; closer study of the pottery, however, has shown it to be somewhat later. The existence of an independent Geometric style in Elis has to be inferred from a handful of sherds found under the Heraeum at Olympia, a few more from Agrapidochori on the Peneus, which surprisingly include fragments of a scene representing a warship, and others known only by report from Kyllini and Agios Andreas; the character and initial date of this school are still beyond conjecture.[44] It is in any case clear that the more advanced Protogeometric schools of pottery did not automatically breed equally advanced Geometric successors, as was demonstrated by the case of Thessaly.

E

28. Elean Protogeometric: neck-handled amphora from a grave at
Ancient Elis. Height 47 cm; later 11th century BC.

ASIA MINOR. It remains to consider the Protogeometric style which grew
up among the Greek settlers at Miletus, and other sites in western Asia
Minor. Here, once again, the material still awaits publication in detail;
but at Miletus the earliest Protogeometric is very early – probably contemporary with the transition from Submycenaean at Athens, and including
elements which could even be classed as Submycenaean – yet locally made.
Again, repeating the pattern of Argos, Iolkos and Grotta on Naxos, there
is a break in occupation just before the beginning of this phase, in this
case marked by a partial burning of the Mycenaean III C settlement, and
possibly involving a slightly longer interruption than on the other three
sites. The subsequent Protogeometric pottery, it is clear, is in an indepen-
29   dent style, but one which owes much to Attic influence; and this is strongly
confirmed by the pottery found long ago at the cemetery-site of Assarlik

29. Protogeometric at Miletus: two miniature oenochoai from the settlement near the Temple of Athena. Heights 9·3 and 11·5 cm; *c.*950 BC.

(the ancient Termera) near the tip of the Halicarnassus peninsula some way further south. The earliest vases again show close affinity to Attic, and stand at the transition to Protogeometric; they and their successors are again locally made with a few possible exceptions at the beginning, and they continue to preserve a resemblance to Attic well down into the Protogeometric period. The main difference from Miletus is that no preceding Mycenaean settlement or tombs are known here; although the site of Müskebi, where a group of Mycenaean chamber-tombs came to light in 1962, is less than five miles distant. Two important and surprising additions have recently been made to the discoveries in this general region: at the inland city of Sardis a stratum containing much Protogeometric and some 'Submycenaean' pottery is reported (this at a place which neither before nor afterwards was to be a predominantly Greek settlement); while at the site of later Stratonicaea, some way further south but also well inland from the Aegean, two 'Submycenaean' pots have been discovered and published. There is thus clear evidence of a local Protogeometric style of great seniority in south-western Asia Minor. The material so far published from the other sites on this coast where Protogeometric has been found – from north to south, Pitane, Phocaea, Mordoğan (perhaps ancient Boutheia), Old Smyrna, Teos, a site near Kuşadasi (probably Pygela), Tsangli, Iasos and Dirmil – is not yet enough to substantiate this picture or extend it further north; indeed the preliminary reports of the Old Smyrna material suggest that the pattern there is different from Miletus and Assarlik, since the affinity to Attic, though real, is said not to appear so strongly in the earliest material as it does later. Nor does the published material from any of these sites go back as early as that from Miletus, which is perhaps natural since none of them, with the possible exception of Iasos, seems to have succeeded a preceding Mycenaean settlement.[45] But the important Milesian school of Protogeometric does not preserve such a clear identity through Geometric times; instead, it becomes eclipsed by a more widespread style which covers the Dodecanese and is most fully to be studied on Rhodes – a region where no such early Protogeometric school had existed as at Miletus. This Geometric school will be considered presently (p. 78).

The Argolid; possibly Corinthia; Thessaly; Naxos, but not the Cyclades as a whole; Elis; Miletus, but not the Asia Minor coast as a whole: these are the diverse and widely-scattered areas which, on present evidence, shared with Athens the necessary artistic impulse to begin producing a more or less independent Protogeometric style, though borrowing the initial technical advances of Attic potters, in close succession to the pottery of the preceding Mycenaean culture. It is no coincidence that in almost every one of these centres, the excavators have spoken of a transitional 'Submycenaean' phase in the pottery-series. But their adoption of the term took place before Desborough's revelation of the chronological position of Submycenaean in western Attica (pp. 31, 33), when it was still held that a 'Submycenaean' phase was an essential element in a continuous ceramic series from Mycenaean to Protogeometric. If this term is henceforward to be strictly defined, in conformity to the limits in shape and decoration observed by the Attic potters, it may be doubted whether any substantial part of the 'Submycenaean' from elsewhere should keep this name. It is also not without significance that the decisive evidence for the early origin of these non-Attic styles has, in almost every case, come to light within the last fifteen years; a warning that other local Protogeometric schools may in due course prove to have belonged to this group.

(ii) THE LATER DERIVATIVE STYLES

To our second group belong those centres of production which at first apparently lacked the incentive, or the contacts, or in some cases perhaps even the population, necessary for them to keep up with ceramic developments elsewhere; but which, before the end of the Protogeometric period, recovered sufficiently to begin doing so, if in most cases only by the direct inspiration of later Attic Protogeometric. Sometimes the resultant Proto-

30. Boeotian Protogeometric: neck-handled amphora from a grave-mound at Vranesi Kopaïdos. The resemblance to Attic products is very close. Height 43·5 cm; *c.* 925 B C.

geometric style shows evidence of having survived long after Athens and other centres had abandoned this style. It is possible for continuity of occupation to have existed in some of the centres belonging to this group, for in certain cases production of pottery continued either in a backward-looking 'survival' style of Mycenaean or Minoan origins, or in a native style owing little or nothing to painted Greek pottery of any period. In other cases, there is no such material; and ceramically speaking, these may fairly be classed as the initially backward areas of early Iron Age Greece. BOEOTIA. To allocate Boeotia to this group may be proved incorrect by later discoveries, but is on present evidence the only justifiable course. Certainly Boeotia in the early Iron Age seems to have been a shattered remnant of the rich and populous region known from Mycenaean archaeology and Greek legend. The late Protogeometric pottery from the western Boeotian sites of Orchomenos and Vranesi Kopaïdos was so hard to

30

31. Boeotian Early Geometric: oenochoe from a grave at Orchomenos, still closely similar to Attic work. Height 16·5 cm; *c.* 825 BC.

distinguish from its Attic models that Desborough was inclined to believe that elements of Attic population had settled there at the time.[46] Thebes itself, however, tells a rather different story: graves there produced a handful of Protogeometric pots and a few others that were very close to Submycenaean; in one case (Tomb 2 at the Electran Gates) a Submycenaean or late Mycenaean III C amphoriskos was found in the same interment with a late Protogeometric lekythos which was probably an Attic import. From this it is safe to conclude that there was close dependence on Attica in Thebes too, if from an earlier date; and while it is going too far to infer, from the tomb mentioned above, that in Thebes pottery of Mycenaean type remained in use down to a date contemporary with later Attic Protogeometric, the earlier part of the Protogeometric period in Boeotia as a whole remains quite obscure. When we pass to the Geometric period we again find a debt to Athens, as great as in any other district of Greece. At Orchomenos the earlier Geometric pottery seems still to
31 depend heavily on Attic models.[47] The skyphos with pendent semicircles (cf. p. 62) appears also in Boeotia, showing that other influences (and perhaps imports) than those from Attica were present from early on. But close if incompetent imitation of Attic remains the dominant theme, and

extends later to the production of figured scenes, with predictably limited success; towards the end, the influence of Corinth shows itself, though perhaps rather later than in the other cases where it occurs. The Boeotian Geometric style has a long after-life, in keeping with the backward character of the pottery of this region throughout our period.

EUBOEA. A Protogeometric school which has emerged very recently is that of the island of Euboea, where evidence for a local style had been sparse in the extreme. Here the excavations at the site of Lefkandi in 1964–6 have revealed settlement-layers of Mycenaean III C, Protogeometric and Geometric; but the evidence of the pottery does not yet support a belief in full continuity of habitation. After an early phase represented by four burials which perhaps belong soon after the end of III C, the Protogeometric element in the series is quite fully represented in its later stages, and reveals that Euboea was indeed producing its own Protogeometric ware, with northern Cycladic connections at least as strongly detectable as Attic. But the most valuable contribution of the Lefkandi series is that it demonstrates beyond all doubt the survival of a Protogeometric school long after the abandonment of the style at Athens: for imported Attic Geometric sherds, covering the whole of the Early and Middle Geometric phases, were associated with the later products of the local Protogeometric style, proving its survival throughout the ninth century and on into the earlier eighth. Numerous sporadic finds of Protogeometric, including a few tombs, have occurred in recent years at sites other than Lefkandi; the distribution of these, which is confined to the northern and central parts of the island, gives a hint of early contact with Thessaly. It is too early to say more than this; but Euboea had already been very tentatively, and possibly rightly, suggested as a possible source for two Protogeometric vases found in a somewhat obscure context at Amathus in Cyprus, the earliest post-Mycenaean Greek imports known in that island.[48] For the Geometric period, Lefkandi may again ultimately prove to be the most important site when its pottery is fully published; but even without this evidence, the later stages of Euboean Geometric have been found to have some interest. The style is not impressive in itself, the resemblance to Attic being close in some of the vases, and the adoption of Corinthian shapes also being in a manner reminiscent of Attic; but there are also features which link Euboea with the Cycladic and Thessalian schools. The foremost of these is the retention of the skyphos with pendent semicircles (p. 27), a shape which is found in stylistically earliest form at Lefkandi, and on Andros and Tenos in the northern Cyclades, and for which a Euboean origin can be argued

32. Euboean Late Geometric: oenochoe from the settlement at
Lefkandi, preserving the old northern Greek feature of the cut-away
neck; *c.*725 BC.

with the greatest historical plausibility; and it is interesting that the jug
32 with cut-away neck also occurs (cf. above, p. 61). A later link with the
Cyclades, central as well as northern, is given by the decorative motif of
rows of small concentric circles round the rims of Geometric skyphoi, a
habit which both areas may have acquired from Cyprus. Indeed, overseas
connections provide the most important aspect of Euboean Geometric,
and must in part reflect the known activities of the chief Euboean cities,
Chalkis and Eretria, in the early phases of Greek colonization. Thus
pottery identifiable as Euboean has been found, alongside Corinthian, in
some of the earliest graves at Pithekoussai on the island of Ischia; but
even earlier belongs an episode unrelated in our historical sources, for the
earliest levels at Al Mina by the mouth of the Orontes contained skyphoi
and mugs of a ware found otherwise only in Euboea and Pithekoussai, in
association with earlier pottery both of native Syrian type and of Greek,
in the shape of the pendent-semicircle skyphoi.[49]

PHOKIS AND LOKRIS. Next comes another region which, as one comes
hypothetically from Athens, is most naturally approached through

Boeotia: Phokis and Lokris, with the great sanctuary-site of Delphi which has produced the bulk of the material. Locally-made Protogeometric pottery here is almost as scarce as in Boeotia, and although continuity of habitation has been suggested for Delphi, the published evidence is not enough to support this view. There is certainly a gap between the very late Mycenaean III c Temenos Tomb and the earlier of the two interments in the tomb near the Museum, whose pottery Desborough classes as Proto-geometric with the survival of some decorative motifs of Mycenaean appearance; and there is a further long gap before the second interment in this tomb, as the excavator saw. The published settlement pottery of Protogeometric and Geometric date is not enough to fill these lacunae, and in any case shows indebtedness to Attic and to Thessalian as well; the slight finds of Protogeometric from a site near Itea do little to controvert this impression, but the graves at Medeon, although they show a gap comparable with that at Delphi, between the latest III c period and the Protogeometric, introduce a new factor at the latter date, with pottery of a very independent style, whose links may be with Ithaka and with the material from a single burial at Derveni in Achaea (below, pp. 85-6). A Corinthian vase of about 900 is reported, from nearby Antikyra. At Delphi there is indeed a substantial Geometric settlement, but the local characteristics of its pottery are not clearly apparent, and it does contain, from about the middle of the Geometric period, a surprising number of Corinthian imports, which remain predominant thereafter. There is also at least one Ithakan piece, and there are several of the skyphoi with pendent semicircles to suggest indirect contact with Euboea or the northern Cyclades—perhaps through Thessaly, since two of the characteristic jugs with cut-away necks of the Thessalian native ware appeared.[50] The Attic contacts become less obvious until late in the Geometric period. But Geometric Delphi, if not yet an international sanctuary, already shows unusually wide connections.

MACEDONIA. In a special category belongs Macedonia. This region, like its neighbour Thessaly, had possessed an indigenous culture to which the Mycenaean element had been intrusive. But the Mycenaean penetration had been shallower than in Thessaly, and the sequel was quite different in Macedonia. Partly no doubt because of its remoteness, but also because of a major wave of non-Greek settlers which arrived at the end of the Bronze Age, Macedonia apparently lost all contact with Greek civilization for a time. But local imitations of Mycenaean III c probably continued to be produced for a while, and when the connection is resumed, the moment

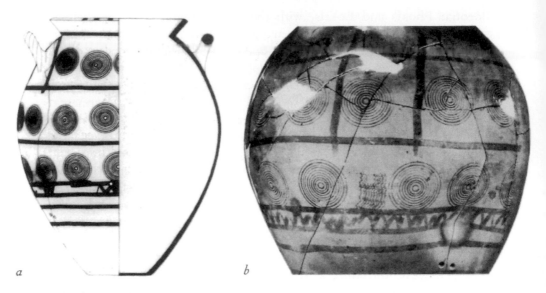

a   *b*

33a, b. Macedonian imitation of Protogeometric: hand-made pithos
from grave L X V *AΞ* at Vergina, showing experimental use of the
multiple brush and compass. Height 60 cm; *c.* 900 B C or rather later.

is marked ceramically by the arrival of Protogeometric pottery, apparently
of a late stage in that style. The richest evidence comes from the great
cemetery-site of Vergina, where excavations have gone on with little
break since 1951. It is clear that some of the vases here are imports, perhaps
from Thessaly, but other Protogeometric pieces are locally made; there is
evidence from half a dozen other sites besides Vergina that this flourishing
school continued at least into the ninth century, and no true Protogeometric
shape is as common in Macedonia as the 'sub-Protogeometric' skyphos
with pendent semicircles. Sometimes the Greek style of decoration is
applied to shapes of native origin, as in Thessaly: perhaps the most
interesting single piece is a large hand-made, unevenly-fired pithos, on
which a painter has experimented with a multiple brush and compass in
a very unpractised way, before falling back on a less ambitious system of
decoration of careless strokes with a broad brush. This pot is a rare
document of the spread of a novel technique to a peripheral region. Equally
interesting is the fact that this Protogeometric school gave birth to no
Geometric; the native Macedonian ware had indeed been heavily predominant throughout, and the taste for fine painted pottery, having been served
for perhaps quite a long time by the local Protogeometric, seems to have

33

34. A Protogeometric tomb-group from Kos, Serraglio tomb 10. In this heterogeneous collection, the large jar in the centre of the bottom row is an indisputable Mycenaean heirloom of the 14th century BC, while two other vases in this row (2nd left and far right) also appear to be of Mycenaean type. Two incised jugs (middle row, far left and 2nd right) are hand-made, but the other similar pots (first three in top row, and bottom row, far left) are apparently wheel-made. The remaining six vases are Protogeometric. All *c.*950 BC.

expired altogether. There is no further datable influence from Greek pottery until near the end of the seventh century, a remarkably late date; although a few imports of around the middle of the eighth century, which are strongly reminiscent of Attic work, have now appeared at Nea Anchialos, some ten miles north-west of Salonika.[51]

DODECANESE. In the Dodecanese we have a clear instance of an apparently late Protogeometric school growing up, largely under Attic influence. The evidence here, as represented by the Serraglio cemetery on Kos, and by Ialysos, Kameiros and Lindos on Rhodes, shows that, at the end of a notable late flowering of Mycenaean culture in the III c period, there is a total break of considerable duration. When Protogeometric eventually appears, it is locally made and develops its own stylistic trends, but its inspiration plainly comes from outside. The earliest material seems to be that from Kos and from Kameiros on Rhodes; it must belong to a stage   *34*

35. Rhodian, transition to Geometric: belly-handled amphora from Marmaro grave 43 at Ialysos. Height 56 cm; *c.* 900 BC.
36. Coan Late Geometric: oenochoe from Serraglio tomb 14, Kos, combining a dark-ground scheme with elaborate zonal decoration in a manner peculiar to this island. Height 25 cm; *c.* 740 BC.

some time before the end of Protogeometric in Athens and elsewhere, and indeed the pottery from Kos shows resemblances to Argive which, reinforced by its association with a characteristic undecorated ware, otherwise not found on this side of the Aegean (see below, p. 95), suggests a link with the Argolid. The starting-point for the Rhodian material is a

35 very late stage of Attic Protogeometric.[52] In the Geometric period, there are again local differences within the Dodecanese, with other complicating factors as well. The prolific child-burials from the cemeteries on Kos apparently reflect the earliest developments in Attic Geometric, and then

36 run on in an unbroken series down to late Geometric. On Rhodes, there is a distinction between the cemeteries of Ialysos and Kameiros

37. Rhodian Middle Geometric: pedestalled krater from a grave at Kameiros (cf. no. *24*). Height 55·5 cm; early 8th century BC.

on the north-west side of the island which faces Kos, and the main central and eastern sites, Lindos, Exochi and Siana. In the former group there are the elements of a series covering the earlier phases of Geometric. But Exochi and Lindos fail to produce any convincing stage of development between late Protogeometric and a late phase of Middle Geometric. There is indeed a hint that features of the former style could have survived to lead directly on to the latter, although the main evidence comes, awkwardly enough, from Ialysos and Kameiros, where the intervening stages also exist. For belly-handled amphorae occur here, of exactly the same late Protogeometric type as those found on Thera (p. 65) which proved to have an eighth-century context, as well as others which look like crude local adaptations of the type; they may be equally late in Rhodes. Then, at a date perhaps a little later than 800, a second wave of Attic influence sweeps Rhodes, most clearly discernible in the pottery from Exochi: richly decorated vases, particularly kraters, suddenly begin   *37*

38. Rhodian Late Geometric: kotyle from Sellada grave 17 on Thera.
The shape is based on the Corinthian form of no. *49.* Height 10cm;
*c.*730 B C.

to appear, distinguishable mainly by their clay from their Attic models.[53]
In the succeeding years, something of an East Greek ceramic *koinē* grows
up, into which are attracted not only the Dodecanese but Miletus (p. 68)
and other cities on the coast of Asia Minor; only Samos and Chios in this
part of the Aegean preserve an individuality which can be discerned
throughout. The main East Greek school develops some clear characteristics in the later stages of Geometric, modifying certain shapes and
decorations to its taste; there is great emphasis on the vertical division of
zones into separate panels, even on small vases, and the dark-ground
36   system is retained to a surprising degree; presently the Corinthian kotyle
38   arrives, and is imitated here too. This Geometric style lives on into a late
and uninspired after-life in the seventh century. But already within the
Geometric period proper, the products of this school are quite widely
cf. 38   exported: first to the Cyclades, in some quantity, with one or two pieces
reaching Aegina and even the Greek mainland; then at the end of the period
5oc   as far afield as Al Mina, and Pithekoussai in the West where a famous
see 111   skyphos has been found with an inscription which challenges the Homeric
Cup of Nestor. The most interesting imports to this area are those from
Cyprus, which re-establish a well-attested Bronze Age link; in an early
grave (Marmaro 43 at Ialysos, which stands at the transition to Geometric)
were 'barrel-jugs' of local ware which closely imitate a Cypriot form;
somewhat later another Cypriot shape, the globular lekythos with a ridge
round its neck, makes its appearance on Kos; and before the end of the
Geometric period Cypriot imports and imitations both become common
in the Dodecanese.[54]

N. CYCLADES. There are other smaller regions which probably ought to be allocated to this group. The only example of which we know anything appreciable is the northern group of the Cyclades, which includes Andros, Tenos and, for a time only (p. 64) Delos and Rheneia, and to which may be added Skyros in the Sporades, which in the Protogeometric period at least seems to show a similar pattern. These islands seem to have been uniquely well placed to retain communications with both Attica and Thessaly, the homes of the two most strongly characterized Protogeometric styles; they must also have been very closely associated with Euboea (p. 71), and when more is known of Euboean Protogeometric it may transpire that that island was in fact the centre of this early cultural grouping. Nevertheless, the evidence for these widespread links belongs entirely to a developed stage of Protogeometric, and later; there is a dearth of material for the earliest stages of the Iron Age, and indeed even the Mycenaean settlement of this region, Delos apart, is still only scantily attested. Its main claim to interest is that the long-lived shape of the low-footed skyphos with pendent semicircles (pp. 27, 62, 70-1) is found   *26* hereabouts in its earliest form, and was presumably developed either in these islands or in Euboea, as a variant of the high-footed Attic skyphos. In the Geometric period the region remained in touch with the outside world, although the Attic influence became heavily predominant. Actual imports from Attica may be rare in the surviving evidence, but the influence of Attic Geometric is felt from early on. There are vases from the Purification Trench on Rheneia, originally interred in burials on Delos, which closely resemble earlier Attic Geometric; from actual graves on Rheneia come oenochoai, cups and skyphoi which imitate Attic even more closely (some of them are indeed imports), as well as a neck-handled amphora which is paralleled at Corinth; from tombs on Andros and Tenos comes a collection of vases, some very close to late Attic Protogeometric, others preserving this resemblance into the earlier part of the local Geometric. Later, as already noted (p. 64), Andros, Delos and Rheneia are attracted more into the orbit of the other Cyclades (although this is another Attic-dominated group); for example, the skyphoi with pendent semicircles, on Delos, give way both to Attic imitations, and to the products of the southern Cycladic schools, with Paros perhaps in the van.[55]

CRETE. In the remaining islands of the Aegean we have no evidence that local Protogeometric styles grew up, with the important exception of Crete. Here there is a special case – or rather several cases, since the course of events was evidently not the same all over the island. The peculiarities arise, first from the presence of the long and unmistakeable Subminoan

39. Cretan Protogeometric: stirrup-jar (with open spout) from
Fortetsa tomb XI at Knossos. The decoration marks the long-delayed
arrival of a truly Protogeometric style in Crete; for the survival of the
shape, contrast nos. *4* and *5*. Height 25·5 cm; *c*. 825 BC.

phase (pp. 40-3), then from the fact that the subsequent Protogeometric
style has itself only a questionable title to the name (p. 26). The areas
where this Cretan Protogeometric, with its direct Attic inspiration, makes
its appearance are also among the prominent centres of production for the
39   preceding Subminoan: in the northern coastal plain of Crete, Knossos;
in the Mesara plain to the south, Phaistos and Gortyn. At Phaistos, there is
continuity of settlement from Late Minoan through into Geometric,
and it might be possible to infer the same for Knossos, where a long
series of tombs has been discovered, ranging chronologically from the
Gypsadhes cemetery (Late Minoan III A to Subminoan), through a Subminoan tomb at Agios Ioannis, to the Fortetsa cemetery (continuous from
later Subminoan to Geometric and later), with further Protogeometric
tombs, some of them early, at Agios Ioannis and Tekke, and other later
examples published long ago by Hogarth and Payne. Near Phaistos there
are also two groups of Protogeometric cremations, each group in a trench,
which show strong connections with the pottery used in and around

40. East Cretan Geometric: krater from the settlement at Vrokastro.
Height 28 cm; early 8th century B C.

Knossos; they include pithoi and stirrup-vases of a kind found at Knossos
and Tylissos respectively, and a piriform jar in an incised ware of which
something will be said presently (p. 96). Several lesser sites, grouped
around Knossos and in or near the Mesara plain, have also produced
Cretan Protogeometric, and fill out the evidence of the major sites. But
so far we have considered only the two regions of Crete most naturally
accessible – the first directly, the second *via* the first – to the influence of
Attic Protogeometric. What happened in the rest of this great island?
Protogeometric is reported from one or two sites in the more mountainous
area to the east of the centres we have been considering, while from the far
west of the island the cemetery at Modi near Vrises has produced evidence
of a local style apparently contemporary with the later Protogeometric of
central Crete. But in the easternmost quarter, which had accommodated
not only some of the most thriving settlements of the Minoan world but a
number of Subminoan ones too – Vrokastro, Kavousi, and the sites using
the graves at Mouliana, Dreros and Olous – there is, in Desborough's
words, 'hardly any trace in this part of the island of the influence of Protogeometric pottery'. The fullest evidence comes from Vrokastro, but even

40

F

here there are only rare signs of the intrusion of any outside influence between the Subminoan survivals and the full Geometric style; the two must have been virtually consecutive, and this is supported by the evidence from Dreros. Not even the curious 'Protogeometric B' style of central Crete (pp. 26-7, and below) penetrates more than marginally to this part of the island. But at Vrokastro at least, continuity of habitation throughout the early Iron Age seems to be indicated.[56]

An important feature of the Cretan series (as of the Euboean) is that it gives positive proof of what in many cases was only suspected, the long survival of a Protogeometric school after the style had ended in Attica and other centres. The cemetery at Fortetsa near Knossos, in what is probably the most advanced locality of the island, produced clear evidence of this time-lag in the form of imported vases in close grave-groups. First, there are two tombs at the very beginning of the Cretan Protogeometric style which contain imports that must belong near the end of Attic Proto-geometric; one of these, the amphora in Tomb XI, is not itself Attic, but a Cycladic imitation of Attic; so that Cretan Protogeometric seems not to have begun until, at the earliest, the time when these other two styles were drawing to an end. Again, a tomb of Cretan Late Protogeometric date
see 121   contained a Cycladic amphora (cf. pp. 64, 125) which derives from Attic Geometric at a stage some way from its beginning; and a recent find in a well at Knossos produced a Cycladic skyphos, of similar or rather later date, associated with Cretan material of Protogeometric and the ensuing phase. Protogeometric at Knossos, and perhaps one or two other sites in central Crete, gives way not to a full Geometric style, but to the remarkable 'Protogeometric B', for which neither this nor any other name yet suggested is fully satisfactory. It has been described as a premature Oriental-izing phase, partly on the strength of its decoration, partly because of its curious experimental shapes, for which metallic origins have been suggested (there are some explicit contemporary copies of non-ceramic objects, such as trees and a boat). Perhaps the most striking feature is the sudden appearance of a figure-style, whose elements range from the purely Cretan, of
41   Subminoan vintage, to a mourning scene for which Attic Geometric has been proposed as a model, since it is painted on a belly-handled amphora
see 122   which is itself a crude copy of the Attic type.[57] Baffling as it is, the Proto-geometric B period is certainly short; it is represented at Fortetsa only by one complete tomb and isolated burials in three others. In the succeeding Geometric period, Crete at last embarks on an era of pottery-decoration which is in keeping with the rest of Greece, and there are a number of

41. Cretan 'Protogeometric B': projected scene of the decoration from a belly-handled amphora (see no. *122*) from Fortetsa tomb OD. Height of whole vase 56·3 cm; *c.* 800 BC.

imported pieces that suggest the inspiration which prompted this. Furthermore, the local differences within the island become less prominent as the Geometric movement spreads across it. The sites in the plain of Mesara and its neighbourhood, which in Protogeometric times had maintained links with the Knossos area, seem to have remained in close touch thereafter. At Phaistos and other sites, including Arkades (Afrati) above the eastern end of the plain, there are found both Protogeometric B and a full Geometric series, with some pieces that are probably Attic imports; but even in this neighbourhood the bizarre pots from Kourtes, perhaps largely contemporary with these phases, suggest a considerable degree of isolation. This is certainly true of the eastern end of Crete, until the time *cf. 40* when Attic imports begin to appear there, of a stage comparable with the earliest Attic influence on the Geometric used at Exochi in Rhodes (p. 77). The Cretan Geometric style, whose start had been so long delayed, finally surprises by its early decline, in the face of new Orientalizing motifs. No part of Greece except Corinth accepted this influence in its pottery so early, even discounting the experiment of Protogeometric B. From first to last the Geometric style of Crete probably lasted less than a century; it was essentially a domestic style which held little attraction outside the island. A class of aryballoi with circles and vertical wavy lines which used to be classed as Cretan, and which is found abroad, is probably of Rhodian origin; more problematical is a group of small closed vases found in the graves at Pithekoussai and Cumae, which were long believed to be of Cretan origin, but which Coldstream would now trace to Euboea. Towards the end of the lifetime of the style, as in Rhodes, Cypriot imports and imitations occur.[58]

So far, it is not easy to see in this group any obvious unifying features, apart from that on which the classification is itself based, the late growth of the local Protogeometric school. Indeed Macedonia and Crete, which on this basis have been included in the group, each present in reality a peculiar and unique case, their outlying location helping to give them a degree of independence from the main developments in the Aegean area which will be found persistent in other fields too. For the other regions – Boeotia, Euboea, Phokis and Lokris, the Dodecanese, Skyros and the northern Cyclades – further research alone can show how far the element of delay in their ceramic development is due to isolation, to inherent backwardness or to actual depopulation; but it can be said that in every region of this group there is either the positive evidence that a Bronze Age survival-style, or an indigenous class of pottery, persisted after the adoption of Protogeometric by the more advanced areas; or else the negative evidence of a palpable lacuna in the pottery-series, succeeded by Protogeometric of a developed stage.

(iii) THE INDEPENDENT STYLES

Our third regional group contains those few Protogeometric schools which seem not to derive from Attic influence, nor from that of any of the other advanced centres. This group shows a clearer geographical pattern than the other two, lying to the west of a line running diagonally from Mount Pindus, across the Corinthian Gulf west of Delphi and down to Cape Malea. Within this area, it is true, lies Elis which we have placed in another category (p. 65), because it seems to show indirect knowledge of the advances made in Attic Protogeometric; but Elis too, after a subsequent interruption in the series, may perhaps have moved into the orbit of this group. There are several signs, as we shall see, that the regions of this group were in touch with each other.[59]

ITHAKA. In one of these regions, Ithaka, continuity of occupation seems assured. The probability here is that a strong resurgence of population, more clearly marked in the neighbouring island of Kephallenia, took place in the Mycenaean III C period, before the contacts with the main centres

42-4. Protogeometric lekythoi, from a grave at Medeon in Phokis (*42*), from the settlement at Aetos in Ithaka (*43*, fragmentary); and oenochoe from a grave at Derveni in eastern Achaea (*44*, height 26 cm). All show a remarkable correspondence in decoration and shape. Probably later 9th century BC.

of Greece lapsed. The local III C style was then allowed to live on; the sites on Kephallenia were ultimately abandoned, but two of those on Ithaka – the cave at Polis, and Aetos – between them show a continuous series; gradually, as the series from Aetos shows, the III C shapes develop into a local Protogeometric style, derived from them without many signs of outside influence. As far as decoration goes, the mere presence of compass-drawn semicircles and circles must depend ultimately on the advances made in Attica. One or two imported pieces, probably from Attica, appeared at Aetos. But in spite of this the Ithakan style cannot be called Attic-derived; the concentric motifs are taken over and treated differently, with fewer arcs; the subsidiary decoration, with marked use of cross-hatched diamonds and triangles, and of zigzags, is sturdily independent. The best parallels are to be found not in the Attic series but in other schools of this group. The development of the Ithakan school from the local Mycenaean III C could have happened quite late, for the evidence of a succeeding style, contemporary with the earlier stages of Geometric at Corinth, has proved weak (see below). It was possibly from Ithaka that the very, very few genuine Protogeometric sherds found in Southern

43
cf. 42-4

Italy came; while the Ithakan style is more closely reflected in the finds from a grave at Palaiomanina in Akarnania on the neighbouring mainland.[60]

In the Geometric style of Ithaka, which undoubtedly follows directly on the Protogeometric, the great problem is to distinguish the Ithakan products from the very copious imports from Corinth, which they imitate from the first. Certainly the Ithakan material for the earlier stages of Geometric is much less full than was at first thought; indeed, in the judgment of the most recent studies of the evidence, the only well-defined class of Ithakan Geometric was that of the late phase.[61] In any case, the Ithakan school leans heavily on Corinthian and shows negligible contact with other schools; in marked contrast with the local Protogeometric, which apart from its marginal debt to Attic was of local development and perhaps even influenced other schools (see below). Yet Ithakan Geometric has its own charm, which greatly increases with the introduction of a figure-style towards the end of the eighth century, and the subsequent growth of an Orientalizing school of real individuality. This Geometric style found no market, so far as we know, outside the narrow confines of the island.

ACHAEA. In the Peloponnese, the first region which seems to belong to this group is Achaea, although the evidence is in no way satisfactory. Achaea has recently been shown to have witnessed an influx of population at the beginning of the Mycenaean III C period, comparable with that which occurred in Kephallenia and Ithaka (see above). The pottery of this latest Mycenaean style may have remained in use in Achaea for a very long time – long enough for traces of influence from Attic Protogeometric to be seen in its later stages: a group of duck-shaped askoi, for which analogies were first sought in Cypriot and Cretan examples, has now found an

15 even closer parallel in grave 114 at the Kerameikos, which is transitional between Submycenaean and Protogeometric. The evidence for the sub-sequent local Protogeometric style is inadequate, consisting in the main

44 of a single pithos-burial which belongs late in relation to Attic, at Derveni on the eastern fringes of this region; a cist of Protogeometric date is now reported at Liopesi near Pharai. It is interesting that the Derveni pottery

cf. 43 shows links with Ithaka, a centre which had perhaps experienced a rather similar course of events at the end of the Bronze Age. But from now on the resemblance to Ithaka ceases, for there is no evidence for continuous development in Achaean pottery after the time of the Derveni burial; and indeed there may also be a gap in time before it, from the end of the Mycenaean III C series. At present the obscurity which covers Iron Age Achaea extends deep into the Geometric period: the existence of a local

Geometric school is attested only at an advanced stage of the style and by few finds, which show, not unexpectedly, the strong influence of Corinth, Achaea's eastern neighbour.[62]

MESSENIA. The case of Messenia at first resembles Ithaka, in that only very slight direct contact with Attica is known to have existed: the pottery from a recently-excavated tomb at Karpophora, and a handful of sherds from the remote upland site of Volimnos seem, from the description of decoration and shape, to be closely influenced by Attic technique. But otherwise the material so far published from Messenia is notable for not copying Attic; concentric semicircles are adopted, it is true, but they are treated in a way similar to that in Ithaka. Messenia had been, on present showing, the most populous settlement-area in the whole Mycenaean world down to the end of III B; but the débâcle thereafter was correspondingly great. Mycenaean III C sites are comparatively few, and the published Protogeometric material is also scarce; however, Protogeometric pottery is now reported from several sites – a tholos tomb at Pylos, a burial at Antheia and half a dozen settlements – whose evidence may in due course be added to the only previously known group of sherds, from a re-used tholos tomb at Tragana near Pylos. The Traganes material is not very early, and the most significant fact that has so far emerged about the new sites is that on none of them, not even Nichoria, the most impressive, is full continuity of pottery-styles from Mycenaean to Protogeometric to be inferred. So there is no reason to believe *a priori* that the style was of early growth; and since the published material shows little close resemblance to Attic, Messenia seems to belong most easily in this group, although the classification must remain provisional.[63] What happened subsequently, in the Geometric period, is even more obscure: there can be no doubt of the existence of a local Geometric style, but it cannot be judged until the material is published; one may expect a modest school to emerge, in view of the developments (or lack of them) in neighbouring Elis, Arcadia and Laconia (pp. 65, 88-90).

LACONIA. Laconia is faintly linked with its neighbour Messenia in the Protogeometric period, by influence and the occasional import; but a more substantial resemblance is that of Laconian to Ithakan and Achaean Protogeometric, which shows itself particularly in the coincidence of decorative ideas, and the love of cross-hatching common to both styles. Yet the development of Laconian Protogeometric cannot have followed a course similar to Ithakan, for there is no stylistic link with a preceding Mycenaean style. Indeed on published evidence there is only one Laconian

45. Laconian Protogeometric: oenochoe from the Heroön at Sparta.
Height 19·5 cm; perhaps about 800 BC.
46. Laconian Late Geometric: fragmentary deep skyphos from the
Chalkioikos at Sparta. Height 9·5 cm; *c.* 740 BC.

site where Mycenaean III C and Protogeometric pottery both occur, the
III C period having witnessed a depopulation here only less drastic than
that in Messenia. This site is Amyklai (Agia Kyriaki); and the most plausible claim for continuity here is in respect of cult, since votive figurines and
sherds of Mycenaean III C date were found below, and sometimes mixed
with, the quite plentiful Protogeometric pottery. But there is no architectural
evidence to suggest continuous occupation; the style of the Protogeometric
pottery owes nothing to Mycenaean; and, as will be seen later, there would
be chronological difficulties in supposing that Laconian Protogeometric
directly succeeded the last Mycenaean pottery, quite apart from the fact
that it may show fleeting signs of the influence of Geometric of other areas.
Laconian Protogeometric has been found in smaller quantities on a few
45 other sites – the sanctuaries and acropolis of Sparta itself, Mavrovouni,
Apidia – but none of these has produced Mycenaean material of the latest
phase. The Geometric school, which demonstrably grows directly out of
this style in Laconia, has wider connections; indeed it is the most considerable of its period in the Peloponnese, after those of Argos and Corinth.
It is a style in which definite stages of development can be detected, all
of which, however, can be equated with later Geometric, by comparison
46 with the Argive series, to which Laconian at first seems to owe most;
the Laconian Protogeometric style must therefore have lasted until a
very late date. The sequence in the Geometric period is that the fabric

and technique of the Protogeometric, with its hard red-brown clay and lustrous paint, is taken over and adapted to a new system of decoration, with multiple concentric circles predominant; this stage is well represented by the finds from the Acropolis at Sparta. A small proportion of the sherds from here (the evidence is nearly all fragmentary) show a different technique, the pots having been covered with a white slip before decoration. From the nearby sanctuary of Artemis Orthia, however, whose use runs on continuously into Classical times, over 90 per cent of the Geometric sherds have this white slip, and many of them show a wider range of more careful decoration. The slip is therefore most naturally seen as a later feature, though its origin, if external, is problematic; of all other schools of Geometric, it is most regular as a feature of Samian, and to a lesser extent Chiot, both of which seem to lie beyond the range of Laconian contacts at this date. A few figure-scenes, reminiscent of Argive, appear on both unslipped and slipped fragments; Corinthian influence is also visible in the later stages. It is clear that the Laconian Geometric school lasted well into the seventh century, mainly by reason of its links with Protocorinthian.[64]

THE REMAINING REGIONS

These are the known centres of production of Protogeometric pottery; and there are some notable absentees from the list. As we have seen, the lack of a Protogeometric phase is not in itself a necessary sign that the pottery-series of a region is not continuous: in east Crete, for example, the absence of this style may be put down simply to lack of communications; and those of the smaller islands of the Aegean which apparently preferred to import Attic Protogeometric rather than make their own – Aegina, Kea and perhaps Siphnos and Amorgos – may have lacked the necessary resources or inclination. Indeed, the mention of Aegina calls to mind the fact that, for much of the Archaic period, all the fine pottery found on this island still seems to be imported. But for other areas, important earlier or later, such as Kephallenia or the Megarid, where no Protogeometric is known, the only reasonable course is to assume provisionally that there was an interruption of habitation, as may be the case with some regions of the second and third groups which did develop a Protogeometric style. Some of these regions re-enter the picture in the Geometric period, and will be considered in a moment; but beyond, there are broad areas, later brought into the circle of Hellenic civilization, which were little touched even at the height of Mycenaean expansion, and were for long left to their own devices thereafter: Aetolia, and points north on the western side of the Greek mainland; Thrace and the islands of the north Aegean; the northern half of the west coast of Asia Minor. In these, Protogeometric and Geometric pottery would not be expected to occur; at Troy, one of the few sites in these areas which had prolonged Mycenaean contacts, a long period of desertion in the early Iron Age is certain.

ARCADIA. There remain those areas where local production of pottery becomes detectable only in the Geometric period. One of these, Arcadia, is associated stylistically, as it is geographically, with the regions of our third, 'independent' group. Practically no genuine Protogeometric has been found here; one of the very few sherds from Tegea may be a Laconian import. Mycenaean material is itself scantily represented, and there is as yet no vestige of continuity. But in the Geometric period Arcadia emerges from the shadows to produce a distinct local school, recognizable in the finds from Tegea, and perhaps discernible also at Asea and Mantinea. The published material seems to belong almost entirely to a late stage of the style, as is suggested by the unusually high proportion of figured scenes, and of rows of birds, on the surviving fragments. This Arcadian school owes much to Argos (where figured scenes were also favoured), and it is no surprise to find that there are several Argive Geometric imports at Tegea, as well as some of the 'Argive monochrome' ware (p. 96) of the late Geometric period; Corinthian imports also occur, though these need not begin at so early a date, and there is some Laconian as well.[65]

E. AEGEAN ISLANDS. Next we may consider the three large islands of the eastern Aegean, Samos, Chios and Lesbos, although they are far from presenting a unified picture. As far as the Protogeometric period is concerned, Samos has been noted (p. 64) for having produced little pottery that is not of Attic type, and the same is true of a single sherd found on Lesbos; Chios, on the other hand, has produced a few sherds whose origin is uncertain, although at the most fully-excavated site, Emborio, there was a total break between Mycenaean III C and Late Geometric. But it becomes clear that Lesbos and the Aeolic mainland opposite lay altogether outside the orbit of Greek painted pottery at this period; the monochrome 'Grey Ware' of the Iron Age in this region merely continued the non-Greek traditions of the Bronze Age, but by the Geometric period at latest it is certain that it is being produced by Greeks; its incised decoration borrows motifs from Greek Geometric. Even at Smyrna, further south on the mainland, the Grey Ware predominates over the Protogeometric and earlier Geometric; while on Lesbos and at the site identified with Larisa in Aeolis, it has almost exclusive currency until well on in the Archaic period.[66]

47. Samian Late Geometric: skyphos from the Samian Heraeum.
Height 9 cm; *c.* 725 BC.

But Chios and Samos fared differently; Samos, having had a direct link
with Attica even in Protogeometric times, has also produced a few vases
which resemble earlier Attic Geometric; in this same period a recognizable *47*
local school really emerges; the smaller vases later show links with the
Dodecanesian style, but there is also a very conscious imitation of the
Attic figure-style; the results are uncouth, but the spirit is more ambitious
than anything visible in the repertory of the Dodecanese. The Chiot
Geometric school is more shadowy, being detectable only in the late phase,
and in fragmentary material; here again there are attempts at a figure-
style, for which Attic must have provided the ultimate inspiration.[67]
SICILY: S. ITALY. In one large area of the Greek world there were special
reasons for the absence of a school of Protogeometric: this was Sicily and
southern Italy, where permanent settlement only began in the eighth
century. It is true that there have been repeated reports of finds of 'Protogeometric' in this region, but only in rare cases has the Protogeometric
character of the pottery been confirmed, and even here it is accepted that
the pieces in question are imported from Greece. Geometric imports are
also virtually unknown for the earlier stages of the style; by the end,
however, they are extremely common. It is an interesting question how far
back in time they can be traced as a continuous sequence, though not one
strictly relevant to our present purpose. Suffice to say that the search for
imports which antedate the historical onset of Greek colonization in the
West, so energetically pursued by Alan Blakeway in the 1930s, for long
failed to produce convincing results; but that now it may prove to have
been vindicated, though for a narrow geographical field, by the discoveries
made in the Etruscan cemetery of Quattro Fontanili at Veii, in the recent

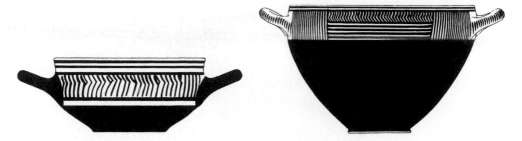

48. Imported Middle Geometric skyphos, perhaps of Cycladic origin, showing use of the multiple brush, from grave G G 14-15 at Veii in Etruria. Height 6 cm; *c.* 775 B C.
49. Imported Corinthian kotyle of the earlier, hemispherical shape; a sporadic find from Pithekoussai on Ischia. Height 11 cm; *c.* 750 B C.

excavations of the British School at Rome. In the preliminary reports so far available, a number of Greek Geometric skyphoi are illustrated which *48* are earlier than almost all the known material from Greek colony-sites; they are numerous enough to suggest an established Greco-Etruscan commerce at this stage. However, it was not this trade with foreign peoples, but the export of pottery to the Greek colonies, some of it perhaps in the possession of the original settlers, which must have inspired the Western Greeks to the production of their own pottery at a date before the end *49, 50b,d* of the Geometric period. Euboean, Corinthian, and to a lesser extent *50c* Cycladic and East Greek are prominent among the exported ware, and it was on these that the potters of the western colonies presently modelled *50a* their products. This, one of the latest of all Greek Geometric styles in origin, survived in a long sub-Geometric twilight in the seventh century, no clearly identified Orientalizing style arising to displace it. In this connection, we may mention an analogous but much more localized and fleeting Geometric style which has been recognized in the material found at Al Mina; but the Greek potters who evidently worked here did not command a wide market, nor did they apparently have successors; whereas the western colonists started a widespread vogue for Geometric decoration when they passed on their ideas to their non-Greek neighbours, particularly the Etruscans and the Sicels.[68]

It will be seen that, in several directions, the production-area of Geometric Greek pottery reached beyond that of Protogeometric, although as far as Macedonia is concerned (p. 74) it was actually narrower. Exports of pottery, most obviously, now covered a far wider area. It should perhaps

50. Four of the vases from tomb 233 at Pithekoussai on Ischia. The oenochoe (*a*) is a local product modelled on Corinthian forms; by contrast the kotyle (*b*, of the deeper form which succeeded that of no. *49*) and the globular aryballos (*d*) are actual Corinthian imports, while the aryballos (*c*) is of Rhodian origin. With them was a Villanovan amphora, not shown here. Heights 19·2, 8·1, 8·5, and 6·3 cm; last quarter of 8th century B C.

be explained that Cypriot pottery has been purposely excluded from this account, as presenting a unique case. Although the island was partly populated by Greek speakers since early in the Mycenaean III c period, if not before, and although the pottery of mainland Greece and Crete shows unmistakable stylistic links with Cypriot pottery down to the very end of that period, and at more than one point thereafter, Cyprus yet embarks on an entirely independent ceramic series from a date close to the end of Mycenaean III c. Thereafter, for the duration of the early Iron Age, she must be treated as an area extraneous to the Aegean Greek world, for all her special relationship with it.

HAND-MADE WARES

We have considered the styles of painted pottery used in early Iron Age Greece; but we must finally recall the fact that not all the fine pottery of this period in Greece is painted, nor even wheel-made. We can, I think, safely assume that we have been dealing up to now with the professional products of potters' workshops. Beside these, there occurs hand-made pottery which bears all the signs of having been made by some kind of home industry: although comparatively rare in Mycenaean Greece, it occurs in Submycenaean graves in the form of coarse jugs and other vessels (p. 37); and such coarse ware reappears in later periods so commonly as not to be worth remark. In some outlying areas such as Thessaly and *cf. 33* Kephallenia it rivals, or in the case of Macedonia predominates over, the wheel-made pottery in quantity. But we have also to deal with the resurgence of hand-made wares which occupy an intermediate position between these two extremes, being conspicuous both for the unusually high standard which they at times attain, and for a certain temporal and geographical concentration which they show. Their quality is certainly high enough to suggest professional workmanship; but it remains very hard to see a direct cause for this resurgence. The occasional coarse pots found in earlier Attic Protogeometric graves provide a link with their very similar Sub-mycenaean predecessors, but the new impetus to produce hand-made ware, quite apart from the differences in quality, seems to derive in part from the Argolid. Two distinct classes appear, along with other material *51* less easily classified: a smooth ware in pale, sometimes greenish clay, *52* which is almost always unpainted; and an even glossier tan-coloured or pinkish ware, with incised decoration of various kinds.

The former is the commoner and perhaps the more significant ware. It is unknown in the earlier phases of the Protogeometric period; when

51. Hand-made oenochoe of plain ware from grave G 1 at Mycenae.
Height 16·5 cm; 8th century B C.
52. Hand-made pointed pyxis of fine incised ware from the rich grave
found in 1967 in the Athenian Agora. Height 10·1 cm; *c.* 850 B C.

it does appear it is most prominent on four Argolic sites, Asine, Tiryns,
Mycenae and Argos itself. At Asine we see it perhaps at its least fine, but   *51*
it is noteworthy that it appears in a settlement here, as well as in at least
six Protogeometric tombs, where it outweighs the true Protogeometric;
a considerable range of shapes is found – amphora, hydria, oenochoe, jug,
bowl, cup, ladle. At the other sites there is less range but greater mastery:
the oenochoai and other closed vases from Tiryns, and especially those
from Mycenae, include some admirable pieces. In date they range from
later Protogeometric downwards, while at Argos was found an unpublished pot of Protogeometric date. This plain ware is also found in two
areas which one may believe to have been in touch with the Argolid,
Corinthia (where it has occurred at Corinth, Vello, Klenia and Perachora)
and the island of Kos, where several vases from the Protogeometric tomb
10 at the Serraglio site bear a resemblance to those from Asine. Laconia,   *34*
too, has produced an analogous, if inferior, local ware, also covering the
transition from Protogeometric to Geometric (which must be later there,

in absolute terms). In the Geometric period, such pottery becomes much more common. It is interesting that two other classes of hand-made ware, which are prevalent somewhat later, are found particularly in the same region, and must surely be connected with the pottery we have been considering: the distinctive 'pie-ware', decorated with the incised wavy lines from which its name derives, which is known over the whole duration of the Geometric style, and is found at Mycenae, Tiryns, Argos and, again, in Corinthia (at Klenia); and the rather later and much more widespread 'Argive monochrome', which was evidently made in Corinthia and perhaps other regions as well as the Argolid, and covers approximately the period 750–600.[69]

The incised ware found in late Protogeometric and earlier Geometric contexts, which we still have to consider, is something quite different; it has also to be distinguished from the darker, coarser pottery on which, especially in Attica, incision is sometimes used. At certain points, incised ware in general comes into contact with the plain ware: at Tiryns and on Kos both occur in one and the same grave, while in the Agora at Athens, and at Eleusis, they are associated in the same cemetery, in graves of not very different dates. Yet both fabric and shapes are quite distinct in the fine incised ware; and its distribution, too, is weighted towards Attica rather than the Argolid. It is used predominantly for small, low shapes like the pyxis and the bowl, but also (at least in Athens) for spindle-whorls, and for toys – dolls, beads and balls. Of these uses, only that of the pyxis can be paralleled in Submycenaean times: incised, hand-made examples of nondescript ware occur in two graves of the Kerameikos and in a well in the Agora. The other shapes appear, without immediate antecedents, in late Attic Protogeometric. Meanwhile a few specimens, in coarser ware, are found outside Attica – cauldrons at Tiryns, bowls and kalathos from Kos, amphoriskos at Klenia, beads at Knossos, and, most interestingly, a piriform jar from Petrokephali near Phaistos[70]; some of these could be the products of independent movements, as the diversity of shapes suggests.

The appearance of these phenomena, whether connected or not, requires some explanation in areas like the Argolid, Corinthia and Attica which had been producing fine wheel-made painted pottery without a break for centuries past. Some of the objects – the whorls and toys – one would expect to be hand-made in any case, but their stylistic models are another matter; and in the case of the vessels both style and technique come as a surprise. But we should remember that the bulk of our evidence comes exclusively from graves, and that these may give an attenuated picture –

often flattering rather than derogatory – of the usages of a community. As far as the incised ware goes, it is perfectly possible that similar objects had been in use for a long period, before a change in fashion led to their being placed in graves; the rare earlier pyxides give a hint of this, and the undoubted persistence of plain, coarse hand-made ware in this same period lends some support. As regards the plain fine ware, there is a useful clue in A. W. Persson's observation about the Asine finds, that they bore 'an astounding resemblance' to the Middle Helladic hand-made ware found on the same site. Since there was copious settlement material at Asine from the intervening period, in which such ware was not represented, it is not possible that it had been produced continuously over the six hundred years between Middle Helladic and late Protogeometric; but the similarity does suggest that, at Asine and no doubt elsewhere, a native art using indigenous materials could have been revived, under the influence of some unknown incitement or pressure. It will be apparent that I see no ground for inferring outside influence, still less migration, from outside Greece, from the evidence of this pottery. It is true that plain hand-made ware had long been, and was still, commonplace in Macedonia; it is also the case that further north in the Balkans the much earlier Unetiče culture had produced clay dolls or idols with incised decoration somewhat resembling the Attic examples.[71] But as I hope to show later, there are few more unlikely periods for such a northern influence to have been operative than the later Protogeometric (cf. below, p. 329).

By this regional division of early Greek pottery-styles, based on the character of the local Protogeometric school, we are inevitably advancing a tentative archaeological model for Greece as a whole. But it is put forward as a working hypothesis only, and indeed there are already clear signs, from the ceramic evidence itself, that such a classification does not remain valid for the whole of the period; some advanced schools of Protogeometric become backward or derivative in Geometric or later times; some active schools of Geometric grow up against a background of slow development, of isolation, or even of total obscurity in the antecedent stages. But the prime purpose of this classification is, first to establish the fact of the great diversity in character and progress of the different regions of dark age Greece; and secondly, to try to illuminate the era of the greatest crisis in Greece's development, the early part of the dark age. We shall see, when other evidence is taken into account, how far the pattern suggested by the pottery can be extended to this period in general.

G

Notes

1] Desborough, *L M S* 20, 115-19
2] Desborough, *B S A* 43 (1948), 260-72; cf. *P G P* 235
3] *P G P* 238, 247-50; J. K. Brock, *Fortetsa* 143
4] G. W. van Beek, *B A S O R* 124 (December 1951), 28, n.8a: adopted by Coldstream, *G G P* 148 etc. For new finds of these skyphoi in eighth- and even seventh-century contexts in Cyprus, see *B C H* 87 (1963), 268 and n.3
5] J. Boardman, *B S A* 58 (1963), 2
6] On the period generally, *L M S* 225-37; P. Ålin, *E M F* 148-50, and *ibid.* 150 on the Granary at Mycenae; but cf. *A R* 1968-9, 13 for more recent discoveries; Tiryns, see *A R* 1963−4, 8; 1964−5, 11
7] See *L M S* 7-8, 192-5 etc., and most recently M. R. Popham, *B S A* 60 (1965), 334-5
8] *L M S* 17-20, 28 n.1
9] J. Deshayes, *Argos, les Fouilles de la Deiras* (*Études Peloponnésiennes* IV) (1966), especially 195, 247, 251; cf. *R E G* 77 (1964), 572-4. C.-G. Styrenius, *Submycenaean Studies* (1967), 125, 127-8, etc.
10] W. Kraiker, *Kerameikos* I, 134-135
11] *L M S* 82; cf. 19. Desborough wrote, however, before the publication of the Tripolis Street graves (*A D* 18, 2 (1963), 61-2)

12] On other finds in Athens, see *Ker.* I, 131-4 and see below, Appendix to Chapter 4, p. 202) for the rest of Greece, note Desborough's remarks on various finds: *L M S* 19 on Argos; 125 on Delphi and Galaxidi; 131 on Ktouri. But elsewhere (*ibid.* 22 (Theotokou), 79-80 (Tiryns), 121-2 (Thebes), 151 and 232 (Naxos)), he is prepared to let the classification as 'Submycenaean' stand
13] A. Furumark, *Chronology of the Mycenaean Pottery*, 22-7. Additional shapes are the 'situla' and ring-vase (*Ker.* I, 111-13), the 'Salbtöpfchen' (*ibid.* 74, pl. 25), the flat-bottomed bottle (*ibid.* 63, pl. 27; *L M S* 27), the carinated cup from Salamis (*Op. Ath.* 4, 115, pl. VII, 3657). But the stemmed cup from Asine and the cup with horizontal handle from Tragana, Furumark's shapes 276, 242, should probably be subtracted. On the frequency of lekythos and stirrup-vase, see *P G P* 69, 117-18. Note that the lekythos takes over from the stirrup-vase the small air-hole to ease pouring, e.g. *Ker.* I, pls. 12,479; 15,451-2; *A J A* 59 (1955), 128 on no. 6. On the trefoil-lipped oenochoe, *P G P* 46, *L M S* 11 (Furumark's shapes 137-8)
14] For the jugs (*Ker.* I, pl. 25,496; *Op. Ath.* 4, pl. V, 3640), compare Furumark, *The Mycenaean Pottery* 602-3, shape 115; the three varieties of cup, *Op. Ath.* 4, 115, nn.5, 6, 8, 10; amphorae, *P G P* 6, 20; pilgrim-flask, *Op. Ath.* 4, pl. VIII, 3647; situla, ring-flask and bottle, see n.13 above; hand-made vases, *Ker.* I, 14, 68, pls. 20,469; 25,427,474, *Op. Ath.* 4, 115; see also *Ker.* 6, 1, 85 and *A J A* 61 (1957), 170-1
15] Furumark, *Op. Arch.* 3 (1944), 216-18. Note also the occurrence of stirrup-vases with conical knob on top

and air-hole, common to Submycenaean and to late Mycenaean III C (e.g.
J. Deshayes, *Deiras* 144-5)

16] For comparable deterioration
outside the Submycenaean area, cf.
O. Frödin and A. W. Persson, *Asine*,
figs. 206 (top row); 207,7; 208,5-6.
For the pithos and other Mycenaean
IIIC shapes, see Furumark, *M P* 585f.,
shapes 38, 63, 148, 155 and 157, 129,
195, 226, 275, 282 and 287, and 291
respectively. Hydriai and kraters are
represented in the Submycenaean
material from the Agora (see Styrenius, *S S* 120 and n.59)

17] Cf. *Ker.* 1, 59, pl. 11, 503;
Op. Ath. 4, 114, 120-1; and the stray
find *Ker.* 1, 53, 77, pl. 5 left, which is
called 'late Mycenaean'. But the stirrup
vase, *Op. Ath.* 4, pl. 3, 3608 is patently
Submycenaean despite its fine Close
Style decoration

18] Styrenius, *Op. Ath.* 4, 118-20,
gives a list of such motifs; it could be
added that elaborate variants like
those on his stirrup-vases 3616 and
3612 (pls. 2-3) are not found in the
Kerameikos

19] See M.S.F. Hood, *B S A* 60
(1965), 97-113, especially 106
(Vrises) and 112 (Melidhoni)

20] Furumark, *Op. Arch.* 3, 229-30;
L M S 179ff., 268; *P G P* 233-71

21] E.g. bowl and kalathos, *B S A*
42 (1947), 38, fig. 16A, B, E; *M P* 51,
n.6 and 54: kylix, *M P* 64: kantharos,
L M S 27, pl. 17b: feeding-cup,
Fortetsa 9, 162, pl. 3, 12: spouted cup,
B S A 53-4 (1958-9), 248, VII.10:
askos, E. Hall, *Vrokastro* fig. 92

22] On these shapes, see *L M S*
179-80; and for amphorae, *B S A* 53-4,
247, VII. 1-2: cups and bowls, *M P* 51,
n.5 and *Fortetsa* 9, pl. 3, 19: stirrup-
vase, *ibid.* 153: oenochoe, *B S A* 53-4,
248, VII. 9: amphoriskos, A. J. Evans,

The Palace of Minos 2, 136, fig. 69 o
and *P G P* 236. On Cypriot links,
L M S 26-8. For finer decoration, see
e.g. *Fortetsa*, pl. 3, 1; *Vrokastro*, figs.
86E, 89A, C, 92; *P M* 2, fig. 69n.;
B S A 53-4, 241, figs. 27-8, 29 top left

23] By 'Late Minoan III B', I mean
Furumark's L M III B I only: see
L M S 167 for a concordance of
terms. On Karphi pottery-decoration,
M. Seiradhaki, *B S A* 55 (1960), 37;
but for a proposed earlier dating of
Karphi, M. R. Popham, *B S A* 60
(1965), 281-2. In general, *L M S* 167,
175, and on Olous, 188-9

24] For Submycenaean grave 108,
Ker. 1, 47-8, 68; for 113, E. L.
Smithson, *Hesp.* 30 (1961), 174-7;
ibid. 165-6 on substitution of clay for
other materials. On range of shapes in
Protogeometric, see Styrenius, *S S* 120

25] *L M S* 258-63: Coldstream
(*G G P* 336) has made the valid point
that 'a new technical discovery does
not in itself constitute a style', but this
does not affect the arguments for
interdependence

26] Multiple brush, Boardman, *Antiquity* 34 (1960), 85-9; for Bronze Age
use of compass, Evans, *P M* 4, 92, n.2,
fig. 59; F. Matz, *Crete and Early
Greece* (1962), 174, 218, fig. 48

27] Kerameikos Submycenaean
grave 114, *A M* 78 (1963), 148-53,
Beil. 54; Heidelberg Tomb B: *P G P*
2, pl. 1, G 82 a, c and G 82 b, d; cf.
L M S 262. For makeshift use of compass, *P G P* 136 etc., pls. 20, 6; 35, XI
1a, and compare the unintentionally
intersecting semicircles, *ibid.* 151, pl.
20, 7, and the uneven spacing, *Ergon*
1961, 57, fig. 57 left

28] Robertson, *J H S* 69 (1949), 93.
Kübler, *Ker.* 5, 1, 182

29] See in general Coldstream,
G G P 11-87, *passim*, and for particular

shapes, H. Marwitz, *JdI* 74 (1959), 69-81 on skyphoi; *ibid.* 81-94 on oenochoai – the change is well Illustrated in K. Kübler, *Ker.* 5, 1, pls. 70-1; hydria, G. Bakalakis, *A M* 76 (1961), 60-6; plate, *P G P* 118, pl. 12; flat-based cup, *ibid.* 101-2; kantharos, *A M* 78 (1963), 152, Beil. 54 – contrast *P G P* 102. Exceptions to the conservatism of earlier Geometric are the 'stemmed kantharos', *Ker.* 5, 1, 62-3, pl. 84,930; the pointed pyxis, *ibid.* 54, 66, pl. 110, 1201; the one-handled plate (*ibid.* pl. 110, 419). For the initial date of the Attic Geometric kotylai, see now T. J. Dunbabin, *Perachora* 2, 51, n.1

30] K. Kübler, *Ker.* 5, 1; P. Kahane, *A J A* 44 (1940), 464-82. The main critic of Kübler's approach is R. Hachmann, *G G A* 215 (1963), 47-67, especially 51-2, answered by Kübler in *A A* 79 (1964), 145-79; others who have found difficulties include K. F. Johansen, *Act. A.* 28 (1957), 114; H. Marwitz, *JdI* 74 (1959), 58, n.26, 76; W. Kraiker, *B Jb* 161 (1961), 119-20. For criticisms of the chronology, see e.g. J. M. Cook, *J H S* 76 (1956), 124-5; E. T. H. Brann, *A J A* 60 (1956), 73-4

31] Cf. the amphorae, oenochoai and cups, *Ker.* 5, 1, pls. 25, 42, 70, 105

32] Protogeometric horses, K. Kübler, *Ker.* 4, pls. 20-1 *Hesperia* 2 (1933) 560, fig. 19, no. 62; Coldstream *G G P* pl. 1k; *Ker.* 5, 1, pls. 20 (bottom), 22 (top, upper right with human mourning-figure)

33] On Attic exports, see *Ker.* 5, 1, 2, n.13, and add Troezen, R. S. Young, *Hesperia* Suppl. 2, 4n.1, 32; Crete, H. van Effenterre, *Necropoles du Mirabello* 37, pl. 20, 4; Euboea, J. M. Davison, *Y C S* 16 (1961), 67f., fig. 101; Smyrna, *B S A* 53-4 (1958-9),

14, 152; later finds in Cyprus, *A R* 1955, 43, pl. 11a; 1956, 26; Hama, *Act. A.* 28 (1957), 107, fig. 207; but J. N. Coldstream, *J H S* 80 (1960), 241 questions whether all these are Attic. The report of Attic Geometric at Perachora is false, *Perachora* 2, 334, but see Coldstream, *G G P* 214, n.4, on Laconia. Delphi, below, n.50; Kapakli: Desborough, *P G P* 132. Nea Anchialos, Macedonia: what are possibly Attic Geometric sherds of the mid-eighth century are shown in *A D* 20, 2 (1965), 421, pl. 472. Veii: *B S A* 35 (1934-5), 204 n.5. Canale: A. Åkerström, *Der geometrische Stil in Italien* (1943), fig. 12, 2. Megara Hyblaea, G. Vallet and F. Villard, *Megara Hyblaea* 2, 93-4, pl. 81.

34] Contrast the judgments implied in the tables of sites in P. Ålin, *Das Ende der Mykenischen Fundstätten auf dem griechischen Festland* (*Studies in Mediterranean Archaeology*, 1), 53, etc., and E. T. Vermeule, *Greece in the Bronze Age*, Appendix 111, 323-5; and note the claims made for Samos and Delos, below, nn. 42, 55

35] *A R* 1964-5, 10-11; (*L M S* 75)

36] W. Kraiker, *Aegina* 25, pl. 1, 24

37] P. Courbin, *La céramique géometrique de l'Argolide* (1966); note especially pp. 500ff. on the relations of Argive with other Geometric

38] For Argive exports, see Courbin, *op. cit.* 1f.: note that he allows only a little of Dugas' 'Argive' at Tegea to be such. For Eleusis and Amyklai, see N. M. Verdelis, *A M* 78 (1963), 45 and 59; for Melos, see also *A D* 16 (1960), 70, pl. 34; for Italy, *N Sc* (n.s.) 18 (1964), 223, fig. 44, 1, and Sicily, G. Vallet and F. Villard, *Megara Hyblaea* 2, 71-2, pl. 59; for Corcyra, *A D* 18, 2 (1963), 182-3, pl. 211α

39] *P G P* 212 on Corinthian Proto-geometric, and *ibid.* 204, 206 on the Corinthian imports in Tomb 25 at Asine. Dunbabin, *J H S* 68 (1948), 62-5 doubts the continuity of occupation at Corinth. On quantity of Corinthian Geometric, S. Benton, *B S A* 48 (1953), 260; for early bird-motifs, *ibid.* pl. 51, 886 and C. M. Robertson, *B S A* 43 (1948), pl. 3, 63. Multiple brush, Boardman, *Antiquity* 34 (1960), 88. Oenochoe, *B S A* 48 (1953), 322. Geometric exports: S. Weinberg, *A J A* 45 (1941), 32, and add Smyrna, J. K. Anderson, *B S A* 53-4 (1958-9), 138-41; settlers in Ithaka, Robertson, *B S A* 43, 113, 122-4; Crete, *Fortetsa* 63, pl. 45, 668; Delos, *B S A* 48, 262, n.42. Weinberg, *A J A* 45, 43: contrast Robertson, *B S A* 43, 53; T. J. Dunbabin, *J H S* 68 (1948), 65, n.55; R. M. Cook, *Greek Painted Pottery* 336

40] N. M. Verdelis, *Ho Protogeometrikòs rhuthmòs tîs Thessalías* (1958); D. Theocharis, *Ergon* 1961, 51-60; cf. 1960, 55-61, inside palace; *L M S* 128-9, 135-6, 261-2

41] *P G P* 174-5 on Thessalian Protogeometric shapes; *L M S* 130-1, 133-4, 278 on sites. Note also the Protogeometric tholos tomb now excavated at Sesklo, *Ergon* 1965, 8, fig. 4, and an amphora from Rodhitsa (*B C H* 91 (1967), 693, fig. 1)

42] *L M S* 149-52 on Naxos finds. Exports, *Fortetsa* 20, pl. 13, 154. Other islands, *P G P* 213-16 and *A A A* 1 (1968), 168-9 (Samos); for the Samian Heraion, full continuity throughout the dark age is claimed in *A A* 79 (1964), 221; the ceramic evidence is now published by H. Walter in *Samos* 5 (1968), 11-13. Kea, J. L. Caskey, *Hesp.* 33 (1964), 333; Melos, E. Kunze, *Ö Jh* 39 (1952), 53-7

43] For earlier Geometric, see N. M. Kondoleon, *A E* 1945-7, 1-21; *P G P* 153f., 213-15. Exports, *Fortetsa* 32, pl. 19, 269 (cf. 31, n.4) and, somewhat later, 38, pl. 24, 364-7; Itanos, *B C H* 75 (1951), 208; Athenian Agora – Dr Smithson has kindly told me of an Early Geometric, perhaps Naxian, amphora among the unpublished finds. For the island schools of later Geometric, R. M. Cook, *Greek Painted Pottery* (1960), 337, 344-5 gives a concise summary of the different authorities and views, to which must now be added O. Rubensohn, *Das Delion von Paros* (1962). Andros, N. Zafiropoulos, *A D* 16, 2 (1960), 249. In general, see Coldstream *G G P* 171-89, with his especially valuable elucidation of the Melian school

44] Agios Andreas, W. A. McDonald and R. Hope Simpson, *A J A* 65 (1961), 224. Ancient Elis, *L M S* 93, 265; *P P S* 31 (1965), 218; *A D* 19, 2 (1964), 180f.; Styrenius, *S S* 139-42, figs. 58-63. Palaiopyrgo, *B C H* 85 (1961), 723; contrast, however, the later dating by Coldstream *G G P* 221-3. Olympia, *A M* 36 (1911), 192, fig. 24; cf. *JdI* 81 (1966), 339 fig. 31. (On the evidence for continuous occupation at Olympia, see H.-V. Herrmann, *A M* 77 (1962), 3-34.) Agrapidochori, *A D* 20, 2 (1965), 217, pls. 250-1. Other Elean Geometric, Courbin, *op. cit.* (n.37), 500, n.1

45] Miletus, *L M S* 21, 162-3; *I M* 9-10 (1960-1), 23, pl. 14. Assarlik, *J H S* 8 (1887), 66-77 and *B S A* 50 (1955), 116-18, 147, 165-7; *P G P* 218-21. Müskebi, *A J A* 67 (1963), 353-7. Sardis, *A J A* 71 (1967), 170-1 and 72 (1968), 52; Stratonicaea, *ibid.* 51-2. Protogeometric sites, J. M. Cook *A R* 1959-60, 40-1; Pitane, *FA* 17 (1962), no. 2226; Smyrna, *B S A* 53-4

(1958–9), 10, pl. 5b and Coldstream, *GGP* 338; Teos, *Türk Arkeoloji Dergisi* 13, 1 (1964), 115; Tsangli, *PGP* 221; Iasos, *LMS* 162, 279 and *Annuario* 43-4 (1956–6), 497f.; Dirmil, *AJA* 67 (1963), 357-61; Milesian Geometric, e.g. *IM* 9-10 (1959–60), pls. 56-62

46] *PGP* 198, 299

47] Protogeometric at Thebes, *PGP* 195-6, *LMS* 121-2, and *AD* 20, 2 (1965), 239, pl. 283α (cremation-amphora from Pelopidas St). Orchomenos, *PGP* 198; and compare at a later stage Haliartos, *BSA* 32 (1931–32), 190. Boeotian Geometric, E. Pfuhl, *Malerei und Zeichnung der Griechen* (1923), I, 73-4; R. Hampe, *Frühe griechische Sagenbilder* (1937), 20f.; F. Canciani, *JdI* 80 (1965), 18-75; Courbin, *op. cit.* (n.37), 521-4; and recent finds in the vicinity of Thebes, *AD* 21, 2 (1966), pls. 205-6.

48] Lefkandi, M. R. Popham and L. H. Sackett (eds.), *Excavations at Lefkandi in Euboea*, 1964–6 (1968), esp. 5 (but contrast 26) on continuity. Vases from Amathus, Desborough, *JHS* 77 (1957), 214-15. Other finds from Euboea, *BSA* 52 (1957), 14 and nn.86-87; 61 (1966), 37-66, summarized by Popham, *ibid.* 106-7

49] See J. Boardman, *BSA* 52 (1957), 5-10 and *The Greeks Overseas* 63-9; *ibid.* fig. 9c and *AS* 9 (1959), 167 for circles on skyphos-rims. Jug with cut-away neck, *Excavations at Lefkandi* 33, fig. 75. For the traditional sway of Eretria in Euboea over Andros and Tenos, see Strabo x, 448

50] Temenos tomb, *LMS* 124; tomb near Museum, L. Lerat, *BCH* 61 (1937), 51f.; cf. 85 (1961), 352-7; *PGP* 200-1. Medeon, *AD* 19, 2 (1964), 223-4: compare *ibid.* pl. 264α with, for example, *BSA* 33 (1932–3),

49, fig. 26, no. 75 (Ithaka) and *AJA* 64 (1960), 16, no. 51, pl. 5, fig. 38 left (Derveni); see *LMS* 130, 227 for earlier links which bridge the Gulf of Corinth. Antikyra, Coldstream *GGP* 197, n.3. Geometric at Delphi, *BCH* 59 (1935), 275, fig. 32 and 85 (1961), 338-52; *RA* 12 (1938), pl. 3; P. Perdrizet, *Fouilles de Delphes* 5 (1908), 133f.; T. J. Dunbabin, *Perachora* 2, 1, n.1; 2, n.5; Ithakan piece, *BSA* 48 (1953), 268; other imports, *PGP* 200 and n.2; Attic, e.g. *BCH* 74 (1950), 322, pl. 39, 1, 2nd from right. Compare the Corinthian preponderance in Geometric finds from Amphissa in Locris, *AD* 18, 2 (1963), 130 pls. 164f.; and the amphora from Medeon, *AD* 19, 2 (1964), pl. 264β

51] For Mycenaean pottery in Macedonia, see Ph. Petsas, *AE* 1953–4, 2, 113-20. Vergina: see *LMS* 143-6, with Petsas, *AD* 17, 2 (1961–2), 218-88 and 18, 2 (1963), 213-32; M. Andronikos, *Praktiká* 1958, 90-5; 1959, 59-70; 1960, 95-103; 1961, 90-4. Pithos, Petsas in *Essays in Memory of Karl Lehmann* (*Marsyas*, supplement 1, 1964), 255-8. See also *PPS* 31 (1965), 238-40. Nea Anchialos finds, *AD* 20, 2 (1965), 421, pl. 472

52] *PGP* 223 and P. Courbin (ed.), *Études Archéologiques* (1963), 71, fig. 7

53] *PGP* 222-3 for the Dodecanese in the earlier Geometric period; for Kos, L. Morricone, *Bollettino d'Arte* 4, 35 (1950), 320-2, figs. 92-3, 95; Exochi, K. F. Johansen, *Act. A.* 28 (1957), 1-192, especially 102-15, 143-6, 189-90, and compare C. Blinkenberg, *Lindos* 1 (1931), 241. Amphorae, *PGP* 33, 35; similarly, the finds from Kameiros, Patelle grave 45 (*ibid.* 228) could be explained by a long Protogeometric survival

54] Exports, J. Boardman, *The Greeks Overseas* 71-3, 182; Coldstream, *G G P* 279, nn.1-2. Nestor cup, *Rendiconti Lincei* 8, 10 (1955), 215-34. Cypriot 'barrel-jugs', *Cl. Rhod.* 8 (1936), 163, no. 6, fig. 149; Lekythoi in Coan graves, Coldstream, *G G P* 268-9; and later imports, E. Gjerstad, *S C E* 4, 2, 262-7

55] See *P G P* 156-8 on this area, including the earlier stages of Geometric: add, for Protogeometric on Tenos, *A D* 22, 2 (1967), 464, and 467 (Dhonousa). H. Gallet de Santerre, *Délos primitive et archaique*, 213-18 has made an energetic case for continuity of pottery and occupation on Delos; but see p. 55 above for doubts in such cases. For Delos, note especially Ch. Dugas and K. Rhomaios, group Aa in *Délos* 15, 13-25, for which J. K. Brock (*B S A* 44 (1949), 74-6) and others argue a Parian origin

56] To Desborough's list of the earlier Cretan sites and material, *L M S* 168-89, 267-9, add further early tombs near Knossos, *B S A* 58 (1963), 34-43, and especially 63 (1968), 205-18. The material from Stous Lakkous Kritsa and the four sites in the Seteia district, *L M S* 187, 268, may when fully published cause some modification in the picture of eastern Crete. See now Coldstream, *G G P* 235-41; U. Jantzen in *Festschrift für E. von Mercklin* (1964), 60-2

57] Dating evidence, *Fortetsa* 213-15; note that Desborough (*L M S* 184, n.4) does not class Brock's Late Protogeometric as Protogeometric. Find in Knossos well, J. N. Coldstream, *B S A* 55 (1960), 161, no.20. Protogeometric B, *Fortetsa* 153; mourning scene, *ibid.* pls. 24, 144, no. 339; other finds, *Kretikà Chroniká* 4 (1950), 441f. (Arkhanes) and

Annuario 39-40 (1961–2), 406f. (Phaistos)

58] Attic pieces, e.g. Arkades, *Annuario* 10-12 (1927–9), fig. 582; Phaistos, 39-40 (1961 a), 409, fig. 51c; Arkades, Kourtes, *P G P* 254, 326; 256-7. Imported krater, *Vrokastro* 173, fig. 106 (Kondoleon, *A E* 1945–6, 19, calls it 'Cycladic or Argive'); later pyxis, *ibid.* 109-10, pl. XXIII; and add H. van Effenterre, *Necropoles du Mirabello* 37, pl. 20, 4. Aryballoi, Johansen, *Act. A.* 28 (1957), 155-61. Coldstream, *G G P* 276; vases found in Italy, *ibid.* 194-5; Cypriot imports, *Fortetsa* 190-1. Note that a skyphos-fragment in Samos may be an import from Crete, *A M* 54 (1929), 13. Beilage 11, 3

59] *P G P* 280-1

60] *P G P* 271-81; for Attic imports, see too S. Benton, *B S A* 48 (1953), 267, 270 (H84, H73) and (Early Geometric) 309, no. 872; on export to Italy, *ibid.* 327, n.491 = W. Taylour, *Mycenaean Pottery in Italy* 118, no. 165. Palaiomanina, Coldstream, *G G P* 223-7

61] S. Benton, *B S A* 48 (1953), 265; cf. Coldstream, *G G P*, 227, n.8

62] E. T. Vermeule, *A J A* 64 (1960), 1-21, esp. 1-3, 5-6, 17-18 on Protogeometric influence; duck-askoi, *ibid.* 11-12, but compare especially no. 43 (pl. 4, fig. 30, right) with the new Kerameikos specimen, *A M* 78 (1963), Beilage 54, bottom left. Derveni burial, Vermeule, *ibid.* 16-17, pl. 5, figs. 38-40; (for links with Phokis, see above n.50; with Laconia, Coldstream *G G P* 222); burial at Liopesi, *A D* 20, 2 (1965), 223; *L M S* 98-101, pl. 10f. Geometric, *A E* 1939–41, parartêma p. 21 (not illustrated); *Praktiká* 1930, 83f.; 1952, 400f.; 1956, 193f.; *A D* 17, 2 (1961–2), 129; 20, 2 (1965), 223, pl. 263α, with Corinthian import

63] *A A A* 1 (1968), 205 for Karpophora; *L M S* 96 on Volimnos and Nichoria; *P G P* 283 on Traganes: *A D* 20, 2 (1965), 208, pl. 222B (Kardamyle); Ålin, *E M F* 77, n.9 (Malthi); *A D* 20, 2 (1965), 207 pl. 215 for Antheia; Hope Simpson, *Gazetteer and Atlas of Mycenaean sites* 68 (Koryphasion). For Geometric finds, *B C H* 20 (1896), 389, figs. 2-3; Coldstream *G G P* 223, with Corinthian and Laconian imports; *A D* 20, 2 (1965), 207, pl. 219γ

64] *P G P* 287-9; Coldstream *G G P* 221-3; *B S A* 52 (1957), 243, 245 for Laconian Protogeometric exports to Messenia; Apidia and Mavrovouni, H. Waterhouse and R. Hope Simpson, *B S A* 55 (1960), 87; 56 (1961), 115, fig. 2. On Laconian Geometric, J. P. Droop in R. M. Dawkins, *Artemis Orthia* 54-68 and E. A. Lane, *B S A* 34 (1933-4), 101-7; dating, J. Boardman, *B S A* 58 (1963), 3

65] *L M S* 87, n.5 (which may be an import anyway), n.7 (perhaps Laconian). It may be doubted whether the 'krater' from Asea, E. J. Holmberg, *A I R R S* 11 (1944), 112, fig. 110a is genuinely Protogeometric; of the sherds from Astros in Thyreatis (*A A* 42 (1927), 365) I know nothing. On Arcadian Geometric, Ch. Dugas in *B C H* 45 (1921), 404-14 and Holmberg, *loc. cit.*: Mantinea, *A D* 18, 2 (1963), 88-9, pl. 103α

66] Protogeometric in Samos, Lesbos, Chios, *P G P* 216-18 (cf. 15-16), and *A A A* 1 (1968), 168; Smyrna and Larisa, *B S A* 53-4 (1958-9), 10-11

67] Geometric in Samos, W. Technau, *A M* 54 (1929), 9-18; R. Eilmann, *A M* 58 (1933), 47-145; H. Walter and K. Vierneisel, *A M* 74 (1959), 10-34; H. Walter, *Samos* 5

(1968), 14-46; Chios, W. Lamb, *B S A* 35 (1934-5), 157-8 and J. Boardman *Excavations in Chios 1952–51 Greek Emporio* (1967), 102-47, with possible Samian imports, 107, 115

68] For reported Protogeometric, see e.g. *N Sc* n.s. 18 (1964), 220-2, figs. 41-2; W. Taylour, *Mycenaean Pottery in Italy* (1958), 118-19, nos. 165-6. A. A. Blakeway, *B S A* 33 (1932-3), 170-208 and *J R S* 25 (1935), 129-49. For Veii, see J. B. Ward-Perkins, D. Ridgway and J. Close-Brooks in *Stud. Etr.* 35 (1968), 307-29, pls. 57-8, comparing the earliest imports at pre-Greek Cumae, in Osta graves 3 and 29. Local Geometric, see especially G. Buchner, *R M* 60-1 (1953-4), 37-55; G. Vallet and F. Villard, *M E F R* 68 (1956), 7-27 and *Megara Hyblaea* 2, 139ff., 189ff.

69] Coarse ware in Protogeometric contexts includes *Ker.* 1, pls. 70, 74-5; 4, pl. 28; *Hesperia* 30 (1961), pl. 30, 52-3; *B C H* 61 (1937), 44f., pl. 6. The main sites for the finer plain ware: O. Frödin and A. W. Persson, *Asine*, figs. 216, 275-6, 279-82; K. Müller and F. Ölmann, *Tiryns*, 1, 128f. and N. M. Verdelis, *A M* 78 (1963), 41ff., Beilage 18,6; 22,6; 25,1-2; 5-6; Mycenae, *B S A* 49 (1954), pl. 46 (53-328 to 335); 50 (1955), pls. 47c, 49a; 51 (1956), pl. 34a; Argos, *B C H* 77 (1953), 260; Argive Heraeum, *A E* 1937, 385-6, fig. 12; Lerna, *Hesperia* 23 (1954), pl. 2c, centre; 25 (1956), pl. 48e, left; S. Weinberg, *Corinth* 7, 1, 3f. (*P G P* 202) and *Hesperia* 17 (1948), 206, pl. 72, B4; R. S. Young, *Corinth* 13, 41, 43; Klenia, *A J A* 59 (1955), pl. 40, nos. 2, 17; *Perachora* 2, pl. 127, 3006; Kos, *P G P* 224; Laconia, *A M* 52 (1927), 48-9; and cf. later Attica, e.g. *Hesperia* 6 (1937), 365, fig. 30 upper left; 18 (1949), pl. 67, 21;

Ker. 5, 1, 140, n.108; on this ware in general, see Courbin, *op. cit.* (above, n.37), 467-8.

For 'pie-ware', see A. J. B. Wace, *Mycenae* (1949), 84, fig. 106b; it is also recorded at Mycenae, Tiryns, Klenia (see references above), Argos (*BCH* 78 (1954), 178, fig. 37). On Argive Monochrome, see most recently T. J. Dunbabin in *Perachora* 2, 314f.

70] *Tiryns* 1, 128 (tomb 6); Kos, *PGP* 224 (Serraglio tomb 10). Agora, see references below. Eleusis, *Ker.* 5, 1, 140, n.108 *ad fin.*; Kerameikos, *Ker.* 4, pls. 30-2; cf. 1, pl. 74 (Submycenaean); Nea Ionia, *Hesperia* 30 (1961), pl. 30, 54-6, and pl. 31, 2168 and 30, P 14873 for Submycenaean forebears; Agora, *Hes-*

peria 2 (1933), 564, fig. 24; 21 (1952), pl. 27c; 30 (1961), pl. 30 (grave 41, P 6695); and now most substantially in the grave found in 1967, 37 (1968), 77f., 103-9, nos. 35-63; Tiryns, Kos, Klenia, see references above, n.69; beads, J. Boardman, *The Cretan Collection in Oxford* (1961), 132, 158; Phaistos, *Annuario* 35-6 (1957-8), 359-61, fig. 216e. Kübler, *Ker.* 4, 5 and 20, argues that the dolls and whorls reflect earlier Aegean types (cf. S. Wide, *AM* 16 (1901), 252 on connection of Bronze Age and later dolls)

71] Persson, *Asine* 279. For Macedonia, see W. A. Heurtley, *Prehistoric Macedonia* (1939), 103f. *et passim*; Balkans, W. Kimmig in *Studien aus Alteuropa* 1 (1964) (ed. R. von Uslar and K. J. Narr), 267, pl. 20

3

The Chronology of the
Early Iron Age in Greece

◆ ◆ ◆
◆ ◆
◆

In our examination of the pottery of early Iron Age Greece, we have seen much evidence for the longitudinal or regional divisions within Greece at this period. In later chapters, some attempt will be made to interpret the pattern of these divisions; but before this can be done effectively, the chronological data must be examined in greater detail. This is a question both comparatively self-contained and complicated enough to merit separate treatment. Chronological schemes for at least part of this period have been proposed in recent years by several scholars, and there is little doubt that they have carried the process as far as is warranted by the present state of the evidence.[1] I do not therefore aim to go beyond their conclusions; my reason for approaching this problem once again is primarily my belief that the first requirement for a chronology, for all or any of this period, has not always been satisfied: it is, that the scheme devised should take account of the period as a whole, extending from the last chronological fixed point for the archaeology of the Aegean Bronze Age, down to the first date in the historical period of Greece for which an archaeological cross-reference is available. Such a scheme must, in the first instance, be based on the Attic series, the only one (apart from the too idiosyncratic Central Cretan sequence) for which every stage is fully and incontestably represented in the published evidence. A study of just one part of that series may point to conclusions which cannot be squared with the evidence as a whole. An example has recently been given by the study devoted to the workshops and painters of the Attic Late Geometric style; this has introduced for the first time such factors as the working life-span of an artist, which, combined with the usual observations and comparisons, have led to a pronounced tendency to compress, in absolute terms, the duration of the whole Geometric style. But the steps used in such arguments are

53. Spouted jar of Philistine ware from Ain Shems, imitating earlier Mycenaean III C pottery. Height 23 cm; *c.* 1175 BC.

inferential; if they involve us in an excessive or improbable lengthening of the earlier phases in compensation, they should be reappraised. The chronological framework has only a limited elasticity. We are fortunate in having ultimate dates, at both ends of the period, which are fairly securely fixed, and we must use them.

PRIMARY DATES, AND THE ATTIC SERIES

Where are these termini to be fixed? At the upper end, there is only one reasonably secure date in the Mycenaean pottery-series which lies close enough to its end to bear on the subsequent period. This is the settlement of the Philistine raiders in their new homeland, which can hardly be dated far from their repulse from the shores of Egypt by Rameses III in the eighth year of that Pharaoh's reign (1191 BC according to the high chronology now favoured by most Egyptologists for this era), and which is signalized archaeologically by their adoption, perhaps a little later again, of a style of painted pottery which is manifestly based on Mycenaean. *53* The resemblance extends to the choice and use of shapes, as well as the scheme of decoration; the Mycenaean influence is strongly felt at the inception of the Philistine style, but barely at all thereafter. It is hard to make a precise chronological equation with a moment in the evolution of the Mycenaean series, let alone to point to an exact locality of origin in the Mycenaean world; but it is clear that the Philistine style presupposes the developments down to a mature stage of Furumark's Mycenaean III C I b stage, but nothing later; there is no sign of contact with the Granary class of the Argolid, for example. Since the function of this date is to provide a *terminus ante quem*, however, such data are enough to push the chronology of later Mycenaean back in time, to a perhaps surprising degree. The main element of uncertainty in this evidence lies in the possibility of a delay between the settlement of the Philistines and their adoption of what was to become the characteristic 'Philistine' pottery; it seems that on the outlying site of Beth Shan, at any rate, the Philistine pottery was not introduced immediately, being absent from an initial stage in which there is other evidence for identifying the inhabitants as Philistines. But from the other excavated sites it is clear that only a short time-lag can have intervened; Desborough considers fifteen years the maximum possible allowance, and adds a possible ten years for a – purely hypothetical – delay between the Philistines' defeat at the Delta and their settlement in Palestine. This gives us, when all reasonable allowance has been made for imponderables, a *terminus ante quem* of about 1165 BC for the earlier phases of the Mycenaean III C I b phase.[2]

But a new element has entered into this question even since Desborough wrote in 1964. In a chapter of the new edition of the *Cambridge Ancient History*, W. F. Albright maintains that Philistine ware has been found at the site of Tell Deir'alla, 'in the same stratum as', and dating to 'the period immediately after', three inscribed clay tablets which were found in 1964. These finds were associated with a broken vase bearing the cartouche of Queen Tewosret, whose reign (again, according to the 'high' chronology) is dated c.1209–1200. The vase gives only a *terminus post quem*, but circumstances make it unlikely that the destruction of the site, which sealed this whole deposit, took place very much later than 1200. The excavator has since stated that Philistine pottery did not occur 'in the same stratum as' the tablets, but in the ensuing phase; nevertheless, he clearly assumes a dating in the first and second quarters of the twelfth century for this later phase. Although final judgment must clearly be postponed, there is *prima facie* evidence here that the characteristic Philistine ware made its appearance appreciably earlier than 1165. This is not all: Albright has also considered the Beth Shan evidence mentioned above, and he concluded that the earliest Philistine settlement in Palestine was in the form of garrison posts occupied *before* the great battle and defeat in the eighth year of Rameses III's reign; he regards the earliest Philistine level at Beth Shan as illustrative of this episode. This, if true, would take away Desborough's main grounds for allowing a fifteen-year time-lag between the post-defeat settlement and the introduction of the pottery. This again is a problematical question, but it gives a further pointer towards the raising of the terminus of 1165. As a final warning against over-confidence in propounding a solution, Albright reminds us that the absolute dating for the reign of Rameses III may still be open to some adjustment: the initial date of 1198, which I have assumed throughout this discussion, is widely accepted today, but there is a possible scope for adjusting it upwards or downwards within the limits of 1205 and 1180;[3] by the latter dating, the great defeat of the Philistines would be brought as low as 1173. It seems wisest, therefore, to retain Desborough's terminal date of c.1165 while recognizing that, at the Philistine end, it has a wide margin for upward adjustment and virtually none at all for downward; while since there is no sign of the direct and immediate influence of the Mycenaean potters of the Greek mainland 700 miles away to the north-west, we are surely safe in concluding that the development of this phase of the Mycenaean III C style happened there considerably earlier than 1165. Yet the evidence suggests that it cannot have happened much earlier than 1200 BC; for some of the latest direct Mycenaean imports to Syria, which belong to the Mycenaean III B style, are dated by their contexts to about 1225 or later still.[4]

What is certain is that there is no absolute date for centuries thereafter which can be introduced into the chronology of the Aegean in a comparable way. The next available terminus of equal dependability is, I think, to be found in the group of sherds from an Attic krater excavated at Hama in Syria, and associated with the destruction of that city by Sargon II of Assyria in the year 720 BC: the upper limit of their context is probably after 800. This could be a misleading piece of evidence in one sense, since there are strong circumstantial grounds for thinking that the krater was made considerably earlier than 720: most obviously, the fact that the krater belongs near the end of the 'Middle Geometric' phase of Attic, while in the same level were found Cycladic Geometric sherds, some in close association; although they belong to a less clearly understood series, these are quite evidently of a later stylistic phase than the Attic krater fragment.[5] But if the date of 720 therefore provides only an extreme *terminus ante quem*, this makes it to some degree comparable with the

54

55

54. Five sherds of an Attic Middle Geometric krater, found at Hama in Syria in a level associated with the destruction by Sargon II of Assyria in 720 BC. Height of joining fragments at top, 12 cm; *c.*775 BC.

previous fixed point in c.1165: the *relation* between the two dates may be more valuable than their absolute force. It is against probability that the length of time which elapsed between the two pottery-phases in Greece, represented by these two pieces of evidence from the Levant, was very different from the interval between these two dates. It is unlikely to have exceeded 450 years; and further, since the range of dating of the later find has just as fixed a 'ceiling' as the earlier one has, it is improbable that the interval was much less than 400 years.

The other fixed points in the chronology of the Greek early Iron Age, between the two that we have been considering, do not compare with these in reliability. Let us, therefore, temporarily revert to the orthodox procedure of constructing a relative chronological scheme before we attempt to give absolute dates to the various phases; we have the initial advantage of knowing that our complete series, down to the 'Middle Geometric' phase of Attic, is to be spread over a period probably between 400 and 450 years in length. The first task is to enumerate this series, and to make it applicable, from as early a point as possible, to Athens and Attica, on which in the later stages we shall depend heavily.

I do not think we can begin in Attica, however, for the III c period there is one of considerable obscurity, whose earlier stages are indeed represented in the settlement material from the Acropolis at Athens, but for whose later manifestations we have to look across to the cemetery-site at Perati on the east coast, which apparently belongs to a different cultural

55. Two sherds of Cycladic Late Geometric pottery found in the same stratum at Hama as the earlier pieces shown in no. *54.* (*a*) is *c*. 730 BC, (*b*) perhaps a little older.

area. Instead, we must turn to the Argolid, where the relevance of our starting point, the transmission of Mycenaean influence to the Philistines, is most likely to be felt. The development of the 'Granary' class here must fall largely after that moment, since it is not reflected in the Philistine style; this class witnesses and survives the final destruction of the Granary at Mycenae; while the later stages of III C in the Argolid are mainly represented by impoverished variants of the Close Style and Granary Class shapes and designs – Furumark's 'III C I c'. Thus far the continuity of the series is not in doubt; and at this point I would make the transition to the Attic series. Desborough is probably right in thinking that the III C period in the Argolid was more or less directly succeeded by the local school of Protogeometric; and he is certainly right to say that neither that school, nor any other local Protogeometric style, can have developed earlier than the Attic Protogeometric from which they all take their inspiration. The likelihood is that the initial date of Attic Protogeometric lies close to the end of Mycenaean III C in the Argolid (cf. p. 56).

If this be accepted, the remainder of the series can be followed without looking beyond Athens – indeed without leaving the Kerameikos cemetery itself, whose use extends down to and far beyond the end of our period. The Attic Protogeometric style is represented by only some fifty-seven graves in the Kerameikos; but the internal evidence confirms what is already strongly suggested by the grouping and funerary rite of the graves, that the earliest stages of Protogeometric take over the newly-adopted rite of cremation for adults which is found in three of the later Submycenaean graves, and briefly continue the use of the Submycenaean burial-ground on the north bank of the Eridanos, on the site of the later Pompeion; and that soon a move is made to a new plot, on the opposite bank and some yards away to the west, where the remaining forty-nine Protogeometric graves are grouped, close together and immediately adjacent to the earliest group of graves of the Geometric period. Neither at the moment of the change of cemeteries, nor at the transition to the full Geometric style, is there any possibility of a break in the pottery-series. The early phase of Protogeometric is still current at the time of the move (indeed there is even a stray Submycenaean grave in the new plot); the middle and later stages are visibly progressive alike in their use of shapes – for example, the successive adoption of the neck-handled and shoulder-handled amphora – and decoratively, in their tendency towards the dark-ground style. The phase of transition to Geometric may have its best illustration in two rich grave-groups from the nearby Athenian Agora, but these help to confirm that the Kerameikos series is uninterrupted.[6] In the classification of Attic Geometric, many scholars today adopt the tripartite division of 'Early', 'Middle' and 'Late', as opposed to the four-stage scheme proposed by Kahane and Kübler (cf. p. 50) which, even if stylistically sound for the Attic series, does not always 'transplant' well to other styles. By this terminology, Early Geometric is represented by only eleven or twelve cremation-graves, most of them immediately adjoining, or even overlapping, the latest Protogeometric burials on the south side, but one or two in a new plot across the stream, at a short distance from the old Pompeion cemetery. Middle Geometric continues the same development in every way: geographically, the graves extend the south bank cemetery yet further to the south and south-west, besides filling out the new plot on the north bank; stylistically, the extreme and perhaps over-disciplined austerity of Early Geometric is relaxed as the painters discover richer decorative patterns based on new principles. Rather more than twenty grave-groups in the Kerameikos can be allocated to the Middle Geometric period, a far from copious representation.[7] At this point our series comes, if rather abruptly, to a halt; for it is a product of an Attic workshop of near *54* the end of this period, a krater of a distinctive class with a maeander panel-decoration flanked by zig-zag bands and triglyphs, whose fragments were found in the destruction level at Hama on the Orontes.

We are faced with this conclusion: the middle and later phases of Mycenaean III C, after the rise of the Close Style, in the Argolid; the Protogeometric and Early and Middle Geometric phases at Athens, which all together are represented by some ninety graves in the Kerameikos cemetery: this brief sequence of periods must be extended over probably about 400 years or more. It is clear that we are dealing with a very slow rate of development in the potter's art in Greece. If we make a provisional hypothesis as to the duration of the styles, and assume about 150 years for the residue of Mycenaean III C, 150 years for Attic Protogeometric, and 50 years each for Attic Early and Middle Geometric, we shall be taking a wholly arbitrary step; but we shall arrive at approximately the right total, without unduly straining credulity in any one case. We can also be virtually certain that no reduction in any one of these figures is possible without a compensatory lengthening elsewhere; indeed, it is likelier that one or more of these figures will require to be increased (cf. below, p. 122).

OTHER EVIDENCE FOR ABSOLUTE CHRONOLOGY

There are several absolute dates indicated for the intervening period, of a different kind from the two primary termini: dates which do ultimately depend on written evidence, but whose reliability is affected either by the indirectness of the dependence, or by the quality of the written sources in question. They are of three main classes: the first group (to which the two primary termini also belong) derives from the finding of Greek objects in dated contexts on Near Eastern sites, and of Oriental objects in Greece; the second is based on similar cross-finds, and also on stylistic links, with Cyprus; the third arises from the Greek material found on colony-sites in Italy and Sicily, for which foundation-dates are given by much later Greek writers. Since these categories are partly independent of each other, a scheme which satisfies all of them has a good chance of being approximately correct. But none of them is fully reliable as evidence on its own: it is particularly worth stressing that the certitude of many Near Eastern dates has been too optimistically assessed by Aegean scholars seeking for chronological fixed points. A closer examination reveals, not only substantial disagreements between authorities on stylistic questions, and on the equating of the archaeological record with historical events, but also in a few cases the demoralizing spectacle of *Greek* imports being used to substantiate the dates of levels in *Oriental* sites. We shall be well advised to proceed cautiously, and to retain as a primary yardstick the data of the two outer termini which do, I believe, rest on secure evidence.

FIRST CATEGORY

In the first, Near Eastern, category come two dates which may be taken together, since they involve Greek pottery found at two sites, in strata which have been judged to be partly contemporary. At Tell abu Hawam in southern Palestine, in level III, a sherd was found from a Greek skyphos of the class with pendent semicircle decoration, frequently mentioned in

H

the last chapter, whose precise geographical origin is not definitely located; in the same level was also a plain flat-bottomed cup of Greek fabric but even less closely classifiable, though its shape would be at home in the earlier phases of Geometric. At Megiddo, in level VA-IVB, two sherds from skyphos-rims were also found, but apparently went undetected until C. Clairmont published them in 1955; in this case they belong near the beginning of Middle Geometric, and look as though they are of Attic fabric.[8] The vital question is, as always, the closing date of the strata in which these fragments lay. At both sites, the levels in question were dated very early by the excavators: the end of Tell abu Hawam III was associated with a destruction at the hands of the XXII Dynasty Pharaoh Sheshonk I, in 926 or perhaps 918 BC; Megiddo V was terminated at c.1000, 'VA-IVB' being a later extension of the period of this level, partly overlapping with it in time but not isolated by the excavators. Later, some scholars came to associate the destruction of Megiddo V with the same campaign of Sheshonk. But a new element entered this question with the excavations at Samaria: the earliest finds at this site, which is known to have been founded by Omri in about 880 BC, proved to have many affinities with Megiddo V; the excavator, Miss K. M. Kenyon, concludes that the final date of Megiddo VA-IVB should come down to about 850, being no longer associated with an identifiable historical event; but although she considers that the two periods at Tell abu Hawam and Megiddo respectively are indeed contemporary in large part, and that the material in them 'corresponds closely', she is prepared to let the excavator's terminal date for Tell abu Hawam III stand. Other scholars, however, have ventured to propose a similar or even greater lowering of the date of the end of Tell abu Hawam III.[9] How will all this affect Greek chronology? Now that the status of the skyphoi with pendent semicircles has become clear, and it can be seen that they date largely or wholly from after the end of Attic Protogeometric, it is not surprising to find that they occur first in an Oriental context apparently contemporary with, or perhaps slightly earlier than, that of Attic pottery of the Middle Geometric phase. Much the more valuable, in view of the clearer pattern of the Attic Geometric series, is the find at Megiddo; if the association – not commented upon by the excavators – is correct, it should mean that Attic Middle Geometric had begun by about 850.

There are a number of later finds of Greek pottery on Oriental sites, some in eighth-century levels, but most of these belong to the class of skyphoi with pendent semicircles, and are thus secondary to the sherd from Tell abu Hawam, merely proving that the production of this vase-type in Greece continued down to about 750 at least. The occasional pieces of East Greek and Cycladic Geometric have, however, in a few cases a valuable *terminus ante quem* provided by their context. Cycladic sherds of developed Geometric style were in the same destruction level   *55* at Hama as the Attic krater mentioned above (p. 109), and must be dated before 720. At Tarsus, the discovery of Greek pottery in both the Early and the Middle Iron Age levels, dated to c.1100—850 and c.850–700 B C respectively by the excavators, opened up the most promising prospects for the dating of the early Greek pottery-styles. But a preliminary examination of the consequences of these dates reveals such difficulties, that one can only suspect that the termini for both these levels have been set too high: 'Early Iron Age' produced not only the expected pendent-semicircle skyphoi, but some much later fragments; 'Middle Iron Age' contained a proliferation of Greek types known from the first half of the seventh century. Furthermore, it is clear that at one point the excavators had relied on the putative date of an imported Greek piece as the basis for the dating of the 'Early Iron Age' phase.[10] It is sad to have to treat with such scepticism one of our richest potential sources of information for absolute dating, but there is no alternative. Lastly, at the Syrian coastal site of Al Mina, where there had been a Greek commercial settlement from perhaps before 800, there is a brief abandonment (but no destruction) of the site at the end of Level VII. It is possible, but far from demonstrable, that this interruption is to be attributed to the campaign of Sennacherib of Assyria in 696, which destroyed Tarsus (during, rather than at the end of, its 'Middle Iron Age' period), and in which it is known from the Assyrian annals that Greek resistance was met and overcome. If so, the great richness of the Greek material at Al Mina would enable a further fixed point to be inserted in the Late Geometric series of Euboea, the Cyclades and East Greece at least.[11]

Objects travelling in the reverse direction in this period are hard to find, and even harder to date: one reason is that they include no pottery; another, that they have most often appeared in Greece on sanctuary-sites, where dating contexts are loose or non-existent. A bronze bowl of North   *56* Syrian origin did appear in Geometric grave 42 of the Kerameikos, which belongs very early in the Middle Geometric period; but the date of the bowl proved harder to determine than its artistic affinities, and could only be fixed relatively to other specimens found in Cyprus, whose dating was in turn based largely on their Cypriot context; no more precise bracket than 'late ninth or earlier eighth century' can therefore be given to it or its

56. Embossed decoration on an imported bronze bowl in Geometric grave 42 at the Kerameikos cemetery, Athens. Diameter 17·5 cm.

associated vases. Many later Oriental objects in Greece provide even less chronological information; and in several cases objects which were once classed as Oriental imports are now cogently argued to be Greek or Cretan adaptations of Oriental forms, which makes their chronological application even vaguer. Even Egyptian scarabs lose their precision value in the early Iron Age: those which reach Greece at this time can often be dated no more closely than to the XXII-XXVI Dynasties, a time-span of over 400 years extending from the tenth century to the sixth. A few specimens can be dated earlier, but there is of course no guarantee that they were not already old when they reached Greece, or at least when they came to be buried there, for scarabs, like other small objects, have an inherent tendency to be kept as heirlooms; they can only provide a *terminus post quem*, and too often this proves to be an extreme one, as with the collection of three scarabs and a figurine found in this 'Isis Grave' at Eleusis. This is dated by its pottery to the ninth or eighth century, and cannot be brought remotely close in time to its Egyptian contents, which include a scarab of the eleventh-century Pharaoh Men-kheper-ra (if indeed it is not earlier still). More usefully, a scarab of the xxiv-Dynasty Pharaoh Bocchoris (c.718–712) was found in a grave at Pithekoussai on the island of Ischia with very late Geometric pottery of local fabric; and a vase with the cartouche of the same king in an Etruscan grave at Tarquinia, with local Geometric pottery of doubtful homogeneity and rather later date. The extreme obscurity of this Pharaoh has been used as an argument for dating these objects, and with them the graves, close to his lifetime; but it is hardly a very compelling one. Even with all these limitations on their use, scarabs can still lead to serious difficulty. In the sanctuary of Artemis Orthia at Sparta, a scarab found with Late Geometric pottery was definitely pronounced to be of xxvi Dynasty date (c.663–525 BC), and other Egyptian and Egyptianizing objects in the same context seemed equally late. This alone could have been explained by the long survival of Geometric in Laconia (p. 89); but the same thing also happened in the Heraeum at Perachora, together with Corinthian and Argive Late Geometric finds, whose dating is far less flexible. Fortunately, however, time has shown that so precise a classification and dating of the scarabs is unwarranted: the recent revelation of the artistic achievements of the xxv Dynasty, which began in the mid-eighth century, has made possible a higher range of dating for such Egyptian products.[12]

SECOND CATEGORY

The second category of dates, those derived from Cyprus, is less valuable in that the chronology of the Cypriot Early Iron Age is itself vague, and only loosely linked with historical events; yet the associations here have the advantage that they show two cultures in definite if intermittent contact with each other, not merely exchanging stray imports; and the Cypriot chronology has the merit of being reached independently of the Greek, after the end of the Mycenaean period. For a long time after the beginning of the Iron Age there are no actual Aegean imports in Cyprus; but it has been found possible to make a looser equation at, and just before, the inception of the Cypro-Geometric period, which is today usually dated at c.1050 BC, and brings in the Cypriot Iron Age. The last three Bronze Age settlement-levels at the site of Enkomi (Enkomi III to I), which belong to the Late Cypriot III B phase, contained imported Mycenaean pottery related to the latest Granary Class, Furumark's III C I c;

similar ware has occurred in a well at Kition, and an unrecorded chamber-tomb at Idalion. Less precise evidence comes from a rather later Cypriot grave, Lapithos tomb 503.1, which contained four small lekythoi of local fabric; their shape is close to that of Attic lekythoi of the later Submycenaean and the transition to Protogeometric. A decorative motif which is found in an equally late stage of Late Cypriot III B (including this same tomb-group at Lapithos) – the semicircle within a triangle on the shoulder of stirrup-vases – recurs in Crete, first on vases from Tombs VI A and VII of the Gypsades cemetery at Knossos, near the beginning of Subminoan, and then in later Subminoan and even Early Protogeometric contexts. Whether or not the source of this motif is in Cyprus, as is probable, it is fair to conclude that the latter part of Late Cypriot III B is at least in part contemporary with Subminoan. In the case of the Greek mainland, the evident connections between the pottery of Mycenaean III C 1 c and Late Cypriot III B give way to the periods, respectively, of the Proto-geometric and the Cypro-Geometric I, in which resemblances, though perhaps detectable, are far less close and direct. These latter phases may therefore have begun at much the same date. There is a piece of positive evidence which suggests the same conclusion: a curious bottle-shaped vase, one- or two-handled, which in Cyprus is characteristic of the transition from Late Cypriot III B to Cypro-Geometric I, is imitated in Athens, if only rarely and not very closely. Examples occur in Kerameikos Sub-mycenaean grave 97, in a squat, two-handled form, and as a one-handled lekythos in the 'Heidelberg' tomb from the Acropolis slope, which is transitional to Protogeometric (pp. 37, 47). The very rarity of the shape in Greece increases the validity of this link; it looks, therefore, as though the change to Protogeometric at Athens may have been contemporary with, or possibly a little later than, the transition to Cypro-Geometric I in Cyprus, at about 1050.[13]

For the latest Bronze Age, the tendency is still to date the Cypriot material by the Aegean; but with this date of c.1050, and for some time thereafter, the rôles are reversed. The absolute chronology of Cypro-Geometric I and III is approximately fixed by a series of finds of Cypriot pottery, particularly on Palestinian sites, associated with scarabs or in levels indirectly linked with historical events, and to a lesser extent by finds of Syrian pottery in Cyprus: E. Gjerstad's dates of c.1050–950, c.950–850 and c.850–700 for Cypro-Geometric I, II and III respectively must now perhaps yield a little to the repeated attempts to raise them. But in any event, these are quite long periods, and within them the pottery tends not to follow a unified development as most Greek styles do, but to fall into a number of technically different classes. The only chronological indicators that occur for some time are in the form of stylistic links, involving commoner and thus less closely datable shapes than the bottles discussed above. When actual imports reappear, they are mostly passing from Cyprus westwards, to Greece and more especially to Crete; but the earliest objects are of metalwork, whose typology is not precise enough to help much chronologically: of the tripods found in an Early Cretan Proto-geometric tomb at Knossos, in two rather later Cretan tombs, and elsewhere, we can only say that such objects had been made in Cyprus during the twelfth century; in at least one instance and perhaps in all, a long time must have elapsed between the manufacture of the tripod and its interment in a Greek grave. Nor do the two clay imitations of a cylindrical stand, found in the Late Protogeometric tomb 48 of the Kerameikos and known rather earlier in Cyprus, give any precise chronological indication. In the reverse direction, two late Protogeometric pieces, possibly of northern Cycladic or Euboean and certainly not of Attic fabric, were found at Amathus with Cypriot vases of Cypro-Geometric II B date, but in a context which did not quite guarantee that the pottery was of a homogeneous deposit; on Gjerstad's chronology, the Cypriot pottery in this group would probably be placed early in the ninth century. When in Cypro-Geometric III more copious Cypriot imports reach the Aegean, particularly Rhodes and Knossos where they are found from the Cretan 'Mature Geometric' period on, this at least confirms the probability that this phase in Crete belongs after c.850 BC. Conversely, in Tomb 13 at Amathus, which is of Cypro-Geometric III B (that is roughly eighth century) date, was found a fine Attic krater of a late stage in the Middle Geometric period, comparable with the fragmentary example from Hama (p. 109 above); other Attic Geometric imports have been found at Cypriot Salamis, in similar contexts. The remaining pieces, giving evidence of trade in both directions within the Cypro-Geometric III period, in each case make equations with the Greek Middle and Late Geometric phases, which anyway would be at least partly dated within this wide bracket. More awkwardly, two Late Geometric cups (possibly Cycladic) and a Corinthian kotyle were found in Tomb 9 at Amathus with vases of the beginning of Cypro-Archaic II, that is c. 600 or later by Gjerstad's dating; here again, even on a somewhat higher chronology, we must assume that a considerable time-lag is involved.[14] It will be seen that the Cypriot chronology can only rarely be used to illuminate that of early Iron Age

see 89

Greece; but it does confirm the soundness of its broad outlines.

THIRD CATEGORY

The third category of dating evidence is in a quite different class; because
it involves no transition from non-Greek to Greek material, it might seem
less susceptible of error. But in fact it introduces fresh elements of weakness:
first, that there is no authority for the dates of the early Western Greek
colonies before Thucydides, who wrote three centuries later; and further,
that foundation-dates of settlements are in general less valuable than
destruction-dates, since only when one is certain that the earliest pottery
on a freshly-founded site has been found, can one make the necessary
equation with a point in the pottery series. In fact there are only three
or four colony-sites early enough to serve our present purpose, which
combine the elements of a foundation-date attested by Thucydides, and
a degree of archaeological exploration which makes it likely that some of
the earliest pottery has been found: Syracuse in 733, Leontini in 729,
Megara Hyblaea in 728, and perhaps Gela in 688, all in Sicily. For the
other colonies, the evidence is defective from one or the other aspect,
or both. These Sicilian sites offer evidence for the dating of the Protocorinthian style, which was the dominant imported pottery of their earlier
levels, and indeed the modern chronology of this style has from the first
been based on the hypothesis that these foundation-dates, with one or
two later ones, are correct. This was a reasonable assumption, especially
when the relative dating of the earliest pottery on each site seemed to
conform to the given order of foundation.

Recent discoveries, however, have brought several difficulties. The
earliest material from Megara Hyblaea was at one stage said to be awkwardly
late, being nearer to the material from Gela than to that from Syracuse:
now, after fresh finds in 1949–51, it is said to *antedate* anything from
Syracuse, and very similar early pottery has also come to light at Naxos
and Leontini. From the later colony of Selinus, in much the same way, a
collection of Late Protocorinthian and Transitional pottery has been found,
earlier than anything known from this site at the time when the chronological scheme for Protocorinthian and its successor-styles was established:
it had been assumed that Protocorinthian was virtually over when
Selinus was founded. In consequence, Thucydides' foundation-date of
628, then accepted as a basis for the chronology, is now widely doubted:
it is argued that the date given in late antiquity by Eusebius, 650 BC,
should be adopted instead; and the resultant uncertainty has spread to
Thucydides' earlier dates, which makes the question relevant to us.[15]

But logically it is rather absurd, when one of the premises for a conclusion is taken away, to alter the other premise too, so as to retain the
conclusion. It would be preferable to adjust the *conclusion*, which was that
the Protocorinthian style came to an end no later than 628 B C, being
supposedly absent from Selinus. This will certainly cause difficulties,
both in extending the earlier, and in compressing the later, phases of
Corinthian pottery; but the former difficulty, at any rate, would be much
reduced, if similar discoveries of earlier and previously unknown material
were to occur at the older sites, as has already happened at Megara Hyblaea
(and indeed Gela). The dating of Protocorinthian could then be brought
down *en bloc*. For the time being I prefer to retain a faith in Thucydides'
Greek Sicilian dates; but the cases of Megara, Gela and Selinus show that
we must be cautious about equating the earliest material so far known
from a site, with the time of its foundation. On this view, the Thucydidean
dates are accurate *termini post quos*, with a margin for downward adjustment in the dating of the early material from their sites. This material in
every case belongs primarily to the Corinthian series; but fortunately there
is elsewhere a whole series of associations of Corinthian pottery with
Attic, Argive and other Geometric wares, beginning at a stage before the
earliest finds from Syracuse and Megara Hyblaea. These associations have
been recently studied, and need not be reiterated here. Coldstream's recent
verdict is that true Protocorinthian begins at about 720; this date would
also serve for the earliest piece from a Greek grave at Cumae, which was
by ancient tradition an earlier colony than the Sicilian sites, although no
plausibly exact date is recorded. On our view, such a dating will make it
just possible to accommodate pieces which may be slightly older from
Naxos, Syracuse, Leontini and Megara, without deserting Thucydides;
at the same time, it will leave an appreciable 'safety margin' from the
presumed foundation-date of Cumae, somewhere in the mid-eighth
century, to allow for possible future finds of earlier pottery there. If this
is correct, then Attic Geometric will have ended at or rather before 700 B C,
and Argive perhaps shortly after Attic: the latter conclusion is
strengthened by the belief, based on late written sources, that the site of
Asine in the Argolid, whose pottery-series ceases with Late Geometric,
was abandoned about 700; but this is an imprecise piece of evidence.

Before we leave the Western sites it should also be admitted that
there is Greek material from other places in this area which could be
brought to bear on this question. Some of it is in a general way favourable
to the trustworthiness of the ancient sources – such as the Geometric

49-50 pottery found at Pithekoussai which is, as it should be, appreciably earlier than the first material from Greek Sicily (but again, no precise foundation-date is available here); some of it is just the reverse, as with the Greek material from the Phoenician sites of Carthage and Motya, which is present in the earliest levels yet discovered, yet is as late as, or later than the first Syracusan material; whereas the *latest* date given in our written sources for the foundation of Carthage is Timaeus' 814 BC, while Thucydides in an important passage implies that Motya and other Phoenician foundations in Sicily antedated Syracuse.[16] In no case, however, does the evidence present a picture both consistent and precise enough to assist with the chronology of Greek Geometric pottery.

ABSOLUTE DATING

THE ATTIC SERIES

The attempt to extract an absolute dating-scheme from this evidence, however provisional and in the long run premature, must now be made. The Attic series being the fullest, let us take first those dates which bear on it, beginning at the lower end. If Attic Late Geometric ended by c.700 (the indirect evidence of the Western sites), and Attic Middle Geometric began by c.850 (Megiddo), then we have some 150 years to apportion between these two phases. We have the assurance of those who have studied the individual workshops of Late Geometric (n. 1) that this phase can barely be extended over much more than fifty years; it is difficult to go against expert judgment, and furthermore the presence of the krater at Hama, which is still Middle Geometric in style yet is in a dated context of 720 BC, discourages us from pushing back the upper boundary of Late Geometric further than we need; while the krater of similar style from Amathus should also by its context be within the eighth century. If therefore Late Geometric is to be concentrated in a span of, say, fifty to sixty years, then Middle Geometric must cover ninety to a hundred years. This may seem excessively long, but we can bear in mind Coldstream's observation that in Middle Geometric the grave-groups do not show the same frequency of overlapping styles or manners, which has led the students of Late Geometric to believe that development was rapid and diffuse in that period.[17] We may also remember that the Megiddo terminus is based on considerations ultimately determined by a foundation-date, that of Samaria; so that it is on the whole more likely that it may one day be required to be lowered slightly, than raised. Moving now, as we have to, to the beginning of the Iron Age, we recall that the links between Attic

Submycenaean and early Protogeometric on the one hand, and Late Cypriot III B and Cypro-Geometric I on the other, point to the transition of styles in western Attica having taken place not very long after the date at which it happened in Cyprus; and that date is placed at c.1050 by the most widely accepted chronology for Cyprus. We now have a further apportionment of roughly 200 years between Attic Protogeometric and Early Geometric; there is no direct outside evidence as to when the division should be made. But if the relative number of graves in the Kerameikos, taken with the comparatively limited Early and Middle Geometric material from all parts of Greece, means anything, it would not be surprising if Protogeometric covered a period much longer than that of Early Geometric, perhaps longer than Early and Middle Geometric together.[18] If the estimate of 90-100 years for Middle Geometric is sound, a division of the earlier period into 150 years for Protogeometric and 50 for Early Geometric may not be far wrong. We now have to address ourselves to the question of the latest Mycenaean periods. If Mycenaean III C I b was in production well before 1165, then we have to allow perhaps 125 years or more for the duration of the Granary Class, and for the degeneration of Furumark's III C I c. This seems quite long enough, for the material is hardly very plentiful: but we may recall that these divisions are valid primarily for the Argolid, and not at all for western Attica, where the main question is the initial date of Submycenaean. The numbers of graves in the two cemeteries where this pottery appears are quite large – over a hundred in each case – but the homogeneity of the pottery in each grave, and indeed in whole groups of graves, is far greater than, say, in Attic Protogeometric; none the less, there are discernible changes in shapes and decoration between the earliest material found on Salamis and the transition to Protogeometric at the Kerameikos. Faced with the evident slowness of ceramic development before and after the Submycenaean phase, one cannot think that these cemeteries had a combined duration of less than fifty years; they could have lasted longer. The initial date of Submycenaean will then be 1100 or rather earlier, perhaps not far from the end of the Argive Granary Class from which it is clearly descended. We thus arrive at some such scheme as this for the initial dates of the Attic pottery-styles after the Mycenaean period: c.1125/1100 Submycenaean, c.1050/1040 Protogeometric, c.900 Early Geometric, c. 860/840 Middle Geometric, c.770/760 Late Geometric, ending c.710/700. This scheme makes no claim to be more than approximate and notional.

THE ARGOLID

Turning to the other regional styles of Greece we can now, in dating them relatively to Attic, at the same time hazard a guess at their absolute chronology. For the Argolid, we have equated the end of Mycenaean III C with the rise of Attic Protogeometric, which is placed in c.1050 or a little later. If the new Philistine evidence is substantiated, this may take the beginning of III C so far back as to give the period a total duration of at least 150 years; but such a conclusion would not be altogether extra-ordinary. The most difficult part of it is the long duration required for III C I c, from fairly soon after the destruction of the Granary at Mycenae (usually placed at c.1150), down to c.1050 or later. But it has been amply shown, by Furumark and others, that the Late Cypriot III B style must be largely coeval with this phase in mainland Greece, and recent evidence suggests that there were probably two major migrations from Greece to Cyprus within this time-span. Late Cypriot III B is a long period – the three settlements of Enkomi III-I cover only a part of it – and there are no signs that it began more than marginally earlier than Mycenaean III C I c; while Protogeometric must be entirely posterior to Late Cypriot III B, as Furumark saw. A length of nearly a century for Mycenaean III C I c is perhaps therefore possible. Thereafter the problems of the Argive series decrease: the Protogeometric style should begin and end very soon after the Attic (for an Attic Protogeometric oenochoe occurred in an Early Geometric grave at Argos), while Courbin has shown that Argive Geometric is susceptible of the same stylistic divisions as Attic, Early, Middle and Late being each divisible into an earlier and a later phase.[19] An exami-nation of the Late Geometric material has convinced Courbin that, as in the Attic series, there is much overlapping of manners, and a short period of time is involved; this although the material (again, as in Attic) is more copious for the Late phase than for the two previous ones together. The end of Argive Late Geometric being presumptively fixed at c.700 (p. 121), and its range of development being more limited than that of its Attic counterpart, Courbin places its initial date at c.740. Middle Geometric he believes to be a long, comparatively sparsely represented period begin-ning at c.820: Early Geometric is more strongly characterized, with features that demand an initial date not far from that of Attic, at c.900. Beyond a tentative suggestion that his two lower divisions may be set a shade too late, it is hard to suggest any improvement on this scheme.

CORINTH

For Corinth, it is better to start at the lower end of the period. We have assumed an initial date of c.720 for the true Protocorinthian style; this once cautious assumption today leaves a bare allowance for the earliest material known from some of the Western sites being later than their foundation. Protocorinthian is preceded by a phase of true Late Geometric, judged by most authorities to be a brief, almost transitional stage; it is unlikely to begin before 750. The kotyle, Corinth's first major contribution to Greek Iron Age pottery shapes, was probably devised just before this date, and imitated in Attic and other styles soon after. The Middle Geometric period may have lasted as long as at Argos, but the Early Geometric at Corinth does not bear the same signs of seniority as Argive; indeed, there are signs of a chronological overlap between Corinthian Protogeometric and Attic Early Geometric, suggesting that at Corinth the full Geometric style began later. For the period before that, the picture becomes shadowy: there is a settlement-deposit at Old Corinth which shows a mixture of late Granary-type ware, apparently of III c I c date, with incipient Protogeometric; if this represents a transition comparable with that at Argos, there is no reason for placing it any later.[20] But before and after this stage, there may well be interruptions in the series available for Corinth; it would not be surprising to learn that there were breaks in occupation there.

THESSALY

For Thessaly, where there is again evidence for the continuity from Mycenaean III c into Protogeometric, but a greater distance for new ideas to travel over, it seems satisfactory to place the change of style at about 1025. At the other end of Protogeometric, there is an overlap, at least at some outlying sites – Theotokou, Marmariani – between the local 'Sub-Protogeometric' and Attic Geometric, so that the former must continue well into the ninth century, if not later still. Thessalian Geometric, apart from a brief phase of Attic influence around the middle of the eighth century, is largely wrapped in obscurity; it may have withered and died quite soon, or it may have survived into the seventh century for an unknown length of time. In any case, a time-lag between Attic and Thessalian seems probable in the later stages of the period.

CYCLADES

This is less true of the Cycladic schools, in so far as it is possible to take them together. On Naxos, there is equally good evidence of an early Protogeometric school, evolving out of the latest Mycenaean, as in Thessaly, with which Naxos indeed appears to have been in contact at this time. Then, an amphora of Cycladic, perhaps Naxian, fabric and later Protogeometric style appears in Tomb XI at Fortetsa, which produced an

Attic Late Protogeometric skyphos too, but in the Cretan series belongs to Early Protogeometric; then after a further interval the well-established Early and Middle phases of Cycladic Geometric are equated, again by finds at Fortetsa, with Cretan Late Protogeometric, a period whose ninth-century date is to be established presently. The earliest context is that of *see 121* Cycladic amphora which so resembles Attic of the transition from Early to Middle Geometric, as to suggest contemporaneity. The equations formed at these two stages are among the most helpful pieces of relative chronology in the period: Attic and Cycladic Late Protogeometric are equated with each other, and with Cretan Early Protogeometric; while Cycladic Early and Middle Geometric, though not quite so explicitly equated with their Attic counterparts, are seen to be, at latest, contemporary with Cretan Late Protogeometric.[21] But at this period, as earlier, it is clear that there were several centres of production in the Cyclades: developments in the Northern Cyclades were clearly later and slower. On Delos and Rheneia, and more especially on Andros and Tenos, the Protogeometric is all of a developed phase; while the earlier stages of Geometric seem to show closer dependence on Attic than in the southern group, where Attic is largely used as a basis for original experiments in decoration. But the situation only becomes clearer with the growth of identifiable island schools towards the end of the period: on Naxos and Paros, independent styles flourished at the same period as the Attic Late Geometric, beginning and ending little if at all later. The finds of Cycladic, perhaps Naxian, sherds at Hama give a precise *terminus ante quem* of 720 for the development of Late Geometric. At Al Mina, too, there are hopes of an accurate chronological indication; but this is likely to be more informative about the Euboean series.

EUBOEA

Identifiable Euboean Late Geometric ware is found at Al Mina, as well as the long-lived skyphoi with pendent semicircles; whereas on the Western colonial sites, including the earliest of them, Pithekoussai, where similar Euboean Geometric pottery is found, these skyphoi are totally absent. The explanation is surely in part a chronological one: production of the skyphoi must have ceased, at any rate in Chalkis and Eretria, at some time between the settlement at Al Mina and the earliest finds from Pithekoussai – that is, after c.800 but certainly before 750. The Euboean Late Geometric series apparently began soon after this happened; imitations of Corinthian kotylai figure conspicuously in it, not necessarily from the very first, but early enough to be imported and *themselves* imitated, in local fabric, in quite early graves at Pithekoussai.[22] Clearly there cannot be much of a time-lag behind the Attic series now and Euboean Late Geometric can be taken to have begun by c.750. But down to this date, as the evidence from Lefkandi makes clear, it was the local Protogeometric and 'sub-Protogeometric' styles which predominated; their beginnings cannot be traced back beyond about 950.

EAST GREECE

From this point, our dating evidence for most other areas of Greece, Crete excluded, deteriorates markedly. Of the Greek settlements in Asia Minor, we can at least say that the pottery from reoccupied Miletus and from Assarlik (Termera) should begin by, or even before, the rise of Attic Protogeometric in c.1050. At Smyrna we await clarification; but in the case of the Dodecanese, it seems clear that even the first Protogeo-metric finds, as found in the cemetery on Kos, date from some time in the middle or later tenth century, while the Rhodian sites on the whole show a derivation from late Attic Protogeometric; their resultant school of Protogeometric may, in the case of Exochi and perhaps Lindos, have lived on down to the arrival of a wave of Attic Geometric influence some-what after 800. But in Kos and north-western Rhodes there was not such marked backwardness; and one of the tombs at Kameiros provides a rare link with the Cretan series, an imported Cretan pithos of perhaps the earlier eighth century being found with Rhodian Middle Geometric. In addition, there are the two imitations of 'barrel-jugs' (p. 78) whose Cypriot originals are most likely to belong in the Cypro-Geometric II to III A periods, that is c.950–800 by Gjerstad's dating; the grave at Ialysos in which they were found stands at the transition to Rhodian Geometric, but the chronological pointer is a vague one. When we arrive at fixed termini at the very end of the eighth century, these show first that when Protocorinthian kotylai of that time were imported to Rhodes, the local Late Geometric style was still very much alive; and secondly, that East Greek skyphoi and imitations of the Protocorinthian kotylai were exported further east in small quantities before c.700, but much more copiously thereafter, when the sub-Geometric 'bird bowl' was the dominant East Greek shape. The true Geometric style in this region therefore lasted into the seventh century, and lived on still longer in a sub-Geometric survival. The startling evidence of the Tarsus finds, in which the 'bird bowls' occurred in levels apparently terminating at 696 BC (p. 115), must surely be reconsidered. Of the East Greek Geometric at Pithekoussai, none so far as I know need be earlier than c.720, as is shown by the Protocorinthian shapes which it imitates and with which it is at times associated.[23]

CRETE

In central Crete we have a unique series, with the merits not only of continuity but of independence, which make it the most valid check on the Attic yardstick which we have used hitherto. The major unknown quantity in it is the Subminoan period with which it begins. The fact that this period must start very early, at least at Knossos, is shown not only by its stylistic connection with the later Granary ware of Mycenaean III C I C in the Argolid but by the substantial overlap with Late Cypriot III B (p. 117); from these links there follows a third chronological equation, partial at least, with western Attic Submycenaean. It therefore seems unlikely that the earliest Subminoan is much, if at all, later than 1100. Yet at the lower end of this period we have, in Knossos, a substantial Early Protogeometric style which is contemporary at least in part with Attic Late Protogeometric and the same phase in the Cyclades, and must therefore begin after about 950 on our reckoning; a Middle Protogeometric phase for which we have no external dating criteria; and a brief Late Protogeometric phase, with an imported Cycladic amphora which is itself influenced by Attic Early or Middle Geometric, bringing the terminal date of this period down to at least 850. The century c.925–825 is a fair estimate of the date and duration of Cretan Protogeometric; and we may recall that for most of this period the eastern extremity of Crete had apparently remained in a Subminoan twilight whose duration cannot have been far short of three centuries.[24]

Returning to Knossos, we have now to accommodate the Protogeometric B phase and the Early, Mature and Late Geometric stages (the first a decidedly brief one), within a limited period; for in Crete the imitations of Corinthian kotylai, which have helped in the chronology of Attic, Euboean and East Greek Late Geometric, seem to appear *after* the end of Geometric. The first of these imitations is indeed of an early type of kotyle which in Corinth could not be much later than 750, and in Athens is probably imitated by c.740; in Fortetsa Tomb VII it is found with an Early Orientalizing pithos, apparently suggesting that the latter style should begin by about 730 at latest. But since imitations of the standard straight-walled type of Protocorinthian kotyle appear, with one exception, not even in this period but in the subsequent one, Late Orientalizing, along with several imported examples of the genuine article, it is clear that something unusual is happening. Either Cretan Early Orientalizing is a brief and precocious style which flourishes only between c.740 and c.710, giving way to a Late Orientalizing which can still overlap with Early Protocorinthian; or the import and imitation of Corinthian kotylai in

Crete took place by a very delayed process. A strong, and I think decisive argument against the former alternative, and in favour of the latter, is the prolific range and quantity of the Early Orientalizing pottery, particularly as represented in the rich multiple Tomb P at Fortetsa; there is also independent evidence that the Early Orientalizing style must continue some way into the seventh century. The imitations of kotylai thus cease to provide an accurate dating guide (including presumably the earliest, in Fortetsa Tomb VII), and remain only *termini post quos*; but it is still a curious fact that the two main types of kotyle arrived in Crete in the order in which they were invented in Corinth, and separated by a considerable interval of time.[25]

This digression was intended to provide a firm terminal date for the Geometric style at Knossos, but its result has been to weaken an apparently secure line of division at about 730. It seems impossible to say more than that the Orientalizing period of Cretan pottery begins, not probably before 730 but hardly later than 700. This in itself is enough to show that the marked time-lag, observed in the early stages of Cretan Iron Age pottery, has gone; a slow tempo has given way to one, if anything, faster than that of the rest of Greece. Such a development was anticipated by the Knossian Protogeometric B period, to which we must now return. J. K. Brock, in proposing a comprehensive chronology for the Fortetsa cemetery, scaled down the dates of Protogeometric B lower than he felt was justified by the evidence, but our dating of Cretan Protogeometric will entail a still lower date for this phase (p. 128). This, and more especially the succeeding Early Geometric, are of limited scope at Knossos and thinly represented elsewhere, and could both perhaps be accommodated in the last quarter of the ninth century. The evidence which had suggested an earlier dating to Brock, consists of imported Geometric pieces in both the Protogeometric B *and* the considerably later Mature Geometric period at Fortetsa; he dated these imports to the ninth century. The skyphoi in Tombs OD and X (and another from Phaistos, chapter 2, n. 58), which are in Protogeometric B contexts, and the oenochoe and pithos in Tomb X, which were probably associated with Mature Geometric, admittedly in no case look later than Middle Geometric; all are of Attic or Cycladic fabric. But for the late eighth century our conclusion was (pp. 128-9) that imports from the rest of the Aegean were reaching Crete after a prolonged delay, or else were kept as prized possessions by generations of Cretans. To suggest that much the same may have been happening in these earlier years too, there are in this period one or two further imported pieces which

I

should be decidedly after 800 – notably a Corinthian Geometric aryballos, probably of the first half of the eighth century, in tomb TFT at Fortetsa; while two kraters from Khaniale Tekke imitate Attic work of the same era. Their association with Cretan Mature Geometric suggests that this phase lies largely or wholly after 800; the Cypro-Geometric III imports, which begin also in this period, provide no close dating-evidence. The Late Geometric style, represented though it is by considerable material at Knossos, must be confined to a fairly short period, after rather than before 750. For East Crete, we have almost nothing in this series after Subminoan which is earlier than Mature Geometric; the earliest imported piece at Vrokastro, probably Attic this time, and of the first half of the eighth century, to some extent confirms the relative dating of the central Cretan series; from this point the chronological divisions for the different areas of the island at this period may perhaps begin to be equated.[26] For the western end of the island, however, and indeed for the south central plain, only the detailed publication of tomb-groups could provide further dating evidence. Despite the distractions and apparent contradictions, the Cretan series can still be dated with more confidence than most.

LACONIA

Crete may have required detailed consideration, but we are now almost at the end of the list of regional Iron Age styles for which there is any chronological evidence other than the generalized and purely stylistic. For Laconia, the independence of the local Protogeometric school and the dearth of evidence for the earlier stages of Geometric make any cross-reference to other regions difficult. The scheme of absolute dates originally advanced by the excavators of the Artemis Orthia sanctuary has not stood the test of time; it has been shown that on *stratigraphic* grounds there is little need to date the earliest material from this site much before 700; we thus fall back on stylistic considerations for evidence of any earlier date. The Laconian Geometric so far discovered seems to owe nothing to outside influences earlier than the beginning of the Late Geometric, when the proximity of the Argive school begins to have effect; later, the influence of Protocorinthian and the evidence of imports from Corinth point to a late survival of Laconian Geometric, perhaps down to c.650. A century of life, beginning at c.750, seems quite long enough for this school, and the only remaining question will be the duration of the Protogeometric style before that. It is most strongly represented not at Sparta, but at the nearby sanctuary-site of Amyklai; but even there the material, though copious, is not impressive in range. It is stratified under the Geometric, and directly over or in some cases in association with the latest Mycenaean dedications from the sanctuary, which evidently already existed at that period. Can we believe that the Protogeometric spans the vast gap in time between the other two eras? Certainly there is almost no sign of stylistic continuity from the Mycenaean to the Protogeometric, and indeed the latter shows awareness of no outside developments, apart from a faint inheritance of Protogeometric decorative ideas. The excavator of Amyklai, who believed in continuity of worship at the site, accordingly held that the Protogeometric developed out of the latest local Mycenaean.[27] We have had reason to doubt the claims of continuity in other areas, and with the example of the time-lag in Euboean and Cretan Protogeometric before us we may easily believe that the Laconian style was of equally late growth. I can see no stylistic ground for thinking that it began before the end of Attic Protogeometric, and it could have done so later, when Protogeometric motifs were still current elsewhere. This conclusion entails a gap of perhaps 200 years in the Laconian ceramic series, during which, on the evidence so far available, Laconia was uninhabited.

ITHAKA

For Ithaka, on the other hand, it seems that the series must be continuous. The hardest question is to determine at what date the Protogeometric school developed from the local Mycenaean III c. I should imagine that this happened some time during the tenth century; the arguments for a high dating of the beginning and end of the Ithakan Protogeometric[28] must be adjusted, now that the subsequent stages of earlier Geometric on the island have been differently interpreted (p. 86). It seems that the production of local ware does not become prominent again before the Late Geometric; if there were real Early and Middle Geometric phases of Ithakan pottery, they could only be reflections of these stages at Corinth, and would have developed at a later date than their Corinthian counterparts. Ithakan Geometric may then have begun as late as 800, and its substantial Late Geometric style rather after 750.

REST OF GREECE

Lack of exploration may in part be to blame for the poverty of our evidence for the rest of Greece, but in many cases there is a real possibility of a break in habitation, as in Laconia. In Boeotia, there is either a gap or a severe stylistic time-lag in the early part of the series; thereafter there are signs that the local Protogeometric survived the end of this style in Attica, and that the various stages of Geometric developed in subservience to Attic. Possibly there was again a slight time-lag at each point, and certainly the

Boeotian Geometric style survives for a time after 700. At Delphi there is a similar lack of continuity in the early phases, but at least there is some daylight from about 800 onwards, when Corinthian imports become common. Elsewhere there is even less evidence. For Elis and Messenia, much of the dark age is at present totally dark even to archaeology; we can only say that Elis was probably in touch with Attica in the eleventh century, and that there are the glimmerings of a largely undated Protogeometric and Geometric style in Messenia. The evidence from Achaea is perhaps a shade more enlightening; for if there are really signs of the influence of Attic Protogeometric on certain vase- and handle-shapes of the local Mycenaean III c style,[29] and if the Achaean duck-vases are contemporary with their nearest analogues elsewhere, then we have proof of such a survival as was inferred in the case of Ithaka. Even so, there must remain a chronological gulf in the Achaean evidence thereafter. In Arcadia, there is a still greater gulf, but the growth of the Geometric school identified at Tegea probably begins, with Laconian, at 750 or soon after. From Chios, there is no Geometric known to me which need be earlier than 800. Samos is more hopeful, for its pottery shows definite links with Attica for a spell in the ninth century, and again from about 750; there is some published material which falls in the intervening period, and a little that is earlier, but whole Protogeometric is thinly covered. Lesbos remains a special case, in that there is no doubt of the continuity of life, but the ceramic evidence on which this depends is, from the earlier Mycenaean III period onwards, in the form of unpainted pottery.

Something of the same situation, though not from so early a date, obtains in Macedonia; but the question of the dating of Macedonian Protogeometric remains an outstanding one. The commonest Greek shape in the cemetery-site of Vergina, which provides the bulk of the evidence, is the skyphos with pendent semicircles; this, as we have seen, is a post-Protogeometric shape, and Desborough found that there was a 'distinct possibility' that in neighbouring Thessaly it survived into the eighth century. It is at least as likely to have done so here, where we must be farther from its region of origin. The remaining shapes at Vergina and other sites also show links with Thessalian Protogeometric, a school where local survivals into the ninth century are undoubted (p. 125); a few pieces are probably imports from that area. I should therefore be inclined to suggest a time-span of, at the earliest, c.900–750 for the Macedonian Protogeometric style, with the interesting pithos from Vergina (p. 74) standing at the beginning of the series and marking the critical advance in technique of decoration. This is not to say that the Vergina cemetery may not extend earlier than 900 (just as there is independent evidence to show that its 'Early Iron Age' period of use continued, if only intermittently, down to about 500 BC); for the Protogeometric made up but a small proportion of the pottery there. Indeed there were two interments which each contained a locally-made, straight-sided squat alabastron, undecorated but plainly derived from a Mycenaean shape. The two vases are, however, difficult to place precisely in the Mycenaean series. I would venture to suggest that they reflect their Mycenaean models indirectly and at some distance in time, and there is some independent evidence for the long survival of Mycenaean shapes in Macedonia, from the site of Vardaroftsa. The stratification here showed, among other things, that at least one stirrup-vase of Mycenaean III c style appeared in the fifteenth half-metre down from the surface; that the fourteenth to tenth half-metres inclusive produced many 'Submycenaean' bowls, which Desborough classes as local imitations of Mycenaean III c; and that after a horizon of destruction in the tenth and ninth half-metres, this same ware still survived into the eighth half-metre. In the seventh half-metre appeared the first sherd of a Protogeometric or Geometric type.[30] Although it is scarcely possible to assign an absolute date to the destruction, it seems highly probable that the local imitations of Mycenaean III c survived long after the end of that style in most of central and southern Greece, perhaps almost down to the arrival of Protogeometric influence around 900. Whatever the truth about this earlier period, the Protogeometric style is succeeded not by a Geometric school but by a period of extreme obscurity, in which datable Greek imports are notably rare until about 600 BC.

SICILY AND S. ITALY

In the Greek sites in Sicily and southern Italy, finally, it is hard to say from what exact date locally-made products begin. It is *a priori* most improbable that any of the colonial pottery could be as early as the first imported pieces discovered at these sites, whether these were brought by traders or the first settlers; we have accepted a conventional date of c.720 for the earliest Corinthian import at Greek Cumae (p. 121), and the first Sicilian material is with some few exceptions no earlier. But there is one site, Pithekoussai, which has produced both imported and locally-made pottery, of which the former, when published, will certainly prove to begin distinctly earlier, and may reach back to about 760 or before.[31] It is therefore very likely that local production also begins by about 750 or earlier on this site; time will show.

The conclusions of this discussion are shown
in diagrammatic form in the table overleaf.

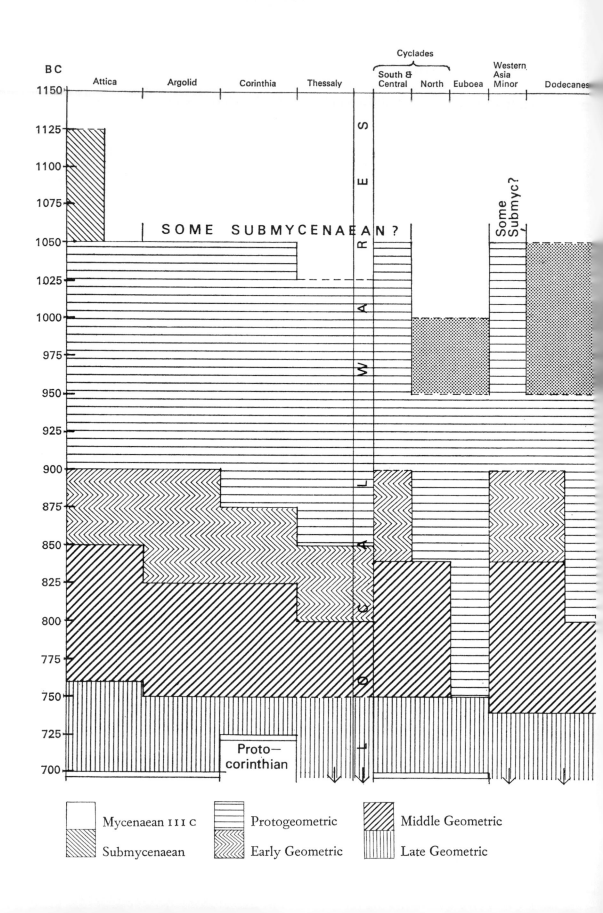

SOME   SUBMYCENAEAN ?

Some
Submyc?

Proto—
corinthian

| Mycenaean III C | Protogeometric | Middle Geometric |
| Submycenaean | Early Geometric | Late Geometric |

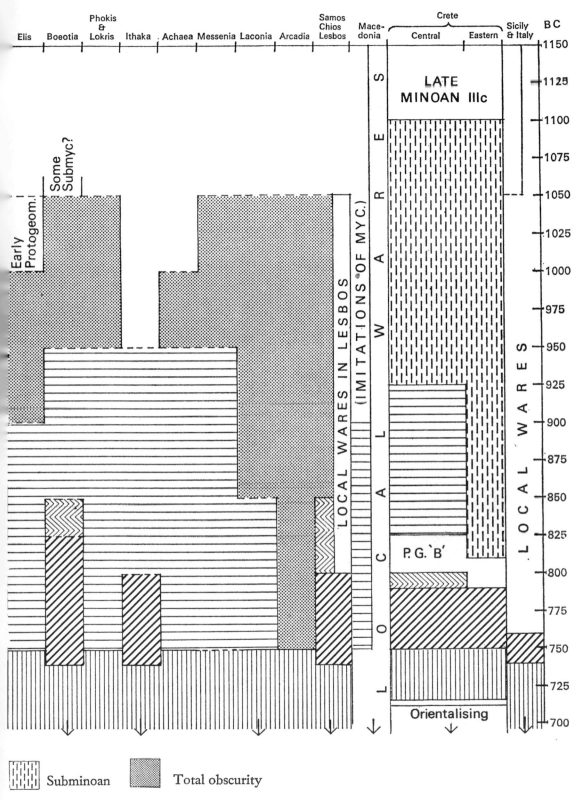

					Crete			
		Phokis & Lokris			Samos Chios Lesbos	Mace-donia	Central	Eastern	Sicily & Italy	B C

Elis Boeotia Phokis & Lokris Ithaka . Achaea Messenia Laconia Arcadia Samos Chios Lesbos Mace-donia Central Eastern Sicily & Italy B C

1150
1125
1100
1075
1050
1025
1000
975
950
925
900
875
850
825
800
775
750
725
700

LATE MINOAN IIIc

Early Protogeom.

Some Submyc?

LOCAL WARES IN LESBOS (IMITATIONS OF MYC.)

S E R W A L A C O L O L

P. G. `B´

Orientalising

L O C A L   W A R E S

▦ Subminoan   ▨ Total obscurity

– – – Extreme chronological uncertainty

Notes

1] W. Kraiker, *Ker.* 1, 132-4; R. S. Young, *Hesp.* Supplement 2 (1939), 1-5 *et passim*; P. Kahane, *AJA* 44 (1940), 464-82; A. Furumark, *Op. Arch.* 3 (1944), 260-1, n.7; F. Matz, *Geschichte der griechischen Kunst* 1 (1950), 37-101; Desborough, *PGP* 291-5 and *JHS* 77 (1957), 216-19; K. Kübler, *Ker.* 5, 1, 70f., 141f., 273-82; J. M. Davison, *YCS* 16 (1961), 122-32; E. T. H. Brann, *Hesp.* 30 (1961), 94-7 and *Agora* 8 (1962), 4-8; S. Foltiny, *AJA* 65 (1961), 295-6; 68 (1964), 255-6; and now Coldstream, *GGP* 302-31, who for the later part of this period offers a more fully-documented account than mine, while arriving at similar conclusions

2] *LMS* 209-14, 238, 240; Albright in *CAH₂*, vol. 2, ch. 23 (fascicule 51) (1966), 27-8. Reports on Deir'alla: H. J. Franken, *Vetus Testamentum* 14 (1964), 377-9 and 417-22; *PEQ* 96 (1964), 73-8, where a date in the first quarter of the twelfth century is suggested; and now *CAH₂* vol. 2, ch. 26b (fascicule 67) (1968), 8-9, where the association of the Philistine ware with the stratum of the tablets is explicitly denied. A further recent study of early Philistine material is that of Jane C. Waldbaum, *AJA* 70 (1966), 331-40, whose conclusions also favour a relatively early date for the arrival of the Philistines (in this case at Tell Fara)

3] Yet in 1948 M. B. Rowton could still suggest c.1170 as the accession-date : *JEA* 34 (1948), 72

4] *LMS* 207-8

5] Hama, *Act. A.* 28 (1957), 107, fig. 207; Davison, *YCS* 16 (1961), 128; for the Cycladic Geometric sherds, T. J. Dunbabin, *The Greeks and their Eastern Neighbours*, 74, and now *Annales Archéologiques de Syrie*, 15, 2 (1965), 80-1, fig. 23; for the general find-circumstances, Coldstream, *GGP* 311

6] *Hesp.* 18 (1949), 275-97; 21 (1952), 279-83

7] See most clearly R. Hachmann, *GGA* 215 (1963), 54ff., figs. 1, 2, 3 and 8; 'Zeitgruppe 1 A', roughly, is Early Geometric, '1 B' and '2' are Middle Geometric

8] Tell abu Hawam, R. W. Hamilton, *QDAP* 4 (1935), 23f.; on the cup, see Kraiker, *Ker.* 1, 164 n.2, and cf. pl. 33, 582; Megiddo, C. Clairmont, *Berytus* 11, 2 (1955), 99, pl. 20, 1-2; cf. Desborough, *JHS* 77 (1957), 217, n.35 and Coldstream, *JHS* 83 (1963), 212

9] Original dating of Megiddo v, R. S. Lamon and G. M. Shipton, *Megiddo* 1, 7; later views, W. F. Albright, *BASOR* 130 (April 1953), 22; G. W. van Beek *ibid.* 138 (April 1955), 34f. Samaria, K. M. Kenyon, *Samaria-Sebaste* 3 (1957), 198-204; B. Maisler, *BASOR* 124 (December 1951), 21-5, conversely kept the high date for Megiddo but brought down Tell abu Hawam III; as did Y. Aharoni and R. Amiran, *Israel Exploration Journal* 8 (1958), 171-84. A useful account of the terminology of these levels can be gleaned from W. F. Albright, *AASOR* 21-2 (1943-4), 2-3, n.1; 6, n.2; 29-30, n.10; he concludes, like Miss Kenyon, that Tell abu Hawam III should end before Megiddo v. Samaria itself produced Geometric Greek imports (*Samaria-Sebaste* 3, 210-13, pl. 18, 1-2, 18), but in curiously scattered contexts

10] Skyphoi with pendent semi-circles, *PGP* 181-5 and *LMS* 270 (Tell Sukas). Hama, see above, n.5. Tarsus, G. M. A. Hanfmann in *Tarsus*, 3, 107f., 127f., 279-82, and J. Boardman, *JHS* 85 (1965), 5-15 and 232

11] J. Boardman, *BSA* 52 (1957), 5, n.22; *The Greeks Overseas*, 62-70; *JHS* 85 (1965), 14

12] Bowl, *Ker.* 5, 1, 201-5, 237, fig. 5 and pl. 162 (Grave 42, M5). Scarabs, J. D. S. Pendlebury, *Aegyptiaca* 11, 39, 80, and add *Fortetsa* 208; on the scarab in the Isis Grave, G. A. Wainwright, *JHS* 52 (1932), 126; Bocchoris scarab at Pithekoussai, S. Bosticco, *Parola del Passato* 54 (1957), 225; Tarquinia vase, see especially A. W. Byvanck, *Mnemosyne* 3, 4 (1936), 181-8; A. Åkerström, *Der Geometrische Stil in Italien*, 77; E. Gjerstad, *Op. Rom.* 5 (1962), 49f., 60f.; Sparta and Perachora, Pendlebury *op. cit.* 109 and *Perachora* 1, 76-7; and T. G. H. James in *Perachora* 2, 463

13] Desborough, *LMS* 22-8, 197, n.2; Lapithos grave, see Gjerstad, *Op. Arch.* 3 (1944), 76-7, Pl. 18, 4-7. Desborough is comparatively sceptical about links between Submycenaean western Attica and Cyprus, and the resemblance claimed for the incised ware found in both areas, J. F. Daniel, *AJA* 41 (1937), 72-4, fig. 7, pls. 2 and 6, is probably illusory; see E. L. Smithson, *Hesp.* 30 (1961), 174, n.22

14] See especially E. Gjerstad, *Op. Arch.* 3 (1944), 84-6 (for Cypro-Geometric I) and *Swedish Cyprus Expedition* 4, 2, 242-57, 421-4; *ibid.* 270-4 for Syrian material in Cyprus.

For support of his dating, Desborough, *JHS* 77 (1957), 216-18 and J. M. Benson, *GRBS* 3 (1960), 14; against, W. F. Albright, *BASOR* 130 (April 1953), 130 and G. W. van Beek, *ibid.* 138 (April 1955), 34-8; G. M. A. Hanfmann, *AJA* 55 (1951), 425; J. du Plat Taylor, *Iraq* 21 (1959), 63, 89; J. Birmingham, *AJA* 67 (1963), 15-42. Stylistic links, Gjerstad, *SCE* 4, 2, 292f. and Brock, *Fortetsa* 143 and n.3, 153-4, 191. On the tripods, see most fully H. W. Catling, *Cypriot Bronzework in the Mycenaean World*, 190ff., nos. 18-20; he includes a fragment (47) plus a clay imitation of a Cypriot stand (p. 214) from Karphi, with which the two Kerameikos stands (*ibid.* n.3) are compared. Amathus find of Protogeometric, Desborough, *JHS* 77, 212-19; Tomb 13, *SCE* 4, 2, 275 and n.4; Salamis, *AR* 1955, 43; 1956, 26; *AA* 78 (1963), 178, figs. 35, 40-1, 43-5; Amathus Tomb 9, *SCE* 2, 55-64, nos. 76, 122 and 19, pl. 139, 7 and 10; cf. *JHS* 77 (1957), 216

15] On Megara Hyblaea, A. W. Byvanck, *Mnemosyne* 3, 4 (1936) 204; contrast G. Vallet and F. Villard, *BCH* 76 (1952), 289-346; the earliest type of cup here is matched by a find from Naxos (which Thucydides dates to 734) (*Bollettino d'Arte* 45 (1964), fig. 41), but it also appears on traditionally later sites – see B. d'Agostino, *Dialoghi di Archeologia* 1 (1967), 22, 32, n.15; Leontini, e.g. *NSc* n.s.9 (1955), 365, fig. 65. Selinus, Vallet and Villard in *BCH* 82 (1958), 16-26; for the view upheld here, cf. J. M. Cook, *BSA* 53-4 (1958-9), 27, n.71. N.B. also Gela, Coldstream, *GGP* 326.

16] On Western dates in general, T. J. Dunbabin, *AE* 1953-4, 2, 247-62.

Note the literary arguments in Thucydides' support by K. J. Dover, *Maia* 6 (1953), 1-20. On Attic associations, J. M. Cook, *BSA* 42 (1947), 153; cf. 35 (1934-5), 203-4; and now C. Brokaw, *AM* 78 (1963), 63-73 and Coldstream, *GGP* 108-11; Argive, P. Courbin, *La céramique géometrique de l'Argolide*, 27-39. For a conventional date of c.725 for the earliest piece from Cumae, Byvanck, *Mnemosyne* 3, 4, 223 (Kübler, *Ker.* 5, 1, 72 works on a date of c.735 for this). On Asine, G. L. Huxley, *Early Sparta* (1962), 21, n.78 and 31. On Carthage and Motya, cf. chapter 1, p. 18 and n.29; the Thucydides passage is VI, 2, 2, where a strict interpretation of the phrase τὰ πλείω implies that Motya, Panormos and Soloeis were included in the original Phoenician settlements. Further evidence based on a colonisation-date may be forthcoming from Corcyra: see V. G. Kallipolitis, *Praktiká* 1955, 187-92; G. E. Dondas, *AD* 20, 2 (1965), 395-6, pl. 442-3

17] *JHS* 83 (1963), 212

18] On numbers of graves, see above, pp. 111-12; and note the plan of the Agora area in Brann, *Agora* 8, pl. 45, which marks 30 Protogeometric, 5 Early Geometric and 11 Middle Geometric graves

19] *LMS* 23-5; Furumark, *Op. Arch.* 3, 257ff.; note that he gave c.205 years to Mycenaean III C, inclusive of Submycenaean however (*ibid.* 262). Later Argive: Courbin, *La céramique géometrique de l'Argolide, passim: ibid.* 66, 553, pl. 148 (C54) for Attic Protogeometric import

20] For Argive, see Courbin, *loc. cit.* (above, n.16); on Corinthian, see especially S. Weinberg, *AJA* 45 (1941), 32, and *Hesp.* 17 (1948), 214-16, pl. 71; T. J. Dunbabin, *JHS*

68 (1968), 68; Coldstream *GGP* 92; and for the beginning of the period in Corinth, *LMS* 20, 85

21] *PGP* 147, 149, 175; *Fortetsa* 20, pl. 13, XI 154; 32, pl. 19, L269 (cf. pl. 143, 311); 213-15; (see Coldstream, *GGP* 165, n.5 on no. 269)

22] *PGP* 194; Dunbabin, *GEN* 30; Boardman, *BSA* 52 (1957), 6-7, n.27 and *The Greeks Overseas* 63-5, 181; for the finds of the 'sub-Protogeometric' skyphoi at Lefkandi, down to perhaps as late as 750, see O. T. P. K. Dickinson in Popham and Sackett, *Excavations at Lefkandi, Euboea* (1968), 28; and for their survival in Cyprus, above, ch. 2, n.4

23] Cretan pithos, G. Jacopi, *Clara Rhodos* 6-7 (1932-3), 123, fig. 135 *bis*, Tomb 39; 'barrel-jugs', *SCE* 4, 2, 264, n.6; cf. 52, 188f.; Corinthian kotylai, *Act. A.* 28 (1957), 15, A8-9. In the West, note especially the Nestor cup (chapter 2, n.54), around 720; Boardman, *Greeks Overseas*, 182

24] *LMS* 15, 26-8, 180; Cycladic amphora, above n.21 (no. 269). Contrast Müller-Karpe, *JdI* 77 (1962), 76 for a much higher dating of Cretan Protogeometric

25] The early kotyle is *Fortetsa* 73, pl. 50, VII, 809 (cf. for Athens, *Agora* 8, 5-6, 50, pl. 9, 153-4); later type with Early Orientalizing, *Fortetsa* 116, pls. 104-5, P 1346; with Late Orientalizing, especially *ibid.* 91, pl. 24, 970, found with the pithos no. 968, but datable around 700 (cf. *ibid.* 166, 190-1). On the position of Early Orientalizing, cf. Brock's conclusion, *ibid.* 216. On order of arrival of kotylai, J. N. Coldstream, *BSA* 55 (1960), 171: a Protocorinthian kotyle is now reported in association with Cretan Late Geometric, *BSA Annual Report* 1966-7, 10

26] *Fortetsa* 38, pl. 24, nos. OD 364-7; 49, pl. 35, X 478; 46-7, pl. 31, X, 454; and 35, X 441; aryballos, *ibid.* 63, 213, n.5, pl. 45, TFT 668; kraters at Khaniale Tekke, R. W. Hutchinson, *BSA* 49 (1954), 222, pls. 25, 19; 21, 20; cf. Fortetsa 63, pl. 44, TFT 671 (Cycladic); *Vrokastro*, 173, fig. 106. T. J. Dunbabin in 1952 believed that Cretan Protogeometric could extend down into the eighth century (*Gnomon* 24 (1952), 195). But for a statement of the case for a high chronology for the Protogeometric 'B' style, see J. Boardman's reconsideration of the Khaniale Tekke finds in *BSA* 62 (1967), 59. In general, Coldstream, *GGP* 238-9, 244, 254-5

27] S. Benton, *JHS* 70 (1950), 17-18; J. Boardman, *BSA* 58 (1963), 3, n.11, 7, n.24. Amyklai, E. Buschor, *AM* 52 (1927), 12; cf. *PGP* 288, *LMS* 42, 88

28] See *PGP* 280

29] E. T. Vermeule, *AJA* 64 (1960), 1-3, 5-6, 17f.; Desborough, *LMS* 98-9, pl. 10f.; 100

30] Vergina: for pendent-semicircle skyphoi, see e.g. M. Andronikos, *Praktiká* 1952, 248, 252, fig. 29; Desborough, *PGP* 193 for date in Thessaly. *PGP* 179-80, *LMS* 143-4 for links with Thessaly. Andronikos, *Balkan Studies* 2 (1961), 96, fig. 5 for a late sixth-century Cypriot import; he has nevertheless stressed the absence of Geometric and Corinthian imports as a sign that this period of the cemetery's use does not extend beyond the earlier seventh century; but this argument from silence would have to be applied to nearly all Macedonian Iron Age sites, since they show the same lack – a conclusion which seems unlikely. Desborough suggested an early ninth-century date for the pithos, Petsas, *Essays in Memory of Karl Lehmann* 258, n.13. On the alabastra (or pyxides), *LMS* 144, n.2; the second is now illustrated, *Praktiká* 1958, 95, pl. 72a; cf. Furumark, *MP* 43, fig. 12, shapes 89-98; a similar piece has now come to light, unfortunately in obscure circumstances, near Elasson in Thessaly (*AD* 18, 2 (1963), 133-4, pl. 170β). Survivals of outdated pottery-shapes in Macedonia are an acknowledged fact (cf. V. G. Kallipolitis and D. Feytmans, *AE* 1948–9, 86, n.1), as in Epirus (below, p. 259). Vardaroftsa, W. A. Heurtley, *BSA* 27 (1925–6), 22, 25-30; *LMS* 141-2. Note now the Geometric imports at Nea Anchialos, *AD* 20, 2 (1965), 421, pl. 472

31] Note the early kotyle mentioned by Miss Benton, *BSA* 48 (1953), 279, n.165; and G. Buchner and J. Boardman, *JdI* 81 (1966), 3-5, 59, 62, figs. 3-5 and *Expedition* 8, 4 (summer 1966), 5-12. An early local piece at Naxos, *Bollettino d'Arte* 45 (1964), 162-4, f.43

4

The Grave

◆ ◆ ◆
◆ ◆
◆

In few periods of antiquity does archaeology lean so heavily on the evidence of graves as in the early Iron Age of Greece.[1] This is a serious disadvantage: one cannot form a balanced picture of the material culture of a civilization without the evidence of the living world of settlement- and sanctuary-sites, and for several areas of Greece these are almost entirely lacking. Nevertheless, we must make what virtue we can of this necessity. The merits of the grave as a source of evidence are several: its universality, in that it is a category which cuts across all racial or social divisions, is one quality whose worth is apparent enough; its survival-value, as a result of the process of concealment which it represents, is high. Equally valuable for historical purposes is the directness of the grave's evidence: to excavate an undisturbed tomb is to have an uninterrupted glimpse into antiquity, such as an occupation-site can seldom offer. One facet of this is temporal directness: all the objects in a single interment, whether old or new, must have been in use at a certain moment of time. Yet these very qualities carry with them their own disadvantages. The fact that the grave tends to be an impartial leveller makes it an unreliable indicator of some aspects, particularly the economic ones, of a civilization; a grave may be richly endowed, but the absence of rich tomb-goods is not a necessary sign of poverty – it may also betoken haste, lack of space, disbelief in an after-life, or none of these. The evidence of the contents of a tomb may be explicit, yet of narrow application: the recurrence of a single vessel of constant shape in the graves of a cemetery may mean only that this shape has funerary associations; it may mean that this was the predominant shape known

Note. Most of the site-references for this chapter are to be found in the Appendix at its end, pages 202-12.

to the community; but equally it could represent a shape of especially transient use which could easily be spared for burials; it may, once again, mean none of these things. Temporal association, finally, should not be confused with practical association: a warrior buried with four swords did not fight with them all at once, and so a group of pots in a grave may not represent a service of crockery.

PRINCIPLES OF CLASSIFICATION

Funerary practice is a multifarious thing, and, if attention is concentrated on one aspect of it only, can be a misleading basis for classification. Burial-rite, with its simple and reasonably clear-cut division between inhumation and cremation, has for long – perhaps too long – been regarded as the primary criterion. Certainly the choice of rite can carry deep implications, and the original adoption of cremation by mankind must have seemed a portentous step; but, the new rite once initiated, its diffusion over the various cultures of the Stone, Bronze and Iron Ages may have become progressively less significant. Further, the broad practices of 'inhuming' and 'cremating' cover a multitude of variants, and indeed this division cuts across other differences which, arguably, can be said to have been more important at certain periods.

These other distinctions of funerary practice fall into several categories, which we may consider in succession. First there is the question of group and single burials; the best division here is not between single and all other burials, but between, on the one hand, single, and more rarely double or more numerous, burials in a small grave with dimensions of more or less constant limits; and on the other hand, true multiple tombs, designed and used for the burials of successive generations, often no doubt of the same family, somewhat after the manner of a family vault. This distinction, which seems to be very widely independent of differences of rite, is clearly an important one. It carries implications as to the situation in which people lived, in that the use of family tombs suggests confidence in the settled order of things, and awareness of heredity; it also involves architectural competence, in the many cases where multiple tombs are of monumental structure, or are built of dressed masonry.

Next comes the classification by tomb-type in the concrete and physical sense, which is no longer dual but multiple. This proves to be, in the main, a refinement of the last distinction: certain tomb-types are regularly used for multiple burials, even if in certain regions they may contain only a single one; others are almost inevitably confined to one or two burials.

For the present, it is enough merely to give a bald list of the types of tomb
64 with which we shall be concerned. There is the chamber-tomb, rock-
hewn normally in sloping ground and approached by a horizontal passage
or dromos, but of very variable plan; there is the tholos tomb, a built
63 tomb of sometimes very large dimensions, vaulted and of circular plan,
also approached by a dromos (whose side-walls may be built); there is
what may be called the vaulted chamber, a fusion of the last two types in
that it is of rectilinear plan, and may in part be rock-hewn both as to the
dromos and the chamber, but has, like the tholos, a built vault; and there is
burial in a natural cave. These four types of tomb are all naturally and
regularly the recipients of multiple burials. Beside them we may range
three forms of structure which are not strictly tomb-types, but which can
have the effect of uniting burials – normally single burials – into a group,
60 although they can also enclose a single grave. These are the tumulus of
65 earth, sometimes bound by a kerb of stones; the cairn of stones; and the
grave-enclosure, a simple perimeter of stones round a group of graves.

Then there are the essentially single tomb-types, which can be located
inside any one of the seven types listed above, but are more often found in
65 open ground. These are, taking inhumation-types first, the pit- or small
shaft-grave (which may have a filling of stones in its mouth) – I shall
scarcely distinguish these two variants, since they seem to be the result
of the same process as applied to softer and harder ground respectively;
58 the cist, a rectangular pit lined and often covered with thin stone slabs; the
slab-covered pit, a fusion of the previous two types which explains itself;
two variants of the cist which are worth isolating, and which may be called
the 'monolith-cist' and the 'boulder-cist', the former being in effect a crude
62 sarcophagus hollowed out of a single block of stone, the latter a pit lined
61 not with fitted slabs but with rough unhewn stones; the burial in a vessel,
or as it is commonly called the pithos-burial, although interments are found
in a variety of vessels besides the pithos; the sarcophagus of terra-cotta
(or larnax); and the coffin of wood, whose perishability is such that its
presence may well be missed by excavators, in graves reported simply as
pits or shafts. The types of cremation-tomb are more limited in range,
and are normally confined to the simple cremation in an open grave (corre-
59 top, 57, 83 sponding to the pit-inhumation), and the urn-burial or 'inurned cremation' (corresponding to the pithos-inhumation). But cremations are also
found, perhaps inappropriately, inside cists and sarcophagi, besides
occurring, in some area of the Greek lands, in each of the seven forms of
cf. 64 collective burial listed in the previous paragraph. An important adjunct

of cremation-burials, where it can be traced, is the funerary pyre, often located at a short distance from the graves, and no doubt used repeatedly; but in some cases the actual incineration took place in the grave itself. Classification by tomb-type is thus a complex matter, making any hard-and-fast distinction seem impossible of attainment.

Other elements of funerary practice, being also associated to some degree with surviving physical remains, can be used as differentiating factors according to their presence or absence. One is the habit of using different burial-practices, or different burial-grounds, for children and for adults, which is almost invariably associated with single types of grave. Secondly, we may note the practice of re-using tombs, of whatever type, of an earlier period, the motive often no doubt being to save labour or compensate for lack of architectural skill. Next comes the almost infinitely variable practice of inserting grave-goods in a burial at the time of interment; it would be impossible to give even a summary account of the kinds of object chosen for this, but it is worth pointing out that they may either be placed inside the grave itself, or be laid close by it, and that they may (even with inhumation-burials) be burned at the time of offering. Last, and often difficult to distinguish clearly from the preceding, is the practice of grave-cult, to which offerings of goods long after the time of burial bear witness. But this, as will be appreciated, is very far from being an exhaustive analysis of funerary practice: among the omissions are the questions of the disposition of the corpse, and of the orientation of the grave, but these and other factors are on the whole too erratic, or too little documented, to be brought to bear on the discussion.

INTERPRETATION OF GRAVE-EVIDENCE

With so many criteria, some interwoven, others independent of each other, how can one use the great body of grave-evidence to determine regional groupings, influences, or successive developments in dark age Greece? If possible, some priorities must be established. The clear-cut distinction of rite, so often invoked as a touchstone since the beginning of scientific excavation, both in Greece and elsewhere, needs to be re-evaluated. The best instance of its limitations is perhaps that singled out and briefly discussed a few years ago by R. M. Cook,[2] that of Athens in the dark age and after. Here we have a community and, more particularly, a single cemetery in the Kerameikos whose continuity in time, and essentially in population, there is no reason whatever to doubt. The people of Athens, habitual inhumers during the Bronze Age like every one else within the sphere of direct Mycenaean influence, continued to inhume

59 their dead after Submycenaean pottery came into use. Of 109 'Submycenaean' graves in the Kerameikos whose remains were sufficiently well
preserved, 106 were inhumations; but in the remaining three were found
the earliest known cremations in Athens, and this was a foretaste of the
situation in the Protogeometric period when the proportions were to be
almost inverted: six inhumations to fifty-one cremations. Within the full
Geometric period, we encounter difficulties because of the disagreement
as to the chronological grouping of the Kerameikos graves (p. 52); but if
we accept the groups proposed by R. Hachmann,[3] adding in the few
Geometric graves not included in his tables, we arrive at these results:
the Early Geometric phase carries on the preference for cremation to such a
degree that all the graves assignable to this period are cremations; in
Middle Geometric inhumation returns in a few cases, though still over-
shadowed by some twenty cremations; and in the much more numerous
Late Geometric graves, the inhumations come to outnumber the cremations
by nearly four to one. The seventh century, however, inaugurates a new
swing to cremation in the Kerameikos, with this rite accounting for some
seventy per cent of the burials; but by the mid-sixth century there are
indications that inhumation, spreading this time from the poorer to the
richer burials, is entering a new vogue.

Here, then, is clear evidence from within the confines of a single cemetery
that one and the same community could repeatedly and wholeheartedly
change its preference in the matter of rite. But if not a racial, can then a
religious significance be attributed to these changes? If so, one would
expect to find simultaneous and equally radical changes in the practices
which are more obviously influenced by religious sentiment, such as grave-
cult, grave-goods, and perhaps the differentiation of child-burials. Such
changes indeed occur,[4] but they hardly coincide with the changes in rite,
being much less frequent. Further evidence might most naturally be sought
in the burial-practices of the same period in other parts of Athens; and
here we do find a degree of cohesion which is enough to suggest that some
strong influences, if only on a purely social level, were at work in the
community. Admittedly we have no other cemetery of the size and com-
pactness of that in the Kerameikos, but there are other assemblages of
graves, particularly those scattered around and under the site of the later
57 Agora, to provide some basis for comparison. Some of these have been
given a preliminary or even a detailed publication by the American
excavators as they have come to light year by year, and at first sight they
show remarkable differences from the contemporary practices in the

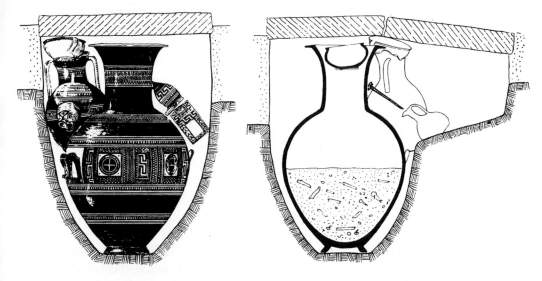

57. Cross-sections of an urn-cremation: the rich female burial of
c. 850 B C, found in the Athenian Agora in 1967.

Kerameikos.[5] But here we must allow of a strong possibility that burials
such as these are complementary to those of the Kerameikos, rather than
examples of local divergence. For example, the incidence of inhumation in
Protogeometric and Early Geometric graves in the Agora is at first sight
very surprising – indeed they comprise a substantial majority of the
burials of the former period so far published. But closer examination shows
that very nearly all these inhumations, in cists and pits, are child-burials;
one is under a contemporary house-floor. Does not this represent 'intramural' child-burial by a community which was cremating its adult dead
elsewhere, perhaps in the Kerameikos, where identifiable child-burials
are very rare at this time? The adult-inhumations in the Kerameikos are
few and early in the Protogeometric period; but it must be admitted that
other Athenian communities at this time were slower to abandon this
practice, as is shown by inhumations, some of them distinctly later, found
at Alopeki Street and Garibaldi Street, and in the suburb of Nea Ionia,
few of which are likely to be of children. In Middle and Late Geometric
times, the practices in the Agora and the Kerameikos begin to show a
closer correspondence, though the former continues to show a detectably
stronger bias towards inhumation for adults; the new rule (for Athens)
of pithos-inhumation for children is common to both regions. Yet, once

K

again, we find further afield in Athens examples of either slow reaction or local divergence: a group of Late Geometric burials on the site of Plato's Academy proved to include a number of cremations, while one of two graves at the junction of Diakos and Anapausis Streets may have been a child-cremation, and contemporary cremations have now come to light at Anavysos and Myrrhinous in Attica.

What we can infer from the case of Athens is not, I suggest, that the changes in funerary rite are without any significance, but that their significance in terms of racial differentiation or religious belief in early Greece – two fields in which they have been adduced as evidence – must be decidedly limited. The strength of mere social fashion should not be forgotten. This was perhaps the root cause for the change which later swept over Roman society, converting it from the earlier practice of inhumation to an era of cremation which covered the later centuries of the Republic and extended into earlier Imperial times. The example of Rome also illustrates another factor which may have operated in many societies, the force of family tradition: some families, among whom the gens Cornelia was especially prominent, continued to inhume their dead even in the greatest vogue of cremation. Perhaps it may also be relevant to observe recent developments in Britain, the country which has moved most rapidly towards the adoption of cremation in the twentieth century. The new rite was not only almost unknown, but also possibly illegal in the earlier nineteenth century, and for a long time afterwards it made an extremely slow advance. As recently as 1935, only 1·7 per cent of deaths in Britain were followed by cremation; by 1945 the figure had reached eight per cent and by 1950 fifteen per cent. At this period, the swing towards cremation received encouragement from the late Lord Dalton, on his appointment as Minister of Local Government and Planning; and in the 1950s the rate of increase rose further, the proportion reaching about thirty-three per cent in 1959, while the latest survey at the time of writing, that for 1968, reports 52·4 per cent of burials in Britain to be cremations.[6] What does this great change, within the span of a single generation, mean? Many would say that it was just one aspect of the secularization of British society; but this is to leave out of account a range of social factors which must have played some part – the effect of a world war (and of the threat of another) on a nation's attitude to the dead, pressure arising from lack of cemetery-space, governmental exhortation, perhaps the climate of austerity prevailing for part of the period, and so on. So if, for example, we were to attribute the first great 'cremation-wave' in the Kerameikos,

over the period c.1050–800 BC, to a reaction against the received religion
of the Mycenaeans, we should have also to admit the operation of other
less permanent and fundamental factors, in answering the questions
which would naturally arise – for example, why did the reaction not extend
to child-burials? Is there a similar explanation of the later but less thorough-
going reversion to cremation in the early seventh century? And what are
the religious links, if any, between Attica and the other cremating regions?
Furthermore, since Greece was clearly not the most advanced area of the
ancient world in this respect, we must admit an additional factor absent in
twentieth-century Britain: the likelihood of foreign influence.

Will any of the other funerary criteria fare better than that of rite?
Rather than answer this question directly, I think the first task is to survey
the evidence from Greece region by region; the material is tabulated in
more detail in the Appendix (pp. 202-12). By repeating the same grouping
of regions as was used in Chapter 2, we can see whether the pattern of
progressive, imitative and isolated areas, suggested by the pottery, has
any support from the evidence of graves.

REGIONAL DEVELOPMENTS

ATTICA

Beginning then with Attica, we may take first the two cemeteries of
Salamis and the Kerameikos, where the earliest burials must lie within the
twelfth century. Here we see the whole-hearted adoption, from the very
outset, of the principle of single burial; and with it the conversion to the
cist (almost universal on Salamis, heavily predominant at the Kerameikos)　*58*
and the pit (quite common at the Kerameikos, but not in the earliest phase).　*59*
The graves are on the whole extremely sparsely furnished; they contain
very few recorded child-burials indeed; and although they are ranged for
the most part in orderly rows, there is little sign of any cult or attention
paid to the earlier dead within the cemeteries. Most of these features show
a departure from the prevailing trend of Mycenaean times, whose significance we shall presently consider. It seems that already the practice of
burying children apart, in the settlement-area, had begun at Athens, but
we do not know of any differentiation in tomb-type or in rite at this stage.
At the risk of anticipating a little, we can say that this acceptance of the
new tomb-type in western Attica is at least as early as any comparable
phenomenon elsewhere in Greece. It is also instructive to compare the
Mycenaean III C cemetery at Perati on the eastern coast of Attica, which
certainly overlaps in time with the two western Attic cemeteries.[7] The vast

58. A typical cist tomb of the Kerameikos cemetery, Athens,
Submycenaean grave 46 (a woman's). The grave, 1·85 m long, is of
c. 1100 BC.

majority of the burials in this prolific site (some 219 tombs in all) were
made in the traditional Mycenaean chamber-tombs; but there were a few
examples of cists or slab-covered pits, some of them child-burials, and it
has been suggested that these show contact with the two cist-cemeteries
to the west. If so, there might be a sign of influence in the reverse direction
in the eighteen cremations so far found at Perati, some in urns, some simply
on the floor of chamber-tombs, which prepare us for the next tide of change
in the Kerameikos. Beginning with a few examples in Submycenaean, the
new vogue of cremation overruns the cemetery in Protogeometric times;
again, both urn- and open-grave-cremations are found, the former heavily
predominant. The inhumations of this period are few, and indeed the true

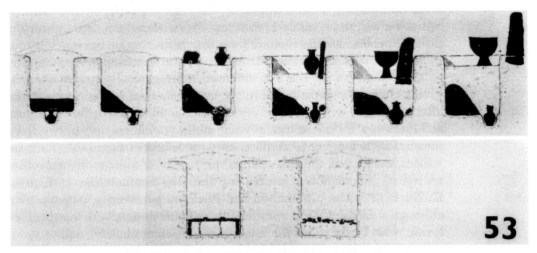

53

59. Cross-sections of the main tomb-types at the Kerameikos, Athens.
Above, Protogeometric and Geometric urn cremations; below,
Submycenaean cist and stone-filled pit.

cist-grave now permanently loses its former ascendancy in the Kerameikos, not recovering even when inhumation becomes the fashion again.
We find cremations elsewhere in Attica from the same period, in Athens
itself and at Marathon; where inhumations occur, they are often child-
burials, as we have seen (p. 145, in Athens; and also on Aegina), but
occasionally of adults. Thus for the second time within less than a century
Athens, followed perhaps more slowly by the rest of Attica, inaugurates a
sweeping change in funerary custom. I would consider the more important
of the two to have been the earlier change, in tomb-types, consequent upon
the adoption of single burial.

In the full Geometric period the Attic evidence becomes much more
profuse. There is first of all the large cemetery at Eleusis, whose evidence
accords fairly well with that of the Kerameikos: that is to say, a continued
ascendancy of cremation in the early phases gives way to a large-scale revival of inhumation, which with the greater number of later graves gives an
overall proportion of about 5:2 in favour of inhumation, down to the end
of Geometric. The Protogeometric type of urn-cremation continues into
the Geometric period here, together with cremations placed in cists or
slab-covered pits, which at the Kerameikos are unknown before Middle
Geometric and perhaps begin contemporaneously at Eleusis. Here, and
in the numerous other Attic cemeteries of Late Geometric date,

child-inhumations become common; they are regularly in the form of pithos-burials, more rarely in cists and slab-covered pits. As a result the pithos-burial, an ancient mode of interment in the Aegean but one long out of fashion in most areas, returns in force to Attica; it remains a very rare type of grave there for anyone but children. More generally, the practice of giving children separate burial in the settlement-area is now on the wane after a currency of some three centuries. The inhumations in the Agora at Athens now include at least as many adults as children, and grave-plots, presumably belonging to families, are now tolerated there. For adults in Athens, the pit and the slab-covered pit heavily dominate this period of revival of inhumation. Outside, we find the communities at Eleusis, Kokkinia (Peiraeus), Marathon and Phaleron persevering with the cist, although at Eleusis there is considerable experimentation with intermediate forms: what I have called the 'boulder-cist' is common here, and so too is a more interesting hybrid, found also in the Kerameikos, in which the cist-walls were built of mud-brick, a form of grave which was to grow to impressive dimensions in seventh-century Athens. On Aegina appears the rarer 'monolith-cist', hollowed out from a single block of stone. Cremation of children, which is naturally difficult to trace with certainty and may never have won acceptance in dark age Attica, nevertheless occurs occasionally in Athens and Eleusis. Respect for the earlier dead, which had weakened markedly since the Submycenaean period, at times gives way to the deliberate slighting or ejection of earlier burials; these might be of Mycenaean, or of much more recent, date.[8] But from late in the Geometric period, both in Attica and elsewhere, this tendency is strongly reversed (see 192-4, below). A factor which emerges in later Geometric times at Athens is the apparent decline in the social status of the main Kerameikos cemetery: perhaps the first sign of this is the abandonment (see note 4) of the provision of 'occupational' grave-goods – weapons and tools for men, housewifely objects for women. This seems to take place around 800 BC, but it is not echoed in other Athenian cemeteries; and similarly, the quality of the larger funerary vases in the Kerameikos is excelled, during the eighth century, by that of other cemeteries; notably those of the near, but distinct, grave-plot found on the modern Piraeus Street in the late nineteenth century, the original 'Dipylon graves'. Here again, the change in custom in respect of grave-goods, which would possibly have been interpreted in terms of religious innovation if we had only the evidence of the Kerameikos, can far more plausibly be seen as the result of extremely localized factors, perhaps economic, perhaps social. A change in the manner of offering grave-goods can also be detected in the Kerameikos: in the first wave of cremations, offerings were placed on a specially-built platform of mud-brick and burned there; the débris (including bits of the platform) was then swept into the still open grave. But with the revival of inhumation in the earlier eighth century, this practice was replaced by digging a pit or trough near the grave, which might be used at repeated funerals; but still the offerings were burned.

THE ARGOLID AND CORINTHIA

The Argolid is one of the few areas of Greece which offers a body of grave-evidence of the early Iron Age to compare with Attica, and it is almost the only region which combines this with a full spread of comparable evidence from the preceding Late Bronze Age. It thus provides the most satisfactory picture of a continuous evolution in funerary practice over more than eight centuries, and the picture is a radically different one from that of Attica. The three, apparently almost simultaneous, phenomena which mark the final break with Mycenaean tradition in Argos itself are the universal adoption of single burial, the shift in location of cemetery, and the appearance of the Protogeometric style. The first of these three changes is that which principally concerns us here, and if we accept the correctness of Desborough's conclusions as to the relative chronology of the two areas (pp. 31-4), this happened distinctly later in Argos than in Attica. But a new element has entered the discussion with the discovery of seven stone-built tombs, most of them what I have called 'boulder-cists', at no. 11 Tripolis Street in the modern town of Argos. The Greek excavator called these tombs Submycenaean, and she illustrates one vase, a lekythos, which certainly carries elements of Submycenaean decoration. However, in his recent study C.-G. Styrenius has classed this vase as 'still Mycenaean' on grounds of its shape – a criterion whose validity is perhaps doubtful.[9] Styrenius has confirmed the Submycenaean character of other unpublished pottery from these graves. The presence of two lekythoi in these tombs does hint at a fairly late date in relation to the Attic series (cf. p. 36); yet it seems certain that the graves are earlier than any of the true cists discovered in P. Courbin's excavations in Argos, the pottery from which Desborough considered to be Protogeometric in character from the first. Whether they are also later than any of J. Deshayes' material from the Deiras cemetery is more questionable; but it seems likeliest, on our view of the relative chronology of the two areas, that they date from well after the beginning of Attic Submycenaean. So Argos would still be well behind Attica in its wholesale conversion to the cist. What is beyond question is that, once the initial radical changes have been made, the situation in Argos as reflected in the grave-material becomes static. This is shown first of all by the funerary rite: single inhumations enjoy a far longer vogue that at any time in Attica, and it is only at the end of the full Geometric period that a few tentative experiments with cremation are made at Argos. Perhaps as a result, the cist suffers no such interruption in its popularity as happened in Attica, but remains the most popular tomb-type through Protogeometric and much of Geometric, alongside the much less common pit; cists are sometimes used for two, or even three successive burials. The pithos-burial, revived for children only in the later part of Attic Geometric, seems to be in unbroken use in the early Iron Age of the Argolid, and not only for children; its popularity does however increase in Late Geometric. The 'occupational' grave-goods, mainly metallic, do not seem to die out here, least of all in Late Geometric. If we compare the extra-mural cemetery in the south-west quarter of the modern town of Argos with the Kerameikos graveyard at Athens, and the burials in the presumed settlement-areas within the town with the analogous ones at Athens, we find a further difference: some child-burials are found at most periods in both localities, and they do not at any time predominate in the settlement-areas as happened in Athens.

Other sites in the Argolid give quite copious evidence, confirming in the main that of Argos itself, and in some cases extending it. Thus at Tiryns, there are single burials in slab-covered pits which definitely antedate the adoption of Protogeometric pottery and belong to a perhaps fleeting 'Submycenaean' phase, substantiating the presumed position at Argos. But soon the cist begins to predominate here, as also in the Protogeometric burials at Asine and Mycenae. Mycenae has interesting evidence to offer about early single burials: it produced a pit-burial, a pithos-burial, a sarcophagus-burial and an infant in a monolith-cist, all belonging – the first two comfortably, the others slightly – before the appearance of Protogeometric. The sarcophagus was inside the citadel itself, where burials became commonplace in the subsequent centuries; so too was a very early Protogeometric cist cut into the remains of the 'Citadel House'. With the full Geometric period, the sites of Lerna and Nauplion offer further assemblages of graves, and there are isolated burials at other new sites. Invariably, as at Argos, the cist, with the pit and the pithos, remains in fashion for the inhumations, and there is no distinctive type of burial for children. Cremations are few and mostly late: a partly-cremated corpse in a cist of Early Geometric date at Nauplion seems to be an early and

isolated experiment; there is a distinct gap before Late Geometric cremations occur at Mycenae and Argos, with a possible example at Asine and
at least one urn-burial, with several pyres, at Nauplion. At Berbati,
Mycenae, Prosymna and perhaps Dendra, as was natural at sites with a
profusion of Mycenaean chamber-tombs, these were occasionally uncovered and carefully re-used, but not until well on in Geometric times.

Taken together, the evidence from the Argolid shows a remarkably
concerted adoption, and retention, of the standard types of single grave,
above all the cist-tomb. This innovation, however, apparently dates from
later than the corresponding phenomenon in western Attica. It is true that
the isolated early pit- and pithos-burials at Mycenae belong before the
destruction of the Granary, and have been placed by Furumark as early
as Mycenaean III c I a; but they are exceptional, for the standard contemporary, and even later, form of burial at Mycenae in the III c period is still
in re-used chamber-tombs of the traditional type, while elsewhere in the
Argolid – at Argos and Asine, and perhaps also Nauplion and Tiryns –
chamber-tombs also predominate, and are more often newly-built than
re-used. The single burials at Mycenae may prove to be better explained as
stray survivors of an older custom in the Argolid (below, pp. 177-84)
than as pioneer forerunners of a new vogue; while the mass acceptance of
the cist and other single grave-types, such as we find on Salamis and in the
Kerameikos, is not detectable in the Argolid until very near the end of
Mycenaean III c at Tiryns and Argos, and later still elsewhere. But if in
this respect the Argolid appears to be taking its cue from Attica, we find a
very different reaction when the second great change in funerary custom
appears in Attica two or three generations later. For whereas Attica
embraces cremation wholeheartedly, there are only very rare signs for
more than three centuries thereafter that anyone in the Argolid even
experimented with cremation; and this although in Argos itself stray
cremations of Mycenaean date seem to have occurred: a chance find of two
cremation-urns with a pithos-burial was of problematical date, and there
were three instances, all of them questionable and two in any case from a
secondary deposit, in the Mycenaean chamber-tombs of the Deiras cemetery (see below, n. 32). Single inhumations remain the rule in the early
Iron Age, with cists predominating until the Late Geometric period,
whereas in Attica the return of inhumation around 800 brought no revival
of the cist; children are not differentiated either in the location or in the
fashion of burial, while in Attica the two methods of distinction prevailed
in successive periods, and the retention of the pithos-burial as the standard

form for children was to last until well beyond the end of the dark age.

The funerary evidence from Corinthia is, for the earliest Iron Age, non-existent; but it shows some independence of the Argolid in the later phases. Single inhumations in pits predominate, but in Corinth itself the monolith-cist is curiously common. The same site also shows a somewhat more enthusiastic acceptance of cremation in Late Geometric times than any centre in the Argolid; by this time, Corinth was of course a totally distinct cultural entity from Argos.

THESSALY

In Thessaly we encounter a new pattern. This had been an area where, in Mycenaean times, the chamber-tomb had been curiously restricted in its distribution, and can hardly have found the favour that it gained further south; the tholos on the other hand had enjoyed a wide currency. Whether for this reason or no, the tholos-tomb retains its popularity long after the end of the Bronze Age. It is not a question, for the most part, of the re-use of existing Mycenaean tholoi; these tombs continued to be built throughout the early Iron Age, and contemporary with them we find examples of the kindred 'vaulted chamber' tombs. Sometimes, as at Chyretiai, the tombs are grouped together under a large communal tumulus. But these are not the only form of burial used in this period, for single cist-graves appear at at least five sites: at Theotokou, the earliest seems contemporary with Attic Submycenaean, and the two tombs at Retziouni may be of similar date; while at Halos, Iolkos and Palaiokastro the examples (more than forty in all) belong within the period of the local Protogeometric style, and at Pherai they seem to be of Geometric date. At Homolion in the far north of Thessaly multiple burials in rock-cut chamber-tombs of the Protogeometric period are reported. The explanation of this mixture of practices would seem to be that the single burials in cists were originally favoured for children: all, or nearly all, the cists at Iolkos were child-burials; so was the earliest tomb at Theotokou; at Halos, six out of eleven cists contained children's skeletons, one that of a youth, and in only one definite case were the remains those of an adult; at Palaiokastro, the only one out of three cists which was adequately preserved contained child-burials. In the cases of Iolkos and Palaiokastro, where the tombs were dotted over the settlement-area both past and current, we have a practice similar to that of contemporary Athens (p. 145): the adult cemeteries are located outside the settlement (no doubt including, in the case of Iolkos, the much-used tholos-tomb nearby at Kapakli), while the children are accommodated inside, if need be under house-floors; but in Thessaly there is the further differentiation by tomb-types. The other sites may have shared this tendency at first – in the Iron Age, that is: for in the Late Bronze Age the cist seems to have been indiscriminately if sporadically used – but there was a refinite relaxation of this rule as time went on. At Nea Ionia near Iolkos, two Late Protogeometric cists contained adults; at Theotokou, the rather later Tomb A contained four skeletons, all of adults; while of the forty-odd cists at Pherai, only half a dozen were child-burials. At Sesklo in the Geometric period, slab-covered pits were dug in the floors of vaulted chambers, and some of these contained cremations; cremation in cists seems to be represented at Homolion, probably at the same period. Cremations placed simply on the floors of tholoi appear at Ano Dranitsa, and probably also at Lestiani. But besides the imposition of cremation on the traditional burial-forms, a more drastic change of practice is found at Halos. The Geometric tombs here are of an entirely new type: cremation-pyres, in which the ashes were burned in the final place of burial, and then covered with an individual cairn of stones: the resultant group of cairns (sixteen in the case examined) was in turn covered by a communal tumulus. All the deceased were adjudged, from their accompanying grave-goods, to have been adults. The Halos pyres are certainly not all as early as the ninth century, in which the excavators placed them, but they probably start early in the eighth. The tumuli are perhaps the least remarkable feature of the complex, since here in Thessaly sepulchral mounds had long been familiar, partly through a tendency to site tholos-tombs on top of natural eminences during the Late Bronze Age;[10] it is the cairns which have aroused most interest, and led scholars to look for parallels outside the central area of Greek civilisation (cf. below, pp. 161-3, 190).

The funerary practices of Thessaly thus show a fundamental divergence from those of the other regions we have considered. The persistence with multiple burials in tholoi and vaulted chambers is the most marked peculiarity of the area. If comparison be made with Attica, the only visible similarity is the tendency in the early phases to segregate child-burials, and perhaps to locate them within settlement-areas. In other respects the contrast is complete, but this does not imply conformity with Argive practice either. The whole-hearted adoption of the cist, in Argos as in Athens, is quite a different matter from its at first selective use, for child-burials, in Thessaly; the late conversion to cremation might seem to recall the Argolid, but the types of cremation show no direct link, and indeed the change of rite apparently developed earlier in Thessaly.

CENTRAL CYCLADES

The next area of the Aegean world which we considered in our study of the pottery was that of the central and southern Cyclades. But here we are faced with an extreme paucity of grave-material in what may have been a significant region. In the case of one island, Naxos, a cemetery has been found whose use follows, perhaps directly, on the series of late Mycenaean graves on the same site, the ridge of Aplomata. But the graves of dark age date were in a ruinous and despoiled condition, and have so far received only a summary publication. Still, certain facts emerge clearly enough. In a region where the characteristic Mycenaean chamber-tomb had been well-established, though not apparently the tholos, the principle of single burial is introduced and as fully accepted as in Attica; but once again, the date of the change is discernibly later than in western Attica, for down to the very end of the Mycenaean III C period, which here must be contemporary with the Attic Submycenaean cemeteries, chamber-tombs remain frequent. A single occurrence of a pit-burial of a child at the site of Kamini, like the comparable forerunners that we noted in the Argolid (p. 153), need not be regarded as the harbinger of the later conversion.[11] Only with the rise of the local school of Protogeometric does this last take place: all the inhumations of this period at the Aplomata site are pit-burials, and the series apparently continues down into Archaic times. More striking, however, is the adoption, apparently roughly simultaneous, of cremation, which is shown by the occurrence of numerous pyres. The chronology of the Aplomata cemetery may ultimately become clear enough to show whether the pit-burials and the cremations appeared together at the beginning of Protogeometric, and whether they enjoyed an alternating vogue in the ensuing centuries as happened in Attica; but they may equally well have flourished simultaneously. Until recently, there has been little independent evidence to show whether the Aplomata site is typical of the central and southern Cyclades in the dark age; but a substantial cemetery of Geometric date on Kimolos consisted of shaft- or pit-graves, containing multiple cremations; and a recent find of two funerary structures at the site of St'Alonakia (near Tsikalario) on Naxos is also interesting. No more precise dating than 'Geometric' has yet been given to these; they consist, in each case, of a sizeable ring of stones, about thirty feet across, which presumably formed the kerb of an earth tumulus. Tomb A had a large central pyre with evident traces of burning, while round the outside of the stone circle were grouped five additional pyres in the form of small stone enclosures, and a sixth structure which may have been a robbed cist-tomb; tomb B, by contrast, has several pyres within its circular area and no external appendages, but the pyres could not be shown to have served for human cremations in this case. Although the appearance of these tumuli raises interesting problems, it is clear enough, in the absence of human skeletal remains, that cremation is still the predominant rite; conceivably the cist attached to tomb A may have housed a child-inhumation from the family to whom the tumulus belonged. There is some indirect support for such a belief in a group of seventh-century tombs at Paroikia on neighbouring Paros, where four child-inhumations were found with two, presumably adult, cremations.[12] Finally, the great cemetery of Thera begins only quite late in Geometric times, and runs on into the ensuing period; here we find a total acceptance of cremation, combined with the use of impressive stone-built chambers in which the urns were grouped in some numbers, again presumably by families. At this point it should be observed that the northern group of the Cyclades, in funerary practice as in pottery, is distinct from the central and southern group, and will be considered presently.

ELIS

Elis is a region which must perforce be considered briefly. The group of fourteen burials at Ancient Elis itself, which provided the only evidence for the early development of Protogeometric in this region, consists entirely of inhumations in slab-covered pits. This variety of single burial is not sufficiently concentrated in distribution to proclaim any obvious affiliations, but the prevalence of inhumation at this time, and the fact that the only other published grave of Protogeometric date, from Palaiopyrgo, was an adult pithos-burial, do generally recall the practices of the Argolid.

ASIA MINOR

South-western Asia Minor, the remaining member of our first regional group, presents a new pattern. Here, as in Thessaly, it seems that the principle of multiple burial survived the fall of Mycenaean power. Such is at least the evidence of the early graves at Assarlik (Termera), where both cairns and circular and rectangular stone enclosures are found; in some cases these are combined with chamber-tombs of traditional type, and where sarcophagi and cists occur, they are generally grouped within the enclosures. But at the same time, cremation is being practised, both in urns and in open graves, as was not the case in Thessaly. Here it may be pertinent to point out that a group of Mycenaean cremations, some certain and some only probable, has recently come to light at Müskebi;[13] their date seems to be early, for the pottery from these tombs is predominantly Mycenaean

III A to B; but had we any well-preserved tombs of the ensuing III C period, it is quite likely that these too would prove to be cremations. The main significance of the Müskebi burials will emerge when we come to consider the sources from which cremation was introduced to the Aegean area (pp. 187-9); meanwhile we may acknowledge the possibility that cremation was an established rite in this region at a time when it made only scattered appearances further west. The fragmentary evidence of later graves from this region gives a complex picture: a vaulted chamber at Dirmil produced Protogeometric vases; at Kolophon the lost evidence of the Geometric cemetery excavated in 1922 at least showed that it consisted largely or entirely of cremations under tumuli; while recent excavations at Iasos have revealed inhumation, in cists and pithoi, in use for children in Geometric times. Graves at Gökçeler, probably of Geometric date, were in the peculiar form of a chamber within a built-up tumulus, which has been recognized as characteristically Carian, and may have had no connection with developments in Greece.

BOEOTIA

The areas we have considered so far, although united in that their pottery shows each of them to have been in early and probably direct contact with Attica, reveal a most variegated pattern of funerary practices that shows little cohesion either with Attica or with each other; and consideration of the remaining areas of the Greek world will only add to the complexity of the pattern. To continue with the sequence observed in studying the pottery, Boeotia at first invites a certain degree of comparison with the Argolid. Here, too, the single cist-inhumation makes an early entry, in the group of ten graves (both of adults and of children) outside the Electran Gates at Thebes, which are probably contemporary with later Sub-mycenaean and earlier Protogeometric in western Attica; and here again its popularity evidently lasted through into Geometric times, as is shown by unpublished cist-tombs at Orchomenos; later still, extending into the seventh century, are tombs at Rhitsona which are also inhumation-burials. Two other small features which find parallels in the Argolid occur in the Mycenaean chamber-tomb cemetery of Kolonaki in Thebes: an early cremation, of probably Mycenaean III C date, in tomb 16, and the re-use of tomb 27 for a dark-age burial, in this case apparently of Protogeometric date. But another Boeotian site, Vranesi Kopaïdos, somewhat disrupts the analogy with the Argolid. For here the burials were in pits, covered by rough stones, under tumuli; and further, a proportion of them (it is not clear how many) were cremations. The life of the cemetery extends from Late Protogeometric down to about the middle of the Geometric period. It is therefore possible that cremation here goes back as far as Protogeometric, and indeed one neck-handled amphora of this style may actually have served as a cremation-urn. The cemetery covered a long period, and it is inherently unlikely that all the cremations were congregated in the latest phase. The tumuli of Vranesi, finally, incline one to look northwards to Thessaly for contemporary and earlier parallels; but this applies to the use of the tumulus only.

EUBOEA, NORTHERN CYCLADES

From Boeotia we pass across to Euboea, where recent finds at Lefkandi have made the picture a little less obscure than it was. The sequence here is as follows: in the town-site, twelve rough pit-inhumations of III c date were discovered under the floors of houses, all very poor and some with pithos-fragments covering the pit. Next come some early Protogeometric cists, which almost certainly contained cremations, the pyres having been located nearby. This appearance of cremation is in fact rather remarkable because at nearby Chalkis a group of Protogeometric cists has come to light which are inhumations. Further evidence for cremation is available to us in a single tomb at Lefkandi, which is perhaps to be dated in the ninth century although its pottery is in the Protogeometric tradition. Then in the Geometric and seventh-century graves from Eretria, we find a combination of practices – cremation for adults, inhumation in pithoi for children in the same cemetery – which in part recalls the example of Attica, though by now the adult burials there would be inhumations. Euboea therefore appears to present a further fusion of the categories which have emerged hitherto. But in this region we may include the nearby islands of northern and north-central Cyclades (Andros, Tenos, Delos, Rheneia) and the Sporades (Skyros), whose pottery suggested such a link (p. 79). In funerary practice there is also harmony with Euboea: Skyros has produced a whole range of cist-inhumations of Protogeometric and Geometric date, including child- as well as adult-burials; Andros (from the site of Zagora) and Tenos (from Kardiani and other sites) have produced cists of a date contemporary with earlier Attic Geometric, also combining child- and adult-inhumations; Rheneia furnished one tomb, and possibly more, of Geometric date which has been conjectured to be of cist type.

PHOKIS

Of Phokis we now know a little. A vaulted chamber-tomb at Delphi of Protogeometric date contained two inhumations, of a man and a child,

60. A view of the remarkable tumulus cemetery at Vergina in
Macedonia. Tumulus VII is in the centre of the picture, with VIII
behind it. Each contains several burials; 9th to 8th centuries BC, with
some much later burials.

and three other such tombs may have belonged to the same period. This
survival of multiple tombs is remarkable, since at Antikyra (Medeon)
nearby a group of cists and boulder-cists of Mycenaean date occurred,
while yet others of the Mycenaean burials at Medeon, of III c date, are in
slab-covered pits. By Protogeometric times, however, cremation had
established itself in this region: this is shown by numerous urn-burials at
Medeon, of this time and later, and by one example from Delphi of Late
Geometric date; a large group of burials recently found at Amphissa in
Lokris, some way to the north, is unfortunately of unspecified type. But
cist-inhumation and pithos-burial for children are also present in the Geometric graves at Medeon; and the whole pattern is hard to match elsewhere.

MACEDONIA

In Macedonia there is no shortage of material: on the contrary, this region
has furnished, in Vergina, one of the greatest cemetery-sites of any date in
Greek lands. In nine seasons of excavation here between 1951 and 1963,
60 over a hundred of the numerous tumuli were opened, and produced some

61. An adult male pithos-burial at Vergina, tomb L X V *A N*. The pithos measured nearly 2 m in height; 9th or 8th centuries B C.

350 burials of early Iron Age date alone, besides many more of the Hellenistic period. The more precise dating of the cemetery has been discussed earlier (pp. 132-3); with only a scattering of painted pottery present in these graves, it is obviously extremely difficult to arrange the burials in a chronological series; at present we are obliged to take the cemetery as a whole. Of the early Iron Age graves, over half are pit-inhumations; the only other common tomb-types are the pithos-burial (used for adults)   61 and the boulder-cist; the true cist is excessively rare at Vergina, and a very   62 few cremation-urns also occur. The tumulus above, which can cover a group of anything up to thirty burials, and in one exceptional case covered sixty, is sometimes replaced by a large cairn of stones. What are the affiliations of this cemetery? Neither the grouping of the tumuli on such an awesome scale, nor their combination with a number of single inhumations

L

62. A closer view of a rich female burial in a 'boulder-cist' at Vergina, tomb L X V *Γ*. The head lay towards the nearer end. Note the two spectacle fibulae, the two belt-bosses beyond them, and one of the sets of spiral tubes worn at the temples, seen beside the left-hand pot. The grave is about 3 m long; 9th or 8th centuries B C.

of these types, can be matched anywhere further south in the Greek peninsula. Nor, again, do they recall the standard mound of the Bronze Age 'Tumulus Culture' of the barbarian Europe to the north, which normally holds one or two burials; but the later tumuli of the Balkans, and especially those of the Glasinac plateau in Bosnia which must in part coincide with the date of Vergina, show certain resemblances.[14] They are multiple, and some of them contain both inhumations and cremations, at times ranging over a long period; but each burial is usually covered by a cairn, and the communal tumulus also seems to be composed largely of stones. Further, the graves are laid on or above the natural surrounding ground-level, and not slightly sunken as at Vergina. Some tumuli in this part of the world also cover cist-burials. Macedonia outside Vergina shows a somewhat heterogeneous pattern: graves near Kozani, of similar date, included both pits and true cists, but the only undisturbed example of the latter proved to be a child-burial (recalling contemporary practice in Thessaly). At a site between Konturiotissa and Kalyvia, a group of small tumuli each covered a cist. The cemetery at Pateli on Lake Ostrovo, dug many years ago by Russian archaeologists, and another at Bohemitza on the Vardar, contained both cist- and pithos-inhumations, the latter probably in a minority. The graves at Chauchitza, close to the Vardar valley, which are probably of the eighth century, confirm that single inhumations were still in vogue here; in this case they are in stone-filled pits, apart from one true cist of unknown date, found a little way off. Indeed, Macedonia kept to this same pattern down to near Classical times. Perhaps the most interesting feature of the Chauchitza graves, however, is the presence of an individual stone cairn over each of them: here, possibly, is a relevant analogue for the cremation-cairns at Halos (p. 155). Altogether the graves of Macedonia, like their contents, are best explained by the durability of the non-Greek cultural element here, in which the phenomena of Greek influence – the Protogeometric pottery, and perhaps the rare cremations at Vergina – are fleeting.

THE DODECANESE

In the Dodecanese, the pattern is a more recognizable one. Here there are several late Mycenaean cremations in chamber-tombs – one from Kos, five from Ialysos in Rhodes – such as were found at Perati, Argos, Thebes and in western Asia Minor. But, after a definite chronological interval, the Serraglio cemetery on Kos offers evidence of exclusive inhumation in the Protogeometric and ensuing periods; further, a resemblance to the practices of the Argolid which was also detectable in the pottery (pp. 76, 95) is reinforced by the funerary practices. In particular, the link with the site of Asine is repeated: both these contemporary cemeteries combine adult- and child-inhumations, but with the latter heavily preponderant; both include many pit- and cist-burials; on Kos we find pithos-burials too, but these are matched on other Argolic sites. However, there is a difference from the Argolid in that there is a differentiation of tomb-type for children, the adult-burials being confined to the pits. It is sad that the published evidence does not tell us how far the practices at Kos were modified as the life of the cemetery ran on into its later phases (a preliminary report mistakenly mentioned Geometric cremations); but fortunately the cemeteries on Rhodes between them give a fairly comprehensive picture of the Geometric period, and they show the imposition of quite a new pattern on that previously established. In the three earliest graves of the Marmaro cemetery of Ialysos, cremation suddenly makes its appearance in the Dodecanese; and in the Patelle cemetery at Kameiros we find, also in predominantly ninth-century contexts, cremation (presumably of adults) being practised alongside child-inhumation in pits, pithoi and sarcophagi, with two remarkable survivals of the chamber-tomb in tombs 82 and 83 near Temple A. In one Geometric cemetery at Ialysos, two adult and twenty-three child-pithos burials were identified beside over thirty adult cremations, which illustrates an apparent transition from the old, 'Argolic' pattern to a new one which closely echoes Attic practice. At Exochi, also an eighth-century cemetery, we find ten cremations beside four inhumations in pithoi, which were all of children – again recalling Attica; at the still later cemetery of Vroulia, thirty out of thirty-two burials were cremations. It is noteworthy that these Rhodian cremations were both in open graves and in urns, predominantly the former: this hardly reproduces the pattern of Attica, where urns are commoner; and still less that of, for example, central Crete, where urn-cremation predominates still more heavily, and is almost invariably combined with the use of a communal chamber-tomb.

CRETE

It is to Crete that we must now turn, and the regions of that island for which we have evidence may be divided, following the indications of the pottery, into central and western Crete on the one hand, and eastern Crete on the other; the border between the two may be placed at the defile on the road from Mallia through to Dreros, close to the modern town of Neapolis. The pottery shows us that communication between these two areas need not have been continuous or close, and the funerary evidence does something to support this. Late Minoan Crete had heavily favoured the chamber-tomb, with the vaulted chamber also common, the true tholos somewhat rarer, and the pit-cave, a type of double chamber-tomb, also known; within these types of tomb, larnax-burials were the standard form, but the pithos-burial also makes appearances; pits or shafts are less common, and cists apparently quite unknown. But perhaps the most striking thing about Late Minoan burial-practices, in relation to the use of these same types of tomb elsewhere, is the fact that in Crete the chamber-tomb and its related forms are very often used for only one or two interments.[15] Genuine multiple burial had been favoured in Early and Middle Minoan times, at a period when it was not yet favoured on the mainland; and it is a feature of the end of the Bronze Age that the use of these tombs for multiple burials begins to *prevail* once more at this date. This sets the whole development of Cretan Iron Age tombs against a radically different, indeed contrary, background from that of mainland Greece and the other islands. However, the central area of Crete, which we may take first, is equally clearly distinguished by another and more familiar change at this period, the adoption of cremation. As in other areas of the Aegean which we have considered, so here there are one or two early examples of cremation in chamber-tomb cemeteries of Middle and Late Bronze Age date: Liliana tomb D at Phaistos provided one example, which is perhaps of the twelfth century BC, and there are others which certainly antedate the late arrival of the Protogeometric style in Crete (p. 128). However, during the long Subminoan period, it is inhumation which remains the dominant rite, usually within a chamber-tomb of traditional type, and sometimes re-using an earlier tomb. This is the case with the scattered burials of the period known at Knossos and Phaistos, but it is worth mentioning an unusual group of pithos-burials, perhaps with cremated remains, further to the west at Atsipades, whose date may in part be Subminoan. Other chamber-tombs are found in use at Siderokefala, south-west of Lasithi, and at Khania and perhaps near Vrises in the western end of the island for which our evidence is hereafter so defective. Tholoi and vaulted chambers of various kinds occur at Karphi, Kourtes and Panagia in the uplands, with pit-caves also surviving at Kourtes; but it is pretty clear that these cemeteries are contemporary with the development of the Protogeometric style on less remote sites, and indeed at Kourtes cremation is present alongside inhumation. With the advent of the Protogeometric style the picture changes as radically as in the comparable stage at Athens, perhaps over a century earlier. The best illustration is from the Fortetsa cemetery at Knossos, where indeed we find that even the solitary late Subminoan burial (tomb *Π*) may have been a cremation. Cremation becomes universal in the Protogeometric tombs, and remains so through the long period of use that the cemetery enjoys, down to the seventh century. But in rather the same way as happened in Athens, inhumation is still known at other cemeteries in the same settlement and at the same period: four occurred in a group of chamber-tombs at Agios Ioannis, interspersed with more numerous cremations, and the Knossos area has produced one or two other examples of Protogeometric date. The cremations, as is most convenient for the multiple use of a single tomb, are invariably in urns of some kind; the number in each tomb frequently reaches ten or even fifteen, and well over thirty such tombs have been found in the Knossos dating to the

63

64

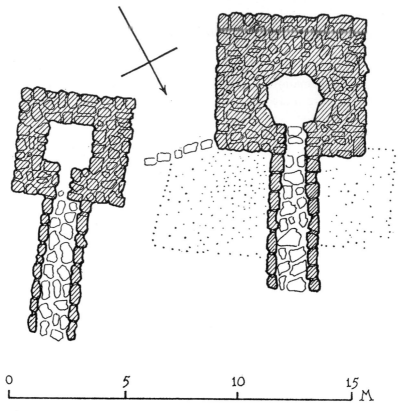

63. Plans of two of the tholoi or vaulted chamber-tombs at Karphi, probably of *c.* 1100 BC.

Protogeometric and Protogeometric B periods alone. It is open to question, however, whether the tombs were specially dug for use as cremation-vaults, or whether they were existing Minoan graves from which the earlier remains were first ejected. At Tylissos, also in the north central plain, an isolated cremation with the ashes stored in a bronze basin is also very early in the series. This concerted pattern of cremation in urns is repeated at Phaistos in the Mesara plain, where two groups of tombs of this period contained exclusively cremations; at Gortyn, where a tholos containing numerous cremations had recently come to light; while at the upland site of Arkades, cremation in tholoi is also found before the Proto-geometric period is over. At Rotasi Monophatsiou in the Mesara the rite used in a tholos-burial is unknown; but further afield the new fashion does

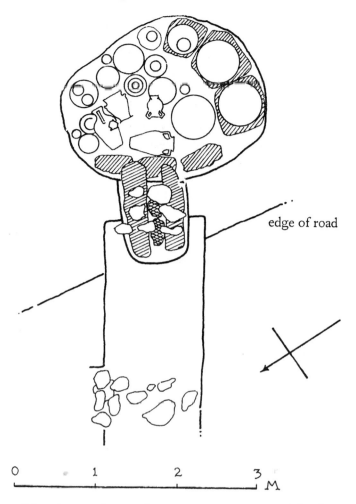

edge of road

0 1 2 3 M

64. Plan of chamber-tomb XI at Fortetsa near Knossos, used (perhaps re-used?) in the period *c.*925-825 BC.

not penetrate. At Kourtes and Panagia, as we have seen, the funerary practices (like much of the pottery) show little change from the preceding age; at Modi in the far west, although few details are available yet, the Protogeometric burials seem to be inhumations in pits and pithoi; while even on the fringes of the north central plain, there is one site, Kollyva Metochi, where inhumation (in re-used chamber-tombs) persists into Protogeometric times at least, although the pottery has to some extent moved with the times. In the full Geometric period, there is little change

in the picture, except that by now (in Knossos at least) the great majority
of the cremations are placed in existing chamber-tombs, or occasionally
tholoi, as secondary burials; elsewhere, where tholoi were more common
and cremation had begun to penetrate more widely, it seems likely that
much the same thing was happening, but the small size and poor architectural quality of most of the tholoi makes it clear that they are of post-
Minoan construction; even so they could on occasion accommodate over
thirty burials. At Mallia, there was a Geometric cremation in the dromos
of a Late Minoan III chamber-tomb; and away in the west, at Khania,
Geometric urn-cremations were simply flanked by large stones. Inhumation, even in outlying areas, is now rare, and certainly enjoys no such
resurgence of popularity as happened in Attica around 800.

Eastern Crete might appear, on the evidence of its pottery, a backward
and remote area by comparison with the centre of the island. Yet it is a
fact that early cremations are here as much in evidence, or more so, than in
see 68,69 almost any part of the Aegean. Perhaps the first example comes in a vaulted
chamber at Praisos where the cremation, inside a larnax, probably belongs
to the earlier twelfth century; there was also a simple inhumation beside
the larnax. Then the problematical tomb A at Mouliana, of the same type
and built originally for an inhumation of the same period, was re-used for
a cremation, the ashes being deposited in a krater whose style for long defied
the search for comparisons, but which most probably belongs in the
eleventh century or the early tenth. Most remarkable of all, there is the
cemetery of Olous (cf. p. 43 for its pottery), where at least fifteen and
perhaps as many as twenty-two urn-cremations occurred, plus three cases
of partial cremation in larnakes, as against twenty-six inhumations of
various kinds, including three pithos-burials of children. This combination
of practices cannot be matched elsewhere in Crete, and indeed it is hard to
find parallels anywhere at the date of these burials, which could conceivably
extend down into the ninth century but no later; and which must surely
begin long before, since the three partial cremations in larnakes are most
naturally grouped with the inhumations of the same type, whose pottery
should belong to Late Minoan III B, four centuries earlier. The evidence
at Olous at least shows that cremation could appear in eastern Crete
independently of any recognizable school of Protogeometric, and this is
confirmed by another group of Subminoan graves, the earlier chamber-
tombs at Vrokastro, in which cremation is about as common as inhumation — more so indeed than in the later chamber-tombs here. Yet in the
majority of Subminoan and even 'Protogeometric' tombs of this region

(see chapter 2, note 56) – tholoi or vaulted chambers, with a few cases of re-use of natural caves which had contained Minoan burials – cremation is still unknown. One possible exception is Anavlochos, a site which lies actually on the route through from the northern plain to the east of Crete, and whose use probably began before the end of the Protogeometric period in the former area; here the burials, in both tholoi and stone-filled pits, may have included cremations.

The arrival of a full Geometric style in eastern Crete, belated though it is, is accompanied by further changes in funerary practice. This is best illustrated by Vrokastro, though the situation there is complicated: in the later chamber-tombs here, nos. 1, 2 and 3, inhumation had begun to come back, and accounts for the majority of the burials, which extend from the Subminoan period deep into the Geometric. The other Vrokastro burials of the full Geometric period include child-inhumations in pithoi, sometimes under house-floors; adult-cremation also makes its appearance, in the unusual form of open burials within rectangular walled enclosures of a type which probably had Minoan antecedents. This shows that (again as in Attica) the two rites could be in use in simultaneous or swiftly alternating phases within the Geometric period. Elsewhere in East Crete, however, it is cremation which perhaps predominates in Geometric times, occurring in most of its known forms: at Dreros, in both urns and pits; at Kavousi, in shafts and, probably, in a small but rich tholos of late date. At the very eastern extremity of the island, inhumation lingers: the early excavators at Praisos found Geometric inhumations in a tholos (perhaps re-opened after Minoan use), in a vaulted chamber which was definitely so re-used, and in a shaft-grave constructed at this time; two other ruined tholoi of Geometric and later times are now reported here; while at 'Stou Koukou to Kephali' near Zakro were two cave-tombs of Geometric date, which may also have contained inhumations.

The division of Crete, at least into two broad regions, would seem to be justified by the evidence we have considered. The concerted adoption of cremation in urns, together with a Protogeometric style, by the communities in the central plains; the association of this rite, in multiple form, with tombs of the traditional, substantial type (where they are not simply old tombs re-used); and the gradual but apparently unresisted spread of this practice to the rest of the region – these find no close parallel in the developments in East Crete. Here we find that cremation is adopted selectively, and independently of any ceramic influence, by the communities at Olous, Vrokastro and perhaps Anavlochos; many of the cremations are in open graves, and many are single burials. Then, perhaps in the late ninth century, there is a distinct reversion to inhumation at Vrokastro and possibly one or two other places; while at others again, cremation still prevails (Dreros, Kavousi). Finally the notion of reserving pithos-inhumation for children, hitherto exceptional in Crete, makes its appearance at Vrokastro, perhaps in imitation of the earlier practice at Olous. But equally it is not impossible that the influence of Attica, as in the contemporary Dodecanese (p. 164), was now being felt.

OTHER REGIONS

For the last group of regions of the Greek world, the evidence from tombs is at its weakest. This is a pity, because such isolated areas might be expected to show interesting survivals of old practices. But from Ithaka we have no material of this period, now that the 'cairns' at Aetos have proved to be best explained by a non-funerary purpose. Two others of the Ionian islands, however, have some light to shed on the developments hereabouts: the late Mycenaean inhabitants of Kephallenia, many of them no doubt immigrants, whose settlements may have lasted well into the lifetime of the Protogeometric style, continued to bury their dead in multiple tombs, some of them tholoi and chamber-tombs of normal pattern, but others – notably at Diakata and Lakkithra – huge chambers or 'dormitories' of a peculiar plan, with each body interred in a pit in a cubicle-like extension from a central passage. These complex tombs are a speciality of the island: they have antecedents in the multiple shaft-burials of the (probably) twelfth-century cemetery at Mazarakata, and modified descendants in graves of Classical date on Kephallenia.[16] The material from this island in general gives a strong impression of independence and insularity, even within this region, and discourages us from applying the evidence beyond its own shores. The only other piece of evidence from the archipelago is a group of cist-tombs on Zakynthos, which are probably of Geometric date; if so, they may show the resumption of contact with the neighbouring area of the mainland, for in Mycenaean times the tholos (and perhaps other multiple tombs) had been at home here.

With Achaea, the evidence is quite rich at both ends of the dark age; in between, as noted earlier, we have to assume either a long survival of Bronze Age features, or a large chronological gap. At the upper end, there is a vast array of chamber-tomb burials in substantial cemeteries, grouped very much towards the western end of the region; it is probable that some of these continued in use down to the tenth century, and if so they provide a rare example of the uncontaminated survival of Mycenaean practices.

Built tombs, on the other hand, had been very rare in Bronze Age Achaea, and this makes it unfortunate that, when they do begin to appear, the first examples are imprecisely dated. Probably they all belong later than the single pithos-burial at Derveni at the eastern end of Achaea, which dates from the close of the Protogeometric period, and may perhaps reflect the influence of the Argolid or Corinthia. At Troumbes near Chalandritsa (one of the two sites so named in this district) three vaulted chambers were found, each under a low tumulus; after much vacillation, the date of their use, and perhaps their construction, was tentatively placed in the Geometric period. To the same period, though equally hesitantly, may be allocated three tholoi found a few miles away at Bartolomio (Mikros Bodias); one of these, most interestingly, contained three inhumations in pithoi, a combination for which I know of no parallel. But the cist – or rather its variant the boulder-cist – also emerges in Geometric Achaea: at Pharai in this same district were found several single examples of this date, one covered by a small cairn, and a contemporary pithos-burial, together with a remarkable stone enclosure unfortunately not certainly datable, with two cists and two pithos-burials set out most regularly inside. At Chalandritsa itself, further Geometric boulder-cists were grouped under a communal tumulus; one of the graves had an apsidal end. The numerous idiosyncrasies of these Achaean graves – the adherence to, and even the re-adoption of multiple types of tomb, and when single graves are admitted, the various attempts to co-opt them into multiple arrangements by housing them in tholoi, enclosures or tumuli; the appearance of the cairn and the round-ended cist; the total absence of cremation; the preference for pithoi and boulder-cists – all these combine to give the region an aura of robust independence, not wholly attributable to isolation.

Messenia is less fully documented, and indeed becomes almost entirely obscure in the latter part of the dark age. But before that we have glimpses of the local trend in funerary practices: as one might expect in this, the richest area of all Greece in Mycenaean tholos-tombs, there is evidence of the re-use of a tholos for Protogeometric burials perhaps 500 years after its original construction at Tragana; evidence, too, for the fresh construction of a tholos, albeit a small one, at Kato Englianos, and another at Karpophora, in the same period. But as in Achaea, so in Messenia the single types of burial came into favour; and at an earlier date, since the burials at Nichoria, consisting of inhumations in boulder-cists and sarcophagi, belong to the local Protogeometric style. The parallel with Achaea can indeed be pressed further, for the boulder-cists at Nichoria had apsidal ends; their priority in date over the Chalandritsa example of similar shape might suggest that the direction of influence was from south to north. In Messenia, once again, there is no definite sign of the appearance of cremation, although this region has produced one of the very earliest known Bronze Age cremations on Greek soil, at Tragana (cf. note 32). A Geometric tomb at Kalamata was evidently a pithos-inhumation.

EPIRUS

We are now confronted with those areas of Greece which offer no funerary evidence for this period. The list is long: it embraces not only some of the fringe-regions to the north of the Mycenaean world, but also Laconia and Arcadia; Lesbos, Chios and Samos, together with many lesser islands in the Aegean; and Al Mina, with its less fully-known sister-settlements in the Eastern Mediterranean. We must, however, turn aside at this point to consider an area which, while definitely lying outside the bounds of the Mycenaean world, was in intermittent contact with it throughout the Late Bronze Age, and has furthermore a particular claim on our attention; this is Epirus, and its interest lies in the appearance there of cist-tombs and other funerary features, in some cases containing datable Mycenaean imports. The first important group of these to become known were the four cists discovered by chance in 1953 at Kalbaki near Ioannina, and afterwards studied in detail by S. I. Dakaris. They include one child-tomb (*B*) and one double adult-burial with an unusual head-to-toe arrangement (*Δ*). In the apparent absence of Mycenaean pottery, the dating of the group rested on typological comparisons for a bronze dagger and spearhead found in tomb *A*; these were said to belong to the transition from Mycenaean III B to III C 1, and Dakaris now prefers a dating within III B. Desborough, comparing this dating with that of cists further south in Greece, has suggested that Kalbaki may represent a possible origin for the spread of this tomb-type to Greece; and Dakaris has since made further discoveries in the area, including cist-tombs at Mesopotamon and other sites which are of roughly the same period as those of Kalbaki, and re-examined a tholos-tomb near Parga. A recently-excavated tumulus at Hexalophos in western Thessaly may also prove relevant here. Furthermore, the region of Epirus extends across the modern frontier into Albania, and here there are further prehistoric sites – notably those excavated and published by F. Prendi in 1954-6 – which became generally known in the West only with the appearance of N. G. L. Hammond's *Epirus* in 1967. The funerary sites here, some of them of Bronze Age date, are chiefly distinguished by the use of tumuli and cairns and, irregularly but from an early date, of cremation. Some of the tumuli, and notably one at Vodhinë, contained cists; at Vodhinë there were sixteen, with two early pit-inhumations; the contents of the earliest burials, in and around a central cairn, ranged from a round-shouldered dagger-blade of a form known in Middle Minoan Crete to a lanceolate or 'fiddle-shaped' spearhead of the same basic type as that found at Kalbaki. A burial near the outer edge of this tumulus contained later objects still – a bronze pin and a spectacle-fibula. It is clear that either such tumuli were in use over very long periods indeed, or objects from further south were very slow in reaching northern Epirot graves – or both. Hammond, in contrast to the excavator, has embraced the first of these two alternative views exclusively: he argues for an initial date contemporary with Middle Minoan III for the tumuli at Vajzë and Vodhinë, their use extending down to the early Iron Age. But this scheme involves him in an impossibly high dating for individual objects: 'Middle Helladic' for the fiddle-shaped javelin-head from Vodhinë must be over 300 years too early; 'Late Helladic III c' for the spectacle-fibula from the same tumulus is almost equally improbable; while the early dating of iron finds in Epirus, on purely typological evidence, must be rejected.[17] (See below, pp. 257-61.) It seems to me far more probable that, as Prendi's dating, 'eleventh to ninth century', implied, there was a very pronounced time-lag in the diffusion and retention of Mycenaean and other metal types and pottery northwards into Epirus. The same lesson may also apply to Kalbaki and the sites in Greek Epirus. With the undoubted prevalence of cist-tombs in this region, it is most unfortunate that the chronology relative to southern Greece should have to be left so imprecisely fixed; but it seems very likely that the preference – by no means exclusive – for cists in Epirus reflects the influence of Middle Helladic and Mycenaean Greece; and therefore the resurgence of the cist in Greece at the end of the Bronze Age is better explained on grounds other than immigration or influence from Epirus (below, pp. 177-84).

WESTERN COLONIES

It remains to deal with one last area of the Greek world which falls under consideration at the end of our period – the western colonies. The evidence from here is, for once, almost embarrassingly full; but it must be remembered that the chronological starting-point for this material is the middle and later eighth century. Only a small proportion of the graves is thus relevant to our purpose. There are four or five sites – Pithekoussai, Cumae, Thapsos, Syracuse and Megara Hyblaea in traditional order of foundations – whose early graves have been excavated; however, Thapsos

65. Excavations in progress at the necropolis of San Montano at
Pithekoussai on Ischia. In the left foreground can be seen unexcavated,
on the right excavated cremation-cairns, while pit-inhumation graves
are visible behind; 8th to 7th centuries B C.

apart, the cemeteries of Geometric date continued in use into the succeeding
periods; the early tombs have therefore to be carefully picked out from the
excavation-reports. At Pithekoussai, the excavations of Dr G. Buchner
are too recent to have been fully published yet, but they have already
yielded one of the most prolific of Greek cemeteries. More than 900 graves
have been opened in what is probably a fraction of the total area of the
San Montano necropolis. It is impossible to say yet what proportion of
these are of eighth-century date; but it is clear that three main types of
burial, each in large numbers, are represented: first, cremations in earth-cut
65   graves under cairns of stone, their associated pyres being so far undetected,

but presumably some distance away; secondly, inhumations in pits; thirdly, child-inhumations in pithoi. Pithekoussai was a Euboean colony, but we cannot match this funerary pattern fully in Euboea or anywhere else in Greece, largely because we can point to no exact parallel for the first mode of burial, in cremation-cairns. The pyres of Halos are the closest analogy, but they are distinguished by the fact that a communal tumulus covered the whole group of cairns, and that the corpses were burned *in situ*, not on a separate pyre. The numerous cremations at Pithekoussai are also interesting because they strike a contrast with other western sites, and even with Cumae which is closest to it in time and space. Here, out of some seventy graves of relatively early date within the Greek period, there were over fifty inhumations in stone-filled pits, and a few other inhumations too, including two in boulder-cists, as against less than a dozen cremations; furthermore, an examination of the relative dating of these reveals that nearly all the earliest graves fall among the inhumations.[18] The cremations, however, show one very interesting feature: eight of them were placed in hollowed-out 'monolith-cists' of a kind that we have rarely encountered on the Greek mainland save at Corinth, where it is used for inhumations. The other three cremations at Cumae were in open graves.

At the three Sicilian sites less precision is possible. The graves of the Fusco cemetery at Syracuse excavated by P. Orsi in 1893 were mainly of eighth- and seventh-century date, and here inhumation was even more heavily predominant than at Cumae; as is perhaps not unexpected in a Corinthian colony, the 'monolith-cists' are very common here for inhumation (some 105 examples), as also are simple pit-inhumations (111 examples) and child pithos-burials (91); with twenty-five inhumations of other types, the total number reached 332, as against only thirty cremations, the majority of them in urns. The somewhat later graves excavated in previous years showed an even greater preponderance of inhumation. At Thapsos, an eighth-century burial in a re-used Middle Bronze Age rock-cut tomb of the native culture contained two skeletons. At Megara Hyblaea, tombs of the earliest years of the colony's life have been sought in vain; but a large cemetery of the seventh to fifth centuries yielded, again, a preponderance of inhumation over cremation of the ratio of very nearly 4:1.

The graves of the early Western Greeks thus display only one general feature: the great preponderance of inhumation everywhere except at Pithekoussai. But more profitable is perhaps the comparison of the funerary evidence from the colonies with that from the mother-cities; here for once

there is reliable literary evidence of close and direct racial connection between two communities, providing an interesting test of the reliability
of grave-evidence as a cultural indicator on a small and local scale. Pithekoussai was a joint colony of the neighbouring cities of Chalkis and Eretria
in Euboea; Cumae, of Chalkis and Kyme in Aeolis. It is unfortunate that
our evidence from Euboea is not strong for the relevant period, and that
from Aeolis is virtually non-existent, although we do know that, at a
rather later date, cremation-burials in urns and under tumuli were the
regular mode at Pitane (Çandarli), a site not far from Aeolic Kyme. But
the combination of modes of burial at Pithekoussai does at least find a
partial counterpart in Euboea at this time (at Eretria, however, rather than
Chalkis), in that child and infant pithos-inhumations and presumably
adult cremations are common to both places in the late eighth century.
But, on the negative side, the peculiar type of cremation at Pithekoussai
has defied comparison anywhere in Greece, and the pit-inhumations are
too widespread a feature (though not, so far as our fragmentary evidence
shows, in Euboea) to be of significance. Similarly at Cumae, the stone-
filled pits are commonplace, and the boulder-cist has proved a frequent
tomb-type in the remoter areas of mainland Greece (Phokis, Macedonia,
Achaea, Messenia), while the notion of putting *cremations* in monolith-cists
is altogether strange to Greece at this date. With Syracuse, the colony of
Corinth, we find our first and only significant correspondence: the monolith-cist, as used for inhumation, is distinctly prominent in both places.
Was it perhaps from Syracuse that this notion spread, to appear perhaps
rather later and in modified form at Cumae? For it represents a very widespread practice in Sicilian colonies of all origins,[19] and these may well have
been following the lead of Syracuse. More generally, the preference for
inhumations may also reflect the practice of Corinth at the moment of the
original colonists' departure, though hardly thereafter. With Thapsos
and Megara Hyblaea, the former a temporary and the latter a permanent
settlement of Megarians, we can only say that the true cist, which was at
any rate in occasional use in the mother-city at the appropriate period, is
so far unknown in either colony. Altogether, the experience of the western
colonies suggests strongly that connections of origin and kinship counted
for less than the pressures of circumstances, and perhaps the mutual
influence between colonists of different stock.

CONCLUSIONS

(i) THE SPREAD OF SINGLE BURIAL

To attempt to draw together the strands of this subject is to face, once again, the need for extreme selectiveness. Extensive as it is, the body of evidence available to us represents such a tiny proportion of the whole, that we can only attribute real significance to those features which are positively and repeatedly apparent. Such features have been seen to exist, most obviously in the tendencies which individual regions of the Greek world show in their burial-practices; but the time has now come to single out the broader features which cut across regional divisions. To do this, we may return to our starting point, Attica. Here may be most clearly observed the two early and lasting innovations in funerary practice which most clearly distinguish the early Iron Age in Greece from what had gone before, the mass acceptance of single burial, predominantly in cists and, almost equally widespread so far as Attica is concerned, the adoption of cremation. In Attica, both fall within the century extending approximately from 1150 to 1050; their reception in the rest of Greece is very far from uniform, but they have repercussions which place them in a different category from any of the later changes or tendencies which occur within the dark age. Among modern scholars, both changes have at different times been hailed as signals of major incursions of new settlers in Greece. Our findings, with their repeated failure to reveal unity of burial customs where unity of racial descent is assured, may appear generally discouraging to such beliefs; but at least in the case of the earlier change, to single burial, the matter deserves closer investigation.

That the phenomenon of the cist-tomb, and of single burial generally, has been brought into prominence and become identified with a probable new element in the population of Greece in the post-Mycenaean period, is very largely the achievement of Desborough. His theory appeared in print as recently as 1964, but it has won swift and widespread acceptance.[20] This is not surprising, for it provides an answer, and a more satisfactory one than that yielded by earlier attempts, to a quest which has preoccupied students of early Greece for nearly a century: the search for a distinct 'horizon' in the material record to equate with the new element of population which, usually in the persons of the Dorians, our ancient sources suggest to have entered central and southern Greece after the Heroic Age. The 'cist-horizon', if we may so call it, satisfies many of the requirements for this rôle: it falls, unlike the era of the destruction of the My-

M

■▼ Vajzë

Vergina ■□▽◉

■ Kozani

Retziouni ■

Iolkos ▣
Palaiokastro ■   ■ Theotokou
Halos ▣

Skyros ▣

Chalkis ■   ■ Lefkandi
Orchomenos ■
                ■ Thebes

Derveni ●
▼ Elis
                Vello ▼   ■□▽▼ Athens
                    Salamis ▣   ▼ Perati
Argos ▣□▼▼   ■□▼ Mycenae
Palaiopyrgo ●   ■□ Tiryns
    Nauplion ▼▣ ▼ Asine

                            ▼ Naxos

●▼ Nichoria

                                    ■●▼ Kos

                                Kameiros □▼

            ◉ Atsipadhes?   Olous □●

CISTS and other single inhumations, c.1125–900 B C

	CISTS	CIST VARIANTS Boulder- Monolith-, Larnax	PITS Incl. slab-covered pits	PITHOS-BURIALS
up to 20	■	□	▼	●
20 or more	▣	▣	▽	◉

cenaean palaces, fairly close to the traditional dates for the advent of the Dorians; it is further a positive feature, implying the occupation of the land, and it has the appearance of a tide moving gradually across Greece, as we should imagine the Dorian (and other) settlers to have done. It is often associated, as Desborough shows, with renewal of settlement after a break, and with a changed location of cemetery. It avoids the fate of some of the earlier candidates proposed for this rôle: for example, the general adoption of cremation or of the use of iron which, as will be seen, can both more plausibly be traced to foreign sources of a different kind; or the concentration on a Geometric system of pottery-decoration, which has been found to be inherent in Mycenaean pottery of the later phases. It appears earlier than any of these last three phenomena in their fully-developed forms; but it does share with them one characteristic which is at variance with the traditional account of the arrival of the Dorians, namely that all of them first become prominent and general (as far as central and southern Greece are concerned) in Attica, the region which above all others claimed to have escaped the infusion of Dorian blood. This, however, is a small defect to set against so many positive and convincing features, and it would be unwise to place great faith in such evidence, in a situation where many an oral tradition has violated the historical facts. Finally, and most fundamental of all, it is a fact that the 'cist-horizon' represents a departure from the practice of the preceding period, such as in some fields of prehistory would be confidently taken to indicate a new racial factor: the Mycenaeans had shown a marked preference for the chamber-tomb and other forms of multiple grave. It is therefore with some diffidence that I venture to question this theory and its implications.

Already in his publication of the Deiras cemetery, J. Deshayes has drawn attention to a serious difficulty of Desborough's account, namely that in Mycenaean Argos single burial was by no means rare, and in particular that a distinct progression in tomb-types, from the simple pit-grave, through several variant stages, to the slab-covered pit (though not to the true cist) can be observed in the Deiras cemetery in the middle and later Mycenaean period. Desborough himself had acknowledged the occurrence of single burials on Mycenaean sites, and given a list of cist-, pit- and pithos-graves from different areas; this evidence he describes as 'very slight indeed'.[21] It seems to me that he has done less than justice to the evidence in the matter of sheer quantity; and it is also true that fresh material has come to light since he wrote. If we may continue to concentrate on the cist-tomb, which is both the commonest and the most distinctive type of

66

66. Distribution map of cists, *c.* 1125-900 BC.

single grave in the earlier part of the dark age, its appearances in purely Mycenaean contexts are really quite widespread. This should not come as a surprise, since the cist is universally agreed to have been the characteristic tomb-type of the preceding Middle Helladic period, and most scholars also support the view that there is a general continuity of culture between Middle Helladic and Mycenaean Greece.

67   Let us consider the incidence of the cist in the full Mycenaean period. It occurs in Attica, but only at Agios Kosmas and Eleusis, where the cist-cemetery extends continuously from Middle Helladic into Mycenaean times, though not apparently as late as Mycenaean III C. It is found in the Argolid, not indeed in its pure form on the central sites, but at Lerna, Asine and the remoter cemetery of Karakasi, of which Lerna provides a closer chronological setting, in Mycenaean I-II, while the Karakasi cists belong in Mycenaean III; however, it is relevant here to remind ourselves that not only Argos, but Berbati and, in the Mycenaean III C period, Mycenae and Tiryns as well have produced pit-burials of various kinds. Three simple child-burials in pits, of Mycenaean II date, appeared at Korakou in Corinthia. In Thessaly the presence of the native, non-Mycenaean pottery creates a special chronological problem. A group of eight cists at Zerelia, for example, were found dug into the remains of a settlement which contained Mycenaean III pottery, and would seem therefore to be of no earlier than Mycenaean date; but their contents were indeterminate. It is in any case likely that, with a time-lag between southern Greece and Thessaly in the earlier Mycenaean period, the characteristic cist-tomb of Middle Helladic would linger on here down to a time contemporary with the Mycenaean I period further south. This is no doubt what happened, for example, with those cists at Iolkos, and with the earlier of two examples at Soufli, which are of this time. But the evidence shows more than this: two cists at Dimini and a further example at Soufli are definitely of Mycenaean III B date; others at Agrilia, Pharsalos and Hexalophos contained pottery probably of the III C class; a cist, a pit and other burials at Ktouri probably bridge the III B-C transition, as does a unique multiple cist at Vardhates, further south.[22] Clearly single burials, predominantly in cists, never altogether died out in the Thessalian Late Bronze Age.

Returning southwards, we may note the roughly contemporary appearance of cists and pits in Phokis – at Medeon, where there are slab-covered pits of late III C date; at Krisa, where the cists seem to be Middle Helladic survivals, while a Mycenaean pit-burial is reported at Delphi – and in

67. Distribution map of cists, *c.* 1500-1125 BC.

CISTS and other single inhumations, *c.*1500–1125 B C

(Mycenean II-IIIC)

■ Cists
□ Boulder- or monolith-cists
▼ Pits
● Pithos-Burials

Map labels:
Kalbaki
Kastritsa
Agrilia
Soufli
Paramythia
Hexalophos
Mesopotamon
Ktouri
Pharsalos
Dimini
Zerelia ?
Vardhates
Delphi
Orchomenos
Gla
Kokkolata ?
Emborio
Eleusis
Korakou
Agios Kosmas
Kafkania
Olympia
Argos
Mycenae
Klidhi
Berbati
Lerna
Asine
Asea
Karakasi
Routsi
Papoulia
Kissos
Agios Stefanos

Boeotia, where an example at Gla is of unspecified Mycenaean III date, and where other single burials occurred in a tumulus at Orchomenos. Several areas of the Peloponnese besides the Argolid offer evidence, particularly Messenia. Here too there are early examples which may simply represent a survival of Middle Helladic practice into earlier Mycenaean times – for example, at Malthi and under the floor of a house at Peristeria. Another feature of the region, suggesting earlier influence from north-west Greece, is the occurrence of cists in tumuli, as at Routsi, where the examples may have occurred alongside pithos-burials, and at Kissos near Chandrino where a tumulus contained very rough boulder-cists, and a child-burial in a true cist, all of Mycenaean III A date. At Papoulia, finally, is a single cist of Mycenaean date, along with other more unusual burials. Further north, the site of Kafkania in Elis has produced a group of cists, one of which contained glass beads of a familiar Mycenaean type, and a tumulus at Klidhi contained burials ranging from Middle Helladic to Mycenaean II. Two pit-graves, together with chamber-tombs, are now reported at Olympia. In Achaea a group of boulder-cists, reported at Tsaplaneika, proved on reconsideration to be more probably collapsed chamber-tombs or tholoi. Lastly, one cist at least at Asea in Arcadia was datable with certainty to the Mycenaean period. Early cists in Epirus have been mentioned (pp. 172-3 above).

In the Late Bronze Age, the cist was almost exclusively a mainland feature within the Greek world, but two occurrences on islands are worth noting. A group of cists at Kokkolata in Kephallenia stands out as exceptional against the characteristic 'dormitory-tombs' of this island (p. 170), but their date may be anything from Middle Helladic to Mycenaean III B; at Emborio on Chios, however, a Mycenaean settlement whose beginnings were scarcely earlier than Mycenaean III B produced a single tomb of this period, which was a cist.[23] Suggesting, as it does, that Mycenaean settlers should have taken this tomb-type with them to a hitherto foreign region at this date, this last piece of evidence seems to me particularly significant.

This list of cist- and other single burials in Mycenaean contexts should of course be seen against its background, in which the chamber-tomb predominated overwhelmingly, and even the elaborate tholos-tombs probably outnumbered these simpler burials. But I hope to have shown that the single burial, and the cist in particular, never altogether died out in the Mycenaean world. It may also be recalled that the pit- and cist-burial enjoyed a sort of secondary existence throughout the vogue of the tholos, and to a lesser extent of the chamber-tomb, since individual interments were often placed in rectilinear pits sunk in the floor of the tomb, and sometimes in lined cists. A more cogent argument perhaps lies in the observation of local trends. The main areas for cist-burial in the early Iron Age were, as we have seen, the Argolid, and other areas of the Peloponnese such as Corinthia and Messenia; Attica, but for a briefer period; Boeotia; Thessaly, but with the peculiarity that at first it was primarily reserved for children; Phokis, in part; Euboea, Skyros, Andros, Tenos; Kos. In Crete and the southern and central Cyclades it is more or less absent. A very similar distribution pattern is shown by the cists of the Late Bronze Age; Euboea *cf. 66, 67* and the other islands do not appear in it, but they may have received new settlers from areas where the cist was in use, in much the same way as Chios had earlier (in the case of Kos there is an especially strong link with the Argolid: pp. 76, 95); Crete and the Cyclades are absent here too. One might indeed make more of this last argument: Crete, throughout the duration of the Minoan civilization, had never adopted the small, slab-lined cist-tomb as Middle Helladic Greece had. Can it be coincidence that she is also conspicuous in refusing to adopt it at the end of the Bronze Age? Does not this suggest a strong element of native tradition in the pattern of distribution of this tomb-type? Finally, there are also physical similarities of detail between the cist-tombs of dark age Greece and the earlier examples – particularly those of Middle Helladic date. One such feature is the very natural tendency to dispose the corpse in a partly or wholly contracted position, which is apparently characteristic of the earliest dark age cist-cemetery on Salamis, though not of later cists;[24] another is the occasional use of mud-brick for the cist-walls (cf. p. 150); another is the occasional practice of placing grave-goods beside, rather than within, the tomb itself; yet another is the predilection for intramural burial.

A separate word should be given to the pithos-burial, a most ancient form of inhumation in the Aegean lands, which had however become rarer in Mycenaean times. Desborough makes the point that its earliest appearances in post-Mycenaean times are in outlying sites, Protogeometric examples occurring at Vergina in Macedonia, Palaiopyrgo in Elis, Nichoria in Messenia and Derveni in Achaea; and that this is an indication against any kind of continuity from Mycenaean practice. But it is also true that a few contemporary, or even slightly earlier, examples have occurred in the very heartland of the Mycenaean world, at Argos and Tiryns, while a very late Bronze Age example has been noted at Mycenae itself (p. 152).[25]

From all of this I conclude that the cist-tomb and its associated forms of single burial, so far from being an indication of a new wave of settlers supervening on the ruins of the Mycenaean civilization, are merely a resurgent phenomenon of pre-Mycenaean Greece which had never been wholly dormant even in Mycenaean times. The case of Epirus (see above, pp. 172-3) no longer seems to me sufficiently exceptional to make a compelling argument for the derivation of cists of early Iron Age Greece from that region. It is neither true that the cist was in exclusive use in the Late Bronze Age of Epirus, nor that it was unknown at such a date further south. The position was, I think, simply that Epirus, as befitted a region on the periphery of the Middle Helladic and Mycenaean cultures, was even more retentive of the burial-forms of the earlier period, and even less receptive of the new types of communal tomb introduced to Greece in the later period, than the outlying regions of the Mycenaean world itself. Miss N. K. Sandars has already pointed out the unlikelihood of any derivation of the cist from further north in the Balkans.[26] But it remains, first to answer an additional argument which has been adduced to support the theory that the cist is intrusive in post-Mycenaean Greece, that from the skeletal evidence; and secondly to attempt to account for the undoubted resurgence in the use of the cist.

(ii) SKELETAL EVIDENCE

The skeletal material of the relevant period has been studied in adequate detail for two sites only, Athens and Argos. From Athens, 18 subjects from the Submycenaean cist-tombs in the Kerameikos were studied by E. Breitinger in 1938, and then used as part of a broader survey of evidence, covering a wide time-span, by J. L. Angel in 1945.[27] Breitinger's conclusions were very circumspect: he found that the dolichocephalic 'Mediterranean' type of skull, which in its various sub-forms had predominated in Greece since Neolithic times, remained heavily preponderant in his sample of Submycenaean remains; several further specimens represented a fusion of this type with others; others again had elements of the Dinaric type, of which he could classify only one, and that after extensive discussion, as 'Nordic'. He showed that, although the sample was a very heterogeneous one, it hardly outdid the known Mycenaean material in this respect: for example, the variation of cranial indices in his sample, ranging from 70 to 85, fell well inside the extremes of 69 and 94, both of which occurred in Mycenaean speciments from the Argolid.

Angel's conclusions from this same evidence, with an added Submycenaean specimen, were rather different. He further increased the sample, to 22, by including three subjects of Early Protogeometric date from the Agora, and was able to compare this with a group of 21 subjects of Mycenaean date, also from Attica. He divided the material into six basic types, of which A and B were those which had been established in Greece since the Bronze Age or earlier, C represented the 'Alpine' type of skull, E showed a mixture of 'Alpine' and 'Mediterranean' characteristics, while D and F possessed 'Dinaric' characteristics. Using this classification, he found a very sharp increase in intrusive types in the Submycenaean sample as compared with the Mycenaean; but this was largely because he included in this element the skulls of his type C (Alpine). The figures in the two samples for his types C, D and F were respectively 3, 1 and 3 in the Mycenaean sample, giving 7 out of 21; and 8, 3 and 4 in the Submycenaean, giving 15 out of 22, an increase from approximately thirty-three per cent to sixty-eight per cent. This indeed appears a most significant change, if the 'Alpine' skulls of Angel's Type C are to be classified within the new and intrusive group. But in his final study of the material from Argos, R.-P. Charles classes the 'Alpine' skulls, along with those of 'Mediterranean' type, under the general heading of 'Cromagnoïde', which he takes to have made up the most substantial element in the established population since before the Bronze Age; and certainly the 'Alpine' type of skull is well represented in later Bronze Age remains from both Athens and Argos. If the type were omitted from the comparative figures in Angel's two samples, the change would be only from 4 out of 21 (nineteen per cent) to 7 out of 22 (thirty-two per cent), which with samples of this small size can hardly be regarded as very significant. It may also be noted that in Angel's Geometric sample of 15 skulls, the 'intrusive' group comprises 6 (forty per cent) with Type C included, or 4 (twenty-seven per cent) without.

To turn now to Argos, Charles published in 1958 an interim study of skeletons of Middle and Late Bronze Age, Protogeometric and Geometric date from this site, as well as material from other Argolic graves; then in 1963 he incorporated the subjects from Argos, with some fresh material of the same periods and from the same site, in a consolidated study. On the basis of the former paper, a conclusion was reached that, in Protogeometric Argos as in Submycenaean Athens, there had been 'a sizable introduction of new people of northern origin' (Desborough's words). But when Charles extended his sample by about half as much again in 1963, the picture came to look rather different. To his 'Atlanto-Nordic' group of skulls (made up of three specific types) were allocated 3 out of 26 Middle Helladic specimens; 4 out of 69 Mycenaean; 1 out of 13 Protogeometric; and 2 out of 14 Geometric – figures which show an actual proportional decline over the first three periods, and a rise which can hardly be of significance, with such a small sample, in the last. Charles' summing-up claims no more than that this group 'gives us important evidence of the advent of northern incursions' – note the plural – which seems a fair conclusion from all the evidence we have considered. For as long as physical anthropologists differ – as of course they are perfectly entitled to do – over fundamentals of classification, as does Charles with Angel (and Angel, incidentally, with Breitinger), and as long as the samples for the crucial periods of the early Iron Age remain small, it seems to me wiser to withhold any more sanguine judgments. It may be added that some recent anthropological study has been devoted to the non-metrical variants in skeletal material, and that these can sometimes give very different results from those reached by craniometric methods.[28]

If the users of the cist-tombs of early Iron Age Greece have not been shown to be intrusive to any unusual degree, how is the massive reversion to this and other forms of single burial to be explained? Any answer must be a tentative one in this deeply obscure period; but it seems to me that a perfectly credible line of explanation is that followed by J. Deshayes, in his study of the sequence of events at Argos (see note 21). According to this view, the cist-tomb is an attribute of the 'substratum' of inhabitants of pre-Mycenaean Greece, the population whose cultural qualities stand out clearest in the Middle Helladic period. On this substratum, the Mycenaean civilization was imposed, so to speak, from the top; although the dominant classes of the new era were perhaps from the same stock as their subjects, many of the material attributes of their culture were drawn from outside. Their choice of tombs provides a clear example; the chamber-tomb very probably, and perhaps the tholos-tomb too, were adopted in imitation of the older civilization of Minoan Crete;[29] the former type in particular had been in regular use at Knossos during the Middle Minoan period, in closely similar form; certainly both types appear foreign to the Greek mainland. Multiple tombs in general, with their emphasis on heredity, may have first commended themselves to the ruling classes, and then spread into general use. But in some cases, as we have seen, single burials were not entirely extinguished; at a non-palatial site like Argos their incidence might be quite high. The collapse of the superstructure of Mycenaean society swept away these multiple tomb-types from much of Greece; indeed the tholos-tomb, as Desborough has pointed out,[30] generally fell victim to the first wave of disasters around 1200 BC. The surviving population, many of whom may have had to move the location of their settlements by a greater or lesser distance, reverted to the simpler form of grave which had never been entirely forgotten. They may not have expected to have any descendants; even if they did, there may have been little reason to suppose that those descendants would still be settled in the same place. A family vault may have come to appear an irrelevant extravagance.

This particular change of burial-practices was in any case very far from universal in Greece. The whole-hearted conversion to single burial of Submycenaean Attica was echoed, perhaps at no great distance in time, by a similar movement in the Argolid, Boeotia and Euboea; sooner or later, much of the Peloponnese – Corinthia, Elis, Achaea, to a large extent Messenia – followed suit, as did Naxos, Skyros, Andros, Tenos and the new settlers on Kos. Thessaly, however, seems to take a different course, in that cists are at first apparently preferred for child-burials: a peculiarity, incidentally, which further argues against the mass incursion of 'cist-folk' in post-Mycenaean times, in this region at least. Yet of all the areas named so far, only one – Naxos – appears to have accompanied Attica even partially in the second great change which she adopted within less than a century, the swing to cremation; and this may not be a case of following the Attic lead (see below, pp. 189-90). Many of these regions are none the less shown to have been in commercial contact with Attica at the relevant time, by their pottery. We have also the converse situation obtaining in at least two areas, south-western Asia Minor and central Crete; here cremation is adopted equally early, but the single burial, and especially the cist, find little or no currency; Crete indeed, perhaps not entirely unexpectedly, takes in this matter exactly the reverse course to that of much of mainland Greece, in that the use of the chamber-tomb predominantly for single burials now gives way to its employment as a multiple cremation-vault.

(iii) THE CHANGES IN RITE

Of the change to cremation which makes such a distinct impact on eleventh-century Attica, and initiates the second major epoch in the funerary pattern of dark age Greece, we have already said something (above, pp. 143-7). Its significance may be far less deep than was once supposed, but even at the level of a superficial change in fashions it can be informative. As a notion, cremation was no stranger to Greece: we have noted some of its sporadic occurrences in Mycenaean times, and the earliest examples in the tumuli of Epirus may have had some part to play in this development; 68

CREMATIONS c.1550–1125 B C
(Mycenean I-IIIC)

while, to look further back, there are Neolithic cremations from the Argolid and Thessaly.[31] But in the more numerous, if still proportionately rare, occurrences in the Mycenaean III C period, it is not difficult to see the direct precursors of the major wave which was so strongly to affect parts of Greece. The most interesting question is therefore the source of these immediate forerunners. Their distribution gives us a strong clue: cremations in chamber- or vaulted-tombs of probable III C date are found at Thebes, Perati, Argos, Langada on Kos, Ialysos on Rhodes, Phaistos, Praisos and Mouliana in Crete; to these we may possibly add some of the contemporary cremations in larnakes at Olous in East Crete. The great majority of these localities are either themselves situated in the eastern Aegean, or else look in that direction geographically or archaeologically. When we add to this the fact that cremation had been established in Hittite cemeteries of the Anatolian plateau–such as Osmankayasi and Ilica–since about 1600 BC, and in the community of Troy VI, with which Mycenaean Greece had close contacts, for some time before 1300 BC, a credible sequence begins to build up. The only substantial gap in time and space lies between the fourteenth and twelfth centuries in the region of the Ionian coast; and now this too may partly be bridged, with the appearance of Mycenaean chamber-tomb cremations at Müskebi on the Halicarnassus peninsula (p. 157) of probable III A-B date. In any case, as has been observed, the inhabitants of Troy VII A (whose cemeteries have not been found) may very likely have continued their predecessors' practice of cremating.[32]

If this account of the spread of cremation has any truth, then the mass acceptance of the new rite in Attica is revealed in rather a different light. *69* No longer does it seem probable that central Crete and Naxos, for example, and still less south-western Asia Minor, waited on a lead from Attica before adopting cremation; more probably, they extended an independent movement which had started before the end of the Bronze Age. Nor is it any longer surprising to find that East Crete shows a partial swing to cremation at a date when there is no sign that Attic influence had yet made itself felt (p. 168). What remains curious, however, is the fact that some of the regions which had made these experiments in cremation near the end of the Bronze Age – the Argolid and the Dodecanese, not to mention Messenia which had produced a somewhat earlier example of Mycenaean cremation – then reverted whole-heartedly to inhumation for centuries afterwards. It is tempting to take this as a sign that there was a major upheaval in the population of these districts at the close of the Bronze Age,

68. Distribution map of cremations, *c.* 1550-1125 BC.

but such a conclusion would hardly be justified from this evidence alone.

It is only in the full Geometric period, and generally towards its end, that cremation finally begins to establish itself in most of these regions; this is true of Thessaly, the Argolid, Corinthia, Euboea, Boeotia and Phocis, but in Achaea it did not happen even at that late date; of Elis and Messenia we know nothing. A somewhat different course of events, however, takes place in the Dodecanese: the first cremations appear at the beginning of Geometric, and their manner and association with child-inhumations recalls the practice of Attica; since Attic influence is reflected in the pottery at two periods, the Late Protogeometric and the Middle and Late Geometric, it is not impossible that this change is attributable to a similar source. It is also possible that a similar Attic influence was operative in Geometric Euboea, where a comparable but less well-documented change seems to have happened.

In Attica, this first wave of cremation enjoys almost universal currency, except for children, between c. 1050 and 800 B C. The eighth-century reversion to inhumation finds only one potential echo in the Aegean area, and this is in East Crete, another area where Attic ceramic influence is detectable at approximately the appropriate period. But apart from the instances we have just considered, and the special case of the western colonies, it is hard to see any new evidence of a clear funerary influence, exercised by Attica or any other region, in Greece after about 1100 B C. The use of the funerary tumulus and cairn, which seems at first sight a promising possibility in this direction, fails to provide any convincing pattern for the Iron Age. The influence of Epirus and north-western Greece, which may well lie ultimately behind the spread of tumuli and cairns to two main regions of the mainland – Macedonia, Thessaly and Boeotia to the north, and Achaea in the Peloponnese – was probably exercised earlier: the phenomenon is already apparent by, and even before, Mycenaean times, when tumuli appeared also in Elis, Laconia, Messenia and even Attica.[33] The presence of tumuli at Assarlik in Caria is probably due to a quite independent local influence, which becomes most clearly detectable in this area a little later (p. 158).

(iv) OTHER INFERENCES

In one further field a unified trend seems to pass over much of Greece within the early Iron Age: this is in the attitude to the dead of earlier epochs. In the earlier dark age, from the Submycenaean period onwards, long-term respect and attention to the grave is almost entirely absent. Of any cult of the dead over the generations, there is little or no sign;

69. Distribution map of cremations, c. 1100-900 B C.

• Vajzë

Vergina ◎

• Vodhinë

Medeon ◎
◎ Lefkandi
Vranesi ◎
◎ Eleusis
• Marathon
Salamis ◎ ● Athens
• Thorikos

• Asine ?

Karpophora ? ? •
◉ Naxos
Assarlik ◎

Tylissos ● ● Knossos Anavlochos ?
Kourtes ◎ ◎ Olous
Phaistos ◎ ◎ ◎ ◎ Dreros
Arkades Kollyva Metochi ? Vrokastro

CREMATIONS *c.*1100 – 900 B C

• 1-4

◎ 5+

● 50+

actual slighting of earlier graves is not unknown. The immediate funerary tributes to the newly-deceased, on the other hand, though drastically reduced, never altogether cease: certain types of object, notably the ubiquitous clay 'goddess' figurines of later Mycenaean graves, disappear almost without trace;[34] the 'occupational' grave-goods, or at least those made of metal or other imperishable material, suffer more than one interruption (cf. pp. 150, 198 n. 4); and a number of graves, particularly in Submycenaean Attica, are devoid even of funerary vases. But the desire to provide some accompaniment, however humble, for the dead was never for long resisted; the traces of an animal-sacrifice or 'banquet of the dead' become very frequent; by Protogeometric times in the Kerameikos at Athens (p. 151) a specially-built platform, and later or elsewhere a trough for the burning of animal-offerings, had become a commonplace; grave-markers of various kinds are used – usually plain stelai of undressed stone, but also, from late Protogeometric times on, large vases often with a hole pierced in the bottom to allow libations to seep through to the dead below.[35] The nature of the grave-goods shows a general concern with the welfare of the deceased in after-life, and at times a specific provision for the journey to Hades – for example, in the miniature clay shoes found in graves in the Athenian Agora and at Eleusis. There are also instances from all periods to show that the sex and age of the deceased were thought to retain significance in the after-life. It is surely legitimate to detect some social differentiation among the dead in the wide variety in standard of grave-furnishings within one and the same period; not only with the comparatively lavish provision of goods in some of the later Geometric graves, but even with the slight qualifications of the general poverty shown by, for example, the Submycenaean tombs of the Kerameikos.

59 top

These developments, however, do little to prepare us for the moment when, at a point late in the Geometric period, several areas of Greece suddenly begin to show a revival of respect for the earlier dead. This does not only exhibit itself in funerary practice, for at this same period appear several new sanctuary-cults, the object of whose worship is not the tomb, but the real or supposed residence of some heroic figure of the Mycenaean era, or some other locality connected with his lifetime: notable examples are the cults of Agamemnon and Menelaus in the vicinity of the Mycenaean citadels of Mycenae and Therapne respectively, where the evidence of cult-offerings in both cases begins rather before 700 B C.[36] But far more numerous are the instances of cult at anonymous Mycenaean graves in several regions of Greece, and these too show a remarkable concentration

70. Terracotta model from Arkhanes in Crete. It has been suggested that the scene could represent the accidental discovery of a Bronze Age tholos tomb; the goddess within would signify that the tomb was taken for a shrine by the discoverers. Height 22 cm; *c.* 800 B C.

in time at the later stages of the Geometric period. From now on, when early graves – and particularly the imposing family-tombs of the Mycen- *70* aeans – are uncovered, their contents are often not only preserved but honoured by simple offerings; if fresh burials are made, they are located carefully so as to avoid disturbance. This is not least interesting because the Mycenaeans themselves had shown scant respect for their own dead – even their comparatively recent ancestors – and virtually never practised any kind of grave-cult. In Attica, there is a notable instance of this revival, near the end of the Geometric period, at the tholos-tomb of Menidi, where offerings were made only in the dromos, the chamber itself being left inviolate; and a roughly similar course of events seems to have taken place

N

at Aliki (Glyfada). At Eleusis appear other interesting practices: a Middle Helladic cist was accidentally exposed in Geometric times and treated with reverence; a further group of cists was discovered and, apparently at the same period, identified with the graves of the Seven against Thebes of the Heroic Age, being honoured at this time with a circular enclosure-wall. At Marathon, a Geometric necropolis may have been intentionally centred on a Mycenaean tholos. At Galataki near Corinth, a Mycenaean chamber-tomb, with at least one skeleton preserved in its slab-covered pit, attracted cult-offerings in the shape of some 1000 vases of Late Geometric and Archaic date. At Mycenae, one chamber-tomb was honoured from a similar period (though on a smaller scale), and another received a carefully-placed fresh burial of Geometric date. In the nearby chamber-tomb cemetery of Prosymna, no less than thirteen cases of offerings of vases from the second half of the Geometric period were noted. Messenia shows several instances of cult-offerings – in the dromoi of tholos-tombs at Akourthi, in the chamber of the tholos itself at Koukounara, and in chamber-tombs such as those of Volimidhia, where a whole group of tombs seems to have been discovered at this period, and Nichoria.[37] In each case the starting-point of the cult is the later eighth century, although later on in historical times there were to be many repetitions of the pattern. What is the reason for this concentration in time, as contrasted with the almost total absence of instances in the eleventh and tenth centuries? Since no one will suggest that there was a substantial change in the population of mainland Greece in the Geometric period, the explanation must lie in the revival of some kind of consciousness in a people who had previously lacked it.

Another development of approximately the same period in Greece, which may perhaps be in some way connected with the sudden growth of cults at earlier graves, is a tendency, in those regions of Greece which had partly or wholly abandoned multiple burial, to revive some of its characteristics in a different form, by incorporating single burials in a plot or group. The natural media for this process – the tumulus, the cairn, the grave-enclosure – have been found to occur intermittently throughout the dark age in certain areas, especially Macedonia and south-western Asia Minor; but it may be significant that certain other areas begin to show a predilection for them in the Geometric period. In Attica, there may be some kind of precedent in the tendency to arrange whole cemeteries of earlier periods in an orderly pattern – examples are the Submycenaean graves of Salamis and the Kerameikos, the group of tombs at Nea Ionia which may even represent a family plot, and the Geometric graves arranged in rows at Marathon. In the Kerameikos cemetery, at about 750 or shortly before, begins the use of a group of carefully-aligned pit-graves, arranged in a plot and associated with a structure partly above ground; while this has been suggested to be a special plot reserved for ephebes, it may equally have had a family connection. So, too, may a group of decidedly later Geometric graves, which continue into the seventh century, in the Agora of Athens: skeletal evidence here supported a belief in kinship. At a slightly later date still begins the use of the cemetery at Anavysos in Attica, where tumuli are used to cover groups of burials. Outside Attica, we may recall the appearance of the cremation-pyres at Halos under their communal tumulus, and perhaps the four or five tholos-tombs grouped in the same way at Chyretiai; of these the former at least belong within the eighth century. At Vranesi in Boeotia, on the other hand, the use of a tumulus to cover a group of single inhumations and cremations seems to begin at a distinctly earlier date. In the Peloponnese, we have already noted that this phenomenon is strongly represented in Achaea (p. 171). Unfortunately, the dating of some of its forms here is obscure – for example, the precisely laid-out enclosure at Pharai, and the grouping of pithos-burials in a tholos at Bartolomio; but a Geometric date seems likely at least for the tumuli which cover cists and tholoi, at Chalandritsa and Troumbes respectively. The significance of these instances would be much increased if Achaea could in fact be shown to have adopted, in a previous period, the practice of simple burial in single graves. From Argos, the phenomenon of cists with multiple burials, of Late Geometric date, is now reported.[38] In at least two further regions of Greece, the Cyclades and East Crete, something of the same kind makes its appearance during the eighth century, although in the latter case the background is somewhat different, in that multiple burials of some kind had been in partial use throughout. The two remarkable tumuli at St'Alonakia on Naxos, however, are certainly of Geometric date and equally certainly an unfamiliar phenomenon in this region; the family cremation-vaults of Thera also begin before 750 BC; and the Geometric bone-enclosures of Vrokastro at least show an entirely new approach to the grouping of burials. It seems reasonable to argue that these phenomena in Greece, somewhat scattered though they are in time and space, do accord well with a belief that the eighth century witnessed the outbreak of a sort of ancestral yearning in Greece, of which the desire to establish a link with heroic ancestors long since dead, and the more practical attempt to reinforce the hereditary principle there and then by reviving the family grave-plot, if not the family vault, are both signs.

71. Attic Late Geometric pitcher in the collection of the British School at Athens, from a grave in the Kynosarges cemetery, Athens. The scene on the shoulder has been interpreted as showing a funerary ritual, with rattles being shaken. We have much evidence for the revival of grave cult at this date. Height of whole vase 36·3 cm; *c.*725 BC.

It is also possible that this phenomenon is connected with a social development now dated to this same period – the formation of the phratry, which must have had its origin as a unit of kinship (below, p. 388).

Concerted trends of any kind, however, are the exceptions: the picture of Greek funerary practices in the dark age has in general proved complex and fragmented. For a typical illustration of this, we need only look back to the numerous variations, for which we have evidence from a wide area, in the treatment and differentiation of child-burials. To seek more general information about the economic and social circumstances of the communities of early Iron Age Greece, one must look rather to the objects interred with the dead than to the graves themselves; and this will be the task of later chapters. The single tombs of the dark age almost entirely lack monumental or architectural quality; almost the only technique that they usefully illustrate is mud-brick construction (see e.g. pp. 150-1), so seldom preserved in the habitation-structures of the period. The larger stone-built multiple tombs of early Iron Age Crete, Thessaly and Asia Minor are mostly constructed out of poor material and at a humble level of competence. Even what would appear the most natural inferences from grave-evidence are fraught with hazards and provisos: how confidently, for example, can we make suppositions about the expectation of life in dark age Greece, when many cemeteries have proved to be restricted in terms of the age-groups for which they were used? It is sad to have to end this long survey in the same tone of depreciation with which it began, but negative conclusions are not always the least valuable ones.

Notes

1] On this general subject, perhaps the most valuable writings are F. Poulsen, *Die Dipylongräber und die Dipylonvasen* (1905); J. Wiesner, 'Grab und Jenseits' (in *Religions-geschichtliche Versuche und Vorar-beiten* 26 (1938)); H. L. Lorimer in *J H S* 53 (1933), 161-80 and *Homer and the Monuments* (1950), 103-10; Desborough in *P G P* 306-7 and *L M S* 32-40; M. Andronikos 'Toten-kult' (in *Archaeologia Homerica*, edd. F. Matz and H.-G. Buchholz, Kapitel W (1968)); for references, P. Ålin, *E M F passim*.

2] *Antiquity* 34 (1960), 178; cf. Kübler in *Ker.* 5, 1, 36-42; 6, 1, 80-4

3] *G G A* 215 (1963), 52f. and fig. 8, where under 'Zeitgruppe 1b', '26' should read '36' and '49' should be deleted; datable graves omitted from this table seem to be nos. 45, 81, 92, 95

4] For example, the abandonment of 'occupational' grave-goods (Hach-mann, *op. cit.* 53, 55) and the reversion to burying children in the main ceme-tery (cf. *Ker.* 5, 1, 6), of which the first seems to have happened half-way through the Middle Geometric period, the second at its end. A clear but over-schematized picture of the develop-ments in the Kerameikos cemetery can be obtained from H. Müller-Karpe's article in *JdI* 77 (1962), 59-129, especially figs. 33-4

5] Cf. the tables in Styrenius, *S S* 89-91, 106-8. I use the word 'intra-mural' loosely, to mean merely 'within the settlement-area'

6] H. Dalton, *High Tide and After* (1962), 357-8; *Economist* 3/9/60, 880; *Observer* 12/3/67, 21; *Antiquity* 44 (1970), 87. Cf. changes in Nubia, W. Y. Adams, *ibid.* 42(1968), 202-3

7] The fullest reports are in *Ergon* for 1954 to 1963 inclusive, and *A D* 19, 2 (1964), 87-95

8] Infant-pithos-burial: three Late Protogeometric examples had appar-ently occurred in the Athenian Agora, Styrenius, *S S* 91. Mud-brick cists, e.g. *Ker.* 5, 1, graves 22, 44; and later, *Ker.* 6, 1, pls. 15-17. Slighting of earlier burials, e.g. *Ker.* 5, 1, 36 (graves 28, 91) and Poulsen, *op. cit.* (see n.1), 17

9] Styrenius, *S S* 132-3; cf. Des-borough's review, *J H S* 88 (1968), 229, on the weaknesses of the criterion of body-profile

10] N. Valmin in *Corolla Archaeo-logica* (*A I R R S* 2, 1932), 216-17; E. T. Vermeule, *G B A* 127

11] See N. Zafiropoulos, *A D* 16 (1960), 249-50. The alleged occur-rence of a cremation of 111 c date at Kamini (see, e.g., *L M S* 151) is doubtful – cf. Andronikos, 'Toten-kult' (see n.1) W 56, n.401

12] *A D* 18, 2 (1963), 273-4

13] *A J A* 71 (1967), 163; cf. 67 (1963), 208, 353-7 and 72 (1968), 133-4

14] See e.g. M. Gimbutas, *Bronze Age Cultures in Central and Eastern Europe* (1965), 282ff., 330ff. (287, fig. 193 for a 'boulder-cist'); Hammond, *Epirus* 403-4; C. Truhelka in *W M B H* 1 (1893), 71-4 and, for cists, 3 (1895), 512-16; A. Benac and B. Ćović, *Glasinac* 1 (1956), 43

15] M.S.F.Hood, *BSA* 53-4 (1958–9), 196; Desborough, *LMS* 186

16] P. Kavvadias, *Preistoriki Arkhaiologia* (1914), 355f., fig. 449

17] S.I.Dakaris, *AE* 1956, 114-53; *Praktiká* 1960, 123-7; *AD* 18, 2 (1963), 153-4; 19, 2 (1964), 312-13; and especially the dagger and spear-head recently found at Paramythia, *PPS* 33 (1967), 30-6 and *AD* 20, 2 (1965), 349-50, where Dakaris speaks of provincial Mycenaean pottery (from Parga) as supporting a dating in the III B period for Kalbaki as well. But, faced with the astonishing evidence for Epirot backwardness in both metalwork and pottery (above, p. 173; Chapter 5, pp. 257-61), I do not think that this conclusion can be secure. Hammond, *Epirus*, esp. 201-4 (Vodhinë), 228-30 (Vajzë), 314-63 for discussion and dating of types; Vodhinë spearhead, 339; fibula, 310; iron, 358-60; also *BSA* 62 (1967), 77-105

18] Among the earliest cremations are perhaps tombs 1, 11 and 56 with their early fibulae; but they need not be substantially before 700

19] See *MA* 1 (1892), 771, n.1 for Selinus, Gela and Camarina. It is possible that, in a quite different context, the appearance of the monolith-cist in Geometric Aegina (above, p. 150) represents Corinthian influence. For Pitane (Çandarli) (p. 176) see *AJA* 65 (1961), 57; 67 (1963), 189; 70 (1966), 157

20] M.S.F.Hood, *The Home of the Heroes* (1967), 126-7, indeed uses this evidence to support the more extreme view that the first Greeks of any group arrived in the post-Mycenaean period

21] Deshayes, *Deiras* 240-2, 249-250; Desborough, *LMS* 33, 39.

Deshayes' view is also upheld by Styrenius, *SS* 161-3; and compare the doubts of R. Hope Simpson, *A Gazetteer and Atlas of Mycenaean Sites* (1965), 198

22] To Desborough's list (see previous note, and add *PPS* 31 (1965), 221), we may add Lerna, *Hesperia* 23 (1954), 9; 24 (1955), 27; 25 (1956), 157; 26 (1957), 145; Karakasi, *Praktiká* 1909, 182-3; Berbati, *AA* 53 (1938), 554-7; C.W. Blegen, *Korakou* (1921), 102-3; Zerelia, A.J.B.Wace and M.S. Thompson, *BSA* 14 (1907–8), 216; *LAAA* 1 (1908), 118; *Prehistoric Thessaly* (1912), 161 (contrast the conclusions of Ålin, *EMF* 145 and Desborough, *LMS* 130); Iolkos, *Praktiká* 1900, 72f.; Soufli, *AA* 74 (1959), 66, fig. 8; Pharsalos, *Praktiká* 1952, 195; Ktouri, *BCH* 56 (1932), 148; for Iolkos now *AAA* 3 (1970), 198

23] Medeon, *AD* 19, 2 (1964), 223 (Styrenius, *SS* 144-6 thinks some of these Submycenaean); Krisa, *BCH* 61 (1937), 311-12, n.1; Delphi, *BCH* 61 (1937), 44; Gla, *BCH* 80 (1956), 298 (Ålin, *EMF* 123); *Excavations at Lefkandi*, 14; Malthi, *BSRL, Lund* 1927–8, 176-8; Peristeria, *Ergon* 1961, 167; Routsi, *BCH* 78 (1954), 124; Kissos (Chandrino), *BCH* 91 (1967), 662, figs. 1-4; Papoulia, *BCH* 79 (1955), 248; Kafkania, *BCH* 85 (1961), 722 and Hope Simpson, *op. cit.* (n.21), 78 no. 264; Klidhi, *BCH* 79 (1955), 253 and *AR* 1955, 17; Olympia, *BCH*, 92 (1968), 824; Tsaplaneika, *Praktiká* 1934, 114f.; 1935, 70f.; Asea, Holmberg, *AIRRS* 11 (1944), 111f.; Kokkolata, *Praktiká* 1912, 250; Emborio, *AR* 1954, 20; Agios Stephanos, *AR* (1960–1), 32

24] Salamis, C.Tsountas and J. Manatt, *The Mycenaean Age* (1897),

388; contrast for the Kerameikos, Styrenius, *S S* 37, 67-8, 118

25] Argos, *B C H* 79 (1955), 312; Tiryns, *A M* 78 (1963), 54-5 and *Tiryns* 1, 128f. For cists and pits in tholoi, see Mylonas in *Studies presented to D. M. Robinson* 1 (1951), 88-90; and for similarities between early Iron Age and Middle Bronze Age practices, Wiesner, *op. cit.* (n.1), 91ff., 121ff.: Vermeule, *G B A* 79, 335, n.3

26] *Antiquity* 38 (1964), 261; cf. Deshayes, *Deiras* 250 and n.2

27] Breitinger in *Ker.* 1, 223-55 (cf. Lorimer, *H M* 341; G. Karo, *An Attic Cemetery* (1943), 7); Angel, *Hesperia* 14 (1945), 279-363

28] Charles, *B C H* 82 (1958), 268-313 (especially 300 on 'Alpine' skulls) and *Étude anthropologique des Nécropoles d'Argos* (*E P* 3, 1963), esp. 70, 72. H. V. Vallois and D. Ferembach, in C. F. A. Schaeffer, *Ugaritica* 4, 584, regard the appearance of 'Alpine' skulls at Ras Shamra as a possible sign of Mycenaean immigration! N.b. *ibid.* 534-5 for 'Atlanto-Nordic' skulls already appearing in graves of the fifteenth century B C. For use of non-metrical variants, see A. C. and R. J. Berry and P. J. Ucko in *Man* 2, 4 (1967), 551-68

29] See M. S. F. Hood, *Antiquity* 34 (1960), 166-76; *The Home of the Heroes* 64, 77; (cf. *ibid.* 64, 76 on pithos-burials); and for 'pit-caves' on the mainland, *B C H* 78 (1954), 119 and Deshayes, *Deiras*, 242

30] *L M S* 34

31] See e.g. Andronikos, 'Totenkult' (see n.1), W 51-2

32] On this topic, the best summary is probably still H. L. Lorimer's in *H M* 103-10; but add *P P S* 31 (1965), 234-5 for references to more recent excavations. For cremations in Bronze

Age Greece and Crete, see Andronikos 'Totenkult', W 52-6; Vermeule, *G B A* 301, 349, n.1a

33] Cf. N. G. L. Hammond, *A History of Greece to 322 B.C.*, 2nd ed. (1967), 42-3; Vermeule, *G B A* 80-1, 127; on Messenia, *B C H* 79 (1955), 248 and 91 (1967), 662 (Turliditsa near Chandrino); in general, M. Andronikos, *A D* 17, 1 (1961-2), 153-76

34] Yet a late 'Ψ' figurine occurs in a Protogeometric stratum on Naxos (*Ergon* 1961, fig. 206, right), another small pointer to the continuity of population. The general absence of funerary idols had also been characteristic of the Middle Bronze Age: Wiesner, *op. cit.* (n.1), 143, 162

35] See Styrenius, *S S* 110-15 on Protogeometric grave-rites in Athens; 95 on early use of amphorae as grave-markers; M. Andronikos, *A D* 17, 1 (1961-2), 176-206 on later practice. Clay shoes: *Hesperia* 18 (1949), 296, pl. 70; *A E* 1898, pl. 4, 4

36] See J. M. Cook in *Geras A. Keramopoullou* (1953), 112-18 and *B S A* 48 (1953), 30-68

37] Menidi, H. G. Lolling *et al.*, *Das Kuppelgrab bei Menidi* (1880); Aliki, *Prakt.* 1955, 96; Eleusis, G. E. Mylonas, *Eleusis and the Eleusinian Mysteries* (1962), 62-3; Marathon, Ålin, *E M F* 111; Galataki, *Ergon* 1958, 112f.; Mycenae, *Praktiká* 1952, 470; Mylonas, *Ancient Mycenae* (1957), 171; for other possible cases, Mylonas in *Studies presented to D. M. Robinson* 1 (1951), 102; Prosymna, *A E* 1937, 377-90; Akourthi, *B S R L*, Lund 1927-8, 201f.; Koukounara, *A D* 19, 2 (1964), 163; Volimidhia, *Praktiká* 1952, 473f.; 1953, 238f.; 1954, 299f.; Nichoria, *B C H* 85 (1961), 697

38] Kerameikos, Hachmann, *G G A* 215 (1963), 65; Agora, R. S. Young, *Hesperia*, supplementary vol. 2 (1939), *passim* and J. L. Angel, *ibid.*, 236-46; Anavysos, *Praktiká* 1911, 110; Argos multiple cists, *A D* 22, 2 (1967), 193-4, pl. 139b

Appendix

Grave-finds from Early Iron Age Greece, mostly mentioned in Chapter Four
SM = Submycenaean; SMin = Subminoan; PG = Protogeometric; G = Geometric

ATTICA

Aegina P G and G cists, W. Kraiker, *Aegina* 11-12,23-5; G monolith-cists,
   A A 53 (1938), 512

Aigaleos G pithos-burial, *AJA* 64,71; *AD* 19,2,70

Anavysos G pits, cists, urn-cremations, *AD* 21,2,97-8: *Prakt.* 1911, 111
   (mostly later)

Athens, Acropolis S M cists, P. Kavvadias and G. Kawerau, *Die Aus-
   grabung an der Akropolis* 77-80, pl.Γ′,22-3,33-4; 95-6, pl.E′,59;
   99-100, pl.A′, no number; 121-2, pl.Z′,72; 143-6, pl.H′, 86; S M/P G
   cist and pit, *Ker.* 1,133

Athens, Agora, S M pits and cremation, *Hesp.* 6,364; 7,325; 21,108;
   Styrenius, *S S* 35. P G pits, cists, urn-cremations, *Hesp.* 2,468;
   5,23; 6,364; 7,325; 21,108,279; 23,58; 24,200-1. G pits, cists, pithos-
   burials, urn- and pit-cremations, *Hesp.* 2,470,552; 9,271,291-2,302;
   16,196; 17,158,166; 18,280; 19,330; 20,82-5; 29,402,413-14; 37,77;
   supplementary vol. 2, *passim*

Athens, Areopagus G cremations, *A M* 21,106; 22,478

Athens, Dipylon (Piraeus St) G pits, cists, pithos-burials, urn-cremations,
   Prakt. 1873–4, 17; *A M* 18,73-191,414; *Hesp.* 21,279,293; *AD* 17,
   2,22-3; *AD* 18,2,29

Athens, Kerameikos S M cists, pits, urn-cremations, *Ker.* 1,8f.; *Hesp.*
   30,174f.; *A M* 78,148. P G pits, cists, urn- and pit-cremations, *Ker.* 1,
   89f.,100f.,184f.; 4,32f.,47f.; *AD* 20,2,40. G pits, cist, pithos-burials,
   urn-, pit- and cist-cremations, *Ker.* 5,1,6f.; *AD* 20,2,40; 21,2,51

Athens, Nea Ionia P G cists and urn-cremations, *Hesp.* 30,151f.

Athens, other localities: Acharnian Gate, *A M* 18,77 (S M cist); Plato's
   Academy, *Ergon* 1956, 10; 1958, 10; 1959, 7 (G urn-cremations and
   pithos-burials); Nymphaion, *Prakt.* 1959, 6 (G burials); Odeion,

Prakt. 1900, 92 (G urn-cremation); near R. Ilissos, *Z E* 22,1 (G cist); Od. Alopeki, *A E* 1911, 251 (P G ?cist); under Metropolis, *A E* 1953 – 1954, 3,89 (P G cremations); area south of Acropolis, *Prakt.* 1955, 36-52; *Ergon* 1957,7; *A D* 17,2,86f. (S M cist, P G and G pit-cremations, G pits); Olympieion, *B C H* 64-5,238 (Styrenlus, *S S* 22) (S M pits, cists and cremation); Od. Lykourgou, *A D* 18,2,36 (P G urn-cremation); Od. Diakou and Anapauseôs, Garibaldi, and Zabeliou, *ibid.* 37,41,42 (G pits, pithos-burials, inhumations in re-used pit and urn-cremation); Od. Ag. Dimitriou, Ag. Markou, Meidani, *A D* 19,2,54f., 55f.,60; Od. Aischylou, Kavalotti, Erektheiou, *A D* 20,2,56f., 75f.,87 (P G and G pits and pit- and urn-cremations); Od. Kriezis, *A D* 22,2,92f. (S M cists, G cremations); Pnyx, *A M* 18,414 (G burial); Od. Amphiktyonos, *A D* 22,2,49 (P G pits); Od. Erysichthonos, Mitsaiou, Parthenônos, Poulopoulou, *ibid.* 79f.,102-10 (G pits and cremations)

Brauron G burials, *Ergon* 1957, 23

Draphi G cremations, *B C H* 82,681

Eleusis G (and a few P G) pits, cists, pithos-burials, and pit-, urn- and cist-cremations, *A E* 1889, 171f.; 1898, 29f.; 1912, 34f.; *Prakt.* 1898, 73f.; 1953, 81f.; 1955, 74f.; *A J A* 44,472;61, 282; *Ker.* 1, pls.42,48; G. E. Mylonas, *Eleusis etc.* 60-3; *A D* 22,2,122

Kaki Thalassa G burials, *A A* 1963, 465

Kallithea G pits etc., *B C H* 87,404f.; *A D* 19,2,65f.

Kokkinia (Piraeus) G cists, pithos-burial, urn-cremations, *Prakt.* 1951, 116; *A D* 17,2,43

Liossia G burial, *C V A* Denmark 2, pl.70,2-8,10

Marathon P G urn-cremations, *A A* 55 (1940), 179 (*Prakt.* 1939, 28f.). G cists, pits and urn-cremations, *A A* 50 (1935), 181f.; 55 (1940), 178f.

Myrrhinous G pit- and urn-cremations, *B C H* 85,626; G pits *A A A* 1 (1968), 31

Phaleron (Old) G and later pits, cists, pithos-burials, sarcophagi, urn- and pit-cremations, *A E* 1911, 246f.; *A D* 2,13f.

Salamis S M cists and urn-cremations, *A M* 35,17f.; ?S M tholos, *A R* 1961–2,7

Spata G pits, *A D* 6, parartêma, 131f.

Thorikos P G and G urn-cremations, G pits, cist and pithos-burials, *Hesp.* 30,299f.; *A D* 19,2,81f.; 21,2, 109; 22,2,138; *Antiquité Classique* 34,16

Trachones G burials, Coldstream *G G P* 403

Vari (Anagyrous) G and later cists and pits, *A D* 20,2, 1 1 2; *B C H* 82,672

ARGOLID

Argos, Deiras ?P G re-use of chamber-tomb, J. Deshayes, *Deiras* 68;
P G (or earlier?) cist, *BCH* 91,840

Argos, Main Cemetery (*S. W. Quarter*) S M cist, *BCH* 78,176. P G cists,
pits and pithos-burials, *BCH* 78,176f.; 79,312f. G cists, pits and pithos-
burials, *BCH* 77,258f.; 78,176f.; 80,376f.; 81,677f.

Argos, Agora area P G cists and pits, *BCH* 83,755f. G cists and pithos-
burials, *BCH* 77,253; 83,755f.; 87,748; *AR* 1966–7,10; *AD* 22,2,193

Argos, Museum area P G cists and pits, *BCH* 78,170; 81,647f.; 83,762f.
G cists, pits, pithos-burials, urn-cremation and pyre, *BCH* 78,410f.;
81,647f.; 83,762f.; 85,675

Argos, other localities: Od. George II, *AD* 18,2,57f. (G cists); Od.
Tripoleôs *ibid.* 6of. (S M boulder-cists); Ag. Petros Square, *AD* 17,2,
55f. (G cists); Od. Danaou, *ibid.* 56 (G cist); Od. Tsôkris, Karaïskakis,
Dagré, Karadzas, Od. Danaou extension, *BCH* 91,833-6,844; Od.
George I, *AD* 21,2,126-7 (G pithos-burials, cists); Od. Presvelou,
Tzoulou, Desmini, *AD* 22,2,170-7 (P G and G cists)

Asine P G cists and pits, O. Frödin and A.W. Persson, *Asine* 422f.
G pit and possible pit-cremation, *ibid.* 152,192f. G ?pithos-burials,
Op. Ath. 6,116.

Berbati G pit in re-used chamber-tomb, G. Säflund, *Excavations at
Berbati* 81f.

Dendra Possible P G and G re-use of tholos and chamber-tomb, A. W.
Persson, *Royal Tombs at Dendra* 41-2,67 and *New Tombs at Dendra*,
101. Cf. also *Op. Ath.* 4,89

Lerna G cists and pithos-burials, *Hesp.* 23,7; 24,27; 25,171

Mycenae (See *L M S* 36 for late Mycenaean single graves). P G cists and
pits, *Prakt.* 1953, 209; 1954, 265; *BSA* 49,258f.; 50,240; 51,128f.
AR 1963/4, 8; *AR* 1964/5, 10 = *PPS* 31,225-6, pl.xxxiii d-e; *AD* 20,2,
165. G cists, pits, pithos-burials, urn-cremation, *AE* 1912, 127f.;
Prakt. 1952, 470 (re-use of chamber-tomb); 1954, 268; *BSA* 49,258f.;
50,240f.; 51,128; K. Müller and F. Oelmann, *Tiryns* 1,134,136, n.1;
G. Perrot and G. Chipiez, *Histoire de l'Art* 7,162, n.1; *AR* 1959–60,9

Nauplion (*Pronaia*) P G pit, *Ergon* 1955, 75. G cists, pits, pithos-burials,
urn-cremations and pyres, *BCH* 78,119; *Ergon* 1954, 73f.;
1955, 75f.

Prosymna (*Argive Heraeum*) G cist, *AJA* 29,427. Possible G re-use of
chamber-tomb (no.34), C. W. Blegen, *Prosymna*, 110f.

Tiryns S M pits, *A M* 78,1f. P G – G cists, pits, pithos-burials, Müller and
    Oelmann, *Tiryns* I, 127f.; *A M* 78,1f.

Troizen G pithos-burials, Müller & Oelmann, *Tiryns* 1,138; *A M* 36,33;
    A D 18,2,52

Xerias (Argos) G pithos-burial, *A D* 21,2,125

CORINTHIA AND MEGARID

Agioi Theodoroi (Moulki) G pits, pithos-burial and sarcophagus,
    A D 17,2,52f.

Athikia G burials, S. Weinberg, *Corinth* 7,1,19; *A J A* 61,169; *Hesp.* 33,91

Corinth G pits, cists, monolith-cists, cremations, Weinberg, *Corinth*
    7,1,9f. G monolith-cist, *Hesp.* 33,89: G pits, cists, monolith-cists and
    pithos burials, R. S. Young in *Corinth* 13,13f.

Diolkos G cist, *A M* 71,57

Klenia G monolith-cists, *A J A* 59,125; 61,170

Megara G cist, *Prakt.* 1934, 54

Vello P G burial, Weinberg, *Corinth* 7,1,3

Zygouries G pit, C. W. Blegen, *Zygouries* 67f.

THESSALY

Ano Dranitsa G cremations in tholos, *Prakt.* 1911, 351

Argalasti ? G tholos, *Prakt.* 1910, 221

Chyretiai G tholoi under tumulus, *Prakt.* 1914, 168

Dimini ? G vaulted chamber, *A E* 1914, 141

Gonnos ? G tholos, *Prakt.* 1910, 246

Halos P G cists, and perhaps rather later inhumation in enclosure, *B S A*
    18,1f. G cremations under cairns, *B S A* 18,16f.

Hexalophos Cists under tumulus, contemporary with L H III C, *A A A* 1
    (1968), 290

Homolion P G chamber-tombs and tholos, *A D* 17,2,175f. Undated cists,
    Prakt. 1911, 287

Iolkos P G cists, *Ergon* 1960, 55f; 1961, 51f. G ? tholos, Desborough,
    P G P 132f.,153

Iolkos, Kapakli P G – G tholos, *A E* 1914, 141

Iolkos, Nea Ionia P G cists, *A D* 18,2,140

Lestiani G tholoi, *Prakt.* 1911, 292

Marmariani P G – G tholoi, *B S A* 31,1f.; C. Tsountas, *Dimini kaì
    Sésklo* 121; and perhaps *A M* 21,247

Melea ? G tholoi and vaulted chambers, *Prakt.* 1906, 125; 1910, 226

Palaiokastro P G cists, *B C H* 56,99

Pherai G cists, Y. Béquignon, *Recherches archéologiques à Phères*, 50f.

Pteleon (Gritsa) P G re-use of tholos, *Prakt.* 1953, 120f.

Retziouni ? S M cists, N. M. Verdelis, *Ho Protogeometrikòs Rhuthmòs tîs Thessalías*, 52

Sesklo P G tholos, *Ergon* 1965, 8f. G vaulted chambers and tholoi, *Prakt.* 1911, 294; C. Tsountas, *Dimíni kaì Sésklo*, 75

Theotokou S M – G cists, A. J. B. Wace and M. S. Thompson, *Prehistoric Thessaly*, 209f.

SOUTHERN AND CENTRAL CYCLADES

Ikaria, Kataphygi G cremations under tumuli, M. Andronikos in *Archaeologia Homerica* (ed. F. Matz and H.-G. Buchholz), W 68,112

Kimolos, Limni G cremations in shafts, *B C H* 78,146

Melos G burials, *B S A* 2,70

Naxos, Aplomata P G – G pits and cremations, *Ergon* 1960, 185 ; 1961, 199 ; 1963, 151

Naxos, Gymnasium area G burials, *Prakt.* 1937 – 8, 117

Naxos, St' Alonakia G cremations under tumuli, and cist, *A D* 18,2,279f. ; cf. 20,2,514f., 21,2,391f., some of these later

Naxos, unknown site P G cremation, Desborough, *P G P* 72,213

Thera G cremations in chambers, *A M* 28,8f. ; H. Dragendorff, *Thera* 2

ELIS

Ancient Elis S M or P G pits, *A D* 17,2,124f. ; 19,2,180f.

Kyllini (Chlemoutsi) G burials, *B C H* 81,568

Olympia G burials, *B C H* 78,128

Palaiopyrgo P G pithos-burial, *A J A* 65,226 ; Coldstream, *G G P* 221

Salmone see *Palaiopyrgo*

WESTERN ASIA MINOR

Assarlik S M – G cremations in chambers, cists and sarcophagi under tumuli and in enclosures, *J H S* 8,66f. ; 16,243

Dirmil (Burgaztepe) P G vaulted chamber, *A J A* 67,208,357f.

Gökçeler ? G chambers within tumuli, *J H S* 16,202,244 ; *C Rh* 1,124 ; *B S A* 50,125

Iasos G cists and probable pithos-burials, *Annuario* 43 – 4,497

Kolophon G cremations, *A J A* 27,68 ; *Hesperia* 13,91,94 ; Lorimer, *H M* 106

Melia G burials in rock-clefts, *A R* 1964–5, 49; G. Kleiner *et al.*,
  Panionion und Melie, 78f.

BOEOTIA

Orchomenos P G – G cists, Desborough, *P G P* 198,318; H. Bulle,
  Orchomenos 1,83; Coldstream, *G G P* 197
Rhitsona G pit-inhumations, *J H S* 53,171; 30,336f.; P. N. Ure, *Aryballoi
  and figurines from Rhitsona*, 17,88
Thebes, Electran Gates S M – P G cists, *A D* 3,25f.
Thebes, Kolonaki P G re-use of chamber-tomb, *A D* 3,203
Thebes, Od. Pelopidou P G pit, *A D* 20,2,239
Thebes, Pyri G pithos-burial, etc., *A D* 21,2,197-8; 22,2,236
Thebes, unknown site G burials, *J d I* 3,247; Blinkenberg, *F G O* 154, etc.
Vranesi Kopaïdos P G – G pits and cremations under tumuli, *Prakt.* 1904,
  39; 1907,109

EUBOEA, NORTHERN CYCLADES AND SPORADES

Andros, Zagora P G – G cists, Desborough, *P G P* 128,161
Euboea, Avlonari G burial, *B S A* 61,73
Euboea, Chalkis P G cists *P P S* 31,228; A. Andreiomenou in *Kharistírion
  eis A. K. Orlandon* (1965) 2,248f.
Euboea, Eretria G pithos-burials and cremations, *A E* 1903, 1f.; *Antike
  Kunst* 9,106f.; 10,134
Euboea Lefkandi S M – P G cists, G urn-cremations, Popham and Sackett,
  Excavations at Lefkandi, 23-4; *A R* 1967–8, 12; *A A A* 2 (1969), 98f.
Euboea, Nea Lampsakos P G burial, *B S A* 61,60
Rheneia G ? cist(s), Desborough, *P G P* 128,156
Skyros P G cists, *B S A* 11,78f.; *A D* 4, parartêma p.41; *A A* 51,228f.;
  A J A 43,131; 55,149
Tenos, Kardiani G cists, *Ann.* 8-9,203f.
Tenos, Exoburgo G cists, *Musée Belge*, 1907, 42 = *Ann.* 8-9,226f.
Tenos, Ktikados G cists, Coldstream, *G G P* 152,165

PHOKIS AND LOKRIS

Amphissa G burials, *A D* 18,2,130
Antikyra (= *Medeon*) G urn-cremations, *Prakt.* 1907, 111f.
Delphi P G and G chamber-tomb, *B C H* 61,44f. G urn-cremation,
  P. Perdrizet, *Fouilles de Delphes*, 5,133; ? other G burials, B C H 59,276
Medeon P G pit-cremations, G pit-cremations, cists and pithos-burials,
  A D 19,2,223

MACEDONIA

Bohemitza Cists contemporary with G and later, *Albania* 4,40

Chauchitza Pits contemporary with G, *B S A* 24,7f.;26,1f.

Konturiotissa/ Kalyvia area Cists of early Iron Age date, *Makedoniká* 1,490 = *A A* 55 (1940), 271

Kozani Cists and pits of early Iron Age date, *Ergon* 1960, 99; *A A A* 1 (1968), 244; and perhaps *Makedoniká* 2,638

Pateli Cists and pithos-burials contemporary with G and later, *Albania* 4, 44

Vergina Pits, boulder-cists, pithos-burials and urn- and pit-cremations contemporary with P G and G, *Prakt.* 1952, 225f.; 1953, 141f.; 1957, 73f.; 1958, 90f.; 1959, 59f.; 1960, 95f.; 1961, 90f.; *A D* 17,2,218f.; 18,2,217f.; M. Andronikos, *Vergina* 1 (1969)

DODECANESE

Exochi G pithos-burials and pit-cremations, *Act. A* 28,6f.

Ialysos P G – G urn-cremations, *C Rh* 8,161f.;3,37f. G pithos-burials and pit-cremations, *Ann.* 6-7,263,288f.,332f.; *C Rh* 8,172

Kameiros, Acropolis G cremation, *C Rh* 6-7,189

Kameiros, near Temple A G chamber-tombs, cremation, and perhaps pithos-burial and sarcophagus, *C Rh* 6-7,193f.

Kameiros, Patelle etc. G pits, pithos-burials, sarcophagi, cremations, *C Rh* 4,341f.;6-7,32f.,119f.

Kameiros, Vizikia G burial, *JdI* 1,136

Kos, Serraglio and Halvagi 'S M' cist, *A A* 51 (1936), 128. P G – G cists, pithos-burials, pits, *BdA* 1950, 320f. (330, n.118 for absence of cremations)

Massari-Malona G burials, *C V A* Denmark 2,47, pl.65,3-8

Vroulia G and later pits and pit-cremations, K. F. Kinch, *Fouilles de Vroulia*, 49f.

CENTRAL AND WESTERN CRETE

Agioi Paraskioi G and later tholos, *A E* 1945 –7, 47f.

Agiou Georgiou Papoura G tholos, *J H S* 57,141

Anopolis G urn-cremation, *A J A* 1,257,260

Arkades P G, G and later cremations in tholoi, *Ann.* 10-12,174f.,202f. G and later vaulted chambers, and cremations in enclosures, *Ann.* 10-12,78f.

Arkhanes P G 'B' burial, *Kretiká Chroniká* 4,441.

Atsalenio G chambers, *B C H* 85,735; *B S A* 63,133

Atsipades S Min and later pithos-burials, *A E* 1915, 48f., perhaps with partial cremation (so Levi, *Ann.* 10-12,544); see also *B S A* 61,178

Episkopi Pediados and region G pithos-burials, *Prakt.* 1952, 628

Gortyn P G cremations in tholos *A D* 22,2,485

Kamares? G cremations in tholoi, *A J A* 5,439

Karphi S Min and earlier tholoi and vaulted chambers, *B S A* 38,57f.

Khania? S Min/P G chamber-tomb, *A A* 45 (1930), 163. G urn-cremations, *J H S* 49,235

Knossos, Agios Ioannis area S Min re-used chamber-tomb, *B S A* 63,205. P G, G and later re-used chamber-tombs and vaulted chambers, some with cremation, *B S A* 55,128 (Ref.[3] in M. S. F. Hood, *Archaeological Survey of the Knossos Area* (1958)); *Kretiká Chroniká* 4,294

Knossos, Fortetsa S Min, P G, G and later cremations in chamber-tombs, perhaps re-used, J. K. Brock, *Fortetsa, passim*[26·7,97]; *B S A* 31,56; 56,68[25]; *A R* 1967–8,22[26]

Knossos, Tekke area P G re-use with some cremations of chamber-tomb, *B S A* 58,34f.[21]; cf. 29,231. G cremations in re-used tholos and chamber-tombs, *B S A* 49,215f.[11]; *Kretiká Chroniká* 1,633[11]

Knossos, other localities: Gypsades, S Min re-use of chamber-tombs, *B S A* 53-4,205-8[156] (cf. Desborough, *L M S* 180): Isopata path, P G chamber-tomb, ? re-used, *B S A* 58,38[1]; Kefala ridge, P G and later chamber-tomb, *B S A* 58,42f.[15·16]; Temple Tomb, G pit. A. J. Evans, *Palace of Minos* 4,1018[148]; Villa Ariadni, P G urn-cremation, *B S A* 58,38[107]; Kefala ridge, P G–G cremations in re-used vaulted chambers and tholoi, *B S A* 6,82f.[15]; 29,224f.,31,98[7]; Unknown area, G cremations, *A J A* 1 (1897), 255f.,260f.

Kollyva Metokhi P G vaulted chamber, perhaps with cremation, *A D* 14,1f.

Kourtes S Min vaulted chambers with some cremations, *A J A* 5,289f.

Ligortino G burial, Coldstream, *G G P* 416

Mallia G re-use of chamber-tomb, *Études Crétoises* 13,122; G burials, *ibid.* 112

Milatos G burial, *Annuario* 10-12,568

Modi P G rock-cut tombs and pithos-burials, *Kretiká Chroniká* 7,485f.

Nea Halikarnassos (Heraklion) G burial, *A A* 51 (1936), 224

Panagia (Kofina) S Min–P G vaulted chambers, *A J A* 5,283f.; *Ann.* 10-12, 389

Phaistos S Min–P G chamber-tomb, *BdA* 1955, 159

o

Phaistos, Liliana ? S Min and earlier sarcophagi in chamber-tombs, *MA* 14,627f.

Phaistos, Mulino and Petrokephali P G urn-cremations, *Ann.* 35-6 (n.s. 19-20), 355f.

Phaistos, Tou Phygiote to Aloni G burial, *Rendiconti Lincei* 1902, 318

Pharmakara G urn-cremations, *BCH* 80,343

Phoinikia ? P G – G chamber-tombs, *AD* 14,2f.; P G cave, *Ergon* 1967, 124

Rotasi Monophatsiou P G   G tholoi, *BCH* 79,304; 80,343; 83,734

Siderokephala ? P G vaulted chamber, *MA* 9,402

Stavrakia G urn-cremations, *AJA* 1 (1897), 257,259; *JdI* 14,37

Tylissos P G urn-cremation, *AM* 56,112

Vrises S Min / P G chamber-tombs, *BSA* 60,106

EASTERN CRETE

Adromyloi G burial, *BSA* 8,249; 12,43

Anavlochos G pit and tholoi, *AD* 14,5f.; *BCH* 55,365f.

Berati-Piskokephalou P G (or S Min) – G burials in re-used cave (see Desborough, *LMS* 268), *Prakt.* 1953, 292

Braimiana ? G tholos, *JHS* 52,255

Dreros S Min vaulted chamber, H. van Effenterre, *Nécropoles du Mirabello*, 17f. G urn- and pit-cremations, *ibid.*

Kavousi S Min tholoi, *AJA* 5,132f. G cremations in tholoi and pits, *AJA* 5,143f.,154; *Annuario* 10-12,560f.

Mouliana L M (or G) cremation in re-used vaulted chamber, *AE* 1904, 21

Olous S Min and earlier sarcophagi, pits, urn-cremations and pithos-burials, van Effenterre, *Nécropoles du Mirabello* 8f.

Patela Sfakia P G (or S Min) vaulted chamber (see above under Berati) *BCH* 80,359

Piskokephalo P G (or S Min – see under Berati) burials in re-used cave, *BCH* 78,154

Praisos G and later re-used tholoi, vaulted chamber and shaft, *BSA* 8, 240f.; 12,24; *BCH* 78,155

Stous Lakkous Kritsa P G vaulted chambers, *BCH* 78,155

Sykia district P G (or S Min – see under Berati) burials in re-used vaulted chambers, *BCH* 79,307; *Prakt.*1954, 365f.

Vrokastro S Min – G chamber-tombs, E. H. Hall, *Vrokastro* 123f. G cremations in enclosures and pithos-burials, and inhumations in cave, *ibid.* 154f.; 106,112,172f.; 174

Zakro (*Stou Koukou to Kephali*) G cave-burials, *BSA* 7,148

IONIAN ISLANDS

Kephallenia, Diakata L H / S M inhumations in 'dormitory' chambers, *AD* 5,92

Kephallenia, Lakkithra L H / S M burials of similar type, *A E* 1932,17f.

Kephallenia, Metaxata L H / S M burials of similar type, and in vaulted chambers, *A E* 1933, 73f.

Zakynthos ? G cists and other burial, *B S A* 32,216

(Ithaka, Aetos – 'Cairns' non-funerary, *B S A* 48,255)

AETOLIA AND ACARNANIA

Kryoneri G burials, *B S A* 32,239

Palaiomanina (*Kalydon*) G pithos-burials, *AD* 17,2,184; 22,2,323

Pylini P G pithos-burials, *A D* 22,2,320

ACHAEA

Asani G burial, Coldstream, *G G P* 229

Bartolomio (*Mikros Bodias*) ? G tholoi, one with pithos-burials inside, *A A* 1932, 142; *Op. Ath.* 5,106

Chalandritsa G cists under tumuli and pithos-burial, *B C H* 85,682; *Prakt.* 1930, 85f.

Chalandritsa, Troumbes ? G vaulted chambers under tumuli, and other G burials, *Prakt.* 1930, 83f. (for dating, contrast 1928, 111; 1929, 91); *B C H* 53,501

Derveni P G pithos-burial, *A J A* 64,16

Katarrakhti, Liopesi (Pharai) P G cist, *A D* 20,2,223. G cists and pithos-burial, and undated tholoi, cists and pithos-burials in enclosure, *Prakt.* 1952, 400f.; 1956, 196f.; 1957, 117f.

Vovodha G pithos-burials, *A R* 1960–1, 14

MESSENIA

Antheia P G burial, *A D* 20,2,207

Kalamata G pithos-burial, *A D* 20,2,207

Karpophora P G tholos, *A A A* 1,2 (1968), 205 (the evidence for cremation seems doubtful)

Kato Englianos P G tholos, *A J A* 63,127

Nichoria P G and perhaps earlier cists and pithos-burials, *B C H* 84,700; 85,697f.

Tragana P G re-use of tholos, *A E* 1914, 99f.

LACONIA

Kythera, Palaiopolis G? burial, *B S A* 56, 158
Mavrovouni P G? burial, *B S A* 56,116f.,n.9

EPIRUS

Elaphotopos Zagoriou Cists of Late Bronze Age date, *A D* 22,2,345
Kalbaki Cists contemporary with L H III, *A E* 1956, 114f.
Kastritsa Cists of similar date, *A D* 19,2,312; *A R* 1966–7, 13
Mesopotamon (*Likouresi*) Cist of similar date, *A D* 18,2,153
Paramythia Pit of similar date, *A D* 20,2,349
Vitsa Zagoriou Cists of 8th century and later date, *A D* 21,2,289f.
    For other sites (Vodhinë, Kakavi, Bodrishtë, Vajzë), see N. G. L.
    Hammond, *Epirus*, 201-5,228-30,346-51,356,362; also *P P S* 31,228,
    addendum (*b*)

WESTERN GREECE

Cumae G (and later) pits and boulder-cists, and cremations in pits and
    monolith-cists, *M A* 22,213-72 and 807-36; also 13,263f.,278f.
Megara Hyblaea G (and later) monolith-cists, boulder-cists, pithos-
    burial, urn-cremations etc., *M A* 1,774f.
Pithekoussai G (and later) pits, pithos-burials, cremations under cairns,
    Atti e Memorie della Società Magna Grecia 1954, 3f.; *Antiquity and
    Survival* 4,255f.
Syracuse G (and later) pits, pithos-burials, monolith-cists and urn- and
    pit-cremations, *N Sc* 1895, 109f.; cf. 1893, 445f.
Thapsos G re-use of native chamber-tomb, *M A* 6,103f.

5

Iron and Other Metals

♦ ♦ ♦
♦ ♦
♦

If there is one incontrovertible fact about the period covered by this study, it is that it witnessed the adoption of iron for practical uses in Greece.[1] The use of the absolute terms 'Bronze Age' and 'Iron Age' has recently, and on perfectly valid grounds, begun to fall out of favour among European pre-historians: to mention only two areas of difficulty, the phases in Central Europe which Reinecke called Hallstatt A and B have 'no justification whatever within the sense of any kind of image based on the material evidence' for their conventional placing at the beginning of the Iron Age of that region;[2] while much of the Italian 'Early Iron Age' seems to be equally undeserving of the name in any literal sense. Yet in both cases these phases represent a cultural break with the preceding Late Bronze Age. With Greece, however, we are presented with no such dilemma: here the beginning of the Iron Age means exactly what it promises, the replacement by a predominantly iron-based economy of an older bronze-working culture.

There are two groups of problems which face one in considering this process, and which will take up the first part of the discussion in this chapter: first, when, from what sources and by what sequence of events did iron reach Greece? And secondly, what did the adoption of iron mean to Greece, not only from the aspect of technological progress, but also in terms of her relations, both external, with other countries, and internal, between the different regions of Greece? Discussion of iron will inevitably involve treatment of bronze and other metals, for as we should expect, the arrival of an Iron Age does not imply a sudden or total conversion to the use of iron.

TECHNICAL FACTORS

We need hardly concern ourselves here with the first tentative steps in iron-working which were taken during the second millennium B C in and beyond the Aegean area. Meteoric iron was perhaps the earliest raw material used, but it was often exceedingly difficult to work; the discovery of a primitive method of direct smelting from ores produced blooms which could be worked into wrought iron, but for a long time this remained inferior in quality and strength. No real iron-working industry, in effective implements and weapons, could be developed until a way had been found to harden the primitive bloomery-iron; and this development did not take place until long after the first use of the metal.[3] Three or four separate new discoveries were involved in the process: first, the ores had to be heated in a furnace to a temperature of not less than 1100°–1150° Centigrade, for although iron will reduce at lower temperatures, the resultant substance cannot be forged. This was hardly a difficult proposition for craftsmen of the Aegean Bronze Age, who must have been used to generating temperatures in excess of 1000° to melt copper, or indeed bronze with a low tin-content, in the process of casting. Second, the function of carburization had to be discovered: this could, and presumably did, happen by pure chance, with the use of charcoal for fuel and a reduced draught to the fire; nor need the early smith have understood why its effects were such, provided that he could go on reproducing them. By increasing the carbon content in this way, from an average of perhaps less than 0·2 per cent in primitive wrought iron to something approaching 0·9 per cent, the smith gave his iron some of the qualities of modern steel, in particular the property of being able to be hardened by sudden cooling and subsequent forging. The mention of cooling brings us to the third and fourth processes, which are those of quenching the carburized metal in water from a high temperature; and of tempering it, by re-heating to a relatively low temperature, and again cooling with water. These are not such simple steps as might appear for, first, they are inapplicable to the forging of copper and bronze implements, which are normally work-hardened simply by hammering; and secondly, the tempering process requires controlled temperatures, and considerable experience or luck in selecting the degree of heat desirable. It is indeed possible to produce quite hard wrought iron without these last processes, and there is plenty of evidence to show that in the early centuries of iron-working, tempering in particular was by no means regularly employed. Quenching, however, is already known to Homer (*Odyssey* x, 459).

Some illustration of the effects of these processes is given by tests of the hardness of ancient and modern metal objects, carried out by the Brinell ball-impression method, or the Vickers diamond pyramid system which

72. Detail of an iron sword-blade from Vetulonia in Etruria, whose structure, in piled laminations, is visible to the right of the indentation (cf. no. *73*). Greatest surviving width of blade, *c.* 4·5 cm; 7th century B C.

gives a roughly equivalent scale of hardness between 0 and 300.[4] The degree of hardness can vary widely even within the compass of a single weapon or blade; the commonest practice is to harden the cutting edge to a degree well beyond that of the base or socket, and the carbon content can also be graded, whether intentionally or otherwise, from one part of an implement to another. An average hardness for wrought iron is 100 Brinell, and even modern low-carbon mild steel often has a hardness ranging between 110 and 150 before forging, and of about 246 when forged. But two early Egyptian iron knives of New Kingdom date, although they had both been air-cooled (i.e. had not been subjected to the third and fourth processes described above), proved to reach a Brinell hardness of up to 302 and 285 respectively at their cutting edges; and two probably tempered Egyptian axes of 'about 900 B C' achieved 229 and 444 Brinell respectively at their cutting edges. There are signs that these were unusually fine products of their kind – also tested, for example, were an Iron Age pick from Lachish which had certainly undergone quenching, and had a highest ascertained hardness of 183 Vickers; while a probably untempered spear-head of the sixth century B C from Deve Hüyük in Syria had up to 153 Vickers. These last specimens may be particularly relevant to Greek practice in the early Iron Age (see below, p. 216). The figures may be compared with those for pure copper, 35 Brinell, and for copper with 10 per cent of tin (a proportion quite commonly found in ancient bronzes), 88 Brinell; but these apply to the metal as cast, and before working; when hardened by hammering, a bronze alloy of the proportions given above, for example, reaches 228 Brinell. Ten per cent bronze, therefore, both before and more especially after hardening, is shown somewhat surprisingly to rival a wide range of irons, and even mild steels, in point of hardness; which makes a most interesting reflection on the motives behind the large-scale adoption of iron for working implements and weapons.

Of the processes discussed earlier, carburization is the most significant; and for the early craftsmen it involved a further difficulty, since their methods could only achieve a slight and shallow penetration of the carbon into the metal – adequate perhaps for a thin blade, but hardly for an axe or a sword. A common remedy for this defect was the process of piling together several thin laminations of iron, already carburized, for forging. It is interesting to find that this was the method used for the Lachish pick and the Deve Hüyük spearhead mentioned above (the latter comprising perhaps fifty separate layers), as well as on other objects tested from the same general region and period, such as a tripod of eighth-century date from Nimrud; and from further west, a seventh-century sword from Vetulonia in Etruria which was examined by Professor Carlo Panseri and others proved to have a similar but more sophisticated structure, being composed of alternating layers of harder and milder metal.[5] Now unfortunately there is no record of early Greek ironwork being similarly tested, but in my own examination of swords and other iron objects of early Iron Age date I have often noticed a layered structure resembling that of the Vetulonia sword as shown in Panseri's detailed view; the poor preservation and severe corrosion of most of the examples actually helps in revealing such features. With contemporary or near-contemporary evidence for the use of this process in two areas on either side of the Greek world, I do not think that we need doubt that this 'piled' or 'compacted' structure was also common, and perhaps preferred, in the forging-work of the early Greek smiths.

The neglect of Greece in the analysis and study of early iron-work is not due merely to chance or oversight: for the generally poor quality of preservation of ancient iron seems to be intensified by the conditions of Greece. Many of the excavated iron objects from early Greece have become so corroded that the metal is entirely converted to oxide; some have quite literally crumbled away into dust. This situation, in one of the major classes of object preserved from dark age Greece, is little short of disastrous; it means that, for details of types and even dimensions, one is thrown back upon the descriptions and illustrations in the excavation reports, and in the case of all but the most recent discoveries, these are usually quite inadequate. However, the mere fact that iron has been used is often the most significant thing, and this is not normally in doubt; while the further indirect evidence that we have considered above will, I think, prove of

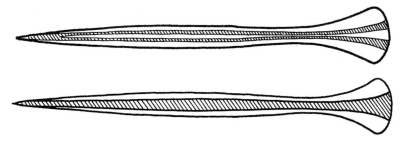

73. Restored cross-sections of sword from Vetulonia (see no. *72*), showing two alternative schemes for the structure in alternating layers of harder (shaded) and milder (open) steel.

some value when we turn to the earliest developments in the use of iron in Greece.

THE INITIAL SPREAD OF IRON-WORKING

The sporadic occurrence of iron on Minoan and Mycenaean sites has long been known,[6] and is not in the main directly relevant to the later growth of a real iron industry. But there is nevertheless a significant development in the last years of Mycenaean civilization in Greece which, since it involves working parts of implements made of iron, is clearly connected with what comes after. Perhaps the most easily intelligible stage in this development is represented by a group of knives with narrow hafts and curved or off-set blades, which are basically of iron but have bronze rivets preserved in the haft, for the attachment of hilt-plates in some perishable material. This retention of bronze seems to be explained by the fact that rivets of bronze could more easily be closed by hammering when cold, whereas iron rivets are commonly closed when red-hot, which early smiths may have found an awkward proposition. The earliest known examples of these knives *74* may belong in the twelfth century: a knife from the Late Minoan III C or Subminoan Gypsadhes Tomb VII at Knossos, two examples from Mycen- *75* aean III C tombs (nos. 28 and 38) at Perati, and one of parallel date at Lefkandi in Euboea; and, from further east, a knife from Level I at Enkomi in Cyprus, of the second half of the Late Cypriote III B period, and a knife from Hama in Syria, of similar period. But other specimens are certainly later: one from the Subminoan chamber-tomb I at Vrokastro (which in this part of Crete may possibly involve a date as late as the ninth century), and one with a wider blade from Kakavi in Epirus which is also likely to be of considerably later date than the first group. There are also instances of

Vajze ?

Kakavi ?
Vodhine ?

Vergina ●

Marmariani ●

Kapakli ●
Theotokou

Skyros

Lefkandi

Athens
Perati

Mycenae ●
Argos ● ● Tiryns
● Asine

Malthi ?

Naxos

Assarlik ?

Kos

Ialysos ?
Kameiros ●

Knossos

Kourtes ● Karphi ●
Virokastro
Mouliana
Kavousi

IRON *c.*1100—900 BC
Early finds of iron utilitarian objects

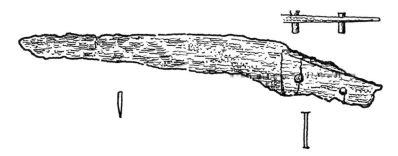

75. Iron knife with bronze rivets from chamber-tomb VII of the Gypsades cemetery, Knossos. Length 15·9 cm; 11th century BC.

other classes of object – swords for example – showing the same combination of materials down to the ninth and even the eighth centuries.[7] The feature is not therefore an infallible sign of early date; but its first appearance in the Aegean is none the less significant. It precedes the appearance of all-iron knives there, and indeed comes at a time when all-bronze knives are still common; and the distribution of the early examples, embracing Cyprus and the Levant, gives the first pointer towards an answer to one of our questions, that of the source of the first use of iron for working implements in Greece. In Cyprus there are also some all-iron knives which belong within or shortly after the twelfth century – two from contemporary tombs at Enkomi, and one from Kaloriziki Tomb 40 which is rather later.[8] No Aegean example is so early, although there are one or two which should belong in the later eleventh century (see below, pp. 222-4). Here then is an instance of typological and material evidence combining to suggest a transfer of types or techniques, in two successive stages, from the region of Cyprus and the Levant to the Aegean. It has been suggested that the knives of the first group, those which retain bronze rivets, are actual imports to Greece, and this may be so: as we shall see, there are few other objects with working parts of iron at this date in the Aegean, and it must have taken time for smiths in Greece to master the new processes described on page 214.

Iron does, however, make an early appearance in one other class of practical implement, the dagger. In this case there is no sign of Cypriot influence, since, as Catling has shown,[9] the dagger of the Cypriot Late Bronze Age is an uninspiring weapon derived entirely from local forerunners, while the early Cypro-Geometric cemeteries show a dearth of daggers of any kind. Iron daggers of twelfth to eleventh-century date do

74. Distribution map of iron objects, *c.* 1100-900 BC.

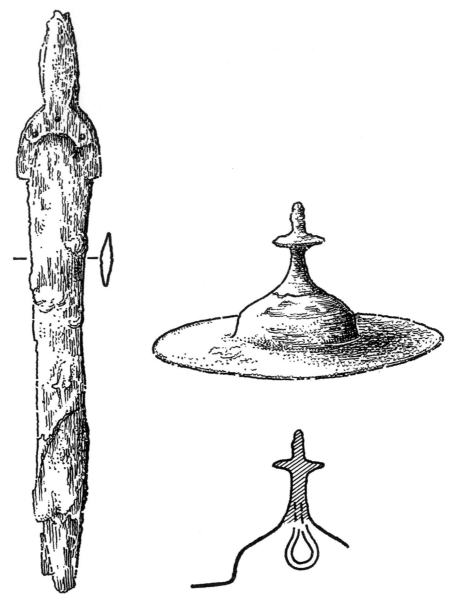

76. Iron dagger from tomb X X V I I I at Tiryns. Preserved length 3 1 cm; mid-1 1th century B C.

77. Bronze shield-boss from tomb X X V I I I at Tiryns. Diameter 10·5 cm.

occur at several sites in Syria and Palestine, as well as deeper into the interior,[10] but these are all of simple, even crude, form, and at present one can point to no clear ancestry for the earliest iron daggers in the Aegean. In chamber-tomb A at Kamini on Naxos, of Mycenaean III C date, there was an example of unknown type; but in tomb XXVIII of Verdelis' excavations at Tiryns, which may not be much later and should date from before 1050 BC, there were two all-iron daggers of the *Griffzungendolch* type, which are as notable for their relationship to the predominant type of sword in this era as for their use of the new material; the larger and better preserved of the two is 31 cm long. These are the only iron weapons so far found which definitely precede the appearance of Protogeometric pottery in the more advanced regions of Greece, those of our first group of local Protogeometric styles (chapter 2, pp. 55-68).[11] A very few other iron objects of substantial size have occurred in equally early contexts: in the collection of objects known as the 'Tiryns Treasure', whose homogeneity is doubtful but which includes material of likely Mycenaean III C date, there was an iron sickle-blade; implements of this type are very common indeed on Near Eastern sites of the early Iron Age, although few are as early as the presumed date of the Tiryns example. A large fragmentary bracelet from chamber-tomb 17 at Ialysos, which is probably of III C date, is differentiated only by its size from a number of other iron objects of personal and decorative use, which are found in much earlier Aegean tombs, and which continue to appear sporadically in later III C (and, in western Attica, Submycenaean) cemeteries: a few rings and two indeterminate objects of iron from the main Kerameikos cemetery, two iron pins (one with an ivory head) from the late Submycenaean grave 113 near by, and a small glass globe pierced by a fragment of iron from Perati, which may well represent an ornamental head to an iron pin. It may be noted that an iron pin with ivory head also appeared in the probably twelfth century Old Tomb 74 at Enkomi in Cyprus.[12] The chief interest of these iron personal objects is perhaps that their much commoner bronze contemporaries were normally cast, whereas these must have been formed by hammering, an awkward operation but one which still did not require the same standards of technique as an iron blade of a working implement or weapon.

Only when the production of real 'working' iron was mastered by Greek smiths could the Iron Age be said to have arrived in the Aegean. The early knives and daggers listed above may have been mostly ready-made imports; so too may some of their successors. Our safest guide to the pro-

76

gress of iron-working in Greece lies, I believe, in the consideration of the factor of *proportion*. Once we begin to find that a certain class of object is being commonly produced in iron, and in particular once iron examples begin to preponderate over bronze in the same class of object, we may surely infer that foreign imports are no longer playing a leading part. If such a situation develops at a time when other evidence for trade contacts with the foreign areas in question is temporarily lapsing – as I think is the case – then we may approach certainty. In our study of the pottery, and in particular of the chronology of the Greek dark age in the light of contacts with Cyprus and the Levant, we found some evidence that the Aegean remained in touch with these areas down to the development of the first local Protogeometric styles (pp. 115-18). The first instances of practical artefacts in iron in Greece fall, as we shall now see, within this key period at, and shortly after, the rise of Protogeometric; but what happens after that is something detectably different.

In Attica and several other regions of Greece the rise of Protogeometric schools of pottery is to be dated somewhere near the middle of the eleventh century. If we consider the appearances of iron in these regions only, a concerted pattern emerges. Attica provides the fullest evidence, but there is a deficiency here in that we have virtually no tools or weapons in any metal from the immediately preceding period, the Submycenaean cemeteries of Salamis and the Kerameikos. This cannot of course mean that these communities lacked such articles; and on the evidence both of other areas of contemporary Greece, and of the predominantly bronze personal objects in these graves, it is a fair assumption that the working implements of Submycenaean western Attica were also of bronze. With the rise of Attica Protogeometric, the custom of occasionally burying weapons and tools in graves fortunately returns, and we can see quite a clear sequence of events.[13] Four graves which stand near the transition to Protogeometric – nos. A, B, 24, and 2 North, in the Kerameikos – produced substantial metal objects. Tomb A (a double cremation) contained an all-iron dagger and knife, and two bronze spearheads; tomb B (also a cremation) had an iron dagger with bronze rivets; 'Protogeometric' tomb 24 (a cremation, rather to be classed as transitional), a bronze shield-boss; and tomb 2 North, the only inhumation, an iron sword. This is a most interesting group of finds, as we can assume the four graves to belong to the same period within a generation's length: the offensive weapons show several different stages of transition to iron-working, while the only item of defensive armament is of bronze – as will remain the rule in the succeed-

74

78

79a

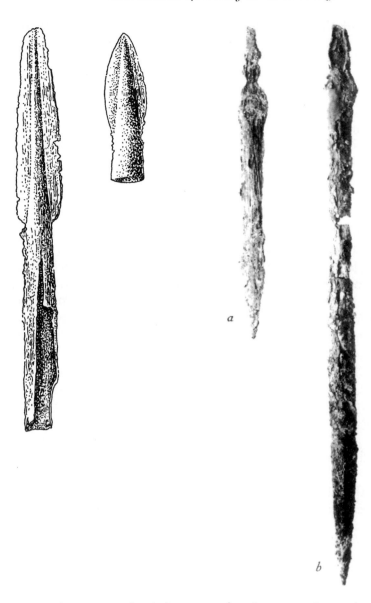

78. Two bronze spearheads from grave A at the Kerameikos, Athens. Lengths 26 and 9 cm; *c.* 1050 BC.

79. Two iron swords from the Kerameikos, Athens. (*a*), 48 cm long, is from Protogeometric grave 2 North, *c.* 1050 BC, and is one of the very earliest all-iron weapons known from Greece. (*b*), 83 cm long, is from Geometric grave 13, *c.* 825 BC.

76

77, 104

78 left

cf. 98a

ing period. With this group we may associate the roughly contemporary warrior-grave XXVIII at Tiryns, already mentioned for its iron daggers, but also containing a bronze spearhead, shield-boss, and part of a helmet; and perhaps tomb A at Assarlik in Asia Minor, which contained a knife and spearhead of iron, but was still in use somewhat later.[14] In all three widely-separated sites, the cutting weapons (knives, daggers, swords) are of iron; but the spearheads mostly remain bronze, perhaps because their sockets were more easily shaped in that metal. Two more detailed observations may be made on individual objects: first, the solitary iron sword, although belonging to the general class of *Griffzungenschwerter* which had become common in thirteenth- and twelfth-century Greece in its bronze form, shows marked divergences from its bronze predecessors there, and bears a marked resemblance only to a small group of bronze and iron swords found in Cyprus, Syria, Palestine and, later, East Crete and Urartu; secondly, the larger bronze spearhead from tomb A at the Kerameikos has a general shape similar to a slightly earlier one from Kaloriziki tomb 40 in Cyprus, and more especially shares with it the feature of a socket formed with a slit running along it for much of its extent. Such a slit is not an infallible sign that the socket was made by beating it round a cylindrical bar or mandril, but in this case I believe that this explanation applies; a perhaps roughly contemporary bronze spearhead from Cyprus with a similar socket was analysed for H. H. Coghlan's study and proved to have been made in this way.[15] As Coghlan remarks, this is a most archaic method of fashioning a socket in bronze, when the casting of such hollow cylinders had been common practice in the Bronze Age, and when the main body of the spearhead was still formed by casting. It is, I suggest, a sign that the art of casting in any but the simplest two-piece moulds was in temporary abeyance in the eleventh century; while the delay in adopting iron hints at further technical deficiencies. As for the bronze shield-bosses, their title to this name has been argued elsewhere, and there is a little further evidence which might have been adduced to strengthen the case[16]; but the question of the likeliest source for their appearance in Greece remains an obscure one. It is unfortunate that all the objects under discussion are of warlike use; we lack evidence for industrial and agricultural tools in Greece at this critical time, and one can only say that, from analogies further east, iron was probably pressed into service for weapons earlier than for tools.[17]

For personal objects at this date in the Kerameikos, we are denied any evidence from the actual graves we have been considering, since these are

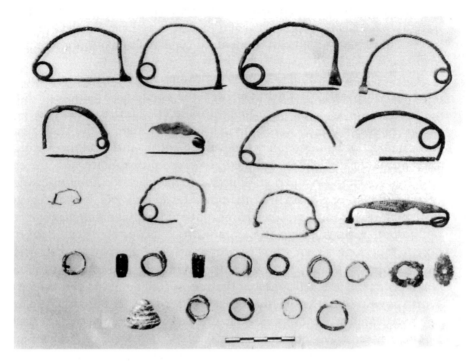

80. Small finds from Submycenaean grave 108 at the Kerameikos, Athens. Besides the numerous bronze arched fibulae of both symmetrical and asymmetrical forms, there are two of the older violin-bow fibulae with flattened bow (2nd row, 2nd from left; 3rd row, far right). Of the bronze rings, one (4th row, far right) is of the 'shield-ring' type. A glass bead appears at bottom left. Scale 1:3; *c.* 1075 BC.

naturally all male burials, and the wearing of pins and fibulae by men, although not unknown in Submycenaean times, ceased almost entirely in Protogeometric Attica. However, there are female graves in the Kerameikos which cannot be far from this group in date; they contain a few pins (mostly of iron, but in one case of bronze), and no fibulae. The latest Submycenaean fibulae, from graves 108 and 113, cannot however be much earlier in date, and are all of bronze; the same types are also present at Perati – a further sign, incidentally, that the use of this cemetery (and therefore the duration of the III C period) overlapped largely or entirely with western Attic Submycenaean. A child-burial at the Kerameikos (114) contained a bronze ring, but rings are absent from the earlier Proto-

80

P

geometric graves here. However, when we turn from Attica to consider roughly contemporary graves at Tiryns, we find bronze still in use for rings and fibulae – both still of identical type to those of Submycenaean Athens.[18]

The first iron pins of the Kerameikos are close reproductions of a bronze type (no. (1) below) which had been the commonest variety in Submycenaean graves, and is also found in late III c burials at Argos. The arched fibulae of this era, too, both in bronze and later in iron, seem to be the products of a purely internal development from the original 'violin-bow' form which had been adopted in Greece probably towards the end of the Mycenaean III B period. This is not the place for a full discussion of the ultimate origin of either the fibula or straight pin in the Aegean; both types seem to appear somewhat abruptly, though at different moments, and in both cases an origin in Central Europe or northern Italy has been accepted by most recent scholars. However, since the pins in their long, bronze form are a later arrival, by a margin of perhaps a century or more, than the first fibulae, and appear at the very threshold of the dark age, it is worth pointing out that J. Deshayes has now shown some serious objections to the accepted account of their source. The commonest type in III c and

81 Submycenaean graves, which we may call type (1), has a disc at its head and a globular swelling a little way down the shaft, and remains predominant in the Protogeometric period in its iron form; it seems to have clear, though remote, Mycenaean antecedents in the long bronze pins with crystal globe found in Shaft-grave circle B at Mycenae. Then an almost

81 equally early, but rarer and shorter-lived type of bronze pin (2) with a more elongated swelling and a series of ring-mouldings instead of the disc, found at Argos, Ancient Elis, in the Gypsadhes cemetery at Knossos and perhaps in Mouliana tomb A, has its most probable antecedents not in Europe but in the Near East and beyond. Thirdly, a pin with spatulate

81 tip from a very late III c tomb at Argos (3) is definitely of Near Eastern

81 type. Deshayes goes on to identify a further type of pin (4) which is not found at Argos but which resembles his no. (2), with shallow incised rings instead of true mouldings, and a rather flatter swelling; this has an interesting distribution – at least four from the town site at Karphi, five in all from four Kerameikos Submycenaean graves, two from a very early Protogeometric cist-tomb at Mycenae and two in a tomb-group of Proto-

87 geometric date from the 'Northern Peloponnese' (see below, p. 244). Its method of decoration and general appearance very much recall the bone and ivory pins found on Late Bronze Age sites (including Karphi itself),

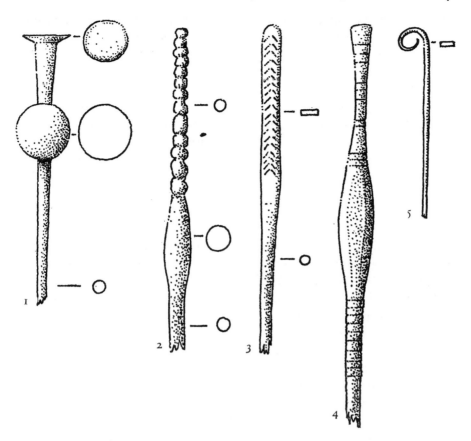

81. Five types of bronze pin, occurring in Greek graves from the late 12th century BC onwards. 1, 2, and 3 are from the Deiras cemetery, Argos; 4 and 5 from Submycenaean graves at the Kerameikos, Athens. Actual size.

and it may well be descended from local prototypes in other materials, although there are roughly comparable pins in northern Italy and Central Europe. Finally, a further variety (5) with much wider distribution is the roll-topped pin, of which Salamis produced two examples, and a Kerameikos Submycenaean grave, one. This form abounds on Near Eastern sites, and can only have reached the Aegean from there.[19] These observations, taken with the fact that Mycenaean tombs had quite commonly contained small pins of bone, ivory and even bronze; with the lack of analogous Central European examples which show any chronological priority; and with the general absence of the earlier types from Greek sites north of Athens, suggest that the origins of the straight pin in Greece need to be reconsidered. In any case, the development of iron versions of these pins in Greece, rather before the middle of the eleventh century, takes the question, from then on, far beyond the reach of any explanation in terms of European influence.

THE ARRIVAL OF THE IRON AGE

We have followed the developments in the use of the new metal in Greece, down to the threshold of a fully iron-based culture. Are we now in a position to give an answer to our first group of questions, as to the date, the source, and the sequence of the first adoption of iron? It is clear that the critical period in this matter is the eleventh century: the earlier instances of iron-use in Greece are not significant, nor even strictly relevant; for they show an attitude to iron, as a rare and even semi-precious metal, which actually militates against its use as a working material. But before 1050 BC there begins a phase which, partly in the light of later events, we can see to be transitional to the full Iron Age. The length of this 'transition' I see in very different terms from those of some other writers on the subject. In a penetrating study of the analogous process in Anatolia, which also treated more briefly of the Aegean, S. Przeworski devised the concept of a 'chalcosideric' period, a long interregnum between the periods of un-opposed dominance of bronze and of iron.[20] In the Aegean he considered his phase to have extended from about 1200 to 700 BC. But such a scheme obscures the true situation *after* the transitional phase, in Greece and the Aegean at any rate; for the fact is that, for long after 700 BC, Greece remained in part a bronze-using civilization; not only is bronze retained for almost all large objects of beaten metal, but it frequently appears in other functional and decorative uses. There are even several classes of object for which bronze is proportionately more often used in the seventh to fifth centuries BC than it is in certain periods of the dark age – fibulae, arrowheads and spearheads, for example. As we shall see, the changes in metal-usage are altogether too complex to be explained by a simple sequence of bronze-based, transitional, and iron-based cultures. I prefer to apply the term 'Iron Age' from the moment that iron first supersedes bronze as the normal material for those functional metal objects for which iron was suitable.

Nevertheless, Przeworski's scheme is valuable for the examples that he gives of seven 'chalcosideric' technical features, characteristic of his transitional period; some of them we have encountered in our earlier discussion.

The seven features are:

1 Imitation of Late Bronze Age types in iron.
2 Simultaneous appearance of bronze and iron objects of the same use and type.
3 Inlay of bronze objects with iron.
4 Combination of iron working and bronze ornamental parts in the same implement.
5 Fitting of bronze products, such as vessels or votives, with iron parts.
6 Use of bronze rivets on iron implements.
7 Repair of bronze objects with iron parts.

Of these techniques, numbers 1 and 2 are both so common and so long-lived that they prevail throughout, and beyond, the duration of the Greek dark age; they are not therefore very precise diagnostic features. 4 and 6 are on the whole more concentrated in their time-range; we have already cited their first appearances in Greece as a sign of the arrival of a transitional stage in metallurgy, and they remain valid as such although 6, in particular, makes some later appearances in Greece as in the Near East. 5 and 7 are rarer among the surviving finds; the examples in the Aegean area seem to be of relatively advanced (9th century and later) date (cf. below, pp. 236 (Marmariani), 273 (Chauchitza)). 3, finally, involves technical attainments which seem to have been beyond the powers of dark age Greece.[21] Przeworski's criteria are mainly valuable for showing that iron-working techniques, in their early stages, followed similar paths in two or more quite independent regions of the ancient world.

The next question is that of the ultimate source of the first iron types in Greece. It was in knife-blades that iron perhaps found its earliest acceptance for functional use in the Aegean, and here clear traces were found of an origin in the eastern Mediterranean area, and perhaps more precisely in Cyprus. Equally likely Near Eastern forerunners exist for the solitary iron sickle-blade in the Tiryns treasure. A Cypriot iron pin antedates the earliest Greek examples, and resembles one of them, from the Kerameikos, in its use of ivory as the material for the decorative head (p. 221). But the case of the iron dagger in Greece proved different; in the absence of likely Oriental models, one may consider a local development from the bronze version of the same weapon-type, the *Griffzungendolch*, to be the possible explanation. The iron finger-rings of this date, for which Mycenaean forerunners in the same material exist, can certainly be explained in this way; and so perhaps can the single iron bracelet from Ialysos. The slightly later appearance of the iron sword in Greece once again, on typological grounds, sends us back to the region of Cyprus and Syria for the source; and this connection is reinforced by a detail of the manufacture of a contemporary bronze spearhead from the same site, the Athenian Kerameikos. Everything tells in favour of the conclusion that it was her contacts with Cyprus and the Levant, already well established and, in the case of Cyprus, quite recently reinforced by migration, which enabled Greece to take the critical step of entering the Iron Age in the eleventh century BC. On the final question of the sequence of the adoption of iron, we have found that quite large cutting- and stabbing-implements (knives, daggers and, a little later, swords) show an earlier and higher incidence of iron than small, mainly decorative objects like rings and fibulae. It is a great pity that the further evidence of agricultural and craftsmen's tools is not available, at the right time and in the right areas of Greece, for comparison; but even without these, it seems that the practical qualities of iron were those which had now impressed themselves on the people of the Aegean, and that in the eleventh century, while iron was perhaps in restricted supply, and particularly while it was coming in the form of ready-made imports, the first call was for working purposes.

Two main difficulties still stood in the way of this conversion to ironusing. First, although iron was potentially a superior metal to bronze for blades and working parts generally, it required considerable skill to make it superior to the *best* hammered bronze; if greater hardness were sought, by quenching the blade, there was a risk of falling into the opposite pitfall of excessive brittleness; if this risk were not taken, the hardness might be inferior to that of a good bronze blade. (One slight advantage that iron had to offer was that of being a little less heavy than bronze, enabling larger weapons to be wielded with equal ease; but this was nullified if, as seems at first to have been the case, the smith's skill was not equal to producing blades longer or broader than their bronze counterparts.) Secondly, a number of Bronze Age implements had been primarily manufactured by the process of casting, and many small personal objects were entirely so made; since cast iron was probably not to be mastered in the West until very many centuries later, and was not in any case suited to most of such products, this meant that iron substitutes had to be shaped exclusively by forging. With some kinds of object this was a great disadvantage: notably those socketed tools and weapons which were not primarily designed to withstand impact, and the more elaborate personal objects which did not require great tensile strength or hardness.

Against these deterrents, we may set a factor whose power as an incentive was evidently overriding: the wide availability of iron. A bronze-based civilization had required large quantities of copper, and a smaller but steady supply of tin. Of these, copper was probably mined in small quantities in the Aegean area, but it is certain that it was also being imported in bulk from Cyprus and the Levantine region, particularly towards the end of the Bronze Age; local supplies were therefore either inadequate or too laborious to extract to be exploited on a large scale. The deposits of tin in the Eastern Mediterranean area as a whole are quite restricted, and the existence of any ancient tin-workings in Greece itself has yet to be proved. The use of arsenic as a substitute for tin in forming the alloy, which is well known in the metalwork of some regions (the Caucasus for example), is not uncommon in early times in Greece, but seems to have died out as the Bronze Age went on. Iron ores, on the other hand, are spread liberally over the earth's surface; although Greece is not especially rich in them, they are quite well represented in the islands of the Aegean, the southern Peloponnese, central Greece and Macedonia.[22] One effect of the mastery of iron-working was therefore, in Greece as in other countries, to increase self-sufficiency and lessen the dependence on outside resources. The same phenomenon has frequently been noted in other parts of the ancient world. It is often assumed that the sharp reduction in trade at the end of the second millennium BC was, in part, caused by this discovery of new internal resources, alike by the peoples of Asia Minor, Mesopotamia, the Levant, Cyprus, Egypt and the Aegean; and that the conversion to iron technology was a powerful advance, the result of free choice on the part of those areas of the ancient world which were able to take this step. While there is probably some truth in this explanation, it seems to me that, in Greece at least, the converse effect was also in operation for a long time: that the reduction in trade had become an established fact and that this drove the people of the Aegean, willy-nilly, to a more widespread use of iron than they would otherwise have chosen to make. To illustrate this, we may consider the developments in the Protogeometric period in certain parts of Greece.

PROTOGEOMETRIC ATTICA

In Attica, to which we must turn once again for the fullest evidence, the progress towards the full use of iron was carried much further in the Proto-geometric era. The earliest group of graves of full Protogeometric date contain only pins in the way of metal finds; these may be of iron or bronze, but they maintain the form of the commonest Submycenaean type (1), with the disc and globe. But perhaps rather before 1000 BC these are

82. Iron pin with bronze globe from Protogeometric
grave 38 at the Kerameikos, Athens. Actual size; *c.*950 BC.

82 replaced by a yet more standardized type of pin, in which the shank is of
iron, but the globe is a separately cast, pierced piece of bronze threaded on
to it; this canonical pin is found in no less than thirteen Kerameikos graves
of middle and later Protogeometric date, in one Early Geometric one
here, and in the rich Agora grave found in 1967 (together with all-bronze
examples); it is nearly always found in pairs, but one grave contained
four and in another case only one survived.

Here we see bronze and iron exchanging their rôles of the Mycenaean era:
it is bronze which now appears as the ornamental material, to be sparingly
used, and iron which does the work. A very few all-iron pins also appear
at this time. Then, in three late graves, bronze pins return to the Kerameikos, and at much the same time arched fibulae re-appear, in both bronze
and iron, (Kerameikos grave 39, Agora grave XIII), and a bronze bowl
is found in Kerameikos grave 48. In all ascertainable cases the graves with
pins were those of women; and the only bronze objects in any of them,
besides the pin-globes, were three finger-rings and a decorative fitting in
the late grave 39. Contemporary male graves, where they contain metal,
show iron reigning equally supreme: grave 6 produced an iron sword to
put beside that from the transitional tomb 2 North and, like it, of very

moderate size; then in graves 17 and 34 appear the first iron spearheads known from Greece proper, some two generations later than the first iron sword. Grave 17 also held an iron dagger, on the hilt of which were traces of 'bronze oxide'; perhaps this represents a survival of the old transitional technique (pp. 217, 222, 229 no. 4). Of tenth-century graves, one (32) had an iron spearhead; one (28) an iron sword, long knife and arrowhead; one (E) an iron sword only; one (43) a bronze shield-boss; and one late grave (40) a bronze shield-boss and fibula with an iron chisel and axe. For the whole of the middle part of the Protogeometric period, the reliance on iron seems to have been almost total: only the globes on the pins, and the rare shield-bosses, are of bronze, until a late reversion brings back bronze for pins, fibulae and finger-rings alike; in the latest Protogeometric graves, too, bronze bowls and decorative fittings re-appear. It is much the same with other Protogeometric graves in Athens: at least two female graves in the region of the Agora (XVII and XXII) produced pins with the same combination of iron shank and bronze globe, together with iron fibulae; a male grave here, and another recently found on Ag. Markos Street, contained iron weapons of canonical type; only a child-burial (XLII) produced bronze personal objects, before the latest phase of Protogeometric. Then, a late female grave (XIV) held a bronze fibula and three bronze rings (just like Kerameikos grave 39); while of male burials, the transitional Agora grave XXVII and a rather earlier grave under the Metropolis cathedral showed a new combination of weapons, with sword and spearhead appearing together for the first time since the Mycenaean period; the former also produced horse-bits, and echoed Kerameikos grave 40 by containing tools as well as weapons. The small burial-plot at Nea Ionia produced three of the standard iron-and-bronze pins, and one bronze and one iron fibula; these burials are fairly late in the Protogeometric series.[23]

83, 84

THE ARGOLID

The pattern that is emerging is by no means confined to Athens and Attica, but can be matched in several of the more advanced areas of Greece. Moving first to the Argolid, we find at least five graves in the old and recent excavations at Tiryns with the standard iron-and-bronze pins, but in the later ones (VI, VII, XVIII of Verdelis' cemetery) there are also bronze pins and finger-rings, and in one case even two gold spiral hair-rings – gold objects of this form had last been seen in three early Protogeometric graves of the Kerameikos, 5, 22 and 25. A grave at Argos produced two further iron pins with bronze globes attached. The rather poor Protogeometric

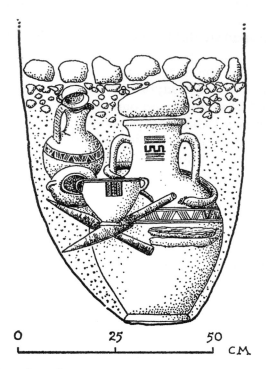

83. Cross-section of a male urn-cremation, Agora grave x x v i i (cf. no. *57*); *c.* 900 b c.

85a graves of Asine produced only two pins of the standard type, and eight or more others of either bronze or iron; in one or two cases the pins were worn by men, a sign perhaps of isolation from the main fashions of the time. An unpublished tomb (184) at Argos contained an iron dagger. At Mycenae, a very early Protogeometric cist held two bronze pins of early type ((4) on p. 226 above), with three bronze fibulae of the simplest arched type; later graves produced pins with iron shank and bronze knob, and bronze rings. Away to the west, the pit-graves at Ancient Elis, which are likely to be early in the lifetime of the Protogeometric style, present an even older metallurgical picture: one grave held a bronze sword and dagger of types which would have been most at home in the twelfth century; two others had arched fibulae of bronze, and others again had pairs

84 (opposite). Metal finds from the same grave as no. *83*: sword, two spearheads, two horse-bits, axe-head, chisel, knife.

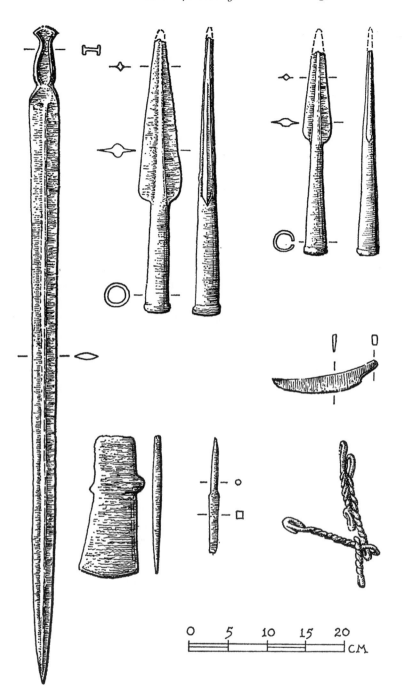

a

b

85. Iron weapons from Argos. (*a*) is a dagger from Protogeometric tomb 184, length 22 cm, 10th century BC; (*b*) is a spearhead from Late Geometric tomb 179, length *c.* 29 cm; *c.* 725 BC.

of bronze pins of the two prime eleventh century types ((1) and (2) on p. 226).[24]

THESSALY AND ASIA MINOR

Another region with an early Protogeometric school which offers some published evidence is Thessaly. The finds from graves of this period at Iolkos include a surprising survival of the violin-bow fibula (in bronze, as always with this type), but otherwise are not yet known. Yet the Submycenaean tomb C at Theotokou had already contained an iron ring, as well as a bronze arched fibula and ring – an assortment very comparable with that of some Submycenaean graves of the Athenian Kerameikos. So too the Protogeometric tomb B at this site held the remains of five or six of the standard pins of this period further south, in iron and bronze, as well as a curved knife-blade like that in Agora grave XXVII at Athens (p. 233), and an arched fibula of iron, with three bronze and one iron rings. From Kapakli and Homolion come several iron swords and other weapons. Cist-tomb 6 at Halos, which is post-Protogeometric in date, had a bronze roll-pin of an old form ((5) on p. 226); while the tholoi of Marmariani, which are still more likely to belong after the end of the Protogeometric style in Athens, have strong connections northwards with Macedonia and the Balkans, as is shown not only by their hand-made pottery, but by the bronze bracelets with tremolo-line decoration, the spectacle-fibulae, and a peculiar type of pin with a pierced, barrel-shaped head. The fact that these and the other metallic finds – knives, a sword, a spearhead and rings – were nevertheless predominantly of iron will not seem surprising when we consider developments in Macedonia; a bronze fibula in tomb VI here had had its pin replaced in iron. The only other published metal objects found with Protogeometric pottery of the more advanced schools come from Assarlik in south-western Asia Minor. Here

84

tomb O, probably contemporary with the transition to Protogeometric at Athens, contained a bronze fibula with swollen arch, covered in silver; tomb A, perhaps rather later, had an iron knife and spearhead as already noted (p. 224); tomb M, not closely datable, had a bronze fibula; tomb G another silvered fibula; and tomb C, which was definitely of Geometric date, three bronze ones; tomb B, also of indeterminate date, held two gold spiral hair-rings and traces of iron weapons.[25]

THE HYPOTHESIS OF BRONZE-SHORTAGE

In total, the evidence from the more advanced areas of the Aegean broadly confirms the evidence of the pottery in suggesting close awareness of developments in Attica; the conformity to Attic practices of metal-use in Protogeometric times is very close at Tiryns, Mycenae and Theotokou, and is more loosely apparent everywhere. Bronze prevails only in the earliest and latest stages of Protogeometric, and in the periods beyond, but still in a restricted field; in between, the dependence on iron is general, with a few exceptions either regular (shield-bosses, and the globes on pins) or irregular (finger-rings); otherwise bronze is used in these years, in so far as the chronology is sufficiently precise to enable us to speak, only where there is independent evidence of backwardness or isolation, either from typology (as at Elis or Iolkos), or from usage (as at Asine). Specific features shared with Attica are the use of the same type of dress-pin, and the tendency to equip only female graves with small metal objects.

A reaction in favour of bronze then develops into the Geometric period; iron becomes progressively rarer for pins, fibulae and finger-rings. Later still there is a marked reversion to bronze in certain classes of weapon: spearheads dedicated in archaic sanctuaries are often made of bronze, presumably partly for aesthetic reasons, since bronze could carry both decoration and inscription, suitable embellishments for show-pieces. Much more pronounced is the resurgence of bronze for arrowheads, in this case for the purely technical reason that such mass-produced objects could be most easily made by casting in multiple moulds. A similar development seems to take place with the spear-butt or *saurotêr*, a weapon whose rare appearances in the early Iron Age are in iron, but which is later much more frequently found in bronze, a metal which could better resist the corrosion to which this arm was exposed when the spear was stuck in the ground. In a different field, the tripod-lebes, one of the most massive types of metal object known to early Greece, also shows overall a higher incidence of iron in its earlier stages.[26] With all these artefacts, whether the reasons for reverting to bronze were technical, aesthetic or precautionary, the fact is that these motives were not apparently operative at an earlier period in the regions we have considered; this, taken together with our finding that the early products of the ironsmith were not by any means necessarily superior to their counterparts in bronze (pp. 215, 230-1), leads me to the conclusion that there was some kind of constraint at work in these areas, which led to a greater dependence on iron, particularly during the middle part of the Protogeometric phases of these regions, after c.1025 and before 950 BC; and which later abated, to allow a gradual reversion to bronze. Such constraint is most likely to have been exercised by the sharp reduction of trade in copper and tin (cf. below pp. 248-9). Another factor may have been at work too: the skill which lay behind the finest bronze products of the preceding age may have perished in the era of disturbance just before the beginning of the Iron Age in Greece; there is indeed the ancient authority of Plutarch (*Moralia* 395 B) for the belief in some 'secret' skill on the part of the early bronze-workers.

It will be objected that the body of evidence on which these observations are based is very small; so it is, although it actually represents a large proportion of the evidence available to us in materials other than pottery. What is certain is that in several areas which were ceramically advanced in the eleventh and tenth century BC, an early mastery of iron-working was also achieved. It also seems to me certain that Attica, perhaps followed by other regions, shows a sequence of transition to iron, then of more intensive use of it, then of a partial reversion to bronze in the latest years of Protogeometric. Very possibly the transmission of the necessary skills was made possible by the same intercommunication which was noted earlier in the case of the pottery; if so, there is a further hint that Athens may have been a leader in the metallurgical as in the ceramic field; the standard iron-and-bronze pins of the tenth century are no more likely to have been devised independently in Attica, the Argolid and Thessaly than is the combined use of compass and multiple brush.

If there was really a period of enforced iron-using in some areas, it will have brought its benefits in the gradual improvement of smithing techniques, especially for those cutting-implements and weapons to which iron was really suited; but the more selective use of iron in later times shows that there were definite limits to the application of these techniques. A more fundamental conclusion on early iron-working seems to be involved, however. Several writers on economic and social aspects of the ancient world have upheld the view that the adoption of iron, as well as being a major technical advance, was a great levelling force. The dramatic fall in the price of iron between Bronze Age and Iron Age is an established fact; but to say that, in Childe's words of 1942, 'Cheap iron democratized agriculture and industry and warfare too' is quite another thing. The historical facts, in some parts of Europe and Asia at least, seem to belie such claims; Childe himself came to write some years later of the same phenomenon: 'It was not however a levelling of societies in Western Europe. On the contrary, the archaeological evidence indicates a greater concentration of political and economic power.' The same might be said of some parts of western Asia, even if it would be going too far to apply this conclusion to Greece, at the early date when iron came to be adopted there. Nevertheless, I find it hard to see any sign that changes in the political organization of the Aegean had their cause in the onset of the Iron Age. If the adoption of an iron-based economy (and that only in certain areas of Greece) was rather a symptom than a cause of the political upheaval at the end of the Bronze Age, an involuntary and in some degree temporary response to circumstances, then indeed we should hardly expect it to have been a very influential factor in the shaping of the new order.[27]

OTHER REGIONS OF GREECE

Meanwhile what was happening in the rest of the Aegean? If the more advanced regions were under some pressure to apply their newly-acquired knowledge of iron-working, what became of their contemporaries who might not have such knowledge? The answer must remain provisional, for apart from two regions which we have already found to involve exceptional circumstances – Macedonia and Crete – we have no evidence to compare in richness with that from Attica or even the Argolid. Indeed, if we were right about the relative chronology of local Protogeometric styles (pp. 68-79, 84-9, 128-32), the period of the most intense iron-using in Attica and elsewhere, within the extreme limits of 1025 and 950 BC, may be for some regions devoid of evidence of any kind. In part at least this is true of Boeotia, the northern Cyclades and Laconia, while the material from Euboea as yet includes no published metal finds of the period. But there is evidence from Phokis, Skyros, the Dodecanese, the Ionian Islands, Achaea and Messenia which should be partly contemporary; there is very copious evidence from the special areas of Crete and Macedonia; and there is material too from Epirus which we shall need to consider.

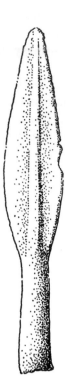

86. Bronze spearhead from tomb near the Museum,
Delphi. Length 22·5 cm.

PHOKIS

86

98c,d

At Delphi, a single object from the tomb near the Museum may prove to be
symptomatic of the conditions in these regions of Greece. It is a spearhead
in bronze, finely made and properly cast; in shape it very closely resembles
a type current in the later Mycenaean period, and even an actual example
found in the twelfth-century Temenos Tomb on this same site. It was
found to be associated with Protogeometric vases, although the group is
difficult to fix more precisely within the lifetime of that style. I would
suggest that this weapon is very probably of late Mycenaean manufacture,
and had been retained in use for more than a century before its burial –
unless indeed it had been recovered from an earlier tomb. The situation
recalls that of the sword and dagger from Ancient Elis (p. 234): the cases
are parallel in that the bronze weapons suggested an early date to the
excavators at each site, but in each instance the pottery has been shown by
Desborough to reflect later, Protogeometric influences. Bronze spearheads of the type found at Delphi are scarcely known from later contexts
in Greece; only two examples from among the dedications at Olympia seem

to belong to the same era, and they too may have been ancient at the time of their offering: they have very worn tips. But also from Phokis, from a tomb at Schiste Odos, comes a bronze *Griffzungenschwert* which resembles so closely another found at Orchomenos in Boeotia, in a Geometric grave, that it has been argued to be a contemporary. Certainly it is of a developed type; but it seems to me almost certain that the Orchomenos sword, and possible that the Schiste Odos one, was already old at the time of its interment; the hilt of the latter is similar to that of a twelfth-century sword from Mouliana Tomb A.[28] From Boeotia, however, there is no relevant evidence of Protogeometric date.

The retention of Bronze Age heirlooms in everyday use is a reaction that we should expect to find in a region where copper and tin had fallen into short supply, but where progress in iron-working lagged behind the more advanced areas. By contrast, the continued reproduction of Bronze Age types, though equally a sign of backwardness, would presuppose a continuing supply of copper and tin such as we have suggested did not exist in other regions of Greece. Can we, at this distance of time, hope to distinguish between heirlooms and reproductions? Certainly it is impossible to confirm the hypothesis made above, that the bronze spearheads and swords are actually of Bronze Age manufacture, rather than made according to a Bronze Age tradition. There is a further factor involved here: one of the beauties of bronze as a material is the fact that it may be melted down and re-used over and over again. In regions which had been thickly populated in Mycenaean times, but were so no longer, it may have been possible to recover or eke out the supplies of bronze acquired in easier days; such supplies might largely consist of ready-made bronze objects for which no use now existed. Whether or not this activity went on in such areas as Phokis, one would judge that in more populous regions like Attica, the Argolid or Thessaly, it would have been impossible to supply life's needs in this way.

SKYROS

The Protogeometric graves of Skyros, although they lie towards the end of the lifetime of this style in Attica, also invite consideration here. Bronze fibulae, still unpublished, were found in a group of tombs excavated by Stavropoullos in the 1930s, and a single grave excavated by J. Papadimitriou held an interesting collection of objects. It was evidently a warrior's tomb, since these included an iron spearhead and bronze shield-boss; but associated with them were small gold-leaf discs in the form of rosettes, numerous blue glass beads, four bronze fibulae and a large bronze bracelet.

Q

The last object has some parallels at this period (as have the gold spiral hair-rings also found on the island); the bronze fibulae are of the type with swollen arch and flanking collars, current since Submycenaean; but the gold discs and the beads can only be Mycenaean heirlooms. Here, yet again, the small finds suggested to the excavator a date at the beginning of Protogeometric, but the pottery tells a different story, for the most characteristic piece is a jug which must belong late in the series.[29]

THE DODECANESE

The earliest relevant evidence from the Dodecanese is that of the Proto-geometric tombs of Kos. The fibulae here are of bronze, mostly of the plain arched type but including at least one example of the somewhat rare stilted form (probably Blinkenberg's type II.15). More interesting however were the pins, for there were about ten examples of the 'standard' Protogeometric type with iron shaft and bronze globe, a most unusual feature in this or any other region outside the advanced iron-working centres. Their presence not only reinforces the evidence for a close connection between this cemetery and the mainland of Greece, particu-larly the Argolid (pp. 76, 95, 163); it must also have a chronological force, confirming that the link dates from before the last years of the Protogeo-metric style, when these pins began to go out of favour with the return of the all-bronze version. Other objects from these tombs included several gold and one iron rings, as well as several bronze ones, and two iron knives. The finds from the Rhodian cemeteries, which begin rather later, provide a contrast: the early fibulae from Ialysos, Kameiros and Lindos alike are all of bronze; pins too are mostly of bronze, although there were two iron ones from Patelle grave XL at Kameiros and two from a predominantly Geometric deposit at Lindos; rings may be of either metal; weapons where they occur (in Marmaro grave 44 at Ialysos) are exclusively of iron.[30] The whole pattern conforms to that expected at and after the latest stage of Protogeometric.

THE IONIAN ISLANDS: ACHAEA

In the Ionian Islands and Achaea alike we have the phenomenon of a sudden access of evidence, presumably the result of immigration, in the Mycenaean III C period. Elsewhere we have inferred that the communities in question, in both areas, lived on until a point well within the lifetime of Attic Protogeometric when a local Protogeometric style, most strongly characterized in Ithaka, eventually developed. What does the evidence of their metal products show? The 'dormitory-graves' of Kephallenia present a fairly uniform picture of Mycenaean survival, in this field as in

their pottery. They contained no iron; the fibulae – of which at least six
are known, together with an example from Zakynthos and another from
Ithaka, to be mentioned presently – are exclusively of the violin-bow type,
which had begun to be replaced by the arched variety by about 1100 BC.
The pins, found only in the Diakata cemetery, are also of early types:
one of them is a roll-pin, two others belong to the commonest twelfth-
century forms (types (5), (1) and (2) respectively on p. 226). Among
other metallic objects were a group of bronze rivets and plate-fragments,
some decorated in repoussé technique, which may be traces of a piece of
body-armour and recall larger bronze strips found at Kallithea in Achaea,
also in a III C context. Lakkithra produced rosettes and other small objects
of gold; two bronze short swords from Diakata and one from Lakkithra
were of the commonest locally-developed Aegean type of the twelfth
and eleventh centuries; two spearheads from Diakata and two from
Metaxata were also of bronze, but the form of the latter two, and the discovery of amber beads in quantity both at Metaxata and at Lakkithra,
suggest that their presence may be the result of Kephallenia's connections
north-westwards up the Adriatic. The fact that no succeeding Protogeometric period is traceable in Kephallenia, however, means that we lack
even an approximate indication of how long these metal types remained in
use. But from the case of neighbouring Ithaka we can infer that a basically
Mycenaean class of pottery was retained hereabouts for a long time.
In the 'Cairns' area at Aetos, a sanctuary rather than a funerary site, the
metal finds included one and probably more bronze fibulae of the violin-
bow shape with twisted wire, a bronze pin which is a peculiar variant of
the early form with disc and globe (type (1)), and no other fibulae or
pins of pre-Geometric type. It is of course possible that these finds are
contemporary with the earliest years of the settlement here, which were
perhaps in the eleventh century, but there is nothing to show that they did
not belong with the later pottery which extends down through and beyond
the lifetime of the local Protogeometric school of Ithaka.[31]

Achaea, as we have seen, is a region whose pottery-sequence not only
echoes the pattern of the Ionian Islands but shows positive links with it at
more than one point. Here, however, there are better grounds for believing
that the local Mycenaean III C phase overlapped substantially with Attic
Protogeometric. It would therefore be illuminating to study the metallic
finds from this time, but unfortunately only a selection has so far been
published. Leaving aside the contents of two rich but relatively early tombs
at Kallithea, we may note that the weapons – swords, spearheads, knives –

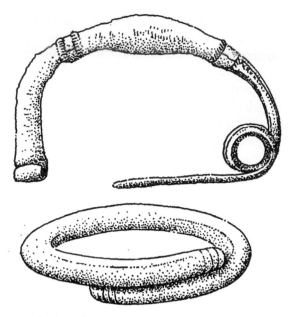

87. Bronze arched fibula (length 10 cm) and bracelet (diameter 7·9 cm), from a tomb-group now in Mainz and found in the 'northern Peloponnese'. Probably late 10th century B C.

from the Achaean graves belong, by type as by material, exclusively to later Bronze Age forms, as also do the glass and amber beads found hereabouts. Precious metals seem to be unknown, and few other personal objects have been published. One interesting object was recently found, apparently in a III c level, at the site of the Dymaean Wall: it is a dagger of the 'Peschiera' type (see below, p. 307), complete with ivory pommel and hilt-plates. Since we have evidence for the use of these Italian daggers in the Aegean at least a century before this time, the find suggests a dependence on out-of-date types. At this point, too, we may mention a tomb-group now in Mainz, recorded only as having come from the 'northern Peloponnese'. Of the four vases in the find, one is loosely related to Attic Protogeometric, and all seem to belong to a developed phase of the style; yet the accompanying small finds are all of bronze, and comprise three fibulae with swollen arch not unlike the Skyros examples (p. 241), two long pins of the modified type with mouldings, not otherwise known so late (type (4) in Fig. *81*), and two bronze bracelets which again find their best parallels in Skyros. Although we cannot be sure that the 'northern Peloponnese' can in this case be equated with Achaea, it seems certain

87

that the tomb belonged to a community that was somewhat backward in metallurgy, and once again it is possible that the bronze finds are actual heirlooms from an earlier age. It may be significant that a bronze spearhead came from an apparently Geometric burial near Chalandritsa. We may finally mention here a discovery from the ill-documented area of Messenia: at Malthi, in company with very late Mycenaean pottery, there occurred an iron dagger and knife, with other fragments. It is impossible to know whether to treat this as an early instance of iron-working or as another late survival of Bronze Age pottery-types, but in either case there is a hint that Messenia did not conform to the pattern of the surrounding regions.[32]

OTHER AREAS

There are other areas where association with Protogeometric pottery may indicate a date either in the later tenth century or later still. Nevertheless, it is worth looking briefly at finds from these regions to see whether they differ from the pattern that has emerged of metal-working in the rest of Greece. With the detectable resurgence of bronze in many regions after about 950 BC, we should expect to find this metal in the ascendant in the 'Protogeometric' periods of these other localities, at least in the field of personal objects. Thus the newly-discovered traces of a bronze-foundry at Lefkandi in Euboea are associated with pottery of the local Protogeo- *101* metric style: but other evidence shows this stage to be contemporary only with a late stage of the Attic style, belonging perhaps not much before 900 BC. Thus, too, the finds from the Kardiani cemetery on Tenos in the northern Cyclades include a bronze fibula of developed type with swollen arch, two bronze pins whose square cross-section proclaims their affinity to new, Geometric bronze types, and two curved iron knives. For Laconia, we have concluded that the Protogeometric style was late in developing; but the metal finds associated with this phase include some strikingly primitive objects. At the sanctuary of Amyklai, the stratum characterized by the local Protogeometric produced two bronze spearheads whose form *88* suggests that they are not the mark of a revived skill in bronze-working: one is small and was cast flat, a very crude socket being formed by beating the lower part of the blade into a tube; the other has a disproportionately wide blade of a kind not found in later spearheads. So too on the site of the Artemis Orthis sanctuary, which has some slight traces of use before the end of this same phase, but virtually nothing of earlier date, there were found fibulae of a violin-bow type (Blinkenberg's type I.2, one of the very earliest). It should be stressed that these objects occurred with others of much more developed type: at Amyklai there were traces of iron weapons,

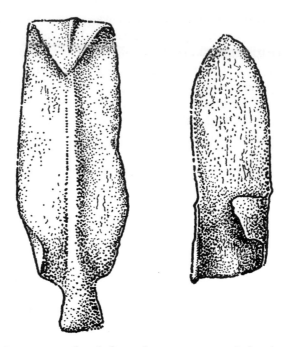

88. Two bronze spearheads from the Protogeometric level at Amyklai in Laconia. Lengths unknown; perhaps about 800 B C.

including a sword, in the Protogeometric levels, and the Orthia sanctuary had innumerable finds characteristic of the Geometric and later periods; while an iron weapon was found at Mavrovouni in association with two fragmentary Protogeometric vases, probably of a late stage. But the fact remains that the bronzes noted from Amyklai and Sparta would have looked very old-fashioned even at the earliest possible date suggested by their associations; and this again suggests such a period of restricted and somewhat primitive metallurgy, with partial dependence on Bronze Age heirlooms, as we have inferred elsewhere. The same conclusion may apply to Samos, an island of whose early Iron Age occupation we know little, but which has produced a bronze *Griffzungenschwert* from a context that is apparently Geometric.[33]

CONCLUSIONS: ISOLATION AND STAGNATION

Can any hypothesis be found to account for the character of the material from all the regions we have discussed so far? I would suggest that it could be explained by a breakdown in communications which left the various regions frozen, so to speak, at the point in metallurgical progress which they had attained at its outset. In some parts of the Aegean world – Attica above all, but also the Argolid, Thessaly and south-western Asia Minor – a partial mastery of iron-working in the eleventh century enabled the population to support itself by an iron-based economy using internal resources, extending the use of iron in the subsequent period of isolation to classes of object which were not well suited to the material. Further, a movement of settlers from one or more of these regions to Kos may have brought the Dodecanese into this cultural enclave during the same period. Other areas – Elis, Phokis, Skyros, Kephallenia, Ithaka, Achaea – seem not to have progressed so far. Where iron weapons were produced, as on Skyros and distinctly later in Laconia, these appear after a perceptible lapse of time by comparison with the more advanced areas. The personal objects from all these areas, on the other hand, are not only exclusively of bronze, but in many cases seem to resemble closely the products of the last centuries of the Bronze Age; sometimes they are definitely heirlooms, but more often we cannot distinguish between long retention and slavish reproduction. Because of the apparently greater communicability of pottery techniques, the pottery finds in some of these localities belie the early date suggested by the associated metal finds: we have found this occurring at Ancient Elis, Delphi, on Skyros and in the group in Mainz from the 'northern Peloponnese'. Other regions again – Kephallenia, and for a time Achaea – show in both pottery and metal types the same characteristics of Bronze Age survival.

The most questionable element in this theory is perhaps the supposed period of isolation, which we may set between the extreme outer limits of 1025 and 950 BC. It is therefore worth adducing some other evidence which may be thought to support a belief in this. Already we have encountered objects of gold, whose occurrence at this time is likely to imply either foreign trade-connections, or more rarely the retention or re-working of precious keepsakes from the Bronze Age. These finds are conspicuously lacking in the 'blank period' that we have posited. Objects of precious metal, although invariably very small, are by no means unknown in the latest Mycenaean III C contexts, nor yet in the Submycenaean graves of western Attica, where glass beads and iron also occasionally appear. Gold hair-rings are still found in three of the earlier Protogeometric graves of the Kerameikos (22, 25 and 5); but thereafter precious materials disappear from that cemetery until Geometric times. A brief examination of such finds from other dated contexts at this time shows that they too fall, without any known exception, either in Submycenaean to early

Protogeometric times (as on Salamis and in tomb B at Assarlik), or at a
stage roughly contemporary with, or later than, the latest Attic Protogeometric (as in Athens, Agora grave xxvi; Tiryns, graves of the old
excavations and vii and xv of Verdelis' cemetery; Corinth, grave C;
Marmariani, tomb 2; Skyros and Kos (see pp. 241-2)). At the same time
it is now clear, from the evidence of two sites, Argos and Thorikos, that
the extraction of silver from lead by a process of cupellation was actually
being undertaken in Greece in Protogeometric times; whether or not this
represents a response to the conditions of isolation from foreign sources,
it is most striking that some of the earliest traces of this process should
belong to this period. Ivory, a material incontestably foreign to Greece,
makes it first re-appearance in post-Mycenaean graves in the late tenth
century BC. The faience and bone necklace from Verdelis' grave xxiii
at Tiryns is of mysterious date: the excavator suggested 'Submycenaean
to Protogeometric' on internal evidence, but the other finds from the
grave belong to Early Geometric, and it may be that we have another
heirloom here; or even a fresh import, since the only parallel find is that
from a rich new Athenian grave of just this period. Then there is amber, a
commodity pointing to connections in a different direction, that is northwards; in this case again, finds of eleventh-century date are not uncommon,
especially along the western coast of Greece, but thereafter there seems to
be a pronounced gap: so far as I know a single find only, that in tomb 1 at
Kardiani on Tenos, is likely to belong even to the ninth century, and only
in the eighth does amber become at all common in Greece again. Faience,
also present in the eleventh century, makes its first re-appearance in contexts rather before 900, chiefly in Crete.[34] Finally, we may briefly glance
at the signs of contact with Cyprus, an island whose production of copper
makes it especially relevant to any question of a break in the trade in metal
ores. We have found that, for a period around 1050 BC, the evidence of
both pottery and early ironwork speaks for a trade-connection between
Cyprus and Greece. But there is no precisely dated evidence of contact
thereafter, with the possible exception of Crete (see below, pp. 251-3 and
331), until a stage contemporary with the end of Attic Protogeometric,
when the Greek mainland resumes the exchange of actual imports with
Cyprus. As an illustration of a device that apparently passed from west to
east, the development of the fibula in Cyprus is informative. As was
noticed by Blinkenberg, but has now been demonstrated in detail by Catling, the Cypriot fibulae develop in close conformity to those of the Aegean
in the earlier stages, down to the emergence of the symmetrical arched

fibula; but then, from rather before 1000 BC, the Cypriot development diverges and on the whole stagnates, ignoring the later changes of form in the Protogeometric and Geometric Aegean, and taking a lead rather from the neighbouring mainland of Asia.[35] This external evidence at least does nothing to controvert the notion of a period of isolation in the Aegean between the late eleventh and the mid-tenth centuries BC.

CRETE, MACEDONIA AND EPIRUS

CRETE

We have still to deal, however, with three areas which in metallurgy as in much else claim special treatment. In Crete, we have found that the Subminoan class of pottery probably prevailed throughout the island between about 1100 and 925, and persisted for considerably longer in the eastern part. The picture of metal-working in this period is unexpectedly rich and varied. There is first of all the settlement- and grave-material from Karphi, but this site is shown by its pottery to have been curiously aloof from many contemporary developments in the island, and it is not surprising to find that the metal objects are almost invariably of bronze, and in most cases belong to types which had become widespread in the Aegean area before about 1050 BC, by which time Karphi was already founded. The bronze fibulae include four of the violin-bow shape, seven of the plain symmetrical arched, and one symmetrical arched with twisted wire – all early varieties; some of the pins, as already noted (p. 226, type (4)), are of a predominantly eleventh-century form, others are of the even older roll-topped type, others again are entirely plain; the finger-rings and spiral rings are of bronze, but they include an example of the 'shield-ring' which is of Submycenaean and later date elsewhere. Also of bronze are the numerous weapons, which include a sword and arrowheads of types which had reached the Aegean in Mycenaean III C. The bronze tools have some rarity value at this period: they include nails, rivets, awls, chisels, saws, sickles, tweezers, a razor and a 'trunnion-axe', many of them in fine condition. Coming as they do from a comparatively well-dated settlement, they would constitute the most precious evidence, but for the fact that Karphi was such an isolated site: we are denied any illustration of the transition to iron in this class of material, or any indication as to when it happened. As it is, the bronze tools from Karphi almost all belong to well-characterized Late Bronze Age types, many of them known from the founders' hoards of the preceding period in the Aegean. A fragment of a bronze pendant has been shown by Catling to have belonged to a

Cypriot type of stand, and there is also a clay imitation of another form of stand, both suggesting a link, past or present, with Cyprus. The Karphi material also included an iron arched fibula, part of an iron knife-blade and other small fragments of this metal.[36] Though representing only a tiny proportion of the metal objects, these finds prepare us for the fact that Subminoan Crete, as represented by sites other than Karphi, was well acquainted with iron.

The evidence is now mainly from tombs: Vrokastro, Kavousi and Gortyn all provide settlement material, but in the former case especially it was difficult to distinguish the Subminoan period of occupation from the later Geometric. But from these sites, and from the burials at Knossos, Phaistos and Kourtes in the central part of the island, and at Vrokastro, Kavousi and Mouliana (if the earlier cremation-material from tomb A can be attributed to this period) in eastern Crete, there are numerous weapons and personal objects which tell a fairly consistent story. The weapons – several spearheads, a finely-preserved sword from Kavousi and several fragmentary ones, and a few knives – are without exception of iron. In chamber-tomb I at Vrokastro were also found an axe, adze and chisel of iron, but unfortunately this tomb probably remained in use deep into the Geometric period, so that indications of date are uncertain; chamber-tomb 3, by contrast, held a piece of a bronze saw, recalling Karphi (p. 249). The even commoner personal objects, on the other hand, are almost exclusively of bronze. The pins are mostly of the two commonest eleventh-century types, (1) and (2); a group from Vrokastro tomb 3 with a biconical swelling was associated by Jacobsthal with later, Geometric burials, but finds from central Crete (below, p. 252) have since shown that this shape had developed there by quite early on in the Protogeometric period. There were traces of an iron pin in the Subminoan tomb *II* at Fortetsa. The fibulae include violin-bow specimens from Gortyn, Kavousi and Vrokastro (there is indeed a Protogeometric example in Crete, from Phaistos), but the great majority are of arched types. Within this category, however, Subminoan Crete offers a remarkable variety, embracing eleven of the fourteen arched types distinguished by Blinkenberg, and known to belong to this early period: in some cases (his types II 4, 9, 12) the examples from these sites are probably the earliest known. This is not the pattern we have found in the metallurgically backward regions; and there is further evidence that Crete was both advanced and independent. Gold 'shield-rings' are found in Vrokastro tomb I and Mouliana tomb A, at a date when precious metals may not be represented on the mainland (p. 247). From the latter grave comes an admirable bronze jug, to whose quality Müller-Karpe has recently drawn attention; while the Vrokastro tombs produced sundry smaller bronze finds, together with a rod-tripod from tomb I, the first that we have so far encountered from Crete but not necessarily the first in date (below). This and its counterparts conform so closely to Cypriot Late Bronze Age products that they were almost certainly made in Cyprus, and very probably at a much earlier date. Their appearance in Crete is therefore doubly interesting: if they had become, in Catling's words, 'highly prized antiques', it seems on the whole less likely that they had been exported from Cyprus as such, than that they had been preserved in Crete after making the journey at an earlier time – perhaps by about 1200, when at least one such tripod formed part of the cargo of the westbound ship wrecked off Cape Gelidonya.[37] It may be significant that no such object has been found in a mainland grave of earlier than the eighth century: the Vrokastro find supports a belief in the comparative prosperity of Subminoan Crete, if not necessarily in its current foreign contacts. The almost exclusive use of iron for practical purposes, like the rarer incidence of cremation in this era (pp. 165, 168), shows that Crete did not have to wait on the arrival of Protogeometric influences from Attica and the mainland in order to avail herself of new ideas; more probably, iron will have come to Subminoan Crete direct from Cyprus. But at the same time the competent employment of bronze for a variety of other products is at variance with anything that we have from the mainland in the later eleventh and tenth centuries. It suggests that Crete had retained a lifeline to an adequate source of copper and tin, and that source again can only have been Cyprus.

When following the development of Cretan metalwork into the period of the Protogeometric style, we have to remember that this period is scarcely a real entity in the eastern end of the island. The earlier Proto-geometric grave material from the central region – from Fortetsa, Agios Ioannis and Tekke in the Knossos area, and from the cremations at Phaistos and Tylissos – will belong somewhere in the region of 900 B C. Here again, we find weapons almost exclusively of iron, by now including a peculiar type of pike- or spearhead whose home is certainly in Cyprus; a further rod-tripod, of the same type as that from Vrokastro, also appeared at Fortetsa. Some all-iron pins occur at this time, in three graves at Agios Ioannis and one at Fortetsa (XI – cf. the earlier grave *II*, p. 250). The fibulae from Cretan Protogeometric graves wear an altogether more primitive and less varied appearance than those from the Subminoan graves

89

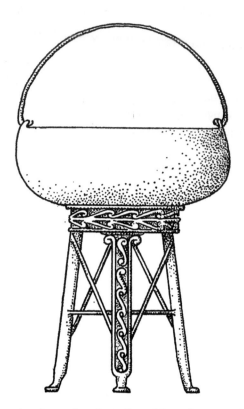

89. Bronze tripod-stand and small cauldron from tomb xi at Fortetsa. Height 17 + 7 cm, without handle.

in the east of the island which must be in part contemporary: those from Fortetsa (though not the probably later ones from Tylissos) are nearly all of the simpler arched symmetrical forms, and from the Mulino cremations at Phaistos comes the violin-bow specimen already noted. But the iron pins do show one innovation which may have been passed on to eastern Crete, and which finds successors but no plausible ancestry outside the island: this is the adoption of a biconical swelling in place of the old globular one, near the head of the pin: two examples occurred in Agios Ioannis tomb 5, a gilt one in the rather later tomb 5 at Tekke, and it is possible that some gold and bronze ones from Fortetsa are related.[38] Then in the brief 'Protogeometric B' phase at Knossos we see further new features: fibulae of an ornate type with three globes on the arch (Blinkenberg's type III. 10), of which the other known examples seem to be Geometric or later, and a delicate bronze pin with biconical moulding and flanking ridges, also known from later contexts (especially in Crete) but nowhere demonstrably as early as this. These finds do something to reinforce our belief in the relatively late dating of the 'Protogeometric B' phase (p. 129). The iron weapons from ninth-century Crete include some bizarre types, showing little contact with contemporary developments in the Aegean: in the case of one further type of spearhead (in addition to the pikes mentioned on p. 251), a link with the Near East can certainly be established, and I should not be surprised if the other weapon-types eventually prove to derive from the same source. Cretan swords are shorter and slighter than their mainland contemporaries; many of them show a tendency to taper evenly to a point, which suggests that they were used mainly for the thrust, and which again is most easily matched in Cyprus. Cretan spearheads are normally long and slim, and often occur in graves in matching pairs: a usage which is usually taken to indicate the use of the throwing-javelin in life, and which is not precisely matched in mainland graves before the eighth century.[39]

MACEDONIA

The case of Macedonia resembles Crete mainly in the fact that the Protogeometric material from there is again, if we are correct in our view of it (pp. 132-3), relatively late in relation to that of the more advanced schools. The finds from the Vergina cemetery are so prolific that, although only a selection has yet been fully published, their character is already quite clear. Elsewhere, only a few scattered finds – a violin-bow fibula from Vardino and several bronzes from graves near Kozani – call for consideration at this point: the comparable material from Boubousti, Chauchitza, Pateli and Bohemitza can hardly begin before the eighth century. The early Iron Age period of use of the Vergina cemetery must have lasted, on any view, for three centuries at the very least. Yet over this period it shows a quite astonishing consistency in metalwork. The weapons so far mentioned in the publications illustrate this for the male graves: they include about twenty swords, nearly all of the *Griffzungenschwert* type now prevalent further south in Greece, and all but one of iron; some forty-odd spearheads and at least one spear-butt (*saurotêr*), all of iron; several arrowheads and at least fifty daggers and knives, also all of iron. But these finds are excelled in quantity, and equalled in consistency, by the personal objects from the women's graves, many of which were more richly endowed than those of *61* their menfolk. The contrast with the meagre offerings of the early Iron Age graves of Greece is amazing: burial after burial yielded whole outfits of bronze jewellery and ornaments – hair-rings (often also of gold) and long spiral tubes which hung from the temples; bead-necklaces, frequently of amber; fibulae or, rarely, pins for the dress; small bronze discs with occasional larger bosses, attached to the belt; finger-rings, bracelets (sometimes in spiral form) and anklets; rarer adornments such as diadems, thin plates in the shape of triple double-axes, and a headdress or veil covered with bronze *tutuli*. The finds from the male and from the female graves indeed show a marked dichotomy: for whereas the small bronze finds in the latter uniformly indicate a source in the Balkan region or even further north (as do the very similar objects in grave XXIII at Kozani), the virtually exclusive use of iron for the weapons cannot possibly be attributed to such a source. As I have argued in detail elsewhere, on the basis of a catalogue of early iron finds in barbarian Europe assembled by Professor W. Kimmig, it is clear that down to about 700 BC iron was only fractionally in use in this region as an industrial metal.[40] Unless the Vergina cemetery were to be dated wholly in the seventh century and later, which few would venture to suggest in the face of the evidence of the pottery, it would be in a literal sense preposterous to trace its iron industry to a northern source.

There are also great difficulties in deriving the iron of Vergina from the iron-using regions of Greece. It is true that the iron *Griffzungenschwerter* seem to be fairly closely assimilated to their counterparts further south, although they are bigger and stouter than most Protogeometric Greek examples; while the spearheads too show some conformity to Greek Iron Age types, and the knives (at least those of the variety with a curved blade) find parallels further south too. But if these weapons are modelled on contemporary Greek products, or even imported, then one is at once led to ask why there are not more widespread signs of Greek connections. In fact, there is only the pottery of Protogeometric style, which composed a small fraction of the ceramic evidence at Vergina (perhaps not more than 5 per cent), and possibly the comparably rare arched fibula (below, p. 256); whereas the iron weapons are evidently standard equipment for all the male graves. Furthermore, one of the rare uncanonical weapons points to connections northwards, that is in the opposite direction: an iron sword with bronze hilt, found in tomb LXVIII z, seems from the published sketch to belong to a different class of weapon, the *Vollgriff-schwert*, extremely rare as far south as this, and unusual anywhere with this combination of metals. Kimmig has listed some dozen examples of different varieties of *Vollgriffschwert* with iron blade, distributed over an area from

Sweden to Bulgaria, and they are datable exclusively to the Hallstatt B$_3$ phase of the Urnfield period, roughly to be equated with the eighth century BC. (They include an example of another variant, the *Antennenschwert*, found at nearby Chauchitza where the other finds do not seem to antedate the eighth century.) This weapon therefore provides both a geographical and a chronological pointer. There is also a single all-bronze *Griffzungenschwert* from Vergina tomb c *Δ*; this belongs near group 1 of H. W. Catling's typology; in both Central Europe and Greece it is prevalent by about 1200 BC, and in neither area is it known to occur after the twelfth century. The Vergina example, at 72 cm long, is unusually large for the type; I should not like to guess from its appearance whether it is likelier to be a survivor of the European early Urnfield period or of the Aegean Late Bronze Age; but survivor it must be, for the cemetery can hardly extend back so far as this date, and indeed grave c *Δ* is located to one side of tumulus c, while the central burial c *B*, a somewhat larger boulder-cist, contained the remains of an iron sword.[41] Two or three other bronze *Griffzungenschwerter* have occurred in the Aegean in Geometric contexts (see above, pp. 241, 246), and these too are best regarded as heirlooms.

If the iron of Vergina is too early to be derivable from further north, and yet lacks the associations to be expected in the case of a Greek origin, then we are forced to look for other hypotheses. Ultimately it could be the result of intercourse with Asia Minor, for which there is possibly some evidence in the matt-painted pottery found in earlier contexts at Vardaroftsa and elsewhere; or else it could be the product of a purely native industry. In support of the latter hypothesis, there is some positive evidence that iron-smelting was at least being attempted in Macedonia at an early date. Iron slags were found at Vardaroftsa in both the pre-destruction period associated with pottery of Mycenaean III c type (p. 133: settlement 10, 21st half-metre), and at a distinctly later date (settlement 20, 4th half-metre). The earlier slag alone is of relevant date: it should belong to the twelfth century or earlier. With its remarkably low metal content, it showed that iron had been extracted by fusion at a very high temperature, a method suited to the production of copper but virtually useless for that of workable iron; it is perhaps the product of an accidental or misunderstood process, but at this early date one would not expect much more than tentative experimentation; with a supply of local iron ore readily available (see p. 231), such steps as this may have led to effective iron-production in Macedonia in the succeeding centuries.[42]

At the same time, the bronzes from the female graves show us that there was an alternative source of this metal available to Macedonia, besides the eastern Mediterranean. For almost every class of bronze object at Vergina, parallels can be given from further north in the Balkan peninsula; taken together, they must indicate prolonged contact with, or more probably immigration from, some such region. It may be that the population of early Iron Age Pieria, the district in which Vergina lies, was Thracian rather than Macedonian in character, in which case these links might be explained. One of the most remarkable features of the Vergina bronzes is the prevalence of the spectacle-fibula: about 150 examples have already been reported from the cemetery. In Aegean terms, the spectacle-fibula is a relatively late form, apparently unconnected with the earlier developments in this class of object: we have not yet encountered an example in the period and geographical area covered hitherto, save for those at Marmariani (p. 236), a site near the borders of Macedonia where other signs of Macedonian influence are present. The predominance of this type at Vergina can only indicate a Balkan origin, and incidentally provides further evidence against a very high dating of the cemetery, for its development in the Danubian region is hardly earlier than Hallstatt B_1 – that is roughly the tenth century – in date. However, a few arched fibulae also appeared at Vergina: two in grave cA, a burial which is in a parallel situation to that of c$\varDelta$, in that they flanked the central burial (*B*) in tumulus c; others were of the symmetrical type with twisted wire, and of the symmetrical and asymmetrical types with swollen arch and collars. Their presence here may, in part at least, result from contacts with Greece: the ascription of the arched fibula to a generally 'northern' source overlooks the fact that it was a type more characteristic of Italy than of the Balkans, where its first appearances are almost certainly due to Italian contacts. Some communication between Italy and Greece is attested for the Mycenaean III c period, and the arched fibula could have been transmitted to Greece then. But it would also be possible to conclude that the arched type developed independently in the two areas; it represents a natural enough expedient, improving the functional efficiency of the 'violin-bow' type by allowing a thicker fold of material to be gripped. Further, in its details of decoration the arched type follows somewhat different lines in Greece and in Italy. The arched fibulae of Vergina do not necessarily involve raising the initial date of the cemetery: if our explanation of their appearance here is right, we may compare the incidence of these same varieties of arched fibula in ninth century and later contexts, in other parts of the

Aegean world – as at Fortetsa (p. 252) and Vrokastro. Indeed, one of the Vergina types (Blinkenberg's 11.10) occurs also in the nearby cemetery of Pateli, which probably contained nothing earlier than Geometric. Even rarer in the graves were apparently the long bronze pins; details of their typology are not yet available, but they may be susceptible of the same explanation as the arched fibulae.[43]

When the pottery and metal finds from Vergina are taken together, the picture emerges of a flourishing community, whose contacts both northern and southern cannot entirely account for its advanced and prosperous air. The northern influence is certainly the stronger; but once its presence is accepted, the most remarkable fact is seen to be the failure of this vigorous element to penetrate to the rest of Greece at this period. The metal objects at Marmariani – which themselves must extend down to the mid-ninth century or later – are the southernmost sign of any such population movement, and they were found in communal tombs of undoubted Mycenaean origin. The often-cited evidence from sanctuary-sites further south in Greece is of a quite different quality, to say nothing of the chronological uncertainties (see below, pp. 275-81).

EPIRUS

One remaining region which must be briefly treated is Epirus, where the almost total absence of Greek painted pottery of the early Iron Age leaves us on even weaker ground chronologically than in Macedonia. That Epirus too had strong links with the Balkan region to the north (and especially with Illyria) at this period, has been demonstrated beyond doubt, largely by reference to the bronze finds. But the existence of any early iron-working industry, such as grew up on the other side of the Pindus, is harder to prove in this case. Since the region to the north of Epirus remained in the Bronze Age throughout the relevant period, such an industry could only have developed either through native resources, or by contact with the iron-using cultures to the east and south – Macedonia, Greece, even perhaps Anatolia. But the first alternative is rendered most unlikely, if not quite excluded, by the fact that there is no apparent trace of ancient iron-workings in Epirus. By far the fullest, as well as the most recent, study of the relevant material is that of Hammond; but in considering his account we have already come up against the fundamental difficulty of chronology (p. 173). To establish even an approximate dating for the Epirot iron finds, the best prospect is to look for a context which combines stratigraphic evidence with clearly-characterized types. These conditions seem best satisfied by the sequence of burials in the great

R

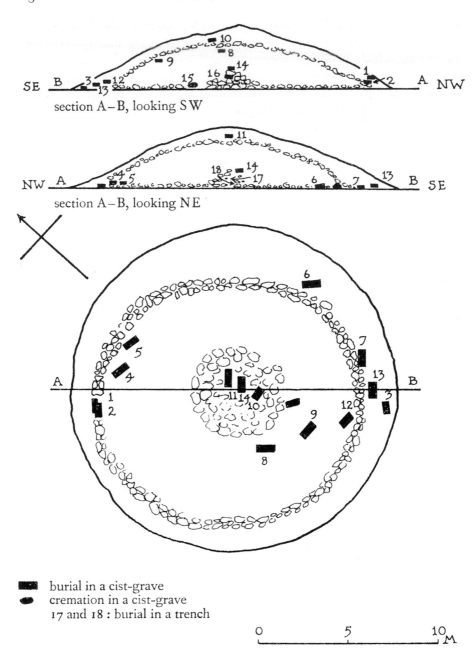

section A–B, looking SW

section A–B, looking NE

▰ burial in a cist-grave
◗ cremation in a cist-grave
17 and 18 : burial in a trench

0   5   10 M

90. Cross-sections and plan of the tumulus at Vodhinë in Epirus; 11th
to 9th centuries BC.

tumulus of Vodhinë. There is little doubt here about the sequence of interments: the two simple pit-inhumations in the body of the central cairn,
18 and 17, came first; of these 18 contained no grave-goods, but 17 held a
bronze spearhead of 'fiddle' shape (with strongly incurved edges). Next
came 15 and 16, which produced several pots which have parallels in Middle
Helladic Thessaly, and a bronze dagger of a type known in Middle Minoan
Crete. To the third phase belong probably graves 14, 4, 5, 8 and 9, of which
14 contained a bronze *Griffzungenschwert* of group I in Catling's classification. The nine remaining graves are allocated to the final phase, and
among them grave 12 produced a bronze spectacle-fibula and a pin with
roughly hemispherical head, and grave 1 a bronze ring; 2, 3 and 12 also
produced pots of classes which can be closely matched at Boubousti in
Macedonia, a site which in turn was occupied for a period extending from
Mycenaean III c to Geometric times and later.[44]

At first sight Hammond's dating of the tumulus, with its four stages,
between approximately the sixteenth and the eleventh centuries BC seems
a natural one. But there are two objects among the metal finds whose
origin lies to the north, and whose chronological context there is clear
enough to undermine this scheme. The spearhead from the first phase is
'fiddle-shaped' or ogival: there is no chronological distinction within this
basically unitary class such as Hammond would make, except that if anything it is the *less* strongly ogival-shaped blade which seems to appear
earliest. The type as a whole is perhaps just detectable in Central Europe
before the end of phase D in Reinecke's scheme – that is by about 1200 BC
– but its widest currency extends through much of the ensuing Urnfield
period. It is barely conceivable that it could have reached a grave in inland
Epirus before the twelfth century. The spectacle-fibula of the final phase
at Vodhinë appears to belong to type 1b in the recent classification of J.
Alexander; as such it is of the earliest variety, but its development still lies
with the Hallstatt B period, roughly the tenth to eighth centuries. The
excavator of the Vodhinë tumulus, Frano Prendi, dated its burials to the
eleventh to ninth centuries; one must accept not only this conclusion,
or something like it, but also its implications, which are wide. The appearance of characteristic Aegean Middle Bronze Age types in Epirot contexts,
contemporary with and even later than that of a twelfth-century spearhead,
must entail a time-lag of at least three hundred years in the survival of
these objects in Epirus. The fact that hand-made pottery 'akin to Early
Helladic III and Middle Helladic' has been shown to survive on Epirot
sites down to about 400 BC will perhaps help us to accept this fact; so, too,

will a yet more pertinent discovery in Tomb 21 at Vitsa Zagoriou, where a violin-bow fibula with flattened and decorated arch (Blinkenberg's type I 8) was found together with an imported Corinthian Late Geometric oenochoë. Also involved, if loosely, is the dating of other Epirot finds, for Prendi and Hammond are agreed that the finds from the Vajzë, Kakavi and Bodrishtë tumuli must in part overlap with the Vodhinë graves. At Vajzë, grave 12 of tumulus A produced pottery similar to the Middle Helladic types at Vodhinë, while grave 5 of tumulus C contained an object typologically later than anything at Vodhinë, a double-shank pin of a widespread class, found especially in the graves of the Glasinac plateau in Bosnia, and datable there after rather than before 600 BC. If the Vajzë burials, therefore, begin at roughly the same time as those of Vodhinë and extend later, this inference becomes significant when we note that four or five graves at Vajzë, in tumuli A (2, 8) and C (2, perhaps 3, and 5), contained iron, as well as two in the tumulus at Kakavi; while there was no iron at Vodhinë. The iron pin and knife in Vajzë A 2 were found with bronze biconical beads of a class known in, and perhaps native to, Macedonia in eighth century and later contexts; the iron sword in Vajzë A 8 was with a bronze spearhead which is probably a European type of the later Urnfield period; the iron pins in C 2 from the same site were with glass beads, which further south would be taken to be Mycenaean in character and perhaps in date – but glass beads are also common in Iron Age Bosnia; an iron spearhead seems to have been found in grave C 3 and to have lacked associated finds, but it is close to a type found further south in Greece in the eighth century and later; the double-shank pin in C 5 (above) is itself of iron, while the buckle found with it is probably a much later intruder as Hammond says. At Kakavi grave 1, an iron knife with bronze rivet (see above, p. 217) was found with a bronze *Griffzungen-schwert* of Catling's group I, and in grave 4 a pair of iron tweezers was associated with fragments of bone and bronze plaques, whose decoration suggests a link with the Urnfield cultures, but no precise dating. The first secure date for Epirot iron-working comes, once again, from Vitsa Zagoriou (see above), where an iron sword was associated with a late eighth century aryballos in tomb 9.[45]

It would seem, therefore, that the iron finds at Vajzë and Kakavi are left in chronological suspense, floating between the twelfth century BC and the sixth; certain of the associated finds (the bronze sword, but not the glass beads) tend to pull their date upwards, but others (the biconical beads, together with the typology of the spearhead and double-shank pin, and the external evidence from Vitsa) indicate a lower dating. I do not think that we are in a position to decide on their precise chronology, but it seems clear that Hammond's case for a very early, perhaps twelfth century, use of iron in Epirus, being partially based on an erroneous belief in a contemporary iron industry further north in the Balkans, cannot stand. Considering the greater proximity of Macedonia, the presence of traits in burial-practice, pottery and metalwork which link the Epirot tumuli with the Vergina cemetery, and the relative lack of features in common with Iron Age Greece, I would tentatively conclude that the early iron finds of Epirus are of Macedonian rather than Greek origin; which, incidentally, will on almost any view involve their dating to the tenth century and later.

THE EARLIER GEOMETRIC PERIOD

With the advance of iron-working, as with other new features of the dark age in Greece, the early stages are the most significant. The development of metalwork in the Geometric period may therefore be treated more briefly: it is the effect, as we shall see, less of further technical advances than of greater material resources. The relative dating of developments, in the still quite clearly distinguished regions of Greece, remains of prime importance: it is not enough to generalize about 'Geometric metalwork', any more than in the fields of pottery or sculpture. We must therefore begin with those regions which provide the most closely dated evidence, in the form of tomb-groups: and this once again means Attica and the Argolid, with central Crete still in a separate category. As time goes on, there begins to be some settlement-evidence too, from these and other areas; but at first it represents a negligible proportion of the total material, and in few cases is there any degree of precision in the dating of it. Much more copious is the evidence of the sanctuary-sites, in metalwork particularly; this calls for a separate discussion (pp. 275-85).

ATTICA

For the grave-series of the Athenian Kerameikos, I continue to accept the groupings and dates put forward by R. Hachmann (cf. pp. 52, 112). The dozen graves belonging to his earliest Geometric group present an almost entirely new picture: grave 7 produced one of the last survivals of a common Protogeometric feature, the pair of standard iron-and-bronze pins, but against this, six burials produced bronze hemispherical bowls, each inserted in the mouth of the cremation-urn to serve as a lid; these bowls have a single predecessor in the cemetery, that from the very late Protogeometric grave 48 (p. 232). Gold finger-rings reappear (as they

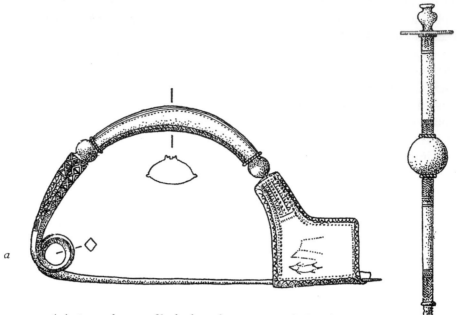

91. (*a*) Large bronze fibula, length 14·5 cm, and (*b*) gilt iron pin, length complete 31·2 cm, from Geometric grave 41 at the Kerameikos, Athens; *c.*850 BC.

do in the rich new Agora grave of this period, and in the roughly contemporary Agora grave XXVI) after an absence of probably well over a
91   hundred years (p. 247); a pair of iron pins in grave 41 were plated with gold, and their form, with a little barrel-shaped knob *above* the previous terminal disc, foreshadows Geometric fashion; and this grave also produced a small plaque probably made of ivory. Of new types, the most significant is the large bronze fibula with massive arch and catch-plate, both often decorated by engraving. A whole array of such fibulae, in two
91   different varieties, appeared in this same grave 41, which Kübler dated soon after 850, and Hachmann places even earlier; part of the interest of this lies in the fact that some had dated such fibulae exclusively to the later eighth century; they are common in Boeotia, somewhat less so in Attica, and an origin in the former region had also been widely accepted. Now, however, the type appears much more likely to have been developed in Attica, and furthermore it would seem to have been confined to Attica
57   for the first century of its life. Further additions appear in the even richer grave found in the Agora in 1967, not only in the field of imports (below,

p. 333), but also in a new and not entirely recognizable type of bronze fibula, and in three all-bronze pins of developed Geometric stage; furthermore, certain details of the fibulae suggest a comparable dating, in the mid-ninth century, for two fine gold fibulae from an Attic grave now in Berlin. The weapons and tools of Athens at this time remain almost exclusively of iron; sword and spearhead may now be found in the same interment, knives with curved blades are still common, but the dagger (as in much of the Protogeometric period) remains virtually unknown in Attica. A single arrowhead has recently been found.[46]

79b

In time, a new factor arises to alter the pattern of Attica, with the progressive decline and impoverishment of the Kerameikos cemetery relative to other Attic sites (p. 150). But the Middle Geometric graves here show a continuance of the features noted: bronze or iron pins and bronze bowls are still present, and the latter class acquires an important addition towards the end of the ninth century, with the Syrian bowl with repoussé decoration in grave 42, whose chronological significance we noted earlier. A much larger type of bronze vessel, the cauldron, makes its appearance (together with a leaden lid) a little later (grave 71); while the bronze bracelet, last seen here in the Submycenaean graves, re-emerges later still. The thin bands of gold foil, decorated by hammering into stone matrices, are a new phenomenon of this same era; at first their decoration is non-representational, consisting of zig-zags or tongue-patterns. Grave 13 contained four iron objects of a somewhat mysterious nature: rings of about 4 inches in diameter, pierced by massive, inward-pointing nails. Müller-Karpe has now shown that these must be for the binding of wheel-naves; they therefore provide our earliest direct evidence for a vehicle of which we see much in later years, the four-wheeled funerary wagon. By now weapons are already becoming rare at the Kerameikos, and during the eighth century, apart from a few knives, they are to die out altogether. The reverse aspect of the decline of the cemetery is the appearance of impressive graves, not only elsewhere in Athens but on other sites in Attica. The rich 'Isis grave' at Eleusis seems to have contained nothing of a date later than 750, and some of its vases are certainly earlier; with them could possibly go some of the small finds, which included not only scarabs and the idol which gave the grave its name, but also further examples of the 'Attico-Boeotian' fibulae (p. 262), a bronze bowl and bracelets, and objects of gold, silver and amber. A group of finds now in Toronto, recorded as having come from an Attic grave, may in fact be heterogeneous in date, but its metal finds – a further 'Attico-Boeotian' fibula and two fine bronze

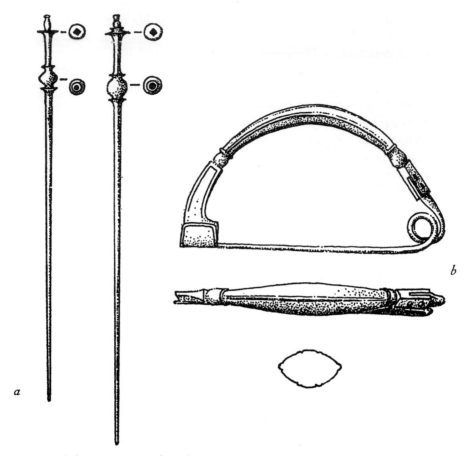

92. (*a*) Bronze pins, lengths 15 and 16·8 cm, and (*b*) bronze arched fibula, length 11·5 cm, from grave G 603 at Mycenae; *c.*875 BC.

pins – could accord with the ninth-century date suggested by some of the pottery.[47]

THE ARGOLID AND CORINTH

Only the sites of the Argolid and Corinth provide a comparable body of evidence from this period and from this part of Greece; but the comparison proves fruitful. There are many differences: the Argive graves contain a few substantial objects of beaten bronze-work, while fibulae remain, as before, rare in this region. But in other respects the graves excel their Attic counterparts: gold, silver and ivory are already known, at least at Corinth, in the earlier ninth century, and a grave at Tiryns (XXIII of Verdelis' excavations) has produced a bead of faience. The pins from

92a

93. Three iron spearheads from a single grave (x x i i i) at Tiryns.
Lengths 31, 26, and 24·5 cm; probably earlier 9th century B C.

Mycenae and Tiryns, which are mostly of bronze with a biconical swelling,
particularly catch the eye: iron biconical pins in Protogeometric Crete
may be earlier in date (p. 252), but these are altogether superior productions
with quite elaborate mouldings; two pins at Tiryns are of iron, with ivory
heads. A solitary fibula from grave G 603 at Mycenae is also of exceptional
quality; while fine bronze pins came from a Corinthian grave of the later
ninth century. Then at a slightly later stage – perhaps around 800 – a more
developed type of pin with a wide disc and multiple swellings makes its
appearance at Corinth. Where weapons occur in these graves, they are
exclusively of iron, but in other ways they differ from Attica, daggers
being quite frequent and swords not represented. One grave at Tiryns
produced three spearheads – one larger (presumably a thrusting-spear),
two smaller which are no doubt javelin-heads; another, at Corinth, contained an iron arrowhead, a great rarity at this time on the mainland of
Greece. In a different region, Euboea, we may note the appearance of a
cast bronze vessel in a cremation-burial of probable ninth-century date.[48]

92b

96b

93

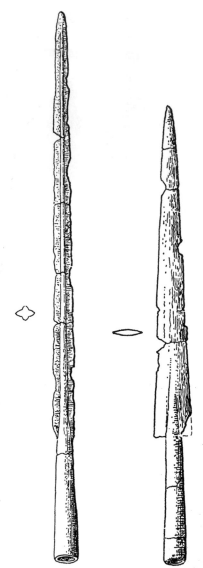

94. Two iron spearheads from tomb P at
Fortetsa, showing typically Cretan forms.
Lengths 32·5 and 40 cm; probably
8th century BC.

CRETE

If we glance across to central Crete, we find that a period of metalwork
no less distinctive than its predecessors is inaugurated during this time,
with the belated adoption of a genuinely Geometric style of pottery-
decoration. Iron retains its full popularity in this region, still being used
for pins as well as for the numerous weapons; among these last, the spear-
94 heads show a continuation of the long, slim shapes which are peculiarly

Cretan, while iron arrowheads are now also added to the warrior's armament. More remarkable is the appearance, in an interment of Mature
Geometric date in grave x at Fortetsa, of a bronze spectacle-fibula, together with gold and amber objects. Although this Balkan type is by now
common in Macedonia, and perhaps known in Epirus, this is its first dated
appearance further south than Marmariani; if the context, on our chronology, need not be much earlier than 750 BC, this is still a remarkable place
and time to find the type appearing. This period may also be represented
in the rich burials in a re-used tholos and two chamber-tombs at Khaniale
Tekke. The pottery, which includes kraters imitating Attic work (p. 130),
proves that the tholos-tomb at least was used in the 'Protogeometric B'
period and on into the first half of the eighth century; but the stratigraphy
was so disturbed that none of the array of small finds – iron weapons and
tools, a bronze vase, pins and fibulae, fragments of amber, crystal, faience
and even ostrich-egg, and above all two small pots full of gold jewellery –
could be assigned to this period, rather than to the repeated later uses of
the tombs, extending into the seventh century. At least two of the types,
however, can be matched by finds of 'Protogeometric B' date at Fortetsa:
two of the ornate fibulae of Blinkenberg's class iii.10, and a fine gold pin
with mouldings like those on the bronze example from Fortetsa tomb L
(cf. above, p. 253). Recently it has been strongly argued that the gold
jewellery likewise belongs to the 'Protogeometric B' phase.[49]

Some of the evidence from Geometric East Crete, though it is hard to
say how much, must date from the earlier eighth century. The 'bone-
enclosures' at Vrokastro were particularly productive: there is a rich
variety of bronze fibulae, as before on this site, among which some types
are known on the contemporary mainland (three of the 'Attico-Boeotian'
type in bone-enclosure 2), while others already familiar in Crete, including
several of Blinkenberg's types iii.10 and 11, cannot yet be matched in
datable contexts outside the island, save that they are reported to have
been present in the material, now lost, from the Geometric cemetery at
Kolophon. Other types again seem to be complete novelties, such as the
large fibulae with high arch and tall, narrow catch-plate (Blinkenberg's
type iv), soon to be found all over the Aegean islands, and perhaps to be
regarded as an insular alternative to the equally massive 'Attico-Boeotian'
class. Geometric tombs at Praisos and Zakro also produced elaborate
fibulae. Pins in this region are now comparatively few and unremarkable.
Iron weapons are still abundant, though the spearheads are not as large
and distinctive as those in central Crete. It is surprising to find, in the town-

site at Vrokastro and in apparently Geometric contexts, bronze weapons – a dagger and some very rudimentary spearheads – and tools, including an axe and a saw.[50]

THE LATER GEOMETRIC PERIOD

As the Geometric period advances thoughout Greece, not only does the evidence of every kind become more plentiful, but it also shows that growth of intercommunication which was the first step in making much of the Greek world once again a single cultural koinê – though never to the same degree as in the last heyday of Mycenaean power in the thirteenth century BC. This does not mean that the regional pattern of archaeological types disappears, for coalescence was never to be carried so far as that; but at a more fundamental level, the economic situation in many areas of Greece begins to show resemblances. For the metal types of later eighth-century Greece, the grave-finds now present only a small part of the evidence, but they are still indispensable for chronology. The geographical spread of the material increases, as does the total number of the graves. Local shifts of emphasis are also detectable: a conspicuous instance is the already noted impoverishment of the burials in the Athenian Kerameikos at this time, but there may be other cases: in the graves excavated by Verdelis at Tiryns, the later ones (mostly pithos-burials) are notably less rich than the earlier, while no subsequent burial at Eleusis matches the 'Isis grave' (p. 263) and its contemporary of the earlier eighth century, grave α. By contrast, more or less rich new cemeteries are inaugurated in fresh places between c.775 and 700: Aigaleos, Draphi, Kaki Thalassa, Kallithea, Koropi, Phaleron, Spata, Trachones and Vari in Attica, the North Cemetery at Corinth, Rhitsona in Boeotia, Eretria in Euboea, the two cemeteries of built tombs on Thera, the tholoi of Praisos and, perhaps a little earlier, Exochi on Rhodes – to name only the most prominent.

FIBULAE AND PINS

The eighth and seventh centuries form the golden age of the fibula in Greece, and it is fibulae which provide perhaps the best illustration of the diffusion of types, for quite apart from their unrivalled popularity as dedications in the sanctuaries, they are still frequent in graves. Two of the most characteristic Geometric types are the 'Attico-Boeotian', for which we inferred an origin in ninth century Attica, and its later contemporary and island counterpart, which we have noted in the eighth-century bone-enclosures of Vrokastro; they are types VIII and IV respectively in Blinkenberg's classification. Between them they spread over much of the Aegean before 700: the 'Attic-Boeotian' is still prevalent in the later Geometric graves of its native region (the Athenian Agora, the Dipylon cemetery and perhaps, in silver, at Thorikos); it is common in Boeotia in eighth- and seventh-century graves; and it appears also in the pyres of Halos, along with a variant class (Blinkenberg's type VII) which appears to be a contemporary and, in the main, a northern Greek alternative. (By contrast, an earlier Thessalian Geometric tomb, A at Theotokou, contained some primitive-looking versions of the much older arched fibulae.) In the other direction, the 'Attico-Boeotian' type reaches a grave on Thera, where the context in terms of date is obscure. The insular type IV, besides its occurrences at Vrokastro, is found at Praisos at a somewhat later period, and at Exochi on Rhodes and Emborio on Chios, while it is much commoner in the Theran graves than type VIII. In a grave at Andritsaina in Arcadia there occurred, more surprisingly, a pair of fibulae of Blinkenberg's type VII.8, together with a further pair belonging to a unique variant of this 'northern' type; the find, reinforced by the undoubtedly Peloponnesian character of the associated pins (see below), probably implies a local manufacture of such fibulae. But all three of these types will have penetrated more widely than grave-finds show: in the Peloponnese, for example, they are known in several sanctuaries, without being common there. There are, however, areas on the outer fringe of the Greek world which they may never have reached: such as the Western Greek colonies, where Italian types of fibula were preferred; Epirus, which also adopts and modifies an Italian type with elongated catch-plate (Blinkenberg's type V) (Hammond dates this development as early as the ninth century, but Sundwall's study of the Italian prototypes has shown that a much later dating – probably sixth to fifth centuries – is necessary); and to a lesser degree Macedonia, which had by now become an almost backward region in relation to Greece proper. Here there are examples of Blinkenberg's 'northern' type VII in contexts which may be of the eighth century, but the fibulae in the graves of this period at Chauchitza, apart from the now abundant spectacle-fibulae, are much more old-fashioned, being variants of the arched type; one Macedonian specimen of these has even occurred in a grave of sixth-century date at Aivasil.[51]

By contrast with fibulae, pins are now quite rare in graves. Where they do appear they are normally of bronze, except in Crete where somewhat crude iron types continue to occur. The finest specimens are again those in bronze from the Argolid and neighbouring regions: two graves at Mycenae preserve the older Geometric type of this region (p. 265), to

which belong also those found in the grave with fibulae at Andritsaina
(see above); two graves at Tiryns show a later and more delicate development, and this type is found also in two Late Geometric graves at Argos.
Contemporary Attic finds are far humbler in execution, although gold
pins have now occurred in an Attic grave. We may also anticipate our
discussion of the sanctuary-material by mentioning the parallel pins from
the Geometric deposit of Hera Akraia at Perachora, which is unique among
such material in that it has a clear *terminus ante quem*; the temple-site was
abandoned, perhaps in about 725, and offerings thereafter directed towards
another sanctuary of the goddess nearby. The pins are mostly of the older
Argolic type found in the graves; they also include examples of the form
with multiple swellings, with or without a broad disc, already noted in a
grave at Corinth (p. 265). More surprising are the associated fibulae,
for the recognizable examples belong to none of the classes we have been
discussing, but to the semicircular variety (Blinkenberg's type XII),
whose origin clearly lies in early Iron Age Anatolia, and which is accordingly
common in East Greek sanctuaries. Only exceptionally is it found in Greek
graves.[52]

   Among the other classes of domestic object, the occurrence of precious
metals now calls for no special remark. Even the rather drab graves of the
later Geometric Kerameikos produced further gold bands, now decorated
with animal friezes (graves 50, 72), and these also appear in contemporary
graves elsewhere in Athens and Attica. Gold and silver are found in some
quantities in the contemporary or slightly later graves at Eretria, while
recent excavations at the same site have produced a rich series of bronze
cauldrons and iron weapons. Of other rare materials, amber is now found
(with what was probably a silver chain) in grave 56 of the Kerameikos, of
the third quarter of the eighth century, as in two possibly earlier graves
at Eleusis. The ivory figurines in grave XIII of the Dipylon cemetery are
less remarkable for their material than for the fact that their workmanship
shows them to have been made in Greece; grave XI of the same group also
produced ivory. Bronze bracelets are now no longer a rarity, and bronze
rings are very common. But the most significant finds for the future are
the vessels of beaten bronze: to the cauldron of the Middle Geometric
grave Kerameikos 71 (p. 263) there now appear several successors from
later graves, in Attica and beyond; one at least of these, from Kerameikos
grave 72, belongs to a special category, the tripod-cauldron: this example,
although of bronze, had been fitted with iron legs and iron handles,
riveted on, of which only fragmentary traces survived. The find is valuable

108

for its chronological context, which is probably early in the third quarter of the eighth century. It is a mark of the rise of a purely Greek industry for the production of such vessels, and it very roughly coincides with the last appearance of the old Cypriot form of rod-tripod – strictly a stand, requiring a separate cauldron – which it was replacing: a Late Geometric grave on the Pnyx contained an example of this, probably already centuries old when it was buried (cf. above, p. 251 and p. 119). Smaller bronze bowls continue to appear in graves.[53]

DEFENSIVE ARMOUR

Beaten bronze finds perhaps its most testing use in the manufacture of defensive armour. We have found no instance of this use of the material for the previous three centuries, with the exception of the bronze shield-bosses (pp. 222-4, 233) which were merely attached to the leather body of the shield; and of a remarkable new find in Athens of a pair of greaves (p.333), which are however imports from further north. But a discovery in a Late Geometric grave at Argos produced both a bronze helmet and the bronze breast- and back-plates of a corslet.[54] The superlative quality of the corslet, shaped to fit the human torso, makes the question of its ancestry a problematical one: this is no prentice piece. My own view is that it can only be modelled on the products of a community acquainted with plate-armour, such as Urnfield Europe: the alternatives involve either the undetected survival of bronze plate body-armour from the fourteenth century BC, when it is last seen in Mycenaean contexts, to the late eighth; or else the fresh development of the corslet in Greece some way back in the dark age. The first of these hypotheses seems to me in principle unacceptable; the second, merely at variance with the evidence that we have for earlier metallurgy. The helmet associated in the Argos burial is of rather different quality, for it is not shaped, in any real sense, to fit the head, but must have been precariously perched on the crown, in order for the deep forehead-guard to be lifted clear of the eyes. Structurally it recalls other contemporary Greek metalwork, such as the hammered tripod-cauldrons, which also consist of several nearly flat parts riveted on to a rounded core. An Attic grave of this period, in the Dipylon cemetery, produced what may have been the remains of the supporting stilt for a crest like the one attached to the Argos helmet. There would therefore be no need to regard this type of helmet as other than a native Geometric Greek creation, but for the fact that its own general shape, and still more clearly the form of the crest-holder attached to it, can be matched in the art of eighth-century Assyria, the home of the most formidably-armed warriors

95

95. Bronze panoply from tomb 45 (Late Geometric) at Argos. Height of helmet and crest, 46 cm; of front plate of corslet, 47·4 cm; *c.* 720-710 B C.

of the day (whose equipment did not however include plate body-armour): the even older crested helmets of Urartu may have been the ultimate common ancestor. Both corslet and helmet stand at the head of a series in Greece – the helmet a short one, the corslet one that lasted all but two centuries – which takes us far beyond the confines of a dark age. By contrast the shield-bosses are now well on the way to obsolescence, thanks to the emergence of a fully bronze-faced shield in these same years; this last is not known to us from grave-finds, but there is other evidence of its

96. Iron weapons from Late Geometric graves at Argos. (*a*) Arrow-head, length 6·5 cm; (*b*) short sword or dirk, length 38 cm; *c.* 720 B C.

presence. Of the later Geometric bosses, one from an Attic grave was, remarkably, made of iron, a very rare experiment in the field of defensive armour at any period of Greek history. Three bronze examples from Chauchitza in Macedonia are of a unique form, with open-work spokes like a wheel; one had been repaired in antiquity with iron rivets. Others, of normal type, come from Crete: one from the town site at Vrokastro, one from a Geometric context (though in obscure circumstances) at Kavousi, and one from a grave of uncertain date at Fortetsana Kamara near Knossos. Late Geometric Crete may also have known a further item of defensive armour, the greave: a pair from Kavousi probably belongs before 700 B C; another from a sanctuary at Praisos is typologically similar and may not be much later.[55]

OFFENSIVE WEAPONS

The offensive weapons of the later eighth century present a much simpler picture. Iron reigns supreme for the last time for some centuries to come: bronze, where it occurs, is as before a sign of backwardness or remoteness. There is much similarity of types: the iron *Griffzungenschwert*, for example, now a stouter weapon than in its earlier stages, is at home in the graves of Attica, the Argolid, Thessaly and Crete. Iron spearheads, now showing clearer signs of mass production, occur in graves in these same regions, and in Rhodes besides; the simpler types, such as a short form with the blade hammered more or less flat, are seen in widely-separated places, including Crete. Bronze swords are found in only two certain cases, in Boeotia and Samos (pp. 241, 246); in a Macedonian grave, however, a solitary bronze-hilted *Antennenschwert* occurred (p. 255), a clear intruder from the north. Bronze spearheads, so far as I know, are unknown in graves of this date: a factor of importance when we come to consider the

96b
85b

S

97. Iron spear-butt (*saurotêr*) from the Potters' Quarter at Corinth. Length 22·5 cm; probably 7th century B C.

97   evidence of sanctuary-finds. The spear-butt or *saurotêr*, also of iron, is found occasionally. The dagger is commoner, reappearing now in Attica after an apparent break. Iron knives are very widespread, and indeed it is they which show the most striking uniformity of type: the tanged knife with curved blade, already found in earlier contexts (above, pp. 236, 253, 263, nn. 46 and 48), is now present in the Agora cemetery and elsewhere in Athens, at Eleusis, Eretria and Corinth, on Thera, and at Vrokastro and Fortetsa in Crete. The only common alternative is a very long hacking-knife or sword, slightly recurved so that the cutting-edge is *convex* instead of concave; this is known in northern Greece (at Halos, where even the women were buried with them, and Chauchitza) and in Crete as well. The only likely ancestor for this curious weapon is the somewhat smaller knife found bent round the cremation-amphora in Kerameikos Proto-geometric grave 28, 27 cm long; the Halos examples reach 49 cm.[56]

There is one field of arms, archery, which provides a probable case of influence by Crete on the mainland. But for a solitary iron arrowhead in the same Kerameikos grave as the long knife just mentioned, two examples of obsidian in a probably Early Geometric burial at Tiryns, and two iron examples in graves of the same date at Corinth and Athens, there is no evidence whatever for archery in Greece proper in the eleventh, tenth and ninth centuries B C. In Crete, by contrast, there is a type of bronze arrowhead whose development can be followed through from its first appearances at the Minoan survival-site of Karphi right down into Classical times; and there are further iron examples of cruder form, found at Panagia in a Protogeometric context, and at Fortetsa and elsewhere from about 800 BC onwards; some of the examples at Fortetsa belong indeed to a particularly Cypriot variety with long narrow head of square section, not to appear on the mainland until much later. But from about 750 onwards, there is clear evidence that the practice of archery had been resumed in mainland Greece, not so much from finds of arrowheads as from the illustrations of the bow in battle-scenes on Attic Late Geometric vases; a few iron arrowheads are also found now – six in a grave at Pherai in Thessaly, one from Argos. Another rare weapon for which we have some   *96a* fragmentary evidence is the sling: stone bullets (in default of the more effective lead) occurred at Marmariani in Thessaly and on Thera. We must probably regard as tools rather than weapons the single- and double-axes, of both iron and bronze, found at Fortetsa and in the settlement at Vrokastro; they find a surprising counterpart on the mainland in the two iron double-axes in the 'Panoply tomb' at Argos (p. 271), and in a single-axe probably from a Dipylon grave at Athens.[57]

THE FINDS FROM SANCTUARIES

We must finally turn our attention to the great sanctuary-sites of Greece. Those which have proved rich in early metal-work include the sanctuaries of Zeus at Olympia, Dodona and near Pherai in Thessaly; the sanctuaries of Apollo at Delphi and Amyklai; of Artemis at Sparta and Ephesus; of Hera near Argos, on Samos and at her two successive temples at Perachora; of Athena at Lindos and Tegea, and of Aphaia on Aegina; the Cretan caves at Psychro on Mt Dikte, and on Mt Ida; and what was probably a sanctuary, though of an unknown deity, at Aetos in Ithaka. Much material from these sites has, in the past, been put forward to illustrate the conditions of Greece during the dark age. Yet at only one of these sites, the Dictaean Cave in Crete, is there a credible case for continuity of worship from the Bronze Age down to the Archaic period; the same claim for Amyklai cannot be supported on the available evidence (p. 131), although genuine Bronze Age dedications seem to be present there; while the case for a continuous cult from Mycenaean times on Delos, although interesting, is not primarily relevant here since on the published evidence the site is not rich in early metal types of the Iron Age.[58] The remaining sanctuaries of the above list have produced some material which is probably of a date before 700, and much else that belong to Archaic and Classical times: the great question is, how far back into the dark age do their dedications extend?

STRATIGRAPHY

Stratigraphical evidence will not help us much, except in the one case of the early temple of Hera Akraia at Perachora which was abandoned during the later eighth century (p. 270). Elsewhere, the dedications found have been not so often stratified in deposits as dumped in pits, heaps or occasionally in wells, together with earlier and later objects: the normal reason for their ejection must have been the congestion of the sanctuary, which could have arisen at any time after their dedication. The best guide to the period of a sanctuary's use would be provided by dedications of pottery closely associated with the metal finds; but in many cases these are largely or totally wanting. At a few sites – Olympia not least – even unstratified and unassociated pottery is scarce; the gods did not apparently share the modern esteem for the ceramic products of early Greece. Architectural remains provide little help, first because a built temple or shrine is not an essential feature of a sanctuary from the first; and secondly because buildings are themselves of too rare occurrence in early Greece to be dated independently of pottery-finds – which brings us back to our starting-point. Basically, therefore, the evidence for dating early sanctuary-deposits falls into two classes:

    (i) on those sites with a sufficient quantity of pottery, we may infer an initial date for the dedications from the date of the earliest pottery;

  (ii) on the remaining sites (the majority) which lack such evidence, we must base our dating on the typology of those of the metal and other finds which are also known from contemporary graves or stratified settlements – or from sanctuaries datable under (i) above.

EVIDENCE FROM POTTERY

Under the first head, we may note the almost total absence of Protogeometric pottery from the sites under consideration. The only full exceptions are Amyklai and Aetos, but both of these are in regions where the Protogeometric style was adopted and retained unusually late. In those cases, like that of Olympia, where early pottery of any kind is rare, the absence of Protogeometric does not necessarily mean much. But at many other sanctuaries later pottery is present, either with the dedications or in looser association: even at Olympia there is some Geometric (p. 65). At Dodona, the remoteness of the site from the heart-land of Greek civilization sets a special problem: certainly the pottery-finds are astonishingly scarce and late, with only a few known sherds and one or two complete pots dating from before the sixth century. At Delphi, there is better evidence in the quite copious finds of Geometric dating from the early eighth century onwards; but the only deposit of Protogeometric consists of a few late-looking sherds found well to the east of the sanctuary of Apollo in an occupation area, which does not prove the existence of a sanctuary at this date, any more than does the earlier tomb near the museum.[59] At Amyklai, the dedications, on the evidence of the pottery, very probably go back into the ninth century. The sanctuary of Artemis Orthia combines the rare features of an observed stratification and a fairly rich yield of pottery; taken in combination, the evidence of these shows that the initial date of the site cannot be taken back beyond the eighth century, and perhaps not even very far into that century. At Ephesus, the main dedicatory deposit, associated with the 'Archaic Basis' and including numerous fibulae and pins, has been re-examined and shown to date from the seventh century, with the exception of one or two pieces which may belong to the eighth; there is a little pottery which confirms this conclusion. At the Argive Heraeum, there is much Geometric pottery, most of it quite late, and no Protogeometric. The Samian Heraeum has produced Protogeometric in a quantity that is minute when compared with the later material; there is some Middle Geometric elsewhere on the island, and much from the Heraeum which is contemporary or later; but the very high chronology adopted by the excavators, beginning with a date of c.900 for 'Altar I' is hardly borne out by the published finds. At Perachora we have unusually clear evidence: the Geometric material from the temple of Hera Akraia belongs exclusively before c.725 (its initial date is vague, but need be no earlier than 800), while the temple of Hera Limenia was built at about the same date of c.725, and its associated dedications begin no earlier than the building itself. At Lindos, there is much Late Geometric pottery, but the little earlier material found was not, it seems, associated with the sanctuary. At Tegea a similar pattern exists: if the minute quantity of Protogeometric here derives from the neighbouring Laconian school (p. 90) then it need not indicate a date earlier than the eighth century; while Late Geometric is plentiful. In the Cretan cave-sanctuaries, pottery is little found; there was enough from the Dictaean Cave to prove its use over a long period, but that from the Idaean Cave is mostly lost in oblivion. In the Ithakan sanctuary, finally, the pottery seems to span the whole of the local Geometric period, as well as the succeeding one: there are even a few pieces of the local Protogeometric.[60]

ANALOGOUS METAL TYPES

On the ceramic evidence, then, the only sanctuaries which need have been in use much earlier than 750 BC are those at Delphi, Samos, Hera Akraia at

Perachora, Amyklai, the Dictaean Cave and Aetos; and of these only the last three need extend back into the ninth century. But at many of the other sites, the quantity of pottery is not adequate to form a final conclusion. We must therefore turn to our second category of dating-evidence, by analogous metal types. The great difficulty here is the long life which such objects as fibulae and pins could enjoy: just how long, is shown by considering first the two sanctuaries with a fairly clear, and relatively late, initial date, Artemis Orthia at Sparta and Hera Limenia at Perachora. At the former site were found 'frequent' violin-bow fibulae with twisted wire – a type that was at home in the twelfth century BC (p. 245); at the latter, more than one example of the violin-bow type with flattened bow, which had also made its appearance before the end of Mycenaean III C, and five examples of the arched type. These specimens are of course heavily outnumbered by later types, but the fact remains that if such types cannot be shown to be exclusively early, their presence (or absence) cannot be used to determine the initial date of a sanctuary. Instead we must weigh them against the quantity of definitely later types: if the latter predominate overwhelmingly, then the early types must be survivals or heirlooms, as is demonstrably the case at Sparta and Perachora. Of the classes of fibula in Blinkenberg's catalogue, type VIII (the 'Attico-Boeotian') has been shown by grave-finds to originate in ninth-century Attica, but it is not known to occur elsewhere before the mid-eighth century; types IV, VII and XII, on similar evidence, are not found before the eighth century; type III, variant 10 is first seen in a Protogeometric 'B' burial at Fortetsa, but its other varieties need not begin earlier than the eighth century; nor are the spectacle-fibula and its derivatives (types XIV-XV) known any earlier except in and near Macedonia. Blinkenberg's type XI may or may not be an Italic intruder;[61] but it is unlikely to have occurred before 750 in either case. Types IX, XVI and the intrusive type V definitely begin even later than the main eighth-century group; types VI and XIII probably do so. Most fibulae in graves before 800 BC, except in Attica and Crete, are of some variety of Blinkenberg's I (violin-bow) and II (arched) types. Looking at Blinkenberg's catalogue of sanctuary-finds, we note that at Olympia there are 2 examples of types I and II as against 48 of other types; at the sanctuary near Pherai, 3 against well over 100; at Delphi, 4 against 16; at Lindos, no example of I and II as against many hundreds of the others; at the Argive Heraeum, 2 against well over 50; on Aegina, 3 against about 20; at Sparta, 2 against about 30 (figures which, with the publication of *Artemis Orthia*, must be adjusted). The fibulae from these sanctuaries thus suggest at the least a heavy weighting of the dedications to the eighth century and later. So too with pins: Jacobsthal in his study noted one pin from Pherai, and two or three from the Argive Heraeum, as having a 'Protogeometric' appearance; but they are very similar to an example, now published, from a later ninth-century burial at Berbati. Even under the Geometric types, only some of the specimens of his second class, particularly from the Argive Heraeum and Aegina, invite a dating substantially earlier than 700, for the third 'Geometric' class, as he points out, proves to be Subgeometric in date. Certain other of the more unusual types of minor object found at the sanctuaries can be shown to date from after 750 BC – in some cases substantially later:[62] others again simply cannot be matched in Geometric grave-finds.

With dedications of weapons and armour, it is equally hard to reach definite conclusions, but the general trend is clear. Protogeometric and Geometric graves show a heavy predominance in the use of iron for weapons, and an almost total absence of metal defensive armour, apart from shield-bosses, down to the time of the Late Geometric grave at Argos. Typologically, their evidence is vaguer: the swords, daggers and knives of these periods are rigidly conservative and show very little development; only with spearheads is there some hope of distinguishing earlier and later forms. But we find that the sanctuaries which attracted the most early warlike dedications – Olympia, Delphi and to a lesser degree Lindos – show a substantial proportion of bronze weapons, and a wide range of defensive armour. Does this then place their contents largely in the post-Geometric period? Too much must not be made of the prevalence of bronze among the weapons: for one thing, its better preservation encourages detailed publication, and corresponding neglect of iron finds; for another, the appropriate qualities for sanctuary-dedications may have differed from those of weapons for everyday use (cf. above, p. 237). In any case at the richest site, Olympia, it is not entirely clear from the original publication of the bronze weapons how large a proportion of the total dedications these represent; since a few iron specimens are also included and specified as such, it is conceivable that there were no other recognizable iron weapons, but in a further large find in 1936, iron actually predominated among the 200 spearheads and swords, bronze among the spear-butts and arrowheads. At Delphi, iron weapons are included in the same volume as the bronzes, and they are few by comparison. What is beyond doubt is that the incidence of bronze weapons at these sanctuaries, so far from being an indication of early date, must rather tend towards a

98

98. Four bronze spearheads dedicated at Olympia, but found without any close dating context. (*a*) is chiefly notable for its primitive method of fabrication, the socket being beaten rather than cast; (*b*) is an example of the quite frequent dedication of foreign (in this case Italian) bronzes at Olympia; (*c*) and (*d*), on the other hand, bear every sign of having been centuries old at the time of their presumed dedication in the early Iron Age, both from their typology and from their very worn tips. Lengths 26, 18·5, 14·1, and 29 cm.

general dating *after* the Geometric period. This is especially true of the
arrowheads, most of which are demonstrably of post-Geometric types.
Among the spearheads, only with one or two specimens is there any
indication that the use of bronze could have any connection with the earlier
heyday of that metal (I exclude here the bronzes from the Dictaean Cave,
among which there were many Minoan dedications). Thus, a bronze
lanceolate spearhead appeared at Delphi, and two bronze heads of an   *98c,d*
equally early, but less clearly characterized, shape at Olympia; but these
could have been centuries old at the time of their dedication, if finds of
bronze swords in graves are anything to go by (pp. 241, 246 above). On
the other hand, a well-defined type of iron spearhead with a sharply-
angled outline to the blade occurs in Protogeometric and Geometric
graves but not, so far as I know, in sanctuaries; and conversely the predominant iron spear-types in sanctuaries, especially Olympia, are larger,
heavier but proportionately slimmer in the blade, and these are seen only
in Late Geometric graves on the mainland of Greece.[63] A further factor
may possibly have operated in connection with weapons: the practice of
burial with arms, though never universal in Greece, dies out with some
abruptness at the end of the Geometric period except in some remote
regions. This change may perhaps be connected, and therefore contemporary, with the rise in the practice of making personal dedications of arms
at the sanctuaries of gods.

TRIPOD CAULDRONS

The evidence adduced above is, of course, very far from conclusive, but
it is at least consistent with the view that a high proportion of the metal
finds from Greek sanctuary-sites are of Late Geometric or later date. But
there is one major class of finds which might be used to refute such a
conclusion, and this is the tripod-cauldrons. All the schemes for classifying   *99*
these objects in a typological sequence – Furtwängler's in the original
Olympia publication, Miss Lamb's in her *Greek and Roman Bronzes*,
Miss Benton's of 1935 and Willemsen's in his Olympia study of 1957 – have
involved the view that the tripod-cauldrons of Iron Age Greece go back
at least to the tenth century BC. The main basis for the conclusion lies in
stylistic arguments: we have encountered little evidence for it from dated
graves or settlements, although it is true that a very recent discovery, at
Lefkandi in Euboea, has produced fragments of clay moulds, probably   *101*
for the casting of tripod-legs, in a context contemporary with Attic Late
Protogeometric.[64] Previously, the arguments for an early chronology had
been indirect; the close resemblance of the earliest Iron Age tripods to

99. Bronze tripod-cauldron (B 1240) from Olympia. Height including handles 65 cm; probably 8th century B C.

the few known examples from the latest Bronze Age, and the presence of clay versions of the tripods, also of analogous shape, in clear Protogeometric contexts, as well as later. The key evidence for the first argument is provided by the partially-restored Staïs tripod from Mycenae, whose find-circumstances are inconclusive but which is very probably of Late

Bronze Age date; and also by the iron tripod-legs, with similar section, which formed part of the Tiryns treasure, a group of objects whose associations are dubious, although it should in part belong to the twelfth century. The material of the Tiryns legs helps little towards their dating: Furtwängler observed that, stylistically, the earliest-looking tripod-fragments at Olympia were those of iron, but Willemsen has shown that the properties of the two metals alone would account for the relative 'primitiveness' of the iron examples, and that a clear chronological division is not possible. Here, too, we may recall that a piece of datable evidence, the bronze cauldron from grave 72 at the Kerameikos (p. 270) which had been fitted with iron legs and handles, belongs perhaps rather after 750. Clearly we cannot conclude that the use of iron for tripods is a token of early, let alone Protogeometric, date. The fine series of cauldrons from eighth-century graves at Eretria provides a further body of evidence; the shape of some of these, and indeed of the Kerameikos cauldron, is particularly important: they are deep and curve evenly inwards at the shoulder, as with the earliest examples in Miss Benton's classification, including the Staïs tripod from Mycenae. These tripods have legs, where preserved, of simple trapezoidal section, and handles of round section ornamented with strokes.[65] If this class is, as it appears, represented both near the end of the Bronze Age and in the third quarter of the eighth century BC, did it enjoy a continuous life between these two periods?

Until the discovery at Lefkandi, the most cogent evidence for such continuity was in the indirect form of the clay copies of tripod-cauldrons. Two such clay tripods were found in the early Protogeometric grave 4 of the Kerameikos, and fragments of another came from the 'Cairns' site at Aetos, where the context was probably that of the local Protogeometric style, although this may mean a distinctly later date than that of the Attic examples; while a further fragmentary find, at Knossos, which may be a handle from one of these clay copies, belongs in the region of 900 BC. Among later finds, an example from the deposit of Hera Akraia at Perachora must belong before c.725, and there are a number of Late Geometric instances. These clay tripods show analogies of shape and proportion with some bronze examples, whether undated (as with finds from sanctuaries, especially Olympia) or probably datable (like the Staïs example) to an early period. Another, and much more indirect, argument comes from representations of a different kind: paintings of tripods on vases from about 750 onwards, some of which show divergent features, apparently more advanced than those of actual surviving tripod-cauldrons;

100

100. Clay copy of a tripod-cauldron from Protogeometric grave 4 at
the Kerameikos, Athens. Restored height 18 cm; later 11th century B C.

but the most positive of these features – additional 'decks', triple handles,
animal feet, new shapes of cauldron – seem to begin only at a date near to,
or even after, 700 B C.[66]

Faced with this body of evidence, I still remain sceptical as to the existence of a continuous industry for the casting of bronze tripods throughout
the dark age of Greece. The picture of metal-usage that has emerged is,
for part of this period, one of the most straitened austerity, with bronze
in especially short supply. The appearance of clay tripods in the Kerameikos, in the vicinity of 1000 B C, may represent not copying of contemporary metalwork, but substitution for it; just as the Cypriot rod-
tripods are copied in clay only when production in bronze has ceased.[67]
The massive bronze legs and ornate handles from Olympia[68] which
Willemsen, on stylistic grounds, has called 'self-evidently Protogeometric'
seem rather to be the successors of the Lefkandi products; they are also
worlds apart in scale, material, technique and decoration from the pattern
of metal-work in that period that we have discerned from the other evidence.
I do not think that we can reach, on such grounds, the conclusion that

101. Fragments of two clay moulds, probably for casting tripod-legs, from the settlement at Lefkandi in Euboea; that on the right had running spirals between vertical ribs. Height of largest fragments *c.*8 cm; *c.*900 B C.

there was a substantial use of Olympia, or of any other sanctuary, for dedications in the Protogeometric period. A more productive line of argument is, I think, one which follows from an observation of Catling's in his preliminary publication of the Lefkandi finds: some of the tripod-legs cast in the moulds, like some actual examples found at Olympia, were decorated with vertical running spirals in relief separated by parallel ridges. *101 right* The motif of the linked spiral is found on the legs of one of the rod-tripods of Cypriot type (above p. 251) which had reached the Aegean, that from Fortetsa tomb XI at Knossos, interred at this time (c.900 BC). Catling *89* himself hints at a natural inference from this: that the iron-founders of Lefkandi were using Cypriot rod-tripods as the model for their experiments in producing a native Greek type. If this was really happening, then it seems likely that they were not heirs to any continuous tradition of tripod-casting in Greece. In any event, the bulk of the associated offerings at the great sanctuary-sites of Greece confirms that the growth of mass-dedication was a development of the later part of the dark age.

Metalwork is a difficult subject, especially so in the case of an iron-using culture; as a result, it is one which for most periods of Greek antiquity has received only a tiny part of the attention bestowed on pottery. Yet metal finds, because of their closer connection with wealth, with technology, with war and even with social structure, should be potentially the more fruitful source of historical evidence; they are the product, too, of factors almost universally applicable, unlike those which shape the work of the potter and painter. The advent of iron-working in Greece, even if its significance has been exaggerated or misunderstood, and even if it is still wrapped in obscurity for us, was still one of the most influential technological changes in four thousand years of Greek history.

Notes

1] Of the numerous studies of this topic in recent years, for Greece and beyond, I would single out H. H. Coghlan's study *Notes on Prehistoric and Early Iron in the Old World* (Pitt-Rivers Museum, *Occasional Papers on Technology* no. 8 (1956)) – hereafter *O P T* 8 – for its usefulness and lucidity. The subject may also be followed in a series of papers by various writers in the *American Journal of Archaeology*: T. T. Read in *A J A* 38 (1934), 382-9; H. C. Richardson, *ibid.* 555-83 and 41 (1937), 447-51; A. Hertz, *ibid.* 441-6; T. E. Rickard, 43 (1939), 85-101 and G. E. Wright, *ibid.* 458-63; and H. Maryon's articles in 53 (1949), 93-125 and 65 (1961), 173-84. Note also R. J. Forbes, *Metallurgy in Antiquity* (1950) and *Studies in Ancient Technology* 9 (1964). R. F. Tylecote's *Metallurgy in Archaeology* (1962) is primarily devoted to the British Isles; T. Burton Brown's *The Coming of Iron to Greece* (1955) somewhat belies its title. I much regret that Dr Radomir Pleiner's excellent study *Iron Working in Ancient Greece* (National Technical Museum, Prague, 1969) appeared too late for me to take it into account. But I have found little in it that I would venture to differ with, save that, like S. Przeworski (above, p. 228), Dr Pleiner believes in a transitional or 'Proto-Iron Age' in Greece, between c. 1200 and 800 BC

2] T. G. E. Powell in *P P S* 29 (1963), 215: for Italy, note that the recent excavations at Veii have shown a sudden increase in the use of iron only towards the middle of the eighth century, *A R* 1966-7, 30

3] See Coghlan's account in *O P T* 8, 38-60

4] Cf. Tylecote, *op. cit.* 314 for hardness tests, and for their results, *O P T* 8, 134-53 (cf. 31), and Coghlan's further paper *Notes on the Prehistoric Metallurgy of Copper and Bronze in the Old World* (*O P T* 4, 1951), 40-44, 105-111

5] C. Panseri, *La Tecnica di Fabbricazione delle Lame di Acciaio presso gli Antichi* (Associazione Italiana di Metallurgia, Milano, 1957), 19-33, esp. 27 fig. 27 and 29 fig. 32

6] Cf. H. L. Lorimer's account in *Homer and the Monuments*, 111-20

7] On knives, see Desborough *L M S* 25-6, n.1, 70; M. R. Popham and L. H. Sackett (eds.) *Excavations at Lefkandi, Euboea* 1964-6 (1968), 14, fig. 22; and Hammond, *Epirus* 358-9 (Kakavi): later swords, cf. Snodgrass, *E G A* 109, and add the sword from Marmariani, *ibid.* 94, no. 1, 9

8] Catling, *C B M W* 103 n.3; 143 n.3; 198 n.5

9] Catling, *op. cit.* 124, 129

10] Cf. the examples listed by D. H. F. Gray, *J H S* 74 (1954), 10-11

11] Kamini, *Ergon* 1960, 191; Tiryns, *A M* 78 (1963), 14-17, Beil. 5, 4. Now, however, an iron sword and bronze spearhead are reported from 'Submycenaean' graves in Athens, *A D* 22, 2 (1967), 92-3

12] Cf. Lorimer, *H M* 68-9, 112 for these finds and Catling, *op. cit.* 188, 297 on the Tiryns treasure; O. Tufnell, *Lachish* 3 (1953), 388-9 on sickles in the Near East; Kerameikos, *Ker.* 1, 87 and *Hesp.* 30 (1961), 175; Perati, *Ergon* 1960, 21, fig. 28d; Enkomi, A. S. Murray, A. H. Smith and H. B. Walters, *Excavations in Cyprus* (1900), 16, 53

13] On the overall incidence of iron and bronze in Protogeometric, see my paper in *PPS* 31 (1965), esp. pp. 230-231. The process is also traced and tabulated by H. Müller-Karpe in *JdI* 77 (1962), 60-2, fig. 33; see Desborough, *PGP* 3, 71 on dating of 'Protogeometric' tomb 24 and of this group generally. Styrenius, *SS* 54-5, 58, 64-5 classifies Kerameikos tombs A, 24 and 2 North as 'Late Submycenaean B'. Further early iron weapons from Athens: *AD* 22, 2 (1967), 92-3

14] Tiryns, *AM* 78 (1963), 10-24; Assarlik, *JHS* 8 (1887), 68; note an iron find from Naxos, *Prakt.* (1967), 117

15] Coghlan, *OPT* 4, 102, 109; swords, *EGA* 94, 107-8; spearheads, cf. Catling, *op. cit.* 123, 125 n.1 – his description of the Kaloriziki spearhead seems at variance with his pl. 14k, and with McFadden's description *AJA* 58 (1954), 139, no. 29 – and *Antiquity* 39 (1965), 152

16] *EGA* 38-51; I failed to notice an important piece of evidence, in the traces of leather found adhering to the underside of one of the Kerameikos bosses (*ibid.* A.9: *Ker.* 4, 42) which sharply reduces the possible range of uses. Note too that a boss from a warrior-grave in Bosnia, A. Benac and B. Čović, *Glasinac* 2 (1957), 75, pl. 30, closely resembles some of the unassociated examples from Greek sanctuaries, notably *EGA* no. A.36 (Olympia)

17] Cf. Gray, *JHS* 74 (1954), 11

18] Pins, P. Jacobsthal, *Greek Pins*

(1956), 95 and *Ker.* 1, 185-8, Protogeometric graves 13 and 11; fibulae, *ibid.* 82-5, pl. 28 and *Hesp.* 30 (1961), 176; Perati, *AD* 19, 2 (1964), 94, pl. 90γ, δ; ring, *AM* 78 (1963), 153; Tiryns, *AM* 78 (1963), 6, 8, 11 (graves XIIIa, b and XXVIII)

19] J. Deshayes, *Deiras* 204-7; n.b. also *ibid.* 101, tomb 25, DB 29 for a Mycenaean pin not closely datable; and add, for types (1) and (2), Elis (*PPS* 31 (1965), 226); for type (4) Karphi (*LMS* 53 and n.5), Mycenae, *PPS* 31, 226, pl. 33e; and G. Säflund's references in *Le Terremare* (1939), 178-9; for type (5), Kerameikos and Salamis, *JdI* 77 (1962), 119, fig. 5, 1 and 128, fig. 32, 4, and in general Catling, *CBMW* 238 and Jacobsthal, *GP* 122-3. On questions of priority, see most recently N. K. Sandars, *BSA* 534 -(1958-9), 235 and n.28; Desborough, *LMS* 50; Styrenius, *SS* 159; and most recently M. S. F. Hood in *BSA* 63 (1968), 214-18

20] S. Przeworski, *Die Metallindustrie Anatoliens* (*Internationales Archiv für Ethnographie*), suppl. vol. 26 (1939), 175-87, and Miss Gray, *JHS* 74 (1954), 1. Cf. also R. Pleiner (above, n.1)

21] For ancient repairs, see also Przeworski's examples, *op. cit.* 144 and n.79; and add *Praktiká* 1911, 298 (Sesklo, of Geometric date)

22] On tin, see S. Benton, *Antiquity* 38 (1964), 138; on arsenical bronze, E. Caley in *Hesp.* suppl. vol. 8 (1949), 60-3. For the location of iron-workings in the Aegean, lists are given by Forbes, *Metallurgy in Antiquity* 384-8 and *Archaeologia Homerica* (ed. F. Matz and H.-G. Buchholz) vol. II, chapter K (1967), 6-10, fig. 6; also in H. Blümner, *Technologie und Terminologie der Gewerbe und Kunst* 4

(1884), 69-87; and add the list of iron slag finds by O. Davies, *B S A* 35 (1934–5), 136-7

23] Kerameikos graves, *Ker.* 1, 220 and 4, 25; graves 11, 13, 14, 22 and 23 represent the earlier forms of pin; graves 5, 15, 16, 26, 29, 30, 31, 33, 37, 38, 39, 45, 47 the canonical form, also found in Geometric grave 7 (*Ker.* 5, 1, 214) and the Agora grave, *Hesperia* 37 (1968), 109 no. 64; graves 18, 29 and the first burial in Geometric grave 75 (*ibid.* 261) contained all-iron pins; graves 9, 20 and 48 see the revival of bronze (for the very late date of these graves, cf. Styrenius, *S S* 88 (gr. 48); Desborough *P G P* 102-4 (Kantharos in gr. 20). Agora graves, *Hesp.* 2 (1933), 468; 6 (1937), 368 and the unpublished grave XIII (Styrenius, *S S* 109); *Hesp.* 25 (1956), 48; 23 (1954), 58; 6 (1937), 365; 21 (1952), 279; Ag. Markos St., *A D* 19, 2 (1964), 56, pl. 51α; Metropolis, *A E* 1953–4, 3, 89-97 (weapons putatively associated with earlier burial); Nea Ionia, *Hesp.* 30 (1961), 173-4

24] Tiryns, *Tiryns* 1, 128 (grave 7) and *A M* 78 (1963), 26, 28, 30, 35; Argos, *B C H* 81 (1957), 656; Asine, O. Frödin and A. W. Persson, *Asine* 425; Argos, cf. *E G A* 98; Mycenae, *P P S* 31 (1965), 225; *B S A* 49 (1954), 259; 51 (1956), 129; *A D* 20, 2 (1965), 165; Elis, *A D* 19, 2 (1964), 180-2, pls. 198-202 and *P P S* 31, 226

25] Iolkos, *Ergon* 1960, 59; Theotokou, A. J. B. Wace and M. S. Thompson, *Prehistoric Thessaly* (1912), 209-14; Kapakli, *A E* (1914), 141; Homolion, *A D* 17, 2 (1961–2), 175f.; Halos, *B S A* 18 (1911–12), 5-6; Marmariani, *B S A* 31 (1930–1), 35-8; Assarlik, *J H S* 8 (1887), 68-77 and H. B. Walters, *Catalogue of Bronzes in the British Museum* (1899),

T

8, no. 118

26] On later bronze weapons, cf. *E G A* 134, n.32, 154 – but the speculations as to the scarcity of iron are possibly misplaced; tripods, S. Benton, *B S A* 35 (1934–5), 80; but cf. p. 254

27] V. G. Childe, *What Happened in History* (1942), 183; contrast *Prehistoric Migrations in Europe* (1950), 222. Similar sentiments to those of the first quotation can be found in F. Heichelheim, *An Ancient Economic History* 1 (translated ed., 1958), 193 (where iron prices are also discussed), 199-200, 204; and G. Thomson, *The First Philosophers* (*Studies in Ancient Greek Society* 2, 1955), 182-3

28] Desborough, *P G P* 200-1 on the Delphi tomb; *E G A* 118, no. A 10 for the spearhead (compare A 4 from the earlier tomb, A 13-14 from Olympia); Catling in *P P S* 22 (1956), 112f., 9 and 10 for the two swords (*ibid.* no. 11 for Mouliana tomb A), and *Antiquity* 35 (1961), 117, 120 for typology

29] See *P G P* 163-6, 308, 310 and H. D. Hansen in *Studies presented to D. M. Robinson* 1 (1951), 57-9 for Skyros; Papadimitriou's grave *A A* 51 (1936), 228-34; Coldstream, *G G P* 149. For earlier fibulae with swollen arch, cf. C. Blinkenberg, *Fibules grecques et orientales* 76, 11. 19f. (Salamis) and *Ker.* 1, 82, fig. 2 and pl. 28; 4, 25, n.24

30] *P G P* 308-12, and site references, 323-4; 230-2 on Lindos; Jacobsthal, *G P* 3, fig. 7 for Marmaro pin

31] Kephallenian fibulae, see Blinkenberg, *F G O* 50, 56; *L M S* 55 and n.4; 104 and nn.7-8; pins, *A D* 5 (1919), 117, fig. 32; bronze fragments, *E G A* 72 with nn.2-3; small finds, *L M S* 104 with references; swords, see esp. N. K. Sandars, *A J A* 67

(1963), 137, 151; spearheads, *A D* 5, figs. 36, 1 and 3 and *A E* 1933, 92, fig. 41. Aetos fibula, *B S A* 48 (1953), 357, fig. 36; pin, Jacobsthal *G P* 3, fig. 8

32] Kallithea graves, *A M* 75 (1960), 42-5; weapons, *A J A* 64 (1960), 13-16; note a knife from Chalandritsa, *P P S* 21 (1955), 183, 189, 195, and others from the Dymaean Wall, *A D* 20, 2 (1965), 227, pl. 273α, β; small finds, *L M S* 98; Dymaean Wall dagger, *Ergon* 1965, 104, fig. 130α (note also the violin-bow fibula, *B C H* 91 (1967), 666, fig. 6). Group in Mainz: *C V A* Mainz 1, 12f. (cf. *L M S* 265, Coldstream, *G G P* 221). Chalandritsa (Troumbes), *Prakt.* 1929, 91, fig. 7. Malthi: N. Valmin, *The Swedish Messenia Expedition* (1938), 371f.

33] Lefkandi, *Excavations at Lefkandi*, 28-9; Kardiani, *Annuario* 8-9 (1925–6), 203f.; *P G P* 308-11; *Ker.* 5, 1, 194; Amyklai spearheads, *E G A* 126 (K.1, cf. Catling, *C B M W* 118, type (c)) and 131 (U.1, cf. *B S A* 48 (1953), 78-9, no. 21 for possible prototype); sword, *E G A* 97 (I.40); Sparta fibulae, R. M. Dawkins *et al.*, *Artemis Orthia* (1929), 198, pl. lxxxiii b; a Late Geometric burial at Kalamata in Messenia, dating perhaps from after the Spartan conquest of this region, held a bronze horse and bronze pins which can be matched at Sparta (*A D* 20, 2 (1965), 207, pl. 213β; cf. Jacobsthal, *Greek Pins*, figs. 29, 39); Mavrovouni, *B S A* 56 (1961), 115-17, fig. 2, n.12; Samos sword, *Antiquity* 35 (1961), 117, no. 24

34] For the incidence of precious metals, see Kübler, *Ker.* 5, 1, 184-5 (note other silver finds in Protogeometric Knossos, *B S A* 55 (1960), 146, and Geometric Exochi, *Act. A.* 28 (1957), 185; early use of Aegean

silver-deposits, K. Branigan, *A J A* 72 (1968), 226-7); silver-extraction at Argos, P. Courbin (ed.), *Études Archéologiques* (1963), 98-100, and Thorikos, *B C H* 91 (1967), 628; ivory, *Ker.* 5, 1, 191, 197; *Fortetsa* 209; *P G P* 208 for date of ivory pin-head at Tiryns; Tiryns necklace, *A M* 78 (1963), 36-7, 42, 58, Beil. 3, 1; Athenian grave with ivory, faience and gold, *Hesperia* 37 (1968), 77-116; amber, twelfth- and eleventh-century finds, e.g. Kalbaki, *A E* 1956, 116, fig. 2, 10, 127-8 (add Hammond, *Epirus* 331 and n.2); Kephallenia, *L M S* 104 n.10; Ancient Elis, Styrenius, *S S* 141; Salamis, *A M* 35 (1910), 30, fig. 30; Tiryns treasure, *A M* 55 (1930), 128, no. 6219; ninth- and eighth-century finds, *Ker.* 5, 1, 197; *B S A* 48 (1953), 260; 56 (1961), 75, no. 33; *P P S* 31 (1965), 238, n.1; on likelihood of Baltic origin, Dunbabin, *Perachora* 2, 521-2; C. Beck and others, *Archaeometry* 8 (1965), 96-109 and *G R B S* 9 (1968), 5-19. For faience in Iron Age Crete, *B S A* 55 (1960), 134, v. 37, pl. 39; *Fortetsa* 208; *Vrokastro* 135-7, 148, pl. 35; and in Rhodes, *C Rh* 8 (1936), 163, fig. 150

35] Blinkenberg, *F G O* 230-3; Catling, *C B M W* 240-1; cf. E. Gjerstad in *S C E* 4, 2, 382-3

36] Karphi, *B S A* 38 (1937–8), 112-21; for 'shield-ring' (*ibid.* 113, pl. 29, 2, 439) cf. *Ker.* 1, 86, fig. 5; weapons, cf. *E G A* 94 (no. 1. 4), 147 (type I (a)); tool-types, see Catling, *C B M W* 78-109 and J. Deshayes, *Les Outils de Bronze* (1960), *passim*; stands, Catling, *op. cit.* 211, no. 47 and 214, with n.4; iron, *B S A* 38 (1937–8), 122-3

37] For chronology of Mouliana tomb A, see most recently Desborough, *L M S* 26, 177, 188. Weapons, cf. *PGP* 311-12; *EGA* 98-9, 103, 118-20, 127, 131, and add an iron spearhead from Phaistos, *Annuario* n.s. 19-20 (1957–8), 359; tools, *Vrokastro* 138, 143; pins, see esp. Jacobsthal, *GP* 1-2, 16 and *Fortetsa* 10, 195, no. 35; fibulae, *FGO* 46-78, and add *Annuario* 33-34 (1955–6), 215 fig. 33 (Gortyn); 35-36 (1957–8), 359 fig. 215 and *BdA* 40 (1955), 159 (Phaistos); 'shield-rings', *Vrokastro* 138 and n.36 above; Mouliana jug, Müller-Karpe, *JdI* 77 (1962), 76, fig. 39; tripod, *Vrokastro* 132 and Catling, *CBMW* 192-9, 217 (*ibid*. 196, no. 12 for Gelidonya wreck)

38] Iron pikes, *Fortetsa* 202, and *ibid*. 22, 200 for a solitary bronze spearhead; pins, *ibid*. 22 and also perhaps 138 (P 1633); 195; Agios Ioannis, *BSA* 55 (1960), 146, graves III, IV and V; tripod, *Fortetsa* 22 (XI. 188); lead, ivory and faience finds, *ibid*. 197, 208-9 (cf. *BSA* 55 (1960), 148 for a contemporary find of faience at Agios Ioannis); fibulae, *ibid*. 195-6 and *AM* 56 (1931), 114, nos. 4-5 (Tylissos); biconical pins, *BSA* 55 (1960), 146, pl. 39 (V. 27); 58 (1963), 43, no. 3; cf. *Fortetsa* 195, type I

39] Fibulae and pins, *Fortetsa* 196, type 5; 195, type 4 (cf. Jacobsthal, *GP* 17-18); weapons, *EGA* 98-9, 104, 110, 123, 126-7, 131-2, type V; twin spears, 135-9, and add *BSA* 55 (1960), 131 (Knossos)

40] Vergina: see publications listed in Appendix to Chapter 4, p. 208 and add M. Andronikos, *Balkan Studies* 2 (1961), 89f. and the full publication, *Vergina*, vol. I (1969), which appeared too late to be considered. Vardino fibula, W.A. Heurtley, *Prehistoric Macedonia* (1939), 231, fig. 104a, a; Kozani, *Ergon* 1960, 99f. See *PPS* 31 (1965), 229-40

41] Iron swords, *EGA* 94 (1. 6-7), to which may be added at least six examples since published; spearheads, *ibid*. 118 (A. 11), 123 – a further example, *Praktiká* 1960, pl. 78α, resembles those found further south; knives, compare *Praktiká* 1958, pl. 73α with examples from Athens and Theotokou (pp. 233, 236 above); pottery, Desborough *LMS* 143 mentions c.25 Protogeometric pieces; Andronikos, *Vergina* (Lund, 1964) 5, gives c.550 as the total number of pots found; *Vollgriffschwert, AD* 18 (1963), 222 fig. 9 (cf. W. Kimmig in *Studien aus Alteuropa* I (ed. R. von Uslar and K. J. Narr, 1964), 275-6); bronze sword, *AD* 17 (1961–2), 241-2 fig. 28, pl. 146α; *PPS* 31 (1965), 239 n.1; Catling, *Antiquity* 35 (1961), 119 fig. 2

42] O. Davies in *BSA* 28 (1926–1927), 197-9; *PPS* 31 (1965), 239, but it was an error to say that the *second* stage antedated the tombs at Vergina

43] See Ph. Petsas in *Essays in Memory of Karl Lehmann* (1964), 255 and n.4 on population elements. Among the bronze decorative objects, cf. M. Gimbutas, *Bronze Age Cultures in Central and Eastern Europe* (1965), pl. 52 a for kindred but different use of spiral tubes; spectacle-fibulae, see most recently J. Alexander, *AJA* 69 (1965), 7-23 and n.4; arched fibulae at Vergina, e.g. *Praktiká* 1958, 91, pl. 67β; *AD* 17 (1961–2), 241-2, pl. 145α (grave C A), and 285 fig. 58; cf. *FGO* 67 (Pateli), and note also the early fibula-types in what must be a comparatively late context at Mesembria in Thrace, *BCH* 91 (1967), 731, fig. 9, and in general J. Sundwall, *Die älteren Italischen Fibeln* (1943), 21 and J. Alexander, *Antiquity* 36 (1962), 123f.

44] Hammond, *Epirus* 352 on lack of ancient iron-working (contra *ibid.* 153 for more recent times); 202-4, 310-11, 320-63 *passim* on Vodhinë (cf. Chapter 4, n.17 above); Boubousti, W. A. Heurtley, *B S A* 28 (1926–7), 167-79 and *Prehistoric Macedonia* 227-9, and for a pin from the same site, Jacobsthal, *G P* 2, n.3; 16 fig. 47. See now Catling's discussion of Epirot swords, *B S A* 63 (1968), 98-104

45] On typology of flame-shaped spearheads, see now Catling, *B S A* 63 (1968), 105-7; spectacle-fibulae, *A J A* 69 (1965), 8-11; Prendi's dating of Vodhinë, *Epirus* 202, 228; pottery survivals, Dakaris *P P S* 33 (1967), 31; and cf. above, Chapter 4, n.17. Vitsa graves, *A D* 21, 2, 289-90, pl. 292; Vajzë, *Epirus* 228-30, 311-12, 320-63 *passim*; double-shank pins, J. Alexander, *P P S* 30 (1964), 173-4, type v; F. Maier, *Germania* 34 (1956), 69f., fig. 1, 10 and 2; beads, *Epirus* 346 n.2 for comparison with Chauchitza, showing that these are of the type dealt with by Maier, *Germania loc. cit.* 70 fig. 1, 3; for the spearhead, *Epirus* 352 (on p. 348 it appears under C 2); compare *E G A* 130, type Q, fig. 8f.; glass beads, cf. *L M S* 92 on Kafkania, but also Benac and Čović, *Glasinac* 1 (1956), 47, 55 (Iron Age); 2 (1957) 75, 77, 81 (seventh/fourth centuries)

46] Pins, bowls, gold rings, ivory, fibulae: *Ker.* 5, 1, graves 1, 2, 7, 38, 41, 74 and Agora, *Hesp.* 18 (1949), 275f.; Müller-Karpe, *JdI* 77 (1962), 65f., figs. 10, 8-9; 18, 1-7; 23-5; 27, 7-11; 29; for weapons, add the grave in the Agora, *Hesp.* 16 (1947), 196f. and those on the Areopagus, *A M* 22 (1897), 478, which produced a solitary bronze spearhead. For later dating of the fibulae, see esp. R. S. Young, *Hesp.* suppl. vol. 2 (1939), 104-5.

Agora grave, E. L. Smithson, *Hesperia* 37 (1968), 77f., 109f., nos. 65-7 (pins) and 68-9 (fibulae); *ibid.* 111 on Berlin gold fibulae, and cf. the Elgin jewellery in London, R. A. Higgins, *B M Q* 23 (1960–1), 101-7. Iron pins and fibulae, e.g. *Ker.* 5, 1, graves 12, 76, 80; *Hesp.* 16 (1947), 196; *A A A* 1 (1968), 22 (T. x, Kriezis St.). An iron knife and possible dagger from Thorikos, *Hesp.* 30 (1961), 303, pl. 64a, a, b: compare a knife from Vranesi in Boeotia, *P P S* 21 (1955), 177 n.3. Arrowhead: below, n.48

47] For these finds, *Ker.* 5, 1, graves 12, 13, 23, 42, 43, 69, 71, 75, 76 (=*Ker.* 1, 107-8, grave α), 80, 86, 87; gold bands, *ibid.* 185-90, pl. 158, and add now *A D* 20, 2 (1965), 40, from grave hS 109; *ibid.* 78, pl. 44α (Kavalotti St.); *A A A* 1 (1968), 22, 26, fig. 5 (Kriezis St); Müller-Karpe, *JdI* 77, figs. 17, 8-13; 19-21; and p. 66 on the nave-rings in grave 13; Isis grave, *A E* 1898, 105ff.; *C V A* Athens 1, pls. 3-6; Toronto group, *JHS* 51 (1931), 164f., pl. 6 and *Ker.* 1, 65-6. For new gold jewellery from Anavysos, see *A D* 21, 2 (1966), 97-8, pl. 95α.

48] Corinth, *A J A* 41 (1937), 543f.; Jacobsthal, *G P* 89, 160, 162; *Tiryns* 1, 128f. and *A M* 78 (1963), 25-42; Mycenae, *B S A* 50 (1955), 242, fig. 2, pl. 49f.; 246, fig. 4, pl. 49c; Corinthian grave at Athikia, *Hesperia* 33 (1964), 91-3; later Corinthian pins, *G P* 7 n.1, 10-11, fig. 33; weapons, see above references for Tiryns, esp. *A M* 78, 35-6, Beil. 5, 3; Mycenae, *B S A* 49 (1954), 262, pl. 45, inv. 53-125; Argos, an iron dirk or long dagger from a Middle Geometric grave (unpublished) is exhibited in Argos Museum; Corinth arrowhead and curved knife, *Hesp.* 17 (1948), 206, pl. 72, B 9, 10; but see now *A A A* 1 (1968), 22 (T. x) for a contemporary Attic parallel. Euboea, *Excavations at Lefkandi*, 23

49] See esp. *Fortetsa* 195-202, with spectacle-fibula *ibid.* 54, 196, pl. 37, x. 558; Khaniale Tekke, *B S A* 49 (1954), 215-28, esp. 227, pl. 29, 49 and 62; and note that J. Boardman now advocates a Protogeometric 'B' date for the two small 'crocks' and their contents (*B S A* 62 (1967), 59). But I cannot follow him in his high dating of the earliest Idaean Cave bronzes and of the Fortetsa belt and quiver

50] *Vrokastro* 154-74 (bone-enclosures), 99-122 (town site); Kolophon, Lorimer *H M* 348; Praisos, *B S A* 12 (1905-6), 33 fig. 10, 64; Zakro, *B S A* 7 (1900-1), 148; Blinkenberg, *F G O* 83-106

51] *F G O* 87-106, 128-85; and for the Agora, Young, *Hesp.* suppl. vol. 2, 87, 92-3, 104-5; Halos, *B S A* 18 (1911-12), 11-14, 24 fig. 14; Theotokou, Wace and Thompson, *Prehistoric Thessaly* 213, fig. 147b, d; Andritsaina, *G P* 4, 7-8, 94, figs. 16-22 and H. G. G. Payne, *Perachora* 1, 71 n.3; Western Greece, see Sundwall, *Die älteren Italischen Fibeln, passim*; Epirus, *F G O* 106-10 and Hammond, *Epirus* 410; (Payne, *Perachora* 1, 170, attributes this to Corinthian influence); Macedonia, *F G O* 135-6 (VII 6c) and 80-1 on Aivasil; *B S A* 26 (1923-5), 7, 25, pl. IV A and *Ant. J.* 1 (1921), 210, pl. VII, 2, 5-7 (Chauchitza)

52] Mycenae, *B S A* 49 (1954), 263, pl. 45, inv. 53-636; 51 (1956), 128, pl. 35a, inv. 55-10; Tiryns, *A M* 78 (1963), 25, 43, figs. 13-14 (contrast *Hesp.* suppl. vol. 2, 86, 104, fig. 73, XVII. 26; gold pins, *A A A* 1 (1968), 26, fig. 11 (T. XII); *Perachora* 1, 70-3, pl. 17 – compare pl. 17, 2 (fig. 11, 3)

with Jacobsthal *G P* fig. 33 (the separate classification of these as 'spits' is misleading, *ibid.* 13-15). A type XII fibula also occurs in a late eighth-century context at Emborio in Chios (Boardman, *Greek Emporio* 210, no. 206); but a Peloponnesian version may later have been developed as Payne suggested (*Perachora* 1, 171); grave-finds, e.g. *Thera* 2, 299, no. 3, fig. 489t

53] *Ker.* 5, 1, graves 6, 49, 50, 55, 56, 72, with 58 and 59 rather later (58 held further nave-rings, *JdI* 77 (1962), 72-3, fig. 21, 9-10); Eretria, *A E* 1903, 1ff. and *Antike Kunst* 9 (1966), 120-4. Eleusis, *A E* 1898, 103, 107; Dipylon, *A M* 18 (1893), 120f. (*Ker.* 5, 1, 180 n.176 for further references to the figurines from grave XIII); Agora, *Hesp.* suppl. vol. 2, 41, 67, 86, 92, 103; Spata, *A D* 6 (1921), parartêma, 138; Pnyx, *A M* 18 (1893), 414-15; Thera, *A M* 28 (1903), 262

54] On the Argos find see *B C H* 81 (1957), 322-86; *E G A* 13-14, 81-4

55] *E G A* 3, 217 on Dipylon crest-holder; 38-51 on shield-bosses (esp. nos. A 24-6, 30-2, 53); 61-6 on metal-faced shields; 87-8 on greaves

56] *E G A* 93-139 *passim* on weapons (the first type of spearhead referred to is type M, *ibid.* 127-8); to the examples there should be added one from Exochi, *Act. Arch.* 28 (1957), 53, 186, fig. 124; saurotêres, *A M* 18 (1893), 107f.; *A E* 1898, 98 n.1; daggers, Mycenae, Argos and Dreros, *E G A* 94, 98, 99; knives, *Hesp.* suppl. vol. 2, 49, 94, with references for Eleusis and Thera; *B S A* 12 (1905-6), 91 fig. 12; Eretria, *A E* 1903, 9; *Vrokastro* 166-7; *Fortetsa* 137, pl. 172, 1594; long knives, *E G A* 100, type II, with *Ker.* 4, 29, 35, pl. 38, inv. M 52

57] *EGA* 142, 148, to which add Tiryns, *AM* 78 (1963), 41; Corinth, above, n.48; Pherai, Y. Bequignon, *Recherches archéologiques à Phères* (1937), 52, tomb 85-6; sling-bullet, *BSA* 31 (1930–1), 9, 38, fig. 16, 25; axe-heads, *EGA* 166 and note the iron-lugged axe from Nea Anchialos in Macedonia, *AD* 20, 2 (1965), 421, pl. 472δ

58] See Desborough, *LMS* 44-6

59] See Hammond, *Epirus* 436 and *AD* 18, 2 (1963), pl. 187β for Dodona; L. Lerat, *BCH* 85 (1961), 352f. on Delphi, and 61 (1937), 44f. for tomb. The occurrence of a tomb actually within a later sanctuary-site surely tells *against* the site having been sacred at the time of burial; on the Nekyomanteion in Epirus, Hammond (*op. cit.* 369) seems to infer the opposite of the truth

60] J. Boardman, *BSA* 58 (1963), 1-7 on Sparta; P. Jacobsthal, *JHS* 71 (1951), 85-95, esp. n.2, on Ephesus; J. L. Caskey and P. Amandry, *Hesperia* 21 (1952), 173-5 on the Argive Heraeum; Desborough, *PGP* 216 on Samos; Heraeum chronology: see the summary by E. Diehl, *AA* 79 (1964), 495-8 with references, and the comments of G. M. A. Hanfmann, *HSCP* 61 (1953), 9, 29, nn.40-42; *PGP* 229-30 on Lindos; Payne, *Perachora*, 1, 112, a dating which should now be slightly lowered; Boardman, *The Cretan Collection in Oxford* (1961), 56-7 on the Dictaean Cave; for the Idaean Cave, see below, Chapter 6, p. 341; M. Robertson and S. Benton, *BSA* 43 (1948), 1 n.3; 48 (1953), 257 on Aetos

61] H. Hencken, *AJA* 62 (1958), 270-1; Delphi, L. Lerat, *BCH* 85 (1961), 340-2; cf. Dunbabin in *Pera-*

chora 2, 439-40 and Boardman, *Greek Emporio* 211, no. 241; but see J. Close-Brooks in *SE* 35 (1968), 327 for a contrary view

62] Sparta fibulae, above, n.33 – the final tally comes to over 70 of the later types, against four or more of type 11 (one in a sixth-century context!) and the 'frequent' type 1 2. *Perachora* 1, 169-70, pl. 72, 7, 15 (Blinkenberg's 1 8); and 2, 433-41, giving a total figure of 7 or more of types 1 and 11 against over 70 of later types (excluding ivory specimens, of which there were well over a hundred). Other sanctuary finds, Blinkenberg, *FGO passim*; and compare the fibulae from the sanctuary of Athena Itonia at Philia in Thessaly, *AD* 20, 2 (1965), 312, pl. 366α, and the late pins, pl. 366β. Jacobsthal, *GP* 3-13; Berbati, G. Säflund, *Excavations at Berbati* 83, 90, no. 48; other objects, *PPS* 31 (1965), 236-7

63] Olympia, H. Weber, *Ol. Forsch.* 1 (1944), 146-65; cf. H. L. Lorimer, *HM* 294. Delphi, P. Perdrizet, *Fouilles de Delphes* 5, 214 for iron finds, 93-105 and 119-22 for bronze. At the new sanctuary at Philia in Thessaly, the iron weapons are said to outnumber the bronze (*AD* 20, 2 (1965), 312). Individual finds, *EGA* 118-19, A.13-14, B.7; *ibid.* 122-3, type G, found in earlier graves; contrast 121, type E; 123-6, type J; 130, type R

64] On tripod-cauldrons, A. Furtwängler in *Olympia* 4 (1890), 75-93; W. Lamb, *Greek and Roman Bronzes* (1929), 44-7; S. Benton, *BSA* 35 (1934-5), 74-130; F. Willemsen, *Ol. Forsch.* 3 (1957). Lefkandi, H. W. Catling in *Excavations at Lefkandi* (ed. Popham and Sackett), 28-9

65] Staïs tripod, *BSA* 35 (1934-5), 76 and n.5; Tiryns treasure, *AM* 55 (1930), 137, fig. 7; Willemsen, *op. cit.*

(n.64), 10-11 on material, cf. 65 ; *ibid.*
4-13, and Benton, *B S A* 35 (1934–5),
76-8, 80-2, 92 on the earliest class; at
ibid. 112, n.5 the Kerameikos tripod is
dated slightly too high; Eretria
cauldrons, *Antike Kunst* 9 (1966),
120-4

66] *Ker.* 1, 95, pls. 63-4; *B S A* 33
(1932–3), 51-2, nos. 88, 95 and 35
(1934–5), 102 n.1, for Aetos; Knossos, *B S A* 58 (1963), 37, no. 18, pl.
12; *Perachora* 1, 55, n.7 for later

finds; *B S A* 35, 102-12 for painted
representations

67] Catling, *C B M W* 217

68] *Ol. Forsch.* 3, 166f.; (cf. pl. 22,
B1248 for a rough parallel with the
form of the decoration at Lefkandi);
H.-V. Herrmann, *A M* 77 (1962), 34.
For similar doubts about the high
chronology of the Olympia tripods,
cf. P. Amandry, *Gnomon* 32 (1960),
461 : C. Rolley, *R A* 1967, 147

6

External Relations

◆ ◆ ◆
◆ ◆
◆

It is one thing to establish, from the material evidence, that an ancient civilization maintained foreign relations in various directions and with various peoples; quite another to interpret the nature of those relations. The former task alone will prove sufficiently complex to take up much of the discussion in this chapter. As for interpretation, I think it is best to establish straight away certain general principles, in as uncontroversial a form as is possible in a hotly-debated field of study.

In the particular period of early Iron Age Greece with which we are concerned, the evidence of material objects is by far the broadest in scope; there is other testimony in the form of oral traditions, evidence from dialect, and even written sources; but these involve quite different ambiguities and problems, and they have little that is worth while to say about, for example, Greek commercial activity abroad. They may therefore be considered presently in their particular contexts. The material evidence embraces objects which appear to have travelled some distance from their place of origin, and other material features which seem extraneous to the areas where they appear. But at this point one almost inevitably passes, in one stride, from platitude to dogma. To say that this evidence comprises two main elements, namely trade and population-movement of some kind, may seem a harmless inference, but it at once involves one in difficulties. First, the two categories are not in fact inter-exclusive: to take a fairly obvious instance, the establishment of a trading-post on a foreign shore is fundamentally a commercial act, but it may involve natives of one country settling more or less permanently in another. Again, the trading activities of the ancient world have been the subject of the most radical reappraisals in recent years, as a result of which many scholars would agree that the whole modern conception of commercial principles, based on the supply-

and-demand market, is so inapplicable to classical antiquity that the very
words 'trade' and 'commerce' should be used and understood in a qualified
sense in ancient contexts: a few extremists have even virtually denied that
trade took place in any sense.[1] This last view may be emphatically rejected;
but I do not think it necessary to venture further into this question, beyond saying that there are overwhelmingly strong grounds for concluding
that, at this period, the appearances of Greek or foreign objects or features
away from home are the result of the activities of *individuals*, and not of
any kind of governmental or state enterprise. It may also be worth observ-
ing here, as a warning, that objects can travel great distances, quite independently of their original producers or owners, by many other agencies
besides commerce: one thinks immediately of gifts sent to sanctuaries and
other destinations by foreign rulers and other notables: of loot brought
back from wars abroad (both of these are categories for which we have
evidence from other periods of antiquity): and of pilgrimages and other
overseas journeys undertaken for non-commercial purposes. As for the
second element in the material evidence distinguished above, that of
population-movement in the widest sense of the term, it embraces a great
variety of activities peaceful and warlike; besides individual travel, we
may enumerate, in their different degrees of bellicosity, colonization,
and settlement of more or less unpopulated regions; mercenary service
abroad; mass immigration, whether unopposed or involving destruction;
and pure military aggression.

We may go on to discuss, and indeed virtually to dismiss for our period,
one aspect of these last activities – the military one. Warlike activity
presents a peculiar difficulty in that the evidence for it, however positive in
itself, may well afford no clue as to the identity or geographical origin of
the aggressors. The prime class of evidence is invariably formed by the
destruction of settlement-sites, and the burning of many of the great
Mycenaean citadels in Greece, near the end of the III B period, provides
a famous example of such a situation: the ruins give no indication as to
whether the destroyers came from within or beyond Greece. Similarly the
destruction of Troy VII A, as an example of what is now presumed to be
Greek activity abroad, would be equally obscure but for the fortunate
presence of a strong oral, and later written, tradition. But when we turn
to our period proper we find that, within Greece, evidence of this kind is in
any case virtually non-existent: from about the middle of the Mycenaean
III C period on, there is scarcely any trace of the violent destruction of a
settlement down to almost the end of the eighth century BC, when the

Geometric settlements at Asine and Lefkandi were apparently burned, and when a recently-excavated house at Miletus seems also to have been destroyed. A house at Argos, found to have been destroyed at the beginning of the ninth century, provides a rare exception.[2] It is legitimate to suggest that this is partly due to the limited scope of excavations: but the fact remains that we can infer no warlike activity, least of all that involving foreign invaders, until we have the evidence for it. There is the less direct evidence of fortification-walls, providing against aggression but, once again, giving no evidence as to whether the anticipated threat came from foreign sources. Even these, however, are very sparse in their distribution

see 125 at this time: the discovery of the early fortifications at Old Smyrna, the first of which dates to the mid-ninth century, the second about a hundred years later, was a revelation in that it finds no counterpart on the Greek mainland: only a probable Geometric wall at Eleusis, and an earlier one found at Phaistos, can be placed with any conviction before the end of the eighth century.[3] The Smyrna fortifications are also informative because, in the technique of their construction, the earliest walls betray no sign of foreign influence. One final potential class of evidence for warfare is that provided by characteristic 'national weapons', occurring in contexts which can be shown to be military: but here we should realize that the diagnostic quality of these weapons is often much less than has been claimed;[4] and here again we find that such evidence is almost entirely absent in the Greek early Iron Age, not least because a rudimentary iron technology is a poor breeding-ground for clear-cut types.

This means that there is virtually no direct evidence that the inhabitants of Greek lands during the dark age engaged in warfare with any external peoples. Warfare there must have been, and this is suggested not only by the few fortifications, and by the inaccessible location of hill-top sites like Karphi, Kavousi and Vrokastro in the eastern part of Crete, but by the far commoner, if still sporadic, provision of weapons in graves, and their occurrence in settlements too. But *a priori* there is no reason to think that these provisions were made against anyone but fellow-Greeks; only when we come to consider other forms of population-movement not immediately accompanied by violence, shall we find any hint that the superficial peacefulness of dark age Greece may have suffered disturbances from without.

We must begin, however, by going back to the widespread destruction of Mycenaean sites late in the III B period; this forms one of the most definite 'horizons' in prehistory, yet its problems are numerous and perhaps insoluble. It concerns us in the main because it raises the question of oral traditions – traditions which, paradoxically, make no mention of it, but which, if they prove *not* to be connected with this era of destruction, must be accommodated at some later point in the sequence of developments. These traditions deal largely with migrations, and are therefore evidence of prime importance for the question of Greece's external links; we may summarize their content in so far as they can possibly be relevant to our period. But we should at the same time admit the quite distinct testimony of the distribution of the Greek dialects, which is in the main the result of these same migrations, and which thus offers incontestable evidence, *a posteriori*, for their reality, and may even tell us something of their date.

The Evidence of Dialect and Tradition

To the Greeks of the Classical period, the population of their country had essentially a common ancestry; yet the greater part of it by far consisted of elements which had reached their homes only by migrations or invasions which belonged relatively late in the sequence of their history – that is to say, at or after the end of the 'Heroic Age'. Since the principle of common ancestry was so strongly held, these population-movements were thought of as essentially internal affairs: Greeks of one tribe or element had moved to displace Greeks of another, and thus set in motion a whole series of similar migrations. The great unifying force was the 'Heroic Age', in which almost all elements claimed a share, unprejudiced by their later movements. The traditions of these movements were, as they had to be, largely in accordance with the distribution of the Greek dialects in historical times; how far are they in harmony with the material record?

Geographically, the three main dialect-groups in historical Greece were spread in three adjacent, roughly parallel bands across the Aegean.[5] The Aeolic dialect was present in the speech of Thessaly and Boeotia, and appeared in a slightly different, if not necessarily purer, form away to the east in the island of Lesbos and the adjacent coast of north-western Asia Minor. The Ionic group of dialects spread from Attica, through Euboea and the northern and central Cyclades to the central part of the west coast of Asia Minor. The Doric/North-West Greek group ran, in the most extensive of the three belts, from Aetolia and Akarnania through Phokis and Lokris into the Peloponnese, and then across the Aegean via Crete and the southernmost Cyclades, to the Dodecanese and south-western Asia Minor: within this belt lay the isolated and distinct area of Arcadia, whose 'Arcado-Cyprian' dialect belongs to none of the three main groups.

Within each of the three bands, Greek tradition posited a generally west-to-east movement of population, by displacement and subsequent migration, and the detailed evidence of dialect supports this. Often, however, these movements spilled across from one band into another; as with the Pylians from the south-western Peloponnese who were supposed to have gravitated to Attica, before partaking in the Ionian migration across the Aegean. But the picture presented by the oral traditions is far more complex than this. For some of the migrant elements were believed to have been already in motion during the Heroic Age, sometimes in quite different directions from the essentially easterly trend of the migrations at the end of that age. The Boeotians who, at some date before the Trojan War, had already settled in the former 'Cadmeïs', were thought of as a kind of advance guard or offshoot of the subsequent Boeotian immigration which was to bring to this region a permanent admixture of North-West Greek dialectal elements; but in contrast, the movements of the Dorians commemorated for this early period were in an apparently aimless anti-clockwise circle, from Phthiotis north-eastwards to Histiaea in Thessaly, then up into the Pindus range, then finally southwards, probably to the small region of Doris which preserved their name; only the last stage could be regarded as a part of their final, concerted move south-eastwards across Greece.

The main spell of migration after the Trojan War was inaugurated, according to Thucydides (1, 12), by the action of the Thessalians: they expelled Boeotian settlers from what was now to become Thessalian territory, a movement which Thucydides dated sixty years after the Trojan War; as a result these Boeotians joined their kinsmen in the Cadmeïs (see above); and then, twenty years later again, the Dorians moved, presumably from their latest area of sojourn in Doris, to their final conquest of the Peloponnese. The same historian dated the Dorian occupation of the island of Melos to around 1116 BC (V, 112,2), without relating this date to that of their other movements. Other historians supply further details: Herodotus (VII, 176,6) that the Thessalians who began this disturbance had come across from Thresprotia in Epirus; that the Dorian conquest of the Peloponnese had been preceded, a hundred years earlier, by an abortive invasion on their part under Hyllos, the son of Heracles (IX, 26,6); and that Achaea received its name from its occupation by Achaeans from the Argolid under Tisamenos, refugees from the Dorian invasion, which led to the expulsion of its earlier, Ionic population to Attica (1, 145). The leadership of the Dorians was agreed to have remained in the hands of the same family of the Heracleidae, who were to form the dynasty of the Spartan kings (cf. Chapter I, p. 11), but who were themselves not Dorian. For Elis, Pausanias adds that Aetolians under Oxylos conquered this region in the wake of the Dorians (11, 18,8; V, 3,6; 4,2, etc.) Smaller tribal movements are also hinted at: such as that of the Dryopes, whose habitat seems to have moved during the era of migrations (compare *Iliad* IX, 484 with Thucydides II, 102,2).

These movements are mainly located within the third and outermost 'dialect belt'; but their repercussions extended deeply into the other two as well. The first onset of the Thessalians was thought to have set in motion the eastward migration in the Aeolic belt, although we have only the authority of Strabo (XIII, 582) for believing that this migration began so early; that Aeolians had at some time passed over from Boeotia and other mainland areas to Lesbos and north-western Asia Minor was however universally accepted (e.g. Thucydides III, 23; VII, 57; VIII, 5,2), and they were also believed to have settled in Euboea, the Ionic dialect of that island being explained by a later wave of settlers from Athens. Yet the evidence of dialect shows that substantial Aeolic elements must have remained behind in their homelands, for both Thessaly and Boeotia show a fusion of Aeolic and North-West Greek forms to a degree which can only be explained on such a hypothesis, and which is not fully paralleled, for example, in the areas of Dorian settlement. It also seems possible, from similar but slighter evidence, that the extent of the Aeolic dialect on the Greek mainland was once much greater in scope, and spread to Phocis, Locris, southern Aetolia and even Corinth; there are fragments of the oral tradition to support this, some of them preserved in Thucydides (III, 102; IV, 42), but the traces are too scanty to have any chronological force.

In the central, Ionic belt the migration of population was believed to have in part arisen from two movements we have already noted: the expulsion of Messenians from Pylos by the Dorians, and of Ionians from Achaea by the refugee Achaeans, both of which groups converged on Attica for refuge. Neither of these movements can be said to find any support from the evidence of dialect, which indeed compels us to add a final stage to the sequence of events in Achaea remembered by tradition, since the dialect of Achaea in historical times, though enveloped in some obscurity, must probably be associated with Doric and North-West Greek. There are other, less specific traditions about the earlier spread of the Ionic dialect – suggesting, for example, that it extended round much of the coast of the Saronic Gulf to include Megara, Epidauros and Kynouriar

(Herodotus VIII, 73,3; Thucydides II, 26,2; Strabo IX, 392) – which find equally little reinforcement in later dialect-evidence, save perhaps that Halicarnassus, traditionally colonized from Troezen and reckoned a 'Dorian' city, spoke an Ionic dialect in the fifth century. However, the ensuing stage in the traditional account, the movement of the Ionians eastwards from Attica and elsewhere, is real enough: Ionic becomes the dialect of Euboea, the northern and central Cyclades, Chios, Samos and the central part of the Asia Minor coast, from Phocaea in the north to Mylasa in the south.

An important question here was the chronological relation between this and the other movements. Greek tradition maintained that there had been a causal connection between the Dorian incursion into the Peloponnese and the Ionian migration across the Aegean; but it combined this, somewhat awkwardly, with a belief that there had been a lapse of two generations' length between the two. A sojourn in Athens, which was supposed to have happened in the case of the contingents from Pylos and Achaea, was sometimes used to explain this delay, but there were also Ionian migration traditions which posited a direct movement eastwards from places other than Athens. During this two-generation interval there was said to have occurred another important event, the unsuccessful attempt of the Dorians to conquer Attica, repulsed by King Codrus; at this time, however, the Dorians did occupy the Megarid, perhaps the last important stage of their main wave of conquest on the Greek mainland. According to the traditions, they had by now already begun their expansion overseas, at least to Thera, whose settlers were led by Theras, the contemporary of the conquerors of the Peloponnese.

The movements described above obviously find some ulterior confirmation in the distribution of dialects in historical times; but how far beyond this point do the traditions invite credulity? Can we accept their testimony for the general picture they present of organized armies, fortifications and pitched battles? Or on the matter of the relative and absolute chronology of the migrations? Or, most specific of all, on the reality and activities of the individual leaders? Archaeological evidence cannot hope to contribute much to the last question, but it is fair to use it in considering the other two. Before we do so, however, we should recognize that there are very strict limits to the scope which we should allow to these traditions in depicting the Greek world at the end of the Heroic Age. These limits have been established by modern scholarship, but they are still ignored or overstepped by some modern scholars. The whole conception of the migrant groups as racially and linguistically distinct peoples, strange to each other, which some authorities have inferred from these traditions, seems to be unjustified. The traditions themselves, after all, assume, though they may not stress, the basic unity of the Greek people in the later part of the Heroic Age, and modern investigation has heavily underlined the truth of this notion.

There is, first of all, the internal evidence of dialect: similarities and differences in word-forms, if studied closely enough, can yield a (purely relative) chronological scheme for the changes involved; these similarities and differences may then be plotted on a map; and if there are rough dates available for the geographical movements which have brought about the distribution, then some kind of absolute chronology for the dialectal changes can even be achieved. In recent years, this combination of methods has been applied with some very interesting results;[6] it has been shown that many of the diagnostic features of the classical dialects are of relatively late development, and in absolute terms can be placed later than c.1200 BC (this being the earliest possible date for the Dorian migration). These findings are particularly interesting in the case of the Doric and North-West Greek group of dialects. The features which distinguish this group from Aeolic are very often features shared with Ionic, which must surely date from the period after the Dorian migration; those which distinguish it from both Ionic *and* Aeolic are in many cases later still. Only those features which unite the Doric and the Aeolic groups, to the exclusion of Ionic, are likely to be the result of early developments (earlier, that is, than 1200); and in most of these cases the innovations took place on the part of Ionic, with Doric and Aeolic preserving the older forms. In other words, not only were the Dorians at the time of their main migration southwards and eastwards across Greece speaking a form of Greek, but their speech may have been perhaps almost indistinguishable from that of a large part of the population of Greece north of Attica, including a substantial element that lay within the bounds of Mycenaean culture. Furthermore, even the dialect of the Mycenaean Peloponnese, if the inferences made from the Linear B texts[7] are correct, was not at this time very different from this 'Northern Greek' speech.

Many centuries later, evidence of a different kind becomes available to us, with the historical development of the peoples belonging to each dialect-group. The antithesis between Dorian and Ionian came to assume almost racial proportions in Classical Greece; but an analysis of the political histories and attitudes of Greek states in the eighth, seventh and sixth centuries, in so far as we know of them, shows a decided absence of this division, apart from isolated prolongations of the Dorian advance such as the Spartan capture of Amyklai and conquest of Messenia; while developments in thought, in art, and even in architecture (for all the nomenclature of the Classical orders) show a similar refusal, with rare exceptions, to flow along the channels suggested by the dialect-division.[8] The growth of the great Doric/Ionic antithesis seems to be to a considerable degree the result of the political climate of Greece after the Persian Wars. This situation does not, to say the least, encourage us to look for a clear distinction in material culture during the dark age between Dorians and Ionians, or any other Greeks. Nevertheless, some effort in this direction must be made. Whether or not we are able to find any cultural differentiation between the various branches of the Greek people at the time of the migrations, we should at least seek to vindicate the migration traditions in the most general way; we should try, that is, to find evidence of the reality of these population movements at roughly the period that the traditions suggest. For if there is any truth whatever in their picture of warfare between organized attackers and defenders, it is scarcely credible that the archaeological record should show no trace of such episodes.

THE GREAT DESTRUCTIONS

The starting point of this whole enquiry (p. 298) was an event most clearly apparent in the archaeological record, unrecorded indeed by any other source: the widespread and roughly contemporaneous destruction of some Mycenaean sites, and the abandonment of many others, at or near the end of the III B period. How can this disaster, and its aftermath, best be fitted into the sequence of events commemorated by the traditions? An armed invasion from outside the Mycenaean world, followed by the settlement of the invaders, would be expected to have left its traces in the form of intrusive cultural features; an armed raid, by attackers who afterwards withdrew, is a second possibility which would avoid this requirement; an internal rising by the subjects of the Mycenaean rulers is another explanation which has been offered; while a fourth suggestion is that of some natural disaster, which led directly or indirectly to the results described. Each of these explanations has its own merits and defects, and we may try to evaluate each in relation to the migration traditions and the other evidence.

To those who would connect the great destructions with the Dorians, the first explanation has long been the most attractive; but it means bringing the Dorians from outside Mycenaean Greece. Others have identified these events with an earlier invasion by certain non-Dorian Greek tribes, succeeded no doubt by a Dorian immigration between fifty and two hundred years later: several have indeed gone further and placed the first coming of the Greeks at this time.[9] Certainly, if one believes that the agents of destruction then settled permanently in Greece, it seems perverse to regard them as other than Greeks: there are enough Greek migrations and settlements in the traditions to be accommodated in this era, without bringing in a foreign element as well. But what innovations did the invaders, whatever their source, bring with them? Or in different words, how does the material culture of Greece in the twelfth century BC differ from that of the thirteenth?

THE EVIDENCE FOR FOREIGN INVASION

It is still quite widely held that there is enough 'intrusive' evidence to satisfy a belief in an invasion, followed by permanent settlement from outside the Aegean area at this time. The relevant material consists primarily of new metal types: first, the bronze flange-hilted, straight-bladed sword known as the *Griffzungenschwert* (or, somewhat less accurately, 'Naue's Type II'); second, the spearhead with a flame-shaped blade and a complete cast socket (i.e. one without a dividing slit) – this somewhat small category may perhaps be enlarged by the inclusion of *all* spearheads with such sockets, irrespective of their blade-shape;[10] third, the type of flange-hilted dagger known as the 'Peschiera dagger'; fourth, the one-edged bronze knife, with or without a curved blade; fifth, the 'violin-bow' fibula, the earliest form of this type of brooch; and sixth, the lugged or 'trunnion'-axe (*Ärmchenbeil*). This list is confined to those types which can claim to be intruders of approximately the date of the destructions at the end of Mycenaean III B, and which are adequately represented in the Aegean area: it excludes rarities like the mould for the casting of a winged axe of northern Italian, or more probably Slovakian, type, found at Mycenae. The objects in the list are united in that they have all, at one time or another, been claimed as Central or Eastern European Bronze Age types and, by some scholars at least, as indications of a massive southward population movement from that region into Greece, closely connected with the destruction of the Mycenaean palaces.[11]

To fulfil this function, the types should appear with some abruptness at the time of destruction; they should become comparatively common in the ensuing period and be rare or unknown in the preceding one. Do all

102
103

U

103. Bronze spearhead with flame-shaped blade in the Ashmolean Museum, Oxford, said to have been found near Thebes. Length 18·4 cm; perhaps 12th century BC.

102. Two bronze swords of the 'Griffzungenschwert' type, from chamber-tombs B and A respectively, at Kallithea in western Achaea. Lengths 67·4 and 81·4 cm; 12th century BC.

or any of the six types conform to these conditions? To take first the *Griffzungenschwerter*, they certainly show a heavy incidence in the III C 　*102* period in the Aegean, and at a similar date further East; but in the latter area there are also found a sword from Tell Firaun in the Nile delta which bears the cartouche of Seti II, a Pharaoh whose short reign belongs in the last twenty years of the thirteenth century BC; and an example from a tomb at Enkomi for which Catling has argued a date equivalent to the transition from III B to III C in the Aegean, which is the latest possible dating for the group. The appearance of these specimens at such a date, on the hypothesis that they were being distributed from Central Europe, suggests that they must have reached the Aegean somewhat earlier; and this inference has now been confirmed by the full publication of Langada Tomb 21 on the island of Kos, where such a sword occurs in an exclusively III B context. Other Aegean specimens whose dating floats somewhat uncertainly between III B and III C may be equally early.[12] The only possible interpretation of this evidence is that the swords were known to, and used by, the Mycenaeans distinctly earlier than the great wave of destructions of the palaces.

Two of the other types, the flame-shaped spearhead and the 'Peschiera' 　*103* dagger, are alike in that no one, I think, will now dispute the fact that they are alien to the Aegean area, and to be derived probably from the northern Balkans and from Italy respectively; but they are also alike in the fairly strict geographical limits of their distribution in Greece. The spearheads are found, in dated contexts of this period, at Kalbaki and Parga in Epirus, at Metaxata on Kephallenia, at Mouliana in Crete and perhaps at Polis in Ithaka; the dagger is strongly represented in Crete (five examples, only one of them even loosely datable), and also occurs at Phylakopi on Melos, and on Naxos (undated). Both types are thus entirely absent, on present evidence, from the heart-land of Mycenaean culture; neither can be reasonably connected with a new wave of settlers in this region. Chronologically, the lanceolate spearheads do seem to date exclusively from after the end of Mycenaean III B: the 'Peschiera' daggers on the other hand must have begun to arrive earlier, for the example in tomb 86 in the Zafer Papoura cemetery at Knossos is to be dated at the very latest in the thirteenth century.[13]

The bronze knives present a more complex picture, since more than one variety is involved: bronze one-edged knives as a whole were no novelty to Late Bronze Age Greece. There are, however, a few examples with features which have been held to be intrusive: they are the handle with a ring-shaped pommel, the handle with a 'swallow-tail' terminal at the pommel end, the stop-ridge at the junction of the blade and handle, the S-curved outline to the blade, and the appearance of incised designs on the blade. But all these oddities appear in rare or unique cases; in Miss Sandars' words they 'might be important were they not peripheral to a large body of well-established, standard knife-types, in itself quite sufficient to account for these idiosyncrasies'. Nor are they clearly concentrated in date: for Tsountas' tomb 49 at Mycenae, the dromos of which produced an S-bladed knife, seems to be of III A date; the ring-handle from New Tomb XV at Ialysos may belong to III C, but the other uncanonical specimens – from Mycenae, the Dictaean Cave and Phaistos – are undated; while Marinatos has pointed out that there are early Aegean knives, of Mycenaean I and II date, which show some of the same features.[14]

The lugged axes, although once again far from common, show some chronological concentration in the Aegean area. An example from House I at Asine should be of III C date, another from the Anthedon hoard in Boeotia can with good reason be placed in this period, while a third from the Serraglio settlement on Kos is no later, although it could equally belong to III A or B. Others from Lindos and Dodona are undated; only an earlier variant from Mallia is a clear outlier in time. But alien as they undoubtedly are to Greece, the origin of the Bronze Age trunnion-axes can with certainty be placed, not in Europe but somewhere in south-western Asia, perhaps in Anatolia; there is now a striking illustration of their passage westwards from this general region, in the shape of the twenty examples found in the Cape Gelidonya wreck off south-western Anatolia. The presumed date of the wreck is in harmony with our chronological findings, while the find also demonstrates one means by which such objects could reach the Aegean: the entirely peaceful passage of cargoes of finished artefacts (in this case together with raw material). At this juncture we may also note that a greater, if less precisely defined, innovation may have passed to Greece from a similar direction and at a similar period: a new and lighter model of war-chariot, based on Egyptian design and first detectable in Greece on representations of the III C period.[15]

The violin-bow fibula represents, together with the *Griffzungenschwert*, the most comprehensive case in this list of types. In their simpler, early variants the fibulae are only less common than the swords; unlike these, they cannot yet be conclusively shown to have reached Greece in the III B period. But examples of more developed types (Blinkenberg's types I.8 and 10) have been found in Langada tomb 20 on Kos, which spanned the transition from III B to C; in tomb B at Metaxata on Kephallenia, where the most closely associated vases were actually of III B date; and in Old Tomb 74 at Enkomi, whose date may be contemporary with an early phase of III C. These finds give a hint that the simpler variants may have arrived some time previously, and it seems highly probable that some at least of the chamber-tombs 1, 8, 29 and 62 of Tsountas' excavations at Mycenae, in which plainer types occurred, will belong well back in the III B period; for the use of this cemetery was apparently associated with the occupation of the extra-mural settlement here, which was terminated by the great destructions at the end of III B.[16]

Throughout this discussion it has been assumed, or in some cases argued, that the types in question really are intruders to the Aegean area. The matter is beyond doubt in the cases of the flame-shaped spearhead, the Peschiera dagger, the trunnion-axe and perhaps some of the peculiar knife-types. But the sources of these types are very scattered geographically, and their total incidence in Greece is slight. With the fibulae and swords it is otherwise; and the question of their origin thus becomes pertinent. For the violin-bow fibulae, it is still impossible to reach a final decision: these objects appear, without any self-evident antecedents, in the Terremare of northern Italy, in Reinecke's phase D of the Central European Bronze Age, and (as we have seen) in the Aegean, probably during the Mycenaean III B period – phases which, according to orthodox chronology, would in each case be partly or wholly equated with the thirteenth century BC. There is thus no clear indication of priority in any of the three regions: the only pointer to a derivation from one of the two northern areas is the likely connection of the fibula with a new and thicker form of dress, and thus most naturally with a cool climate. On the other hand, the roughly simultaneous acceptance of the fibula in each region has suggested to some scholars a major climatic change, affecting Greece as well as the central regions of Europe, and perhaps leading to a large southward population movement. For the climatic change there is indeed some independent evidence, although hardly enough to encourage confident assertion. The question has recently been covered in a symposium, *World Climate from 8000 to 0 BC*, of the Royal Meteorological Society;[17] in a paper contributed to this under the title 'The Atlantic/sub-Boreal Transition', B. Frenzel sums up the developments in our period thus: '(Observations) . . . show that between 1500 and 700 BC, but most of all between 900 and 700 BC, climate tended to become cooler and moister in vast regions of the Northern

Hemisphere'. He adds that 'It can be shown conclusively that this deterioration took place', but warns that its 'intensity . . . should not be exaggerated'. On a later page he comments that 'mean annual temperatures seem to have decreased a little'. Now these findings are very far from providing a sufficient explanation for a widespread change of dress in the thirteenth century BC: the climatic change is neither intense enough nor abrupt enough. Indeed, much the same evidence had already led Professor Rhys Carpenter, in his J. H. Gray lectures delivered at Cambridge in 1965,[18] to almost exactly the opposite conclusion as to the effect of climate on Greece at the end of the Bronze Age. It was, he believes, not the onset of the new, cooler and wetter climatic era which influenced events at this time, but the culmination of the long preceding period of hot and dry weather; he goes on to attribute the very break-up of Mycenaean civilization to the drought and famine which these conditions eventually engendered.

With so much chronological latitude in the climatic evidence, certainty is impossible; but this digression is in any case relevant only to the fibulae. It must suffice to say that the apparently swift diffusion of the fibula, as of any new article of everyday dress of both sexes, is hard to associate with armed conquest or immigration, since it could only be a coincidence which led this diffusion to follow so immediately upon the first invention of the article; whereas the alternative explanation, that this was a form of dress-fastening acceptable in several areas of Europe at that time, involves no such coincidence: the humble merits of the fibula will have secured its own popularity. Its contemporary, the *Griffzungenschwert*, is in a different case, first because the sword is a weapon of war and can thus be more easily believed to have been diffused through conquest; and secondly, because this particular class of sword (unlike the violin-bow fibula) has now been clearly shown to have an unbroken and intelligible ancestry in earlier sword-types of Central Europe.[19] It is still true that, on the Mycenaean side, no explanation has yet been given as to why the Aegean bronzesmiths should have had to wait on an outside source to furnish them with a sword-type which simply represented a combination of features well known to them – the flanged hilt, made in one single casting with the blade, which in turn has roughly parallel edges and a flattish elliptical cross-section, interrupted by shallow ridges or channels – some of which features were represented on swords, and more especially on knives, throughout the Aegean Late Bronze Age. Even the earliest *Griffzungenschwerter* found in the Aegean may have been actually made there, and furthermore the type soon came to be produced locally in several variants, some of which may have been exported northwards.[20] Although there can now be no question of the type having had a purely Aegean origin, these difficulties still lead me to believe in some kind of parallel development in Central Europe and in the Aegean, rather than to suppose that the type was simply donated in its finished form from the one area to the other; which in turn makes the possibility of an armed invasion of Greece from the north, by sword-bearing warriors, recede even further.

THE DORIAN HYPOTHESIS

We have dwelt for a long time on the innovations of the period around 1200: this is, I think, justified by the fact that this era presents the most widespread horizon of destruction in Greece over many centuries of her history. If a massed invasion of Greece took place at any time in this period, it was surely then. Furthermore, we have at this time the undoubted phenomenon of mass-emigration by Mycenaeans to regions where they had hitherto formed a much smaller element in the population: this is shown by the sudden appearance of new cemetery-sites at the beginning of the III c period in Achaea, particularly in its western regions, and on Kephallenia; by the vast new cemetery at Perati on the eastern coast of Attica, and perhaps by smaller developments like the predominantly III c cemetery at Agios Ioannis near Monemvasia; by fresh settlement at Lefkandi in Euboea and Emborio on Chios, and by the clear signs of a new and specifically Mycenaean wave of settlers in Cyprus, and to a lesser extent at Tarsus in Cilicia. In Crete, there are cases of desertion and occasional destruction of lowland sites, and it is possible that Karphi and other refuge-settlements were occupied as early as this. Here, too, must be mentioned a piece of evidence of a different category: the fortification-wall built at the Isthmus of Corinth some time in the latter half of the III B period. It is northward-facing, and probably ran right across the isthmus, despite some earlier views to the contrary.[21] It is thus most easily intelligible as a barrier against a land invasion from further north, although the threat could as well have been from within the Mycenaean world as from beyond it.

And yet, our conclusions about this period in the Aegean have been largely negative. Many of the local destructions at this time are followed by prolonged desertion; in other cases, where re-settlement occurs, its predominant characteristics are those of a Mycenaean survival. The weight of evidence from the architecture, tomb-types, grave-offerings, dress-buttons, necklaces and, above all, pottery (see above, p. 29; below, pp. 360-1) far outweighs that of the few novelties in bronzework. Nowhere do we find destruction at this time followed immediately by the signs of a new cultural element. Faced with this baffling situation of an invasion without invaders, some scholars have turned to the other possible explanations that we noted earlier (p. 304). But there is yet another course which, to me as to many others, seems more promising: it is to try to relate our findings, in the most general way, to the record of the traditions of the Dorian, Boeotian and Thessalian migrations. The hypothesis that the destructions around 1200 were caused by these movements is only possible if linked with another hypothesis: that the Dorians and other immigrants were essentially indistinguishable in their material culture from Mycenaean survivors. But such an assumption appears by no means unlikely after our consideration of the dialectal and historical evidence (pp. 299-304); and indeed such an explanation as this would exempt us from the difficulty of searching for other causes for the disasters around 1200. But it must be said at once that this will also mean a very substantial modification of the details of the oral traditions: to take two obvious examples, the necessary signs of an early wave of disturbance in Thessaly are very hard to detect; and the fact that an area of Dorian settlement like Laconia shows a long period of apparent desertion after the end of Mycenaean III B will throw grave doubts on the legend of a swift occupation by the newcomers of their future homelands over much of the Peloponnese.

ALTERNATIVE EXPLANATIONS

We must therefore at least acknowledge the other possible interpretations of these events. The theory, that the destructions were the work of raiders who afterwards withdrew, is not new: this is the epoch of the 'Land and Sea Raiders' of the Egyptian documents, as was noted long ago. Desborough, however, has put forward a convincing series of arguments against attributing the disaster to this or any other sea-borne agency. The areas of refugee settlement which receive a prominent influx of Mycenaeans after the destructions lie in the very path of the putative maritime raiders – Kephallenia and western Achaea on the western seaboard of Greece, Perati, Lefkandi and Chios in the eastern approaches. These regions share another striking feature with the Cyclades and the Dodecanese: they all seem to have escaped the great wave of destructions. Is it credible, either that sea-borne raiders should have spared those regions which lay in their path, or that the survivors of their victims should then have taken refuge in the jaws of danger? The alternative of an overland raid seems far more likely, and for this the wall at the Isthmus (p. 311) again adds its powerful evidence. The idea of a raid from barbarian Europe, followed by the withdrawal of the attackers to their starting-point, taking certain metallurgical skills with them, was accordingly put forward by Miss Sandars in a discussion of Desborough's book.[22] There is much to be said for this suggestion, and little to invoke against it; only, perhaps, the law of economy of hypotheses. If the bronzes of northern origin in Greece, and the developments in metallurgy in barbarian Europe now and later, can both be explained in terms of peaceful communication; and if the tradition of an armed invasion by certain groups of Greeks can be even partially reconciled with the archaeological record in the Aegean, then we have no need to posit an unrecorded barbarian raid.

On the other potential explanations of the disaster, I shall have to be brief. The theory of an internal rising against the Mycenaean rulers, on the part of either the nobility or the masses or both, has proved attractive to modern minds, and it may also be thought to derive some support from the words of Thucydides in 1, 12 (see Chapter 1, pp. 8-9). But, as Desborough once again shows, it is very hard to reconcile this with the desertion of many, and the destruction of a few, of the non-palatial sites at this same period. What class stood to gain if Messenia was almost wholly depopulated? How can a mass emigration, such as that to Kephallenia, be linked with internal risings in the several Mycenaean states? Any revolution should yield fruits for somebody, and in the Aegean of Mycenaean III c they are scarcely detectable. As for the hypothesis of a great natural catastrophe at this date, the lack of secure grounds for it has been exposed in our earlier arguments (p. 310). When the same phenomena are explained as consequences, both of excessive heat and drought and of a sudden increase in cold and precipitation, it is surely clear that the present state of the evidence is unripe for assertion. Famine and drought, plague and flood alike could have bred the violence which the record reveals: but none of them can yet be treated as more than a surmise.

THE SECOND WAVE OF DISTURBANCES

We now move on in time to the only other likely period in the Late Bronze Age for a large-scale immigration into Greece, the later twelfth century, where we find evidence of a rather different kind. There is virtually no sign now of preparation to meet attack; perhaps few of the centres of settlement were in a position to take such steps. Nor, in the event, does very much violence appear to have taken place: in central and southern Greece there is only the destruction by fire of the Granary at Mycenae, somewhere in the region of 1150 BC, and that may have been accidental (p. 29); beyond, we have the burning of the palace – and only of the palace apparently – in

Iolkos at some unspecified date after the beginning of Mycenaean III C; the burning of the settlement at Lefkandi in Euboea some considerable time after the beginning of the same period; the destruction, with some use of fire, of the fortified settlement at Miletus, perhaps at roughly the same date as the end of the Granary at Mycenae; and the destruction of Emborio on Chios. These events make up a much less impressive horizon than the great earlier wave of destructions; they invite comparison not with these, but with the sporadic fires detectable at a slightly earlier period still, during the course of Mycenaean III B but well before its end, at Mycenae, Tiryns and Miletus (to name three important sites only). Since in each case these are followed by an intensive period of rebuilding and re-fortification in later III B, no one has supposed them to be other than the effects of local warfare. Are there any grounds for treating the events during III C period differently? The sequel is admittedly somewhat dissimilar, though uneven: the destruction at Mycenae is followed by a resumption of occupation at the same humble level, and that at Lefkandi by a fresh laying-out of the site at a rather superior level of architectural skill, and with other signs of increased prosperity; but those at Iolkos and Miletus lead to a detectable gap, during which the sites are temporarily abandoned, and the next settlement-level is in each case characterized by pottery at or near the beginning of Protogeometric; while that at Emborio is succeeded by a vacuum of four centuries' duration. There may also have been some further dispersal of Mycenaeans to remoter areas at this time: for pottery closely resembling the Granary style of the Argolid appears in Cyprus, notably in the settlements of Enkomi III, II and I: while in Crete there is some ceramic and other evidence, though much less direct, to suggest that there was an influx of population from the mainland at this same period.[23]

THE EVIDENCE OF THE CIST-TOMB

But the most impressive argument advanced for the appearance of a new population element at this time is perhaps that based on the mass adoption of the cist-tomb, and of other forms of single burial. Before saying anything more about this, let us note that there is no evidence for a close chronological association between the later destructions and the adoption of the new burial practice. On the contrary the cist-tombs make their first appearance *en masse* in the cemeteries of Salamis and the Kerameikos, after no detectable destruction: and there they are accompanied by Submycenaean pottery that is a clear development from the Granary style, which itself remained in use at Mycenae for a substantial period *after* the destruction of the Granary. So an interval of time seems to be involved here; and this is yet more clearly true of the Argolid itself, where the advent of the cist-tomb is less concerted and on the whole later than in Attica: only at Argos and Tiryns does it antedate the rise of the Protogeometric style, while in the other direction, an early pit-burial and pithos-burial at Mycenae both belong *before* the destruction of the Granary (pp. 152-3). There is hardly, therefore, any question of a wave of 'cist-users' encompassing the final destruction of Mycenaean culture and immediately moving in to take its place; so far, the most that could be posited is that the latest wave of destructions created a vacuum of desolation, into which the cist-tomb users, themselves perhaps quite unconnected with the destructions, presently moved. This is indeed very much the position that Desborough has adopted; but its foundations rest upon a hypothesis which I cannot accept, that the cist-tomb is, in the Late Bronze Age of Greece, an intrusive feature (see pp. 177-84). If, as has been argued, it rather represents a revival of an old, never entirely forgotten custom, on the part of people who no longer felt the need for the laborious practice of excavating family vaults, then this still leaves several possible interpretations of this change open: the cist-users could be merely the old inhabitants in a new guise; or they could represent migrants or refugees from other parts of Greece near or far – possibly even from the open country round the sites in question; or they could perhaps be, in contrast to the view expressed earlier, the Dorian, Boeotian and Thessalian invaders themselves, coming from the common Greek stock among which the cist-tomb had earlier been at home. This last equation is very tentatively made by Desborough, with the different implications which his view of the cist-tomb involves. But this, like all attempts to recognize these invaders in the archaeological record of the era, including our own (p. 312), can only be accepted at the cost of deserting the oral tradition at many points. Why is the mass conversion to the cist-tomb first visible on Salamis and in Athens, in a region which according to the unanimous verdict of the traditions the Dorians never penetrated, let alone settled? How is it that the islands of Crete and Thera, by tradition early Dorian conquests, totally reject the cist? And how does it come about that Messenia, overrun by the Dorians in the initial advance according to tradition, only adopts cists and other single burials in Protogeometric times? It seems that the association of the cist with Dorians, Boeotians and Thessalians can only be very loose: too loose to allow of the identification of the invaders by the new burial practice.

The cist-tomb cemeteries do, however, show another feature which seems more impressive: this is their tendency to break away from the established location of burials. There is quite a long list of sites where, after the end of Mycenaean occupation, the new tomb-type is found on a fresh cemetery-site in the same neighbourhood: these include Argos, Asine (with perhaps Lerna and Nauplion, though only apparently in Geometric times); Athens (the Kerameikos, Nea Ionia, and perhaps the area south of the Acropolis) and Eleusis; probably Lefkandi in Euboea; Nichoria in Messenia; and perhaps Chalandritsa in Achaea and Ialysos and Kameiros on Rhodes, though again scarcely before Geometric times. To these is to be added the shorter but even more significant list of sites where the new tombs are actually cut into the former Mycenaean settlement levels: Mycenae, Tiryns, Athens (Acropolis), Thebes (Electran Gates), Palaiokastro and perhaps Iolkos in Thessaly, and the Serraglio site on Kos. This evidence speaks strongly for some disturbance or movement of population at the time of changing the burial practice; it is hardly credible that, in each of these cases, the existing inhabitants could have decided simultaneously to change their tomb-type and to start a new cemetery.

In most of these instances, the appearance of the new tombs comes after a gap in time, of varying duration; it is the end of the old order, not the beginning of the new, which comes nearest to presenting a concerted horizon of change across Greece. The character of the change does not mean that the people using the new cemeteries were intruders to Greece: since their distribution so strongly resists any arrangement in accordance with dialect or oral tradition, the tombs must at times represent the refugees as well as the instigators of these moves; indeed, if the main influx of Thessalian, Boeotian and Dorian Greeks had really taken place in the region of 1200 BC, the situation of all groups may by now have become very similar. That there were further upheavals at this time is shown not only by the fresh exodus to Cyprus and perhaps Crete (p. 314), but by the fact that a further scatter of Mycenaean sites is decisively and semi-permanently abandoned during the III C period: Korakou and probably Gonia in the Corinthia; Delphi, which had probably suffered from a catastrophic landslide; Phylakopi on Melos; and several cemetery-sites of which we can only say that burials cease at this time, such as Spata in Attica, Ialysos and Kameiros on Rhodes, Volimidhia in Messenia and the sites near Monemvasia in eastern Laconia.[24] The Aegean world must have undergone a further wave of convulsions, with a few scattered outbreaks of violence, but with a much more widespread tendency simply to desert one's home for a final destination which, to judge from the evidence, may in some cases only have been reached by one's descendants several generations later. The refugees from the earlier disaster had taken the chamber-tomb with them, in some cases at least, to their new homes: to Achaea, Perati, Cyprus and perhaps the Dodecanese; the new wave of refugees may have done the same with the cist-tomb within Greece, although we know that they did not take it to Cyprus or Crete.

THE EVIDENCE OF METAL-TYPES

But the claim that these disturbances were connected with a further influx of population from outside Greece does partly rest on other evidence besides that which we have considered; there is first of all the skeletal material (on which see pp. 184-6), and also the evidence of a 'second wave' of intrusive material, originally assembled by V. Milojčić in 1948 together with the 'first wave' that was discussed earlier (pp. 305-11): to his collection there can now be added some more recent finds. The new types belong once again almost exclusively to the field of metallurgy, being bronzes of warlike, and to a lesser degree of domestic, use. They consist of further *Griffzungenschwerter*, flame-shaped and other spearheads, shield-bosses, long bronze dress-pins, arched fibulae and bronze spiraliform and 'shield' finger-rings; rarer novelties are the votive wheel (perhaps from a pin-head) found in a chamber-tomb of the Deiras cemetery at Argos; the embossed helmet, part of which was found in a grave at Tiryns (p. 224);   *104* and the spiral gold wheel-shaped ornaments, and the bird perched on the rim of a bronze beaker, in the Tiryns treasure.[25]

Precise chronological evidence, such as was used in the discussion of the earlier bronzes, is absent here: there is no clear horizon, marked by destructions and broadly valid throughout Greece, to match that of the transition from Mycenaean III B to III C. All that can be said is that most of these phenomena make their first appearance within the III C period (or its local contemporaries in Crete and Western Attica), within a time-span of not more than fifty to a hundred years, and perhaps much less. Some of the new bronze types have been discussed already: for the pins, recent studies of their connections suggests an element of native inheritance, a marked element of eastern derivation, and no clear evidence for a northern origin (pp. 226-8). For the arched fibula, the most likely direct source lies not in Central Europe or the Balkans but in Italy: but such a derivation of it is far from demonstrable (p. 256), and even if it is correct, it remains difficult to see in the appearance of this type any significance in terms of population movement. The swords and spearheads are in a different case, for with these the passage of the III C period sees no radical changes in the types from what they had been when first apparent in Greece; if they

104. Bronze embossed helmet-attachment from grave XXVIII at
Tiryns (cf. nos *76* and *77*). Height 34 cm; mid-11th century BC.

represented a new population element then, they can hardly do so now. The slight modifications in the Aegean *Griffzungenschwerter* at this time, principally the addition of a pommel-spur to the hilt, seem to be of purely local inspiration. Three other rare items on the list can also be briefly dismissed: the votive wheel or pin-head from Argos (along with two closely similar but undated specimens, one of them in lead, from Mycenae) is probably of northern Italian origin; its presence at this time could be taken to strengthen the case for a similar source for the arched fibula. The gold spiral wheel-ornaments from Tiryns, which have amber beads threaded on their spokes, are probably of Central European origin and can be matched in the Urnfield culture: the only problem here arises from the nature of the Tiryns treasure in which they were found (cf. p. 221), which makes it impossible to establish the date at which they reached Greece. Of the finger-rings with spiral discs, which also have Urnfield connections, half a dozen examples have occurred in Greece: one in Submycenaean tomb 108 at the Kerameikos, one in the Salamis cemetery, one in the earliest cist at Mycenae (p. 226), one in tomb 74 at Perati, and a recent find at Hexalophos in Thessaly.[26] It will be noted that the first three were in cists of comparatively early date for their regions, but the fourth was in a chamber-tomb of traditional Mycenaean type; and in terms of chronology, while the Perati and Salamis examples may belong around 1100 BC (and the Hexalophos find even earlier), the Kerameikos grave is late in the Submycenaean series and the Mycenae grave later still – perhaps after 1050.

The remaining classes of object – the shield-bosses, the Tiryns helmet, the 'shield-rings' and the beaker from the Tiryns treasure – may seem a heterogeneous collection, but they prove to have qualities in common. To take them first singly, the shield-bosses make their first appearance in the Aegean in tomb B at Mouliana, where they probably belong to the late twelfth century; subsequently they are found in the tomb with the helmet at Tiryns (XXVIII), in the rich tomb 40 at Kaloriziki in Cyprus, and in the 'Protogeometric' (or more accurately transitional) tomb 24 at the Kerameikos – all probably in the period c.1100–1050. These objects are a novelty in the field of Aegean armour, but a search for foreign prototypes has failed to reveal anything of similar shape, with a domed centre and flattened rim, serving this purpose at a comparably early date. The helmet in the Tiryns grave is incomplete, but its best-preserved component, the cheek-piece, has been shown to conform quite closely to the tradition of Aegean metal helmets, represented by one or two earlier examples. The 'shield-rings' of this period include two from the Submycenaean graves

80, lower right

in the Kerameikos, one from Karphi which is contemporary or later, one from Mouliana tomb A, which could belong to the twelfth century but could equally well be far later, and two from the Dictaean Cave which have no dating association. But this basic shape of ring, with a roughly elliptical bezel set at right-angles to the hoop, had been the standard type of the Aegean Bronze Age, and was again to become common in the Geometric period. The beaker from Tiryns, finally, for all its uncertain date, is of an unimpeachable Mycenaean shape, found in both clay and metal.[27]

It is when we turn to the decoration of these objects that a striking pattern emerges. The earliest shield-bosses, from Mouliana, are decorated with small embossed dots round the outer edge, and larger protuberances on the rim inside them. The Tiryns helmet has concentric circles of small dots round single larger ones, and a double row of dots round the edge of the surviving head-piece, which also makes use of open-work decoration. The Kerameikos 'shield-rings' and two others from the Dictaean Cave, which may or may not be among the earliest of our group, are decorated with rosettes or swastikas in impressed dots. These embossed and impressed designs are much more of a commonplace of Urnfield metalwork than in the Mycenaean world; it is noteworthy that violin-bow fibulae with flattened bows also appear at this period in Greece with dot-designs. In a different way, the Tiryns beaker tells the same story: itself of a Mycenaean shape, it carries on its handle a perched bird, whose upturned beak corresponds closely to Danubian representations. In each case, we seem to be witnessing a transient phase of northern influence on a class of object which is essentially of native origin: both shield-bosses and 'shield-rings' revert to a plain form afterwards, in which they occur during the dark age. At the same time, the Tiryns treasure contains objects decorated in the granulation technique, whose sources are also probably foreign, but lie in a very different region, the Levant.[28]

It will, I think, be clear that this assemblage of objects cannot be taken to represent a new and extraneous population element at this time in Greece. All that we have found is that, between the outer limits of approximately 1125 and 1050 BC, a few small objects showing origins either in the Urnfield culture of east-central Europe or in northern Italy appear in Greece: that the influence of the former region is also represented by the decoration on some other metal types: and perhaps that developments in Italy are reflected by the change, within Greece, in the form of the fibula. Nor do these features materially strengthen the case for regarding the cist-tomb as extraneous to Greece, for they are not consistently associated with cists (one need only recall the finds from Argos, Perati and Mouliana); while the cist, let us remember, is a tomb-type which cannot have derived from any part of the Balkan peninsula north of the Pindus, nor yet from Italy, since it is of very rare occurrence in both regions (see Chapter 4, p. 184).

THE SIGNIFICANCE OF METALWORK IN GENERAL

This protracted discussion of metal-types raises, I think, a more general point of archaeological principle. Metalwork, because of the very fact that it was so fundamentally linked to the necessities of human livelihood in antiquity, seems to have obeyed certain laws. In its production, the demands of functional merit and practicability, always present to some degree with artefacts, seem to have been overriding: any good new idea in the metal-lurgical field seems, as a rule, to have won acceptance wherever it was both understood and capable of being put into practice. Racial, cultural or geographical differences were often not strong enough to interrupt the spread of such notions. We may substantiate this statement with one or two examples in Greece, taken from outside the range of this study. First, the true sword was introduced to Greece near the end of the Middle Bronze Age: when it appears for the first time in the Shaft-graves at Mycenae, the great majority of the examples there – at least 11 out of 15 in Grave Circle B, 30 out of 41 now identifiable from Circle A – are of one type of rapier, Karo's Type A, which had almost certainly developed to its full size in Minoan Crete before this time, and which is found in closely similar form there. But it is doubtful whether anyone would now argue from this that the dead of the Shaft-graves were immigrants from Crete; there is too much evidence to the contrary. Then let us consider a fundamental piece of utilitarian furniture in Greece of some centuries later, the bronze tripod. The characteristic one-piece tripod-cauldron of Geometric Greece (pp. 281-5) was rather abruptly replaced in popularity, beginning at around 700 BC, by a new form of Oriental tripod-stand with separate cauldron. Many of the earliest finds of this class in Greece (which mostly consist of detached fittings from the cauldrons) have been shown to be definitely of Oriental manufacture; and they begin a tradition which dominates the production of cauldrons in Greece for some generations. Yet the adoption of this type in Greece can have no significance, at this date, in terms of population movement. The bronze 'Scythian' arrowheads, as an instance of the 'national' weapons referred to earlier (above, note 4), would serve as a further illustration here: in Greece as in many other countries they become the very commonest form of arrowhead used.

99

x

I do not think that there is any reason to treat the intrusive metal types, which won acceptance in Greece at and after the end of the Late Bronze Age, any differently from the other types that we have just considered. The evidence of metalwork, when it conflicts with that of other material objects and especially that of pottery, must in this matter at least give way. The essential quality of the painted pottery series in Greece is for long its continuity: against this background, there could be no danger of missing major intrusive elements if they existed. Even in the two periods covered by the examples we have just considered, the pottery, although it shows some influences from the very quarters as the sources of the intrusive metalwork, again provides a check on the too absolute conclusions which might have suggested themselves on the basis of the metalwork alone: the lustrous dark-on-light pottery of Mycenaean I is patently developed out of the burnished Yellow Minyan ware of Middle Helladic; the Orientalizing styles of seventh-century Greece clearly grow out of Geometric. And if, following this argument in reverse, we take as our starting-point a moment at which mass immigration into Greece and subsequent settlement *are* believed to have happened, we find a complete contrast. At the time of the onset of the Early Helladic III and Middle Helladic invaders, who were perhaps the first direct ancestors of the historical Greeks to reach their future homeland, the evidence for their arrival is based on changes in pottery and architecture, supplemented by the destruction of sites of the preceding era. It does not consist even fractionally of new metal objects, and indeed the incursion seems to bring in a marked recession in metallurgy, with widespread reversion to such materials as antler and flint.[29]

THE VARDAR VALLEY INVADERS

A similar contrast is exemplified by the evidence, from a very localized region, of an incursion which may be roughly contemporary with the second body of evidence discussed earlier (pp. 317-21), but which at no point shows signs of direct connection with it. The region is the Vardar valley in Macedonia, and the invasion is now generally accepted as a reality; the evidence consists primarily of a new class of fluted, hand-made pottery, and on two sites it is associated with a deep and conspicuous stratum of burnt debris; a further site (Chauchitza) has the destruction but not the pottery, while at Saratse this situation is exactly reversed. Metalwork plays no significant part in the distinction of these invaders. To trace the source of the new element has proved a harder task: in a careful treatment of the problem, W. Kimmig has argued that there are chronological difficulties in the traditional derivation of the invaders from further north in the Balkan peninsula: but they do seem to be intrusive to the native Macedonian culture, and their apparent use of the Vardar route makes it hard to believe in any but a Balkan origin for them; further, Marija Gimbutas has now cited comparable pottery of approximately the right period from the Middle Danube region. This invasion is not only sharply confined to a few sites in the Vardar valley, but its impact even on these sites seems to be of a transient nature: locally-made pottery of Mycenaean III C type continues to appear for a time after the destruction, while the native hand-made wares, having adopted one or two features from the fluted pottery of the invaders, thereafter only very rarely show traces of its influence. More interesting implications might follow from this invasion if only it could be closely dated: estimates have ranged from the excavator's original date in the mid-eleventh century to Milojčić's in the late thirteenth, which is certainly too high.[30] If in fact it could be shown to belong in the second half of the twelfth century, then we should have a plausible occasion for the passage further southwards into Greece of the European objects and techniques of this period that were discussed earlier.

RETROSPECT

After this time, a change comes over the evidence from Greece. Signs of violence or insecurity become rare: almost the only instance likely to belong in the eleventh century is a partial destruction of the houses in the second III C settlement at Lefkandi in Euboea. Intrusive metal objects and new decorative techniques for metalwork die out. Major innovations still occur, but they are different in kind. The cist-tomb continues its unhurried and limited spread, with whatever implications that carries; before the first advent of Protogeometric, it has made appearances in the Argolid and at Thebes, while the former region, with Lefkandi, produces other single burials; in Thessaly and Phocis, as in Epirus, the cist had never gone wholly out of fashion and is well represented at this same time; the slab-covered pits at Ancient Elis cannot be much later. Meanwhile the general use of cremation, also gradual and limited in spread, extends over Greece; and the practical mastery of iron-working also spreads, fractionally but detectably later, no doubt from roughly the same geographical direction, but not always to the same regions of Greece. These too are important changes, but they are the last of their kind for many years. Let us therefore look back from this point at the material we have surveyed; we have been concerned to examine, and finally to exclude, the possibility of mass immigration from outside Greece between the early twelfth and the middle of the eleventh centuries B C. What sort of picture is left for those external influences and objects which undoubtedly do exist at this time in Greece?

POTTERY

Peaceful communications, however reduced their scope, had continued in the central and eastern Mediterranean during the Mycenaean III c period. This is shown first and foremost by the distribution beyond Greece of the III c pottery itself. Early in the period, it is found at Tarsus and at least eight other sites in Cilicia, in Level v at Enkomi and on other Cypriot sites too; at Tarsus and Enkomi it is in quantities that have suggested a migration of Mycenaeans to these places, a hypothesis which is reinforced by the presence at Enkomi of architectural remains in fine ashlar masonry, recalling Mycenaean work. At much the same period, a little Mycenaean pottery reached Tell Sukas in Syria and Beth Shan and Ashdod in Palestine; and we have also the indirect evidence of the Philistine pottery, which clearly has Mycenaean III c as its starting point in both shapes and decoration, although it is not yet clear what part actual migration may have played in the transmission, nor yet which regional style of the Mycenaean world served as the source. Later, probably about the time of the destruction of the Granary at Mycenae, and corresponding with levels III-I at Enkomi, a further infusion of III c pottery and perhaps of Mycenaeans carrying it is detectable at this latter site, and in smaller finds at Kition and Idalion (cf. above, p. 314). In western Asia Minor there is certainly one site, Troy VII B, where communication with Greece persisted until a very late date in the III c period. Away to the west, III c pottery is present on Lipari, and at Scoglio de Tonno, Leporano and Torre Castelluccia in the region of Taranto; at the two last-named sites this is almost the only period at which Mycenaean ware is represented, and the material mostly falls late in III c, showing affinities with the pottery of Kephallenia; while at Scoglio del Tonno it has been suggested that there may have been a Mycenaean settlement extending from the III A to the III c periods, although the excavator's brief reference to 'ruined oval huts' hardly abets the identification of Mycenaeans here.[31]

METALWORK

But on the continent of Europe there had long been a tendency for Mycenaean artefacts of other kinds to penetrate much more widely, and exert a far deeper influence, than did their pottery. Now in the twelfth century this process was certainly still at work, and indeed it provides a further key to the problem of how extraneous European objects could have found their way to Greece, down to a point late in the III c period, without any mass immigration. G. Säflund has pointed out a number of analogies, mostly in the field of metalwork, between the finds from the Terremare of northern Italy and those of the latest Bronze Age in the Aegean. In some cases there may be an element of doubt as to the direction in which the influences and traffic were passing, the periods being substantially contemporaries; but some steatite dress-buttons in the Terremare show a remarkable affinity with a long-established Mycenaean type, and another clear case is provided by an arrowhead illustrated by Säflund, which certainly derives from the Eastern Mediterranean area, and which in this particular variant is first known in xix Dynasty Egypt. Säflund also shows bronze pins with incised rings on the head which are close to an Aegean form (type (4), p. 226); if in this case the direction of the transmission is less than certain, the date is not: it can only have taken place in the iii c period, and probably during its second half. The appearance at Scoglio del Tonno in Calabria of several metal types which derive from the Terremare is also notable, forming a natural link between the two terminal regions. Against this background, it is easy to see how the development of the arched fibula could have proceeded, along similar but not identical lines, at roughly the same period in Italy and in Greece, and how isolated rarities like the 'votive wheel' at Argos may have found their way southwards. Another phenomenon that may be explained in the same way is the appearance in Umbrian hoards of two fragments of rod-tripods of the Cypriot type which reached Greece in the twelfth century and perhaps later (pp. 119, 251). Their date here is strikingly late (perhaps about 900 bc), but then so is that of some of their appearances in Greek graves (Chapter 5, p. 271). In Sicily, by contrast, Mycenaean iii c pottery has not so far been found, although its influence may possibly be detectable on local wares; but here again, metalwork tells a more positive story, for Miss Sandars has shown that two Sicilian weapons, a dagger and a miniature sword, are very probably derived from a late Aegean sword-type with T-shaped pommel, which is well represented in two of the regions of Greece that face Sicily, Epirus and Kephallenia.[32]

In the Eastern Mediterranean, the picture of late Mycenaean activity may seem disappointingly faint by comparison. No Scoglio del Tonno has yet been found on the Asiatic coasts, where in the thirteenth century the Mycenaeans had been so active: Mycenaean metalwork may no longer have commanded much custom in this region, but the undoubted influence on the Philistine pottery suggests that unseen forces could have been at work; so, in the other direction, does the appearance of scarabs, cartouches, cylinder seals, faience figurines, ivories and other objects of Eastern Mediterranean origin in the III c tombs at Perati in Attica and Ialysos on Rhodes; these cannot all be explained as heirlooms.[33] With Cyprus, however, the links of Greece in the III c period are so strong that they can serve on their own as a basis for important conclusions: this is a relationship that is attested bilaterally, for the influences of Cypriot pottery on the Late Minoan III c and Subminoan of Crete, and even on the later Submycenaean of Western Attica, seem real enough (pp. 41, 117-18). It is thus legitimate to derive the first practical iron artefacts in Greece, during the late twelfth and early eleventh centuries, from Cyprus and if necessary from Cyprus alone: there is corroborative evidence (pp. 217-19) which hardly requires us to look for a direct Oriental source beyond it.

CREMATION

With cremation, the other major innovation of the period between c.1150 and 1050, it is otherwise. Neither a Cypriot origin nor even a Cypriot share in the transmission of the rite to Greece can be regarded as possible on present evidence: cremations in the Cypriot Late Bronze Age are almost unknown, and indeed Cyprus shows a complete divergence from Greece in the sphere of burial practice from this time on, retaining for example the Mycenaean fashion of inhumations in a rock-cut chamber-tomb approached by a dromos (often with inward-sloping sides) for long after this practice had ceased in Greece; other Cypriot tombs of the period are of varieties native to the island but unknown to Greece.[34] We must therefore look elsewhere for a possible outside source for the swing towards cremation in Greece; but it should be stressed that a fully comparable external model is not absolutely necessary. A community, once acquainted with the notion of cremation, may as we have seen differ profoundly from another community in similar case, in the degree of acceptance of the rite; and further, it may itself vacillate over the use of the rite without being subject to any further outside impulse. There is thus no need to seek for a habitually cremating culture outside Greece, with which Greece was specifically in close contact during the eleventh century BC. There is no difficulty in explaining how the notion of cremation was accessible to Greece at this time: the occurrence of cremations in Mycenaean chamber-tombs of fourteenth and thirteenth century date at Müskebi in Caria; the stray cremations of probable twelfth-century date in the Aegean; the links with a community, Troy, which had formerly cremated and presumably still did; the substantial movement of Greeks into western and south-western Asia Minor which seems to have taken place by the mid-eleventh century (see

p. 127) – each of these could be a stage in one or more lines of transmission to Greece. The sequel is an extraordinarily variegated picture of burial rites in early Iron Age Greece: the enthusiastic embracing of cremation by eleventh-century Athens; the more selective adoption in Greek Asia Minor, Naxos, Central and Eastern Crete, and even Phokis (in the last case definitely later than at Athens); the still later spread, also partial, of cremation to Boeotia and Rhodes; the long resistance, probably extending down to the eighth century, of Thessaly and the Peloponnese to the new rite. It is tempting to say that no 'blanket' explanation for this pattern will ever be found.

THE ADVENT OF PROTOGEOMETRIC

We are now at the threshold of the appearance of the Protogeometric style in Greek pottery: each of the last two innovations discussed, practical iron-working and large-scale use of cremation, marginally but perhaps significantly antedates that event in Athens, and in some other parts of Greece too. If the advent of Protogeometric cannot therefore be closely linked with either of these changes, how far can we ascribe it to external influence? Only, I think, to a slight degree. Certain correspondences between Cypriot, Cretan and mainland Greek pottery have been noted, which fall at approximately the time of the transition to the Protogeometric style at Athens (pp. 117-18): but the link is hardly strong enough to provide any credible explanation of the profound change which now sweeps over the pottery of Attica and other areas. E. Gjerstad, approaching the question from the Cypriot side, has indicated some of the most telling signs of influence on earlier Protogeometric pottery. A few shapes, including a common and important one like the belly-handled amphora, show a correspondence with those of the Proto-White-painted pottery of Late Cypriot III B. Other shapes are distinguished by their rarity in the Protogeometric repertoire, but have even clearer links with Cyprus: a good example is the flat-bottomed bottle noted earlier on (p. 118), which in one occurrence at Athens already carries the compass-drawn semicircles of Protogeometric. To it we may add the ring-vase, which is briefly present near the beginning of Attic Protogeometric and then seems to have temporarily faded out; its appearances in graves of the Kerameikos were fragmentary until the discovery of a complete example in Submycenaean grave 114; although it has late Mycenaean antecedents, it is not impossible that Gjerstad is right in seeing the link with Cyprus as lying behind its brief period of popularity. More doubtful is the case of the bird-shaped askos, also found in Kerameikos grave 114 and, in a debased form, in the slightly later Protogeometric graves 1 and 13; here continuity from Mycenaean times is a distinct possibility. These are really the only plausible signs of Cypriot influence on Greek shapes in this important early stage of Protogeometric; while the links in decoration proposed by Gjerstad are less convincing, and it may be noted that few if any of the Greek specimens illustrated by him are of fully-fledged Protogeometric style.[35]

There remains, however, one aspect of Protogeometric in which outside influences may possibly be at work: this is in the use of the multiple brush, and the likeliest source is once again in Cyprus. This instrument had been used in decorating Cypriot pottery for a very long time indeed: it is traceable on the island in Neolithic times, it remained common in the Bronze Age, and it was used on at least two wares, 'Base-ring 11' and 'White-Slip 11', whose life extends down into the twelfth century B C. But throughout this time it was used freehand in Cyprus, and there is therefore some slight difficulty in supposing that its sudden adoption in Greece in association with the compass, which inaugurates the Protogeometric style there, is a simple case of borrowing. It is most interesting to find that Cyprus adopted the same practice at this time: during the ensuing Cypro-Geometric period, the multiple brush is used only with the compass.[36] But we have found no evidence that the beginning of Cypro-Geometric antedates that of Attic Protogeometric, so that we are hard put to it to say in which direction this specific notion is travelling; the fact that the same practice prevailed in the Early Iron Age of Syria and Palestine hardly helps.

But we now enter on a period when the Cypriot link, and all other external communications with mainland Greece, seem to die away for a time. It is my thesis that in the central part of the duration of Attic Protogeometric, a period which should fall between the extreme outer limits of 1025 and 950 B C, Attica and much of the rest of the Aegean area, with Crete the only likely exception, were virtually isolated from the outside world. This conclusion was initially based on the evidence of metalwork, and reinforced by that of precious or other exotic small finds (pp. 237-9, 246-9). The evidence of pottery and other material hardly conflicts with it. The Protogeometric style at Athens, once it has received the considerable impulse needed to get it started, seems to proceed by its own momentum for some time: the decorative repertoire seems to grow from internal sources, and it is only in the late phase that further new shapes are added.[37] At first the other more advanced styles seem to have fared no differently in this respect; although it is important to note that among these new schools is that of the Greek settlements on the western coast of Asia Minor: the finds at Miletus, Assarlik and elsewhere suggest an early dispersal of pottery, and probably of actual migrants carrying it, beginning in the first half of the eleventh century (p. 127). This is perhaps our material testimony for the beginning of the Ionian migration; but there is as yet no evidence that Smyrna and the other settlements of Ionia go back so early.

HAND-MADE POTTERY

The next innovation which comes is of some potential significance: this is the emergence of hand-made pottery, in quite a wide range of practical shapes, on sites in the Argolid; and of the (perhaps unrelated) incised hand-made clay objects found in Late Protogeometric graves at Athens and elsewhere (pp. 94-7). Neither ware can be traced back to the early stages of Protogeometric: the fine Argive hand-made is of somewhat indeterminate date at Asine and Argos, but at Mycenae and Tiryns, and further afield in the Serraglio tombs on Kos, it definitely belongs to an advanced stage of the style. At such a moment, what meaning can we assign to this new phenomenon? Clearly it cannot be derived from the same impulse which started the Protogeometric style, or else it would be detectable earlier. It also seems most unlikely that the Argive ware has a major ethnic significance, for not only is its own distribution very localized, but the other, roughly comparable hand-made wares which seem to form its natural successors, and which are still in production over two hundred years later, show a similar geographical concentration in the north-eastern Peloponnese. It seems, in short, to represent no more than a local industry, originating perhaps at some time and place of technical impoverishment (the wheel-made vases at Asine are sometimes inexpertly made) and deriving from some ancestral craft, but rising to a high degree of competence. The miscellaneous hand-made products at Athens, except for the incised dolls which are frankly a mystery, have some precedents and are anyway unremarkable. If we are to suppose that the dolls are in any way connected with the considerably earlier clay idols of the northern Balkans, then we must believe that there is a major chronological gap in the chain of transmission as known to us: the gap may be filled in several ways, but it is plain that these isolated objects cannot testify to any communication with the north in the later tenth century, to which they belong. It is perhaps simplest to believe that such curious objects had existed for some time in Greece before anyone had the notion of putting them in a grave; it has indeed been argued that they are but a survival of Bronze Age terracotta idols, and the ancestors of the later bell-shaped Boeotian dolls.[38]

The Revival of Communication

By the time that these last phenomena appear – that is, in the later years of the Attic Protogeometric style – there are beginning to be signs of communication, and even migration, between different regions of the Aegean world once again; at the same time, more tentatively, the old links with other parts of the Mediterranean are apparently being resumed. Let us briefly consider the internal movements first. One of them may be isolated immediately, both for its restricted scope and for its undisputed nature: it is a migration of settlers from central Macedonia to the outlying Thessalian site of Marmariani, where they provide a rare illustration of the absorption of a new element, their characteristic pottery (and spectacle-fibulae? p. 256) surviving for a time alongside native hand-made wares and the peculiar painted pottery in the Protogeometric tradition (p. 62), all ensconced in small tholos-tombs of obvious Mycenaean derivation. The most doubtful aspect of this migration, once again, is its date: the Protogeometric influence reaches Marmariani very late in relation to the Attic series, but the continuous use of the cemetery may extend back somewhat further in time than this. Recently Desborough has argued that the migration from Macedonia to Marmariani should 'precede . . . or be caused by' the migration into western Macedonia which he posits to coincide with the beginning of the Vergina cemetery; our findings (pp. 132-3, 256) would suggest a tenth-century date for that movement, if such it is.[39] These changes are to be clearly distinguished from the earlier incursion of the 'fluted ware' invaders into the Vardar valley (p. 322).

A migration, this time by sea, seems to be indicated at about this date in the case of Kos: the new settlers using the Serraglio cemetery are distinguished by their partial use of plain hand-made pottery and of iron dress-pins with bronze globes – both of them features current on the Greek mainland but unparalleled in this part of the Aegean. Detailed resemblances in the pottery to finds at Asine suggest that the starting point for the movement may have been the coast of the Argolid. Other movements may be traceable hereabouts, not very far distant in time: the pottery from Ialysos and Kameiros on Rhodes suggests that these settlements began a new life in the closing period of the Attic Protogeometric style. Back on the mainland, there is comparable evidence from certain Boeotian sites: here an actual migration of late tenth-century date from Attica has been suggested. A similar migration, though not perhaps from Attica, could perhaps lie behind the new and extensive settlement which grows up at Lefkandi in Euboea at this period.[40]

Contact of a different kind is involved elsewhere. In Central Crete, it is clear that continuous occupation had existed at Knossos, Phaistos and perhaps other sites: but there is still a major injection of influence from the Attic Protogeometric school in the later tenth century, which launches the pottery of this region, and ultimately that of the whole of Crete, on a new course. Later, about the beginning of Middle Geometric, Attic potters exert a similar wave of influence on the Cyclades; but there is unlikely to be any question of migration in either case. Nor is it any more strongly indicated in the case of another series of contacts, in the western part of the mainland of Greece, which may either have grown up a little after this time, or else remained in existence throughout. There is a dearth of chronological evidence, but it can be said that the solitary pithos-burial at Derveni in Achaea must belong very late in relation to Attic Protogeometric: the pottery from this tomb shows clear links with that from Medeon in Phokis, *42-4* just across the Gulf of Corinth, from Amyklai in Laconia, and from Ithaka: while before long there is an independent link between two of these regions in the shape of an Ithakan import at Delphi (pp. 73, 84-8). In Ithaka, though not probably in the other regions, there had been continuous habitation since the end of the Bronze Age: these links may therefore represent a resumption of sea-going contacts between four regions rather remote from the more active centres of the Aegean shores; on present evidence, they should probably be dated to the ninth century.

This marked access of communication within Greece, in the period before and after 900 BC, in part coincides with a revival of contacts with the Eastern Mediterranean. For it is at this time that Cypriot influence once again shows itself in Attic Protogeometric pottery. The very late tomb 48 of the Kerameikos contained not only fragments of ring-vases, not seen since the beginnings of this period (above, p. 327), but also two clay openwork stands which seem to be directly modelled on Cypriot metalwork (p. 119); while tomb 26, only slightly earlier, produced a belly-handled amphora whose traditional shape is curiously combined with three loop-supports on which the foot rests, an imitation of Cypriot (or perhaps Syrian) models. In metalwork, this period sees the appearance at Athens (in Agora grave XXVII) of a type of spearhead which has clear *84* Cypriot ancestry – the first sign of such a link since the very beginning of Protogeometric. In Crete, meanwhile, the Cypriot link had perhaps never been broken; whether or not the rod-tripod in Fortetsa tomb XI testifies *89* to commerce with Cyprus at the time of its burial (the late tenth century), the appearance of the Cypriot iron pikes in this and another grave of the same period cannot be explained otherwise: these are serviceable weapons of war of a peculiar kind, not found earlier or later in the Aegean but characteristic of the Cypriot early Iron Age, and they must have been imported at this time. Beside them we may put the lead lion and faience ring from the same two tombs; when we add the Cypriot-influenced pots in Marmaro tomb 43 at Ialysos on Rhodes, and in the opposite direction the rare appearances of Late Protogeometric and later pottery in Cyprus and the Levant (for these see Chapter 3, pp. 113, 119, 127), it is clear that from the late tenth century on into the ninth, Greek communications with the Eastern Mediterranean were operative once again. Certainly the establishment of a bronze-foundry at Lefkandi in Euboea, probably also in the late tenth century, must ultimately be attributable to the overseas commerce, presumably in this direction, which brought in the necessary tin.[41]

How far did Greek horizons extend in other directions? Isolated but none the less striking evidence comes from the pottery-series at Sardis, which apparently covers the Protogeometric period; the city lies fifty miles inland from the Aegean and was not to become Greek in any sense until six centuries later. The Greek hold on the western coastline of Asia Minor must have been already stronger than the discoveries so far made there would lead us to suppose. Not less remarkable is the fact that this penetration into Anatolia, unlike the other signs of expansion at this time, did not apparently follow in the path of Mycenaean enterprise. To the Late Protogeometric period we must date the short-lived wave of Greek influence on Macedonia, to which the pottery from Vergina and elsewhere bears witness (p. 132). In Macedonia it is notable that this phase of contact is succeeded by a period in which there are almost no signs of such communication with southern Greece. Finally, away to the west of Greece there may be one or two pieces of genuine Greek Protogeometric pottery in Calabria, which are perhaps of Ithakan fabric (p. 85), and which suggest yet another tentative re-opening of old commercial routes.

These links, however, are very far from signifying the opening of the floodgates of foreign trade, travel and experience to Greece, a development which was not to follow until more than a century later. Throughout the ninth century BC and for the earlier part of the eighth, the development of material links with overseas cultures is gradual, localized and unspectacular. It is possible that the distinct reversion to the use of bronze in ninth-century Greece (p. 237) reflects a strengthening of contact with sources of copper and tin: in Cyprus there had been no pressing signs of the shortage of bronze, and possibly Greek smiths could now begin to supply themselves through Cyprus, as some of their Cretan counterparts had probably been doing throughout. The ninth century does see the occasional appearances in Greek lands of such substances as ivory and amber once again; and gold and silver are more often found now, although for silver, at any rate, we cannot assume that Greece depended on external contacts (p. 248 and n. 34); while fragmentary Greek pottery now appears in the East. Yet the most positive proof of foreign traders in the Aegean, in the shape of identifiable artefacts, remains curiously elusive: I have argued earlier (pp. 275-85) that the main sanctuary-deposits of Greece, which contain many objects both of European and of Asiatic origin, need not and in many cases cannot extend back beyond the eighth century in date. In this situation our only reliable guide to the date of revival of commercial links comes from the graves of Early and Middle Geometric date; and these, although not always austere in their provision of grave-goods, are generally unproductive of foreign objects, except in Athens and central Crete. The embossed bronze bowl found in 1938 in Kerameikos grave 42 (Middle Geometric, perhaps of about 850 BC), which is certainly an import and probably of Syrian manufacture, was until recently still conspicuous by its isolation in mainland Greece; the glass pendant found in a well in the Agora, probably of similar origin, may be as early as this but could be in the early eighth century. A new find of quite different origin is the remarkable pair of greaves which came to light in a re-used Mycenaean grave, apparently together with Early Geometric pottery, on the slopes of the Athenian Acropolis. The full impact of this, as yet, isolated find cannot be assessed until it is fully published; but it is clear that the greaves, which so closely resemble examples from Hungary and Bosnia, must be of actual barbarian manufacture; and it is notable that they were accompanied by knives and razors of bronze, not iron, which is so untypical of this period at Athens (cf. p. 263) as to suggest that these too could be intruders. Finally, the rich Agora grave of about the end of the Early Geometric period, found in 1967, has filled out the picture still further. Here were found a necklace composed of numerous faience and other beads, which at this date are likely to be of Levantine origin, and which suggest a similar history for a roughly contemporary find at Tiryns (p. 248); also ivory stamp-seals, an ivory plaque, and a whole range of gold jewellery which, although said to be of local workmanship, must be made from freshly imported metal.

Nevertheless, to find objects of Levantine influence, let alone origin,

98b

56

plate 1

in any quantity we have still to look to Crete; and even here we might expect to find more Oriental objects of this time than there actually are. Such shapes as the duck-askos are common enough in the ninth-century pottery of the island, but their diffusion in other parts of Greece since the end of the Bronze Age is too wide (cf. p. 86) to make a continuous Eastern influence necessary. The next clear occasion for such influence in Crete perhaps comes with the baffling 'Protogeometric B' phase of pottery which briefly prevails in the central part of the island. Some of the shapes of this phase are new arrivals (or revivals) in Crete: the straight-sided pithos with flat bottom, for instance, has obvious Cypriot analogies but could yet have developed from internal models, such as the smaller straight-sided jars; the splaying mouth of jugs and aryballoi is another feature which can be matched in Cyprus. More striking is the decoration of the period, in which a precocious and even premature figure-style makes its appearance; but here the direct evidence for Eastern inspiration is lacking. A belly-handled amphora which carries a mourning scene is itself manifestly a copy, perhaps indirect, of an Attic shape; but the attempt to derive the figured scene from Attic prototypes encounters an insuperable chronological obstacle: our proposed dating of the 'Protogeometric B' phase to the last quarter of the ninth century is later than is generally allowed, but is still some fifty years earlier than the earliest possible date for an Attic Geometric *prothesis* scene. The figures on the Cretan vase are in the silhouette technique of the later Geometric schools, but most of them are disposed horizontally, that is at right angles to the main axis of the vase; it is conceivable that this motif is inspired by some Oriental source, for the sudden reappearance of running spirals and cable-pattern decoration on other vases of the period could have such an origin, perhaps in metalwork. But the figures of goddesses painted under the handles of a contemporary pithos are not susceptible to this explanation, for they resemble too closely the clay figurines of Subminoan date which have occurred on several Cretan sites. The element of spontaneous native revival at this time may be stronger than we can yet realize.[42]

One of the most significant developments in the opening up of overseas communications comes when Greeks again settle permanently on foreign soil, and this is very probably to be dated to this time. The advent of the Greeks at Al Mina, their first settlement on the Levantine coast since the thirteenth century BC, was claimed some years ago as a Euboean-led enterprise, and subsequent discoveries, first of some analogous Geometric wares at the traditionally Euboean colony of Pithekoussai, and now of a

41, 122

more fully comparable range at Lefkandi, have proved this claim correct. What is still not entirely clear is the initial date of the Greek settlement: it partly depends on whether the town was in existence for any substantial period before the arrival of the Greeks. There was Greek pottery in the earliest levels (x-ix), but it seems to have become mixed with that from level viii; the evidence of the associated Oriental wares does suggest that the Greeks were there by about 800 BC, if not rather earlier. A partial parallel to Al Mina may be provided by the site of Tell Sukas, about fifty miles further south, where Greeks probably settled in later days, and which has produced a few of the cups with pendent semicircles, whose main vogue in this region seems to belong in the earlier eighth century (see p. 126).[43] Yet the first half of the eighth century hardly shows evidence of significant increase in communication between the Levant and Greece, except in restricted areas such as central Crete and western Attica. For most classes of imported object in Geometric Greece, the indications suggest an initial date of around 750, as we shall see, and the same is true of many of the reflections of Oriental influence in Greek art.

By this period, however, communications in another direction, destined to become equally important historically, had been re-opened. Some of the earliest finds of Greek pottery in dated contexts in Italy are those of the early eighth century in pre-Greek graves at Cumae; roughly contemporary are the more numerous examples from the Quattro Fontanili necropolis at Veii in southern Etruria; and slightly later, but still within the second quarter of the eighth century, begin the first bulk finds, indicating permanent settlement, in the cemetery of San Montano at Pithekoussai on Ischia. This last site provides us, not only with a date for the advent of the first Greek colonists on these shores, but also with a strong hint of what may have been one of their prime motives in going there: for iron slag has been found in some quantities at Pithekoussai (once in an eighth-century context), together with other finds which unequivocally attest the existence of iron-foundries on this island, which itself possesses no iron-ore. Analysis of the slag has now proved that its origin is on the island of Elba further north. The 250-mile sea-voyage, over which the extravagant and bulky ore must then have been brought, shows even more clearly than the 800-mile journey of the colonists from their Euboean homeland the lengths to which some Greeks in the eighth century were prepared to go in pursuit of metals. It could indeed be argued that the Pithekoussai finds speak only for the situation of these colonists in their new home, and do not represent any commerce in iron-ore with the Greek mainland. But the occurrence

48

49-50

of early pottery in Etruria and at pre-Greek Cumae, and the fact that these slightly antedate the settlement on Ischia, should tip the scales against this explanation: when we recall that there were also iron-ore deposits on the Etruscan mainland, and that Etruria produced much copper as well, it seems quite credible that it was the metals of this region which first attracted the Greeks – perhaps predominantly from Euboea and Corinth, as is suggested by the pottery, and by the known interest of Corinth on the western coast of the Greek mainland by this time (see below, p. 339). The most surprising implication of all this is that the supply of iron-ore available from the quite copious deposits in Greek lands (p. 231) must have begun to fall short of demands; but when we come to consider the question of population increases, this may no longer seem so remarkable. The evidence for Greek penetration in the West is at first almost entirely uni-lateral; there are few objects of Italian or Sicilian origin to be found in Greece at this date. Etruscan imports (notably at Olympia) do not begin before the seventh century; but long ago a Villanovan bronze belt, almost certainly of eighth-century date, was acquired privately in Euboea, and said to have been found there. The importance of metallurgy in the western contacts of Greece naturally gives rise to other questions: for example, is it possible that it was the Greeks who finally brought Italy into a true Iron Age? The generally southern distribution of early Italian iron finds might at first seem to favour such a theory, but there are grave difficulties – not least the chronological one, that some of these finds seem to have a definite ninth-century date, and Greco-Italian communication at this time was, on present evidence, virtually non-existent. The discovery of links, apparently direct, between the metallurgy of Sicily on the one hand and Cyprus and the Levant on the other, suggests an alternative possibility for the diffusion of iron to Italy, for these links should go back to an earlier date than those with Greece.[44]

THE FINAL EMERGENCE

In the mid-eighth century, the picture of Greek activity in every direction overseas changes fundamentally. There is the sudden intensification of colonization in the West, which in the second half of the century reaches a pitch never exceeded in later years; there are the first substantial signs of contact with the barbarian peoples in the European hinterland; and above all there is the dramatic increase in communication with Cyprus and the Levant, with the inland cultures of Anatolia and (in the main only indi-rectly) with those of Mesopotamia, Iran and Egypt. This shows itself in the form of imported objects and Eastern artistic influences in Greece, and to a much lesser extent in the appearance of Greek pottery on Oriental sites. But this is not only a period of expansion outside Greece. Within the Aegean too, the eighth century sees a detectable quickening of the process of populating deserted areas – or rather re-populating them, since in nearly every case the new penetration followed paths trodden by the Mycenaean centuries earlier. There is also a discernible tendency for areas already populated, but hitherto rather isolated, to be brought back into the fold by the revival of communications with the more advanced regions. Neither of these developments is in the least surprising in itself, but in some cases their pattern was to be of lasting significance historically. Clear examples of the first process are given by the distribution of cemeteries: in the Late Geometric period there is a sudden growth in their number and diffusion (p. 268). In the countryside of Attica, for example, there are perhaps three times as many cemetery-sites known at this period as there had been in Protogeometric and earlier Geometric times. In the Argolid and Corinthia there is a fresh wave of burials at this time, sometimes at sites like Lerna, Berbati, Prosymna and Zygouries which had been established Mycenaean centres, and there are signs of re-settlement on the peninsula of Methana, at Perachora, and on the offshore island of Poros. To the West, there is a proliferation of eighth-century cemeteries in Achaea, and part of what seems to be a vast necropolis has been discovered at Kyllini (Chlemoutsi) in Elis. In Thessaly the spread of the cemeteries in places now exceeds the uneven Mycenaean penetration of the region. Elsewhere, there are important sites such as Sikyon, Eretria, Thera, Ephesus and Colophon where, on the evidence of burials or settlement finds, it is only in the eighth century that occupation is resumed and the swift advance to prosperity begun. Then there are apparently fresh sites, such as Exochi on Rhodes, where communities now begin burying their dead for the first time. Much more satisfactory evidence is that provided by the excavation of a settlement itself, but this is still too rare. As an exemplar we may take Emborio on Chios: the site of a thriving Mycenaean settlement in the III C period, it lies deserted thereafter until a date around 750 when it is re-occupied in strength. This must represent not the first arrival of the Ionian settlers on Chios but their subsequent expansion over the island: the revival of the site of Phanai in the same part of the island may not have been much earlier. A similar explanation will apply to cemetery-sites like Exochi, and to the rather later settlement excavated at Vroulia, also on Rhodes; while, further west. the sequence of events at the

Y

CEMETERIES *c.*760–700 B C

● Graves with Late Geometric pottery

◉ Cemeteries with 10 or more burials of this period

○ Indicates cemeteries without Late Geometric pottery, but of contemporary date

Kastro site on Siphnos, and probably at Zagora on Andros, was evidently similar, and Naxos and Kimolos have produced fresh cemetery-sites at this time. Meanwhile, on the Greek mainland, the swift rise of the major sanctuary-sites in areas like Laconia, Arcadia and Elis tell a similar story in less direct terms: and even on Samos, if at a somewhat earlier date, it is the sanctuary of Hera which first gives evidence for the revival of civilization on the island.[45]

The quite distinct process of the re-establishment of contacts with remoter Greek communities is also conspicuous in the eighth century, and in at least one instance it begins very early in the century. The regions bordering on the Gulf of Corinth – Achaea, Phocis and further west the island of Ithaka – are shown by their pottery to have been in intermittent contact with each other, but on the whole isolated from the rest of Greece (pp. 73, 85-6, nn. 50, 62; p. 331). Into this enclave the Corinthians broke, and the evidence from Ithaka shows that their goods probably begin to arrive there by 800 or a little later: some have inferred, from the quantity of pottery and the absence of other imported ware, a permanent Corinthian settlement. Comparable evidence from Phokis, and Lokris, appears at the same period: at Delphi and Amphissa, where again the predominance of Corinthian pottery is almost overwhelming, the initial date seems to be early in the eighth century. The re-settlement of Thermon in Aetolia may be of similar date and origin, and the establishment of the first sanctuary of Hera at Perachora appears to point in the same direction. In Achaea, where the evidence begins later, it is simply a matter of the growth of a local Late Geometric style under strong Corinthian influence, and with a modicum of imported Corinthian ware.[46] This early example of Corinthian enterprise cannot be matched elsewhere in Greece, but we may credit Attica with the recovery of another major isolated area, East Crete; and at much the same period, the first half of the eighth century, her pottery also exercises a marked influence on the products of Rhodes. A more fleeting illustration of Greek enterprise may be given by the finds of Geometric pottery at Nea Anchialos in Macedonia – perhaps the only sign of southern Greek activity in this corner of the Aegean between the Late Protogeometric period and the seventh century BC (Chapter 2, n.33).

But it is the Near Eastern contacts which, more than any other single factor, herald the end of the dark age in Greece, and thus take us beyond the scope of this work. The material evidence for these has been discussed in countless publications, many of them recent,[47] yet some brief account of it must be given here, if only to indicate its scope and chronological con-

105. Distribution map of cemeteries, *c.*760-700 BC.

106. Bronze decorated shield-facing from the Idaean Cave, Crete.
Diameter 34·5 cm; probably earlier 7th century BC.

centration. We may begin with Crete, the senior Orientalizing culture of
the Aegean whether in the Bronze or the Iron Age. The whole pattern
of the process here is, as will emerge, fundamentally different from that
in the rest of Greece. A first sign of this is the absence of Cretan products
among the Greek artefacts on Oriental sites, which suggests, although it
does not entail, a special explanation for the undoubted Oriental goods in
Crete. Such an explanation is further supported by the nature of those
goods: the most important group of Orientalia in Crete is formed by a
106   series of objects in beaten bronze, mostly shields, and mostly dedicated at
the sanctuary of Zeus in the Idaean Cave, of a more or less unified style
which nevertheless shows considerable internal development and must
extend over several generations. A few of its products have a purely
Oriental character in both style and content, but most of them draw on
local decorative elements, and some illustrate Cretan features. The most

natural explanation of this phenomenon is that a guild of immigrant crafts-men, perhaps from northern Syria, settled in Crete and gradually imbibed more and more elements of Greek art; it is almost certainly correct in this instance, but should be most sparingly applied to other cases. The dating of the shields and other bronzes of this group has been much debated, but today it is hard to see any reason why they should begin much earlier that 750. The main find-spot, the cave on Mt Ida, also produced a few ivories, of two clearly-distinguished Oriental schools, normally classed as Phoenician and Syrian respectively: these appear to be straight imports. The Eastern connections of the Phoenician group (to which also belong some ivories from Samos), are with the Layard ivories from the North-West Palace at Nimrud, whose find-context is probably of the late eighth century, but which in turn have many connections with a series from Arslan Taş in North Syria, a few pieces of which seem definitely to date from the period c.850-830; it is often therefore argued that some or all of the Layard ivories were already old at the time that they reached Nimrud. The second group in the Idaean Cave, together with a few finds from Ialysos and Lindos on Rhodes, is closest to the Loftus series of ivories from the South-East Palace at Nimrud. These are certainly of non-Phoenician origin, but in other respects their circumstances somewhat recall those of the former group: once again, they almost certainly represent loot carried off from a subjected region, and once again the likeliest date for their arrival in Assyria is at the time of Sargon II's conquests in the late eighth century; but, again, they have stylistic connections with finds of ninth-century date. All that one can say is that, if more than a century's time-lag is indicated between the manufacture of such ivories in Phoenicia or Syria and their installation in a conqueror's palace at Nimrud, then their journey west-wards to a Cretan sanctuary may have been equally dilatory; the find-circumstances of the examples on Rhodes and Samos strongly support this view (below, pp. 346-7).[48]

Distinct from the main Idaean Cave series of bronzes are other reliefs, in bronze and in gold, which are agreed to be of Cretan manufacture but which are pervaded by Oriental motifs. Their initial date probably goes back as far as that of the Idaean group, for they include a gold strip found in a Mature Geometric grave, that is of the first half of the eighth century according to our reckoning. Crete has produced further Oriental finds which distinguish it from the rest of the Aegean. There are, for example, a few bronze statuettes which seem to be imports from Syria, and others which are close to them, yet are certainly Cretan products. Imported

Cypriot pottery, too, makes its appearance here in the first half of the eighth century, which is probably earlier than its occurrences elsewhere, apart from the finds at Ialysos (p. 332) and elsewhere in the Dodecanese. At the same time appear some blue paste beads, and the first Iron Age amber in Crete (p. 267), and by the end of the century there are imports in almost every characteristically Oriental material, as well as bronzes whose shape or style links them with Egypt and Luristan. The most important feature of the Cretan series of Oriental and Orientalizing objects is perhaps the evidence that it begins distinctly earlier than 750: this, following on the phenomena of the 'Protogeometric B' period (p. 334), makes up a credible picture of early Cretan accessibility to Eastern Mediterranean influences. It is not surprising to find that the Cretan alphabet presently emerges as the closest to the Phoenician original.[49]

But Crete, in this as in other periods, is a law unto herself. Elsewhere in the Aegean, we find an Orientalizing movement whose first stage, in the shape of imported artefacts, is datable before the mid-eighth century only in two prominent centres – Athens, and the Dodecanese with its special predilection for Cypriot pottery (p. 78). The initial date in other regions – notably Samos and Chios – seems distinctly later. Both in Attica and in the eastern Aegean, ivories play a more significant part than in Crete; indeed, as media for the transmission of the more refined artistic styles and motifs they almost outweigh metalwork in importance. There is nothing comparable with the Idaean Cave series to suggest resident Oriental craftsmen. In Athens, it is true, there are some faint signs of the presence of 'invisible' Eastern imports in the first half of the eighth century, reflected in shapes and motifs of Attic Middle Geometric pottery. Yet several of these features may represent simply the retention of ideas acquired from the Levant at the time of the first wave of Oriental contact in the Late Protogeometric period: the cylindrical clay stands imitating Cypriot metalwork, and the loop-supports on the feet of certain vessels, both fall under this heading (p. 331). There is also, however, the evidence of the Isis Grave at Eleusis, whose exotic contents have been mentioned more than once before (pp. 117, 263): the huge deposit of pottery in this tomb (69 vases in all) covers a considerable time-span, from perhaps the earlier ninth century to the second quarter of the eighth. There is no clear reason to doubt that the date of the imported Oriental objects is the same as that of the latest pottery: the fact that some of them were themselves centuries older does not help with the prime question, that of the date of their reaching Greece; but this must still be decidedly earlier than 750, as must that

107. Two bands of thin gold foil, decorated with zig-zag patterns, from Geometric grave 13 at the Kerameikos, Athens. Lengths 9·3 and 38·1 cm; later 9th century B C.

of the finds from the nearby grave α. A clear development in Attic pottery-decoration which belongs in the vicinity of 750 is the adoption of plant-leaf motifs, particularly on skyphoi: Oriental metalwork has been suggested as the inspiration of this, but it is a largely invisible factor. We may more confidently detect its effect in the change which comes over the decoration of gold bands in Attic graves at this time. These had been produced in a plain form, or with Geometrical patterns, since about the middle of the ninth century (p. 263), but they now begin to be decorated with representational scenes of animals, in a style which at this date can only derive from the Near East. The earliest such gold bands were in Geometric graves 50 and 72 at the Kerameikos, where they need not be earlier than about 750 B C, although Kübler has argued that the intaglio moulds on which they were shaped were of somewhat earlier date.[50]

But in Athens, as elsewhere, there is a very sharp increase in the quantity of Oriental goods and influences after 750. The sudden entry of the human figure into vase-painting, just before that date, and the gradually increasing importance given to representational scenes generally, cannot in themselves be called an 'Orientalizing' development, for their style is of purely native, Geometric inspiration, and they have real if isolated forerunners in the occasional representations, usually of horses, on Middle Geometric and even Late Protogeometric vases, and in the scenes engraved on the larger 'Attico-Boeotian' fibulae from the first half of the ninth century (Chapter 2, n. 32; p. 262). Yet one doubts whether the concerted movement of the years after 750 would have taken place but for the presence of figured scenes on imported Oriental works of art at this time. Indeed, it is not long before unmistakably Eastern elements enter these scenes: a man in combat with what seems to be a lion, an animal which the artists can have known only through Oriental art, and which had made a rather

19-20

107

108. Ivory figurine of a girl from grave XIII of the Dipylon cemetery, Athens. Height 24 cm; *c.* 740-730 BC.

earlier appearance engraved on an Attic fibula; full-blown plant-motifs and a representation of a sphinx; deer and poultry in what seems to be Eastern guise. Even more tangible is the evidence of the superb ivory figurines of naked girls, found in a Dipylon grave whose pottery belongs in the third quarter of the century, definitely of Greek workmanship, and of a quality which already excels that of the Astarte statuettes which they imitate. Of Near Eastern, rather than Egyptian, manufacture are several scarabs and faience objects which appear in Attic graves with contexts no later than the third quarter of the century.[51]

The rest of the mainland and islands show a detectable time-lag by comparison with Attica. The other Geometric styles are slower to adopt Eastern motifs; the graves at first contain few foreign objects; the sanctuary-deposits, even given the relatively low dating of them that we have proposed, are unproductive in their early years. The rather few Eastern imports at Olympia include nothing that need be much earlier than 700: a bronze tripod-handle which incorporates a crouching lion would be dated far back into the eighth century on F. Willemsen's chronological scheme, but this we have had reason to question before (pp. 281-5). At Perachora, there is a striking contrast between the material from the Hera Akraia sanctuary dating from before c.725, and that of the later Limenia sanctuary: the former produced only three scarabs, a few glass beads and one amber pendant. Other sanctuaries only come into their own as depositories for Oriental dedications in the seventh century: the largest single class of object is that of the attachments from cauldrons of the new Oriental type which suddenly swamped Greek markets from about 700 onwards (above, p. 321 and n. 29). Bronzework of a different kind makes its appearance in an Argive grave of about 720 BC (p. 271): a bronze helmet which I believe to be related to an Assyrian type, and a two-piece metal cuirass whose ultimate origins must be sought in a very different region, that of the great bronze-working cultures of Central Europe and northern Italy. In the same grave were two iron fire-dogs, whose earliest analogues are perhaps those found in roughly contemporary Etruscan tombs. That the Argolid soon became accessible to both Oriental and northern traffic is demonstrated by the copious small bronze finds from the nearby sanctuary of Hera; but earlier, if less direct, evidence is provided by the resumption in Greece of the native art of gem-cutting, for which Near Eastern inspiration can alone be responsible. Some of the earliest Greek products, datable on stylistic grounds to about 750, are found at Perachora and the Argive Heraeum, and sites in this region remain richly productive of seals in the

1 cm

109. Two red serpentine seals of the 'Lyre-player' group, found in tombs 637 and 73, respectively, of the cemetery at Pithekoussai, Ischia. Last quarter of the 8th century B C.

succeeding period, although Boardman has argued that the first steps in the process of revival were taken in the Cyclades.[52]

The most interesting finds, however, are perhaps those from the eastern Aegean islands of Rhodes, Samos and Chios: not only did these have rather easier access to the products of the same regions as served Crete and Athens, but they also, for the same geographical reasons, established especially close connections with some quite different areas. Thus the import of scarabs and faience objects to Rhodes was so intense that Pendlebury in 1930 omitted the island from his study of Egyptian and Egyptianizing objects in the Aegean, there being over 1500 finds of Late Bronze and Early Iron Age date reported by that time; yet there is little sign that the revival of traffic in these objects begins before the Late Geometric period.

109 More precisely studied are the seals of the 'Lyre-player' group, whose centre of production must lie in the Near East, perhaps Cilicia or North Syria: from grave-finds at Pithekoussai, their initial date can be securely fixed in the third quarter of the eighth century, although they still appear in the seventh. Over 60 examples have been found in the Aegean area, with Rhodes (18), Chios (7) and Samos (4) among the main find-spots; curiously, they seldom seem to reach Attica, and in the eighth century not at all. Later, East Greece comes to play a part in the revival of native gem-cutting. Two classes of object paralleled in Attica may serve to illustrate the time-lag mentioned just now: gold bands appear in Rhodian graves, first with zig-zag and other abstract decoration, later with animal-friezes, just as in Attica, but each stage seems to belong at least fifty years later in time than there; while ivories are most richly represented at the Heraeum on Samos, where neither they nor any of the other Eastern imports can be shown to have arrived before 700. But the eastern Aegean islands also show strong predilections of their own in the matter of foreign trade: Rhodes and Kos, as we have seen, had been importing Cypriot pottery during the ninth and eighth centuries on a scale which no other part of Greece emulated; Samos shows a particular taste for another Cypriot product, terracotta figurines, in a rather later period. The Iranian 'Luristan' bronzes are also well represented here; one of the very few objects in Greece which H.–V. Herrmann, in a sceptical recent study, will allow to be genuine products of the distant kingdom of Urartu is a bronze statuette found in the Samian Heraeum; while the same site has produced a bronze lion-headed situla of Assyrian type. Geographically, the most convincing link is that established between the eastern Aegean islands and their mainland near-neighbour, Phrygia, whose greatest flowering came at this very period, the end of the eighth century. A handful of sherds from the Samian Heraeum have been claimed as showing Phrygian influence: conversely, it has been argued that the Phrygian Geometric style was in general based on Greek models. More widespread are the dedications of bronze belt-attachments, which occur at two sites (Emborio and Phanai) on *110* Chios, at the Samian Heraeum, and at Old Smyrna and Ephesus on the Asiatic mainland: this accoutrement was almost certainly derived from Phrygia, although the Greek examples show distinctive features, and the transmission may have taken place around 700. Emborio has also produced a single fragment from a characteristically Phrygian type of vessel, the dinos with swivelling ring-handles: the context is seventh century. But there are several other bronze types, more widely found on Greek sites, whose Phrygian origin, although often argued in recent years, is still very far from certain. They include the shallow bowl with ring-and-spool handle, and the phiale with a central omphalos surrounded by ridges, of which we can as yet only say that they are well represented in Phrygia, but could well be derived from further east; and the fibulae of certain 'Anatolian' types (Blinkenberg's XII. 3, 7-9, 13-4 especially), which are also found in huge quantities at Gordion, but may yet be of East Greek origin – some of them had penetrated to Perachora, we may recall, before c.725 (p. 270). Altogether there is little sign that Greco-Phrygian relations

110. Two bronze belt-handles of Anatolian type, dedicated in the Harbour Sanctuary at Emborio on Chios. Lengths 10·2 and 15·5 cm; early and mid-7th century B C.

– which in fact almost exclusively concerned the Eastern Greeks – began to operate before the last years of the eighth century. The correspondences in decoration between Phrygian pottery and Greek (mainly East Greek) Geometric ware of the second half of the century are not close: the strongest supporter of this link has written of 'inspiration, not imitation', and others have considered an independent, parallel development possible. Definite Greek imports are not visible on Phrygian soil until the seventh century.[53]

But the 'Phrygian question' cannot be left here. For in recent years Phrygia has been brought to the centre of the stage by the remarkable discoveries of the American excavators at the capital city, Gordion, and by the claims that Phrygia played a prominent part, sometimes as originator, sometimes as intermediary, in the 'Orientalizing' process which did so much to bring Greece out of the dark age. For example, perhaps the most important single development of this whole period, which we have yet to discuss, was the adoption of the Phoenician convention of alphabetic writing in Greece; the discovery of early Phrygian alphabetic inscriptions at Gordion has led to the theory that the alphabet came to Phrygia not via Greece, as hitherto assumed, but by a wholly independent route; and even to the more tentative suggestion that it was the Phrygians who first transmitted the alphabet to Greece from its Phoenician source.[54] Let us, however, leave aside the question of the alphabet for a moment, and consider the more general issue of the precise function of Greece's relations with Phrygia at this crucial period.

As so often, the vital prerequisite for any such consideration is an agreed chronology for the two areas. Professor R. S. Young, the director of the recent excavations at Gordion, had in his earlier work on Geometric Greece supported an unusually low chronology, and his conclusions as to relative dating now tend to favour Phrygian priority. In particular, by placing the rich and important burial in the Great Tumulus ('MMT') at Gordion at c.725, he gave its finds a significant margin of precedence over the many features of Geometric Greece which he dated to the very end of the eighth century (including the first alphabetic inscriptions there). Since he has stated the argument for this dating of the tumulus in some detail, it is worth examining it closely, hazardous though it is to venture into an archaeological field of which one has little first-hand experience. Professor Young argues that the king buried so richly and laboriously in the Great Tumulus must have died at a time of security and prosperity: he cannot therefore be identified with the Midas who was the last king of the great period of Phrygia according to Greek tradition, and who was said to have committed suicide at the time of the disastrous Cimmerian invasion, which in turn tradition and archaeology agree in placing in the first quarter of the seventh century. But this King Midas is also known from the royal annals of Assyria, which mention one Mita, king of Mušku (a country identifiable with Phrygia) under several different years; the earliest of these years is 717 BC, and so the burial in the Great Tumulus must have taken place some time before then. Without this written testimony, I think it is true to say that the archaeological finds in the grave, and the scientific aids of Carbon$_{14}$ dating, would not justify a more precise dating than to the late eighth or early seventh century; all that is certain is that this and other great tumulus-burials at Gordion must antedate the Cimmerian invasion.[55]

This argument of Young's rests in part on certain unexpressed hypotheses: the most obvious of these is perhaps that the Greek traditions of Midas, first recorded even in general form some 250 years later, are so reliable in detail that they can be used in a common-sense historical reconstruction of this sort; but there is the further assumption that the name 'Mita' in the Assyrian annals, being identifiable with the great historical Midas of the Greeks, is therefore the name of one individual ruler only. Here there are definite grounds for doubt. Not only does it seem clear from Greek tradition that the names of the Phrygian kings were recurrent, and perhaps semi-titular, for the numerous and irreconcilable references to 'Midas son of Gordios' and 'Gordios son of Midas', from Herodotus on-wards, forbid any other conclusion; but there is another occurrence of this very name 'Mita', that of the king of Pakhuwa in a late Hittite docu-ment of the end of the Bronze Age – five centuries earlier in date, it is true, but referring to a geographical area so close to that of the later Phrygia that the identity of name is unlikely to be coincidental.[56] When a ruler's name which is transliterated as 'Mita' is attested twice in the same region, in a period as obscure as this, then who knows how often it may have occurred unknown to us, or how many bearers of it contributed to the multiple and composite figure of 'Midas' which Greek tradition cherished? It is, for example, possible that the 'Mita' of the Assyrian annals, last heard of in 709, was not the great Midas who perished in the disaster of perhaps c.675, but his father or grandfather. It is a sounder method to ignore the Midas tradition as dating evidence for the burial, and I should prefer, with E. Akurg al,to date the Great Tumulus at Gordion to the region of 685–80 BC, without following him and others in identifying the deceased ruler with a historical Midas.

If such a course is followed, the position of Phrygia vis-à-vis Geometric Greece begins to appear radically different, for it is the Great Tumulus which in many ways offers the most spectacular evidence for the develop-ment of Phrygian culture, including alphabetic inscriptions which are among the earliest yet known here. Whether or not Akurgal is right in holding that the first establishment of Phrygian power at Gordion dates from only c. 725 or a little earlier,[57] we may doubt whether this civilization can have played a great part in the Orientalizing movement of Greece. For it could only have done so through the cities and islands of East Greece, and we have found little evidence that the Greeks of this region were in the forefront of the movement in its earlier stages: on the contrary, it seems that both Crete and Attica were in continuous touch with the Near East from a significantly earlier date than Ionia, while Euboea, through her now substantiated activity in the early days of the settlement at Al Mina (pp. 72, 334), has equally as good a claim for priority in this field.

Let us come briefly back to the subject of the alphabet. The date of the

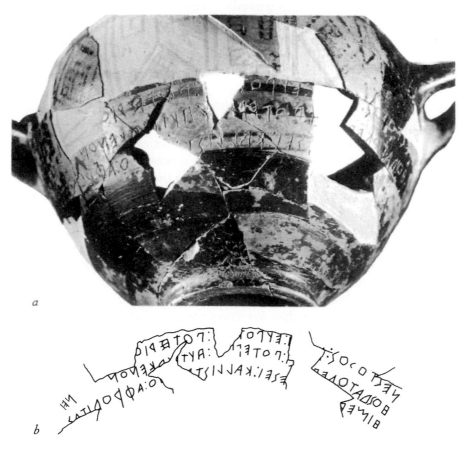

111. (*a*) Late Geometric skyphos of East Greek fabric, found in tomb
282 of the cemetery at Pithekoussai on Ischia, with an inscription in
the Chalcidian alphabet. (*b*) The inscription transcribed. The approximate sense is 'I am Nestor's cup' [or possibly 'To blazes with Nestor's
cup'], 'good to drink from. But whoever drinks of this, he will be
struck at once with desire for fair-crowned Aphrodite'. Height of cup
10·3 cm; *c.* 720 B C.

adoption of this form of writing in Greece has been debated for many years,
and many different conclusions reached. But today we are surely justified
in arguing from the steadily increasing number of inscriptions of a date
near the end of the eighth century, and the contrasting lack of any earlier
ones, that the event took place during the years around or after 750 B C.
The graffito, incorporating a hexametric line, on an Attic Late Geometric

oenochoe from the Dipylon, is normally given pride of place among early Greek inscriptions, not only on the evidence of the pot (which in terms of ceramic typology should belong to the third quarter of the eighth century), but also because the inscription itself shows peculiar anomalies of letter-forms. But greater precision may now be possible, for another very early inscription, also in verse, is that on an East Greek Late Geometric cup found in a grave at Pithekoussai (p. 78); the inscription itself is in the Chalcidian alphabet and may have been scratched after the pot had reached Ischia. Thanks to the completeness of the grave-series here and the close stratigraphic observation of the excavator, it is now possible to date the grave to about 720; and a sporadic discovery on the same site produced a graffito which seems yet earlier. If alphabetic writing could reach this, the most far-flung Greek community of its time, by so early a date and in such a degree of familiarity, then it can hardly have become known to the Greeks in general much later than 750. The means by which this borrowing took place has been almost as controversial a question as that of its date. In the days when scholars saw Phoenician traders everywhere in the eighth-century Aegean, bringing their goods to Greece and instructing the Greeks in the higher arts of civilization, it was easy to regard the alphabet as one product of this activity, and a recent writer has still upheld this view.[58] Today, however, it has been shown that many of the earliest imports in the Iron Age Aegean are not Phoenician but North Syrian and, in Crete and Rhodes, Cypriot; that early Phoenician activity both in the Aegean and in the West (cf. p. 18) has been systematically exaggerated by ancient tradition; and that Greeks from Euboea and elsewhere were residing at Al Mina, an entrepôt where Phoenician goods were also undoubtedly present, from at least 800 B C onwards. It therefore seems wiser to conclude that the initiative in this matter lay with the Greeks – perhaps with the Euboeans who were at first dominant at Al Mina, and whose colonists wrote the Pithekoussai inscription by about 720 B C and passed alphabetic writing on to the Etruscans not later than the early seventh century – and that it was they who sought out this vital innovation at or near its source. Whatever the precise sequence of events, it is a symptom of the predicament of Iron Age Greece that she should have had to wait until so relatively late a date in order to acquire from outside so fundamental a perquisite of civilization as the art of writing.

Notes

1] On this general topic, see the contributions of M. I. Finley, C. Mossé, E. Will and C. Roebuck to the *Second International Congress of Economic History* (Aix-en-Provence, 1962), I, 1-115; Finley, *ibid.* 32 on the extreme position reached by J. Hase-broek, with which compare T. Burton-Brown, *The Coming of Iron to Greece,* 23

2] O. Frödin and A. W. Persson, *Asine* 437 etc.; M. R. Popham and L. H. Sackett, *Excavations at Lefkandi,* 5, 35; *Istanbuler Mitteilungen* 9-10 (1959–60), 38 (Miletus). The destruction of about 700 B C at Old Smyrna seems due to earthquake: see J. M. Cook and R. V. Nicholls, *B S A* 53-4 (1958–9), 14, 124; but Akurgal, *Die Kunst Anatoliens* 11-12, also speaks of an earlier destruction-level in the first half of the eighth century. P. Courbin, *La ceramique géometrique de l' Argo-lide,* 161-2, n.1 (Argos)

3] See R. V. Nicholls in *B S A* 53-4 (1958–9), 39f., 68f., 82, 122f.: Eleusis, *Archiv für Religionswissen-schaft* 32 (1935), 63-6: Phaistos, *A R* 1960–1, 24. The walls at Siphnos (*B S A* 44 (1949), 9) and Emborio on Chios (*Greek Emporio* 4-5) *may* belong before 700; so may those now excavated at Zagora (Andros), Iasos and Panionion-Melie (ch. 7, nn. 56, 60, 61)

z

4] A good example is that of the 'Scythian' bronze arrowheads, whose distribution was discussed in *E G A* 148-51

5] Recent summaries of this evidence are those of C. D. Buck, *The Greek Dialects*$_2$ (1955), 3-9; A. J. Beattie in *A Companion to Homer* (ed. A. J. B. Wace and F. H. Stubbings, 1962), 311-24; Desborough in *L M S* 244-57. For a confident account of the Dorian and other wanderings, see N. G. L. Hammond in *C A H*$_2$ 2, chapter 36 (b) (Fascicle 13, 1962)

6] See especially W. Porzig in *Indogermanische Forschungen* 61 (1954), 147-69 and E. Risch, *Museum Helveticum* 12 (1955), 90-105

7] J. Chadwick in *Greece and Rome* n.s. 3 (1956), 48-50

8] See E. Will, *Doriens et Ioniens* (1956), esp. 75-98 and R. M. Cook, *Proceedings of the Cambridge Philo-logical Society* 188 (1962), 19-20

9] F. Hampl, *Museum Helveticum* 17 (1960), 85 has the bearers of the Arcado-Cypriote, Ionic and North Aeolic dialects arriving at this date; A. Heubeck, *Glotta* 39 (1960–1), 171, the 'Achaeans'. For the first arrival of the Greeks at this time, see also M. S. F. Hood, *The Home of the Heroes* (1967), 126-30; and lectures by the late Prof. E. Grumach, now published in *Bulletin of the John Rylands Library* 51, 1 (1968) and 51, 2 (1969).

10] This hypothesis was advanced by Miss N. K. Sandars, *A J A* 67 (1963), 142 and a list of examples given in *Antiquity* 38 (1964), 261-2. But of these, one at least, from Langada tomb 21 on Kos, belongs to the III B period (cf. above, p. 307), while another, from the Epano Phournos tholos at Mycenae, seems from its find-circumstances to be of

Myc. II date (Hood, *B S A* 48 (1953), 78-9, no. 21)

11] See most recently W. Kimmig in *Studien aus Alteuropa* I (1964), 220-83, citing earlier studies; and M. Gimbutas, *Bronze Age Cultures in Central and Eastern Europe* (1965), esp. p. 339, 'This was not an "Aegean migration", but basically a "central European expansion", during which the most powerful units of Bronze Age Europe fell upon the South with crushing force ... the Middle Danube people upon the whole eastern Adriatic area, south-eastern Italy and Sicily, Greece, Crete and the Eastern Mediterranean area, and Tisza people upon the southern Balkans, Greece and Anatolia'.

To the list of intrusive objects, M. S. F. Hood would now add the fragments of a vase found in an unstratified deposit at Mycenae and associated by him with the *Buckelkeramik* of Troy VII B (*Europa: Festschrift für Ernst Grumach* (ed. W. C. Brice, 1967), 120-31). But even the tentative conclusions that he draws there seem too narrowly based

12] See H. W. Catling's fundamental articles, *P P S* 22 (1956), 102-125 and *Antiquity* 35 (1961), 115-22. V. Milojčić, *Germania* 30 (1952), 95-7, doubts whether the Tell Firaun sword should be classified here. For Langada tomb 21, L. Morricone, *Ann.* 43-4 (n.s. 27-8) (1965-6), 137-9, figs. 122-4

13] Spearheads, see *L M S* 66-7; *E G A* 119, 208 (type B), and see above Chapter 4, n.17, for doubts about the dating of Epirot specimens to III B. Daggers, see most recently J. Boardman, *The Cretan Collection in Oxford* (1961), 13-17, esp. 16, n.1, and note the Achaean example, above, p.244, n.32; Zafer Papoura chronology, A.

Furumark, *Chronology of the Mycenaean Pottery* (1941), 95, 105

14] V. Milojčić, *Jahrbuch des römisch-germanischen Zentralmuseums in Mainz* 2 (1955), 153-69; N. K. Sandars, *P P S* 21 (1955), 174-97, esp. 185; Sp. Marinatos in *Atti del VI Congresso Internazionale delle Scienze Preistoriche e Protoistoriche* (Rome, 1962), I, 170-1; Boardman, *Cretan Collection* 17-18; H. Müller-Karpe, *Germania* 41 (1963), 9-13 on bird-headed knives

15] Catling, *C B M W* 87-8 for the type, with references; to which add Hammond, *Epirus* 407-8, fig. 28, 2 for Dodona; and Stubbings, *Mycenaean Pottery from the Levant* (1951), 21-2 and R. Hope Simpson and J. Lazenby, *B S A* 57 (1962), 171 n.157 on date of Serraglio settlement. Chariot, Catling in *A J A* 72 (1968), 46-8

16] Blinkenberg, *F G O* 41-58 and Desborough, *L M S* 54-7; add *Ann.* (1965-6), 134, fig. 119 (Kos) and Catling, *C B M W* 240 (Enkomi); Ålin, *E M F* 21 for date of cemeteries at Mycenae

17] International Symposium at Imperial College, London, in April 1966: B. Frenzel, *ibid*. 99-123, esp. 113, 118

18] *Discontinuity in Greek History* (1966), esp. 63-75: note the comments of H. E. Wright in *Antiquity* 42 (1968), 123-7

19] This is thanks largely to J. D. Cowen's article, *P P S* 32 (1966), 262-312; but also to S. Foltiny's lists of swords of the 'Sauerbrunn' and '(Keszthely-)Boiu' types in *A J A* 68 (1964), 247-57 and *Archaeologia Austriaca* 38 (1965), 21-30. As a result, certain views which I had upheld on the origins of the *Griffzungenschwert* in 1964 (*E G A* 205-8) are now untenable

20] This argument is followed by
Marinatos, *op. cit.* (n.14), 169; for
Aegean manufacture and re-export of
Griffzungenschwerter see Catling,
Antiquity 35 (1961), 120 and E.
Vermeule, *A J A* 64 (1960), 14 (cf.
Cowen, *P P S* 32 (1966), 310-12 for
earlier Aegean types which found their
way northwards). Further evidence
of links in metalwork between
Mycenae and northern Europe is given
by E. Randsborg, *Acta Archaeologica*
38 (1967), 1-27

21] On 'centrifugal' migrations, see
Desborough *L M S* 34-5, 226-8;
Achaea, *ibid.* 98-101 (*contra* R. Hope
Simpson, *Gazetteer* 84, 86, nos. 289
and 297); Kephallenia, *L M S* 103-8;
Perati, 115-16; Emborio 159; Monem-
vasia area, 89; Cyprus, 198-200;
Tarsus, 206; *Excavations at Lefkandi*
22-3, 34. Crete, M. R. Popham, *B S A*
60 (1965), 281-2, 334-5 and for other
refuge-sites, M. S. F. Hood and others,
B S A 59 (1964) 92-3; 61(1966),178-9.
Isthmian wall, O. Broneer, *Hesperia* 35
(1966), 346-62 and 37 (1968), 25-35

22] Desborough, *L M S* 221-5;
N. K. Sandars, *Antiquity* 38 (1964),
259-60

23] *L M S* 75, 230 (Mycenae); 128,
227 (Iolkos); 159, 162, 233 (Emborio
and Miletus); *Excavations at Lefkandi*,
11, 34. Earlier destructions, Ålin,
E M F, figures on p. 24 (Mycenae)
and 36 (Tiryns); *L M S* 162 (Miletus);
23-4 (Cyprus); 192-4 and 235-6 with
Popham, *B S A* 60 (1965), 335 (Crete)

24] Ålin, *E M F* 56-7 (Korakou,
Gonia), 130 (Delphi), 109 (Spata), 81
(Volimidhia), 96 (Monemvasia);
L M S 149 (Phylakopi), 156 (Rhodes)

25] V. Milojčić, *A A* 64-5 (1948–9),
12-36, esp. fig. 2: I here omit the
spearheads from Delphi and one-
edged sword from Halos (*ibid.* 25-6,

fig. 2, 15-18) because their date is
probably or certainly much later; the
violin-bow fibula, *ibid.* 25, n.1, fig. 2, 7
seems to be that from Kerameikos
Submycenaean grave 108 (*Ker.* 1, pl.
28). See *E G A* 247, n.34 for other
criticisms. 'Wheel', J. Deshayes, *Deiras*
60, 203 (Tomb XXII, DB 11), pls. 24,
8; 60, 5; helmet, *A M* 78 (1963), 21-4,
fig. 10; Tiryns wheel-ornaments, Sp.
Marinatos in *Theoria* (*Festschrift für
W. H. Schuchhardt*) (ed. F. Eckstein,
1960), 151-7 and beaker, G. Karo,
A M 55 (1930), 130, Beilage 34, 1.
On the Tiryns wheels, see now C.
Beck, *G R B S* 9 (1968), 5-19

26] Desborough in *P P S* 31 (1965)
224, 228 with references; Hexalophos,
A A A 1 (1968), 290; Elaphotopos
Zagorion, *AD* 22, 2 (1967), 345.

27] Shield-rings from Dictaean
Cave, Boardman, *Cretan Collection* 37,
41, nos. 189-90, fig. 18; and *Island
Gems* (1963) 156-7 and *Antike Kunst*
10 (1967), 5 on the general shape. For
Tiryns beaker, cf. Furumark, *The
Mycenaean Pottery* (1941), 56, type
226, fig. 15

28] Violin-bow fibulae, e.g. two
from Kerameikos Submycenaean
grave 108 (*Ker.* 1, pl. 28); Tiryns bird,
cf. V. G. Childe, C. F. C. Hawkes,
P P S 14 (1948), 186, 202. Granulation, *A M* 55 (1930), 124-5, nos. 6212,
6210, fig. 1, pls. 4 and 2, 4; Boardman,
Cretan Collection 136-7 and n.7

29] Karo's type A swords: N. K.
Sandars in *A J A* 65 (1961), 17-29,
esp. 23, nn.54, 56; on origins of
Mycenaean I pottery, F. H. Stubbings
in *C A H₂* 2, chapter 14 (Fascicle 18,
1965), 8-9. Cauldrons, H.-V. Herrmann, *Ol. Forsch.* 6 (1966) (*Die
Kessel der Orientalisierende Zeit*), 30-
32, 57-8, 91-2, 102, who counts 37
imported 'Siren'-attachments against

12 made in Greece. Vermeule, *G B A*
75 on Middle Bronze Age recession

30] Kimmig, *op. cit.* (n.11), 257-62;
Gimbutas, *Bronze Age Cultures of
Central and Eastern Europe* (1965),
331, fig. 233 B; dates, W. A. Heurtley,
B S A 27 (1925–6), 63 – c.1050 BC,
changed to c.1150 in *Prehistoric
Macedonia* (1939), 125; Milojčić, *A A*
64-5 (1948–9), 24

31] Eastern Mediterranean, *L M S*
23-5, 197-205, with V. Seton-
Williams, *A S* 4 (1954), 134 on
Cilicia and V. Hankey, *B S A* 62
(1967), 114, 128, 143 on Syria and
Palestine; Troy, *L M S* 164; southern
Italy, Lord William Taylour, *Mycenaean Pottery in Italy* (1958), 134 and
n.1: F. Biancofiore, *La Civiltà Micenea
nell' Italia meridionale*, 1: *La Ceramica*
(1963). Two of the Mycenaean sherds
from Luni, in later Etruscan territory,
are assigned to the III C period by
C. E. Östenburg, *Luni sul Mignone e
problemi della preistoria d'Italia*
(1967), 128-45, 245-54, figs. 31, 32,
1-5

32] G. Säflund, *Le Terremare*
(1939): to the observations of Taylour, *op. cit.* (see previous note) 135-6,
172-4, add Säflund 161, pl. 55, 6
(arrowhead) and 178, pl. 60 (pins);
tripod-fragments, Catling, *C M B W*
223; swords, Sandars, *A J A* 67 (1963),
137-9

33] *L M S* 52, 116, 156: note also
the faience at Iolkos, *Ergon* 1961, 58

34] Gjerstad in *S C E* 4, 2, 431-2

35] For precedence of iron and
cremation over the first Protogeometric, see Styrenius, *S S* 154, 156.
Shapes, Gjerstad in *Op. Arch.* 3
(1944), 92, fig. 5, 1 and 3 (but the
example of Attic Protogeometric is of
a relatively late stage); ring-vase, *Ker.*
1, 112-13, pl. 39; 4, 46, pl. 36; *A M* 78

(1963), 152, Beilage 54 bottom right;
(there is a loose correspondence in
decoration between this last and *S C E*
4, 2, fig. v, 8); Gjerstad, *ibid.* 293.
Decoration: in *Op. Arch.* 3, fig. 7
(p. 96), nos. 7-8 are of Cretan Geometric style, no. 20 is from an exceptional Attic vase which is transitional
to Protogeometric (*Ker.* 1, 121, 148,
pl. 39, lower right), while nos. 13 and
17 are, as Gjerstad says, Subminoan

36] Boardman, *Antiquity* 34 (1960),
85-9; cf. *A S* 9 (1959), 166; Gjerstad,
Op. Arch. 3, 76 on date of Cypriot
wares

37] For new shapes in Late Protogeometric, see Desborough, *P G P*
106f. and *Europa: Festschrift für
Ernst Grumach* (ed. W. C. Brice,
1967), 75-9, (globular pyxis); *P G P*
114f. (kalathos), 101f. (flat-based
cup); Styrenius, *S S* 89-91, 120

38] For poor wheel-made vases at
Asine, see *P G P* 204. Kerameikos
'Protogeometric' grave 48 is classed as
transitional to Geometric by Styrenius
S S 88. For internal ancestry of Kera-
meikos dolls, see Kübler, *Ker.* 4, 5, 20

39] Protogeometric at Marmariani,
P G P 147 (cf. *L M S* 133); quotation,
L M S 145. Coldstream, *G G P* 158-60,
places the main *floruit* of the Marmariani pottery in the ninth century

40] *Excavations at Lefkandi*, 23-8

41] Cypriot influence in pottery,
P G P 27, 301; cf. *S C E*, 4, 2, 292, and
for Geometric successors, *Ker.* 5, 1,
55, 107, 168 fig. 4. Spearheads, *E G A*
122, 191, G 3-4, fig. 7g (cf. 120, D2,
fig. 7d). Metalwork in Crete, Brock,
Fortetsa 15, 22, 202, V I 108, X I 188,
192, 203. Foundry, *Excavations at
Lefkandi* 27-9

42] Kerameikos bowl, *Ker.* 5, 1,
201-5, 237, fig. 5 and pl. 162; pendant,
R. S. Young, *Hesperia Suppl. Vol.* 8

(1949), 427-33; Greaves: *AD* 21, 2 (1966), 36, figs. 1-2, pls. 59, 60a; and 20, 2 (1965), 30-2. For European parallels, G. von Merhart in *BRGK* 37-8 (1956–7), 91-147, especially figs. 2, 2 (Rinyaszentkirály) and 5, 1-2 (Ilicak). Agora grave, *Hesperia* 37 (1968), 77f., 111-16, nos. 71-81. Crete, *Fortetsa* 153-4, 191 on duck-askoi; 143, especially pls. 24, 444 (OD 339) and 77, 163 (P 1440) on Protogeometric B; Boardman, *Cretan Collection* 131 doubted the connexion with Oriental metalwork, but see *BSA* 62 (1967), 57-75 for his revised view, involving a guild of Near Eastern immigrants

43] Al Mina, see Boardman, *BSA* 52 (1957), 5-6, 24-5 and now *Excavations at Lefkandi*, 33; date, G. M. A. Hanfmann in *The Aegean and the Near East* (Studies presented to Hetty Goldman, ed. S. Weinberg, 1956), 175; cf. C. M. Robertson, *JHS* 60 (1940), 2, n.1; and now Coldstream, *GGP* 310-16. Tell Sukas, P. J. Riis, *Annales Archéologiques de Syrie* 8-9 (1958–9), 107-32; 10 (1960), 111-32; 11-12 (1961–2), 133-44

44] On Cumae finds, see Chapter 2, n.68 and most recently D. W. R. Ridgway in *JRS* 57 (1967), 270-1 and *Stud. Etr.* 35 (1968), 311-21; Pithekoussai, chapter 3, n.31; iron slag, G. Buchner in *Expedition* 8, 4 (summer 1966), 12 and his article 'Ischia: aggiornamento' in *Enciclopedia dell' Arte Antica*, Supplementary Vol.; sources of metal in this region, Blümner, *Technologie und Terminologie* 4, 64, 78: Forbes, *Metallurgy in Antiquity*, 304. Etruscan finds in Greece, G. Karo, *AE* 1937, 316-20; E. Kunze in *Studies presented to D. M. Robinson* 1, 736-46; Villanovan belt, J. Close-Brooks, *BICS* 14 (1967),

22-4; links between Sicily and the Levant, H. Hencken, *PPS* 22 (1956), 213-15; cf. J. Birmingham, *PEQ* 95 (1963), 102-3

45] For links with barbarian Europe, see *PPS* 31 (1965), 229-40; but add the greaves from Athens, above, n.42. For references to cemetery-sites, see the Appendix to Chapter 4; other site-references, Ålin, *EMF* 52, nn.289-92; 57, n.24; *Perachora* 1, 30, 51; Chios, *LMS* 159 and Boardman, *Greek Emporio* 250; K. F. Kinch, *Vroulia* (1914); Siphnos, J. K. Brock and G. Mackworth Young, *BSA* 44 (1949), 6-16; Zagora, see *Ergon* 1967, 75-82; sanctuary-sites, above, pp. 275-85

46] Ithaka, see esp. Robertson, *BSA* 43 (1948), 122; Benton, *BSA* 48 (1953), 259 and Coldstream, *GGP* 353 for date; Phokis and Achaea, above, Chapter 2, pp. 73, 86, nn.50, 62; Thermon, *AD* 1 (1915), 270f. etc.

47] Among recent works on this subject are, for Crete, J. K. Brock's *Fortetsa* (1957) and J. Boardman's *Cretan Collection* (1961), but E. Kunze's *Kretische Bronzereliefs* (1931) is still fundamental. For the mainland, see especially K. Kübler in *Ker.* 5, 1, (1956), 159, n.121 and 168-78, esp. nn.160 and 171; for Olympia, Kunze in *Ol. ber.* 5 (1956), 81-2; for Samos, H. Walter and K. Vierneisel in *AM* 74 (1959), 35-42. Export of Greek pottery eastwards, T. J. Dunbabin, *The Greeks and their Eastern Neighbours* (1956), 72-4, and C. Clairmont in *Berytus* 11 (1954–5), 85-137

On particular classes of find, to the references given in the following notes add, on early figurines, Kunze in *AM* 55 (1930), 141-62; on cauldrons etc. P. Amandry in *Syria* 35 (1958), 73-109: on faience, F. W. von Bissing in

Sitzungsberichte der Bayerischen Akademie der Wissenschaften (1941), 7, 98ff.

48] Lack of Cretan finds in the Near East, Boardman, *Cretan Collection* 151, 155; but note his revised views on chronology and origins of Orientalia in Crete, *BSA* 62 (1967), 57-75; Idaean Cave series, Kunze, *Kretische Bronzereliefs*, and *Cretan Collection* 79-84, 138-9; ivories, Kunze in *AM* 60-1 (1935–6), 218-33 and R. D. Barnett, *A Catalogue of the Nimrud Ivories* (1957), 49-52 (Loftus series), 128-9, 133-5; Arslan Taş finds, see esp. J. W. and G. M. Crowfoot, *Early Ivories from Samaria* (*Samaria-Sebaste* 2, 1938), 5-6; and now G. Turner in *Iraq* 30 (1968), 67-8

49] Reliefs, *Cretan Collection* 134-8; statuettes, Dunbabin, *op. cit.* (n.47), 36, pl. 8, 1-3 and *Cretan Collection* 118-19, pl. 44; Cypriot pottery, and glass and amber, *Fortetsa* 190-1, 218; 208; other imports, *Cretan Collection* 150-2, but the context of the glass bowl Fortetsa *1567* (151, n.1) was about 700, not 800. Alphabet, L. H. Jeffery, *The Local Scripts of Archaic Greece* (1961), 310

50] On the Isis grave, see now N. Himmelmann-Wildschütz in *Marburger-Winckelmannsprogram* 1961, 6-9, who upholds a pure ninth-century date; gold bands, Kübler in *Ker.* 5, 1, 185-90 (esp. 189), and J. M. Cook, *BSA* 46 (1951), 49, who rightly propose a lower chronology than that of D. Ohly, *Griechische Goldbleche des 8 Jahrhunderts vor Chr.* (1953); plant-leaf motifs, *Ker.* 5, 1, pls. 97-9 – his dates should, however, be lowered

51] *Ker.* 5, 1, 174ff.; lion, 177, pl. 77, inv. 2160 (inv. 407, pl. 69 is surely a boar as Kübler says); fibula, *BMQ* 23 (1960–1), 105, pl. 46; sphinx and plants, pls. 126-7, inv. 301-3, grave 98

– these may be rather later than the period c.745-30 to which Kübler dates them. Grave with ivories, *ibid.* 92-3 (Piräusstrasse 13); Boardman, *GO* 81-2, pl. 1a and fig. 12 (d). Scarabs etc. J. D. S. Pendlebury, *Aegyptiaca* (1930), 78; *Ker.* 5, 1, 159, n.121; and add *AD* 20, 2 (1965), 78, pl. 44β,γ

52] Olympia, see Kunze, *Ol. ber.* 5, 81-2; lion handle, Herrmann in *JdI* 81 (1966), 132-3, fig. 47 (inv. Br. 11340, *Ol. Forsch.* 3, 99, 172 etc.). *Perachora* 1, 33-4. Cauldron-attachments, Herrmann, *Ol. Forsch.* 6 (1966), *passim*. Argos finds, *EGA* 14, 73-83; see Courbin, *Ceramique géometrique de l'Argolide* 174, 177 for date of grave; fire-dogs, S. Piggott, *Ancient Europe* (1965), 192 and n.60; cf. 247; C. Waldstein, *The Argive Heraeum* 2 (1905); gems, Boardman, *Island Gems*, 110-16; cf. 116-22, 129-32

53] Pendlebury, *Aegyptiaca*, p. vii; Lyre-player seals, Buchner and Boardman, *JdI* 81 (1966), 1-62; East Greek gems, *Island Gems* 136-42; gold bands, Johansen, *Act. Arch.* 28 (1957), 175-80; ivories, B. Freyer-Schauenberg, *Elfenbeine aus dem Samischen Heraion* (1966); Cypriot pottery, *SCE* 4, 2, 262-7, and figurines, *AM* 65 (1940), 57-65 and 66 (1941), 1ff.; Luristan bronzes, Boardman, *GO* 89; *Iraq* 18 (1956), 163, pl. 34, 4; J. Birmingham, *AS* 11 (1961), 191-2, figs. 7-10; Urartian (?) figurine, Herrmann, *JdI* 81 (1966), 126-7, figs. 37-9; Phrygian sherds, E. Akurgal, *Phrygische Kunst* (1955), 33, pl. H.1 (see M. Mellink in *AJA* 61 (1957), 393); belts, Boardman in *Anatolia* 6 (1961), 179-89; dinos-handle fragment, *id.*, *Greek Emporio* 224, no. 383. For an exchange of views on Greek and Phrygian art, see E. Akurgal, R. S. Young, P. Amandry in *VIIIème Congrès Internationale*

d'Archéologie Classique (Paris, 1963)
(*Le Rayonnement des Civilisations grecque et romaine sur les Cultures Périphériques*) 467-74, 488-9; 481-5; 485-8 respectively; earliest Greek import, *ibid.* pl. 122, 3. Note now Coldstream's observations, *GGP* 379

54] For Gordion reports, see R. S. Young in *AJA* 59 (1955), 1-18; 60 (1956), 249-66; 61 (1957), 319-31; 62 (1958), 147-54 with report of excavation of the Great Tumulus; 64 (1960), 227-43; 66 (1962), 153-68; and *Proceedings of the American Philosophical Society* 107, 4 (1963), 349-64; Phrygian transmission of the alphabet to Greece, R. D. Barnett in *CAH₂* 2, chapter 30 (Fascicle 56, 1967), 20

55] This argument is given in summary form in *Archaeology* 11 (1958), 231; it was also lucidly expounded by Prof. Young at the VIIth International Congress of Classical Archaeology in 1963, but is not included in the transcript of his paper (above, n.53); Carbon$_{14}$ dates, *AJA* 65 (1961), 360-3

56] See W. Kroll in Pauly-Wissowa, *RE* 15, 2 (1932), s.v. Midas, on the incompatible references in Hdt. I, 14, 2-3; 35, 3; VIII, 138, 2. On the significance of Mita of Pakhuwa, see O. R. Gurney, *LAAA* 28 (1948), 46. On Gordion tumulus, E. Akurgal, *Die Kunst Anatoliens* (1961), 118; Barnett, *op. cit.* (n.54), 12 also identifies the dead ruler with the famous Midas

57] Akurgal, *op. cit.* (see previous note), 119

58] The early alphabetic inscriptions are discussed by L. H. Jeffery, *The Local Scripts of Archaic Greece*, 16-17; other late eighth-century examples may be added, e.g. *Excavations at Lefkandi*, 33-4; K. Schefold, *Meisterwerke griechischer Kunst* (1960), 131, no. I 59; *BSA* 59 (1964), 40 (Smyrna). Dipylon oenochoe, Jeffery, *op. cit.* 68, no. I; Pithekoussai inscriptions, 235, no. I and Buchner, *Expedition* 8, 4 (summer 1966), 9; (Rhys Carpenter's arguments for a much lower dating of the inscription, *AJP* 84 (1963), 83-5, seem answered by H. Metzger, *REA* 67 (1965), 301-5); earlier graffito, M. Guarducci, *Archeologia Classica* 16 (1964), 129. Alphabet brought to Greece by Phoenicians, J. A. Bundgård in *Analecta Romana Instituti Danici* 3 (1965), 56-8; Phoenician presence at Al Mina, J. du Plat Taylor, *Iraq* 21 (1959), 88f.

7

The Internal Situation

◆ ◆ ◆
◆ ◆
◆

The purpose of this final chapter is twofold. First, there are many broad aspects of Greek culture at this period which have been barely touched on so far; in some cases this omission cannot be made good simply for lack of evidence, but there are other fields – architecture, art, religion, political organization, to name only the most obvious – of which something can and must be said. Secondly, the attempt must be made to draw together the disjointed and disparate evidence amassed in the previous chapters, so as to frame some kind of answer to the central question with which this study is concerned – what was life really like in Greece between the eleventh and the eighth centuries BC? The general character of the evidence from this period is already well known, and I cannot claim to have modified it in any significant way. The vital element comes in assessing the *competence* of the evidence. Can we accept the picture that it presents at face value? Can we supplement the picture with information drawn from other regions or other periods, or even reject it as fundamentally distorted? The problem could be posed in different words, but the basic decision remains the same.

DECLINE: THE TWELFTH AND EARLIER ELEVENTH CENTURIES

That our period begins with the decline of a great civilization, a decline which in spite of the fact that sudden violence played a major part in it, was nevertheless gradual and prolonged, will by now be generally agreed. We have illustrated its gradual character already by the high quality of some of the twelfth-century pottery (pp. 28-30), by the more widespread conservatism in tomb types and burial practices (pp. 153, 182), and by the undoubted survival of Mycenaean overseas connections in this same period (pp. 313-21, 324-7). Further evidence is provided by the picture of the architectural remains and general living conditions at this time on Mycenaean sites. The results of the recent excavations at Lefkandi[1] give an unusually clear example. On the sparse remains of occupation of this site in the Mycenaean III B period, the supervenes a fresh and basically re-planned settlement early in III C. If the new builders were immigrants, they were Mycenaean immigrants, perhaps from Aeolis as later Greek tradition suggests (p. 301). Their settlement was not very prepossessing, but it consisted of rectilinear houses, with walls of pisée or of mud-brick on stone socles, and of more than one storey in height. More striking is the fact that when this settlement was destroyed, at a rather later date but still within the twelfth century, a further rebuilding took place, presumably by the erstwhile destroyers, with a detectably higher standard of planning and workmanship; the stone footings of the walls are well constructed, and once again it is clear, above all from their pottery, that the newcomers were still Mycenaeans. The new settlement survived for a considerable period; perhaps the most telling sign of the changing times is the fact that a number of intramural burials were dotted over the habitation area. The picture at Lefkandi shows clearly enough that Mycenaean communities lived on, sometimes moving to fresh sites, and inevitably accommodating themselves to changed circumstances, probably for well over a century after the great wave of disasters had struck their civilization. This evidence is substantiated by that of several other sites: we may mention, in the heartland of Mycenaean culture, the III C occupation of the citadel of Mycenae itself, with its close-packed stone-built houses and paved yards; the recently-discovered III C settlement of Tiryns, which apparently continued to make use of the two subterranean passages leading to springs outside the fortifications; the apparently undisturbed continuation of life at Argos; and the settlement at Asine, which seems to belong very largely in the later part of the period. Further afield, we have the well-known arrangements made at Athens in the early part of III C, enabling the population to use the underground fountain in the north face of the Acropolis rock; the survival, apparently unharmed, of the III C settlement surrounding the destroyed palace of Iolkos, and of that at Grotta on Naxos; and the temporary survival of the massively fortified settlement at Miletus.[2] At nearly all these sites, the atmosphere of insecurity is unmistakable: we see it in the abandonment of the extramural houses at Mycenae and Athens, in the emergency water-supply provisions at Athens and Tiryns, in the partial or eventual destruction at Iolkos, Miletus and Lefkandi. We may also detect a quite different reflection of it in the diffusion

112

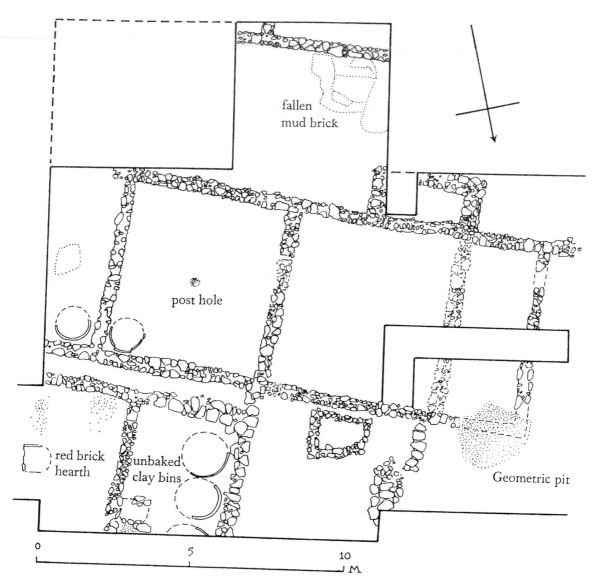

fallen
mud brick

post hole

red brick
hearth

unbaked
clay bins

Geometric pit

0   5   10
                                         ᴊ M

112. Plan of part of the rebuilt Mycenaean III C settlement at Lefkandi
in Euboea. Later 12th century BC.

of Mycenaean refugee-elements in other parts of Greece (pp. 316-17). But the indications are equally clear that Mycenaeans for a time succeeded in enduring insecurity, and often in recovering from actual disaster, without losing the arts and practices which distinguished their culture in its heyday.

In due course there came a time when this was no longer so; and it may be that the best demonstration of this is to be found, not in the positive appearance of new phenomena – the use of cists and other forms of single burial, the Submycenaean pottery of western Attica, the growth of extra-mural settlement in the same region and elsewhere – but in the sheer negative evidence of the disappearance of the old. At most of the sites we have mentioned, the end of the career of the III C settlements comes in a curiously obscure form: at Lefkandi a third rebuilding, still within the III C period, apparently proved necessary, but its end seems to be marked only by slow decay, and then probably by a temporary desertion of the site. At Tiryns the situation is not clear, but burials presently began to take place within the Mycenaean house-ruins; while at Argos the settlement area was definitely re-sited at some time, perhaps about 1100, after only the briefest interval in occupation. In both these cases there is a suggestion that the former III C population had either disappeared, or had tired of its existence among the relics of ancestral glory. At Asine too the last Mycenaean occupation fades out before any attempt at re-settlement occurs. At Mycenae, the destruction of the Granary did not bring the occupation of the citadel to an end, but presently it faded away nonetheless, leaving a probable gap before the next settlers make their presence known by burying in the ruined houses. By contrast, across the Aegean at Miletus the destruction of the fortified settlement seems to have terminated occupation for a time. The III C inhabitants eventually moved down from the Acropolis at Athens, although we cannot say whether they are the same people as those who now settled and excavated wells in the Agora below, or who inaugurated the Kerameikos cemetery. At Iolkos, there is also an interruption of settlement during Mycenaean III C; the excavator estimated this to be of only one generation's length, but there are grave difficulties involved in this assumption, since the succeeding style is characterized as 'Protogeometric'. Even on Naxos, despite the excavator's claim of total continuity of occupation, there is some circumstantial evidence to suggest a brief interval between the latest III C and the first Protogeometric occupation.[3]

We seem to have clear evidence of a general tendency of III C settlements to decay and run down, and finally to be abandoned or at least

re-sited. In most cases the decay must occupy the later part of the twelfth
century, while the desertion extends into the eleventh, and the eventual
re-occupation falls in the eleventh or even, as at Lefkandi and Asine, in the
tenth. Only very rarely is this process accompanied by traces of further
violence. What explanation of this pattern can be given? The answer may
best be sought by turning away from the handful of sites we have been
considering, and looking at Greece as a whole. These sites were chosen
because they tell a positive story, even if it is an interrupted and unim-
pressive one, in this dark period; but how much greater is the impression
of decline and desolation when we consider the rest of Greece. Although
we are no longer able to speak, with even the limited confidence assumed in
the earlier cases, of the sequence of events, the bare statistics of the occupation of other sites are sufficiently eloquent. For this purpose we may take
the ceramic phase of Mycenaean III B to be equivalent to the thirteenth
century BC and deduce, from the discovery of that class of pottery on a
site, that it was occupied in that century. Similarly the occurrence of the
well-established earlier and middle classes of Mycenaean III C pottery –
the Close Style, the Granary class and their contemporaries – may be taken
to indicate twelfth-century occupation; while for the eleventh century we
may include all varieties of late and degenerate III C or Submycenaean
pottery, together with the earlier stages of Protogeometric in all regions
where that style was of early growth. Working on this basis we may examine the list of sites and their pottery-yields in a valuable and quite recent
publication, R. Hope Simpson's *A Gazetteer and Atlas of Mycenaean Sites*
(1965). Its survey covers the whole Mycenaean Greek mainland, the
Aegean and Ionian islands (Crete excluded) and the western coast of
Asia Minor; it embraces settlement-, cemetery- and sanctuary-sites, besides
many others undifferentiated and known from surface finds only. It
includes sites in regions such as Epirus, Macedonia and Lesbos where the
occurrence of Mycenaean finds is often taken to indicate commercial
links on the part of a non-Mycenaean population, but these are omitted in
the figures given below. Adding to Hope Simpson's list the entirely fresh
sites discovered since 1964, the existing sites where material of a new period
has occurred, and the post-Mycenaean sites probably first occupied in the
eleventh century and not listed by him – all of them small categories – we
obtain figures of the following order[4]:

> Occupied in the thirteenth century: c.320 sites
> Occupied in the twelfth century: c.130
> Occupied in the eleventh century: c.40

The figures cannot be precise, as they involve many uncertain factors such as the occurrence of pottery of a transitional phase. But it may be said now that the eleventh-century figure includes a number of distinctly   *113* questionable sites, where the reports of unpublished 'Submycenaean' or 'early Protogeometric' material have been given the benefit of the doubt; while on the contrary the thirteenth-century figure, and perhaps to a lesser extent the twelfth, stand to be substantially increased by the many sites where undifferentiated 'Late Helladic' pottery is recorded, none of which has been included.

DEPOPULATION

In terms of absolute population, no doubt these figures are misleading or meaningless. But in relative terms I believe they are unanswerable. The years of Mycenaean decline must have witnessed a drastic fall in the population of Greek lands. Depopulation can have many causes, not all of them necessarily associated with disaster. But one factor which can hardly be allowed to have played a decisive part here is mass emigration, for the simple reason that the geographical scope of these figures covers most of the areas to which Mycenaeans are likely to have emigrated – that is to say, the Ionian coast and the Aegean islands. It is true that the survey excludes the islands of Crete and Cyprus; of these, it is likely, if not yet demonstrable, that there was some intrusion of new settlers into Crete during the twelfth century, and equally probable that such settlers came from the Greek mainland. In Cyprus it is almost certain that Mycenaean elements made their appearance near the beginning of the III c period, and again during its later part.[5] But Cyprus was itself racked by major disasters at both periods, and is unlikely to have attracted whole communities of settlers. The material from the two islands – expecially that of the relevant Cypriot sites of the twelfth and eleventh centuries, Enkomi, Sinda and to a lesser degree Kition and Idalion – is not enough to suggest that they can have accommodated more than a small fraction of the missing population of Mycenaean Greece.

The striking depopulation of these years cannot then be attributed, except in a small part, to emigration from Greek lands. And indeed when one considers the other internal phenomena which are present – widespread violence at the end of the thirteenth century with intermittent recurrences later, a definite shrinking of overseas communication, the disappearance of the more elaborate building-forms and precious artefacts – it is a natural and obvious conclusion that this depopulation is a symptom of economic disaster. It may be objected that 'disaster' is too extreme a

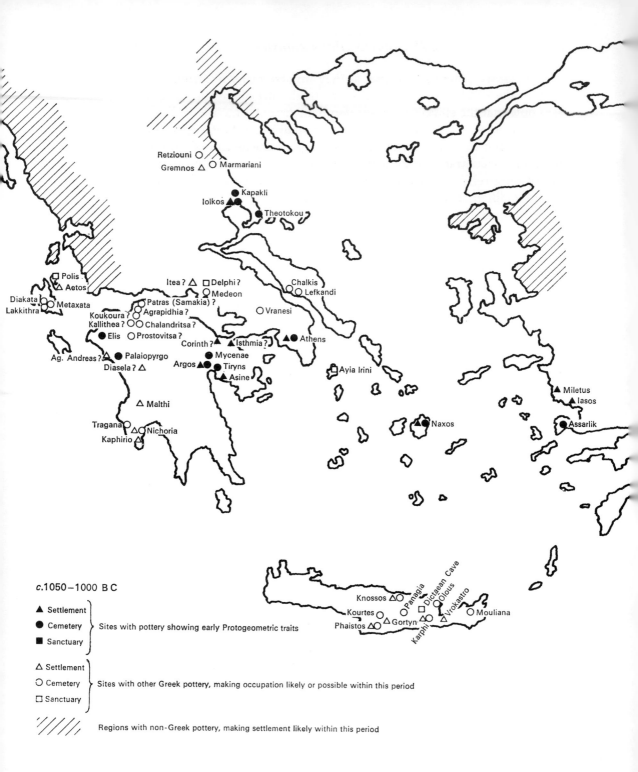

Retziouni ○
Gremnos △ ○ Marmariani

● Kapakli
Iolkos ▲▲●
● Theotokou

Polis □
Aetos △
Diakata ○
Lakkithra ○ ● Metaxata

Itea ? △ □ Delphi ?
○ Medeon
Patras (Samakia) ?
Koukoura ?
Agrapidhia ?
Kallithea ? ○ ○ Chalandritsa ?
Elis ● ○ Prostovitsa ?
Corinth ? ▲ ▲ Isthmia ?
Ag. Andreas ? ○ ● Palaiopyrgo
Diasela ? △ Argos ▲▲ ● Mycenae
● Tiryns
● Asine

Chalkis
○ ● Lefkandi

○ Vranesi

▲ ● Athens

□ Ayia Irini

▲ Miletus
▲ Iasos

▲ Malthi

Tragana ○
△ ○ Nichoria
Kaphirio △

▲ ● Naxos

● Assarlik

c.1050–1000 B C

▲ Settlement
● Cemetery ⎫ Sites with pottery showing early Protogeometric traits
■ Sanctuary ⎭

△ Settlement
○ Cemetery ⎫ Sites with other Greek pottery, making occupation likely or possible within this period
□ Sanctuary ⎭

////// Regions with non-Greek pottery, making settlement likely within this period

Knossos △○
Panagia
Dictaean Cave
Kourtes ○ ○ □ Olous
Phaistos △○ △ Gortyn ▲ Vrokastro
Karphi ○ Mouliana

word for a process which evidently lasted over 200 years; but what I wish to argue is that the depopulation figures add a fresh dimension to the picture of steady decline which has already emerged. If it were merely a case of decline in the *quality* of the material remains, it would still be possible to argue[6] that this was largely because Greece had dispensed with the obsolete centralized autocracy of the Mycenaean civilization; but when we add to this such a drastic decline in quantity as to suggest a reduction by over three-quarters in the population, then it is surely inconceivable that total prosperity remained constant. We have to assume not only some extreme unpleasantness in living conditions which must have put this process in motion, but also the almost equally inexorable consequences which depopulation generates once it is an established trend. Skills are lost; the standards of technology and, most important, of agriculture fall; the horizons of each community shrink. We may, finally, set the numbers of known settlements in Greece in these centuries against a wider background. Hope Simpson's survey also lists the sites in the Greek mainland and islands at which Early and Middle Helladic remains have been found: they number, respectively, nearly 200 and nearly 250. It will be rightly observed that these are periods of several centuries' duration, but against this must be set the fact that they are cultures of a more limited geographical extent than those of the Mycenaean and post-Mycenaean eras: they barely extend beyond the peninsula of the Greek mainland, being replaced in the islands and Ionia by their Cycladic, Minoan and Anatolian counterparts. There is therefore no reason to doubt that the population of Greek lands in the eleventh century B C was lower than it had been for a thousand years. Similarly, it was probably never so low at any later time in antiquity: a rough count of later Protogeometric and Early and Middle Geometric sites is enough to show that, without any spectacular increase, the numbers of known occupied sites in the tenth and ninth centuries are certainly higher than in the eleventh. Then in the eighth century, as has been noted elsewhere, there is something of a 'population explosion' in Greece. The catastrophe of Greece in the two centuries before 1000 B C, whatever form it took, was surely a most profound experience. The suggestion that many regions of Greece, particularly the islands, were for a time totally depopulated, should not shock us to the point of incredulity: as recently as the fifteenth and sixteenth centuries A D, much the same thing can be traced in many Aegean islands.[7]

113. Distribution map of occupied sites, *c.* 1050-1000 B C.

ISOLATION: THE LATER ELEVENTH AND EARLIER
TENTH CENTURIES

But the surviving communities of Greece, however scattered and demoralized, were the basis for the eventual revival of Greek culture. When we look more closely at them, the picture is not without its relieving features. The last lifeline to the outside world was that to Cyprus, perhaps preserved by the latest groups of Mycenaean emigrants, and this had already provided Greece with the means of making the crucial technological change to iron-working in the first half of the eleventh century; but the way in which this change was received illustrates the disjointed state of Greek society which the breakdown of internal communications – itself accentuated by the thinning-out of population – had brought about. The regions of Greece where a proper iron-working industry now comes into being are scattered geographically, and are not linked by any obvious feature beyond the fact that they share an Aegean seaboard. They include Attica, the Argolid, Thessaly, south-western Asia Minor, Naxos and Crete; elsewhere we have no proof that iron-working was yet mastered and, in several areas, definite evidence to the contrary. Nor are the early iron industries distributed according to the deposits of iron ore; rather, the better-organized and more accessible communities of Greece were able to adopt this timely advance at the moment when they most needed to become self-sufficient in order to survive the even greater isolation of the late eleventh and earlier tenth centuries. The fact that these regions are not contiguous territorially, and include some islands, confirms that in this as in other eras the prime mode of communication, internal and external, was by sea. We have no direct knowledge of the types of shipping in use at this date, but there are representations of oared ships dating from both the Mycenaean III C and the Cretan Early Protogeometric periods which show some similarities – roughly symmetrical build, with high bows and stern, and a ram. Later, eighth-century ships show a revival of other Mycenaean features, and we need not doubt that throughout the intervening period the Greeks had the use of such oared vessels, which could no doubt serve as combined warships and transports.[8]

But to carve timber is one thing, to work in masonry another. When we turn to the architectural features of this period, we see the full extent of the fall in standards which the years of depopulation had brought. Only at one or two places in Greece is there any sign that good stone-built constructions of eleventh or tenth-century date existed; they are all in the regions already recognized as being the most advanced. Beside the site of the former Mycenaean palace at Iolkos, there were the remains of quite a substantial Protogeometric settlement, which passed though four building-phases, with stone-built rectangular houses. Then at Grotta on Naxos the Mycenaean III C settlement was rebuilt in Protogeometric times, also in stone, and incorporating at some stage a building of 'megaron' type.[9] At both these sites the reconstruction may be dated to the eleventh century; but even here there is no sign that the full range of Mycenaean constructional ability was preserved. The finest structures of the Late Bronze Age were composed either of huge fitted and smoothed boulders, or of sawn limestone blocks, retaining a rubble core; probably the normal tool for this latter work was a bronze saw in whose cutting edge pieces of emery were set.[10] As far as we know, neither this tool, nor either of the two techniques, survived the Mycenaean decline. Early Iron Age stone house-walls in Greece (as distinct from socles for mud-brick, often consisting of totally unworked stones) are all small-stone constructions; at best they are formed of two rows of blocks with a squared outer face, backing so closely on to each other that only very small stones can be fitted in between. But even this technique is mostly found in the full Geometric period; before that, we may suppose that the commonest building material was mud-brick of the kind used in the early oval house at Old Smyrna, of about 900 BC; here the wall is of a thickness of only one of these large bricks, about 30 centimetres, and the choice of material and dimensions imposed strict limitations on the scope of the building.[11]

114

Clearer proof of the essential discontinuity with Mycenaean architecture is given by the types of house-plan; as H. Drerup has shown, the forms most favoured in early Iron Age Greece are the apsidal and, perhaps slightly less often, the oval. Of these the second provides a decisive case, since it almost entirely lacks Bronze Age predecessors in Greece; its walls may be of stone or mud-brick, but in either case it is a simple, one-storey and even one-room structure, normally no doubt with a steeply-pitched, thatched roof. The apsidal house by contrast has a long pedigree extending back to the Middle Bronze Age and continuing in the outlying regions of the Mycenaean world. But the Iron Age examples of both the apsidal and the rather rarer rectilinear plans have at first a curious tendency to exhibit slight, but deliberate, convex curvature in their long sides, a feature which links them to the oval plan and dissociates them from their Bronze Age forerunners.[12] It is possible, therefore, that it was the oval-plan house which was the dominant form in the years around 1000 BC; and certainly the prevalence of thatched roofs in the ensuing period strengthened the

2A

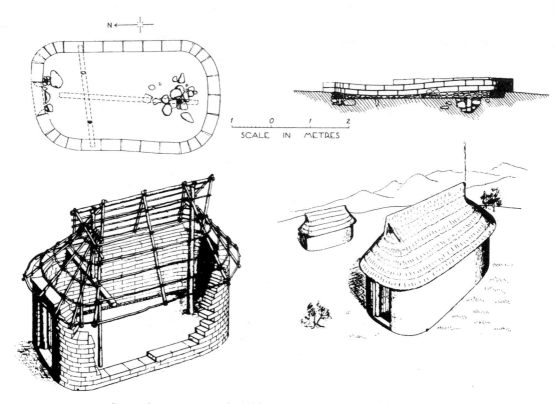

SCALE IN METRES

114. Plan and restoration of oval house of *c.* 900 BC at Old Smyrna
(R. V. Nicholls).

114   tendency towards rounded corners. The oval house at Smyrna has been
mentioned above; the apsidal and rectilinear forms are found in structures
which may be dated to the ninth century (see below, pp. 408-13). The gap
in the evidence before these buildings may be partially filled by the publication of the Protogeometric settlements at Iolkos and Naxos, but from
the dearth of other surviving remains one suspects that the more perishable
mud-brick predominated in the structures of the eleventh and tenth
centuries; especially since this technique occurs in the sacrificial platforms
beside contemporary graves and later in the walls of the grave itself
(pp. 150-1, 196).

To all of this, however, Crete provides an exception. Buildings in stone
survive at several sites, some of them from the period which for the remainder of Greece is almost blank; while among the types of house-plan

the rectangular is predominant, although a few rounded or oval structures apparently existed. The evidence of Karphi must, as always, be put forward with qualifications, not only because of its general cultural isolation but also because the date of the building of the settlement may well go back further than the excavators thought, perhaps to the mid-twelfth century. Nevertheless it is probable that the Karphi houses remained occupied down to about 1000 BC or later, and this means that, despite the forbidding nature of the site, with its rocky outcrops and steep gradients which necessitated terracing, the inhabitants of this city of refuge were distinctly better housed than most of their contemporaries in other parts of the Aegean. True, the houses are largely dry-built, with split but undressed stones; but the thickness of the walls, and the size of many of the blocks, are greater than is found elsewhere for some time afterwards; while the regular presence of such features as thresholds, door-jambs and chimneys puts these houses on an altogether higher level than we shall find in Greece as yet. Rectilinear plans were universal; second storeys are perhaps a possibility in some houses, and frequently changes of level made communi-cation-stairways necessary; roofs were certainly flat, as commonly in Crete, with rafters and planks topped by beaten earth. The streets between the houses were carefully paved. The accompanying tholos-tombs, how-ever inferior to their Bronze Age predecessors, are competently built structures, of a rather higher standard than the houses. There are new settlements in the Cretan plains which must be contemporary with Karphi – for instance, the fresh re-building of Phaistos and the new foundation of Gortyn, which belong in the twelfth century – but for any preserved architectural remains we have to turn to other upland sites, similar to Karphi.[13] Vrokastro, built on equally steep terrain but not nearly so high as Karphi, had housed a Middle Minoan settlement; but after a consider-able gap settlers returned to the site, at a date which must be placed in the eleventh century if not before, and they remained for several centuries. The houses excavated, although still occupied in the eighth century, must retain the form of their predecessors, for no changes of plans or clearly-distinguished strata could be observed. But if the re-building was in part contemporary with Karphi, the standards were appreciably lower. The Vrokastro houses are small-stone constructions, with thin walls and no door-jambs; streets are scarcely provided between the houses; curved walls are tolerated where convenient, and in general terracing has been avoided. At Karphi, rock outcrops are often split to form a vertical wall for an abutting room, whereas at Vrokastro they are either incorporated

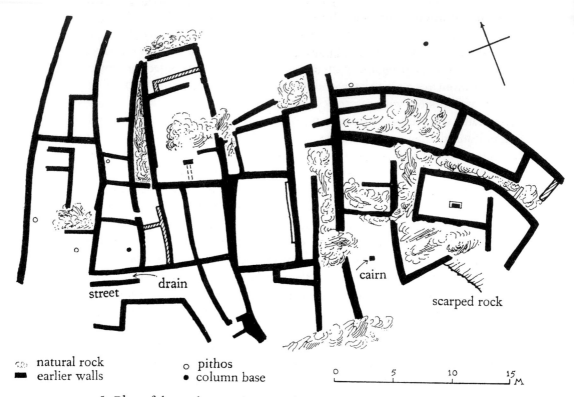

natural rock   o pithos
earlier walls   • column base

115. Plan of the settlement site at Vrokastro in East Crete.

in their crude state, or else masked by a built wall. There is a marked contrast between the basically early houses and a superior structure of presumed eighth-century date, which accompanies the 'bone-enclosures' at Vrokastro. At nearby Kavousi, there is the same chronological uncertainty arising from continuous occupation of the site from Subminoan to Geometric times; but at any rate the house and associated structures on 'Thunder Hill' near the Subminoan cemetery can lay claim to an early date. The main building was evidently quite imposing, with a forecourt, while the surviving walling of another building near by is described as 'excellent'. Whatever insecurity compelled their recourse to such sites, it is clear that the settlers of Karphi and Kavousi were still in possession of the basic architectural skills of the Bronze Age. Since they were heirs to the Minoan rather than the Mycenaean tradition, their structures took a different form from those of their only comparable contemporaries, at Iolkos and Naxos; but in both cases it is clear that their skills were inherited. There is indeed an eloquent illustration of this in the survival of masons' marks on a piece of Protogeometric walling at Iolkos, of a form which resembles sign number 24 of the Bronze Age Linear B script.[14] It is equally clear that the survival of such hereditary skills was the exception; their loss, and the consequent experimentation with simpler forms that we find elsewhere, was the rule.

THE IONIAN MIGRATION: REGIONAL DIVERSITY

Such a conclusion, that quality stood in direct relation to the strength of Bronze Age survival, is clearly not universally true of life at this period. The development of iron technology, in the more advanced regions of Greece, has already provided a direct instance to the contrary. There is the same air of fresh initiative about the one great historical development which we can date with certainty to this period, the Ionian migration (a term which I now use in its widest sense, to incorporate Aeolic and Doric settlers as well as Ionians). On present chronological evidence, one cannot do better than repeat the conclusion of J.M.Cook that 'Ionic settlement . . . should go back at least to about 1000 BC, and perhaps still earlier at Miletus' (p. 127).[15] The material from Assarlik and other sites in the region endorses this last judgment on Miletus, and we can only conclude that the initial wave of settlement took place in the eleventh century. Equally justified, and even more important, is the claim that 'the Dark Age migrations were not a reinforcement of already existing Greek settlements'. Even if the picture of Mycenaean settlement in western Asia Minor is considerably extended in future years, it is doubtful whether that could invalidate this statement: the silence of Homer about the Ionic coast in heroic times, and the archaeological evidence of the choice of fresh Iron Age sites, and of the distinct breaks in occupation at the rare exceptions such as Miletus and Emborio, all tell in its favour. This makes the Ionian migration a remarkable testimony to the vitality of the Greek communities in the eleventh century: to carry groups of settlers a hundred miles or more across dangerous seas to a potentially or actually hostile shore requires some organization and resources, as well as courage. But despite the implication of Thucydides, who closely associates them with the later process of colonization (1, 12,4), we should not imagine these migrations as an official enterprise, dispatched or even sponsored by a state; there is no likelihood of such processes as we hear of in accounts of historical colonization, when selection by lot might be employed by the state, and pressure applied to reluctant emigrants. These migrants were clearly independent groups, led by individual aristocrats such as were later remembered as the founding fathers of the Ionian cities; the location of the starting points from which they sailed is a question of largely geographical interest. Later Ionian belief combined two elements of remarkable persistence: that the settlers had a diversity of origins, but that in most recorded cases they actually sailed from Athens, and were led by members of the Athenian royal family. Whatever worth we may be inclined to allow this last element in the tradition, we may probably accept the two main tenets, which accord well enough with the archaeological record. For example, the fact that Messenia was heavily depopulated in the twelfth century could lie behind the tradition that Pylians fled for refuge to Athens before crossing to Asia; but the discovery that a Protogeometric style did exist in Messenia (p. 87) at least makes it possible that a movement, perhaps later, of settlers direct from Pylos to Ionia took place, such as was recalled by Mimnermus of Colophon in the seventh century. The tradition that Euboeans, Boeotians and Phocians partook in the migration (e.g. Herodotus I, 146) is consonant with the current impression that these regions were still populated in the III C period, but that they then fade into temporary obscurity before the appearance of somewhat late or derivative Protogeometric schools. Above all, the fact that Athens seems to have been as active and populous a centre as any in Greece in the dark days before 1000 BC makes it credible that she should have provided the focus for much of the migration.

In all our discussions of Greek culture at this period, a constantly recurring factor has been the dichotomy between certain relatively advanced, active and accessible regions, and the rest of the country. The division was first formulated on the basis of the pottery styles, and if it rested on no other foundation we might hesitate to attribute significance to it. But even then it would remain true that the Protogeometric style represents both an entirely new artistic current, and a fairly high standard of technique based on certain purely mechanical attributes – a fast wheel, a pair of compasses, a multiple brush; and therefore we concluded that its early spread constituted a genuine and direct transmission from one centre to certain others, but no further (pp. 45-68). But when we find that a very similar grouping of regions plays the same role in the other categories in which we can assess material progress at this time, we can only believe that the pattern is not illusory. Protogeometric styles of early growth appear in Attica, the Argolid, Thessaly, Naxos, western Asia Minor, and perhaps

Corinthia and Elis. The early adoption of cremation as a common rite   69
occurs in Attica, Naxos and western Asia Minor – but also in Crete. The
early mastery of iron-working occurs in Attica, the Argolid, Thessaly,
Naxos, western Asia Minor – and again in Crete. Competent stone building
of later eleventh- and tenth-century date is known only from Thessaly,   74
Naxos and Crete. The emergence of Crete as an advanced area materially,
despite the fact that she was impervious to the influence of Protogeometric
pottery until a century later than the other regions, is perhaps not so surprising: she was, after all, uniquely well placed to benefit from such ideas
as were transmitted from Cyprus and the eastern Mediterranean, while
as regards those inherited from the Bronze Age, she was heir to the basically independent Minoan tradition, which any immigration from mainland Greece, whether in the fifteenth century or the twelfth, had only super-
ficially contaminated. She could therefore progress on her own resources
in a way which was perhaps impossible for other areas of the Aegean; if
her advance, both at this time and again with the fresh onset of Oriental
influence centuries later, seems at times to be curiously in step with that
of Attica and other regions, this need not be a pure coincidence; the
same external ideas could reach their destinations simultaneously, yet
independently.

The other more advanced regions are mostly united in that they share a
natural and easy access to the Aegean Sea. Although it is hard to distinguish
between cause and effect here, the fact must possess some significance in
connection with the Ionian migration. It is perhaps as likely a reconstruction
as any to say that the general drift of population from west to east on the
Greek mainland, recorded by the traditions and confirmed in the material
and dialectal record (pp. 299-304), was already established, and that the
Ionian migration merely carried it a stage further. Thereafter, the links
with the new settlements across the Aegean, and perhaps the swift prosperity of these last, preserved the pattern for a few generations. The more
active communities in Greece, and all those in Ionia, turned their faces to
the Aegean and their backs to the hinterland; the Aegean became what it
had never been even at the height of Mycenaean power, a Greek sea. This
was of course a permanent development; from now on the focus of Greek
civilization increasingly became the Aegean, and the appearance of foreign
military and even commercial power in it became exceptional, a matter
for remark if not for resistance. But much less permanent were some of the
side-effects of this move: in particular the neglect of the Greek hinterland
to the west. The disused land-routes across the peninsula, and a natural

waterway like the Gulf of Corinth, could not be ignored indefinitely. In due course the pattern broke up; and indeed in many ways the picture of Greek civilization in the eleventh and early tenth centuries is unique and somewhat extraordinary. Already before the mid-eighth century we find that Thessaly has withdrawn to a lasting obscurity and backwardness; that Corinth has found an equally lasting focus of interest in western Greece; that other fresh powers are arising, such as Sparta which also looks westwards for further expansion; that religious centres of panhellenic importance are growing up in neglected territories like Elis and Phokis; and that the new wave of traders and settlers are looking to the far west. But the hard core, to which Greek culture shrank at the lowest point in its fortunes, had been centred on the Aegean.

Something of this was clearly remembered by Greek tradition, and indeed we have cited tradition in support of this picture. The general sense of indebtedness to Athens for her part in the Ionian migration is surely a genuine element in this, rather than a political fiction invented by later Athenians. But the migration was the one great and positive achievement of the era; apart from this, the Greeks in my view remembered astonishingly little about this period of quiescence, once the wars and movements which marked the end of the heroic age were completed.

In the first chapter (pp. 10-16) we considered how, by means of genealogical tables and other documents ultimately based on genealogy, the later Greeks tried to span this period and link themselves with the heroic age, with results that are quite unacceptable as historical fact. But rather than reject their efforts as pure invention, we attempted to reinterpret them on the assumption that the more credible sections of their pedigrees were genuine, and that the main error had arisen in the conversion from generations into years. On this view, several recorded pedigrees from different parts of the Greek world – those of the Spartan royal families, of the Philaids at Athens, of Hecataeus of Miletus, of Heropythos of Chios and of the Asclepiads of Cos – suggest that genuine memory of lineal descent went back to approximately the tenth century BC, but stopped there. The Spartan royal genealogy, if it records a genuine succession going back to the last years of the tenth century, apparently conflicts with our surmise that the earliest Iron Age pottery from Laconia, the Protogeometric of Amyklai, is unlikely to begin at so early a date (p. 130). But the Asclepiad pedigree, which on our interpretation would date its eponym to about 950 BC, provides a quite striking concordance with the archaeological date reached for the beginning of burials at the Serraglio on Kos (p. 127). Chios, where Protogeometric finds so far seem few and late, may possibly not have been reached by the Ionian settlers until the end of the tenth century, to which Heropythos' first recorded ancestor may belong; if so, this will mean that the Ionian migration was a long-drawn-out process, and it is perhaps easier to believe that some more localized movement brought this worthy to his new home in Chios, such as that which took new settlers to Emborio in the late eighth century. With the Athenian and Milesian pedigrees, in cities where continuous occupation from at least 1050 BC seems assured, I think we can only conclude that the Philaids and Hecataeus were stopped short in their genealogical reconstructions by a barrier of pure ignorance, unaffected by movements of peoples. Hecataeus' fourteenth ancestor had to be made the son of a god, Miltiades' eleventh ancestor the son of Ajax, simply because not even a name could be recovered from the oblivion that lay beyond them.

That nothing should be remembered of this period would be natural if, in fact, nothing worth remembering had happened. A society whose very survival may have been threatened by depopulation was now given the peace and isolation needed for its slow recovery: its activities, of pressing concern and perhaps not uninspiring to its members at the time, would hold little interest for a richer and more enlightened posterity. The important changes and advances of the mid-eleventh century did not, as we have seen, inaugurate a steady or unified advance; on the contrary, they gave way to a period of perhaps two or three generations' length, in which isolation reached its peak and apparent stagnation came in its wake. The technique of iron-working was not yet diffused over the rest of Greece; the influence of Attic Protogeometric pottery was for the time being confined to the areas which had originally accepted it; even the first wave of migration across the Aegean may not have been supported in strength until later, although this last is no more than a surmise. More certainly, the commodities for which Greece depended on foreign suppliers – the most conspicuous are gold, ivory, amber and faience, but much more basic materials such as copper and tin seem to be involved too – run short in Greece in the middle years of the Protogeometric style of the advanced areas (pp. 246-9). Only Crete is a likely exception; her access, perhaps unbroken, to Cyprus is probably responsible. The rest of the Aegean was certainly heavily depopulated; apparently isolated from the outside world; apparently also stagnant in its material culture. What is this likely to mean in terms of contemporary life?

Once again, the picture must not be painted too black. Since the Greeks were able to row and sail across the Aegean, their disinclination to go further may be in part put down to the sheer unattractiveness of more distant shores at this time. Further, they did not entirely lack internal resources: iron may have been the most important of these, but the discovery of two Protogeometric furnaces, evidently used for the extraction of silver from lead, at Argos and Thorikos (p. 248) gives a surprising hint of the potentialities which isolation may even have encouraged them to realize. Once again, however, let it be noted that these sites are located in the advanced regions of the Argolic and Attica; conclusions drawn from one area are not to be applied to Greece as a whole, least of all at this time. It is a cliché of later history that isolation spells poverty for Greece, and not many years ago a powerful illustration of this was given.[16] We should not assume that the same consequences would follow at a time when Greece must not only have had an immeasurably smaller population to support, but also possessed far greater natural resources than now, for instance in timber. But we may well wonder how the communities of the eleventh and tenth centuries kept themselves alive, and then shook off the unhealthy symptoms of depopulation.

AGRICULTURE

The answer must lie largely in agriculture. Not even the austere evidence of agricultural tools and field-systems is available to throw direct light on this subject during the dark age – except in Crete, where we can at least see that the people of Karphi must have descended from their mountain fastness to reap their crops with sickles.[17] The existence – as in the Late Bronze Age – of metal hoes, picks and plough-shoes would not normally be doubted, but for the fact that Hesiod's prescription for making a plough, centuries later, seems not to include a metallic share. Perhaps a better source of information is the general comparison between the stages of agriculture which preceded and followed the dark age. As the Linear B tablets, from both Knossos and Pylos, make clear, the breeding of livestock was carried on on a large scale in Late Bronze Age Greece; the 'D' tablets at Knossos alone record, in whatever precise context, a sheep population of 'something approaching 100,000 animals'.[18] Bones of every kind of domesticated animal are found on Mycenaean sites. Although grain, vegetables and olive oil are by no means unknown, it seems clear that stock-breeding held first place in Mycenaean agriculture; when one adds to this the evidence of art – and once again of animal-bones – for the popularity of hunting game, it follows that a meat-based diet was at least very common. All of this makes a striking contrast with the farming

116. Terracotta chest and lid decorated with model granaries, from
the rich grave found in the Athenian Agora in 1967 (see no. *57*).
Another separate granary-model was in the same grave; *c.* 850 B C.

methods advocated later by Hesiod.[19] He is an arable farmer through and
through, and he instructs his audience from the basic first principles
onwards. And in fact the efforts of Hesiod and his contemporaries were
ultimately successful: Greece in the historical period, with much of the
Mediterranean world, did increasingly adopt arable farming, and a grain-
based diet. As with many other aspects of life in which such a contrast is
visible between the Mycenaean and Classical periods, we are left wondering
how far and how fast the change progressed during the dark age. In this
case there is some evidence that the conversion was slow and late. The
very energy of Hesiod's advocacy suggests that in about 700 BC Greeks
still needed exhortation and elementary instruction in arable-farming.
The factor of land-hunger is an uncertain one: stock-breeding in Greece
must always have been extravagant in land-usage, each animal requiring
quite a large grazing-area on that soil; but it is only in the eighth century
that we begin to have proof of the shortage of land in the onset of colonization. Perhaps livestock helped to crowd the colonists out of Greece;
certainly the dedications at sanctuaries, which are also predominantly of
eighth century and later date, include many terracotta figurines of domestic
animals. Finally, the traces of the funerary meals which often accompanied
burials in dark age Greece (p. 192) mostly consist of animal-bones,
apparently from specially-cut joints of meat: in the Protogeometric period

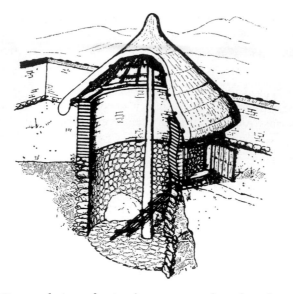

117. Restored view of a circular structure, thought to be a granary, at Old Smyrna. Earlier 7th century B C (R. V. Nicholls).

of the Kerameikos cemetery, bones of sheep and goats predominate, but the remains of these and other animals continue to occur through the ensuing Geometric period, both here and elsewhere. Meat was thus an esteemed form of food, and relatively widely available, thoughout the dark age; and perhaps we may tentatively conclude that Greeks had continued to subsist rather by stock-breeding than by arable farming after the fall of Mycenaean civilization.[20] If the Dorians and other immigrant Greeks were really nomadic herdsmen, then their advent would have strengthened this tendency. But in the later dark age there begins to be evidence of a contrary trend, at least for Attica and Ionia: a number of Attic graves, ranging in date from about 850 to 700, have produced circular terracotta models which have been convincingly argued to represent granaries; and further, the circular foundations of what are probably real granaries have been uncovered in the yards of Geometric houses at Smyrna.[21] Perhaps we have here the early signs of a major change of course in agriculture, which subsequently spread to the rest of Greece.

116

117

INTIMATIONS OF POVERTY

Some features that have emerged seem at variance with the generally humble picture of dark age Greece presented here: ship-building and silver-

extraction are not the activities that one expects to find among impoverished villagers. Can we set against these any other, stronger factors,
intimations of the poverty of a true dark age? The many *argumenta e
silentio* are easily rehearsed, and just as easily controverted by those who
hold the opposite view. Most scholars today concede the loss of the art of
writing, as a casualty of the fall of the Mycenaean palace bureaucracies
with which it had been closely, perhaps exclusively associated. Representational art is another sacrifice which many appear to accept, holding
perhaps that it is not an essential ingredient of prosperity. It is on the
more purely material aspects of life that argument centres. On the question
of architectural standards, for example, it can be maintained that our knowledge of settlement-sites lags far behind that of graves, and that perfectly
adequate stone-built settlements will yet be found. Such a view certainly
wins some support from the discoveries on Naxos (in 1951) and at Iolkos
(in 1960); but before and since those dates, the search for Protogeometric
settlement-structures has continued unabated, with otherwise slight
results. The elusiveness of such settlements, it is now clear, arises in part
from the fact that they were relatively so few in number; this in itself
requires explanation. Again, grave-finds may not be a fair index of the
prosperity of their times if they simply reflect changing fashions in the
provision of grave-goods. We may try a concrete instance: when, after
generations of Protogeometric urn-burials in the Kerameikos which lack
bronze utensils, we find that one transitional grave and six Early Geometric ones produce bronze bowls, placed in the mouth of the urn in an
otherwise identical form of burial, the most natural and surely the likeliest
inference is that such objects had now become more freely available. It
could be explained as a temporary funerary vogue; and indeed temporary
it certainly is, in that such bowls are not a regular feature thereafter. This
does not mean that there was a corresponding recession in prosperity:
there is too much evidence to the contrary. But in Protogeometric times,
such contradictory indications are lacking, and there is much supporting
evidence. These questions cannot indeed be argued in terms of single
categories: it is the overall pattern that counts, and there comes a point
beyond which this cannot be dismissed as illusory.

A few positive arguments for the poverty of these times might be
interjected here. One is that of the choice of material for certain classes of
object. In some cases this is an uncertain element: the occurrence in Protogeometric graves of clay versions of objects, which one would expect to
be made of wood, leather or wickerwork, might be due to the particular

demands of funerary dedications; although we have questioned this in
the case of the clay imitations of bronze tripod-cauldrons (p. 284). We
are on safer ground with objects of a clear practical function, which had
presumably been used by the deceased in life. Blades and weapons of
obsidian, for example, can at this date only represent a shortage of metal:
we find an obsidian arrowhead, and flakes from knife- or implement-
blades, in Geometric graves at Asine, in the Isis grave at Eleusis, and in the
Subminoan chamber-tomb V at Vrokastro; two arrowheads in a ninth-
century grave at Tiryns were also of obsidian. Other primitive materials
re-appear as apparent substitutes: the bone spacer-beads in another grave
at Tiryns, for which I have also argued a ninth-century date (pp. 248,
333), are of a form once familiar in amber; bone finger-rings are found in
Protogeometric Athens and Asine; the clay beads of the early Iron Age,
which so widely replace the Mycenaean examples in richer materials, surely
betoken poverty; one of the rare dark age examples of sling-bullets, which
in the Late Bronze Age had existed in their ideal material, lead, is a stone
example from Marmariani, and later sling-bullets from Thera are also of
stone. Again, when we consider the practical question of the use of weapons
in warfare, it is notable that the sword and the spearhead are very seldom
found together in graves of the eleventh and tenth centuries, the dagger
being the only common accompaniment of the spear, and the sword
normally found alone; whereas from the end of the Protogeometric period
onwards sword and spear are quite often associated in the same burial,
as they had been in Mycenaean times. This suggests strongly that the
equipment of the warrior had been curtailed by circumstances, with sword
and spear serving as alternative rather than complementary weapons, until
resources increased once again.[22]

   The fondness for heirlooms is another hint of deprivation. Here certain
qualifications are necessary, for heirlooms, particularly precious ones, have
been prized at most periods of man's history, and have indeed proved a
constant source of difficulty to archaeology. But it is the mark of an impoverished age to cherish quite humble objects over the generations, and
to think enough of them to place them in graves. In the scanty material
relics of early Iron Age Greece, older objects are relatively frequent;
particularly those artefacts which it was apparently beyond the power of
contemporaries to produce at all. Thus, engraved sealstones form perhaps
the commonest category of all: a list of such finds has recently been given
by Boardman, who observes that for centuries their original function
was ignored by people who treasured them simply as relics. Rather more

surprising are the numerous instances of Bronze Age pottery being retained or recovered centuries later; surprising, because the ceramic art
was one in which dark age Greece, relatively speaking, excelled. But it is
likeliest to imply practical use, since there is little evidence for the aesthetic
appreciation of pottery In early Greece; and thus it is surely a token of
impoverishment. A substantial instance is that of tomb 10 in the Serraglio
cemetery on Kos where, somewhere about 950 BC, three Mycenaean vases
were placed in the burial, one of them an amphora which cannot have been
much less than 400 years old. The excavator suggested that they had been   *34, centre, foot*
recovered from the underlying Mycenaean settlement. At roughly the
same period, a similar case occurs in tomb 3 at the Electran Gates of Thebes,
with a jug of Mycenaean III B date; and in the previous century in Protogeometric tomb 1 at the Kerameikos, with a stirrup-jar of III A style. It
also seems likely that a jug from tomb 1 at Marmariani in Thessaly was an
heirloom, if use of the cemetery did not begin earlier than the tenth
century (p. 330). A late ninth-century grave at Eleusis contained a Protogeometric amphora; but in the later part of the dark age these pottery
heirlooms become less common: a tomb of the full Geometric period at
Pherai in Thessaly produced a Mycenaean drinking-jar, and it may be
that some of the problematic survivals of pottery of Protogeometric type
in Thera (p. 65) are accountable for in this way. Keepsakes in other
materials show a similar weighting towards the earlier part of the dark
age: among them are the gold-leaf ornaments and glass beads from Papadimitriou's grave on Skyros (p. 241); and such humbler finds as a crude
marble figurine in a Protogeometric grave at Argos, some pieces of glass
beads in a contemporary or earlier burial at Tiryns, and fragments of rock-
crystal in a Cretan Protogeometric grave at Knossos.[23]

Some of the features of the dark age, as here presented, strike an echo
with an earlier period of Greece's past, the Middle Helladic. The analogy
between the two eras is not perhaps a very original one, but it will bear
some scrutiny. Recent discoveries, especially those of Early Helladic II and
III date at Lerna, have shown that on the Greek mainland the Middle
Bronze Age brought in a period of marked recession. The great achievements of the Early Helladic age – architectural works like the tholos at
Tiryns and the House of the Tiles at Lerna, fortification-walls, delicately
shaped and patterned pottery, carved stone seals, work in precious metals
– all seem to fade away. Middle Helladic begins as a world of small,
unfortified village-settlements, their houses built of mud-brick on rough
and rather flimsy stone foundations, with pitched roofs; apsidal plans are

quite common, curved walls and irregular angles ubiquitous. Thus far
there is a loose conformity to the pattern of the eleventh, tenth and ninth
centuries in Greece. But in fact it is grave-finds which provide our fullest
evidence for both periods, and it is in their burial practices that the closest
resemblance appears. The single cist, as we have seen in an earlier chapter,
is the most characteristic form in both eras: many an excavator has hesi-
tated in his dating when confronted by such a burial without distinctive
grave-goods. Both in the earlier part of Middle Helladic, and in Submycenaean Salamis, the cist is usually too small to receive the body in any
but a contracted position; but in both cases a desire for extended burial
evidently existed, and in later years it prevailed, the cist being lengthened
accordingly. Other more detailed analogies have been noted earlier
(p. 183): the occasional use of mud-brick as an alternative material for
the walls, and the depositing of grave-goods outside the tomb. At both
periods the pithos-burial, particularly for infants, is a common alternative
form of grave. Most symptomatic of all is the resort to intramural burial
– again, mostly for children – which gives a powerful suggestion of
demoralization and stress. In their material culture, the two eras show
further correspondences. The fact that the matt-painted pottery of Middle
Helladic Greece had a dark-on-light decoration which often took the
form of geometric patterns may probably be dismissed as a chance, and
not very close, repetition of a very widespread tendency; although it may
not be without significance that the wheel-made pottery in general forms
by far the most impressive class of the material remains from each of the
periods. There are also close analogies in other fabrics, particularly the
hand-made; we mentioned this earlier (p. 97) in the case of the fine pale
hand-made ware of the Argolid where, in Asine at least, there proved to
be an 'astounding resemblance' to the corresponding Middle Helladic
pottery. Elsewhere in Greece, too, one finds difficulty in distinguishing
the fabric and shapes of the coarser hand-made wares of the early Iron
Age from their prehistoric forerunners; Middle Helladic Greece, for
example, also produced incised hand-made ware similar to that of dark
age Attica. Even in metallurgy, there is a faint echo of the much stronger
recession at the beginning of Middle Helladic, in the occasional resort to
obsidian, bone and stone for implements in the early Iron Age. Predictably,
too, the privation and isolation of both periods, and with it some of their
security, dissolved when the Aegean was gradually opened up to Near
Eastern influences, with Crete in the forefront. But I have no wish to gloss
over the differences between the two eras: the legacy of the Mycenaean

civilization made a total reversion impossible. Thus the cultural homo-geneity of the dark age, although far shallower than that of Middle Helladic and permitting of greater regional diversity, is more widely spread, thanks to the expansion of Mycenaean influence over the Aegean islands to the coast of Asia Minor. Thus, too, if dark age Greece was in the main a world of herdsmen living off their flocks (above, pp. 379-80), then this was another Mycenaean legacy, making a contrast with the crop-raising com-munities of Middle Helladic.[24]

This analogy, if it is at all sound, carries a more important implication: the fundamental continuity of Greek life from the Middle Bronze Age to the Iron Age. There is, I think, much to be said for that view of the Mycen-aean culture which regards many of its more spectacular attributes – Cyclo-pean walls, palace bureaucracies, built family-tombs, large-scale painting and miniature glyptic – as exotic and essentially intrusive features, trans-planted to the soil of Greece and never to become deeply rooted there. Beneath all this there lay a substratum which we may now recognize as essentially Greek. As a kind of test-case for the reality of this substratum, we have repeatedly cited the question of the single cist-burial in Greece: a feature characteristic of the periods before and after the Mycenaean, over-shadowed yet never entirely hidden from view by the very different prac-tices of the Mycenaean era. But this, and other aspects of the issue, are matters of conviction rather than proof; and even those who accept the notion of Mycenaean Greeks with alien cultural features may well baulk at another implication of this view. In most historical and archaeological reconstructions of the post-Mycenaean age, it is the great immigrations, particularly that of the Dorians, which dominate the picture; but the account given in these pages will be found almost barren of such powerful intrusive elements. I am far from denying that this period was one of upheaval, migration and re-settlement in Greece: all the evidence confirms the Greek tradition that it was. It is simply that the sharply-differentiated pattern of dialect-groups, which many scholars have accentuated by bring-ing some of these groups freshly into Greece from outside, seems to me to find no echo in the pattern of the material culture of Greece in the early Iron Age. No doubt there were some diversities of dialect among Greek-speakers already in the thirteenth century BC; no doubt the movement of groups in the following centuries, and the subsequent lack of communi-cation between the groups when they had settled, did much to sharpen and perpetuate these divisions. But to treat the various groups as culturally and almost racially distinct was a step which the Greeks, so far as one can

2B

see, did not take until well down into historical times; and for modern scholarship to read such a distinction into the very beginnings of the migratory period seems to me a fundamental mistake. If the attackers who struck the main death-blows to Mycenaean civilization around 1200 BC were to a large extent the ancestors of the later Dorians, Thessalians and Boeotians, as seems most likely (pp. 311-12), then we need believe no more than that these were Greek-speakers from the outer fringes of the Mycenaean world, belonging to the same cultural milieu. If the invaders came from the region of the Pindus, as Greek tradition suggests (though without specifying how long they had been settled there), then we should look for their traces not in the form of an alien, non-Mycenaean culture, since in the event no such intrusive culture was to impose itself on southern and central Greece. Rather, we should see their presence in the spread of the Middle Helladic and Mycenaean culture to this region which, although relatively late in the case of Macedonia (pp. 73-4), and subject to a massive time-lag in the case of Epirus (pp. 172-3, 257-61), is nevertheless genuine for both these areas. Alternatively, we can perhaps without dishonour resort to the old explanation that the Dorians and Thessalians were pastoral nomads, who used tents instead of houses and skins instead of pottery, and whom we can therefore scarcely hope to trace. We may even believe that such nomadism persisted after the immigrants had moved into central and southern Greece, and attribute to this some of the paucity of material remains in the eleventh and tenth centuries.[25] Yet even nomads have to die, and are usually buried; whereas a very high proportion of the graves of this period are in concentrated cemeteries that imply prolonged settlement; and nomadic life is in any case hardly compatible with migratory sea-voyages to small islands or foreign shores.

POLITICAL AND SOCIAL STRUCTURE

If then the Greek way of life in these years was generally based on settled communities, however small and humble, we must inevitably speculate on the political, social and spiritual aspects of those communities. There are perhaps no other fields for which we have so little direct testimony as these, apart from the important category of the Homeric evidence (see below, pp. 388-94); our line of approach must be once again the indirect one of comparing the situation before the dark age with the situation after it, and guessing at the speed and course of the intervening changes. Politically, for example, it is certain that the dark age witnessed a shift in power from the centralized monarchies, some of them served by a literate administration, which we can detect in Mycenaean times, to the smaller and at times more mobile units, each dominated by an aristocrat and his family. The identity of interests among such aristocrats would produce larger groupings of population, spread over wider areas, and these were in due course to produce the historical phenomenon of the city-state, often comparable in size with a Mycenaean kingdom. Equally commonly, these groupings large or small were still ruled by a king, *basileus*, until the eighth century or even later. But the *basileus* was not the same as a Mycenaean king; on the contrary, from close study of the texts of the Homeric poems, it is possible to deduce that the word *basileus* had gradually 'climbed the social ladder' in the post-Mycenaean period, as the older word for king, *wanax*, dropped out of political currency.[26] The interpretation of the Linear B texts, which seems to reveal *wanax* as the ruler and *basileus* as a subordinate figure of obscure status, accords well with this; and the 'gift-devouring *basileis*' of whose injustice Hesiod complains in eighth-century Boeotia presumably represent the process near its culmination. One would like to know how far Hesiod's *basileis* were distinguished from other aristocratic chieftains, and from what precise starting-point their rise had begun, but the general pattern is not in doubt. Modern society tends to think in terms of horizontal class-divisions, and tries to imagine a similar structure in early communities; but in a world like that of early Greece for which we have some objective evidence, our information suggests that such lines of distinction were faint or blurred: even such apparently clear-cut issues as those of freedom, serfdom and slavery, or of the ownership of the land, may have been far from straightforward in contemporary eyes. Much more prominent in the extant evidence are the vertical divisions: Greek society at the beginning of the historical period was formed of units, in many ways independent of each other, each headed by an aristocratic family of greater or lesser eminence. Because these units were small, the system was both durable and flexible: it could be combined with a tribal structure of society such as is clearly present in the background of early Greece; it could provide a focus for migration, and must indeed have been the instrument for the launching of the Ionian migration in the dark days of the eleventh century; it could even to a great extent survive the growth of the city-state, and dominate the activities of its early days.

 Recent research has suggested that this pattern of 'pyramidal' groups was systematized, perhaps at a time towards the end of the dark age, around 800 BC, by the creation of a recognized social unit, the phratry, which could operate in military as well as in civilian life. It may have originated as a pure kinship-unit, but by historical times it extends far more broadly and deeply through the social scale;[27] we may see a reflection of it in the tendency to adopt family grave-plots during the eighth century (p. 196). Before then, we have to imagine the situation developing *de facto*. A monarch can survive the destruction of his capital, but he cannot continue to rule his subjects if they uproot themselves and migrate in different directions. The descendants of the Mycenaean kings could no doubt maintain their power for a time in those cases where the population remained in their homeland (as traditionally happened in Athens), or where they migrated *en bloc* (as with Tisamenos who was believed to have led his people from the Argolid into Achaea). But then what happened? We may suspect that the days of the old-style monarchy were numbered; indeed tradition also records that Tisamenos was killed in battle, and when we hear of his family again two generations later (Pausanias VII, 6,2) there are several grandsons of equal importance in Achaea, the eldest having significantly gone to take part in the Ionian migration, and there are other unrelated *basileis* (as Pausanias calls them) on an equal footing; while in Athens the monarchy was traditionally usurped by Melanthos, a Neleid refugee from Pylos. Were these new men – if real, they lived in the late twelfth and eleventh centuries – in fact the first of the ruling *basileis*? If so, they may sometimes have had to share the territory with others who had no claim to royal blood, but could muster the necessary retinue to challenge them. But nomenclature may be a poor guide to the true situation, since the domain of the *basileus* could apparently vary greatly in size. We are safe in assuming that the fragmentation of the Bronze Age kingdoms into smaller, mutually independent political units was well under way by the period of the migrations – when, indeed, the growth of regionalism in the material culture of Greece would lead us to a similar conclusion. But there is no justification for thinking that the rulers and nobles of the ensuing dark age lived in any sort of affluence. Among the hundreds of burials known from Greece in this period, some few at least must be those of aristocrats and rulers; yet, south of Macedonia, there is barely a single grave between the early eleventh and the late tenth century which can be called rich.

THE HOMERIC WORLD

Many scholars, however, would avoid the need for such indirect inference about society in the earlier dark age by calling on a direct witness, the Homeric epic. There is a growing body of opinion which would find a historical basis for many important features of the Homeric world in the earlier part of the dark age; the political and military system of the *Iliad* has been given a provisional place in the period of the Ionian migration; the social system has been assigned to the immediately succeeding centuries. This is a sorely vexed question, but it cannot be shirked. It remains as true today as it has been for some years past, that there are only two positively and widely identifiable historical 'strata' in the world described in the Homeric poems: that of the full Mycenaean era (if at a point near the end of its development), and that of the poet's own day, commonly placed in the eighth century for the *Iliad* at least. These two form, respectively, the third element and the basis for the second in Rhys Carpenter's *Folk tale, fiction and saga in the Homeric epics* (1946), from which work this observation is taken. There have been constant shifts in the relative emphasis accorded to these elements, and the depth of the Mycenaean stratum is particularly hotly debated; but however much the division needs to be modified in detail – for instance, it is wrong that the boar's tusk helmet of *Iliad* x should still be regularly presented as a relic of the *early* Mycenaean age, years after the publication of an example in a pure twelfth-century context – its hard, indestructible core will always be there.[28] To take the political issues we have been considering, the kings in Homer are autocratic rulers, set in general in the political geography of the Mycenaean world and against some identifiably Mycenaean trappings; yet there are discordant features which show that the picture is not purely Mycenaean, and these cannot all be very happily accommodated in the world of the eighth century. The likely conclusion is that the Homeric political system, like other Homeric pictures, is an artificial amalgam of widely separated historical stages. And yet there is a natural and almost irresistible urge to look for a single period in which as many features as possible of the picture can be credibly and simultaneously set. In the case of the king's political and military status, it is argued that the era of the migrations – roughly, the Mycenaean III c period – was a time when a king might be known as *wanax* and live in a palace of megaron plan, maintaining a large household owning considerable treasures, as is true of Homer's kings; but when his throne might also be threatened by any one of several *basileis*, his political authority potentially diluted by councils and assemblies, his military command disrupted by the loose structure of his army and by the individual antics of subordinate chieftains, each with his own following – as also happens in Homer. In this case, the arguments sound convincing enough; but there is little point in putting them forward unless it is consistently maintained that a faithful picture of the actual situation in the Mycenaean III c period had come down to the poet who reproduced it in the eighth century. Perhaps it had; but the abstract nature of political and military structure make it unlikely that our evidence will ever give a decisive answer on this matter. What we can do is to examine the testimony of the poems in fields where our external evidence is more eloquent, and see whether it encourages us to believe that the poet had access to such faithful images of a period after the break-up of Mycenaean culture, yet substantially earlier than his own day; we should also remind ourselves that the migration era was a very different thing from what followed it, a more settled but still obscurer time; even a demonstrably migration-period monarchy would do nothing to make a tenth- or ninth-century social system more likely.

These other fields are inevitably those of material life, and the scrutiny of Homer's material background has been close, and constantly revised in the light of fresh waves of archaeological discovery.[29] Since even a brief summary of the results would be impossible here, one must be dogmatic: the scrutiny has revealed some points of concrete detail which seem purely Mycenaean, many more which must be taken from the poet's own times, and still others which could well be of the same inspiration (I exclude here the question of later interpolations). It has failed almost entirely to isolate single features which belong in the twelfth, eleventh, tenth or even ninth centuries – let alone major aspects. We may briefly consider two such large aspects for which our other evidence is quite full, metallurgy and funerary practice. The Homeric pattern of metal-using, as was shown in a fundamental article by Miss D. H. F. Gray, is a comparatively clear-cut but totally artificial one.[30] In the matter of weapons of war, the poems archaize with a stern and almost unbroken consistency: the exclusive use of bronze for swords and spearheads would be totally out of place in Greece at any time after the earlier eleventh century. But the frequent use of iron for agricultural and craftsmen's tools, and the familiarity with working and even trading in iron, point to a much later period; and the two practices never overlapped in fact. Here then is proof of a diversity in background within the same general aspect; there is nothing to suggest that the earlier dark age inspired any part of the picture, and indeed there is one positive discouragement to us to look in that direction: in an allied matter, the use of twin throwing-spears on the battlefield, we find that such a practice was known, if hardly common, in the Late Bronze Age, including the twelfth century; common if not characteristic in the ninth and eighth centuries;

but on present evidence almost unknown between about 1100 and 900 BC.

The very mention of Homeric burial-customs is almost enough to bring a smile to specialist faces today. Scarcely a year goes past without the discovery of some grave or cemetery whose practices are remarked on for their resemblance to those of Homer. Multiple cremations and inhumations under tumuli in Bronze Age Epirus; single cremations in chambers under tumuli in twelfth-century Moravia and Slovakia; multiple cremation-pyres under tumuli at Halos in eighth-century Thessaly; multiple urn- and pyre-cremations under tumuli in contemporary Colophon; single crema-tions (not in urns) under cairns in eighth- and seventh-century Pithe-koussai; chamber-tomb inhumations in seventh-century Cyprus; single urn-cremations under tumuli in sixth-century Samos – all of these have been claimed to bear a significant resemblance to Homeric custom; and indeed by a *tour de force* of advocacy it has been argued that the Homeric picture essentially reproduces that of the chamber- and tholos-tomb burials of the full Mycenaean era.[31] In every case the resemblances are substantial; yet the very multiplicity of these claims induces a sceptical reaction. Such scepticism is however only justified where it is claimed that the problem of Homeric burial-customs has been 'solved', that a historical model has been found on which Homer's picture is entirely based. Signifi-cantly, the closest approximation in the list given above is probably that of sixth-century Samos, where the inference is of course that, if anything, the practice was modelled on epic and not *vice versa*. Everything suggests that the problem is insoluble because the model never existed; that the different features of the burials – two multiple, half a dozen single – described by Homer, are taken from different periods and regions, united only in that they are all designed to impress. The rich goods committed to the grave, the slaughtered animals and even occasional human sacrifice, other rarer features such as the erection of cenotaphs – these were presum-ably a reminiscence of Mycenaean practice. On the other hand, the appar-ently exclusive use of cremation and of the tumulus could have been inspired by the customs of Ionia in the poet's day, although there was probably no time at which they were the regular practice throughout Ionia (let alone all Greece), and although the common provision of a tumulus over a single cremation may be dictated by the form of the story. Once again, it is hard to see what the earlier dark age can have contributed; even in a region like Attica where the heyday of cremation fell between about 1050 and 800, the humble burials find no echo in Homer save the rite itself, and perhaps the erection of a *stele*.

In the cases where we can apply some sort of check, therefore, it seems that the Homeric epic has little to tell us of the immediate post-Mycenaean period and the earlier dark age. But the claim that little was remembered of this period must not be thought to conflict with an evident fact, that memory of an earlier age survived *through* this period, even if it was kept alive largely or entirely in Ionia; this, it is safe to say, will never be denied. From this, it is a significant step forward to suggest that this period witnessed the first major impetus in the creation of the epic tradition that culminated in Homer; that narrative poetry about Mycenaean Greece began to be composed now rather than in the lifetime of Mycenaean civilization; and that the bards of this age, rather than merely passing on inherited songs for their more talented successors to expand and improve, created many of the passages of Mycenaean content which we can read in Homer. This further claim need not conflict with our main argument, although I doubt once again that it can be shown to be more than a possibility; there is indeed evidence that some Greeks of this period did cherish some memory of the Late Bronze Age, if not nearly so intensely as their descendants in the eighth century, and the development of religion will provide a little more (below, pp. 394-9). But there is no justification for going further still, and saying that the poets of this time put much of their own world into these compositions; that, for example, the world of Odysseus should be placed in the tenth and ninth centuries BC. This was the conclusion of M.I.Finley,[32] who delineated some of the most important and pervasive features of that world: in particular, the giving and exchanging of gifts in an almost endless variety of situations, which was no mere function of good manners, but practically the life-blood of heroic society; and the ceremonial eating which occupied such an important place in the heroes' leisure hours. But can we really follow him in deriving this picture from the real world of tenth- and ninth-century Greece? Once again, the answer must ultimately be based on personal conviction, and I can only say that such a pattern of behaviour seems to me unimaginable in dark age Greece. A society of this kind almost certainly did exist at that very period, but not in Greece: if we look at the material traces from Urnfield Europe, and particularly at the rich graves from the Hungarian plain, we shall find all those heroic attributes which are missing in the Greek world – lavish single burials in large tombs, with the paraphernalia of war, feasting and sheer acquisitive wealth generously provided. The surviving evidence from dark age Greece, by contrast, is simply too shallow a foundation for such an edifice. A positive equation can occasionally be extracted: the

oval house of about 900 BC at Smyrna, for example, may not have been   *114*
unlike the hut erected for Achilles at Troy (*Iliad* XXIV, 448), or the house
of Eumaeus the swineherd (*Odyssey* XIV, 45);[33] but it is not clear why we
should make such an uneven comparison between the humble structures
of one world, and what appears to be the standard accommodation of
another.

So the contribution of the Homeric poems, though of priceless worth
for eighth-century Greece if it is sifted carefully enough, can in my view
not yet be admitted to the story of the dark age. It is true that many of the
seeds of Homer's own world were present in the eleventh and tenth centuries, once Greece had settled down after its upheavals: the launching of
the all-important Ionian migration was, among other things, the first step
in its creation. But a misleading or excessive emphasis has sometimes been
laid on other advances of that period. The decisive change in pottery-
decoration came without doubt in the birth of Protogeometric in the mid-
eleventh century; but the criterion of ceramic style as an indicator of major
cultural changes is less than satisfactory. We have found it misleading for
the period of Mycenaean III C, and again at the end of the Geometric
period (pp. 33-4; 27), and it may be so here as well. The roughly simultaneous mastery of iron-working makes an equally clear dividing-line,
but we have tended to see in this as much a response to the force of circumstances as a major technological break-through (pp. 237-9); nor, be it
remembered, did all Greece profit from it as yet. Like the earlier adoption
of the cist-tomb, and perhaps that of cremation too, it seems to represent a
re-organization of life along modest and rational lines. Existence might no
longer be so constantly perilous as it had been for the past few generations;
but nor would the world for a long time be safe for grand households,
carefully amassed treasures, monumental tombs, or sea-borne trade in
foreign metals. The realities were recognized, and sights were lowered
accordingly. Life need not have been too unpleasant in these years; houses
of mud-brick, timber and thatch are seldom intolerable in the Greek
climate; dark age Greece had no doubt inherited the vine and its products
from the Mycenaeans; the deeds of the heroic age were a consoling memory,
even where no specific poetic tradition had lingered on, but communion
with that age was wistful, rather than deliberate as it became in the eighth
century; a few slaves no doubt remained in the possession of the better-off;
there was no risk of starvation while the population remained so drastically
reduced, even if there is little sign that the Mycenaean taste for hunting was
still indulged. One small but not trivial question which arises is whether

the dark age was literally dark, in the sense of lacking means of artificial lighting; and certainly objects which are recognizable as lamps, either by shape or by traces of use, are altogether missing from Greece between the Mycenaean III c period and the later stages of Protogeometric. But in a world where a single-room house with a large central hearth is the standard form of dwelling, the function of lamps would in any case have been much curtailed. Even in Homer's palaces, firelight, braziers and torches normally suffice.[34] Writing, reading and the more intricate arts and crafts were, after all, a thing of the future (and the past). Clothes and shoes were of the plainest: the pinned Doric peplos, a one-piece woollen garment which did not require cutting or sewing, was gradually winning acceptance among women in Submycenaean Athens, to judge from the sparing pro- vision of pins in the graves, and then became a common if not the regular female dress in Protogeometric Attica, the Argolid, Thessaly, in contem- porary Crete, and later in the Aegean islands, in all of which areas we find pins in enough graves to represent a high proportion of the adult women. The garment that it was replacing was probably a shaped, sewn and buttoned dress, worn perhaps by all but the richest women in Mycenaean and even Middle Helladic times. For men, the short tunic or chiton, with its somewhat longer variants, is the only standard dress for which we have evidence at either end of the period; but in the dark age it can hardly have been made of linen, as the chiton was at those periods when communica- tions were open with the Near East.[35]

THE PROBLEM OF CONTINUITY IN RELIGION AND ART

It remains to consider the spiritual and artistic life of these years. The two aspects are intertwined: in the general absence of religious architecture, it is from crude figurines and other such offerings that we learn most about cult; while purely secular art is for a time virtually non-existent. Never- theless, the sites which later became sanctuaries figure prominently among those for which continuity of use from Mycenaean to Archaic times has been claimed; and in one or two cases it is further held that the function of the site was sacred in the Bronze Age as well. We have already examined the circumstances at some of these sanctuaries (pp. 275-85); many show no real evidence of use in Protogeometric or even earlier Geometric times; few indeed are those where the claims for continuity rest on architectural evidence. But here it should be pointed out that a place of worship in the Bronze Age Aegean was a very different thing from the great sanctuaries familiar from historical times. Both Minoan and Mycenaean religion tended

to favour either natural sites, or others that were insubstantial architectur-
ally, for their cult: a natural cave, a tree, an isolated pillar, a small open-air
shrine or enclosure, or a specially consecrated room in an otherwise
secular building. This being so, we should hardly expect to identify many
places of worship except by means of dedicated offerings. But we may
briefly survey the sites where such evidence of Bronze Age cult is succeeded
by the growth of a sanctuary, including the very rare instances where
an actual building seems to have preserved its sanctity. Perhaps the most
impressive case of the latter has come to light quite recently at Ayia Irini
on the island of Keos: a long, narrow stone building, demonstrably a shrine   *118*
and continuously in use through the last three centuries of the Bronze
Age, survived in partial repair when the surrounding town was abandoned:
Protogeometric and Geometric sherds were found in the vicinity; the head
of one of its large terracotta female statues was even resurrected as a cult-
image in Archaic times, and worship continued down to the fourth century
B C. No such clear sequence of events has been recovered at any of the
greater sanctuaries. At Eleusis, the sixth-century Hall of the Mysteries
was built exactly on the site of an unusual Mycenaean megaron-building
in an enclosure which may itself have been a shrine; but the long interval
of time is not fully bridged by the pottery found here or elsewhere on the
site; and a possible oval or apsidal temple which might be of Geometric
date, also sited over the Mycenaean building, has left only the most fragmentary traces. In the case of Amyklai, the fact that there is no ceramic
continuity between the Mycenaean and the Protogeometric (p. 131)
must surely outweigh the other considerations; although there is a strong
case for believing that a Mycenaean cult-place was here, and although an
Archaic sanctuary was established on the same site, the finds of the intervening period suggest no more than that, in the ninth and eighth century,
some vague memory of the sanctity of the place survived. At the site of
the later Artemision on Delos, there is also a long hiatus in time, which a
few Protogeometric sherds in the area hardly fill. But the excavator, Gallet
de Santerre, has claimed that this gap was spanned in a unique way: the
Mycenaean building Ac, which he believes to have been a shrine, somehow
remained standing, with numerous dedications in gold, ivory and other
materials still revered, until a date around 700 B C when it was dismantled, a
new temple of Artemis (E) built on its site and with the same alignment,
and the precious Mycenaean objects carefully buried as a foundation-
deposit. By the same token, he suggests that another Mycenaean structure
on the site (H), close to which a later Greek temple (G) was built, experi-

118. The temple at Agia Irini on Keos, seen from the north-west
(1964). Built at least partly in the Middle Bronze Age, it remained in
use, perhaps continuously, until the 4th century BC, retaining its sacred
character throughout. Its length, even after erosion by the sea at the
further end, is *c.* 25 m.

enced a similar history. More than one scholar has found this reconstruction
of events somewhat improbable, and sought alternative explanations:
Desborough has questioned the certainty both of the identification of
building Ac as a shrine, and of its intact preservation through four disturbed centuries; he suggests the possibility that the deposit was buried
by its owner at the close of the Mycenaean period, the great period for
the deposition of hoards. Boardman has pointed out that the deposit
contained Mycenaean sherds as well, and rightly doubts whether these
would have been prized until Geometric times; he proposes intermittent
cult-usage over the intervening period.[36] I can only share the scepticism
of these scholars over the detailed picture of an unbroken temple-series;
but at least the coincidence of siting and the Protogeometric pottery
suggest that some Greeks of the early Iron Age *believed* that they had
found a genuine holy place of the heroic age.

But it was not necessary for such 'holy places' to have been, in actual fact, Bronze Age sanctuaries. Against the handful of instances we have been considering, all of them in some way doubtful and none of them earlier than about 700 BC in the definite re-establishment of cult, we may set a whole range of sites where early Iron Age cult was centred on purely secular Mycenaean sites. The evidence for cult at Mycenaean graves has been considered earlier (pp. 192-4), and may be set on one side; this merely shows that, within the Geometric period, cult took place at numerous Mycenaean tombs in widespread areas of Greece; but these were clearly recognized – and sometimes re-used – as tombs, and in the very nature of the case there can be little question of continuity of religious observance. Equally numerous, and in this context more interesting, are the cases where Greek sanctuaries of historical times were sited over, or close to, Mycenaean domestic structures: the shrines of Agamemnon at Mycenae, and of Menelaus at Therapne near Sparta, have been mentioned before because of their explicit associations, and the fact that their initial date, the late eighth century, coincides with the greatest resurgence of grave-cult (p. 192). But at approximately this period, many of the greater sanctuaries over-lying Mycenaean sites were coming into prominence. In a few cases there is some evidence of Bronze Age worship, but nowhere can continuity be shown. For example, in the sanctuaries at Delphi, and at the sites of the temples of Aphaia on Aegina and of Apollo Maleatas near Epidauros, there were human and animal figurines among the Mycenaean finds, but at none of them is there any sign of cult-revival before the later years of the Geometric period. At Mycenae itself, a temple of Archaic date was built over a room of the Mycenaean palace which may have been a shrine, preserving its north-south orientation; Geometric pottery-finds suggested that cult was already taking place here at that period. But here again the lapse of time tells against any conscious revival of worship at a spot known to be sacred. At Olympia, where Middle Helladic and Mycenaean settlements underlay the Altis, it has been argued in a recent study by Herrmann that cult-features also existed in the Bronze Age, and that the survival of certain of these – the mound revered in later days as the Pelopion, and perhaps a Mycenaean cult-pillar which later Greeks associated with Oenomaus – helped to stimulate the growth of the sanctuary. But, as was noted in an earlier chapter, the stratification and typology of the dedications do not confirm the claim that Olympia was the scene of continuous worship through the dark age (pp. 276, 279-85): the strongest argument used is that based on primitive terracotta and bronze figurines, whose qualities are considered to point to a pre-Geometric date. A similar but weaker case has been made for continuity of cult at the Heraeum on Samos. But at a site on the outskirts of Athens, later made famous as the location of Plato's Academy, something different and indeed remarkably interesting was taking place: the surviving ruins of an Early Helladic house apparently attracted enough notice for a special cult-building to be erected alongside it in later Geometric times, and to receive numerous sacrifices; further, the general area may have acquired an aura of sanctity at an earlier date, for a deposit of some 200 or more Protogeometric vases, also designated as sacrificial offerings, was found about 150 metres away.[37]

Much more often, however, it was Bronze Age structures of apparently purely domestic nature – which after all were much more likely to leave architectural traces, however fragmentary, than were places of worship – that seem to have attracted temples and sanctuaries, after a fairly long interval of time, simply because they were visible or their location was somehow remembered. The list of such sites is long, and includes the Acropolis of Athens, the sanctuary of Iphigenia at Brauron, the Heraeum of Argos, the Isthmian sanctuary, the Temple of Zeus Thaulios near Pherai in Thessaly, the Temple of Apollo at Thermon, perhaps the Temple of Athena Alea at Tegea, the Heraeum of Perachora and that on Samos, and the sanctuary of Zeus at Dodona (although in this case the Bronze Age remains are not truly Mycenaean); other temples at Kalydon, Elatea and Nemea were sited close to Mycenaean settlements, and there is a possible but problematical case at Tiryns. In Crete, too, about which we shall have something separate to say, a temple of Dictaean Zeus was sited on the Minoan settlement at Palaiokastro, and other possible temples built over the west wing of the palace of Knossos, and beside the palace at Phaistos. It was, then, clearly exceptional for the Greeks of the earlier dark age to keep up observances at a sacred site of the Bronze Age; much more often, a cult was re-established after a prolonged lapse of time, which made any precise memory of sacred localities impossible; the Bronze Age remains were sanctified by virtue of their mere existence. There are even one or two cases of the converse process, pointing to the same conclusion: at Asine, an undoubted Mycenaean shrine in House G was apparently quite forgotten, even though the site was generally re-settled in Protogeometric times; while other places of Bronze Age worship such as the Cave of Pan at Ninoi near Marathon, or a possible temple at Mouriatadha in Triphylia, were equally ignored in the dark age.[38]

Many persuasive arguments have nevertheless been deployed to show that the origins of historical Greek religion, as with mythology, lay in

Minoan and Mycenaean cult.[39] Yet we find a distinctly tenuous material link between the two. There is, I think, a possibility of explaining this in part by the strength of the conscious revival in eighth-century Greece – revival not only of the memory of the heroic age, prompted by the diffusion of the Homeric poems, the rediscovery of Mycenaean tombs, the re-settlement of Mycenaean sites; but a specifically religious revival in which faint recollections of the rites of the heroic age, kept alive but not on the whole practised in the subsequent period, were put into practical service. That a revival of some kind took place in religion is surely clear from the prodigious growth in the number and size of sanctuary-sites in the eighth century. Again, a major element in historical Greek religion was composed by festivals and cults which originally held little connection with officially organized worship, but of whose great antiquity there is no doubt, even if it has to be inferred *a posteriori*. Such practices seldom leave a substantial material record, even in a well-documented period; they are known to us largely from literary sources. We should not therefore doubt the possibility of their transmission through the dark age, simply because we cannot find proof of it in the material evidence. A further factor may have been the regional disparity of early Iron Age Greece; if a Mycenaean survival-culture persisted, as we have inferred, down to about 1000 B C or even later in places like Achaea and Ithaka, then Mycenaean religious practices may have continued with it, which would increase their chances of being remembered later. But some features which are prominent in the *material* record of Mycenaean religion conspicuously failed to survive: the ubiquitous terracotta 'goddess'-figurines, for example, found in both sanctuaries and tombs down to and including the III c period. The latest unadulterated version of this known to me is a crude but recognizable specimen from the Protogeometric stratum at Grotta on Naxos. But it is possible that a distorted or half-understood reminiscence of the Mycenaean figurines of '*Ψ*' shape lies behind the 'epiphany' pose of some early male figurines at *127* Olympia; just as the resurrected female head at Ayia Irini on Keos apparently became the centre of a cult of Dionysos in later days.[40]

  Stray survivors like the Naxos figurine show that some faint echoes of Bronze Age representational art still existed in the dark age. But the great technological recession placed most of the Mycenaean art-forms beyond the reach of their successors: carved stone reliefs, engraved gems, work in precious metals, bronze-casting in complex moulds, painting on wall-plaster, inlay work – none of these, it seems, could be attempted any longer. Only the humble art of modelling in clay, which would come naturally

119. Clay rhyton in the shape of a stag, from Protogeometric grave 39
at the Kerameikos, Athens. Height 26·1 cm; *c.* 925 BC.

to a skilled potter, seems to have survived, along with the even rarer use of painted representations on pottery. From Athens there is a solitary and fragmentary figure of an ox with painted decoration in Mycenaean III C or Submycenaean style; while the Protogeometric material from the Kerameikos included one or two small fragments of animal-figurines, and a fine barrel-bodied stag from a late tenth-century grave, whose artistic qualities still look back to Bronze Age figurines. One of the fragmentary pieces came from a horse's head, and we may recall that two Late Protogeometric pots (p. 54) also show a small and inconspicuously-placed painting of a horse, which may have a partly social significance (below, pp. 414-15). As so often, however, the evidence from Crete is in marked contrast to this near-vacuum, both religious and artistic, in mainland Greece. This seems due almost entirely to the strength of Minoan survival in both fields. The shrine at Karphi was furnished in a purely Minoan tradition, and its bell-skirted cult idols suggest that Minoan religious beliefs were retained unchanged; while down in the plains, the shrine at Gazi might be a simple rectangular hut, but it yielded idols of similar form. Nor were Minoan cult-places forgotten: the Dictaean Cave sanctuary, although in its nature difficult to study stratigraphically, was very probably in use throughout the early Iron Age; certainly it received dedications in the period of the occupation of Karphi, and again by the ninth century. Another Cretan speciality was the making of model buildings – houses, shrines or tombs – often with figures incorporated in them. The Cretan duck-askoi show crude modelling that is not without charm, and representational scenes on vases upheld a late Minoan tradition down into the tenth century – Cretan wild goats, ships (p. 368) and a unique mounted warrior on the problematical krater from Mouliana Tomb A, which Desborough now (rightly I think) classes as a late Subminoan survival, perhaps even of the tenth century.[41] In a modest way, the dark age brings Crete some requital for the premature decline of her Bronze Age civilization. But for the rest of Greece, the evidence of religious and artistic activity in the eleventh and tenth centuries strengthens the feeling that, despite the contrary appearance of iron technology and Protogeometric pottery, the changes from the latest culture of the Bronze Age had been mainly negative ones. Greece was not forging ahead in a new direction; she was reappraising her way of life in a realistic mood, and waiting.

119

70, 132

The Beginnings of Recovery: The Late Tenth to the Early Eighth Centuries

In the second half of the tenth century, a change comes over this picture, not so far-reaching as to affect every region of Greece, but clearly to be seen in the more accessible areas. There is indeed a case for regarding this as the end of the true dark age,[42] for it represents a distinct easing off in many of the symptoms we have been considering – depopulation, isolation, metal-shortages, architectural and artistic impoverishment, sharp regional disparities. Yet in other ways the development of these years looks more like a false dawn; certainly the rate of improvement was apparently too fast to be maintained, and the slow progress of Greek culture in the ninth and early eighth centuries comes as a disappointment after this. Furthermore, it is difficult to speak of a 'Greek Renaissance', or even of the end of the Greek dark age, while some of the historically important centres of Greek civilization are still wrapped in obscurity. But first let us consider what were the elements of this change, and how much of Greece they affected.

Movements of traders and settlers within Greece, although no doubt on a modest scale, had perhaps continued sporadically through even the darkest years, but the evidence suggests that they were mainly confined to the shores of the Aegean Sea. Now in the second half of the tenth century we begin to find more substantial proof of such movements in the form of freshly-established cemeteries and settlements, and of influences on pottery and other artefacts. These changes affect a wider area than the 'advanced' regions of the previous century (pp. 374-6), but their operation is still, by and large, confined to the Aegean and its coasts. That this should still be so confirms the strength of the earlier trend; the swing of the pendulum has not yet been corrected. It is worth mentioning that one of the inter-state federations or religious leagues of later Greek history for which a high antiquity can be argued is the Kalaurian Amphictyony; centred on the island off the coast of the Argolid from which it took its name, it embraced Athens, Prasiai on the east coast of Laconia, Aegina, three sites in the Argolid (Nauplia, Hermione, Epidauros) and Orchomenos in Boeotia. R.M. Cook has pointed out that the notion of a community of interest between these places goes well with the pattern of Late Protogeometric pottery-styles; on several of these sites, however (and on Kalauria (Poros) itself) the extant remains belong to the Mycenaean and Geometric periods, and a slightly later origin is perhaps equally possible.[43] But such a confederacy, centred on the Saronic Gulf and adjacent waters, would fit the pattern of the early Iron Age better than that of any other period.

DIFFUSION OF POTTERY-STYLES

If we consider pottery-styles, we find that Attic Protogeometric in its later stages exercises a marked and direct influence on Boeotia; that it still maintains a close and dominant relationship with the products of the Argolid and Corinthia; that it is sometimes imported, and more often imitated, by the communities in the Aegean islands – the Cyclades, Aegina, Samos, Rhodes; that it begins to have a stronger influence than hitherto on the Protogeometric pottery at Smyrna; that it inspires a sudden and permanent change in the decoration of pottery in Central Crete; but that its effect is only faintly detectable elsewhere, in Delphi and perhaps Ithaka. But Attic is no longer the only school of Protogeometric to spread beyond its original bounds. To the north and east, there is an enclave embracing Thessaly, northern and central Euboea, Skyros, Andros, Tenos and Delos. Since the Thessalian school of Protogeometric is the earliest and best-attested in this area, we may see its influence as initially the predominant one: the spread of the jug with cut-away neck, a clear Thessalian adaptation, touches Delphi as well as Lefkandi in Euboea, and a new settlement on the latter site, dating perhaps from the mid-tenth century, may have emanated from Thessaly. Nevertheless, the most characteristic single vase-form in this region, from the end of the tenth century onwards, is the low-footed skyphos with pendent semicircles, for which a Euboean or north Cycladic, rather than a Thessalian, origin seems likeliest. It is from this region, too, that the influence of Protogeometric spreads northwards to Macedonia – very possibly by sea, since the Macedonian sites where the style is found are congregated in the plain at the head of the Thermaic Gulf. A third source of influence, slighter in this case, is to be found in the Protogeometric of the Argolid; it penetrates in some degree to Corinthia and Aegina, but its clearest and most interesting reflection is in the finds from the Serraglio cemetery on Kos. All these developments show themselves clearly in the second half of the tenth century and almost all, it will be noted, involve transmission across the Aegean or along its shores. The communities in the western half of the Greek mainland, sparsely scattered as they seem to have been, were still largely left to their own devices; some of them may have re-established contacts among themselves at about this time, to judge from the resemblances of the Protogeometric pottery at Derveni in eastern Achaea, Medeon in Phokis, Aetos in Ithaka and Amyklai in Laconia (pp. 73, 85-8); but their connections eastwards were still, it seems, of the most tenuous. The Protogeometric school of Messenia, which like that of Laconia may in large part be later than this phase, has

42-4

most in common with the Ithakan school. Other small finds from these regions do nothing to dispel the impression of isolation and backwardness.

So too when we look to the new features of this period which must stem from outside Greece, we find that their presence is confined to the areas bordering on the Aegean. A recent discovery may typify this: in the Late Protogeometric settlement at Lefkandi, the traces of a bronze-foundry, with moulds for casting tripods, prove that a source of supply for copper and tin was once again open to some Greeks at least; stylistic details give a firm hint that Cyprus was playing a part (p. 285). At approximately the same time, in the vicinity of 900 BC, objects of gold begin to appear in some numbers, but only on a geographically limited range of sites. Athens, Corinth, Tiryns, Marmariani, Skyros, Kos, central Crete produce gold finds (p. 248): the few contemporary objects of ivory show a similar but narrower distribution. The agency of Cyprus, which may once again be suspected, is clearly apparent when pottery and metallurgy show Cypriot influence; but on the published evidence, this seems to happen only in central Crete, Rhodes, Attica and Euboea as yet (p. 331). Finally, the rare instances of Greek pottery in Cyprus and the Levant in the tenth and ninth centuries involve only Attica, Euboea and the northern Cyclades.

In the immediate Aegean area, one can see something of the benefits that this increased accessibility brought in its wake. But Greek culture in the ninth and early eighth centuries is still represented by a relatively thin scatter of material: only in certain areas did the pottery pass through recognizable Early and Middle Geometric phases, and these wares are seldom found in profusion; elsewhere, the dominant strain is still that of Protogeometric survival, with its accompanying chronological vagueness. Such advances as are made, in pottery and other minor arts and in the visible acquisition of wealth, are still the province of one or two centres.

ATTICA

For Athens and Attica, this is undeniably an impressive period: the latest stages of Protogeometric had witnessed the diffusion of that style to a few outlying sites in Attica where it was produced locally, recognizably Attic yet distinct from the finest Athenian; perhaps this era, the late tenth century when Miltiades' ancestor Philaios may have lived (p. 12), witnessed a crucial stage in the political and cultural unification of Attica, a process which tradition credited entirely to the heroic age and to Theseus. At all events, in the ensuing generations, Attica leads the way for much of Greece. Attic potters of the Early and Middle Geometric periods retain most of the influence of their Late Protogeometric predecessors, and even

120-2. Original and derivative, *c.*850-800 BC. *120,* Attic Middle
Geometric amphora from Geometric grave 41 in the Kerameikos,
Athens (height 69·5 cm); *121,* a quite close Cycladic adaptation,
exported to Crete and found in tomb L at Fortetsa (height 65 cm);
122, a free Cretan version, debased in shape although hardly in decoration
(see no. *41*), Fortetsa tomb OD (height 56·3 cm).

extend it in new directions: Thessaly and Euboea, it seems, had little new
to offer in decorative ideas, and Attic products are, in due course, imported
or imitated in their former sphere of influence, as on Andros, Tenos,
Delos, Rheneia and very markedly at Lefkandi and Eretria. Similarly,
the short initial era of Argive influence in the Dodecanese gives way to a
more general imprint of Attic influence, re-inforced by a second and clearer
wave of Atticism in the region of 800 (p. 77). On the Greek mainland, too,
earlier Attic Geometric makes ground; deservedly, for some of its products,
such as the 'severe style' grave-amphorae of Middle Geometric, are deeply
satisfying. It is revealing to compare such robust products of a craftsman's   *120*
inspiration with the competent but dull copies being executed in a deriva-   *121*
tive school like that of the Cyclades, and again with the uncouth approxi-   *122*
mation to the same shape and style by a contemporary Cretan.[44] The

other material from Attica in most ways lives up to the pottery. The grave found in the Agora in 1967, dating from about 850, is the richest known from the area since the thirteenth century; it has a near-contemporary in Geometric grave 41 at the Kerameikos, and its finds suggest a comparable date for two rich tomb-groups from unrecorded excavations, now in Berlin and Toronto respectively, both said to have come from graves in Attica – perhaps outside Athens itself? A rich and recently-discovered cemetery at Vari, 15 miles south-east of Athens, is also said to have begun in Middle Geometric times, and has produced gold fibulae and impressed bands. The finds from these graves show that Attic craftsmen were beginning to engrave the catch-plates of their new and elaborate fibulae with

91a　simple designs, sometimes representational: a ship, partly preserved on a fibula from the Kerameikos grave, is the most significant of these, a forerunner of the great ship scenes of the following century. It is also possible that the sumptuous gold jewellery from the new Agora grave was locally-made, as was certainly true of the fine gilt pins and fibulae and the impressed gold bands. Other hesitant steps in creative art are taken: the incised face on an ivory plaque looks like a piece of local work; cup-handles in the form of a human leg, one of them from yet another newly-found grave in Athens, surprise us with their naturalism; a bronze pin with a finial shaped like a shod foot shows a similar venture in a new medium. The faience and ivory from the Agora grave, and the bronze embossed bowl from the rather later grave 42 of the Kerameikos, confirm that both raw materials and finished products from the Near East were now reaching Athens. Finally, the greaves from the Acropolis grave (p. 333) show that Athens was even in touch with the barbarian north.[45]

REGIONAL LIMITATIONS

Beyond Attica, we find comparable enterprise only in the fine bronze jewellery of Argive graves (pp. 264, 269), and in the peculiar finds of the Aegean frontier-zones, Macedonia in the north, Crete in the south. Of Macedonia little need be said: although the rich material from Vergina and other sites shows that the gates were thrown wide open to the north, the Macedonian plains in combination with the mountain barrier to the south formed a remarkably effective buffer to the passage southwards of intrusive influences. The areas of overlap with the culture of the Greek Iron Age are slight: the Protogeometric imports of ninth- and eighth-century date on Macedonian sites are balanced by the spread of Macedonian hand-made pottery and other finds, no doubt through the vale of Tempe, to the sites of Marmariani (p. 236) and, perhaps rather earlier, Rakhmani,[46] in the extreme north-eastern corner of the Thessalian plain. The local iron-working industry at the most may have owed some of its initial impulse to Greek prompting, and may have repaid this by supplying ore for use further south, if only briefly. But beyond this, Macedonia simply has no part in the process of the revival of Aegean culture in these years; indeed this era in Macedonia apparently gives way to one of stagnation and obscurity in the eighth and seventh centuries. This isolation, with the late emergence of the country in Greek historical records, and the unexplained situation of the Macedonian language, must justify us in excluding it from the story. The same conclusion applies *a fortiori* to Epirus, a region whose isolation from Iron Age Greece in material culture persists to almost as late a date, and is interrupted by no such episodes of communication as occurred in Macedonia.

Crete, although comparable in that it dissociates itself from the main-stream of Greek development, cannot be treated in the same way. For one thing, the outside influences which it so eclectically receives in the ninth century, as in the eleventh and tenth, are ultimately from the same quarter as those which will presently swamp the Aegean – the Levantine coast and Cyprus. Again, Cretan pottery and other small finds show that the island was from now on continuously in touch with other parts of the Greek world, most obviously the Cyclades and Attica. Yet Cretan art of this period is unlike anything found elsewhere; the other Greeks, it seems, were neither attracted by its end-product nor, on the whole, inclined to follow the Cretan course of accommodating immigrant foreign craftsmen in their midst. The series of bronzes from the Idaean Cave has long been credited, in part at least, to such an Oriental guild, and it has been suggested that a further instance lies behind the outbreak of Orientalism in the 'Protogeometric B' phase (p. 334; Chapter 6, n. 42). Even if this explanation can be applied from so early a date, the results are too complex to be attributed to any one cause; for the art of 'Protogeometric B' shows some remarkable revivals of Bronze Age features, in vase-shapes, patterns and occasional painted figures, another development which it would be hard to imagine anywhere else in Greece at this date. If the rich finds from the two 'crocks of gold' in the Khaniale Tekke tholos are really to be dated to this phase – which I have argued to be the end of the ninth century – they add greatly to the aura of wealth in central Crete, and mark the revival of such refined crafts as filigree, granulation and inlaying of gold jewellery with rock-crystal and amber.[47] Even so, this injection of Oriental craftsman-ship cannot be felt over the island as a whole until much later.

ARCHITECTURE

There is one field in which a more general and less uneven advance is detectable, and that is architecture. The ninth century sees a marked increase in the number, size and quality of preserved domestic buildings; it also probably witnesses the first stages in the growth of the independent sacred building or temple, that characteristically Greek institution. At first it is often difficult to distinguish between the two classes of structure: not only was there no clear differentiation in plan, but there may even, according to a recently advanced theory, have been at first no absolute distinction in use.[48] Many of the earliest temples may have been converted dwelling-houses or dining-halls, whose prime function was now to provide a setting for sacrifices and sacred meals and not, as in later days, to house the cult-statue of a deity. In many early instances, the sacrificial altar or hearth was located centrally, inside the temple; although the important early buildings at the Samian Heraeum (see below) form one of the exceptions. In these circumstances it would naturally be difficult either to identify a newly-built structure as a temple, or to place the moment at which an existing one was consecrated to sacred use. The more substantial isolated buildings of this period are commonly claimed as temples, and the absence of recognizable votive offerings need not tell decisively against this. Apsidal plans are now prominent for all purposes; they may even be reflected in the grave, with the appearance of round-ended cists in Messenia and Achaea (pp. 171-2). A securely-dated house at Argos, which was involved in a conflagration early in the ninth century, will serve as a starting-point; there is no suggestion that this was other than a domestic structure. At Mycenae, a roughly contemporary and quite impressive apsidal building was found in the area of the rich Mycenaean houses outside the walls, well to the west of the Acropolis; its size (9 metres long), its outlying situation, and the appearance of some miniature, presumably votive, pots all provide grounds for regarding this as an early temple; and it would then provide yet another case of an Iron Age sanctuary sited on the ruins of a Bronze Age domestic complex (cf. above, p. 397). Another more equivocal case is that of the earlier of two superimposed buildings at Antissa on Lesbos; the date of its construction should be lowered since the underlying 'Protogeometric' pottery is probably later than the excavator thought, but it was replaced by the later, apparently oval building in the late eighth century, and its life may just possibly begin in the ninth. Its building-technique is competent, a fore-runner of the carefully-fitted 'Lesbian' style of masonry in which the joints describe curving lines. Finally we have the first unquestionable occurrence of an apsidal temple, that of Hera Akraia at Perachora, which was also (though less directly) replaced by a fresh structure in about 725, and whose initial date is again uncertain, but could well be as early as 800 (pp. 270, 277). Among the offerings dedicated here was a terracotta model of an apsidal building, generally agreed to represent the temple itself, which – as restored – gives a clearer picture than any description of the mud-brick or rubble walls, timber facings and upper works, and steep thatched roof. The oval-plan building, whose heyday perhaps belongs in the earlier dark age (above, p. 369), survives into this period and beyond: we have noted that the second building at Antissa was probably of this form. Earlier, we find an isolated house of oval plan and ninth-century date in the Agora at Athens; both here and at Antissa, later structures were found to abut on the outer faces of the walls. It seems possible that temples of oval plan also came to be erected: besides the extremely fragmentary building of uncertain purpose and date whose curving wall was discovered on the site of the Hall of the Mysteries at Eleusis (above, p. 396), there is the Archaic temple at Gonnos in Thessaly which preserves the form of a truncated ellipse. Two models from the Samian Heraeum – one of terracotta and apsidal in plan, probably of Late Geometric date, the other of limestone, oval and probably Archaic – may perhaps represent temples.[49]			*123*

But the lasting trend of early Greek architecture, both sacred and profane, was away from such curvilinear plans; and before long we can see the resurgence of the rectilinear form in both fields. A central place in this development is usually given to the impressive structure at Thermon in Aetolia, known as Megaron B; but most unfortunately its chronology remains problematical. The 'Protogeometric' pottery which is said to date its construction is far more probably a later native ware and, even if genuine Protogeometric, would not imply a date earlier than 800 in this remote region; it is only certain that Megaron B had stood for some time before its replacement by a Temple of Apollo in the late seventh century, and that it acquired in this time, if not at its first construction, a row of bases for a colonnade or stockade of apsidal plan, running round the very slightly curved side- and back-walls of the basically rectangular megaron. This is not the first re-appearance of the characteristic Mycenaean megaron-arrangement of a symmetrical hall, with or without ante-room, entered from one direction only, by a central door in one of its short sides. Such an arrangement is perfectly compatible with an apsidal plan, and is indeed found in the buildings at Mycenae and Perachora mentioned above. What

123. Terracotta model of an apsidal temple or house, from Well F at the Heraeum, Samos. Height 13·3 cm; *c.* 725 BC.

is striking about the Thermon building is its size (21·5 metres long), its symmetry and its quasi-rectangular plan: the surrounding bases may have been for posts to support the eaves of a curving thatched roof, as Drerup has suggested, rather than for a true colonnade or peristyle. This last feature, which is to all appearances the exclusive property of the fully-fledged temple, is nowhere attested before the eighth century. The status of Megaron B at Thermon is therefore obscure or, perhaps better, ambivalent.[50]

124   We must turn now to a greater sanctuary, the Samian Heraeum, where the sacred function of the earliest temple 'Hekatompedon I', is beyond question, but where chronological difficulties once more impede us. The excavators' view remains that the first open-air altar on the site belongs at the latest to the region of 900; and that the subsequent era saw the building

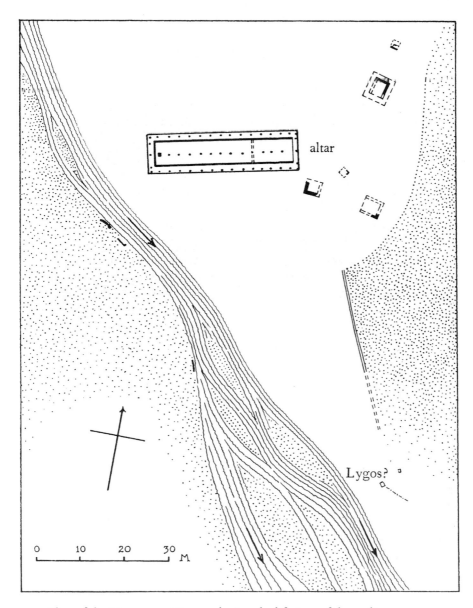

altar

Lygos?

0 10 20 30 M

124. Plan of the Heraeum at Samos during the lifetime of the earliest temple (Hekatompedon I). Late 8th century B C.

of Altar II, Hekatompedon I, Altars III, IV and V, and Hekatompedon II, probably in that order of construction. Two of the main fixed points in the series are provided by deposits, one under Altar II ('Fundgruppe A'), of which the terracotta figurines only were published, and the other under Hekatompedon II ('Fundgruppe H'). The first deposit is said to be Early Geometric in character and to belong no later than 850; the second one is dated to the earlier seventh century, but its latest contents seem to belong in the region of 650. Thus the dating of Hekatompedon I is set within fixed limits on both sides; with Altars I and II we are not here concerned, but it must be said that the stylistic arguments from the material of the first deposit do not justify such a high dating as is proposed; while the apparently elliptical plan of Altar I is matched by that of a stone structure in a Late Geometric shrine since excavated at Miletus. Hekatompedon I, however, is the outstanding surviving building of its era in Greece, a long narrow hall (33·5 metres long on its foundations) with a single row of columns down the centre; it acquired a complete peristyle at some time during its life, and also saw three re-buildings of the altar which faced it, at a distance of some 15 metres. No doubt it stood for a considerable time, but I do not see that there are grounds for dating its construction before the eighth century – in which, indeed, its excavator at first placed it.[51] A third structure of rectilinear plan which has been dated to the ninth century or earlier is that whose remains were traceable under the Oikos of the Naxians on Delos.[52] This is a smaller and proportionately broader structure, with two rows of internal columns instead of one; once again, its dating is determined only by that of the building which replaced it, around 700 BC; and again its function, as at Thermon, is obscure. One can only say that on present evidence a building-plan of this kind seems hardly likely before the eighth century. In the cases where we can with certainty point to rectangular Geometric temple-structures of undoubted date and purpose, we find that none of them is earlier than c.750 (below, pp. 422-3).

The evolution of the temple-plan thus proceeded along a fairly natural, if far from unified course. But there came a point when the development of the domestic house, with which it had hitherto marched roughly in step, had to diverge from that of the temple. Temples were required more and more to be isolated and imposing structures; the creation of the peristyle enhanced both these qualities, and the retention of curvilinear plans was for a time compatible with them. With houses, however, the growth of population made greater density necessary in town-sites; isolation was less tolerable, and curvilinear plans less convenient in closely-grouped

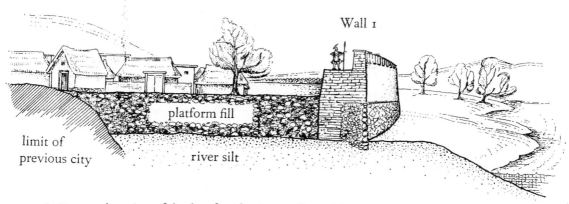

125. Restored section of the first fortification-wall at Old Smyrna. Mid-9th century B C.

housing. The natural development was for blocks or rows of rectangular houses to be adopted, and it is interesting to find that this was already taking place in ninth-century Smyrna. In one excavated sector, several such houses were found, stone-built for at least the greater part of their height, still one-roomed but with several times the ground-area of the earlier oval house which stood near by (p. 369); their roofs were now apparently flat.[53] At Smyrna itself these structures were rather surprisingly replaced in the eighth century by somewhat inferior houses, largely of mud-brick construction and in many cases of apsidal plan. But the earlier tendency towards grouped rectangular houses was a lasting one, which we shall find strongly represented on other eighth-century sites (pp. 426-7 below). Contemporary with the ninth-century houses at Smyrna is the first circuit of fortifications on the site, a still more remarkable development *125* (p. 298). The wall was basically constructed of mud-brick, and had an overall thickness of 4·75 metres; but it had an outer facing of large stones with rubble behind, and it boasted projecting bastions whose upper facing was no longer in rough blocks but in dressed ashlar masonry of white tufa, a striking token of the recovery of lost skills.

GENERAL INFERENCES

When all is said, the period between the mid-tenth century and the earlier part of the eighth hardly qualifies for the title of a renaissance. There are marked differences from the darker era that preceded it, but the contrast with the later eighth century is much broader and sharper. There is no doubt that prosperity was reviving, but its rise was uneven geographically

126. Fragmentary Argive Late Geometric krater, from the settlement
at Argos, with a scene showing a warrior breaking-in a horse. Height
25·7 cm; *c.* 740 B C.

and perhaps socially as well. The supplies of metals and luxury goods now
available – some of them intrinsically precious, others of great practical
possibilities – may well have served to increase the differentiation in wealth;
in a primitive society where land was the principal form of capital and where
the hereditary claims to its ownership were (to judge from later evidence)
deeply entrenched, it is hard to see how most of the people could share in
the limited opportunities for enrichment such as we can detect at this time.
The hereditary landowner was still probably as powerful economically as
he was politically. We may briefly digress to consider that partly symbolic
standby of aristocratic societies everywhere, the horse. A horse was not
only valuable as a vehicle that would multiply a man's speed in travel and
in battle, and as a pedestal that would literally raise him above his fellow-
men; the intricacies of its breeding also reflected the almost mystical
quality that aristocrats find in human breeding. Its significance in early
Greece lies partly in the fact that the Mycenaean and Minoans appear to
have used it, especially in war, almost exclusively as a traction-animal and
not for riding. The rise of equitation, and thence of cavalry in warfare,
took place in Greece at some time in the early Iron Age, and it may therefore have had a significant effect on society in the period of this study. We
know that it had reached by the mid-eighth century a stage where the horse,
often on its own but sometimes held and occasionally ridden by an armed

man, had become a dominant motif in art; this is especially true of Argive Late Geometric pottery, where it is ubiquitous, and we may note the *126* appearance of plastic horses, forming the handles of Attic pyxides, in the *18* first half of the eighth century. But the earlier stages in this process are hidden in ambiguities; we have noted that in Protogeometric Athens (p. 401) two of the earliest representational vase-paintings show horses, and a terracotta horse-figurine was also found; but more than one interpretation of such scenes is possible, in a funerary context. We may also recall that an Athenian warrior's grave of about 900 BC produced two iron *84* bits (p. 233); but the fact that there were two of them points to what is, in the light of earlier and later parallels, the likeliest explanation: the bits represent the pair of horses which had pulled the funerary wagon (in more spacious days the horses were sometimes slaughtered and buried by the grave). This in itself is a hint that the deceased was an eminent man, but for positive proof of the mounted aristocrat, we have from before the mid-eighth century only the solitary painting from Mouliana (p. 401) and a figurine of a mounted man, apparently a warrior, from a Middle Geometric well at Miletus. No doubt the advances in riding were slow; and if, as seems likely, one most important element in this process was the introduction of a stronger breed from outside Greece, then this probably did not happen until the seventh century.[54] Efficient cavalry was thus probably beyond the powers of dark age Greece; but peaceful equitation, which leaves few material traces, apparently prevailed increasingly down to the eighth century; it may well have enhanced the predominance of the landowning classes.

But increased social differentiation was not incompatible with political advance. That the ninth century saw some considerable change in the direction of state organization seems extremely likely. It is possible that a vital step in the co-ordination of town and country life, which was to prove so effective in the form of the fully-developed city-state, had already been taken in Attica (p. 404), and that this to some degree explains the relatively advanced and prosperous state of Attica at this time. What is much more certain is that the decision to fortify the town of Smyrna, and to carry out the project with a higher standard of architectural skill than can be found anywhere else in Greece for generations afterwards, cannot have been taken by a chance confederation of aristocrats and their followers; nor do the carefully-orientated and competently-built houses inside the wall look like the products of any but a corporate enterprise. If it is really true that East Greece led the way in the development of the *polis*, as some historians have long since held, then it must be stressed that neither this, nor even her architectural advances, can be in any way the result of her greater proximity to the Oriental civilizations. The maritime links with Cyprus and the Levant are not conspicuously strong in Ionia before the late eighth century; while Phrygia and the other territories of the Ionian hinterland show no close analogies for such developments in their material remains. What was happening in Greece was still largely the concern of Greeks alone.

THE GREEK RENAISSANCE: THE MIDDLE AND LATER EIGHTH CENTURY

The changes which came over the Aegean in the eighth century are so profuse that it is hard to enumerate them in any logical order. For a time, we may try to preserve the chronological sequence; some of the developments are detectably earlier than the main wave of the mid-century.

COLONIZATION

One of the most important is the change in the character of Greek activity overseas. Such exploits as the Corinthian expansion along the shores of the Gulf of Corinth, to Ithaka, whose onset dates to perhaps the end of the ninth century (p. 339), and the establishment of a Greek entrepôt at Al Mina in the Levant, which probably belongs slightly earlier (p. 335), have many elements of permanence. In each case it seems that Greeks decided to settle away from home; in Al Mina's case at least the motives seem to have been commercial and the community became sufficiently entrenched to justify resident Greek potters in setting up their business there; while much of the earlier Geometric in Ithaka could have been made locally by Corinthian potters, and was in any case profoundly under their influence. Since some of the earliest Greek colonies in the West seem also to have sprung from commercial motives (pp. 335-6), it might well be asked how they differed from these forerunners. The measure of the difference is shown indirectly by the sequel: the Greek colonies in southern Italy and Sicily shaped the history of this region for the next five centuries, while the Corinthians in Ithaka and the Euboeans in Al Mina created so transient an impact that their activities are virtually unrecorded in Classical written sources. More relevant to this period, however, is the difference in status: the commercial enterprises of the ninth century were clearly, on occasion, successful enough to be supported for a considerable time, but they remained in origin voluntary and spontaneous ventures, motivated presumably by private economic aims. The colonies of the eighth century were the work of organized bodies: they might be led by an individual aristocrat, as even the expeditions of the Ionian migration had been, but they were not entirely of his creation; they might sometimes be commercial in purpose, but they were not manned by traders only. They were complete communities, detached from the population by some selective processes, of which in most cases we know nothing, but which on occasion carried more than a hint of compulsion. In other words, they imply some degree of state organization. The lapse of time between the early trading settlements and the first colonies is not long, but it exists: in the first quarter of the eighth century we find stray Greek imports in graves at Veii and Cumae; and then during the second quarter a permanent colony is seen to be established at Pithekoussai. It is likely that the search for metals played some part in both types of venture, and in the case of Ischia (p. 335) iron ore seems to have been an attraction. Behind this, we may see another factor, the growth of population in the Greek homeland. The importance of this factor is widely agreed, but its operation is usually explained in terms of land-hunger: the increase in population is thought to have caused a crisis over land-ownership as well as a serious shortage of food-supplies. Such developments may well have happened, but we are justified in adding to them a shortage of metal-ores, when we find that the metal being shipped to Ischia was the one of which Greece had most substantial native resources, on which she had perhaps hitherto subsisted. Perhaps it was the same pressure which brought eighth-century Atticizing pottery to another iron-bearing region, Macedonia (Chapter 2, n.33).

REPRESENTATIONAL ART

Even though many of the changes that followed stemmed from outside sources, the task remains of seeing how far they were reflected in Greece. The revival of representational art presents an interesting case; for although we have encountered likely instances of Oriental craftsmen working in Greece, and although their influence is even more certainly detectable in the first Greek essays in bronze- and ivory-work, the fact remains that the earliest media in which we find widespread representation are the simple terracotta figurines of men and animals, found in such quantity on the sanctuary-sites, and the pictorial vase-paintings. The figurines are the product of a purely native development, whether we choose to emphasize those of a recognizably 'Geometric' style, especially human and horse-figures, in bronze as well as terracotta, or the other more primitive, but not necessarily earlier examples; while neither the style nor the technique of the early vase-scenes owes much to outside sources. With the figurines,

2D

127. Frontal and profile views of a male figurine from Olympia, whose 'epiphany' gesture may indicate that it represents Zeus. Height *c.* 10cm; perhaps 9th or 8th century BC.
128. One of the few early Greek figurines for which accurate dating evidence is available, this bronze warrior was found at Delphi in a deposit with Corinthian pottery of *c.*740-730 BC. Height 7cm.

cf. 128 the abiding problem is that of chronology; as so often, there is little correlation between sanctuary-finds and grave-finds, and the grounds for the dating of the terracottas and bronzes are, in most cases, not only purely stylistic but indirect, in that they are ultimately based on comparisons with the figures in vase-scenes. The 'styleless' primitive figurines, most
127 strongly represented at Olympia, have no automatic claim to early date. But we can state that the revival in representational painting begins in
21, 138 Attica rather before the end of the Middle Geometric style, in the second quarter of the eighth century: the masterly restraint of these early silhouette-scenes and their deceptive air of simplicity have been well described by others. A clear illustration of the changed conditions of the new age is

the way in which, during the middle and later years of the century, this experiment in representational painting is taken up by the other schools of Geometric, one after another: Argive, Corinthian, Laconian, Arcadian and even Elean in the Peloponnese; Boeotian and Euboean to the north and east; Ithakan, and the schools of Pithekoussai and other early colonies to the west; and, over the Aegean, Naxian, Parian and other Cycladic styles, Rhodian, Milesian, Samian, Chiot and in a more independent way Cretan. Such influences are reflected in many other elements besides the figure-scenes: in the later stages of Argive Geometric, for example, Courbin has been able to show that this school was involved in a complex pattern of borrowing and lending of motifs and shapes with half a dozen other regional styles, some of them geographically quite remote from the Argolid.[55]

REGIONAL PATTERNS

As the scattered settlements grew and multiplied, the geographical 'regions' of which we have so often spoken were divided into units on a new scale, the *poleis* with their surrounding territory, small or large. These new states were rapidly in touch both with each other and with those of other regions. And yet, as later events show, the regional grouping of these states, first roughly detectable in the local pottery-styles of Protogeometric times, was always to remain an overriding force. Sometimes, as in Attica, a whole region coalesced into a single state; sometimes one city achieved a lasting domination of its smaller neighbours in the region, as at different times did Thebes and Argos, while with Sparta these processes were carried much further, and indeed already in the eighth century led on to the conquest of a neighbouring region, Messenia; sometimes the cities of a region formed a league or association of equals, although the most famous early instance of this, the Ionian league of twelve cities of East Greece grouped round the Panionion, seems not to have developed until near the end of the eighth century, to judge from excavations on the site of the federal sanctuary;[56] sometimes a purely tribal or cantonal state continued to exist, embracing a region without any major urban concentration.

INTERCOMMUNICATION

This pattern is therefore one of the many lasting and fundamental features of Greek civilization which were a legacy of the dark age; but in the purely material culture of eighth-century Greece it is accompanied by signs of intercommunication between most areas of Greece, and by a much more widespread evenness in prosperity. The evidence of metallic finds, no

SANCTUARIES c.760–700 B C

Italic indicates sites where finds other than pottery constitute the evidence for the existence of a sanctuary at this date.

less than that of pottery-styles (p. 68f.), testifies to the greater accessibility of the regions to each other. The spread of population in these years, as shown most clearly by the appearance of new cemetery-sites, extends significantly into hitherto backward regions like Achaea, Elis, Phokis and Lokris. But this picture is greatly extended by the other great material phenomenon of the age, the growth of the sanctuary-sites. We have seen   *129* (pp. 408-12) that built temples were already in existence in some places during the previous century; we have also found that a few other sanctuaries produced pottery or small finds which indicate that they had been receiving dedications for some time (pp. 285-95). But for the great mass of the offerings, the eighth century is the earliest possible date. At Olympia, the traditional date of 776 B C for the first celebration of the games, whatever its reliability in absolute terms, is consonant with the sharp increase in the volume of the dedications which must have taken place at roughly that time. But the sanctuary itself had clearly been in existence for some time before; while although the testimony of the victor-lists suggests that the festival of the games was for much of the eighth century an affair of largely local interest, the evidence of the rich and varied dedications suggests that pilgrims were by now visiting the place from far beyond the confines of Elis. Nor was Olympia alone in having such a wide clientele: the Geometric pottery at Delphi, for example, indicates firm contacts with Corinth, Athens and Thessaly, while the special relationship of that sanctuary with Crete must also begin by the eighth century. But the growth of certain other sanctuaries, whose finds show a more local colour, has a different significance: the rise of the Artemis Orthia sanctuary at Sparta, in the later part of the eighth century, is still our earliest substantial proof of the growth of the town of Sparta. Much the same is true of the sanctuaries at Tegea and, from a somewhat later date, at Ephesus. Imported goods, especially bronzes, were now finding their way to some of these sanctuaries, coming ultimately from barbarian Europe as well as a wide area of the Near East (pp. 339-48). The spread of alphabetic writing, which would seem to have reached Greece first somewhere between c.750 and 720 B C (p. 352), was fast enough for inscriptions of probable eighth-century date to appear in Attica, Euboea, Aegina, Ithaka, Thera, Smyrna, Rhodes and Pithekoussai.

ARCHITECTURE

But it is the architectural evidence which again gives the most direct and tangible evidence of the advances of society, in organization as well as in prosperity. It cannot be coincidence that surviving buildings of eighth-

129. Location map of sanctuaries, *c.* 760-700 BC.

130. Terracotta model of a rectangular temple from the Heraeum, near Argos. Height 54 cm; *c.* 700 BC.

century date are so much commoner, and on the whole so much better constructed, than those of the preceding centuries; we must believe that building-standards had rapidly risen, and skills been diffused over a wider area. Some structures still have the shape or materials of the previous era: this seems particularly true of sacred buildings, in whose planning tradition would be a powerful factor.

SACRED BUILDINGS. A small apsidal temple at Galataki near Corinth, the centre of a cult evidently inspired by a nearby Mycenaean chamber-tomb (p. 194), was built in the late eighth century but represents no detectable advance; its contemporary, the later building at Antissa (p. 408) may be a temple too. But by now the rectangular megaron-plan is more widely used: examples which can be dated to the second half of the eighth century are the Temple of Apollo Delphinios at Dreros in Crete, a most competent dry-stone structure, and the Temple of Hera Limenia at Perachora, also a simple megaron but of cruder workmanship, even though it represents a marked advance on its nearby predecessor. A temple in the recently excavated town-site at Zagora on Andros (of which we shall have more to say, p. 425), has proved to be later than the settlement. In each of these modest buildings (the Perachora temple is the smallest, 9·5 by 5·6 metres) the central place is taken by a hearth or altar, which evidently had precedence over a cult-statue (p. 408). Once again, we have the evidence of a contemporary terracotta model for the appearance of this form of temple: it is from the Argive Heraeum, whose first actual temple-structure was perhaps of similar date and form.[57] Two examples of a different type of sacred building have been found, both in Attica: one of these, that excavated near the site of Plato's Academy (p. 398), served as a covered place of sacrifice, confirming the demand for structures of this purpose in eighth-century religion. This and, more especially, its contemporary building at Eleusis, are both of somewhat irregular polygonal plan, with several rooms opening off a connecting corridor; this is the first testimony that we have for such a house-plan, which emerges in Classical times as the standard form of a superior town-house or farmstead.[58] The Eleusis building had the normal wall-construction, but the Athenian house was built entirely (including the foundations) of mud-bricks, somewhat shorter and broader (45 cm by 45 by 10) than the Ionian brick used at Smyrna (p. 369). If domestic structures of this size and plan existed yet in Greece, we know nothing of them.

DOMESTIC ARCHITECTURE. It is, however, the domestic and utilitarian architecture which most clearly shows how times were changing. The ninth-century experiment in grouped, and perhaps axially-planned, housing at Smyrna seems isolated and, as we have seen, succeeding generations of Smyrnaeans apparently went back on it (p. 413). But in the later eighth century genuine town-sites, with grouped houses of rectilinear plan, quite suddenly become common: the clay jars and chests which are sometimes found, sunk in the house-floors, are naturally taken as evidence of cramped or crowded living, and may be concomitant with the growth of fortification-walls, which set a premium on close-packed living – the two features are contemporary at Smyrna. A few village-sites have more loosely-grouped housing: at Lefkandi, the Geometric houses included at least one of apsidal plan, and several curved walls. At the Acropolis site

130

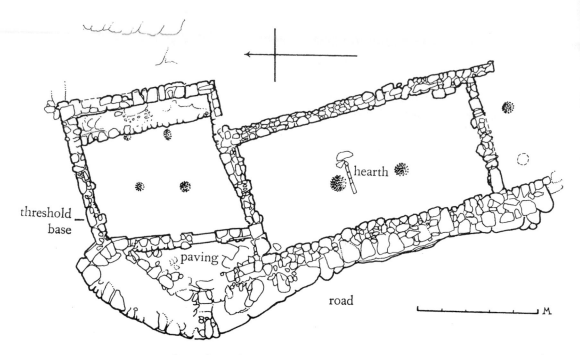

131. Houses of Bench- and Megaron-types at Emborio, Chios. Late 8th to 7th centuries B C.

of Emborio on Chios, the steepness of the ground prevented regular

131 planning; the houses were of two main types, both rectangular in plan – the orthodox 'megaron', which is apparently the earlier form here, and which by now has recovered its regular Bronze Age attribute of a porch with two columns *in antis*; and the squarish 'bench house', often with a

cf. 132 raised stone sleeping-bench across its inner end. Both types had all-stone walls, probably flat roofs, and in some cases at least clay chimneys. Most interesting in terms of plan and siting is the 'Megaron Hall', built into the

133 fortification-wall round the crown of the hill and over 18 metres long: there can be little doubt that this is the residence of the local chieftain, a concrete illustration of the kind of social system which we would infer from literary and historical evidence (pp. 386-8).[59] Several other village or small town settlements have been recovered, particularly in the Cyclades; and here must be noted a feature of the construction of these Cycladic houses. They are almost entirely built in a dry-stone construction with schist slabs, a time-honoured technique in these islands, most conspicu-

132. Terracotta model of a house from the tholos tomb at Khaniale Tekke, near Knossos. There is a chimney, not visible here, and inside is perhaps a representation of the wall-bench found in a type of Greek house of the 8th century. Height, at front, 29·7 cm; probably *c*. 800 B C.

ously found in the built tombs of the Early and Middle Bronze Age, but also present in the shrine of Mycenaean date on Keos (p. 395). That it should reappear in the same area in the eighth century, and at a relatively high standard of competence, will no doubt be taken to suggest an unbroken local tradition; the possibility of continuous settlement down to Geometric times at Grotta on Naxos shows how this could have existed, but the certainty of the survival of the shrine on Keos equally hints that the practice could have been revived, from observation of extant Bronze Age buildings. But it remained, if only for geological reasons, a buildingstyle of limited applicability. The sites now in question were all fresh settlements: the most impressive of them, that at Zagora (Palaiopolis) on Andros, has been tentatively linked with the Ionian migration, but the bulk of the finds, and with them the visible structures, seem to date from the late eighth century, after which the site was apparently deserted again. Despite the different building-techniques, Zagora shows several resemblances to Emborio: there are two intercommunicating 'megara' of modest

118

134

135

133. The Megaron Hall at Emborio on Chios, from the north. 18·25 m
in length, it stood against the inner face of the Acropolis wall, which
ran down its right-hand side, and faced the main gateway. It was
presumably the chieftain's house. Late 8th century B C.

cf. 134

dimensions, side by side. Otherwise, a squarish house predominates, of
similar dimensions to the bench-houses of Emborio and likewise containing sleeping-benches in several houses. The temple has been mentioned
already (p. 423). Perhaps the most interesting quality of the Zagora site
is the regular orientation of its closely-grouped blocks of houses; no
streets have however yet been positively identified. Similar but less well-
preserved settlements are those of Kastro on Siphnos, and Exoburgo on
Tenos.[60] An even more regular piece of town-planning, if of slightly later
date, is the town of Vroulia on Rhodes, a place apparently established as a
colony of Lindos at the end of the eighth century, and so yet another
example of how expansion within the Aegean was still proceeding at this
date. Here the fortification-wall, protecting the site on the landward side,
ran dead straight for no less than 177 metres in one stretch, and against its
inner face were ranged 39 square houses, of uniform one-room size save
that some were provided with an ante-room or court; another similar
row ran parallel to it at a distance of 25 metres, giving what must have been

134. Zagora on Andros. View, from the north, of the central room of a
housing complex (see no. *135*). It is roughly square in plan, about 8 m
across, with a raised stone bench running most of the way round three
of its sides, and a central hearth. For the building technique, compare
no. *118*. It is not clear whether such a room comprised a whole
dwelling-unit. Late 8th century B C.

an almost unpleasantly regular effect. At Lindos itself, only one ruinous
contemporary house could be traced, rectangular in plan and with storage-
jars sunk in its floor, as earlier at Smyrna. At Vrokastro and Kavousi in
eastern Crete, we have late survivals of the Cretan hill-top refuge-city into
Geometric times: in the case of Vrokastro at least the houses of the Subminoan era were simply being retained in use, although a building of
Geometric date shows that standards had begun to rise (pp. 371-2). But
at Kavousi the Acropolis site was freshly built over in the eighth century,
and here there is a radical change, with sizeable houses of megaron plan
crowding on to the inhospitable site. Other more or less fragmentary
examples of Geometric housing have survived on several sites, including
Asine, Delphi, and Miletus and Iasos in south-western Asia Minor.[61]
    Both in the newly-established towns and in the countryside, there are
independent signs of the higher standard of living now achieved. Wells,

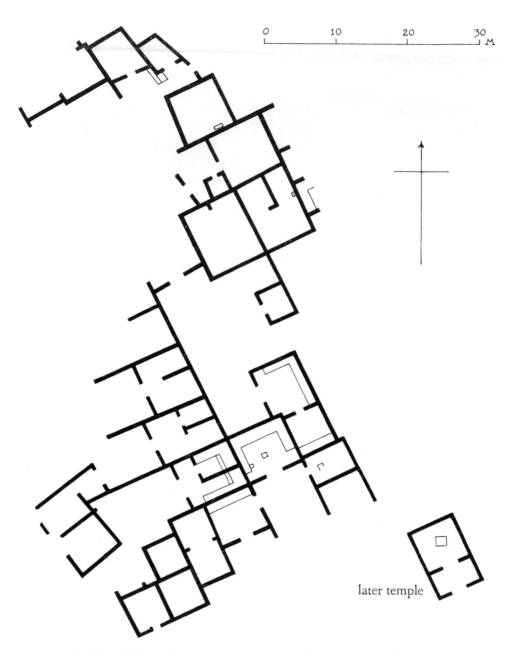

135. Plan of the settlement at Zagora on Andros, as excavated up to
1969. Late 8th century BC.

an invariable accompaniment of settlement-sites in most parts of Greece, were not new; Submycenaean and Protogeometric examples have been found in some numbers in the Athenian Agora and elsewhere, and the quite numerous Geometric wells show no very great advances in technique. But an **impressive** innovation is the appearance of slab-lined street-drains outside the town-houses at Delphi and, rather earlier, at Miletus; a harbour- mole at Delos may belong to the Geometric period and testifies to the growth of regular maritime traffic; one or two Geometric bridges or cause- ways in the Argolic plain show that land-communications were now being improved; some enigmatic constructions at Lefkandi are probably the foundations of olive-presses or granaries, close up against the house- walls, and there are more definite granaries in Geometric Smyrna (p. 380); a paved courtyard at remote Agrapidochorion in Elis reminds us that material advance was now widespread. At the same time, the siting of the fresh settlements on Chios, Andros, Siphnos and Rhodes, all on high, fortified or easily defensible sites above the sea, no less than the retention of places like Vrokastro and Kavousi and the massive rebuilding of the Smyrna fortification-wall in the mid-eighth century, remind us that material progress by no means went hand in hand with security.[62] One effect of the end of the dark age was indeed to bring an increase in the internal perils of Greece: the earliest recorded warfare of Hellenic history – the Lelantine War, the First Messenian War and other struggles – belongs at just this time.

HISTORICAL CONSCIOUSNESS IN POETRY AND ART

These years of reviving fortunes also witnessed a revival in the other sense of the word: the new and intense enthusiasm for establishing links with the heroic age. So far we have found the clearest evidence for this in the religious and funerary practices of the eighth century (pp. 192-6, 397-9); but there can be no doubt that one of its major causes lay in the diffusion of epic. The Homeric poems, the culmination of the epic tradition, are now widely held to have reached their final form in the eighth century, with the *Iliad* at least belonging well before its end: I do not propose to go into the complex evidence that forms the basis for this conclusion, which I fully support. But the diffusion of the Homeric epic is an issue closely bound up with this, and here agreement is harder to reach. In Ionia, where the poems as we know them were fashioned, it is certain that an unbroken tradition ran from the time of the Ionian migration down to Homer. But how did the rest of Greece fare? Were there flourishing local schools of epic, of comparable antiquity, in many places? It has been argued in recent

136

136. Miletus: a drain of the Geometric period, originally covered with further stone slabs, running beside the wall of a contemporary house. Average width *c.* 30 cm; earlier 8th century BC.

years that there had been continuous traditions of native poetry in mainland Greece: in particular, one centred on Boeotia which specialized in
passages of catalogue form.[63] Our views on the discontinuity of occupation
in many regions are obviously hard to reconcile with such notions; and
in the context of Boeotia we should remember that even Hesiod himself
was the son of an immigrant from Ionia. There is no obvious reason why
a community like Athens, which had an unbroken record of occupation
of its homeland, should not have preserved memories of the heroic age
in the form of saga and perhaps of poetry; but equally it is clear that the
Homeric poems in their finished form enjoyed a swift and permanent fame
and popularity in Greece. Since the revival of interest in the Bronze Age,
as shown by the evidence of the cults at Mycenaean graves and the conse-
cration of former Mycenaean sites as sanctuaries, seems in some cases to
begin before the Homeric poems can possibly have been diffused, we should
most naturally infer that there was first an era of general interest and pride
in the heroic age, and later a specific and increasing familiarity with the
Homeric epic and the themes that it comprised.

Just such a sequence has been discerned by some scholars in an independent medium, the representational scenes on Attic (and other) Geometric
vases. Many of these scenes, and all the grandest of them, are painted on
large vessels of evident funerary purpose; some have therefore interpreted
them as, in general, scenes of contemporary life, more or less relevant to
the career of the deceased man. But there comes a point – and in temporal
terms it must lie well before 700 BC – when such an explanation, if universally applied, would lead to ridiculous results. We must accept a mytho-
logical or heroic significance in a number of Late Geometric scenes which
represent centaurs, or an exploit identical with one of those of Heracles,
or Siamese twins in battle. These do not yet provide proof that the painters
knew of Homeric or any other epic; but in a different field, the verse-
inscriptions on late eighth-century pottery show familiarity with the metric
form of epic; and one of them, the lines from Pithekoussai which favourably
compare the cup on which they are written with that of Nestor, suggests
something more. It is surely simpler to accept that this inscription was
written by someone who knew the eleventh book of the *Iliad*, than to
argue for the survival of an unknown epic which became in some way – in
geographical terms it is difficult to see now – ancestral to both. Another
episode from the epic cycle, the death of Achilles and the rescue of his
corpse by Ajax, is surely represented in a seal-impression on a vase from
the same site, which belongs no later than about 700.[64] There are, then,

137. Fragments of an Attic Late Geometric krater, some of them now
in Warsaw. The naval exploits, for a time much favoured by Attic
painters as a subject, do not always end well; here, two of the survivors
seem to be lowering the mast; *c.*750 B C.

independent grounds for thinking that, from the earliest group of representational vase-scenes in the second quarter of the eighth century onwards, the painters might wish to depict some heroic subjects; by the last
quarter of the century there is certainty that they are doing so, and a great
probability that the Homeric poems are already in circulation to stimulate
their interest further.

But subject and content are different things: even if it were firmly
established that the recurrent types of scene on the earlier pictorial vases –
funerary processions, chariot-scenes, battles (in many cases round a
137   beached warship) – are intended to be of heroic import, it would still be
possible for the painters to have illustrated them entirely from the material
background of their own times. That they did so with one major field,
that of the ship-representations, is certain: the long, oared warships so
lovingly drawn on these vases are beyond question those of the eighth
century, developed entirely in Greece and ancestral to the vessels of
Archaic times; they differ from those described in the Homeric poems and
from those of the Bronze Age, even though they show revivals of some
Mycenaean features (p. 368). The 'chariot'-pictures are a more complex
matter. It is now an established fact that the habitual funerary vehicle in
Attic burials of Geometric date was a four-wheeled wagon (p. 263): the
wheel-naves from two Kerameikos graves, and two very late Geometric
models of four-wheeled hearses, prove this.[65] It is therefore almost certain
138, top right   that the rare Attic paintings of hearses represent four-wheeled vehicles.
I have argued elsewhere that many of the 'chariot' representations, which
show two wheels, one behind the other, and share other common features
with the funerary wagons, are similarly portrayals of four-wheeled wagons,

138. Detail of an Attic Late Geometric krater from the Dipylon cemetery, Athens (the Hirschfeld krater), which portrays, upper right, one of the very rare surviving scenes of an actual funerary procession (*ekphora*), with the bier borne on a hearse. Height of whole vase 1·23 m; *c.* 740 B C.

rather than two-wheeled war chariots drawn in disregard of perspective; only near the end of the Attic Geometric style do we encounter either definite two-wheeled chariots (that is, with one wheel only shown in the painting), or scenes of chariots in actual combat. We have not found any material evidence for the use of war-chariots during the dark age, and indeed such practice would be entirely out of keeping with the picture of Greek society that has emerged in the earlier part of the period. But the memory of chariot-driving Mycenaeans would persist where saga persisted. What appears to have happened is that at first, with their reviving interest in the heroic world and its trappings, the painters usually portrayed the chariot in the form of a vehicle that they did know, the four-wheeled wagon; then, perhaps a little later, revival was carried altogether further and the chariot itself was re-introduced to Greece for a strictly limited range of purposes – racing and processions, but not warfare.[66]

2E

The chariot-race as an event in the Olympic games is said to have been included for the first time early in the seventh century. That the latest Geometric painters should have represented the chariot accurately is in keeping, not only with a growing familiarity with their models, but with the increasing tendency to draw on the contemporary world as it became more interesting. A clear example of this latter trend is the appearance of mounted warriors in very late Geometric scenes. Riding into battle had no place either in the epic tradition or in Bronze Age reality, but by the late eighth century it had become too important to be ignored. One newly-published vase combines such an illustration with another feature that I believe to have been adopted just at this time: the bronze plate-corslet (p. 271), recognizably shown in silhouette on the body of a mounted man. The appearance of organized groups of men in uniform equipment was another feature that presumably went hand in hand with the evolution of the city-state in the eighth century, and in due course this too affects the Geometric painters' portrayal of warfare. Indeed, nothing could demonstrate the essential dichotomy between the two sources of their inspiration than those vases which give their principal scene to a 'heroic' battle with the attributes, more fanciful than faithful, of heroic warfare, and which have a subsidiary decorative frieze of a file of warriors, uniformly armed and marching in step. Both may be equally intended to convey the world of saga – even the specific world of the *Iliad* perhaps; but the warriors below are essentially incompatible with the battle above.[67] Such considerations as these detract from our confidence in the Geometric vase-paintings as illustrations of life at the end of the dark age; artistic convention introduces a whole new field of ambiguity, and the analysis of the different elements is even more hazardous and conjectural than it is in the case of literary epic. But if the ships are real and contemporary, then so in part may be the use to which they are most often put – a sea-raid, in which the ship is beached and an amphibious battle ensues. The growing insecurity of the age, and the maritime predominance which Athens may have enjoyed in more recent times, are in accordance with such events as these, and could well have coloured the Attic artist's view of the heroic past. In a world where real life was apparently so profoundly overshadowed by the growing interest in the heroic age, it might have been hard even for the painter himself to analyse for us the factual basis of his creations.

Since Homer, too, has emerged as a witness of the material developments of the eighth century, it is appropriate to look to the poems for some reflection of them. Our earlier difficulties (pp. 388-94), no less than those involved by contemporary art, serve to show how difficult it is to isolate those passages which are derived from the world of Homer's day. Apart from the broad category of similes, whose content is naturally but not inevitably taken to be derived from first-hand experience, we have to search through the poems line by line, sometimes phrase by phrase, in our attempt to distinguish contemporary features. Even among the similes, the very common occurrence of images involving lions is on several grounds more likely to derive from Bronze Age tradition than from the new accessibility of the regions to the east where lions were still common. But we can safely detect the world of the eighth century in the more homely images of hunting deer, wild goat and boar; of fishing and diving for oysters; of horse-riding and ivory horse-trappings; of ploughing, reaping, winnowing, milling, irrigation and other activities linked with arable farming; of vine-growing; of tree-felling and ship-building; of stock-breeding, tanning and working in wool; of fairly advanced metallurgy in gold and silver as well as iron; and of trading by sea.[68] Other features are of greater historical importance however; and none more so than Homer's recognition of the great social and political advance of his day, the rise of the *polis*. The town in Homer is most easily understood as the developed version of Geometric times; it is comforting that his native Ionia has provided our earliest secure archaeological evidence – Smyrna indeed has perhaps as strong a claim as any to be his home-town. Homer envisages towns with walls, docks, temples and a market-place; although his kings live in palaces amid splendour that can only be of Mycenaean inspiration, and with other features, such as staircases and basements, which must be of equal antiquity, it is still true that the technical building-knowledge which Homer shows is recognizably that of contemporary constructions – rough stone walls and roofs with high pitched rafters; one detail, the circular 'tholos' in the courtyard of Odysseus' house, is closely matched by the structures in the yards of Geometric houses at Smyrna. The growth of fortification in these years suggests a contemporary inspiration for Homer's references to the siege, sack and burning of towns. The city in Homer functions as the political and economic hub of its district; his nobles for example live in it rather than on their estates. This is the picture which the material evidence of the eighth century – and of no earlier period of the dark age – suggests to us. We may note, too, that in Boeotia a little later Hesiod centres his interests in the *polis*, and in its function of justice which should override the faction or corruption of aristocrats; he too seems to know of walled towns and sea-trade (p. 4).[69] In many other ways

117

too the Homeric background shows its affinity with the eighth-century world: it is enough to mention the factors already familiar from the material evidence – the presence of Phoenician traders on the fringes of the Aegean (cf. p. 18); the growth of more organized military tactics in place of the spontaneous duels between heroes; the common use of twin spears, one at least of which is thrown; the prominence of tripods as prizes for contests.

The finished literary masterpieces of the *Iliad* and *Odyssey*, like the curiously sophisticated and analytical mentality behind the contemporary Late Geometric paintings, show the magnitude of the renaissance that now enveloped Greece. Their very existence, more even than what they tell us of their times, is the proof that we are now dealing with a vigorous and outward-looking civilization. Where exactly we place the critical turning-point in time is perhaps a matter of personal inclination. For me, the decisive moment comes when the Greek world can be seen to be moving forward *as a whole*; when the beneficial or disruptive developments in one centre are swiftly reflected in most parts of central and southern Greece, in the islands and in Ionia. Such a state of affairs cannot be detected before the beginning of the eighth century; yet it is patently in existence before its end. Whatever category of progress we choose, there is little doubt that the years around the mid-eighth century witnessed many of the decisive developments. The predicament from which Greece then emerged, the period which was now permanently set behind her, seems to me to deserve the title of a dark age.

Notes

1] *Exc. at Lefkandi*, 11-23, 34-5

2] Mycenae, *AR* 1964/5, 9-10; 1966/7, 8-9; Tiryns, *AR* 1963/4, 8; 1964/5, 11; Argos, Asine, Athens, Iolkos, Grotta, Miletus – see *LMS* 80-1; 82-3; 113; 128-9; 149-50; 162-3 respectively

3] *LMS* 129, 135-7 (Iolkos); 149 (Grotta)

4] Figures that differ in detail but not in general proportion have been given by Desborough, *PPS* 31 (1965), 213-17, and in a paper given to the Hellenic Society in London on 17th March 1966

5] *LMS* 23-5 (Cyprus), 192-4 (Crete); cf. Chapter 6, p. 314 above

6] So R. M. Cook, *Antiquity* 34 (1960), 179. On depopulation, one thinks of the 'landmark in economic history' of the steady decline in Ireland's population since the great potato famine of 1847, following the equally constant increase before that date – see Alfred Marshall, *Principles of Economics* (9th ed., 1961), 191

7] Growth of population in eighth century: see above, pp. 268, 337, and compare J. M. Cook, *The Greeks in Ionia and the East* (1962), 33-4 for overcrowding in eighth-century Smyrna. For Athens, the count of wells in the Agora is informative, Coldstream *GGP* 360, n.1. Aegean island depopulation: F. W. Hasluck, *BSA* 17 (1910–11), 151-75

8] J. S. Morrison and R. T. Williams, *Greek Oared Ships* (1968), 7-12, 37-8, pl. Ic-d; but G. S. Kirk, *BSA* 44 (1949), 118 considers the Knossos picture to represent a merchantman, and its projection not a ram but a steering-oar

9] Iolkos, *Prakt.* 1960, 49-59; Grotta *Prakt.* 1951, 214-23; 1960, 258-62; 1961, 191-200; cf. 1967, 114, fig. 2

10] Cf. W. M. F. Petrie, *Tools and Weapons* (1917), 45

11] Smyrna, E. Akurgal, *Die Kunst Anatoliens* 9-10, Abb. 1 and Fig. 1; the brick-dimensions were 51 cm. by 30 by 13, with slight variations. The primitive hut at Corinth, *AJA* 43 (1939), 596-9, will be rather earlier than this

12] Drerup, *Marb. W Pr.* 1962, 1-9 and *AA* 79 (1964), 180-8; D. M. Robinson in Pauly-Wissowa, *RE* Suppl. vol. 7, 235, 244 on Bronze Age apsidal houses

13] Note the simple hut-shrine at Gazi, *AE* 1937, 278-91. Karphi, *BSA* 38 (1937–8), 66-8, 100-9; for dating, above Chapter 2, n.23. *Vrokastro* 86-8, pl. xviii; cf. 170-2, fig. 104. Kavousi, *AJA* 5 (1901), 131-6

14] *Ergon* 1960, 58, fig. 69

15] Cook, *CAH₂* II, chapter 38 (fascicle 7) 13 and 15; cf. above, Chapter 2, p. 66

16] Cf. B. Sweet-Escott, *Greece, a Political and Economic Survey, 1939-53* (1954), 93-4

17] *BSA* 38 (1937–8), 116, pl. 28, 2

18] J. T. Killen, *BSA* 59 (1964), 5 and n.23

19] Cf. K. Vickery, *Food in Early Greece* (1936), 61ff., and on the special topic of Hesiod and agriculture, Thalia P. Howe, *TAPA* 89 (1958), 44-65.

Note J. Deshayes' remarks on agricultural tools in the Aegean Bronze Age, *Études Archéologiques* (ed. P. Courbin, 1963), 171, fig. 2

20] On funerary feasts, see *Ker.* 1, 260; 4, 4; 5, 1, 24-5; *Hesperia* Suppl. Vol. 2, 19 n.1, 236; *A M* 28 (1903), 273. Cf. M. I. Finley, *The World of Odysseus* 63-4 on Homeric farming

21] Granary models, E. L. Smithson, *Hesperia* 37 (1968), 92-7; Smyrna, J. M. Cook, *The Greeks in Ionia and the East* 32, and cf. *Excavations at Lefkandi* 30, fig. 69 for other possible granary-foundations of the eighth century

22] Obsidian, *Asine* 193 and *Op. Ath.* 6 (1966), 127, 135; *A E* 1898, 107; *Vrokastro* 151, no. 6; *A M* 78 (1963), 41-2. (Obsidian had been used for arrowheads in earlier Mycenaean times, but apparently died out during Myc. 111 – see H.-G. Buchholz, *JdI* 77 (1962), 24-8.) Bone, *A M* 78, 36; *Hesperia* 21 (1952), 286, no. 13; *Asine* 425 (tomb 44). Clay beads, Boardman, *B S A* 55 (1960), 146-8 with references. Stone, *B S A* 31 (1930–1), 9, 38, fig. 16, 25: *A M* 28 (1903), 225: Weapons, see *E G A* 94-132 *passim*, and add *A E* 1953–4, 111, 89-97

23] Boardman, *Island Gems* (1963), 110, n.1; other survivals down to Subminoan times include *B S A* 53-4 (1958–9), 249, tomb VII, 20-1 (Knossos, Gypsades), and *B S A* 38 (1937–8), 131 (Karphi). Serraglio tomb 10, *P G P* 224, pl. 30; Electran Gates tomb 3, *A D* 3 (1917), 28, fig. 24; *Ker.* 1, 89, pl. 62; Marmariani, *B S A* 31 (1930–1), 7-8, 19, no. 30 (cf. *P G P* 136); Eleusis, *A E* 1898, 86, pl. 3, 4 and Coldstream, *G G P*, 16f.; Pherai, *P G P* 133; Thera, *P G P* 34 and especially 215 on skyphos from

tomb 17E; Skyros, *A A* 51 (1936), 228f.; Argos, *B C H* 79 (1955), 313; Tiryns, *A M* 78 (1963), 24; Knossos *B S A* 55 (1960), 134, tomb v, 33. I exclude the dish in Agora tomb XIV (*Hesperia* 6 (1937), 365, fig. 30 upper left – see *P G P* 119), and the rhyton from Karphi (*B S A* 55 (1960), 28, M 123), on grounds of the chronological uncertainties. See also Kübler, *Ker.* 5, 1, 184, n.182.

24] See E. T. Vermeule's survey of Middle Helladic, *G B A* 66-81 and especially 335, n.3 on graves, with C. W. Blegen and A. J. B. Wace, *Symbolae Osloenses* 9 (1930), 28-37; above, Chapter 4, n.24 on Salamis; on hand-made ware, *Asine* 279 and *Ker.* 5, 1, 139-40 n.106; Middle Helladic incised ware, e.g. *A J A* 36 (1932), 113-14

25] On nomadism, C. G. Starr, *The Origins of Greek Civilisation* (1962), 79-80

26] Starr, *op. cit.* 326-9 on *basileus*, and M. I. Finley, *Historia* 6 (1957), 141-2 on the word in Homer and on Linear B tablets.

27] See A. Andrewes, *Hermes* 89 (1961), 129-40 and *The Greeks* (1967), 79-82 on phratries. On dark age society in general, W. G. Forrest, *The Emergence of Greek Democracy* (1966), 44-65

28] Early dark age features in Homer: see above, Chapter 1, n.33 and Andrewes, *The Greeks* 45 (political and military system), 41 (social system), the latter following Finley, *The World of Odysseus*, 51 etc. Carpenter, *Folk Tale* etc. (1946), 89. Boar's tusk helmet, *A M* 75 (1960), 44, Beilage 31, 4

29] Here it will be enough to mention H. L. Lorimer's *Homer and the Monuments* (1950), *A Companion to*

Homer (ed. Wace and Stubbings, 1962) and the new German-edited *Archaeologia Homerica*, which began appearing in 1967 (see n.35 below)

30] *JHS* 74 (1954), 1-15; and cf. *EGA* 173-4. On throwing-spears, *ibid.* 136-9

31] Hammond, *Epirus* 387-8; M. Gimbutas, *Bronze Age Cultures in Central and Eastern Europe*, 321; Lorimer, *HM* 108-9 (Halos), 106 (Colophon), 108 (Samos); Pithe-koussai, *Expedition* 8, 4 (1966), 5-6; Cyprus, *BCH* 87 (1963), 378; the Mycenaean era, G. Mylonas in *AJA* 52 (1948), 56ff. and *A Companion to Homer* 478-88

32] Finley, *The World of Odysseus*, esp. 68-73, 106-8, 134-7. Elsewhere (*Historia* 6 (1957), 146-7, n.1) he says that archaism in material details can be combined with 'modern' institutions. See also G.S.Kirk, *The Songs of Homer* (1962), chapter 6

33] Cf. Cook, *CAH*₂ 11, chapter 38 (fascicle 7), 25; Drerup, *AA* 79 (1964), 184. Miss N.K.Sandars first pointed out to me the analogy with Urnfield Europe

34] On lamps, cf. Desborough in *BSA* 51 (1956), 129-30, and for other potential dark age examples, S. Benton, *BSA* 48 (1953), 329; Lorimer, *HM* 509 on Homeric lighting

35] See Kübler in *Ker.* 5, 1, 192 on the possible introduction of shoe-latchets in about 900. Pins and peploi, Lorimer, *HM* 340-1; on Sp. Marinatos' very different conclusions in *Archaeologia Homerica* (ed. F. Matz and H.-G.Buchholz), Kapitel A (1967), see my criticisms in *Gnomon* 41 (1969), 389-94. Sewn and shaped women's dress, *HM* 366-9; men's chiton, *ibid.* 358-9, 369-70

36] For a comparable survey see Desborough, *LMS* 42-7. Keos, J.L.Caskey, *Hesperia* 31 (1962), 278-83; 33 (1964), 326-35; Eleusis, G.E.Mylonas, *Eleusis and the Eleusinian Mysteries* (1961), 33-49, and 56-9 on possible Geometric temple; Amyk-lai, E.Buschor, *AM* 52 (1927), 12f., and *LMS* 88; Delos, H.Gallet de Santerre, *Délos primitive et archaique* (1958), 89-91, 216, 278; 93ff. on building H; Desborough, *LMS* 45-6 and Boardman, *Island Gems* 110, n.1. On Mycenaean cult-places, see R. Hägg, *Op. Ath.* 8 (1968), 39-60

37] Desborough, *LMS* 43-4 (Delphi), 119 (Aegina), 42-3 (Epi-dauros), with references. Mycenae, A.J.B.Wace, *Mycenae* (1949), 82-6. Olympia, H.-V.Herrmann, *AM* 77 (1962), 18-23; there is also the claim that one of the Middle Helladic apsidal houses must have survived in part to form the model for the construction of the first Bouleuterion in c.600 (*ibid.* 26, n.103); figurines, cf. Herr-mann's series, *ibid.* Beilage 2, and E. Kunze, *Ol. ber.* 8 (1967), 213-24, on which see *Gnomon* 40 (1968), 390-1. Samos, E.Homann-Wedeking, *AA* 79 (1964), 220-5; cf. D.Ohly, *AM* 65 (1940), 82ff. Plato's Academy, Ph. Stavropoullos, *Ergon* 1956, 10-13; 1958, 5-15; 1959, 5-9; 1960, 5-10; 1961, 3-9; 1962, 6-16

38] On these sites, see Hope Simpson, *A Gazetteer and Atlas of Mycenaean Sites*, nos. 348, 368, 4, 63, 498, 313, 89, 75 and pp. 190 (Samos), 171 (Dodona); Kalydon, Elatea, Nemea, *ibid.* nos. 311, 458, 46. Tiryns, see M.P.Nilsson, *The Minoan-Mycenaean Religion* (2nd ed.) 475-9; *ibid.* 462-5 with references for Cretan sites. *Asine* 74-7, 308-10 (House G); Hope Simpson, *op. cit.* nos. 379 (Cave of Pan), 236 (Mouriatadha)

39] See especially Part 11 of Nilsson's *The Minoan-Mycenaean Religion* (2nd ed, 1950), 447-633; and his *The Mycenaean Origin of Greek Mythology* (1932)

40] Naxos figurine, *Ergon* 1961, 199, fig. 206, right. Olympia figurines, E. Kunze, *Antike und Abendland* 2 (1946), 95-113; *Ol. ber.* 7, 138-41 and 8, 213-24, pl. 106

41] Attic ox, G. Hafner, *JdI* 58 (1943), 183-98; stag, *Ker.* 4, 20, pl. 26; cf. 1, 203, n.4, pl. 60; I disagree with Hafner's view (*op. cit.* 198) that this has 'nichts gemeinsam' with the earlier ox; horse-fragment, *Ker.* 1, 203, pl. 60; paintings, *Ker.* 4, pls. 20-1. Dictaean Cave, J. Boardman, *The Cretan Collection in Oxford* 1-5, 56-7. Idols, *BSA* 38 (1937-8), pl. 31 (Karphi) and *AE* 1937, 278-91 (Gazi); see also H. E. Schmid in *Gestalt und Geschichte: Festschrift für Karl Schefold* (1967), 168-71, pl. 58, 2. Models, e.g. A. J. Evans, *The Palace of Minos* 2, 129 fig. 63, and Boardman, *BSA* 62 (1967), 59 fig. 2 and 64-6 fig. 3. Paintings, *Fortetsa* pl. 4 (VI, 45); *AE* 1904, pl 3 (Desborough, *LMS* 27, 177, 188 on its dating)

42] G. S. Kirk indeed has written (*PCPS* 187 (1961), 42) that 'by 1050 possibly, 1000 probably, 950 certainly the true Dark Age in Greece has ended'.

43] R. M. Cook, *PCPS* 188 (1962), 21 (cf. 20 n.1). For the tentative conclusion reached here, cf. Coldstream, *GGP* 343; for a later, seventh-century date, T. Kelly, *AJA* 70 (1966), 113-21

44] Attic influence, *Excavations at Lefkandi* 28. Compare *Ker.* 5, 1, pl. 46 (inv. 2146) (Attic) with *Fortetsa* pls. 19, L 669 (Cycladic) and 24, OD 339 (Cretan)

45] Agora grave and contemporary finds, *Hesperia* 37 (1968), 110-16 and Chapter 5, nn.46-7 above; Vari, a first report in *AD* 20, 2 (1965), 112-14; ship on fibula, *JdI* 77 (1962), 126, fig. 24, 5; leg-cups, *AM* 43 (1918), pl 1, 2 and *AAA* 1 (1968), 22, fig. 3; pin, *Ker.* 5, 1, 219 pl. 161 (grave 13); bowl, *ibid.* 201-5, pl. 162; greaves, *AD* 21, 2 (1966), 36, figs. 1-2, pl. 59

46] On Rakhmani see *LMS* 133, 138

47] Oriental guilds, above Chapter 6, nn.42, 48, especially Boardman in *BSA* 62 (1967), 64, who would incorporate the gold treasures and other finds from Khaniale Tekke. On techniques, R. A. Higgins, *Greek and Roman Jewellery* (1961), 18-20: E. Bielefeld in *Archaeologia Homerica*, Kapitel C (1968), 26, n.185; 48, n.425

48] H. Drerup, *AA* 79 (1964), 199-204

49] Argos, Courbin, *La Ceramique géometrique de l'Argolide* 161-2 and n.1; Mycenae, N. M. Verdelis, *Ergon* 1962, 106-8; Antissa, W. Lamb, *BSA* 32 (1931-2), 41-4, fig. 3 (cf. R. L. Scranton, *Greek Walls* (1941), 25-44 on 'Lesbian' masonry); H. Payne, *Perachora* 1, 27-30, pls. 116 upper and 139; the model, *ibid.* 34-51, pls. 8-9, 117; Samos models, *AM* 55 (1930), 16f., fig. 6, Beilage 4; 74 (1959), 18, Beilage 29, 2

50] On Thermon, see Drerup in *Marb. W Pr.* 1963, 1-12 and *AA* 79 (1964), 187 with references; *ibid.* 194-5, fig. 7 for roof-posts; the pottery which he classes as 'Protogeometric' is that shown in *AD* 1 (1915), 265, fig. 31

51] The evidence is clearly set out by E. Diehl, *AA* 79 (1964), 495-8; cf. G. M. A. Hanfmann, *HSCP* 61 (1953), 9, 29 nn.40-2 and Coldstream, *GGP* 293 on the need for a lower

chronology, and Drerup, *A A* 79
(1964), 196, n.35 on original dating;
Miletus, *I M* 9-10 (1959–60), 79-85,
fig. 2

52] Gallet de Santerre, *Délos primitive et archaïque*, 215-16

53] Akurgal, *Die Kunst Anatoliens*
9-11, Abb. 2; *B S A* 53-4 (1958–9),
plan at back, squares E-G, xi-xiii;
Wall I, *ibid.* 40ff., 96ff., 122-3. H. F.
Mussche, *Thorikos* 2 (1967), 25f. for
a contemporary house

54] See M. S. F. Hood, *B S A* 48
(1953), 84-93 on Mycenaean equitation; Courbin, *La Ceramique géometrique de l' Argolide* 403-13 on the horse
in Argive Geometric painting; Attic
pyxis-handles, Coldstream, *G G P* 23;
L. Malten, *Jd I* 29 (1914), 179-255 on
funerary symbolism of the horse;
Vermeule, *G B A* 298, pl. 47B and V.
Karageorghis, *B C H* 87 (1963), 282-6,
378-80 on horse-burials; J. K.
Anderson, *Ancient Greek Horsemanship* (1961), 16-17 on new breeds.
Miletus figurine *I M* 9-10 (1959–60),
58-9, pl. 61

55] On 'styleless' figurines, cf.
Kunze, *A M* 55 (1930), 142 and above,
n.40: for two Geometric figurines,
dated by their context, at Delphi
(c.750–25), Coldstream, *G G P* 366,
n.2. On Argive Geometric pottery,
Courbin, *op. cit.*, 500-544

56] On the Panionion, see J. M.
Cook, *A R* 1959–60, 47f.; 1964–5,
49f. G. Kleiner, *Panionion und Melie*
(1967)

57] K. Müller, *A M* 48 (1923), 52-
68; G. Oikonomos, *A E* 1931, 1-53

58] Athens, Ph. Stavropoullos,
Ergon 1958, 5-15; 1961, 3-9,; cf. 1962,
5; Eleusis, G. E. Mylonas, *Eleusis and
the Eleusinian Mysteries* 59-60;
Drerup, *A A* 79 (1964), 198-200

59] *Excavations at Lefkandi* 30,

fig. 68 (compare the eighth-century
apsidal house-model from Samos,
A M 72 (1957), 18, Beil, 29-30);
J. Boardman, *Greek Emporio* (1967),
31-51, 250-1

60] Zagora, Greek excavations in
A D 16 (1960), 248-9; and now Prof.
A. Cambitoglou's in *Ergon* 1967, 75-
82; Siphnos, J. K. Brock in *B S A* 44
(1949), 2-10, pls. 4-5; Tenos, N. M.
Kondoleon, *Prakt.* 1949, 122-34;
1952, 531-40; 1953, 259-66

61] K. F. Kinch, *Vroulia* (1914), 2f.,
91f.; C. Blinkenberg, *Lindos* I
(1931), 57-8; *Vrokastro* 86-8, pl.
xviii; Kavousi, *A J A* 5 (1901), 137-43,
fig. 5; *Asine* 64, fig. 42 and 81, fig. 61;
Delphi, *R A* 12 (1938), 191, 207f.;
B C H 74 (1950), 320-2 and 85 (1961),
338f.; Miletus, *I M* 9-10 (1959–60),
38; Iasos, *Annuario* n.s. 39-40
(1961–2), 527f. For Cretan sites, see
also L. Renard, *Ant. Cl.* 36 (1967),
566-95

62] Wells, e.g. *B S A* 55 (1960),
159, 163 (Knossos), *Annuario* 43-4
(1965–6), 502, fig. 131 (Iasos);
drains, *B C H* 64-5 (1940–1), 259,
fig. 26 (Delphi) and *I M* 9-10 (1959–
1960), 40 (Miletus); mole, Gallet de
Santerre, *Délos primitive et archaique*
220; bridges, *A J A* 43 (1939), 427-8
and A. J. B. Wace, *Mycenae* 27; *Excavations at Lefkandi* 30, fig. 68;
Agrapidochorion, *A D* 20, 2 (1965),
217, pl. 249β. Eighth-century wall at
Smyrna, *B S A* 53-4 (1958–9), 123-4

63] Boeotia, see e.g. D. L. Page,
History and Homeric Iliad (1959), 152
and n.93; and in general J. A. Noto-
poulos, *Hesperia* 29 (1960), 177-97

64] The position is well and amusingly summarized by R. T. Williams
in Morrison and Williams, *Greek
Oared Ships*, 41-2; add Kirk's arguments in *The Songs of Homer* (1962),

283-5. Inscriptions, above, Chapter 6, n.58; Webster, *BSA* 50 (1955), 39 on the implications of the Dipylon jug verse; Nestor's cup, *Iliad* XI, 632-7. Seal-impression from Ischia, *Expedition* 8, 4 (summer 1966), 11-12

65] Ship-representations, G. S. Kirk, *BSA* 44 (1949), 134-41; wheel-naves, above, Chapter 5, nn.47, 53; models, *AJA* 61 (1957), 281, pl. 84, 9 (Vari) and *BCH* 90 (1966), 743, fig. 5 (Boeotia)

66] Arguments for a four-wheeled vehicle, *EGA* 160-3; hard to steer such a vehicle might be (so J. K. Anderson, *Classical Philology* 61 (1966), 280), but its existence at least for funerary purposes is certain. Cf. also H. W. Catling, *AJA* 72 (1968), 48-9

67] Note the important argument of Webster that the 'Dipylon' shield in the 'heroic' battle-scenes was a romantic archaism, *BSA* 50 (1955), 41-3 and *From Mycenae to Homer* (1958), 169-70; cf. *EGA* 58-60. For detail of the newly-published amphora in Buffalo, N.Y., see A. Alföldi in *Gestalt und Geschichte–Festschrift für Karl Schefold* (1967), pl. 7

68] On lions, see Webster, *From Mycenae to Homer* 82, 224-5 and F. H. Stubbings in *A Companion to Homer* 526; on similes in general, Webster, *op. cit.* 223-38

69] Building in Homer, see H. Bagenal in *Perachora* 1, 42-51; tholoi, *Odyssey* XXII, 442, 466, and cf. J. M. Cook, *The Greeks in Ionia and the East*, 32; siege and sack, e.g. *Iliad* XVII, 737; XVIII, 207, 220. Hesiod, n.b. especially *Works and Days*, 269. Note too that Homer's knowledge of carpentry extends to the drill and the lathe, of which the latter at least was probably re-adopted only in the eighth century, when representations of furniture with turned legs begin to prevail in vase-paintings: see S. Laser in *Archaeologia Homerica*, Kapitel K (1968), 24, n.96; 30-2

General Index

Site Index